'This is the most compelling and convincing indictment of the Attlee Government we are ever likely to see.'
Andrew Roberts, THE TIMES

'Excellent . . . particularly interesting is Barnett's attempt to concentrate on the first five years after the war. This is a valuable book. Barnett draws on meticulous research into cabinet papers over the past fifty years, much of which remains unpublished. In addition, he mines veins of social psychology and political philosophy to illuminate the changes that occurred. It might be hoped that the hindsight he offers will help to improve foresight.'
Eric Roll, senior adviser of SBC Warburg, FINANCIAL TIMES

'A heartfelt, anguished analysis of a succession of wilfully stupid decisions made by an over-centralized government, written in the implicit fear that the lessons might not have been learned, and the same errors may still be being perpetrated.'
Simon Heffer, DAILY TELEGRAPH

'Few writers exercise political influence, but Correlli Barnett's *Audit of War* converted some powerful people to his brand of economics. Barnett is a good thing. He cares for England and his books have stimulated useful debate.'
Terence Kealey, THE SPECTATOR

'Correlli Barnett's blunt and combative study of the Attlee government is an almost irresistible indictment of postwar thinking and absolutely well worth anyone's time and money to read in order to understand the wasted opportunities of Labour's too reverently recalled finest hour. A long and distinguished career as a military historian has given Barnett an exciting style of writing. [*The Lost Victory* is] delivered with Barnett's customary panache and argumentative power.'
Martin Kettle, GUARDIAN

'Barnett writes with brutal candour . . . there is stuff here to make the blood boil about how badly we have been governed. Read it . . . and you will learn more about the causes of our postwar decline than in most other studies of Britain's social and economic status put together.'
Andrew Neil, THE SUNDAY TIMES

'An important book . . . Barnett excels at the exploding of myths. The book is well written and, above all, possessed of a considerable narrative force . . . wonderfully readable.'
Toby Buchan, LITERARY REVIEW

'Clear lines of analysis, diligent research in the public records should stimulate a constructive debate. Even his most trenchant critics will warmly welcome this disputatious book . . . a serious, well researched academic argument.'
Kenneth O. Morgan, NEW STATESMAN AND SOCIETY

THE LOST
VICTORY

BRITISH DREAMS, BRITISH REALITIES
1945–1950

CORRELLI BARNETT

PAN BOOKS

First published 1995 by Macmillan

This edition published 1996 by Pan Books
an imprint of Macmillan Publishers Ltd
25 Eccleston Place, London SW1W 9NF
Basingstoke and Oxford
Associated companies throughout the world
www.macmillan.co.uk

ISBN 0 330 34639 3

3 5 7 9 8 6 4 2

A CIP catalogue record for this book is available from
the British Library.

Typeset by Parker Typesetting Service, Leicester
Printed and bound in Great Britain by
Mackays of Chatham plc, Chatham, Kent

For my younger grandchildren
Olivia, Georgia and Helena

in the hope that the meteor flag of England
may yet terrific burn

Contents

LIST OF ILLUSTRATIONS

(Between pages 178 and 179 and 370 and 371)

Photograph number 3 reproduced courtesy of National Monuments Record; photograph number 32 reproduced courtesy of Centris Coal Benefits Ltd; *Daily Telegraph* newspaper photographed in number 33 loaned by John Frost Historical Newspaper Service. All other photographs reproduced courtesy of The Hulton Deutsch Collection.

Acknowledgements

FIRST AND foremost, I wish to thank my wife Ruth for acting once again as a first-class quartermaster and one-woman general staff. Without her help this book certainly could not have been completed.

I would like to thank Mr Meredith Pickford for checking certain figures and calculations, thus saving me from error, but not, alas, from such that remain. I wish to express my gratitude to my editor, Ms Claire Evans, for her care and diligence in preparing the book for publication; and I am especially grateful to my copy editor, Mr Peter James, for his meticulously detailed scrutiny of the text. I also wish to express my gratitude to Mr William Armstrong, my publisher, for his support, constructive ideas and forbearance during what has inevitably proved a long gestation; and to Ms Suzanne Reeve, who, as the then Secretary of the Economic and Social Research Council, first encouraged me to undertake the work. I would also once again like to thank my agent, Mr Bruce Hunter, for all his wise counsel.

The present book being the final product of a research contract awarded to me by the Economic and Social Research Council, I would like to thank the Council for commissioning the work and the Council's staff for their cordial collaboration.

I wish yet again to express my indebtedness to the professional knowledge, courtesy and willing help of the Search Room staff at the Public Record Office, where so much of the research was carried out; to my colleagues in the Churchill Archives Centre (Mr Alan Kucia, Mr Victor Brown, Mrs Margaret Williams, Mrs Josephine Sykes, Miss Kathryn Beckett, Miss Monica Halpin, Miss Moira MacKay, Mr Martin Taylor and Mr Jonathan Draper); to Miss Mary Kendall, the

Librarian of Churchill College; and to the staffs of the following institutions: the University of East Anglia Library; the London Library; the Library of the Royal United Services Institute for Defence Studies; the *Statistisches Bundesamt*; and the Library of the Bank of England. I would also like to give thanks to Mrs Joan Revel-Walker and Mr and Mrs Alan Eden-Green for their help.

I am indebted to the following for permission to quote from works or documents in their copyright:

Mrs B. Jeffrey: the Robinson Papers in the Churchill Archives Centre. Sir Alexander Cairncross: letters to the author. Professor C. H. Feinstein: letters to the author. The London School of Economics: the Dalton Diaries. Jonathan Cape: *The Motor Makers: The Turbulent History of Britain's Car Industry* by M. Adeney. HarperCollins: *Memoirs* by Jean Monnet. Heinemann: *Ernest Bevin: Foreign Secretary 1945–1951* by A. Bullock. Patrick Stephens Ltd, an imprint of Haynes Publishing: *The Rootes Brothers: Story of a Motoring Empire* by J. Bullock. Weidenfeld & Nicolson: *Our Age: The Generation That Made Post-war Britain* by Noël Annan, and *Nye Bevan and the Mirage of British Socialism* by J. Campbell. BBC Worldwide Limited: *On Britain* by R. Dahrendorff. Oxford University Press: *Dictionary of National Biography: H. Dalton* by N. Davenport. *The Location of Industry and the Depressed Areas* by S. R. Dennison. Croom Helm: *The Decline of the British Motor Industry: The Effects of Government Policy 1945–1979* by P. J. S. Dunnett. Routledge & Kegan Paul: *Social Mobility in Britain* by D. V. Glass (ed.). Chatto & Windus: *The Uses of Literacy: Aspects of Working Class Life, with Special Reference to Publications and Entertainments* by R. Hoggart. Bloomsbury Publishing: *Typically British? The Prudential MORI Guide* by E. Jacobs and R. Worcester. Macmillan and Cambridge University Press for the Royal Economic Society: *The Collected Writings of John Maynard Keynes, Vol. XXIV, Activities 1944–46: The Transition to Peace* by D. Moggridge (ed.). The Clarendon Press: *Labour in Power 1945–1951* by K. O. Morgan. Hutchinson: *Small Wonder: The Amazing Story of the Volkswagen* by W. H. Nelson. Penguin Books: *The Stagnant Society* by M. Shanks. The Lord Wilson of Rievaulx: *New Deal for Coal* by H. Wilson. Random House: The Gallup International Opinion Polls. The author also wishes to thank the following newspapers for permission to quote from their columns: the *Independent* and *The Times*.

Extracts from Crown Copyright material are reproduced with the permission of the Controller of Her Majesty's Stationery Office.

Author's Preface

*T*he *Lost Victory* seeks to explain how and why it was that between the ending of the Second World War and the outbreak of the Korean War Britain let slip a unique and irrecoverable opportunity to remake herself as an industrial country while her rivals were still crippled by defeat and occupation. Although written as a free-standing narrative, the book is the third in what has become the 'Pride and the Fall' sequence exploring the causes and course of Britain's decline in the twentieth century.

The sequence began in 1972 with *The Collapse of British Power*, the first historical work to demonstrate that between the world wars the British Empire, far from being an asset to Britain (as national myth would have it), was a political and military liability; in fact, 'one of the most outstanding examples of strategic over-extension in history'. The book traced the resulting diplomatic, strategic and financial dilemmas from the 1920s up to the nemesis of 1941–2, when a now bankrupt Britain became an American pensioner under Lend–Lease, when the British Empire in Asia and the Pacific collapsed under Japanese attack, and when the Dominions of Australia and New Zealand fell under American protection. *The Collapse of British Power* argued that one root cause of this débâcle lay in the nature of the British governing elite between the world wars. It accused this elite, the small-'l' liberal product of a late-Victorian upbringing, of seeing international relations too much in terms of romantic ideals and moral purpose, too little in terms of power and strategic calculation. Hence followed their misplaced faith – brutally mocked by the actual course of events – in the myth of Empire, in the League of Nations as a guarantor of world peace, and in conciliation as a means of resolving conflict, even with dictators. *The Collapse of British Power* further contended that this same romantic idealism had also been responsible for the anti-technical bias of general education in Britain and the neglect of vocational training from the mid-Victorian age up to the outbreak of the Second World War – principal factors in Britain's industrial decline over the same period from leader into laggard. The book showed how in turn this decline served only to aggravate the fundamental problem of strategic over-extension, since the defence of the Empire overwhelmingly depended on the wealth, productiveness and military strength of the United Kingdom herself.

The second work in the 'Pride and the Fall' sequence, *The Audit of War* (1986), drew on a mass of once secret and hitherto unpublished Whitehall and Cabinet-committee files to document how the demands of total war between 1939 and 1945 found wanting Britain's backward industrial system. It showed that, behind the deceptive façade of victory and the propaganda about the scale of the national effort, the symptoms of the 'British disease' of the 1960s and 1970s were already present in wartime: a largely ill-educated, ill-trained and ill-motivated workforce; chronic overmanning; obdurate union resistance to new production methods; poor management; a too narrow base in advanced technologies, with consequent dependence on imports from abroad (in wartime, from America under Lend–Lease). The book searched back for the historical roots of these weaknesses, with special reference to the British failure for a century adequately to educate and train the nation for industrial success.

The Audit of War examined Government planning for the postwar era, and analysed the conflict of priority between modernising the out-of-date industrial machine and fulfilling the people's yearning for a 'New Jerusalem', a Britain cleansed of pre-war evils like unemployment, poverty and ill-health. It showed that this yearning was encouraged and given shape by just the same kind of small-'l' liberal idealists in the governing elite and intelligentsia who before the war had preached the cause of the League of Nations. It narrated how by 1945 these evangelists of the 'Brave New World' of the welfare state had triumphed over those in Whitehall who were bleakly aware of the 'Cruel Real World' of a bankrupt Britain with a ruined export trade and vanished overseas investments. The book drew the sorrowful conclusion: 'By the time the British people took the bunting down from the streets after VE-Day and turned from the war to the future, they had, in their dreams and illusions and their flinching from reality, already written the scenario for Britain's postwar descent.'

The fulfilment of this scenario during the first five years after the Second World War provides the theme of *The Lost Victory*. As with its predecessors, the book is an operational study — its purpose to illuminate Britain's present and future by the light of her history. Again as with its predecessors, the standpoint of *The Lost Victory* is throughout that of 'total strategy' (as I have termed it): that is, strategy conceived as encompassing all the factors relevant to preserving or extending the wealth and power of a human group in the face of rivalry from other human groups. The book therefore ranges from technology to national myth; from the influence of religion to foreign policy; from grand strategy to social welfare; from the cultural values of the governing elite and the intelligentsia to industrial productivity; from economic policy to the character of the nation itself.

The Lost Victory carries forward a major motif of *The Collapse of British Power*: that of global overstretch, political, strategic and financial. It describes how in the postwar era this overstretch was eagerly resumed by a Labour Government under the illusion that Britain, at the centre of the Commonwealth, was, and would remain, 'the third world power', thus laying an immense burden on an economy kept going only by borrowed dollars. *The Lost Victory* likewise carries forward a principal motif of *The Audit of War*, that of 'New Jerusalem', showing how the postwar fulfilment by the Labour Government of this wartime dream loaded a second crushing burden on the economy. And the book demonstrates how these double demands on scant resources served to starve investment in modernising British industry and infrastructure, shown by the 'audit of war' to be so urgently needed.

The continuing theme of the 'Pride and the Fall' sequence lies in the contrast between British pretensions and desires and Britain's actual wealth and weight; in the clash in the British mind between realism and a romanticism in moralistic garb, between reason and emotion. *The Lost Victory* freshly interprets this theme by showing that British total strategy between 1945 and 1950 was shaped less by the realities of Britain's postwar plight than by the nation's dreams and illusions. For it was these dreams and illusions which, with calamitous long-term consequences, set the limits of the politically possible and dictated the imperatives of the politically inevitable.

Prologue

ON 24 AND 25 July 1945, days of clear weather after storms, the fast carrier groups of the United States Third Fleet in the waters off the Japanese home islands struck at the remnants of the Imperial Japanese Navy lying immobilised in Kure naval base. Japan was now on the point of collapse as an industrial society capable of waging war, her factories either smashed by American heavy bombers or starved of fuel and raw materials thanks to the destruction of her merchant marine by American submarines.

On the 26th, on the far side of the globe, in a war-crumbled, war-shabby London, the results of the British general election held earlier that month were announced. The Labour Party had won 393 seats as against the Conservative Party's 213, the Liberal Party's 12 and Independent candidates' 22. In the late afternoon Winston Churchill resigned as Prime Minister at the head of the 'caretaker' Conservative Government which in May had replaced the wartime coalition, whereupon King George VI sent for Clement Attlee, Leader of the Labour Party, and asked him to form a government. Labour's stunning electoral victory, which buried the pre-war political landscape and created a new one, resulted from the electorate's eagerness to see a 'New Jerusalem' built in Britain after the war – a society in which poverty, ill-health, slums and unemployment would all be abolished by beneficent state action. The Labour Party manifesto had offered a detailed prospectus for New Jerusalem, including social security from the cradle to the grave, a free national health service, a promise to maintain full employment, and a programme of building 4–5 million houses in the first ten years of peace. It unambiguously committed a Labour government to bringing all this about. As the manifesto

1

ringingly put it with reference to the victory already won over Nazi Germany and the national determination to defeat Japan: 'The people will have won both struggles. . . . They deserve and must be assured a happier future than faced so many of them after the last war.'[1]

On 28 July the United States Third Fleet took final revenge for the Japanese strike on Pearl Harbor on 7 December 1941 by sinking the last seven major ships of the Imperial Japanese Navy at their moorings in Kure naval base. On 6 August the United States Army Air Force opened the nuclear age by dropping an atomic bomb on Hiroshima; and on the 9th a second bomb was dropped on Nagasaki. From the 9th to the 14th the Third Fleet's carrier groups and United States Army Air Force heavy bomber forces subjected the Japanese home islands and their flimsy cities to a climactic onslaught of fire-bombs and high explosive. On 14 August the Japanese government announced that it accepted the allied terms of unconditional surrender. The Second World War was over – many months sooner than Labour or Conservative ministers in the British wartime coalition had expected when drawing up plans for the transition from national mobilisation for war to peacetime economic life.

On that same day, 14 August 1945, the Chancellor of the Exchequer in the new Labour Government, Hugh Dalton, circulated to his Cabinet colleagues a memorandum written on the 13th by Lord Keynes (the principal Treasury economic adviser) on what Dalton called 'a most grim problem'.[2] Although Keynes's paper was entitled 'Our Overseas Financial Prospects', it covered much more than that. It was, indeed, a penetrating and comprehensive analysis of the 'total strategic' situation in which the United Kingdom found herself at the end of the Second World War. It coldly pointed out the economic and strategic realities so blithely ignored in the successful marketing of New Jerusalem.

> Three sources of financial assistance [stated the very first paragraph] have made it possible for us to mobilise our domestic man-power for war with an intensity not approached elsewhere, and to spend cash abroad, mainly in India and the Middle East, on a scale not even equalled by the Americans, without having to export in order to pay for the food and raw materials which we were using at home or to provide the cash which we were spending abroad.[3]

In the present year, 1945, Keynes continued, these three sources – Lend–Lease from the United States; Mutual Aid from Canada; and other credits, mostly from Sterling Area countries – 'are enabling us to overspend our income at the rate of about £2,100 million a year'. Of that total more than half, £1100 million, was accounted for by Lend–Lease. Although Keynes did not choose to mention it in his paper, this 1945 figure for Lend–Lease was less than half the figure for 1944, the crowning year of the war against Germany as well as Japan.[4]

In other words, the wartime mobilisation of British manpower and industrial resources (proportionately so much greater than that of any other belligerent); the British and Imperial armies which had marched and conquered in the latter years of the war in North Africa, in Italy, in Burma, in Normandy and North-west Europe; the great bomber fleets which had smashed and burned German cities; the navy which had defeated the U-boat; all these were not manifestations of British power at a new zenith, but only the illusion of it. Instead they represented American power and wealth – and the decline of Britain into a warrior satellite of the United States, dependent for life itself on American subsidies. This was the gruesome truth which the British people, under the spell of victory celebrations and the blowing of trumpets about their wonderful war effort, failed to grasp, and of which even their political leaders found all too easy to lose sight. In Keynes's own anguished words:

How vividly do Departments and Ministers realise that the gay and successful fashion in which we undertake liabilities all over the world and slop money out to the importunate represents an over-playing of our hand, the possibility of which will come to an end quite suddenly and in the near future unless we obtain a new source of assistance?[5]

Unfortunately, as Keynes pointed out, much of the British expenditure overseas at present being covered by foreign (mostly American) subsidies was not related to the war with Japan, but represented Britain's worldwide strategic overstretch in general.

We still have a vast number of men in the three Services overseas, and the Government cash expenditure outside this country, which this involves, is still costing more than the value of our total exports.

3

It might be supposed that the defeat of Japan would bring most of this rapidly to an end, subject, of course, to the inevitable time-lags. Unfortunately, that is a long way from the truth. Out of the £425 millions cost of the Services overseas in the current year the South-East Asia Command is responsible for only £100 millions. We have got into the habit of maintaining large and expensive establishments all over the Mediterranean, Africa and Asia to cover communications, to provide reserves for unnamed contingencies and to police vast areas eastwards from Tunis to Burma and northwards from East Africa to Germany. None of these establishments will disappear unless and until they are ordered home; and many of them have pretexts for existence which have nothing to do with Japan. Furthermore, we are still making loans to Allies and are incurring very large liabilities for relief out of money we have not got.[6]

Asked Keynes: 'What happens on the morrow of V-J [Victory-Japan] day? We are led to expect that Lend–Lease and Mutual Aid (amounting this year to £1,350 millions altogether) will cease almost immediately. . . .'[7]

In the event, it was just a week later, on 21 August, that President Truman announced the ending of Lend–Lease.

A predicament unique in British peacetime history now abruptly confronted the new Labour Government: national bankruptcy, yet imperial and world commitments at their grandest and most costly ever.

Yet this predicament was not the inevitable product of the Second World War, let alone a testimony to Britain's willingness in wartime to sacrifice herself for the cause of liberty. It had been brought down upon the British people by themselves and by the elite they had allowed to manage national policy in their name – the final reckoning for illusions too long cherished and the calamitous errors of total strategy that had followed therefrom.

PART ONE

The Dream of World Power

If we are to carry our full weight in the post-war world with the US and the USSR it can only be as a united British Commonwealth.

(C. R. ATTLEE, DEPUTY PRIME MINISTER, 1943)

It is in brief the problem whether, after the economic exhaustion of the war years, we have the power and the resources to maintain the armed forces . . . required to permit us to play the role of a Great Power.

(A. V. ALEXANDER, MINISTER OF DEFENCE, 1949)

CHAPTER ONE

'The Strength of England'

I T WAS THE most beguiling, persistent and dangerous of British dreams that the Empire constituted a buttress of United Kingdom strength, when it actually represented a net drain on United Kingdom military resources and a potentially perilous strategic entanglement.[1] The myth of Empire had originated in the 1880s when the United Kingdom found herself facing the rivalry of newly arisen great states such as the German Empire. Henceforward the British turned to the idea of a British Empire both as an economic refuge from German and American competition and as a psychological prop. Propagandists for the imperial idea such as Sir John Seeley (Professor of Modern History at Cambridge, whose book *The Expansion of England* was reprinted ten times between 1883 and 1899) counted up the white populations of what were later to become the Dominions – Australia, New Zealand, Cape Colony and Natal (South Africa) and Canada – and showed that this created a British world race on a par in numbers with the new continental super-states like Germany or even America. At Queen Victoria's jubilees in 1887 and 1897 the imperial myth (together with the newly contrived ceremonial of an imperial monarchy) was launched like some richly decorated hot-air balloon. This pink-on-the-map Empire to be sold to generations of British schoolchildren comprised not only the future Dominions of European race, but also India (of which Disraeli had had Queen Victoria proclaimed 'Empress' in 1876), and a litter of colonial possessions left over from eighteenth-century wars with France (like Caribbean sugar islands) which had been regarded by the mid-Victorians as mere anachronistic encumbrances. The bounds of the pink on the map would be set

7

wider yet during the so-called 'scramble for Africa' in the closing years of the nineteenth century.

The Great War served to enthrone the imperial myth in glory. Had not the young Dominion 'lion cubs' rallied loyally to the aid of the embattled Mother Country, and sent expeditionary forces to fight under British command in France and in the Mediterranean and Middle East theatres? Had not India too contributed splendid fighting divisions? The victory parade of 1919 had been a heart-lifting march-past of Empire. And then, in 1923, had come the British Empire Exhibition at Wembley, its numerous and fanciful pavilions bringing to life for the man in the street and his children the Empire upon which the sun never set, and its romantic variety of race, religion, natural resources, crafts, climate and culture.

Yet it was not only the man in the street who had come to believe in the imperial myth. Politicians talked in public and private about 'the Empire'; kings talked about the 'Empire', not least during the 1930s novelty of the royal Christmas wireless broadcast to, yes, the Empire. Every few years between the world wars imperial conferences were held to discuss, though only rarely to solve, imperial problems. There was a Committee of Imperial Defence and an Imperial General Staff (in fact both of them exclusively United Kingdom bodies). At King George V's Silver Jubilee in 1935 and George VI's Coronation in 1937 the Empire was again made splendidly manifest to the British public by the military contingents from all the Dominions, from India and from the colonies marching in the processions.

Thus the imperial myth continued to confirm the British up to the outbreak of the Second World War in a belief that the Empire provided the buttress of British power and importance in the world. Not only the British themselves, but also foreign countries, be they friendly or hostile, took the British Empire at the face value placed on it by myth, and assumed that Britain was indeed a world power, with resources to match the responsibilities.

Since the myth served as a necessary psychological crutch to the British, it is hardly surprising that neither as a whole nor in its constituent parts was the Empire ever subjected to a critical cost-benefit analysis. Yet, when measured in terms of economic or strategic advantages balanced against entanglements and obligations, the Empire was not so much an asset as a liability, one of the most remarkable examples of strategic over-extension in history.

Even at the apogee of imperialism before the Great War the Empire had remained more a matter of rhetoric, more of a façade of power, than hard political reality. The imperialists' hope of a federal empire on the German model, with a customs union, a single foreign office and single imperial army and navy, had been finally dashed by 1911. The white colonies – Australia, New Zealand, South Africa and Canada – were far too keen on growing into independent nation-states to accept the role of pieces in an imperial mosaic arranged in London. Nor did the Empire then or later form a coherent economic bloc. There was never any close correlation between the imperial pink on the map and the pattern of British global trade and investment. India ('the jewel in the crown' according to Lord Curzon), though a key British economic asset in the nineteenth century because of her opium exports to China, had lost her value by the 1930s. In 1931 she took only 7.4 per cent of British exports,[2] and thereafter the hitherto favourable balance of trade between Britain and India swung decisively against Britain.[3] In 1938 British investment in India represented merely 12.5 per cent of total British overseas investment, and about a third less than in South America,[4] for which latter continent Britain incurred no political or strategic entanglements on the grand scale as with India. Nor was India ever a source of important raw materials. As for the colonial Empire – a rummage-bag of Crown colonies or League-of-Nations mandates in the Middle East, Africa, Asia, South and Central America and the Caribbean – it provided just 11 per cent of Britain's total imports of raw materials in 1937.[5] Only Malayan tin and rubber constituted really valuable commercial assets. In 1930 the Iraqi and Iranian oilfields under British control accounted for only 3 per cent of world output, and Britain drew most of her supplies of oil from the United States and Venezuela.[6]

Nor were the Dominions of European race decisively more important economically to Britain than regions outside the Empire such as Europe or the United States. In the 1930s Australia and New Zealand rated only just above Argentina as fields for British investment, while New Zealand rated below Brazil, and Canada below the United States.[7] The most valuable Dominion sources of minerals, South Africa and Canada, were at the same time strategic backwaters for Britain, making little call on British naval and military strength.

And it is when the Empire is considered from a strategic point of view, in terms of British power, that it becomes still clearer that even in the heyday of imperialism before the Great War the Empire belonged more to the realm of romantic myth than to reality. Even by 1914 the Dominion armed forces were too weak to defend their own territories. The Indian Army's contribution was more than counter-balanced by the British garrison tied up in India, to say nothing of the sprawling strategic commitments in the Mediterranean, Middle East and Africa which Britain had had to shoulder in the nineteenth century in order to secure her main line of communication with India. Moreover, it was the British taxpayer who overwhelmingly paid for the naval power which protected this worldwide imperial sprawl: in 1902 nearly thirty shillings per head of population as against an average of less than three shillings in the future Dominions.[8] Even so, by this time and in the face of the growing strength of other naval powers, the Royal Navy was no longer strong enough to defend both the United Kingdom and the worldwide Empire. After 1904 the Royal Navy became largely a home-waters navy, concentrated in the North Sea against the menace of the new German High Seas Fleet. The security of the British Empire in the Far East and Pacific had come to depend on the Japanese Navy, thanks to the Anglo-Japanese alliance of 1902. Thus even before the Great War Britain had already reached the paradoxical situation where she could not find the resources to defend the Empire that was supposed to be the prop of her world power.

It happened that during the Great War the Empire did not come under direct attack by a great power, only Britain herself by Imperial Germany. This fact alone enabled the Dominions and India to send military aid to Britain rather than the other way about, so making possible all that wartime propaganda about the Empire's wonderful contribution, propaganda which served further to foster the delusion that the Empire was a source of strategic strength to Britain. Yet the truth was that in any war where Britain and the Empire were attacked by great powers at the same time, Britain would face the gigantic task of defending both herself and also vast territories scattered across the world. As Billy Hughes, the Australian Prime Minister, told the 1921 Imperial Conference:

Look at the map and ask yourselves what would have happened to that great splash of red down from India through Australia to New Zealand, but for the Anglo-Japanese Treaty. How much of these great rich territories and portions of our Empire would have escaped had Japan been neutral? How much if she had been our enemy? It is certain that the naval power of the Empire could not have saved India and Australia and still been strong enough to hold Germany bottled up in the narrow seas. . . . Had [Japan] elected to fight on the side of Germany, we should most certainly have been defeated.[9]

Between the 1880s and the 1920s, therefore, Britain locked herself into an imperial role which she simply lacked the naval and military (and, of course, financial) resources to sustain.

Yet in this same period the real foundation of the United Kingdom's power and prosperity – that is, her own industrial machine – was becoming more and more outdated and uncompetitive.[10] Britain's share of world trade in manufactures fell from 31 per cent in 1870 to 14 per cent in 1910. By the outbreak of the Great War Britain's steel production was only about half Germany's, and Britain was particularly weak in carbon and alloy steels needed for modern machine-tools.[11] According to the official *History of the Ministry of Munitions* Britain would have lost the Great War by 1916 had it not been for huge imports of American steel.[12] The munitions crisis in the first years of the Great War brought home to the Government just how dependent Britain had become on foreign imports of advanced technology – machine-tools, aero-engines, sparking-plugs, ball-bearings, magnetos, dyes and drugs, scientific instruments and much else.[13]

Britain's loss of technological leadership dated from as far back as the 1840s, when her unique world monopoly as the first and only industrial nation began to be challenged by newly industrialising countries such as the United States, France and Prussia.[14] As early as 1835 Richard Cobden had warned after a visit to the United States that 'our only chance of national prosperity lies in the timely remodelling of our system, so as to put it as nearly as possible upon an equality with the improved management of the Americans'.[15] Just two years after the Great Exhibition of 1851, Dr Lyon Playfair foretold in his book *Industrial Education on the Continent* that, unless Britain altered her whole industrial outlook and methods, she was bound to be overtaken by other countries. Thirty-three years later the Royal Commission on Technical Instruction reported that the Europeans had now clearly passed Britain in the application of science to industry, had clearly passed her in the efficiency of their industrial organisation.[16] Leadership of the second, science-based, industrial revolution from the 1870s onwards – complex precision machine-tools, electrical equipment, the large-scale manufacture of dyes and drugs – belonged not to Britain but to America and the continent of Europe, and, within Europe, to newly united Germany above all. In the early 1900s only 5 per cent of Britain's industrial labour-force were working in the new technologies, which accounted for a mere 7 per cent of her exports; 25 per cent of her industrial labour force was locked up in older technologies such as coal, iron and steel, and textiles, which still accounted for 70 per cent of her exports.[17] She had begun to retreat from the highly competitive but fast-growing markets of the industrialised world such as Europe and North America into the refuges offered by less exacting but slow-growing markets in backward regions of the world, such as the British Empire or South America.[18] In other words, Britain as an industrial society had failed from the 1840s onwards to adapt fast enough and radically enough to meet the challenges of new technologies and new competitors. Instead she had remained stuck fast in the patterns of that primitive stage of industrialism in the late eighteenth and early nineteenth centuries which had witnessed her initial triumph. For the unique nature of the supremacy which she then won had bred arrogance and self-satisfaction, leading British industry to believe, like an army after a victorious war, that it had found the formula of success; and, like such an army, it clung to the formula with blinkered stubbornness.

The formula consisted in the individualistic competition of self-taught 'practical men' leading workforces also of self-taught 'practical men'. Entrepreneurs and machine-builders alike had carried into the first stage of industrialism the craft traditions of learning by experience on the job, of proceeding by rule-of-thumb and trial-and-error. Even science in the late eighteenth century had been a matter of private experiment by self-taught amateurs. During the nineteenth century, however, British industry's continued faith in this formula, or myth, of the 'practical man' carried with it a deep mistrust of the application of intellectual study or scientific research to industrial questions, a total disdain for systematic technical training for the workforce or even sound general education. And yet, as perceptive critics like Cobden and Playfair were pointing out in the 1830s and 1850s, and royal commissions demonstrated with fearsome weight of evidence from the 1870s onwards, Britain's rivals were fast adopting a much more sophisticated approach to industrial development, based on applied science and on thorough training at all levels.[19] Moreover in Europe and America it was the state which provided the key piece of equipment in achieving this new professionalism – complete national education and training systems: primary, secondary, vocational and technical. By the 1850s close collaboration between industry and university research institutes in these countries was already resulting in new products and processes, especially with regard to chemicals.

No comparable developments in education, training or research took place in Britain between the Great Exhibition and the Great War. Instead Britain trailed after foreign examples at up to fifty years' delay, and even then on a dismally inadequate scale. It was not for want of warnings that Britain would be wrong to take for granted that her existing domination of world markets would always continue; wrong to delude herself that she could coast along for ever on the income from her vast accumulation of overseas investments. In 1868 the Schools Enquiry Royal Commission reported:

> our evidence appears to show that our industrial classes have not even the basis of sound general education on which alone technical education can rest. . . . In fact, our deficiency is not merely a deficiency of technical education, but . . . in general intelligence, and unless we remedy this want we shall gradually but surely find that our undeniable superiority in wealth and perhaps in energy will not save us from decline.[20]

In 1884 the Royal Commission on Technical Instruction remarked: 'The one point in which Germany is overwhelmingly superior to England is in schools, and in the education of all classes of the people. The dense ignorance so common among workmen in England is unknown.'[21] Of the German polytechnic system the same Royal Commission reported:

> To the multiplication of these polytechnics may be ascribed the general diffusion of a high scientific knowledge in Germany, its appreciation by all classes of persons, and the adequate supply of men competent, so far as theory is concerned, to take the place of managers and superintendents of industrial works. In England there is still a great want of this last class of person.[22]

13

In the 1890s the odds against an English child in an elementary school going on to secondary education were 270 to 1.[23] Not until 1902 did Britain inaugurate state-sponsored secondary education. In 1909 three-quarters of young people in England and Wales between fourteen and seventeen years of age were receiving no full-time or part-time education or training whatsoever.[24] As for further education, England and Wales in 1902 had seven universities for a population of 31 million; Germany twenty-two universities for a population of 50 million. In 1908 when Germany possessed (in addition to her polytechnics) ten technical high schools with over 14,000 students, Britain still had no equivalent institutions – only a ragbag of thirty-one technical schools with a total of fewer than 3000 students.[25] Only in the field of pure scientific research had Britain begun to catch up, since the founding of the Clarendon Laboratory at Oxford and the Cavendish Laboratory at Cambridge in the 1870s.

One cause of this failure to match Britain's competitors in creating a skilled nation lay in the cult of the 'practical man' itself, which meant that there was little demand from industry for educated and trained personnel at whatever level of qualification. This proved especially true of technical training, as the Board of Education reported in 1908-9: 'The slow growth of these technical institutions is, however, in the main to be ascribed to the small demand in this country for the services of young men well-trained in the theoretical side of industrial operations.'[26] But there were other causes too. According to the Liberal economic and social doctrine of laissez-faire which prevailed in Britain from the 1840s until the middle of the Great War, education should be left to private enterprise or private charity, and training to the 'practical man' on shop-floor or in office. The idea that the state should create a coherent and elaborate national structure of education and training thus appeared to the Victorian political consensus as positively un-English, not to say Prussian: hence the spasmodic and disconnected nature of British governments' reluctant initiatives in this field. Moreover, despite the doom-laden warnings of royal commissions, these governments – unlike European – regarded expenditure on education and training as a painful and politically unpopular load on the taxpayer rather than as a key investment in the country's future prosperity.

Yet there was yet another factor, one which at the same time bore directly on Britain's general loss of technological dynamism – the nature of the British governing elite and intelligentsia created by the Victorian public school (as remodelled by Dr Arnold and his followers) and Oxbridge. For these institutions saw their purpose not as turning out technocrats to lead an industrial nation, but as forming Christian gentlemen, knights in a stained-glass tableau by Sir Edward Burne-Jones, to serve in public life, the Church, the law or the civil service, or bring enlightened administration to the Empire.[27] It was to be such Christian gentlemen in the governing elite and intelligentsia who between the world wars would espouse such romantically ideal causes as the League of Nations, disarmament and appealing to Adolf Hitler's better nature; who in regard to Indian demands for dominion status would think more in terms of India's interests than those of the United Kingdom; and who in the 1940s would evangelise the vision of New Jerusalem.[28]

The public school and Oxbridge moreover taught the future governing elite and intelligentsia to despise 'trade' as beneath a gentleman, equally to despise any form of education that might be deemed vocational (such as technology) rather than 'liberal' (like the classics). These highminded snobberies were to shape the character of the new university colleges founded in the late nineteenth century as well as the development of the grammar schools. In the persons of senior civil servants at the Board of Education the same snobberies were after 1902 to devise the curricula of the new state-funded secondary schools on the model of the Victorian public school. These calamitous civil servants also ensured that even elementary schools steered clear of vocational or technical education in favour of a useless and irrelevant cut-price version of an academic 'liberal' education.[29] No wonder the President of the Royal Society in 1903 attributed government neglect of scientific research to:

> the absence in the leaders of public opinion, and indeed throughout the more influential classes of society, of a sufficiently intelligent appreciation of the supreme importance of scientific knowledge and scientific methods in all industrial enterprises and indeed all national undertakings. . . . In my opinion the scientific deadness of the nation is mainly due to the too exclusively medieval and classical methods of our higher public schools.[30]

The pursuit of the ideal of the 'gentleman' and loyalty to the myth of the 'practical man' between them therefore go far to account for Britain's failure between the 1840s and the Great War to adapt fast enough to the second industrial revolution and match the dynamic advance of her rivals. Yet there remains a third factor in this failure: the nature of the workforce.

It is impossible to exaggerate the long-term consequences, social and psychological, of the experience of the workforce in the foul industrial slums of late Georgian and early Victorian Britain under conditions of ferocious competition and uncontrolled exploitation.[31] Here was created the enduring nature of the British urban working class as a culture apart, an alienated group with its own strong sense of tribal solidarity, embittered and hostile towards the rest of society and in particular towards those who employed it. The national neglect of even primary education (let alone secondary) until after 1870 compounded the brutalising effects of life in slum and factory by ensuring that 'dense ignorance' (to quote the Royal Commission on Technical Instruction in 1884) became a widespread working-class characteristic to be passed on from generation to generation.

From the very beginning of the industrial revolution British workpeople regarded the machine as an enemy, technical progress as the destroyer of status, independence and employment. It followed that British trade unions from their birth saw their principal role as the defence of existing crafts and existing industrial technology against replacement by new machinery and new methods. As the trade unions gained strength in the course of the nineteenth century they became an ever more potent factor in retarding or even preventing technical change.[32] By the time of the Great War, according to the official *History of the Ministry of Munitions*, the craft unions:

> had built up a system of rules and customs, written and unwritten, which hampered production [such as] the limitation of the number of apprentices, the insistence that skilled men only should work certain machines, the restriction of output, the regulation of overtime, the exclusion of men and women who had not been initiated into the mysteries of the craft, the sharp demarcation between the operations proper to the various trades. . . .[33]

This now obsolete and arthritic industrial system, with its inability to manufacture the advanced technology needed for modern warfare, presented Britain with a national emergency after the outbreak of the Great War in 1914. In the next four years and under the aegis of government she embarked on a remarkable and breakneck industrial revolution financed by the state (a radical breach of laissez-faire orthodoxy) and heavily dependent on imported American equipment. By 1918 an impressive array of new industries had been created – for making shells and fuses, aircraft, aero-engines, dyes and drugs, optical instruments.

Yet, with the exception of the new chemical industry, this forced growth largely wilted with the return of peacetime. Worse, the disruption caused by the Great War to world trading patterns finally destroyed Britain's privileged Victorian place at the centre of a global network of finance and free trade. Henceforth she rapidly lost world-market share to new local industries (such as the Indian cotton industry) or to more efficient competitors. From 1920 onwards her traditional Victorian staples like shipbuilding lay in deep slump. Even in the late 1920s when other industrial nations were enjoying a boom, Britain still remained in chronic slump, with 1.3 million unemployed, and with industrial production below the 1913 figure.[34] In 1929 the Balfour Royal Commission on Trade and Industry, perhaps the most thoroughgoing investigation of British industrial shortcomings ever undertaken, painted a dismal picture of worn-out machinery and outworn attitudes and methods. The cause of the malaise was diagnosed by the report as:

> The conservative habits of mind which prevent many British employers from pursuing so energetic and (as it appears to them) so ruthless a policy of scrapping old plant and replacing it by new as their competitors (say) in America or Germany, and the corresponding qualities of mind which led many workmen to cling tenaciously to obsolete trade customs and lines of demarcation and thus prevent them from cooperating to the full in getting the best value out of machinery at lowest cost.[35]

During the 1920s, therefore, the contradictions in the British 'total strategic' situation were deepening: contradictions between the United Kingdom's imperial obligations and her own resources, between delusions of imperial grandeur and real strength. Back in 1883 Sir John Seeley had written:

17

we have here by far the largest of all political questions, for if our
Empire is capable of further development, we have the problem of
discovering what direction that development should take, and if it is
a mischievous encumbrance, we have the still more anxious problem
of getting rid of it. . . .[36]

Yet in the 1920s not even the Labour and Liberal parties saw the
Empire as a mischievous encumbrance to be got rid of, for progressive
opinion in Britain had come to believe in its own version of the
imperial myth. It saw the 'white' Empire as a happy family of free
peoples, a smaller League of Nations, and the 'coloured' Empire as
inhabited by younger brethren whose future constituted for Britain a
sacred and noble trust.[37] Labour and Conservative governments alike
therefore sought in the 1920s to tighten rather than loosen (let alone
sever) the political and military links of Empire, even though at
successive imperial conferences this purpose was thwarted by Canada
and South Africa, who were resolved on complete national freedom of
action and hence refused to be drawn into an imperial 'alliance'.[38]
After the Imperial Conference of 1930 and the Statute of Westminster
of 1931 (transforming the 'white' Empire into a 'Commonwealth' of
independent nations each with the same monarch), Britain as the
Mother Country was left with an unlimited obligation to defend the
Dominions but enjoyed no guarantee of Dominion support,
diplomatic or military, in Europe (her own area of direct concern)
in return; hardly a good bargain.

By historical accident, the Dominions most 'loyal' to the Mother
Country and closest to the British people in kinship, Australia and
New Zealand, were also the furthest away, settled in the South Pacific
in that vanished era when the Royal Navy was unchallenged mistress
of the world's oceans. No great power would have chosen to have two
weak and dependent allies on the far side of the globe, especially when
it entailed the ultimate risk of having to fight a major war in their
defence, perhaps at a time when the great power itself was also
engaged in a war for its own survival. But weak and dependent kin,
though an encumbrance, cannot be got rid of; ties of affection and
moral responsibility forbid it. So Britain entered the 1930s with a
commitment to send her main fleet to Far Eastern waters should
Australia and New Zealand ever come under threat from Japan (the
Anglo-Japanese alliance not having been renewed in 1922).

18

India, however, was another matter altogether. She was certainly, in Sir John Seeley's phrase, a mischievous encumbrance since she swallowed a large garrison of British troops for internal security and for the defence of the North-west Frontier. Moreover, the mischievousness of the encumbrance went far beyond India herself: it embraced the sprawling structure of British political, naval and military involvement in the Mediterranean and Middle East that had been erected to protect the Suez Canal route between the United Kingdom and India – Malta, Cyprus, Palestine, Egypt, the Sudan, Aden. But in this case no ties of kinship existed to inhibit the British from seeking to get rid of the encumbrance. Nevertheless, other ties did so exist to inhibit them: the seductive romance of the Raj; the belief that India constituted the very keystone of the imperial arch; the pride in having brought unity and good government to a turbulent and divided sub-continent, and the anxiety lest this achievement should come to nought in Indian hands. And India more than any other British possession offered the British governing class that opportunity for imperial service for which the late-Victorian and Edwardian public school was the designed preparation. The British rulers of India – and their colleagues in Whitehall and Westminster – felt a moral responsibility for the future of India and the welfare of her peoples which would have astonished Lord Clive. For all these reasons there was therefore no question between the world wars of the British coming to the conclusion that India was an encumbrance, let alone deciding to get rid of her. Between 1928 and 1935 Conservative, Labour and National governments even threw away a splendid opportunity to do just that, when they rejected the demands of the Congress Party and the Moslem League (backed by mass demonstrations and civil disobedience) for immediate dominion status for India and a new Moslem state to be called Pakistan.[39] Moved by a concern for the good of India (as they perceived it), the British chose to hang on in India for the very reason which, on a clear view of their own interests, should have prompted them to get out – that India depended on British forces for her defence. This meant, so went the curious logic, that British forces would have to remain there. However, they could not be handed over to an independent Indian government to use at home or abroad as it thought fit, but must remain under British control. Therefore it was out of the question to grant India her independence at that time.[40]

19

So Britain continued to shoulder the strategic burden of India and its corollary, the British presence in the Mediterranean and Middle East.

Yet even while British governments were thus seeking to perpetuate and indeed enhance Britain's military obligations to the Empire they had to accept that Britain could not afford the armed forces – especially a navy – large enough to protect the Empire against all threats. Indeed, by 1931 the armed forces had been slashed into impotence in the name of economy and disarmament. Moreover, on top of the existing burden of imperial defence had been added since 1919 the altruistic duty to implement the Covenant of the League of Nations, and to do so in the last resort by the deployment of armed force anywhere in the world – even where the United Kingdom's interests or security were in no way threatened.[41]

The British governments of the 1920s (abetted by the progressive intelligentsia) sought to resolve these fundamental contradictions in total strategy by maintaining Britain's world role on the cheap by means of the League of Nations and universal disarmament. It was their fervent hope – more, an article of faith – that the existence of the League of Nations and its Covenant had put an end to traditional power struggles based on armed strength. Since the British Empire could survive only in a peaceful and law-abiding world, then a peaceful law-abiding world it had to be. And the most effective way of ensuring the success of the League of Nations, so the British believed, lay in general disarmament, with Britain of course giving a lead.

As a total strategy this had one fatal flaw – it absolutely depended on nations respecting the Covenant of the League. The Japanese invasion of Manchuria in 1931 brutally demonstrated this to be idealistic wishful thinking. Now Britain along with other members of the League had to decide what to do about Japan's act of breaking and entering. The problem immediately exposed the disharmony between two key components of British total strategy. The foreign-policy component was supposed to consist of full-hearted support of the League of Nations, even to the point of deploying British forces. Yet the military component was, or had been, one of economy and disarmament, the pursuit of which by Conservative and Labour governments had in particular left the Singapore naval base (originally supposed to be operational by 1925) still nowhere near complete.[42] And without a base it was quite impossible to send a fleet to Far

Eastern waters. As a consequence of this disharmony in her total strategy Britain was reduced to moralising at Japan at the League of Nations, which did nothing to remove Japanese troops from Manchuria, but did serve to alienate the Japanese.

From this time onwards the contradictions in British total strategy, the gulf between the façade of world power and the reality of the United Kingdom's military and economic weakness, began to deepen year by year. After Hitler came to power in 1933, the German threat to Britain herself emerged once again. In February 1934 the Defence Requirements Sub-Committee of the Committee of Imperial Defence (appointed in November 1933 to examine the whole field of British total strategy) reported that, while Japan posed an immediate threat to the Empire in the East and Pacific, Germany was 'the ultimate potential enemy against whom our "long-range" policy must be directed'.[43] Yet the two threats, pointed out the committee, were not separate but linked, because Japan might be tempted into aggression if Britain herself were endangered by events in Europe. Britain thus now faced an insoluble strategic dilemma. For the rest of the 1930s the opposite pulls of Britain's own security (necessarily tied up with the fate of Europe) and the security of the Empire (especially Australia and New Zealand) supplied the basic theme of Whitehall's agonising over British grand strategy.

To meet the twin threats from Germany and Japan the Defence Requirements Sub-Committee Report in February 1934 recommended a five-year programme of rearmament. But this proposal necessarily embraced the economic factor in total strategy. In 1934 Britain was still struggling out of the world slump, with her income from foreign investments and invisible earnings more than halved between 1929 and 1932.[44] Rearmament would compete with the export trade for Britain's all too scarce resources of modern technology, such as the automobile, electrical, radio and light-engineering industries. The National Government therefore chose to give priority to economic recovery, meanwhile putting its faith in the possibility of some kind of arms-control deal with Nazi Germany.

But, in any case, the question of large-scale rearmament involved yet another of the factors in total strategy: public opinion, which in a parliamentary democracy cannot readily be flouted by government. In 1934 British public opinion ranged from outright and fervent pacifism to the merely pacifistic; it refused to contemplate the idea of rearmament and with it the possibility of another Great War, another Western Front, plus this time the destruction of London and other cities in a few days by enemy bombers, as promised by air-power pundits and believed by politicians. The Labour and Liberal parties, for their parts, vehemently opposed British rearmament. In 1933–4 the National Government lost six by-elections, all fought by opposition candidates largely on the issue of 'peace', by swings of up to nearly 25 per cent.[45] It took until the general election of 1935 to steer opinion round to accepting a modest measure of rearmament, supposedly in support of the League of Nations. It was only at the beginning of 1936 that Britain at last embarked on a programme of large-scale rearmament – a fateful delay of at least two years which was to emasculate British foreign policy in the critical period ahead.

By now, 1936, the contradictions between the façade and the reality of the British world position – the dilemmas of British total strategy – had become even more acute. Fascist Italy was no longer a friend (if a somewhat unreliable one), but a potential enemy threatening Britain's main imperial lifeline through the Mediterranean and the Middle East. This development had been gratuitously brought about by British foreign policy.[46] In 1935 Italy had threatened to conquer Abyssinia, a primitive state in east Africa, and finally had done so. The fate of Abyssinia could not conceivably affect Britain's own interests. Nonetheless, British foreign policy, pushed by an idealistic – not to say moralistic – public opinion, was publicly committed to upholding the Covenant of the League of Nations and what was called 'collective security', whereby all members of the League were supposed to turn out together to stop an aggressor. As the Abyssinian crisis deepened, and the Cabinet anxiously pondered the question of applying League of Nations economic sanctions to Italy, the possibility of a shooting war in the Mediterranean loomed closer. 'Collective security' was now revealed to be yet another romantic illusion of the time, because in the event Britain found herself virtually alone in preparing for the contingency of war.[47] Yet the Chiefs of Staff warned the Cabinet again and again that the Royal Navy was not sufficiently strong to fight such a war and at the same time retain enough ships in hand to parry a Japanese move in the Far East and also provide cover against the German Navy in home waters.[48] So once again the disharmony in British total strategy between foreign policy and military strength reduced the Cabinet to wagging its fingers at the aggressor, though this time accompanied by League of Nations sanctions hopefully calculated not to be effective enough to provoke him into war. This did nothing to save Abyssinia, but did serve to affront Mussolini and push him into Hitler's camp.

In the meantime, Hitler too had been on the move, taking advantage of a British diplomacy which fatally combined weakness, sermonising and attempted ingratiation.[49] In 1935 the Nazi government reintroduced conscription and embarked on a major expansion of the German Army, hitherto limited to 100,000 men under the Versailles Treaty; announced the existence of the Luftwaffe (another breach of the Treaty); and browbeat the hapless British into agreeing to a naval treaty by which Germany could build up to 35 per cent of the Royal Navy's surface strength and up to parity in submarines.[50] In March 1936, when British deployment in the Mediterranean and Egypt over Abyssinia was at its height, Hitler ordered his troops into the demilitarised zone of the Rhineland in outright defiance of a key security provision of the Versailles Treaty. France and Britain took counsel of each other's nerveless irresolution and did nothing. The hard-won allied victory of 1918 had finally been thrown away.

In their Annual Review for 1937 the Chiefs of Staff bleakly summed up the predicament in which Britain was now imprisoned:

> we are in the position of having threats at both ends of the Empire from strong military powers, i.e., Germany and Japan, while in the centre we have lost our traditional security in the Mediterranean.
> . . . So long as that position remains unresolved diplomatically, only very great military and financial strength can give the Empire security.[51]

But such military and financial strength simply did not, and could not, exist. The countries of the Empire being themselves little industrialised, the task of imperial rearmament, like all other aspects of imperial defence, was to fall overwhelmingly on the United Kingdom.[52] Back in 1879, when imperialists were first propagating the myth of Empire, Gladstone had shrewdly told an audience:

> I wish to dissipate if I can the idle dreams of those who are always telling you that the strength of England depends, sometimes they say upon its prestige, sometimes they say upon extending its Empire, or

23

upon what it possesses beyond these shores. Rely upon it, the strength of Great Britain and Ireland is within the United Kingdom.[53]

Now, nearly sixty years later, the course of events was proving Gladstone entirely right. But the strength of the United Kingdom was relatively no longer what it had been in Gladstone's day, when she still remained the most powerful of industrial nations, the 'Workshop of the World'. By the mid-1930s the United Kingdom, with a population of some 45 million as against America's 200 million and Germany's 70 million, and with a now dwarfed and outdated 'workshop', was really only a second-rank power. Her financial and industrial strength simply could not carry the load of imperial rearmament about to be imposed on it. According to a report by the Defence Policy and Requirements Committee in November 1935: 'The most serious factor in the completion of the proposed [rearmament] programme is the limited output of our existing resources. The key to the successful completion of the Service programmes lies in the solution of the industrial problem. . . .'[54]

The problem, in short, was to equip modern high-technology armed forces out of a largely low-technology industrial machine. To solve the problem demanded first of all – just as during the Great War – a breakneck major programme of capital investment in advanced-technology industries to manufacture aircraft, aero-engines, instruments, fuse mechanisms, guns. Because of the British machine-tool industry's limited output and old-fashioned designs, the rearmament programme critically depended on imports of foreign machine-tools, mostly American, but also German, Swiss and Hungarian. Between 1935 and 1937 these imports rose from less than 8000 tons to more than 31,000.[55] As a stop-gap while the new factories were being built and equipped Britain also had to import large quantities of foreign military technology – Browning machine-guns from America, Oerlikon guns from Switzerland, Bofors guns from Sweden, aircraft instrumentation from America and Austria, armour plate for new aircraft carriers and cruisers from Czechoslovakia.

By 1938 the volume of all of these imports was running Britain straight towards a balance of payments crisis. In October that year the Chancellor of the Exchequer, Sir John Simon, warned that the Royal Air Force programme alone was 'so costly as to raise serious doubt whether it can be financed beyond 1939-40 without the gravest danger to the country's [financial] stability'.[56] In other words the strategic component of British total strategy was by now dangerously out of phase with the financial-cum-industrial component.

Only a single means existed whereby with one bound John Bull could be free – free, that is, from the dilemma of having to parry the triple threat to Britain and the Empire from Germany, Italy and Japan while going bankrupt in the process. The means was 'appeasement': to reach a deal with one or more of the Empire's potential enemies, and preferably Germany, the nearest to the United Kingdom and the most formidable of the three. The Chiefs of Staff favoured 'appeasement' for obvious strategic reasons. So too did Neville Chamberlain, Prime Minister from 1937 onwards. But Chamberlain also genuinely aspired to 'appease' Europe by negotiating a general political settlement with Hitler. A small-'l' liberal by upbringing, imbued with the moral values and unworldliness of the Victorian public school (Rugby in his case), Chamberlain believed that the key to relations between states lay in mutual goodwill, reason and compromise. But this belief amounted to optimistic fantasy when applied to Adolf Hitler, whose character, ambitions and admiration of brute power were already well known to Chamberlain and his Cabinet. Indeed, just at the time in 1937 when Chamberlain was embarking on his foredoomed attempt to settle the affairs of Europe, he and his colleagues decided that the British Army should in future have no continental role as in 1914, but be equipped for a colonial campaign in the Middle East and for the anti-aircraft defence of the United Kingdom. Thus foreign and defence policies marched smartly away in opposite directions, a nonsense of a total strategy which left Chamberlain's attempts at 'appeasement' backed only by the leverage of the prime-ministerial umbrella. Chamberlain's consequent surrender at Munich in September 1938 disarmed Czechoslovakia by handing over her powerful frontier defences to Germany, swung the military balance in Europe decisively in Hitler's favour, and paved the way for Hitler's occupation of the rest of Czechoslovakia in March 1939.[57]

It was only after the German entry into Prague and an alarm – false, as it turned out – that Germany was about to invade the Low Countries that Britain reversed her isolationist strategy of the previous twenty years and decided that the territorial integrity of France and the Low Countries was after all vital to the United Kingdom, in fact more so than ever in the age of the bomber. The 1937 decision not to prepare the British Army for a continental campaign alongside the French was abruptly reversed. At the end of March, panicked by another false alarm about an imminent German attack on Poland, Chamberlain proceeded to give a guarantee to Poland which Britain had no military means of directly fulfilling – yet another negation of total strategy. Instead he committed Britain to going to war with Germany whenever the Poles should decide that they must defend their independence against German aggression.

When in April 1939 French and British politicians and their military advisers met in London belatedly to recreate the alliance of 1918, the British Chiefs of Staff spelt out the plight into which the existence of the British Empire and the incoherence of British total strategy had finally placed the United Kingdom:

> We are considering a position in which we, allied to France, would be engaged in war with Germany and Italy simultaneously and when Japan would also be a potential enemy. . . . The British Empire and France would thus be threatened at home, in the Mediterranean and in the Far East at the same time, and it would be hard to choose a worse geographical combination of enemies.[58]

The Chiefs of Staff saw the allies' only hope of victory as lying in a war protracted over several years. However, the Under-Secretary at the Treasury warned at the same time that 'if we were under the impression that we were as well able as in 1914 to conduct a long war we were burying our heads in the sand'.[59] Here then was the ultimate disharmony between two essential elements of total strategy, the military and the financial. Whereas Britain could only hope to win a long war, she could only afford a short one.

In other words, once a European war broke out, Britain's total-strategic bankruptcy must inevitably follow. And this it did in 1940–2. Firstly, France, condemned to fight the German Army in May and June 1940 virtually on her own (ten British divisions in the field, ninety-four French), collapsed under the German onslaught. This wrecked Britain's existing war strategy and left her alone (except for a handful of Empire warships and divisions, and the Empire's moral support) against Germany and Italy, and facing the menace from Japan as well. By the turn of the year 1940–1, Britain's overseas assets and her reserves of gold and dollars were near exhaustion. Yet she had committed herself to vast purchases of industrial and military equipment from the United States. By March 1941 Britain's financial resources were utterly at an end. She was, in a word, bankrupt.

From the catastrophic consequences that must follow from this she was rescued at the last moment by the Lend–Lease Act passed by Congress. Henceforward she became, like a patient on a heart–lung machine, dependent for life itself on American subsidies.

The collapse of the actual structure of British world power – it would be more accurate to say façade of world power – took place later, after the Japanese onslaught in the Far East in December 1941. The story is briefly told: two heavy ships, HMS *Prince of Wales* and *Repulse*, despatched to Singapore by Churchill instead of the battlefleet intended under pre-war plans, and soon sunk; the loss of the British Empire in the Far East up to the borders of India; the merciful passing of Australia and New Zealand under American protection. Even so, the United Kingdom was still left with the obligation to fight a major war with Japan for the recovery of her lost colonies (especially Burma) and in defence of India, that famine-stricken burden on scarce shipping resources which she could have dumped in the laps of Indian politicians in the 1930s. Nor was this the whole burden imposed by India, for the United Kingdom also continued to be embroiled in a major war with Italy (aided by German contingents) which would not have occurred but for the British presence in the Mediterranean and the Middle East, a presence the *raison d'être* of which had always been the need to protect the main imperial line of communication to India via the Suez Canal. Yet between 1940 and 1943 this route could not in any case be used because of enemy air and sea power in the Mediterranean. Equally Persian Gulf oil, another reason for the British presence in the Middle East, served only to fuel this imperial theatre of war, while the United Kingdom's own war effort, together with the Royal Navy in Atlantic and northern waters, the Royal Air Force (especially the bomber offensive) and the British Army's campaign in North-west Europe in 1944–5 all depended on oil from the Western hemisphere.[60]

Moreover, by a sour irony, these wartime imperial burdens imposed a heavy financial as well as strategic cost on the United Kingdom, which by 1945 had run up a sterling debt of over £1 billion to India and £475 million to Palestine, Egypt and the Sudan in respect of supplies and services purchased from them. These figures represented no less than 82.6 per cent of the total sterling debt incurred by the United Kingdom in the course of the war[61] – a major item in the terrifying balance sheet of national bankruptcy confronting the new Labour Government after the Japanese surrender.

In his memorandum of 13 August 1945 Lord Keynes, having analysed the total-strategic mess into which Britain had finally got herself by the end of the Second World War, proceeded to discuss the possible ingredients in a new total strategy for getting out of it. The first of these ingredients lay in drastically reducing Britain's costly global overstretch. In Keynes's own words, 'our external policies are very far from being adjusted to impending realities'.[62] Yet to adjust them would not be easy:

> There is likely, however, to be a considerable time lag in reducing such [overseas] expenditure, for three reasons. In the first place, bills for much of the expenditure are received considerably in arrear, and we are responsible in India and Australia (as we are not in the case of Lend Lease supplies) for winding up our munition contracts just as at home. In the second place, the withdrawal of our forces will be protracted on account both of lack of transport and of the slowness of the administrative machine. In the third place (and above all) a substantial part of existing Government expenditure overseas has no direct or obvious connection with the Japanese war and will not, therefore, come to an end merely because the Japs [sic] have packed up. . . .[63]

Then came the nub:

> retrenchment in these other directions will require quite a separate set of Cabinet decisions. Merely as a personal judgement, I should guess that *without any change of policy* [emphasis added] good and energetic management might bring down the annual rate of £800 millions to (say) £300 millions by the end of 1946, although the cost during that year as a whole may not be much less than £450 millions. Any further substantial reduction *will require drastic revisions of policy* [emphasis added] of a kind which do not automatically ensue on V J [sic].

Keynes himself was quite clear that the time had come to shrink Britain's war-bloated world and imperial role and its extravagant annual military cost of £725 million as quickly as politically feasible:

> To an innocent observer in the Treasury very early and very drastic economies in this huge cash expenditure overseas seem an absolute condition of maintaining our solvency. There is no possibility of our obtaining from others for more than a brief period the means of maintaining any significant part of these establishments. . . . These are burdens which there is no reasonable expectation of our being able to carry. . . .

The second ingredient in a new total strategy would consist, wrote Keynes, in 'extreme energy and concentration' on expanding exports while holding down imports. Yet the omens for exports were hardly encouraging despite the present total eclipse of Britain's most formidable pre-war rivals, Germany and Japan, and the hunger of war-starved world markets for goods. For, Keynes pointed out, the limiting factor would lie in 'our physical capacity to develop a sufficient supply . . .'.

CHAPTER TWO

'A Financial Dunkirk'

IN 1943–5 VARIOUS Whitehall committees dealing with what was called 'post war reconstruction' had carried out detailed investigations industry by industry into export prospects.[1] The findings were uniformly gloomy. In June 1944, for example, the Board of Trade turned in a 27-page report which drew the overall conclusion that the export outlook was, in the words of Hugh Dalton (then President of the Board of Trade), 'pretty bleak'.[2] On the assumption that British industry failed to improve its competitive efficiency, and that international trading conditions remained as in the 1930s, the Board of Trade reckoned that 'we cannot expect any appreciable long term improvement of the import/export position for at least two thirds of British manufacturing industry, and there may be some worsening to offset the improvement from the remaining third'. Before the war, the report glumly continued, some British industries had been beaten in world markets on design and cost, others because of the growth of new industrial countries. Moreover, the evidence received from industries over the previous year showed that 'few seem to be contemplating any considerable increase of production or export trade, and many are apprehensive about foreign competition'.

Even more defeatist was an annex to this report summarising the views of individual British industries of every type, from motor-vehicles to clothing and photographic equipment, on likely postwar foreign competition. Almost all pleaded for government protection; almost all feared American competition and a revival of German and Japanese competition; many referred to the growth of new industries making their products in the Commonwealth; many even doubted their ability to hold on to their own home markets. Of the fifty-three industries canvassed, only two, cosmetics and sewage-disposal plant, expressed optimism.[3] It might have been a survey of French Army units in May 1940.

Here is a striking contrast with the legendary wartime industrial effort that inspired so much pride in the British people – the greater degree of mobilisation of resources, human and material, than any other belligerent, the prodigious output of tanks, guns, aircraft, ships;[4] the national genius for invention, as exemplified in the Spitfire, radar, the jet aircraft. And yet the once secret wartime files of the Cabinet and its specialist committees and of the Admiralty and the Ministries of Production and Aircraft Production make clear that in reality, as opposed to propaganda and national legend, British industry's wartime record was all too congruous with the Board of Trade's pessimistic surveys of postwar prospects.[5] The gamut of industries, from old Victorian staples like coal and shipbuilding to advanced technologies like aircraft, machine-tools and even radar, displayed the depressing characteristics of what was to become known in the 1960s and 1970s as the 'British disease'.

In the first place, British wartime productivity per employee lagged behind German and American. In 1944 British coal output per wage earner was only 84 per cent of German, even though the German mines in the Ruhr had long been subject to heavy bombing; in machine-tools British productivity overall through the war amounted to only four-fifths of German. In aircraft, British peak annual productivity in structure weight per man-day was again only four-fifths of German, but less than half of American. In aero-engine output Rolls-Royce in 1944 reached only seven-tenths of Daimler-Benz's productivity, even though the German firm was suffering from the allied bomber offensive and the effects of dispersal of plant.[6] Even that supreme legend, the Spitfire, provides a poor advertisement for British productivity. Partly as a consequence of a design originally derived from a hand-built racing seaplane and ill adapted to mass-production, it took three times as many man-hours to build a Spitfire Mark VC as to construct its equivalent, the Messerschmitt ME 109G.[7]

Because of the desperate wartime need for maximum output from available resources of plant, manpower and machines, the various ministries concerned with production carried out urgent field investigations in order to discover the causes of disappointing productivity. The reports of these teams reveal some familiar villains. The first was the low average quality of British management – partly a matter of poor personal and educational calibre, owing to the unattractiveness of an industrial career in Britain; partly a matter of lack of thorough professional and technical training.

In the coal industry, for example, a Cabinet committee in 1942 investigating falling output and productivity was told by an expert witness: 'It is well-known that for some years it has been found difficult to attract to the Industry a sufficient number of well-educated young men likely to develop into first class mining engineers.'[8] Instead there were too many 'practical men', able by rule-of-thumb to manage a colliery on traditional lines from day to day, but quite incapable of planning and directing a large-scale modern colliery operation as a single integrated machine. In the shipbuilding industry, field investigations in 1942–3 equally found many managements to be 'practical men' of the traditional kind, in this case elderly and timid, deeply resistant to new methods of standardised prefabricated construction, and quite unable to mastermind complex flows of components into the production process, or the production flow through the yards. According to the author of one report: 'The planning of the work and the operation of the shipyard does not appear to have made much progress in the last twenty years. The work proceeds with the maximum effort, and methodical handling of material is rare. . . .'[9]

Nor was the quality of management in the aircraft industry always better, even though in mass-production terms this was an entirely new industry created since 1936. A Whitehall study in November 1944 drew the conclusion: 'Probably the most outstanding single cause of failing to reach a maximum production efficiency in wartime is scarcity of skilled management.'[10] At worst, the aircraft industry's management could offer appalling examples of the survival of the traditional self-taught 'practical man' even in a new technology. At Vickers Armstrong (Aircraft) at Weybridge, a team of Ministry of Production experts found that the assistant to the production manager was a solicitor with no engineering qualifications, while the production manager himself refused to delegate, and insisted on controlling every detail of the factory's operations himself. Labour relations were poor, as was productivity, with skilled labour employed on simple tasks, much idle time, and shifts completing their work quotas hours before the end of the shift. According to this team of experts there existed 'no system of line production throughout the whole organisation'.[11] This was not an exceptional case: the development of the jet engine had to be removed from Rovers because of, according to an official study, the 'chaotic condition of the production organisation'. In any case, Glosters, the makers of the airframe for the new jet aircraft, were, according to the same study, equally chaotic.[12] That same year a team of inspectors from the Ministry of Aircraft Production found the Bristol-group parent aero-engine factory at Bristol to be badly organised, with no proper layout of production lines.[13]

By contrast, a British aircraft industry mission in 1943 to the United States led by Sir Roy Fedden reported enthusiastically on management in the American aircraft industry:

The various production operations are broken down into stages and planned more elaborately in America than in this country. Much time and effort is put into pre-preparation work of scheduling, process planning, machine loading, labour-loading and shop layout, and this is carried out in greater detail in America than is customary in many of our factories. This is considered to be an essential part of obtaining efficient production.[14]

But of course such an approach required an abundance of fully qualified production engineers and technicians, not just the shop-trained ex-apprentices typical of the British aircraft industry.

Across the gamut of wartime industries British management also proved inept, tactless and weak in its leadership of the workforce; and this served only to worsen the other great cause of lagging productivity – the obstructiveness of the trade unions and the lack of commitment of the workers, whether in shipyard, in mine or on the engineering shop-floor. There took place a continual warfare of mostly wild-cat unofficial strikes (official ones being illegal in wartime) and go-slows. There was also a near universal tendency to shorten shifts and lengthen breaks at both ends. These particular symptoms of 'the British disease', which were to become so notorious in the 1960s and 1970s, are bluntly documented in the war years of the 1940s by field investigations into various industries, and tabulated in the weekly 'strike chart' kept by the Ministry of Labour and National Service. More working days were lost through strikes every year from 1942 to 1945 than in 1938, the last full year of peacetime.[15] Coal was far and away the worst offender, with no fewer than 1.2 million man-days and 2 million tons of coal lost in the first quarter of 1944 alone.[16] Usually a coal strike was about wages, which really meant the miner's place in the industrial pecking-order. But one local strike during the Normandy invasion year of 1944, costing 1000 tons of production, took place simply because the miners wanted to get rid of the canteen lady.[17] But strikes only reflected a deeper disgruntlement. In 1944 a visiting team of American mining experts reported that the key to the British problem of lagging production and productivity lay in:

> the bad feeling and antagonism which pervade the industry and which manifests itself in low morale, non-cooperation and indifference. In almost every district we visited, miners' leaders and mine owners complained of men leaving the mines early, failure to clear the faces and voluntary absenteeism.[18]

In mid-1942 a special Cabinet committee on the coal industry was informed by expert witnesses that 'absenteeism, particularly among Coalface workers, was responsible for a greater loss of output than any other single factor . . .' and that it was well known to colliery managers that 'there is a tendency among certain men to take a few days' rest on account of having sustained a very minor accident'.[19] As Harold (later Lord) Wilson put it in his 1945 book *New Deal for Coal*: 'What statistics cannot record, however, is the persistent guerrilla warfare which continued in the majority of pits between management and men.'[20] But neither the nation's dire wartime needs for coal nor the reorganisation of the industry under state control proved enough to solve the problems of poor management and an alienated workforce. Coal output dropped by 4.5 million tons in the second half of 1944 compared with the second half of 1943, while output per man-shift underground sank from 1.44 tons in 1942 to 1.33 tons in 1945.[21] Harold Wilson acknowledged in his book:

> It must be admitted that apart from magnificent efforts in particular districts, the miners did not fully co-operate in securing maximum production. Strikes, ca'canny, and a lower effort all proved that

more could have been done, in spite of the difficulties and the inefficient layout and organisation of the industry.[22]

Here, then, was a classic case of a British industry in every way still fixed in the patterns set during the first stage of the industrial revolution a century and a half before.

With shipbuilding and shiprepairing workforces, the principal problem lay in 'who does what' disputes and stoppages, which abounded in wartime even though Britain stood in desperate danger of losing the Battle of the Atlantic for want of new warships and merchant vessels to replace those sunk by the U-boat. In 1942 an investigating committee on labour in the shipyards reported:

> In certain yards we found an atmosphere based upon an inadequate appreciation of the urgency and gravity of the national situation. In some cases the Management appeared content with the existing position and . . . did not appreciate the need for greater effort. A similar outlook was observed also in the attitude of the Union representatives. . . .[23]

The chairman of this committee, the industrialist Sir Robert Barlow, expressed himself far more bluntly in a private memorandum to the Minister of Production in July 1942, saying that he was convinced 'that a degree of complacency among all concerned permeates the whole field of production'.[24]

Once again poor man-management, an aspect of poor management in general, was much to blame. According to another expert report (the Bentham Report) on shipbuilding in 1942, shipyard managers tended to be older than in other industries, and 'it has not been easy [for them] to shake off the inevitable lethargy of the slump period . . .'.[25] The equivalent legacy of the pre-war slump to the workforce, according to the Barlow Committee in 1943, was a 'not unnatural reluctance . . . readily to admit of a future great expansion of the people in the industry'.[26] In such a defensive attitude, together with the tyranny of traditional custom, lay the roots of the 'who does what' disputes and the stubborn resistance to new technical methods or to 'dilution' of skilled labour by unskilled, even when the nation was in peril of final defeat at the hands of the U-boat. In the words of a Ministry of Labour memorandum in October 1943:

Few industries require the skills of so many different types of craftsmen (each necessarily working in the same confined area) or experience so much difficulty in keeping them continuously employed; it frequently happens that some of the skilled craftsmen are unable to get their work through to time whilst other types of craftsmen are insufficiently occupied. Owing to demarcation restrictions, however, the latter cannot help the former, although technically equipped to do so.[27]

In unrelenting pursuit of such absurdities, worthy of a weird land of nonsense visited by Gulliver, the Amalgamated Engineering Union and the Boilermakers' Society refused to allow appropriately skilled members of the National Union of Railwaymen to work in shipyards; the Electricians' Union in one shipyard refused to work with a non-union electrician and threatened to strike; and the Boilermakers did go on strike in December 1944 in a dispute with the Shipwrights' Union over who should operate a flame-cutting machine. Even day-to-day interchangeability, like an electrician boring the hole for his own wiring, was not achieved on any scale. In the fabrication of ships' ventilators alone, no fewer than seven crafts were involved, some more than once.[28] The men and the unions objected to interchangeability for much the same reasons that they objected to dilution, but even more keenly, for if a skilled man could do another's job then the mere labourer could do it too, and, they feared, at a labourer's rate of pay. Furthermore, they also feared losing the 'ownership' of some part of the production process to another union.

The craft unions in the shipyards also fought strenuously to prevent new technology being introduced that would render their traditional skills and manning levels redundant; and it was the Boilermakers' Society which provided the Old Guard in this largely successful last stand. A Ministry of Labour official groaned in May 1943: 'Whenever dilution is raised, we seem to be brought up against this ghostly squad of unemployed boilermakers.'[29] The opening of a government riveting school was delayed for more than a year because the Boilermakers demanded a promise that the ratio of apprentices to journeymen should not exceed one to five.[30] When and where pneumatic riveting replaced hand-riveting, employers and unions agreed that an additional man, as needed on pre-war hand-riveting, should also be employed. As a Mass-Observation report noted at the time, this man 'has nothing at all to do now, except sit all day beside the riveters. He draws full wages.'[31]

And shipyard workers were not notorious for zeal. One investigating committee reported in 1942:

> We have evidence of a lack of discipline, particularly among the younger men, and of a reluctance to work agreed overtime, and our attention was drawn to what has become a custom whereby workers delay starting work until 10 or 15 minutes after the due time, and begin making their way to the gates 10 or 15 minutes before stopping time.[32]

Nor were the workers and unions in advanced-technology industries such as aircraft or precision engineering more conspicuous for zeal and concern for productivity. As early as 1941 sloth in aircraft factories was causing anxiety. A report on de Havilland at Castle Bromwich, for instance, found 'a marked absence of discipline', 'slackness' and 'difficulty in controlling shop stewards'.[33] In April 1943 the new Production Efficiency Board reported after visiting Coventry firms on Ministry of Aircraft Production contracts that there would be no need for extra labour if the existing labour-force did its stuff. But timings and prices for piece-work made it possible to enjoy 'high earnings without a correspondingly high effort'. Wrote the board: 'in each factory there is evidence of slackness and lack of discipline. Operators are slow in starting work at the beginning of each shift and after each break, and there is a complete stoppage of work from 15 to 30 minutes before each break. . . .'[34]

And then there were the wild-cat strikes, usually over the same parochial grievances as bedevilled the 1970s car industry – for example, over an efficiency check on the use of a machine; or because two fitters had been transferred by management to a different section of the same shop; or over piece-rates for a new machine; or over canteen facilities; or because of the alleged victimisation of a shop-steward.[35]

Meanwhile the craft unions in the aircraft industry and its sub-contracting firms hung on to their demarcations and restrictive practices as stubbornly as their brothers in the shipyards, and likewise despite the 1940 Restoration of Trade Practices Act, which guaranteed that the privileges of the craft unions everywhere would be fully restored after the war. Of all absurdities, the sheet-metal unions sought to maintain that, because for centuries metal had been shaped by craftsmen banging away with hand-tools, then metal shaping for the fuselage of a Spitfire or Lancaster by the power-press and automatic tool in a mass-production factory must be rated as craftsmen's work, and manned and paid as such.[36] It is therefore no wonder that the rise in aircraft output during the Second World War was achieved not by a surge in productivity, but simply by deploying over 100,000 extra machine-tools and over a million extra workers.[37]

Thus even a total war for survival had failed to remedy in British management and the British workforce that smug, stubborn conservatism of outlook and method that had been first identified a century earlier by Cobden and Lyon Playfair, and documented by royal commissions from the 1870s to the 1920s. In fact these failings had actually been encouraged by wartime conditions. For firms on government contracts were subject to no discipline of international or even home-market competition. Those working for the War Office or Ministry of Supply cruised comfortably along on a 'cost-plus' basis, whereby they received a fixed but certain profit on top of whatever their costs turned out to be. Even the fixed-price contracts preferred by the Admiralty and the Air Ministry (later the Ministry of Aircraft Production) were frequently negotiated after production was well advanced – hardly the most effective way to keep costs low and efficiency high.[38] The workforce, for its part, enjoyed 'full employment' to the point where firms were poaching scarce labour from each other. This decisively swung the balance of industrial leverage from management to unions and shop-stewards, and left no effective sanctions to spur efficiency and effort.

Yet the Second World War reveals the survival of other long-standing British industrial weaknesses: a cripplingly narrow base in high-technology resources and skills; a concomitant difficulty in 'technology transfer' from original invention into series production of equipment; and hence a strong dependence on imports of foreign technology. In the first place, the British machine-tool industry proved quite unable to tool Britain's new wartime factories, whether aircraft and aero-engine, munitions, general engineering products or radio and radar.[39] Because the industry's total output was too small and its designs mostly old-fashioned, Britain had to import from the United States some 120,000 American tools. In the peak years of 1940 and 1941 such imports amounted to half Britain's own output. But Britain depended even more on America for highly sophisticated automatic machine-tools. In 1942 imports of automatic lathes amounted to two and a half times Britain's own production; of turret lathes, three times; of vertical drillers, twice. In 1941 Britain found herself totally dependent on America for over twenty types of machine-tool.[40] Without these massive imports British wartime production of high-technology products, from aircraft to radar, guns to instruments, would have been impossible.

It was and is a key facet of Britain's national myth about her marvellous wartime technological achievements that British scientists were responsible for inventing successive generations of radar, of electronic navigation and target-finding devices for Bomber Command such as Oboe and H2S, and radio-proximity fuses for anti-aircraft shells. There is no question that British original research was brilliant, thanks to small groups of world-class scientists recruited from the university research departments that had been created from the late-Victorian era onwards, especially the Clarendon Laboratory at Oxford and the Cavendish Laboratory at Cambridge. But the problem lay in the gulf between these scientists and the industries that were asked to manufacture their inventions. For the British radio industry in peacetime had been largely a backwater compared with the German or American, mostly assembling simple radio sets from imported components. Its technical staff and production management were too often of the classic British model – their knowledge and skills acquired, to cite a 1943 Whitehall report, 'by practical experience in the Industry, though they may have no academic qualifications'.[41] The problem of 'technology transfer' was rendered the more difficult because the scientists, fresh from their ivory laboratories, had little concept of designing products in terms of easy manufacture. Moreover, the shortage of highly trained production engineers and managers competent to plan and control complex production flows led to severe muddles and hold-ups in the factories. Immense delays therefore occurred between original research and development and the subsequent delivery of radio and radar kits to the armed forces, delays not so much of months as of years. To cite one example, the Mark III Identification Friend or Foe radar originated as an idea in 1939, was ready for series production by the end of 1941, but a year later was still meeting (according to a Whitehall committee) a 'serious setback' owing to 'delays in production of certain vital components'.[42] Similar

39

delays occurred with Oboe and H2S for Bomber Command, 3cm radar for U-boat hunting, and VHF (Very High Frequency) radios.[43]

Caught short again by the deficiencies of her own industrial base, in this case the radio and precision-engineering industries, Britain had no alternative but once more to turn to the United States for rescue. Without huge supplies of American thermionic valves and radio components, the vaunted British inventions in the radar field would have remained useless laboratory toys. In April 1943 it was estimated that imports of electronic items from the United States in that year would equal four-fifths of British production by volume. For certain special categories, like the magnetron, Britain was particularly dependent on North American supplies.[44]

The roots of this problem of technology transfer, so widespread in British industries – the gulf between the handful of world-class scientists and the second-class ruck of ill-qualified industrial managers and technicians – lay deeper than industry itself; it lay in the continuing failure between the world wars to provide an education and training system comparable to those of Britain's trade rivals. For example, German output of graduate electrical engineers in the one year 1937, at 448, amounted to more than half the cumulative British total for the fourteen years 1925–39, of 781.[45] The number of students studying science and technology in British universities actually fell between 1918 and 1939; and in 1939 those studying technology amounted to less than 10 per cent of the total student body.[46] Britain still had no equivalent of the German *Technische Hochschulen*. With regard to the quality of the 'NCOs' and rank-and-file of industry, Britain just before the war had proportionally less than half the German total of youngsters between the ages of sixteen and twenty-one in full-time vocational training.[47] Worse, Britain had still failed to provide that adequate basic education to the nation on which alone, as the Schools Enquiry Commission pointed out in 1868, technical education can rest. The overwhelming majority of British youngsters were dumped into the job market at age fourteen with no vocational qualifications at all, and little hope of further part-time education and training. The 1938 total for England and Wales of about 20,000 youngsters in day-continuation schools compares with the German total of over 1,800,000.[48] These are the statistics of the 'dense ignorance' (to use the words of the Royal Commission on Technical Instruction in 1884) that still remained a disabling feature of the British workforce. Thus British technology rested on shoddy human foundations, in a stark contrast with the brilliant ornaments of world-class science at its apex.

The audit of war thus plainly demonstrates that Britain as an industrial society needed fundamental reforms and reconstruction, all long overdue; massive capital investment in rebuilding and re-equipping obsolete plant and infrastructure; a huge expansion of education at all levels, especially vocational and technical. It no less plainly demonstrates that the British people and their governing elite needed to shed the double illusion, too long cherished, that the existence of the British Commonwealth buttressed the strength of the United Kingdom, and that thanks to this the United Kingdom constituted a world power. And what sharper spur to the adoption of a realistic total strategy could there be than Britain's immediate postwar plight of bankruptcy?

Lord Keynes, grappling with this immediate plight in his paper of 13 August 1945, bravely strove to be optimistic about Britain's medium-term export prospects, writing that if 'to cheer ourselves up, we make bold to assume that by 1949 we have reached the goal of increasing the volume of exports by 50 per cent, the value of exports in that year, at double pre-war prices, would be £1,450 millions'.[49] When invisible income was added in at a guesstimated total of £150 million, he went on, and assuming that the growth of imports had been kept down and government overseas expenditure had been steadily cut, 'we can produce the following pipe dream': to wit, that the balance of payments could be brought into equilibrium by 1949.[50]

Unfortunately, according to Keynes's calculations even this 'pipe dream' would still leave Britain facing a truly enormous cumulative net deficit of £1250 million over the three years 1946, 1947 and 1948. 'Where, on earth,' Keynes asked his Cabinet readers, 'is all this money to come from?'

> The conclusion is inescapable that there is no source from which we can raise sufficient funds *to enable us to live and spend on the scale we contemplate* [emphasis added] except the United States. . . .

Keynes therefore reckoned that Britain would have to cadge a loan of about $5 billion from the United States. But spending 'on the scale we contemplate' included the extra future load of costs on the British economy represented by New Jerusalem, that 'happier future' for the British people promised by the Labour Party's election manifesto. Keynes did not go into this in detail, merely remarking that, if the Americans refused to be touched for $5 billion, it would render 'the economic basis for the hopes of the public non existent'.

Keynes summed up his outline 'total strategy' for the United Kingdom thus:

> there are three essential conditions without which we have not a hope of escaping what might be described, without exaggeration and without implying we should not eventually recover from it, a financial Dunkirk. These conditions are (a) an intense concentration on the expansion of exports, (b) drastic and immediate economies in our overseas expenditure, and (c) substantial aid from the United States on terms which we can accept. They can only be fulfilled by a combination of the greatest enterprise, ruthlessness and tact.[51]

Keynes made it clear that the most urgent of these conditions lay in negotiating an American loan to fill the gap left by the early ending of Lend–Lease. But if Britain failed in this 'tough proposition', how could she cope with the resulting 'financial Dunkirk'? Wrote Keynes:

> Abroad it would require a sudden and humiliating withdrawal from our onerous responsibilities with great loss of prestige and an acceptance for the time being of the position of a second class Power, rather like the present position of France. From the Dominions and elsewhere we should seek what charity we could obtain. At home a greater degree of austerity would be necessary than we have experienced at any time during the war. And there would have to be an indefinite postponement of the realisation of the best hopes of the Government [this was clearly a reference to New Jerusalem]. . . .

Another government economic adviser, J. E. Maude of the Economic Section of the Cabinet Secretariat, agreed with Keynes that to carry on without an American loan would mean 'a withdrawal from the part of a major power in the strategic and diplomatic affairs of the external world'.[52]

Thus even such objective minds as Keynes's and Maude's failed to draw the logical conclusion from their own analyses (let alone from the historical record) that the United Kingdom was indeed only in the second rank of nation-states; or draw the further conclusion that she should therefore abandon the costly and distracting attempt to play the role of 'a major power in the strategic and diplomatic affairs of the external world'. On the contrary, Keynes and Maude both assumed that, if the Americans would lend Britain $5 billion to tide her over until her exports recovered, then she could, and moreover *should*, go on fulfilling this role. In other words, an unquantified portion of the loan would be used to bolster British pretensions to world-power status rather than to invest in modernising the real source of the United Kingdom's strength and wealth, the British industrial machine.

Nor was this the only diversion of borrowed dollars from industrial reconstruction to other purposes clearly implied by Keynes's outline total strategy. A further unquantified portion of the loan would be used to enable a start to be made on constructing New Jerusalem, as well as to improve the British people's austere living standards. Even the poet Blake, who had first coined the phrase about building New Jerusalem in England's green and pleasant land, had never imagined doing so on foreign tick.

It was hardly likely that the Labour Cabinet themselves would dissent from Keynes's views on Britain's present and future. Its members stood committed to New Jerusalem by their general election manifesto and a lifetime of idealistic faith. Half of them had served as ministers in the wartime coalition when Britain waged war apparently on an equal footing with the United States and the Soviet Union. The Foreign Secretary, Ernest Bevin, was a robust working-class patriot resolved to maintain Britain's traditional place in the world. Within the Whitehall bureaucracy, too, all wartime planning by the Foreign Office and the Chiefs of Staff with regard to Britain's postwar foreign policy and grand strategy had assumed that Britain, at the centre of the Commonwealth, was and would remain the 'third world power' alongside the United States and the Soviet Union, complete with the traditional pattern of garrisons, bases, fleets and air forces scattered across the Mediterranean, Middle East and Far East.[53] The Chiefs of Staff themselves in August 1945, Field Marshal Lord Alanbrooke (Chief of the Imperial General Staff), Admiral of the Fleet Lord Cunningham of Hyndhope (First Sea Lord and Chief of Naval Staff) and Marshal of the Royal Air Force Lord Portal (Chief of the Air Staff), had all held their present appointments during the Second World War, responsible for conducting British strategy at the highest level and meeting their American opposite numbers as equal partners. It was not to be expected that now in the afterglow of victory they would suddenly perceive that the United Kingdom was in reality a second-rank power, and that her world and imperial commitments represented not assets but expensive liabilities. In any case the present generation of the governing elite – senior politicians (including the Conservative Opposition led by Churchill), civil servants and military leaders – were all late Victorians and Edwardians by upbringing and education. It would have been hard, perhaps impossible, for them now to question the presumptions about Britain's place in the world which had been stamped into their minds in childhood and young manhood and by which they had lived ever since.

Therefore 'drastic revisions of policy' of the kind hinted at by Keynes were unthinkable – and certainly unthought by the Labour Cabinet and their advisers. Even when the Americans were demonstrating the warmth of the 'special relationship' by driving the hardest possible bargain with the British loan negotiators in Washington,[54] the majority of an anguished Cabinet came to the conclusion that to do without a loan would demand unacceptable sacrifices.[55] As Hugh Dalton, the Chancellor of the Exchequer, pointed out to his Cabinet colleagues in one such discussion, 'failure to reach agreement with the United States, with the consequent shortages of food and luxuries, such as tobacco, would be disastrous for the Government'.[56] In the 1930s Reichsmarschall Göring had coined the slogan 'Guns Before Butter'; here instead was a new variant, 'Tobacco Before Machine-Tools'. Britain therefore swallowed the American terms: a loan of $3.75 billion, instead of the $5 billion originally hoped for, at an interest of 2 per cent per annum; the capital sum to be repaid in fifty annual instalments starting on 31 December 1951. The Americans imposed the condition (harsh enough in view of Britain's financial straits and uncertain economic prospects) that sterling should be freely convertible into any currency twelve months after Congress formally approved the loan.[57]

And so in the course of the painful debate over national bankruptcy and the related negotiations for an American loan, the Labour Cabinet and its advisers had settled almost by default on

44

Britain's total strategy for the postwar era – that is, to persist in the ruinous make-believe that the United Kingdom was a first-class world power, and at the same time pursue the dream of New Jerusalem: a double burden of costs to be loaded on the back of a war-impoverished, obsolescent and second-rank industrial economy.

CHAPTER THREE

'Our Position as a Great Power'

the picture was a very gloomy one. An economic survey which had been made of our position in the year 1946 showed that we would be nearly one million men short of the minimum needed to revive our export trade, and to carry out the other necessary tasks in the civilian field. He was very much worried by the very large expenditure overseas, and he had had a letter from the Governor of the Bank of England, who was also extremely disturbed. . . . Could we possibly afford to continue in this way?

Thus, according to the minutes of the first meeting that year of the Cabinet Defence Committee, on 11 January 1946, did the Chancellor of the Exchequer, Dr Hugh Dalton, warn his colleagues.

It appeared likely [he proceeded in answer to his own question] that the total sum which the Service Departments and the Ministry of Supply would ask the Treasury to find would be in the neighbourhood of £2,000 million. This was a figure we could not possibly afford. It should be viewed in relation to the £500 million which the examination conducted by the Coalition Government had shown to be the figure which we should aim at for our peacetime expenditure on defence. . . . The whole picture of defence manpower and expenditure appears out of scale, and if there was no quick drop, particularly abroad, in the expenditure, he could not promise anything but economic disaster.[1]

How then could this fact of Britain's bankruptcy be reconciled with the make-believe that she was and would remain 'a great power' (in the words of the Foreign Secretary and the Chiefs of Staff in 1946 and the Defence White Paper of 1948)[2] and 'a centre of world influence and power' (as the Minister of Defence was to put it in 1949)?[3] In this self-inflicted dilemma the Labour Government and its military advisers were to wriggle and writhe year after year.

At this first 1946 meeting of the Cabinet Defence Committee the Prime Minister asked the First Sea Lord (Admiral of the Fleet Lord Cunningham) how long it would be necessary to maintain 'a comparatively large fleet in the Pacific'. The First Sea Lord answered that 'the object of keeping the fleet there in its present strength was to show the flag. The Americans had a very large fleet out there, and it was not thought right to reduce our fleet too much. . . .'[4] The Foreign Secretary agreed; he 'felt that the British Pacific Fleet should be kept at good strength until the Control Council in Japan had got into its stride' – in the event, a vain hope and a vain expense, because General MacArthur was to rule Japan as an American proconsul, paying no heed to the Control Council, let alone to the pretensions of the British. The Chief of the Air Staff, Marshal of the Royal Air Force Lord Tedder, justified the stationing of twelve squadrons of bombers in the Mediterranean theatre as 'our striking force in case of need in any of the countries where trouble might take place, such as Italy, Greece, Palestine etc. It was a political question whether or not a striking force might be dispensed with.'

The last comment equally applied of course to all the land, sea and air forces left dumped across the world by the subsiding flood of war. But the Foreign Secretary, Ernest Bevin, took the view that Britain should cut her commitments only when and where outstanding international questions were resolved, even though he assured his colleagues that 'the cost of settling this war gave him as much anxiety as it did the Chancellor of the Exchequer . . .'.[5]

When the Cabinet Defence Committee met again on 21 January, Dalton pointed out that the likely financial deficit in 1946 'would be very largely covered' if the manpower in the armed forces could be cut by half a million men and the bill for munitions trimmed by £150 million.[6] At this point, Attlee, shrewd and matter-of-fact as a solicitor or accountant advising a profligate family, pronounced that

> there was no doubt that the nation could not afford either the
> manpower or the money for forces of the size suggested by the

47

Chiefs of Staff. A cut in the size of the forces was unavoidable. The cut could not be large in June, mainly for the reasons of foreign policy which had been explained by the Foreign Secretary at the previous meeting, but it would have to be drastic after that date.[7]

Cunningly the Prime Minister sought to avoid becoming bogged in swamps of argument over details of strategic commitments and the force levels needed to meet them: 'better', said he, 'for Government to lay down ceilings for June and December 1946 . . .'. This, to the dismay of the listening Chiefs of Staff and service ministers, he proceeded to do:

> In estimating those ceilings, he had taken into account the fact that there were [sic] now in existence no foreign Navy worthy of the name other than that of the United States. Similarly, there was no Air Force worth speaking of other than the Russian and the American. It seemed therefore that in the immediate future we could afford to make more drastic cuts in these Services than the Army, where there were a great number of commitments that could not be liquidated.

He therefore proposed total manpower ceilings for all three armed services of 1,900,000 at 30 June 1946, and 1,100,000 at 31 December, as against the COS's figures of 2,068,000 and 1,440,000.[8] This pronouncement had something of the agitating effect of a hand-grenade rolled down the table. The First Lord of the Admiralty, A. V. Alexander, doubted whether the Royal Navy could be slimmed as much as the Prime Minister wished because the Navy 'had considerable commitments, particularly in the Far East. There were more than 190,000 men East of Suez, and a large number of assault craft were still being used in the Far East to fetch and carry. . . .' The Chief of Air Staff, Lord Tedder, similarly argued that the Royal Air Force 'were faced with occupational commitments, with commitments in the Far East and the Mediterranean and a large transport commitment . . .'. With regard to the Army, the Prime Minister himself remarked that he had suggested a cut of only 35,000 men at 30 June 1946 'because of the many commitments with which we were faced'.

But which of these 'commitments' of all three armed forces

derived from the hangover of war, which of them was essential to the security and prosperity of the United Kingdom itself, and which merely furthered Britain's costly pretensions to 'world influence' as a 'great power'?

In 1945–6 the hangover of the war with Japan found British forces in French Indo-China and the Dutch East Indies (sometimes with Japanese troops under command) holding the fort for European empire until the former rulers could return in sufficient strength to resist local demands for independence. In Indo-China this happy event (for the British military) occurred as early as October 1945; in the Dutch East Indies not until November 1946. In any case the numbers of United Kingdom forces were small, and subsumed in the total for South-East Asia Command (including the British colonies of Malaya and Borneo) in May 1946 of 12,700 soldiers, 21,600 airmen and 177 aircraft.[9] In Japan the British occupation contingent consisted of some 3000 soldiers, 1200 airmen and fifty-two aircraft, plus that other hangover of the Japanese war, the 'show the flag' British Pacific Fleet of two battleships, two carriers, seven cruisers, sixteen destroyers and thirty-four other vessels.[10] Except for this impressive fleet, all these various Far Eastern legacies of the war amounted to little enough when measured against a total of over 2 million men in the armed forces as at 30 June 1946.[11]

In the case of the Mediterranean and Middle East theatre it is harder to distinguish the military detritus left behind by the Second World War from commitments arising either from the sharpening Cold War with the Soviet Union or from the British desire to play the world power. In Iran the British occupation force was down to only 600 men by March 1946 and due for early withdrawal, but in the former Italian colony of Libya the garrison of over 20,000 soldiers plus an air component[12] now constituted a part not so much of the hangover from the Second World War as of the postwar British binge on 'world power' (see below, pp. 62 and 80). In Greece two divisions (successors to the occupation forces which had entered the country on the heels of the German withdrawal in 1944) were shoring up the Greek government against Communist rebels.[13] In Italy the campaign of 1943–5 had left as its residue a British occupation force of three divisions (some 50,000 soldiers) stationed in the province of Venezia Giulia. However, in 1946 the Western allies were disputing with

Communist Yugoslavia and the Soviet Union whether the province, and especially the city of Trieste, should belong to Yugoslavia or Italy. They were also arguing long and hard with the Soviet Union over the terms of a general peace treaty with Italy. These troops had therefore now become a useful tool of diplomatic leverage, potentially even a defence against Yugoslav aggression. It could therefore be argued that they (and perhaps even the divisions in Greece) were indirectly serving the United Kingdom's own security, which, as the pre-war period had painfully taught reluctant British statesmen, could not be separated from the security of Europe as a whole.

This applied even more strongly to the British occupation forces north of the Alps: 60,000 soldiers in Austria and some 200,000 in Germany (together with over 200 aircraft and some 20,000 air personnel). Facing Soviet armies in dismaying strength across the zonal borders, they constituted the diplomatic front line between Western hopes of a general European settlement (including peace treaties with Germany and Austria) and surly Soviet intransigence.[14] Finally, stationed at home were some 200,000 soldiers and another 200,000 air personnel (with over 1000 aircraft),[15] together with a Home Fleet of two battleships, two fleet carriers and two other carriers, seven cruisers, sixteen destroyers, twenty-five submarines and sixty-two other types of vessel.[16]

Such, then, was the sum of the military detritus of the Second World War plus those other forces at home or on the continent of Europe which, in the context of the 'cold war', could be deemed essential to the security of the United Kingdom herself.

However, to support British pretensions to be a world power the Labour Government (and a Conservative Government led by that inveterate late-Victorian romantic, Winston Churchill, would hardly have done otherwise) was directly committing in 1946 something like a fifth of the total trained strength of the British army, a third of the Royal Air Force's total number of squadrons,[17] and between a half and two-thirds (depending on the class of ship) of the Royal Navy's total active fleet. In round numbers the Mediterranean Sea, the Middle East, India, South-east Asia and the Pacific were swallowing up over 140,000 soldiers and over 78,000 air personnel and 700 aircraft;[18] two battleships, a fleet carrier, four light fleet carriers, twenty cruisers, forty destroyers, twenty submarines, and 102 other types of vessel, plus four cruisers and four escorts giving cocktail parties in the America and

West Indies Station and the Africa Station.[19] To these figures of fighting forces have to be added the disproportionate costs of resupply, reliefs and base facilities so far from home and in backward countries.

It is therefore clear that the crux of the problem of reconciling military costs with national impoverishment lay in this fantasy of the United Kingdom as a present and future 'centre of world influence and power'. Nonetheless, Bevin at the Foreign Office, the service ministers and the Chiefs of Staff were to go on cherishing this fantasy in the years to come, even though the resulting commitments were to be keenly questioned by realists in Whitehall (not least by the Prime Minister) on both strategic and financial grounds.

With the logic of a fairy story, belief in the world-power fantasy depended on a continuing belief in another fantasy – that the British Empire (now bowdlerised into 'Commonwealth') constituted a total-strategic asset to the United Kingdom rather than a liability.

In Attlee's own words as wartime Deputy Prime Minister back in 1943, one year after Britain had proved unable to defend the Empire against simultaneous attack from Germany, Italy and Japan:

> I take it to be a fundamental assumption that whatever post-war international organisation is established, it will be our aim to maintain the British Commonwealth as an international entity, recognised as such by foreign countries. . . . If we are to carry our full weight in the post-war world with the US and the USSR it can only be as a united British Commonwealth.[20]

Already during the latter years of the Second World War Whitehall had begun to frame a postwar global strategy along these traditional lines, in defiance of all-too-recent wartime proof that this imperial connection represented not strength, but enfeebling over-stretch.[21] The postwar Labour Government followed suit, seeking to reforge the strategic links between Britain and the Commonwealth rather than allow them finally to rust apart. In particular it sought to build anew that very United Kingdom–Australia–New Zealand axis which had placed the Admiralty in such a quandary from the mid-1930s until the final débâcle in Malaya in 1941–2, when the burden of defending Australia and New Zealand had mercifully passed from Britain to America. This neo-Edwardian vision of Empire even inspired postwar British policy towards civil aviation. Could not air transport draw the scattered Dominions and colonies together in a new Commonwealth unity? In 1945 Whitehall revived the Edwardian fantasy of an imperial army and navy in the new guise of a Commonwealth airways corporation. The fantasy quickly faded in the cold light of the Dominions' determination once again to go their own independent way.[22] Nonetheless, the question of Commonwealth air routes and British aircraft to fly them was to continue to dominate British civil aviation policy for years to come.[23]

However, as early as September 1945 (in the midst of the crisis caused by the abrupt end of Lend–Lease) Attlee himself had begun to doubt whether the traditional Commonwealth strategy based on a British military and naval presence in the Mediterranean and Middle East really fitted the facts of the postwar world:

> the British Commonwealth and Empire is not a unit that can be defended by itself. It was the creation of seapower. With the advent of air warfare the conditions which made it possible to defend a string of possessions scattered over five continents by means of a fleet based on island fortresses have gone. . . . The British Empire can only be defended by its membership of the United Nations Organisation. If the new organisation is a reality, it does not matter who holds Somalia or Cyrenaica or controls the Suez Canal. If it is not a reality we had better be thinking of the defence of England, for unless we can protect the home country no strategic positions elsewhere will avail.[24]

In February 1946 the Prime Minister told the Cabinet Defence Committee that 'he hoped that the strategic assumption that it was vital to us to keep open the Mediterranean, and that in fact we would, should be re-examined'.[25] But the First Lord of the Admiralty, A. V. Alexander, who had also served as First Lord in the wartime coalition, demurred: 'As to the Mediterranean, the cost to us of its closure during the war had been so great, in terms of shipping, that if it was at all possible we ought to keep it open. . . .' Next month a now deeply perturbed Attlee again questioned this key assumption shared by the First Sea Lord, the Foreign Secretary and the Chiefs of Staff that, in Attlee's words, 'strategy demands that there should be no potentially hostile power flanking our sea or air communications through the Mediterranean and Red Sea':[26]

This assumption, which is in my view based on a strategy formulated in the past, is that this line of communication is vital to the interests of the British Commonwealth and Empire and that it is possible under modern conditions of warfare to render it secure. In my opinion neither of these propositions is self-evident. . . .

He again pointed out that the British Empire, including the British presence in the Mediterranean and Middle East, had been built up in the era of the Royal Navy's maritime supremacy. Yet in the Second World War the Mediterranean Fleet had lost control of that sea in the face of enemy shore-based airpower, compelling Britain to switch her imperial line of communication to the Cape route:*

> The advent of airpower means that instead, as in the era of navalism, of being able to maintain the route [through the Mediterranean and Suez Canal] by the possession of Malta and Gibraltar and by a friendly attitude on the part of Egypt, we must now provide very large air forces in North Africa, large military forces in Egypt and Palestine and also large sums of money for the [balance of payments] deficit areas, such as Cyrenaica and Libya, if we wish to occupy them as air force bases.
>
> In the Red Sea, where formerly we had only to maintain Aden we have now to keep on good terms with Ibn Saud [King of Saudi Arabia], and also apparently to occupy Eritrea and Somaliland, which are also deficit areas.

Attlee therefore 'considered that we cannot afford to provide the great sums of money for the large forces involved on the chance of being able to use the Mediterranean route in time of war . . .', and he therefore queried 'whether the benefits which we should have to purchase at so great a cost are worth while'. As for the oilfields of South Persia and Iraq, '. . . I suggest that we are not in a position to defend this area against a determined attack from the North.'

What in fact Attlee was offering in this paper was nothing short of an alternative grand strategy for the postwar era founded on realistic appraisal of the United Kingdom's economic strength and its own security needs: a strategy of timely retreat from traditional commitments and ideas.

* From 1940 to late 1943.

In the changed conditions of the world and in the modern conditions of three dimensional warfare, it is, I think, necessary to review with an open mind strategic conceptions which we have held for many years. In the present era we must consider very carefully how to make the most of our limited resources. We must not, for sentimental reasons, give hostages to fortune. It may be we shall have to consider the British Isles as an easterly extension of a strategic area the centre of which is the American Continent than [sic] as a Power looking eastwards through the Mediterranean and the East.

Attlee therefore requested the Chiefs of Staff to furnish the Cabinet Defence Committee with a fresh grand-strategic appreciation.

The Prime Minister's paper must be accounted one of the most penetrating and percipient written by any British statesman in the twentieth century. It tackled the fundamental problem shirked by all pre-war British governments and indeed all postwar British governments up to the 1990s – that of getting British politico-military commitments and British resources into proper proportion. But it evoked a swift counter-attack by Ernest Bevin, who in regard to his battering-ram espousal of the 'world role' throughout his term of office was to prove an altogether disastrous foreign secretary. Bevin acknowledged that Britain could indeed do without the Mediterranean route in a future war just as in the last war, but then went on to assert:

> a very great political issue is involved which affects us more from the peace-time point of view. The Mediterranean is the area through which we bring influence to bear on southern Europe, the soft underbelly of France, Italy, Yugoslavia, Greece and Turkey. Without our physical presence in the Mediterranean we should cut little ice with those States, which would fall, like Eastern Europe, under the totalitarian yoke. . . . If we move out of the Mediterranean, Russia will move in, and the Mediterranean, from the point of view of commerce and trade, economy and democracy, will be finished. . . .[27]

Britain, averred Bevin, was 'the last bastion of social democracy' between United States capitalism and Soviet Communism. In the event of conflict between them in the Mediterranean after a British withdrawal, 'we, having forfeited our position, should lack the power to bring conciliatory influence'.

Two things may be noted about this effusion. The first is its enunciation of what might be called the 'vacuum theory' of world strategy, to become a favourite with the United States in the 1960s: that is, the alleged necessity to hang on to a region for fear that otherwise the Soviet Union would move in to fill the vacuum. However, it follows that if such a region constitutes an expensive exercise in overstretch for the existing incumbent, then it must equally do so for the usurper – as was to be demonstrated by the self-defeating Soviet penetrations of south-east Asia and Africa in the 1960s and 1970s. The second interesting point lies in Bevin's iterated use of the word 'influence', which – along with 'prestige' and 'status' – was to become part of the language of the world-power lobby (or, at least, great-power lobby) in British government from the 1940s to the 1990s. Neither Bevin in 1946 nor anyone ever afterwards cared to define exactly what 'influence', 'status' and 'prestige' actually mean in hard terms of leverage. It is fair to suggest that, for the no-longer-strong, such vague though grand language serves as a delusive but psychologically reassuring substitute for real power.

On 30 March 1946 the Chiefs of Staff (Cunningham, Alanbrooke and Tedder) sketched a resplendent vision of a global Commonwealth defence system. It would consist of four 'world zones' each with its own co-ordinated command structure and inter-service headquarters – a Mediterranean and Middle East Zone, an Indian Zone, a South-East Asian Zone and a combined Australian and New Zealand Zone (although this, they wrote, might be divided into two zones, as the Dominion governments chose).[28] Three days later they submitted the fresh grand-strategic appreciation requested by Attlee, except that far from being 'fresh' it proved to be intellectually stale. Entitled 'The Strategic Position of the British Commonwealth',[29] it trotted out the familiar clichés unquestioned. The basis of Commonwealth strategy against the Soviet Union ('the only possible enemy'), wrote the Chiefs, would lie in 'main support areas' containing 'concentrations of manpower, industrial potential or sources of food or raw material . . . essential to our war effort'. These comprised the United Kingdom, the American continent (including South America), Africa south of the Sahara (including East Africa), and Australia and New Zealand.

The position of the United Kingdom is peculiar in that it contains 63 per cent of the white man-power of the British Commonwealth and an even greater proportion of its industrial potential. . . . Eventually it may be possible to build up the war potential of the Dominions to such an extent that the relative importance of the United Kingdom will be diminished, but short of mass immigration, which at present appears impracticable, the United Kingdom's contribution in war-making potential will remain high.

Needless to say, the Chiefs of Staff did not draw from this analysis the obvious conclusion that, just as in the past, the Commonwealth served not as a boost to British power but as a drag on it. Instead they swept on to express the hope that India too (after independence) would become a 'main support area'.

With regards to the Middle East, wrote the COS,

It may be argued that we can afford to abandon this area, that we should thereby place between ourselves and a potential enemy large tracts of difficult country, and thus compel him, in order to extend his influence further, to fight at the end of long and difficult lines of communication, and that we are unlikely in any case to be able to hold the area in war.

But on the contrary the Chiefs of Staff believed that the Middle East was vital on both strategic and political grounds. It was the land-bridge between the continents of Europe, Asia and Africa. It controlled the eastern Mediterranean and one main gateway to the Indian Ocean. It offered the easiest route for a European–Asian power to penetrate Africa. Moreover, if the Soviet Union could gain control of Egypt and Palestine, it would enjoy a ready-made base area for moving on into Africa. 'Such an extension would prejudice our position both in North-west Africa . . . and in the Indian Ocean. It would be the first step in a direct threat to our main support area of Southern Africa.' Then again, the COS pointed to the vital importance of Middle East oil,[30] although it turned out in later discussions of this topic that the principal function of the oil would be, as in the Second World War, to fuel allied forces in the Middle East theatre rather than in the United Kingdom and the European theatre.[31] In any event – and here the COS quoted from the paper written by their principal ally, the Foreign

Secretary – from the political point of view 'our presence in the Mediterranean is vital to our position as a great power. On it depends our influence on Spain, France, Italy, Yugoslavia, Greece and Turkey, and with that goes all we stand for as the last bastion of social democracy.'[32]

The COS had not, however, entirely forgotten the question of Britain's own survival. In yet another reprise of a pre-war theme they wrote:

> In view of the direct threat to the United Kingdom which would result from the loss of France and the Low Countries, and of the threat to our sea communications which would result from the loss of Scandinavia, it is clearly of the greatest importance to us that Western Europe should not fall under Russian domination. . . .

By way of finale the COS trumpeted: 'Our main strategic requirements are based principally upon facts of geography and the distribution of man-power and natural resources which do not change.' Since they had earlier acknowledged that Britain herself supplied the bulk of the industrial and human strength of the Commonwealth, this is an astonishingly illogical statement for them to have made. No less astonishing is the complacent certainty of their closing utterance: 'We consider that the basic principles of strategy set out above will not be radically altered by new developments in methods or weapons of warfare.'

The Chiefs of Staff had thus done their best to shut the door against the Prime Minister's unwelcome cold blast of reality. In its combination of grandiosity of vision with dubious but unquestioned assumptions, their report resembled a prospectus issued by some fraudulent company promoter – even though in the present case the authors were deceiving themselves as much as others. Its gravest flaw lay in the COS's 'basic principles of strategy', which, when coupled with their earlier proposal of four 'world zones' of strategic responsibility, could only signify a disastrous return to the pre-war opposite pulls between the United Kingdom's own defence (including the defence of Western Europe) and her far-off imperial commitments. In any event their global design as a whole took no note of Britain's current condition of poverty, debt and industrial backwardness. Therefore the true leitmotiv of their paper was that of total-strategic overstretch prolonged into the far future.

On 5 April the Cabinet Defence Committee debated this COS appreciation along with the design for a global British Commonwealth military structure based on four 'world zones' of responsibility.[33] Alanbrooke (the CIGS) and Tedder (CAS) argued that Britain must retain her military presence in the Mediterranean and Middle East not only as a kind of buffer to absorb Soviet attack while Britain was mobilising her resources, but also as a base in which to station bombers with atomic bombs to serve as a deterrent, or from which in case of war to launch a nuclear offensive against Soviet territory. The Foreign Secretary agreed with the COS that:

> we must maintain our influence in the Mediterranean. It was impossible to retain the necessary diplomatic strength if military support was withdrawn, and in his view, Russia only respected nations which had the power to command respect. At the same time, our presence in the Mediterranean served a purpose other than military, which was very important to our position as a great Power. . . .

Bevin then repeated his claim that this presence enabled Britain to have 'influence' on every state round the shores of that sea, from Spain to Turkey. Moreover, the Middle East was, in his opinion, of great economic value to Britain: 'a thorough development of the Middle East trade area, particularly in a belt stretching from West Africa to East Africa, could offset the cost of retaining the small defence commitment in the Mediterranean'. Here again was a positively late-Victorian vision, in this case economic, wherein vast tracts of territory inhabited by peoples described by a 1948 Colonial Office report as 'on the margin of subsistence'[34] were perceived as assets.

The Dominions Secretary, for his part, declared that in view of the 'magnificent military and political advantages (in peace and war) he could see no reason for withdrawing our influence from the Mediterranean'.[35]

The Prime Minister rowed as best he could against this tide of nostalgic illusion. He pointed out that what could be termed the 'protective' zones (lying outside the COS's 'main support areas') in Europe, the western Mediterranean and the Middle East included:

> groups of comparatively weak nations. If the security of these groups was to be assured, they were in need of a strong defensive

organisation to support their resources. Would the British Empire be able to provide sufficient forces to guarantee this support? He considered that Russian policy in the Middle East might take the form of gradual infiltration of political influence and ideologies. We might be faced with a gradual series of political intrigues. . . . In his view it was very doubtful if we could provide the forces on such a scale as would be necessary to support a 'forward' policy in the Mediterranean and Middle East.[36]

However, the Prime Minister could do no more than persuade his colleagues that there ought to be further study before a final decision was taken over issues with such far-reaching consequences, where-upon the Defence Committee turned to the more congenial question of where best to locate the British forces in the Middle East. The Foreign Secretary put forward his new wheeze of establishing a new main base in East Africa instead of Egypt; a wheeze which he was to go on forcefully selling to his colleagues over the coming years, and which he himself did not think would add to overall costs. Alanbrooke tactfully acknowledged that the COS's proposals were 'nearly in line' with the Foreign Secretary's, especially in regard to locating reserves and base installations. Nonetheless, he said, the tri-service headquarters must be in the Canal Zone, for the sake of co-operation between the Army, Air Force and Mediterranean Fleet. The Prime Minister thought that the argument for developing bases on British territory in Africa was 'a strong one.' It was finally decided to approve both the COS's proposals for a main base in the Canal Zone and (in principle) the stationing of military reserves in East Africa – potentially, then, yet further strategic overstretch.

Moreover, the committee also approved the COS's visionary plan for four 'world zones' of strategic responsibility within the British Commonwealth, and agreed that the Dominions should be asked to accept this plan as the formal basis for military co-operation via mutual joint staff missions. Canada (the one Dominion which in the Second World War had actually proved to be indispensable to Britain's survival) was, however, to be omitted because 'she tended to stand out of Commonwealth defence commitments for fear of prejudicing her position vis-à-vis the United States'. Yet in the event the Labour Government was to prove no more successful in getting the Dominions to pull their military weight than its National Government predecessor before 1939 or its Liberal predecessor before 1914. In the glum words of the Secretary of State for Commonwealth Relations in 1949:

> it is clear that (with the shining exception of New Zealand) the old Commonwealth countries have not yet come to think that it is their duty to develop adequate forces for their own local defence in peacetime, and to make their full contribution towards wider Commonwealth defence against external aggression. In other words, they still unconsciously rely in large measure on the Royal Navy and the British taxpayer.[37]

As late as spring 1950 the Commonwealth Secretary was still to be pondering how best to persuade them 'to assume a greater share of the financial burden'.[38] Australia was at that time spending 3.3 per cent of GNP on defence, New Zealand 2.5 per cent, South Africa 1.2 per cent, Canada 3.3 per cent – and the United Kingdom 7.7 per cent.[39] So much, then, for the stubborn belief of the Foreign Secretary and Chiefs of Staff (even the sceptical Attlee) in the postwar version of the old mirage that the Commonwealth served, or could serve, to augment British power.

In contrast to its unanimous faith in the Commonwealth, Whitehall continued to be deeply split between fantasists and realists over the other, though related, question of the hugely expensive British military and political presence in the Middle East, sprawling from Cyrenaica in the west to the Persian Gulf in the east; from Palestine and Egypt in the north to Aden, Somaliland and (if the Foreign Secretary had his way) Kenya in the south. The argument smouldered on against a setting of boundless political complications. In 1946 Cyrenaica, a former Italian colony, was the object of rival bids by Britain and the Soviet Union for control via a United Nations trusteeship (which had now replaced the old League-of-Nations mandate as a convenient device for acquiring colonies on a long lease). With Egypt, a fully sovereign state, Britain was engaged in negotiating a new treaty which would enable Britain to turn the Suez Canal Zone into a major military base after the evacuation of British forces from Cairo and the Nile Delta. In Palestine (ruled by Britain since 1922 under a League mandate) the British government, prodded by the United States, was striving to find some formula for partition that would reconcile the irreconcilable: that is, the claims of Arab and Jew to the same land. In the meantime two British divisions and support troops, some 60,000 soldiers, were stuck in Palestine adding to the balance of payments deficit, carrying out clumsy and ineffective sweeps against the Jewish terrorists who were murdering their comrades, and otherwise doing nothing but guard their own barbed wire.[40]

What was more, the British government was also engaged in 1946 in a no less hopeless attempt to reconcile the rival political demands of the Indian National Congress and the Moslem League, and to reach an agreed political formula for a united independent India. For the Labour Cabinet had resolved that Britain at long last must dump that immense imperial liability, at present sucking in a British military commitment of 7000 officers and nearly 34,000 soldiers.[41] But, when India went, so too would go the historic reason for the British entanglement in the Middle East. However, the Chiefs of Staff did not appear to notice this. Far from it: they wished Britain still to remain strategically entangled with India herself even after India had become independent. In June 1946 the COS were writing that 'in any future war our strategic requirements in India are that she could be a main support area (i.e., we should be in a position to have recourse to her industry and man-power potential) and that we should be enabled to use her territory for operational and administrative bases, and air staging posts . . .'.[42] In September that year the COS were still urging 'the importance of India to our Imperial strategy'.[43] She was needed for control of the Persian Gulf and, in the event of war with the Soviet Union, for air attacks on the Urals and western Siberia. 'The continuance of India's co-operation with the Commonwealth in defence is therefore essential.' In October the CIGS (by then Field Marshal Lord Montgomery) told the Cabinet Defence Committee that the COS 'wished to emphasise the importance of taking every possible step to persuade India to remain within the British Commonwealth. The strategic advantages of her so doing were beyond question.'[44]

So when the Union Flag was finally hauled down in New Delhi on 15 August 1947, marking the ruthless liquidation of British rule by Lord Mountbatten (fully backed by Attlee) and the partition of the former Indian Empire into the two Dominions of India and Pakistan, it did not at all mean that Britain had thankfully dropped the sub-continent from her strategic concerns.

Neither, therefore, did the end of the Raj imply that as a

consequence the United Kingdom's embroilment in the Middle East would be liquidated. For, according to the stubborn belief of the Foreign Secretary and the Chiefs of Staff, this embroilment provided the keystone to the arch of Britain's world influence. In May 1946, the COS, anxious about the consequences of having to evacuate Egypt and of the possible end of the British mandate over Palestine (an Anglo-American Committee of Enquiry on the country's future had just reported), anxious too about uncertainties over the future of Libya and the Sudan, reported on Britain's future minimum peacetime requirements in the Middle East theatre.[45] These embraced firstly full military rights in Palestine, freedom to locate there 'such forces as we wish', and complete control over the defence organisation of the area. In the second place, Egypt must give an effective guarantee that base installations would be developed, and made available to British forces 'as soon as the British Government considers that a state of emergency has arisen'.[46] Thirdly, Britain must have rights to maintain garrisons and air bases in Libya, in order to command the route through the Mediterranean. The COS hammered away in their report on how essential Egypt was to the entire structure, especially for locating General Headquarters and the theatre reserves, for they judged Bevin's preferred option, East Africa, to be too distant. In the COS's conviction, 'Egypt and Palestine are interdependent; without both it would not be possible to defend any of our vital interests in the Middle East.'[47]

When this report came to be discussed by the Cabinet Defence Committee on 27 May, the COS explained that it was 'an attempt to show the relationship between the problems at present under separate negotiations, namely, those in Egypt, Palestine, and Cyrenaica, and brought out the position not previously examined of the relationship of Cyrenaica to our Middle East strategy . . .'.[48] Attlee was not impressed: Egypt was a foreign country, he remarked, and Britain would have to respect her sovereignty in regard to British military requirements; the future of Cyrenaica was 'doubtful'; the problem of terrorism in Palestine 'emphasised the insecurity of developing that country as a main base'. When Bevin backed Attlee in questioning why the Middle East GHQ had to be as far forward as Egypt or Palestine, the COS replied that in any future war just as in the last war a central GHQ would be essential for control of a major conflict, and that it must be as near as possible to the centre of communications:

'The Middle East Communications Centre [at present in Egypt] was the focus, not only for the Middle East but for the whole Empire Communication system. . . .' If GHQ could not be located in Egypt in peacetime, then some other place near by must be selected, because 'a Headquarters far to the South of Egypt would find it impossible to conduct naval operations in the Mediterranean . . .'.

Then the Defence Committee touched on the topic of oil, a favourite justification of the continued British entanglement in the Middle East. Bevin averred that it was 'one of our most important strategic interests and would be vital to us in time of war'. However, the Vice-Chief of the Imperial General Staff (Lieutenant-General F. E. W. Simpson) had to acknowledge that, though plans existed for defending the oil supply in time of war, 'we did not possess in peace sufficient troops or facilities in the areas concerned to guarantee the security of the oil fields in Persia and Iraq in the event of large-scale attack. Present plans dealt only with the security of the oil fields against sabotage attempts.'

It was left to the Chancellor of the Exchequer, Hugh Dalton, to introduce into these high strategic considerations the vulgar matter of cash:

He was greatly concerned at the adverse sterling balance existing in Egypt and the implications that the administrative forces were still being maintained in Egypt when they could be located elsewhere. Unless expenditure was greatly reduced in the future we should be in the impossible position of borrowing money from the Egyptians in order to maintain our forces in Egypt.

Again, however, no fundamental decision was reached. The committee simply agreed with the Prime Minister that the COS report could not be endorsed as it stood, and that, in Attlee's words:

our whole position in the Middle East required re-examination to determine our exact strategic requirements . . . with particular reference to what in the Middle East would it be essential for us to defend in a possible future war, to determine what would be our wartime requirements [in forces] to defend those essentials and what would be our peacetime minimum military requirements on which we could expand in war.

But prise away as he might, Attlee could not open the closed minds of the Chiefs of Staff and let in the cold light of present-day total-strategic reality. Their report on 1 June 1946 in response to his request to re-examine 'our whole position in the Middle East' began by asserting: 'The fundamental basis of Commonwealth Defence is the security of the United Kingdom, of the Dominions and of the communications between them.'[49] Although they therefore accepted that the security of the United Kingdom was 'vital', they went on to contend that to limit our strategy 'to the local defence of this country would permit an enemy to concentrate unimpeded his entire effort against us . . .'.

Here is a statement remarkable for its omission of any mention of Western Europe, which in two world wars had supplied the United Kingdom's forward defensive zone and the decisive battle-front, or of the possibility that Britain might once again have allies. Turning to the main topic of their paper, the Middle East, the COS clothed in up-to-date air-force blue in place of traditional navy-blue the lure of this fringe theatre which in two world wars had so dispersed British strength. Since air forces based in the United Kingdom would not suffice for strikes against the Soviet Union, they argued, then the Middle East 'provides the only air base from which effective offensive action can be undertaken against the important Russian industrial and oil-producing areas in the Caucasus . . .'. After disingenuously remarking on the importance of Middle East oil to Britain's war effort, the COS then provided a grand-strategic survey of the imperial pink on the map that might have come out of a drawer in the Victorian War Office: 'By holding the Middle East we shall obtain defence in depth for East and Southern Africa, and may also secure the through route of communication via the Mediterranean, Suez Canal and Red Sea.' It remained for them only to draw the overall conclusion 'that it is essential to maintain our position in the Middle East in peace and defend it in war'.

When this report came before the Defence Committee on 19 July,[50] it provoked fresh argument between the realists and the victims of nostalgic delusion. The realists questioned whether any sovereign country in the Middle East would provide base facilities from which British aircraft might strike at the Soviet Union. They pointed out with regard to Middle East oilfields that, given 'our present inability fully to provide for their defence', it was of 'first importance' to associate the United States in their protection. In general, argued the doubters, 'the complexities of international politics could not safely guarantee acquiring all those facilities in the Middle East we needed in peace and war'.

But once again the committee put off making a decision, concurring with the Prime Minister's view that it was impossible to arrive at definite conclusions 'without being aware of other general factors governing the overall strategy of the British Commonwealth'. Instead, therefore, the COS's report would be examined again after the pending European peace conference (in the event, abortive), and when the future status of European and Middle Eastern countries could be foreseen − and also after yet a further examination of 'the overall Commonwealth strategic concept'.

After three months had seeped away, the COS asked the politicians to make essential decisions as to where British forces should be based if and when Egypt was evacuated. They put in an ambitious bid for a base in Palestine for a divisional HQ, two brigade groups, base troops and air and naval support.[51] On the assumption that Britain was going to maintain her present position in the Middle East, they 'tentatively estimated' that the ultimate peacetime strength of the Army in the Middle East would be 'in the nature of' a corps headquarters, one armoured division, one infantry division, a parachute brigade, internal security battalions, plus corps and base troops. Yet again, however, the politicians proved not to be in the deciding mood. The Prime Minister reasonably enough thought that it was premature to agree to forces being permanently located in Palestine since this depended on the nature of a final settlement of the country's future. This time it was the Lord President of the Council, Herbert Morrison, who touched on the matter of cost, pointing out that married quarters in Palestine would cost £4000 each compared with £1200 in the United Kingdom.

Come late October 1946 and discussion of the current state of negotiations for a new Anglo-Egyptian treaty[52] found the Foreign Secretary still plugging East Africa as the site of the main Middle East base after the evacuation of Egypt − say in 1949. The CIGS (Montgomery) remarked that under the present form of the treaty, 'we should depend entirely for any military rights in Egypt on the goodwill of Egypt'; and he stressed how important it therefore was to retain such rights in Palestine because these 'must assume a growing and vital importance in the defence of the Middle East'.

Next month the COS put in another of their global strategic surveys, this time in relation to the strength of the armed forces as at 31 December that year and at 31 March 1948.[53] They stuck to it that the first task of the forces in war would lie not only in the defence of the United Kingdom, but also in the defence of 'the main support areas and the [Commonwealth] communications between them'. It is noteworthy that, with the exception of garrisoning ex-enemy countries, all the peacetime tasks of the armed forces now listed by the COS had to do with maintaining the world and Commonwealth role. The forces were needed, they wrote, to uphold law and order 'in territories for which we are responsible'; to protect British lives and property 'in the event of disturbances'; to foster British trade throughout the world (a doubtful one, this); to provide forces for the United Nations if asked; and, most notable task of the lot, 'to maintain British prestige, to provide adequate backing to our diplomacy and where necessary to ensure that in areas still under dispute we shall not be faced with a *fait accompli*'.

Although the Chiefs accepted that by March 1948 British forces would have retired from Cairo and the Nile Delta to a new base in the Suez Canal Zone, they still believed that 'we have to maintain generally our position in the Middle East in support of our foreign policy . . .':

> We therefore consider that we must plan on providing strong land and air garrisons for Palestine and small garrisons for the Sudan, Iraq and all British colonies. Naval and air forces will be required in the Mediterranean and Middle East both to support these garrisons and to safeguard British interests there. They will also be necessary as a backing for British policy, particularly in the eastern Mediterranean.

Annexes on the Army and Royal Air Force make it plainer still that the size of the armed forces (and hence of the resulting burden on the economy) was to go on being determined by the world and imperial role rather than by the needs of Britain's own security. In the case of the Army: 'It is clear that the size of the army at this date [March 1948: that is, in eighteen months' time] is governed by the necessity of meeting our overseas commitments rather than the need to maintain a nucleus for expansion for war.' And with regard to the

Royal Air Force: 'We consider that some fifty squadrons [out of a total of 150] will be necessary for our garrisons in the Mediterranean, the Middle East, India and the Far East. To these squadrons will fall most of our active peacetime commitments.' As for squadrons in Britain or Germany, these must be earmarked for reinforcement of overseas garrisons in local emergencies.[54]

On through 1947 the Foreign Secretary, the service ministers and the Chiefs of Staff continued bravely to pipe the imperial march and beat the world-power drum. During a Defence Committee discussion on New Year's Day about the political future of Palestine Bevin argued:

> our whole position in the Middle East had weakened, and the impression seemed to be growing that we had lost the ability, and indeed, the will, to live up to our responsibilities. Without the Middle East and its oil and other potential resources, he saw no hope of our being able to achieve the standard of life at which we were aiming in Great Britain. If, as he believed, the retention of Palestine was strategically essential to the maintenance of our position in the Middle East, we should have to make up our minds on what solution we were going to impose and recognise that any solution which we might think it right to impose would be met by opposition from both Jews and Arabs – a situation which the Chiefs of Staff had hitherto regarded as unacceptable. . . .[55]

The Minister of Defence (A. V. Alexander) backed him: 'on the long-term issue he was convinced that the retention of our position in Palestine was a strategic necessity . . .'. A week later the COS offered their written support: 'If we are unable to obtain these requirements [to locate a main British base in Palestine], our ability to defend Palestine – and therefore our whole strategic position in the Middle East – will be gravely prejudiced.'[56] If a plan for the partition of Palestine should be opposed by the Arabs, they wrote, then one extra division would be required on top of the two already there; if opposed by the Jews as well, then two extra divisions.

In the same month of January 1947 the Minister of Defence is found broadly pleading 'the need to meet current operational requirements and to provide the requisite backing for our foreign policy . . .'.[57] In February the COS urged that a new oil pipeline to the Mediterranean from Iraq should be located within Britain's future Middle East defence perimeter in North Palestine and Syria, which offered the best defence of Egypt. Whether the British eventually evacuated Egypt or Palestine or not, argued the Chiefs, they would have to return in time of war.[58] In June the Defence Committee approved the COS's recommendation that military stores evacuated from India and Egypt (in Egypt alone Britain was stocking £300 million of such stores)[59] should be located in a new Store Holding Area for two corps, each of two divisions, in East Africa, at a total cost in transport and base facilities of £50 a ton, or, in the case of ammunition, double that.[60] This marked a decisive step towards fulfilment of Bevin's dream of a new British main Middle East base in East Africa.

Not until September 1947 did Bevin with teeth-clenched reluctance come round to recommending to the Cabinet that Britain should withdraw from Palestine by 1 August 1948. The Chancellor backed him on the grounds that, if an agreed settlement could not be reached in Palestine, then 'that country was of no strategic value . . . and the maintenance of forces in it merely led to a heavy drain on our financial resources . . .'.[61] But no broad strategic lesson was drawn from the dumping of Palestine any more than from the dumping of India. In this same month Bevin was telling the Cabinet Defence Committee that he would be 'most reluctant to see any weakening of our forces in Cyrenaica',[62] while the First Sea Lord (Admiral Sir John H. D. Cunningham) and the Parliamentary Secretary to the Admiralty were likewise telling the Committee that a reduction 'of our Naval strength in the Pacific and West Indies, for example, might have far-reaching political and economic effects'. And on the 18th, the Chiefs of Staff were putting a fresh lick of paint on their rickety global Commonwealth defence structure:

The planning of our overall strategy and policy for the defence of the Commonwealth must be carried out in London and Commonwealth capitals, since the overall picture in regard to resources, political information, intelligence and scientific developments, will not be available to individual zones. The defence organisation in each zone would perform a complementary function to the higher defence machinery in London and the Commonwealth capitals. . . .[63]

And at the beginning of October the Foreign Secretary was again demanding that 'the foreign policy of His Majesty's Government must be backed by adequate armed forces . . .'.[64]

In 1948, despite the final abandonment of Palestine on 15 May, the Chiefs of Staff continued to pursue their fantasy of a Commonwealth strategic structure based on four 'world zones'. They now proposed that a British Defence Co-ordination Committee for the Far East should be set up under the Governor-General of Malaya to co-ordinate all matters bearing on defence, with a remit embracing Malaya, Singapore, British North Borneo, Brunei and Sarawak, Hong Kong, the Andaman and Nicobar Islands, Ceylon, Siam, French Indo-China, Java, Sumatra and Dutch possessions, China (including Manchuria and Inner Mongolia), Korea, Outer Mongolia, Tannu Tuva, Tibet, Nepal Bhutan and the British Pacific Fleet station (including Japan). Observers from Australia and New Zealand, the COS suggested, might be invited to the committee.[65] The proposed Middle East Defence Co-ordinating Committee's remit was hardly less ambitious, extending as it did from Greece and Turkey in the north to Ethiopia, Kenya, Uganda and Northern Rhodesia in the south, and from the Gulf states in the east to Malta and Tripolitania in the west.[66]

The persistence of such *folie de grandeur* marks the Prime Minister's failure from the beginning of 1946 to impose his own total-strategic realism on his colleagues in the masterful manner of Chamberlain in the case of appeasement or Margaret Thatcher later in regard to most matters. For instead Attlee had sought (in concert with his Chancellors of the Exchequer) to outflank the world-power fantasists by ruthlessly reducing the overall size and cost of the armed forces. Interwoven with the purely strategic argument between the realists and the fantasists in Whitehall in 1946–8 was, therefore, a second argument, about price-tags and purses, national, contents of.

CHAPTER FOUR

'We Cannot Afford Either the Money or the Men'

W HEN IN THAT first Cabinet Defence Committee meeting
of 1946, on 11 January, Attlee had stung the Foreign
Secretary and the Chiefs of Staff into indignantly
justifying all Britain's current 'commitments' (see above p. 47), Bevin
of all people put his finger on the fundamental issue at stake by
remarking that it was 'necessary to weigh up whether our future
prosperity depended more upon a satisfactory clearing up of the
international situation in the coming year, or upon an additional build-
up of our productive capacity'. Herbert Morrison, the Lord President,
had no doubts about the proper order of priority, insisting at the same
meeting: 'a really sound economy was of great importance in relation
to our foreign policy and would also give a firm foundation on which
to build future defence measures. He felt that although the arguments
were nicely balanced, the emphasis should be laid upon building up a
sound economy.' Unsurprisingly, Dalton as Chancellor 'supported this
view and said he would like to see a sharp drop in expenditure on
defence in the coming year, even if this meant a rise in defence
expenditure in two or three years' time'.

The meeting came to no final decision, but instead agreed to take
the Prime Minister's suggested manpower ceilings for all three services
of 1,900,000 at 30 June 1946 and 1,100,000 at 31 December (as
against the COS's figures of 2,068,000 and 1,440,000) as the basis for
planning. At the beginning of February the Chiefs of Staff, having
unhappily pondered the operational implications, reported that the
proposed reductions 'will necessitate the abandoning of certain of
our hitherto accepted commitments', such as withdrawal from
Venezia Giulia and Greece by the end of 1946 and brutal cutbacks

of the Royal Navy in the Mediterranean and Far East.[1] In particular, the Navy east of Suez would have to shrink from 140,000 men to 34,000. The Pacific Fleet would have to lose both its battleships, its fleet carrier and about half its strength in cruisers and destroyers by the end of 1946. The East Indies Fleet would have to lose all eight destroyers, eight out of twenty-four fleet minesweepers and sixteen out of twenty escorts. The America and West Indies Station and the Africa Station would each lose one of their two cruisers, while the planned build-up of the training fleet in the Mediterranean would have to be postponed.[2]

These reductions to a 'minimum' would still, for instance, leave the Royal Navy with a strength east of Suez of four light fleet carriers, seven cruisers, eight destroyers, sixteen escorts and twenty submarines. Nonetheless, the Admiralty wagged a doleful head over the 'consequent effect' which the cuts would have on 'British *prestige* [emphasis added], fostering of trade and readiness for emergencies'.[3] When the Defence Committee came to discuss this COS report on 15 February 1946, the Prime Minister tersely reminded his colleagues: 'There was no possibility of war with America, and in his view, there were no hostile fleets in being, or in sight within the next few years, to cause us alarm. . . .'[4] The First Lord, A. V. Alexander, warned shrewdly enough that it was 'not entirely safe to assume that [the Soviet Navy] would not emerge as a menace'.[5] Bevin, for his part, hunched his massive weight behind the Chiefs of Staff, telling his colleagues that the proposed cuts:

faced him with grave difficulties in obtaining the support which he thought necessary as a backing to the Government's foreign policy. At the moment difficult problems such as the revision of the Treaty in Egypt, the Greek Elections, the Balkan situation, the Peace Treaty with Italy, and the disposal of the Italian Colonies [in Africa], were in the process of discussion and solution. With all these factors before him, and realising full well the financial and manpower implications of maintaining the forces at their present levels, he asked that their strengths should not be reduced appreciably over the next three months. This would provide him with the necessary strength in the most delicate period, and providing a satisfactory solution were found to his problems he would support reductions in the second half of the year.[6]

71

He was also, he reminded the committee, 'in the process of the formulation of a Far Eastern policy', and for this reason he 'considered it dangerous to weaken our naval forces further at present, as we should not then succeed in influencing decisions in this area to the extent we desired . . .'.[7]

The upshot of the debate was that the Defence Committee accepted that 'we shall not be called upon to fight a major war during the next two or three years'; that in any future trouble the United States 'will probably be on our side, and will certainly not be against us'; and that no fleet capable of being a menace would exist in the next few years. Given these assumptions, given too that 'certain political commitments' could be liquidated in the course of the year, and accepting 'certain risks', the proposed force levels should be confirmed as 'targets'. Even so, 'in certain eventualities' some reductions might have to be postponed and supplementary estimates presented.

So apparently Attlee had had his way. And yet when it is borne in mind that this was the aftermath of war with no immediate enemy in sight and that Britain was desperately hard-up, even his chosen total of 1,100,000 men in the armed forces by the end of 1946 seems inflated enough in comparison with the total of 681,000 on the outbreak of war with Germany in 1939. The projected 1946 bill for defence still amounted to £1100 million even after a 10 per cent cut proposed by the Chancellor.[8] And in the event the strength of the armed forces at the end of 1946 proved to be 327,000 above Attlee's target figure.

The financial cost of such forces (especially those overseas) was not the only burden laid on the British industrial economy by the scale of the defence effort required by the pretensions of British foreign policy. That effort bit directly into the nation's productive resources – manpower, the technological base, research and development – at a time when it was so desperately urgent to expand output, boost exports and find a margin for investment in the modernisation of industry. As Attlee observed to the Cabinet Defence Committee in April 1946, 'he could not possibly see how the country, if it was to expand trade to meet its financial obligations, and return at the same time to economic stability, could possibly afford to maintain armed forces over a million strong . . .'.[9] In October 1946, fourteen months after V-J Day, the armed forces still totalled 1.76 million men and women,[10] while defence industries swallowed another 590,000, making a grand total of 2.35 million. This was equal to one and two-thirds of the manpower engaged in export manufacturing.[11]

Fifteen months later, in January 1948, the Board of Trade was expressing keen anxiety that defence production should not be allowed 'to involve any considerable diversion of manpower, capacity or scarce raw materials from other important production', and warning that 'until the consequences of the present crisis in our export trade can be seen more clearly, it will be very difficult to provide iron and steel for the re-opening of the production of arms and equipment for Commonwealth countries and those foreign countries . . . which look to us for supplies'.[12]

Worse still, the defence demands of the world role particularly overloaded Britain's narrow base in high technology and research and development.[13] In another victory by Bevin over fierce opposition by the Chancellor of the Exchequer, a Cabinet inner circle secretly decided in October 1946 on a technically novel but enormously expensive (in R and D and engineering resources as well as money) expedient for perpetuating Britain's status as a first-class power: the development of a British nuclear deterrent.[14] In January 1947 the total cost of defence R and D and production stood at £180.4 million.[15] Although the Minister of Defence contended that nearly a third of the £66.1 million of that devoted to basic and applied research actually served civil needs, such as in the fields of radar and radio, metallurgy, aerodynamics, and jet-engine design,[16] the Chancellor nonetheless reckoned that the £66.1 million were still 'excessive'.[17]

From spring 1946 onwards a new question enriched the familiar Whitehall arguments about Britain's role in the world, the related size of the armed forces and the impact of their cost on the economy – the question whether or not conscription should be adopted as a permanent peacetime policy.[18] Only once before in her history had Britain introduced conscription in peacetime, and that was in the spring of 1939 in the face of apparently imminent danger of war with Germany. It had then been justified, like conscription in the two world wars themselves, as necessary for national defence and survival. But in October 1946 a Manpower Working Party reporting to the Cabinet Defence Committee on 'The Introduction of a Permanent Scheme for Compulsory Military Service' offered a further, and novel, justification:

Our peace-time commitments require the maintenance of effective armed forces and the lessons of the years between the two wars reflect the disastrous consequences of attempting to play our part in world affairs without the necessary backing of armed force. . . .

It seems to us essential that we should back our foreign policy with sufficient military force to carry out our commitments and to live up to our responsibilities as one of the three leading powers of the world.[19]

The working party therefore defined overall peacetime requirements as the manpower, in the first place, to enable Britain to be adequately strong at the outbreak of a war, and secondly to meet 'normal peacetime requirements'. At the top of Britain's 'inescapable permanent commitments' was put, reasonably enough, the defence of the United Kingdom. But then followed a shopping-list comprising such old favourites as maintenance of garrisons and bases overseas; strategic reserves overseas as well as at home; forces and bases in the United Kingdom for training and for administration of 'our forces throughout the world'; contributions to the United Nations; and of course 'The maintenance of British prestige abroad – "showing the flag" [sic]'. The working party then did its sums on the basis of these alleged needs, found that likely voluntary recruitment would not meet the total, and concluded that compulsory military service 'is essential in peacetime'.

Nonetheless, when the working party looked five years ahead, it had to admit that if average productivity in 1952 were the same as in 1939, and 'there is at present no evidence that output per man-hour over the whole range of production of goods and services is greater now than before the war',

. . . it is evident that it will be impossible simultaneously –
a. to meet the requirement of the Armed Forces as estimated in this paper;
b. to meet by 1952 the contemplated degree of expansion in exports, investment, housing and in Government service, as compared with 1939;
c. to regain by 1952 even the 1939 volume of goods and services for civilian use – a volume which cannot itself be considered satisfactory as a target for 1952.

> The deficiency in terms of man-power in 1952 would be between 400,000 and 830,000 if the period of compulsory military service were fixed at 1½ years. If the period of service were kept down to 12 months, the deficiency would be reduced by just over 100,000.[20]

The impact of conscription on Britain as an industrial society was not, however, just a matter of the sheer number of young men locked away from the labour market, many of them overseas consuming scarce foreign exchange. As the working party pointed out, the resulting late entry of conscripts into professional training:

> involves a serious qualitative loss to the man-power resources of the country, affecting as it does practically all men taking courses at Universities or higher technical institutions and many apprentices. The loss will be felt particularly acutely at the present time, because it is generally recognised that the country has fewer men than it needs in nearly all those occupations for which a long period of education and training is required.

The working party ended its report by trying from another angle to guesstimate the economic cost of half a million conscripts. Given that the average net output of a young man in industry was about £400 a year, then the loss of production would equal about £200 million a year, or 22 per cent of the expected level of fixed investment in 1946–7, and likewise 22 per cent of expected exports.

In the light of these gruesome prognostications about the impact of conscription on Britain's frail economy, it does seem astonishing that the working party should nevertheless still choose to give priority to 'the maintenance of British prestige abroad' and to living up to 'our responsibilities as one of the three leading powers of the world'.

When the Defence Committee came to discuss this report on 16 October 1946, it split as usual between the Foreign Secretary, service ministers and the COS all wordily arguing for the world role and for the size of armed forces which they reckoned necessary to maintain it, and the Chancellor of the Exchequer and the President of the Board of Trade warning about the cost to the economy.[21] Unsurprisingly, all the talk ended in 'general agreement that compulsory national service should be adopted as a permanent measure in peace-time in order that this country might make the minimum necessary provision for security in war and to carry out its other international responsibilities'. But for how long should these peacetime conscripts be removed from the productive economy – one year or eighteen months? The Minister of Labour and National Service (George Isaacs) in pleading for a one-year term 'stressed the manpower requirements now vital for the development of industry'.[22] But the COS were adamant that eighteen months was the minimum term which would give them the use of conscripts (especially overseas) for six months on top of training. The Chancellor surrendered at discretion, and eighteen months' service it was to be.

Taking all factors into account, not least the formidable weight of the world-power lobby in Whitehall and Westminster, it therefore hardly astonishes that the burden of the world role on the buckling British economy was lightened only very slowly year by year. The net total cost of the armed forces in 1946-7 amounted to £1091 million,[23] no less than 15 per cent of gross national product (compared with 7 per cent in 1938, when Britain was rearming for war),[24] while the estimates submitted by the Minister of Defence for 1947–8 still stood at £989 million (itself a reduction from the original total of £1064 million put up by the service departments). 'This is a terribly slow rate of decline,' complained the Chancellor in a memorandum in January 1947. 'At the end of 1947–8 we shall be three years from V. E. Day.'[25] The wartime coalition Government, he went on, had thought the defence budget would soon drop to £500 million, 'and that even this might be more than the country could, or would, tolerate . . .':

> I recognise that we cannot get so far as this next year, but I was counting on not having to find more than £750 million. . . . It is most disturbing that the Minister of Defence now asks for more than £200 million (the equivalent of nearly 2s [shillings] in the £ on the income tax) in excess of this figure. We cannot afford either the money or the men for which the Minister of Defence asks.

The Chancellor pointed out that the British economy was short of nearly 650,000 workers, and yet here was a demand for military manpower of nearly 1,200,000 and another 323,000 in the munitions industries (nearly 1,600,000 in all) as at 31 March 1948.

In particular, I cannot accept the proposed manpower of 189,000 for the Navy, as compared with only 94,000 in 1935 and 119,000 in 1938. Then, we had to deal with the German, Japanese and Italian fleets, now all liquidated; and no one claims that the Russians have, as yet, a fleet as strong as any of these three in 1938.

Tromboned the Chancellor:

I take a very serious view of the vast size of these estimates. We are vainly trying in every sector of the national economy to do more than we can. Unless we relax, the result will be rupture. We must think of our national defence, in these hard and heavy years of transition, not only against the more distant possibility of armed aggression, but also against the far more immediate risk of economic and financial overstrain and collapse.

He therefore called for a total of £750 million for 1947–8. But after exhaustive argument in the Defence Committee and the Cabinet[26] a compromise figure of £899 million was finally struck on 28 January 1947. This time the Prime Minister threw his weight behind the world-power lobby – the Foreign Secretary, the Minister of Defence and the Chiefs of Staff – saying that 'the Cabinet must keep in mind the importance of preserving an armed strength sufficient to support the foreign policy which the Government had undertaken'.[27] Such a choice of priorities appears the more wayward since it was made just at the time when, on top of all the customary postwar economic shortages and difficulties, the country was being crippled by one of the worst winters on record, with blizzards paralysing road and rail transport, the power stations about to run out of coal, and the shivering populace barely able to cook their miserable rations (see below, pp. 198–9).

Throughout the summer and autumn of 1947 the Government continued to agonise over the cost of playing the world power, not least because by July Britain was running a balance-of-payments deficit of $500 million a month, with consequent alarmingly rapid exhaustion of the 1945 American loan. Yet in accordance with the terms of the loan, sterling had to be made freely convertible into any currency as from 15 July 1947. This resulted in a torrential outpouring of Britain's dollar reserves, forcing Britain to draw $400 million of the loan in the first three weeks of July alone. In the six weeks up to 14 August the dollar drain averaged $115 million a week. By now a mere $400 million out of the original $3.5 billion loan remained.[28] Only two years after the 'economic Dunkirk' following V-J Day, Britain once again faced imminent bankruptcy. Some 'great power'! Some 'centre of world influence'! And yet in continued pursuit of this make-believe, 500,000 men in battle-dress or khaki-drill or jungle-green, mostly conscripts, were still eating their rations and 'sweating on demob' in overseas garrisons and airbases across the globe, or in white ducks serving in ships whose main current purpose was 'to show the flag': a direct deadweight cost of £140 million a year laid on the balance of payments[29] at a time when Britain as an industrial economy was faltering towards catastrophe.

Nevertheless, in September 1947 the Minister of Defence was hopefully putting forward defence requirements for 1948–9 costing £711 million.[30] Of the British Army's proposed strength at 31 March 1949 of 339,000, no fewer than 80,500 would be stationed outside Europe sustaining the world and imperial role, as against only 70,000 in Germany facing the Soviet menace.[31]

All things considered, British total strategy in this period is best summed up by the graphic Yorkshire expression 'all fur coat and no knickers'. No wonder Attlee returned to his old unwelcome theme when on 18 September 1947 the Defence Committee discussed these proposed defence requirements for 1948–9, telling his colleagues that 'in his view, there had not been sufficient appreciation of the need to bring the strength of the Armed Forces within the limit of what the country could afford in terms of money and manpower . . .'.[32] But the Foreign Secretary as usual forcefully opposed the further cutting of the armed forces, and he too returned to a familiar theme: 'He recognised the economic difficulties, but if the United Kingdom Government were to have any influence in international affairs he must have an adequate backing of armed force.' The Chancellor of the Exchequer, for his part, no less forcefully expressed a wish to avoid national insolvency:

> he recognised the risk involved in assuming there would be no major war for five years, but . . . in his view, the greater danger was the possibility of early economic disaster. . . . This was the situation against which the Committee had to consider what we could afford to spend on defence, whether in money or manpower.[33]

This time the Prime Minister did prevail, for the committee accepted his view that it 'had no option but to recommend to the Cabinet that the strategic risks and the political consequences . . . should be accepted, and that the proposed run-down in the strength of the Forces be approved': that was, to a total of 937,000 men by 31 March 1948 and 713,000 by 31 March 1949.[34] But this did not at all imply that Britain was in parallel to run down the world and imperial role, except for the forthcoming evacuation of Palestine. For by now Attlee's politically clever tactic of going for the cost of British world-power pretensions rather than the pretensions themselves had initiated that pattern of 'salami-slicing' the armed forces which would be followed by all governments in the next half-century. In other words, instead of drastically cutting the defence budget by means of liquidating major overseas roles in good time (India being the singular exception), governments clung on to the roles while calling on the armed services to fulfil them with weakened and overstretched resources.

The beginning of 1948 saw the struggle in Whitehall still continue between the victims of the hallucination that the United Kingdom was 'a Great Power'[35] and the financial realists, such as the new Chancellor of the Exchequer, Sir Stafford Cripps, who believed, in his words, that the 'prime necessity' was that 'the country should recover economically . . .'.[36] In the COS's recommendations in January on the future size of the armed forces, the demands of the world role accounted for almost a fifth of the projected strength of the British Army. The Mediterranean and Middle East (including East Africa) would, the COS predicted, require a garrison of over 40,000 soldiers (over 20,000 in Cyrenaica alone), and the Far East nearly 9000, most of them in Malaya.[37] In all, the world and Commonwealth role would suck in 53,000 soldiers, as against 64,205 in Germany confronting the Soviet Army, and 183,870 in the United Kingdom itself. In weighing these projected figures it must again be borne in mind that the costs of maintaining large garrisons in primitive countries thousands of miles from England were disproportionately high.

But when the Defence Committee came to discuss the defence estimates for 1948–9 the Prime Minister yet again failed to impose his own clarity of vision on colleagues dazzled by neo-Edwardian imperial fantasy. Instead he chose to play the chairman's balancing role:

The amount that would have to be spent on the overseas commitments of the Forces must vary according to the Foreign Policy pursued, but if it were found that they were absorbing an undue share the Foreign Secretary would no doubt be prepared to consider in what areas they might be reduced with least detriment to our interests.[38]

Once more Attlee preferred simply to lay down a ceiling on cost, this time of £600 million.[39] Such a sum would nevertheless still represent a quarter of the total national budget and 7 per cent of gross domestic product, as against the 1934 figures for defence expenditure of 14 per cent of national budget and 3 per cent of GDP.[40] The committee accepted the figure of £600 million – but only as a target for the years after 1948–9.

On 15 May 1948 there trundled into the British base area in the Suez Canal Zone from Palestine the last of 62,000 personnel (down from a peak of 100,000 in 1947), 257,500 tons of stores and 19,700 vehicles,[41] so completing the evacuation of a territory so long proclaimed by the world-power men in Whitehall to be an essential bastion of the British Middle East 'world zone'. Yet no lesson had been learned even now from the Palestine experience about the ultimately disposable nature of allegedly essential military commitments. On the contrary, only a month earlier the Cabinet Defence Committee had freshly expressed the same kind of convictions about the indispensability of Cyrenaica as had the Foreign Secretary and the COS in 1946–7 about the indispensability of Palestine: 'From the strategic point of view it was essential that we should secure for ourselves in Cyrenaica a position which would enable us to do exactly as we liked in that territory. Without this we should be unable to maintain a firm hold in the Middle East. . . .'[42] Thus the Middle East fantasy and with it the entire world-power fantasy continued to exert their spell nearly three years after the end of the Second World War.

Britain had in fact paid a double penalty, military as well as economic, for the failure of the Prime Minister and his Chancellors to induce the world-role lobby to abandon their nostalgic dreams and devise a new total strategy based on the United Kingdom's true weight and wealth. For by 'salami-slicing' the armed forces and their budgets without *pari passu* liquidating commitments, the fudges between the world-role lobby and the economic realists had left the United

Kingdom with the worst of total-strategic outcomes. On the one hand Britain's obsolescent industrial economy had been burdened with defence expenditure starting at 15 per cent of GDP in 1946 and falling only to 7 per cent in 1948 (as against 3 to 4 per cent before the war) – to say nothing of the demands of defence on real resources such as manpower, high-technology industries and R and D. On the other hand, this bloated expenditure had merely paid for military 'presences' in desert and jungle and on blue water in furtherance of those mystical advantages so cherished by the Foreign Secretary and the COS, 'prestige', 'status' and 'influence'. What it had not bought were armed services capable of fighting a war.[43]

According to a memorandum by the Minister of Defence in July 1948, the Army in Germany 'is primarily equipped not for war but for an internal security role and units consist mainly of young soldiers'. In the Middle East none of the Army 'is complete for war' and only a single weak division could be deployed east of the Canal Zone. The Far East forces 'are also not organised on a war footing'.[44] The Royal Air Force, with a strategic bomber force of just 144 aircraft and a fighter force for the defence of the United Kingdom of only 160 aircraft, was in hardly better case.[45]

It was no mere chance, however, that July 1948 witnessed this audit of the British armed forces' fighting capability. For, in a dismaying echo of the 1930s, immediate threats had now appeared at opposite ends of the British global strategic sprawl, together with a latent menace in the Middle East as well. No longer was it a question of seeking to lighten the burden of defence on the British economy; it was one of confronting the possibility that the burden might have to grow heavier yet again.

CHAPTER FIVE

The Cold War and Total-Strategic Overstretch

O N 16 JUNE 1948 a state of emergency was declared in Malaya because of the guerrilla war being waged against British rule by the Communist Malayan Races Liberation Army (which in fact drew its support exclusively from the Chinese population). Dollar-earning rubber and tin rendered Malaya that rare phenomenon among British colonies, a valuable asset to the United Kingdom, and so was considered worth investing large forces in what were to prove counter-insurgency operations protracted for more than a decade. Then, barely more than a week later, the Soviet Union finally cut all land links between West Berlin and Western Germany – the climax of a series of gradually tightening impediments to traffic. This aggression fell into the same category as Nazi Germany's reoccupation of the demilitarised zone of the Rhineland in 1936, confronting the Western powers with an apparent choice between timorous surrender and the risk of war if they attempted to send escorted convoys up the Berlin autobahn. It announced a disquieting new phase in the so-called Cold War between the Soviet Union and its satellites and the Western powers, in which Stalin was prepared to expand Communist tyranny by openly aggressive forward moves instead of rigged elections as in the case of Poland in 1945 or *coups d'état* as in the case of Czechoslovakia as recently as February 1948. It clinched – if clinching were necessary – the belief of the Western powers that they were confronted by a cunningly devised global Communist strategy aimed at bringing down democracy and the capitalist system. After all, quite apart from the Soviet takeover of Eastern Europe in 1944–8 in the wake of occupation by the Red Army, the proof seemed brutally evident. There had been the Soviet attempt to obtain permanent squatters' rights in the northern Iranian province of Azerbaijan in 1946 and the Soviet-backed Yugoslav demand for Trieste in 1946-7 (both successfully thwarted by a Western diplomatic palm of hand firmly shoved in the Communist face). There was the Soviet support for the insurgents in the still continuing civil war in Greece, as well as for the menacingly large Communist parties in France and Italy. There was the current Communist uprising in Malaya and the increasingly successful war being waged by the Chinese Communists against Chiang Kai-shek's Nationalist regime.[1]

As the Cold War had deepened in frigidity so its importance as a theme in the Whitehall justifications of the British world role had swelled. No longer was Britain (with the Commonwealth) to be a 'great power' simply as a self-evident good thing and because of history, but more and more in order to fulfil the role of equal partner with the United States in the global struggle against Communism. This had given a new perspective to the Chiefs of Staff's grandiose structure of four 'world zones' from the United Kingdom (and Western Europe) through the Mediterranean and Middle East to the Far East and, on the other side of the world, Australia and New Zealand. The United Kingdom and European zone now lay under direct Communist menace; so too did the Far Eastern zone, including Hong Kong and British commercial interests in mainland China as well as Malaya. Moreover a latent threat to the Middle East zone existed in the form of possible Soviet subversion of, or direct military intervention in, Turkey or Iran.

Yet this new Communist version of the 1930s Fascist triple threat did not alter the fact that it was once again the existence of the British Commonwealth, plus the consequent British involvement in the Mediterranean and Middle East, which entangled the United Kingdom in strategic obligations remote from its own direct security as a North European island; obligations too costly for its national resources to bear. In particular the Labour Government now had to try to reconcile – like its National Government predecessor in the 1930s – the opposing demands made by British and European security on the one hand and Commonwealth defence on the other.

Unbelievable as it must seem in retrospect, the Government chose exactly to repeat the folly of Chamberlain's isolationist grand strategy, and decided (in January 1949) not to send reinforcements to Europe if war broke out, but instead to give overriding priority to the Middle

East.[2] Even less excusable was the concurrence of the Chiefs of Staff (now Marshal of the Royal Air Force Lord Tedder, Admiral of the Fleet Lord Fraser and Field-Marshal Lord Slim) in rehashing this 1930s strategic escapism in defiance of the lesson taught by its catastrophic outcome. In their own words in June 1949:

> From the purely tactical point of view, it would be clearly not sound . . . to commit any additional forces [on top of the two divisions of occupation troops] to the Continent for the defence of Western Europe if war broke out in the period 1951–53. Our first concern must be for the vital elements in our strategy, namely, for the security of the United Kingdom, of our essential sea communications and of the Middle East. Our plans for the Middle East in an emergency require the dispatch of two Infantry Divisions and an Armoured Brigade from the United Kingdom *at the earliest possible moment* [emphasis in original]. . . . If the first two formations were sent to the Continent instead of the Middle East, the defence of the Middle East would certainly be jeopardised. . . .[3]

In a sentence that might have been penned by a CIGS in the mid-1930s, as if, indeed, the European battles of 1940–5 had never happened, the COS averred: 'To promise additional forces means to be committed to a Continental campaign. . . .'

They would concede only that if ministers judged that Britain must not fail to make a further contribution to European defence lest 'serious weakening' be inflicted on Western Union (an embryo integrated allied command created by the Brussels Treaty of March 1948), then 'from the broadest strategic point of view it would be right to commit ourselves to reinforce the British Army of the Rhine . . .'.

It did nothing to ease the British dilemma that, in another historical echo, the Commonwealth was again to prove all too ready to free-ride on the United Kingdom in terms of defence, in so far as it was not also free-riding on the United States. In October 1948, for example, the Australian Prime Minister, Chiffley, privately told the British High Commissioner in Canberra (but soon officially confirmed) that Australia would furnish no help to the British in the struggle against the Chinese insurgents in Malaya, even though what was the Far East to Britain was the Near North to Australia.[4] Nor did

Britain's other 'kin' in New Zealand, let alone the new Dominions of Pakistan and India, prove any more willing to join up in the cause of containing Communism in South-east Asia, or, to put it in less high-minded terms, the cause of propping up European colonial empires in that region.[5]

From the summer of 1948 onwards therefore the old familiar problem (in its new Cold War guise) of total-strategic overstretch confronted the Labour Government more urgently and more intractably than ever. As early as 26 July of that year the Prime Minister was warning colleagues that a major revival of arms production:

> would involve demands on our resources which would make it impossible for us to carry out our present policy of achieving economic viability by 1952. The adoption of a policy of rearmament even if accompanied by considerable reductions in production for export and for civilian use, and consequently by abandonment of the present policy of economic recovery, is not possible unless large American assistance is assured from the outset.[6]

In fact, Britain's economic situation was at that moment much happier than it had been the previous summer during the convertibility crisis (which had been solved by the simple expedient of reneguing on the terms of the 1945 US loan, and stopping sterling convertibility: see below, pp. 199–200). For she was now yet again on an American life-support machine, this time the European Recovery Programme (or Marshall Aid, after General George C. Marshall, the US Secretary of State who had fathered the programme), so freeing her from immediate anxieties about foreign exchange (see below, Chapter 19). Nonetheless the Cabinet Defence Committee had gloomily to agree with Attlee:

> if the United Kingdom were to embark on major preparations for war it would be necessary to obtain from the United States, not only assistance on the scale now being provided under the European Recovery Programme, but also raw materials for the re-armament programme and compensation for the loss of income from the diversion of production from exports to munitions.[7]

A report by the Joint War Production Staff at the end of July further hammered home the economic reality behind the illusion of Britain as a great power in the Cold War: 'no major improvements in production for the Services could be made without serious dislocation of the national economy . . .'.[8]

On 13 August 1948, with the allied air bridge between Berlin and the West now shifting bigger and bigger tonnages of supplies over the heads of the baffled Soviet blockaders on the ground, the battle between the world-power lobby in Whitehall and the economic realists was renewed over a report by the COS on 'Preparations for Defence' – meaning the contingency of war with the Soviet Union.[9] Bevin, deep in 'top-table' diplomacy, urged the overriding need to put the armed forces in order:

> While it might be necessary to take measures which would involve some diversion of our resources, we could not afford to run the risk of any further losses or retreats. For example, if, through military weakness, we were forced to give way in Germany or Malaya, the resulting economic loss would be far greater than the cost of bringing the Armed Forces to an effective state.[10]

But Cripps as Chancellor of the Exchequer noted that Britain faced possibly unavoidable extra commitments in regard to the creation of the new Western European Union defence scheme. He pointed out that the COS's proposals for rearmament suggested that as many as 400,000 men might be taken off civilian work by the end of 1949. If so, it would cut production for export and the home market by £200 million, as well as using 160,000 tons of steel and 100,000 tons of brass and copper. All this would have an effect on Britain's hopes under Marshall Aid of achieving a narrow balance of payments surplus in 1948–9.[11] It was left to the Minister of Defence, A. V. Alexander, in the chair admirably to sum up the British total-strategic dilemma:

> If we were to maintain our position in the West, in the Middle East, and in the Far East – and it was essential that we should from an economic as well as from the political and strategic point of view – and play our part in these momentous issues, we must be able to deploy greater armed strength. The crux of the problem was how

much it was possible to do in the present economic circumstances. . . .[12]

In August the question how much it was possible or desirable to do was only very partially answered by decisions to arrest the planned decline in the size of the armed forces by prolonging National Service for three months and to adopt an emergency scheme for rebuilding ammunition stocks, overhauling communications systems and refitting certain vessels.[13] On 6 December 1948, in a memorandum on defence requirements for 1949–50, the Minister of Defence glumly looked back at events in the year that had elapsed since he had submitted a budget of £692.6 million for 1948–9. British forces were still stuck in Austria, Trieste and Greece instead of being withdrawn as hoped, and, according to the Foreign Office, they were likely to go on being stuck there at least until the end of March 1950. Then there was the unforeseen new commitment in Malaya. And while a year ago the assumption had been that there would be no major threat of war before 1957, the Berlin crisis had occurred instead. After traipsing through the details of service requirements Alexander drew the conclusion that the defence budget for 1949–50 could not be less than £770 million, and that to drop it to £712 million (as the Chancellor wished) 'would compel us to abandon many present commitments' (an oft heard song), as well as reducing the forces and denying them new equipment.[14]

When this offering came up for discussion by the Defence Committee the Chancellor of the Exchequer sang his familiar song too, although in his case more the doom-laden squawk of a raven:

> unless the Cabinet were prepared to make drastic cuts in other sections of the Budget, it would not be possible to devote more than £712 million in 1949 to defence services. In the present economic position of the country, the only proper policy was to decide what total provision could be made for defence, and to bring the individual programmes of the Service Departments into line with that figure. But the proposals contained in [the Minister of Defence's paper] approached the problem from the opposite point of view; and the provision of £770 million for which the Minister of Defence had asked seemed to him to be simply the aggregate of the separate requirements of the three individual services.[15]

But once again hard choices were put off. Instead the Chiefs of Staff were asked to submit tri-service proposals (including R and D) which 'would cost no more than an average of £700 million a year during each of the three years from April 1950 onwards, and which would, within the limitations of this figure, give the greatest possible measure of security against foreseeable threats'. The COS in turn appointed a working party to study the problem.

For the first time since the war, therefore, strategy was to be looked at from the starting point of cost instead of the other way round. Chaired by a senior civil servant, Sir Edmund Harwood, the working party consisted of a sailor (Rear Admiral Charles Lambe), a soldier (Major-General Joseph Poett) and an airman (Air Vice-Marshal Ronald Ivelaw-Chapman). Although the Harwood Committee rendered its report on the 'Size and Shape of the Armed Forces' on 28 February 1949, it was not circulated to the Cabinet Defence Committee until 21 June.[16] And no wonder! – because this document constituted that radical rethinking for which Attlee had long called in vain about what armed forces, and in consequence what pretensions as a power, could really be afforded by Britain without imposing breaking strains on the economy.

The report struck the vitals of the target with its very first salvo by observing that there were two methods of approaching the problem:

> The first consists of calculating the shape and size of the armed forces needed adequately to support and implement a given policy and strategy and converting this into terms of money. The second consists of calculating, in relation to the various risks, the shape and size of the force which can be provided for a given sum of money and converting it, so far as it will go, into terms of policy and strategy. We have adopted the second approach because the fixed quantity in our terms of reference is money. . . .[17]

The report took it as a basic fact that Britain was finished as a world seapower of the first rank, and that her naval contribution in war 'must be complementary rather than competitive [with the United States Navy] and be confined to those tasks which are essentially a domestic responsibility'. It also accepted that the British nuclear deterrent could not be operational before 1953, and that in the meantime Britain would have to rely on the United States nuclear bomber force. It then proceeded to state what could and should be bought for £700 million a year. First and foremost was the security of the United Kingdom, both in itself and as an offensive base. 'This task includes the air defence of Great Britain; the defence of our coastal waters and sea communications to this country; and, as a measure of self-protection, such assistance as we can afford to the forces of Western Union. . . .' The report then went on: 'In so far as it can be done *without prejudice to our primary duty* [emphasis added] we must endeavour to hold covering positions in the Middle East to enable the deployment of Allied reinforcements with a view to its use as a base for offensive operations.' The Army would be cut to a three-year average of 308,660 men: two divisions in Germany; two brigades in Austria and Trieste, one and one-third infantry divisions and three armoured regiments in the Middle East; one division in South-east Asia and Hong Kong. The Royal Air Force (with an average strength of 190,000) would consist of a 'small bomber force', a gradually expanding day and night fighter force, a nucleus tactical air force for Western Union, and small maritime and transport forces. Beyond Europe it would consist only of a weak component to support the Army and for use in maintaining internal security. But it was the Royal Navy which would suffer the most drastic change of character. With a three-year average strength of 102,500 men, it would consist of a 'small but mobile carrier force', an anti-submarine training squadron and other training ships in home waters, a small mixed force in the Mediterranean and the Persian Gulf and another such on the China Station. The dockyards at Sheerness and Chatham would be closed. All these total proposed cuts in service manpower would give a net gain of 100,000 to the civilian economy.

The Harwood Committee concluded its report with a crisp restatement of the dilemma which had haunted Whitehall arguments about total strategy ever since the beginning of 1946:

> There is no insuperable difficulty in producing a balanced modern force at a cost of £700 million a year. But its size may well be deemed insufficient to support in peace the position in the world which we desire to occupy and provide in war a contribution to the Allied effort commensurate with that position.

As it happened, just four days before the Harwood Report was sent on its way to the Cabinet Defence Committee the Chancellor of the Exchequer, Sir Stafford Cripps, had reported to another Cabinet Committee that Britain was now once again facing the very real prospect of national bankruptcy.[18]

Between the first and second quarters of 1949 the fall in dollar reserves had accelerated from £82 million to £157 million, and this despite the inflow of Marshall Aid funds. In the one week of 10–16 July alone $39 million drained away, at which rate Britain's total dollar reserves would last only another forty weeks even with Marshall Aid. Throughout the summer the drain continued – $86 million between 27 July and 3 September. This then was the horrifying background to Whitehall arguments about the recommendations of the Harwood Committee. Yet the world-power lobby – the old alliance of the Foreign Secretary, the Minister of Defence and the COS – still shrank from the clear implications of Britain's habitual economic weakness and recurrent fits of apparently imminent bankruptcy. In the wistful comment of the Minister of Defence on the Harwood Report, 'It is not difficult to see that the Harwood proposals as they stand would lead to such a catastrophic decline in our influence as would bring very close our extinction as a first-rank Power.'[19]

The Chiefs of Staff themselves, clearly horrified, sought to demolish the Harwood Report completely in so far as Britain's commitments outside Europe (especially naval) were concerned. The proposed 'peripatetic task force' to provide naval support wherever needed in the world 'would almost inevitably be split up to meet recurrent local emergencies and would thus ultimately find itself permanently disintegrated into small detachments, leaving no fleet to continue training for war'.[20] The recommended naval forces in the Mediterranean and Middle East were 'inadequate and ill-balanced, and their severe reduction might well be taken by the Americans as an indication of our abandonment of the present accepted doctrine that the retention of the Middle East is vital to our strategy . . .'. Furthermore, 'the abolition of the East Indies Squadron would create a void in South-East Asia and the Indian Ocean. Ceylon has no naval force of her own and could be expected to view the withdrawal of the Royal Navy from Trincomalee with disquiet. . . .' Much the same, wrote the COS, applied to the Harwood Committee's proposed withdrawal of naval forces from Simonstown in South Africa, which they reckoned 'would have political effects in the Union of South Africa, where the presence of these forces is the only tangible sign of the benefits which South Africa receives in the defence field for remaining a member of the Commonwealth'. It would also mean that there would be no British naval forces available to deal with an emergency in the West African colonies. Then again, the peacetime naval strength in the China Sea proposed by Harwood would be 'quite inadequate to support our policy in normal times, quite apart from the growing Chinese Communist threat'. The proposed withdrawal of the Americas and West Indies Squadron meant that there would be 'no naval forces in the Caribbean to meet an emergency either in British Honduras or the Falkland Islands'.

As for land and air forces, the COS reckoned that the Harwood Committee's suggested strength in the Middle East 'would probably be just sufficient for garrison purposes', provided Britain could be quit of all former Italian colonies (except Cyrenaica) and cut her forces in Greece, while the proposed reductions in Far East garrisons were 'completely out of accord with recent developments in the area'. If the Harwood Report were accepted, wrote the COS, 'almost the whole of our strategic reserve' would have to be devoted to this area, not least because there was 'little prospect that Australia will be willing, or able, to take more than a very small part in the defence of South-East Asia in peace . . .'.

With regard to the Harwood Committee's suggested force levels in Europe, the COS justly opined that they were 'quite insufficient', and would have 'a disheartening effect in the Western Union, and may even undermine the whole defence structure which has been built up'. But in fairness to the Harwood Committee, it had had no alternative under its terms of reference but to ration out its £700 million worth of forces over the complete spread of Britain's global entanglements.

Concluded the COS patronisingly but dismissively: 'The Harwood Report is a valuable analysis of the position, but we cannot recommend the Defence Committee to accept it as it is. . . . the forces it describes are inadequate to carry out the Government's policy.' And so the COS, quite unable to free themselves from the prison of their assumptions about Britain's place in the world even with the aid of the hacksaw provided by yet another financial panic, thankfully left it to ministers to 'indicate which of the risks and implications [of the Harwood Report] they are not prepared to accept. We can then work out and submit a plan. . . .'

In making his own comments both on the Harwood Report and on the COS's gloss, the Minister of Defence, A. V. Alexander, began by not shirking the fundamental total-strategic issue before the Government. In his words, the report had offered:

> an honest and penetrating examination . . . of problems which touch vitally the whole future, not merely of the Services, but of the United Kingdom itself as a centre of world influence and power and, as I believe, of our ability to maintain in these Islands a tolerable standard and way of life for all our people. . . . it is the whole problem of our ability adequately to support our policies throughout the world . . . in the next decade. . . . It is in brief the problem whether, after the economic exhaustion of the war years, we have the power and the resources to maintain the armed forces equipped to modern standards required to permit us to play the role of a Great Power.[21]

Quite so. But although the Minister had not shirked stating the problem, he now proceeded to shirk the only answer warranted by the evidence, to wit, that postwar Britain indeed lacked the resources to permit her to play the role of a great power. Instead he sought escape in rhetorical assertion: 'it does not admit of doubt that any such wholesale abandonment of commitments is unthinkable . . .'. Apart from Western Union and the North Atlantic Treaty (which it may be agreed were unquestionably related to the United Kingdom's own security), the Minister was thinking above all of British commitments in the Middle East, 'hitherto accepted as one of the major pillars of our defence strategy', where unless Britain was able to support the Arab states, she might well see 'this whole area, with its oil resources and its control of communications, pass under Soviet influence'. The resultant knock-on effect 'could scarcely fail to be the elimination of our influence in the whole of the rich territories of the Far East which lie beyond Suez'. And then, of course, there was the Empire and Commonwealth:

> The burden of continuing to maintain forces which are adequate for Imperial purposes will undoubtedly be heavy, but I must remind my

colleagues that it would be quite inconsistent for this country to be providing large sums for the development of overseas territories if concurrently we were unable to keep on foot adequate forces to defend these territories against possible attacks.

Here Alexander achieved a remarkable double, justifying the cost of defending the colonies (currently over £16 million a year, the bulk of the colonies being so poor that they could not even pay for their own internal security[22]) by reference to the cost of British financial handouts to them. It was a double example too of the long-lasting tendency among British politicians to mistake the burden of Empire for an asset. Alexander even looked hopefully to the new Dominions (India and Pakistan) taking up their share of responsibility for Commonwealth defence in the future:

in the interim it is quite vital, in the interests of the Commonwealth and all it stands for in the world, that we should not permit present economic difficulties to stampede us into withdrawal of our outposts throughout the world. History shows many examples where the withdrawal of such outposts has been the preliminary to the decline and fall of great States.

The Minister of Defence had his own ready answer to the total-strategic conundrum analysed by the Harwood Committee: he simply reversed the committee's order of priorities: 'the central problem is not so much how much can we afford to spend on defence over the next few years, but what must be spent on defence adequately to discharge our responsibilities to our own people . . .'. At this point he added the remark (already quoted) that the Harwood proposals, if implemented, would lead to such a catastrophic decline in Britain's 'influence' as to bring very close her extinction as a 'first-rank Power'. In other words, never mind about your overdraft or the profitability of your business, much more important to go on playing the squire and impressing the neighbours.

Indeed the Minister of Defence advocated that, given the ever increasing cost of advanced military technology (with guided weapons and nuclear bombs to come), Britain should spend at least £800 million a year on defence – say 9 per cent of GNP, as against 8 per cent in 1938. After an inconclusive discussion chaired by the Prime

Minister on 5 July 1949, the Minister of Defence set on foot further studies on the basis of his figure of £800 million. On 29 July the Cabinet agreed that sterling must be devalued in order to stop the present lethal bleeding away of Britain's dollar reserves; on 29 August it formally endorsed this decision, and on 18 September announced it.[23] On 8 October, when the prospect of national bankruptcy was receding again, the reports asked for by the Minister of Defence were finally circulated.[24] The first of them, by an Inter-Departmental Committee on the Defence Estimates, recommended a provisional defence budget for the three years beginning April 1950 of £810 million per annum – more than a sixth larger than the figure given to the Harwood Committee in their terms of reference, and bigger even than the Minister of Defence's own figure back in June. The second report, by the Chiefs of Staff on 'The Size and Shape of the Armed Forces over the Next Three Years',[25] took no more note of the Harwood Report than a battleship of a trawler on a foggy night: 'Any substantial reduction in the suggested annual allocation of £810 million can only result in unacceptable defence risks, or in our inability to meet some of our present commitments *with the political consequences that this would entail* [emphasis added].'

The COS laid much emphasis, reasonably enough, on the Communist threat in the present Cold War and in a possible hot war, and therefore on the defence of the United Kingdom. However, in yet another historical echo of the 1930s, they gave priority to the retention of the Middle East over the provision of forces for Western Europe, grudgingly acknowledging that a promise of British reinforcement for Western Europe 'sooner or later' was 'probably a political necessity if Western Union is to develop effectively'. They recommended that two divisions should be held against this eventuality, but if Western Union were to collapse before they could embark, they might be sent to the Middle East instead. In fact, this entire report shows how the COS continued to lie under the enchantment of the world-role illusion. For instance, the Royal Navy, far from being drastically reduced in size and function as in the Harwood Report, was to remain the same size as at present in order to 'maintain the same support to our Foreign and Colonial policy as now, continue to play its present part in the cold war and carry out training as a preparation for war'. This meant stationing fleets in the Mediterranean and Far East each little smaller than the Home Fleet.[26] The Army similarly would have in 1951 the same infantry strength in the Middle East and also in the Far East as in Germany (where there would, it is true, in addition be an armoured division).[27]

In a fresh paper of his own, the Minister of Defence commended these reports to his colleagues as 'an important advance towards securing a practical and acceptable policy for defence'.[28] He repeated that any reductions in overseas commitments would lead to 'a sharp decline in our position as a world power', but happily went on to note that the level of forces now proposed 'would not cause the frustration, if not the abandonment, of some of the major objectives of our foreign policy [as under the Harwood Report]'.

When the Defence Committee met to discuss these matters on 9 October, Alexander dismissed not only an annual defence budget of £700 million as relegating the United Kingdom 'to the position of a second-class power',[29] but also the Chancellor of the Exchequer's compromise figure of £760 million, which he argued would have the same effect. The Chancellor for his part said that he saw no possibility of finding £810 million in each year 'unless the whole of the present policy of the Government were recast'. The Foreign Secretary reckoned that 'any abandonment of our overseas commitments could hardly fail to lead to an intensification of the Cold War and this he was not prepared to contemplate'.

The argument trundled on, the world-power fantasists opposed by an alliance between Cripps as Chancellor and Herbert Morrison as the Lord President of the Council. In a paper on 3 November 1949 Morrison shrewdly identified the total-strategic trap into which the Government was running:

> The Chancellor of the Exchequer has told us that such expenditure [that is, £800 million per annum] would gravely endanger our economic recovery, on which all else, our defence included, must depend. Yet the Forces provided would still be unsatisfactory. As the Minister of Defence has said, if a major war came without adequate warning our risks would be particularly grave. We are, in fact, in danger of paying more than we can afford for defences that are nevertheless inadequate, or even illusory.[30]

All Alexander could say in return was that a little over £800 million a year must be spent 'if we are to maintain our present position as a world power', and that once Britain started to scale down her commitments as Morrison urged, 'it is difficult to stop. I believe that the end of that road to be the loss of the position which we at present hold in many parts of the world and with it the standard of living to which this country has become accustomed. . . .'

At the Defence Committee on 15 November the Chief of Air Staff, Marshal of the Royal Air Force Lord Tedder, provided the star turn with another of those global strategic surveys which justified British entanglements by sweeping assertions about such unquantifiables as Britain's 'stabilising influence' in, and 'the vital economic importance' of, this or that region menaced by the 'spread' of the 'Communist threat'.[31] For Tedder, an outstanding wartime air strategist but now unable to adjust his mind from past imperial power to present national penury, was not the man to question such Bevinian givens. Having noted first of all that the security of the United Kingdom 'was of course fundamental', he vaulted straight to the other side of the world:

> Then there was the Far East where the Armed Forces were holding the Communist threat and preventing its spread over South-East Asia. He felt Ministers would agree that this was far more than a purely military responsibility, inasmuch as United Kingdom Armed Forces were the only stabilising influence in areas of immense economic consequence to the Western World and to the United Kingdom in particular. Then there was the Middle East. The Committee well knew that the Chiefs of Staff attached vital importance to this area from the military point of view, but in fact the United Kingdom Armed Forces in this area were fulfilling a far wider function. Not only did they bring a similar sense of stability into an area which again was of vital economic consequence to us, but they held a position which was at the centre of the Commonwealth and the centre of the Moslem world, withdrawal from which could hardly fail to lead to the disintegration of the Commonwealth and the eventual fall of Africa to the Communists.

Then, in an extraordinary ordering of priorities, Tedder remarked:

> *Finally* [emphasis added] there was Western Europe, in which the Armed Forces were discharging the responsibilities which flowed

from our victory in the recent war and at the same time contributing in no insignificant way to the unity of Western Europe as the first line of our defence against another war. . . .

The Chancellor could only point out that if he had to find the Minister of Defence's £810 million (plus £20 million for development costs) then £70 million would have to be cut from the social services. Here was a moral dilemma – world power or New Jerusalem; a choice for the hard-up between an illusion and a dream. The Foreign Secretary for one, however, 'did not feel that he should be called upon to choose between foreign policy and defence on the one hand and Social Services on the other'. It supplies a poignant footnote to this continuing debate about Britain's ability to afford the world role that on 21 October the big decision was taken by the Cabinet's Economic Policy Committee to increase the British people's tea ration to, yes, just two and a half ounces a week as from 4 December.[32]

The arguments on paper and across the table rolled on through November, the 'first-class power' lobby unshaken by opponents who pointed out that Britain was spending more per head on defence than any other Western European state.[33] In particular, the new German Federal Republic, already perceived in Whitehall as posing a future menace to British export markets, was spending nothing at all on defence; nor for that matter was Japan, also by now seen as a reviving commercial threat.

Just as in the 1930s it was the opposing pulls between the defence of Europe (embodied in Western Union) and the entanglements of the world-and-Commonwealth role which racked the Government's collective mind. Thus in the very same meeting on 25 November 1949 which agreed to maintain the British garrison in the Middle East at a strength of one and one-third divisions Bevin argued that to reduce the defence budget to £760 million as the Chancellor now urged would be taken as a 'repudiation' of Britain's obligations to Western Union.[34] The Prime Minister thereupon told his colleagues that, 'in his view, the case had been made out for some increase in defence expenditure over £760 millions, to have regard for Western Union commitments . . .'.

And so the Defence Committee finally settled on a budget for 1950-1 of £780 million. This was more than a tenth larger than the target figure given to the Harwood Committee, £20 million more than the Chancellor had thought possible without radical changes in the Government's overall policy, and £30 million less than the Minister of Defence had thought essential to uphold Britain's existing global commitments – in other words, a classic Whitehall fudge. It promised exactly what Morrison had warned against barely three weeks earlier: 'paying more than we can afford for defences that are nevertheless inadequate, or even illusory'.

Of this total of £780 million no less than £245 million related to production programmes for the armed forces – a measure of how deeply the double demand of playing the world power as well as defending the United Kingdom and Western Europe bit into Britain's industrial resources.[35] Indeed it was yet another expensive aspect of Britain's pretensions to the status of 'first-class power' that she was striving to be self-sufficient in the procurement of military hardware at a time of accelerating complexity of design and therefore cost. This was especially true of aircraft, where in mid-1950 no fewer than thirty different models, from jet fighters to troop transports, were in current production and twenty-seven in the development stage.[36] On top of these military orders the British aircraft industry was building in mid-1950 four different models of airliner and developing three more.[37] For the conviction that Britain was, and should remain – and, what was more, *could* remain – a player in the same league of *technological* power as the United States shaped the policies of the postwar Labour Government towards civil aviation[38] (see below, Chapter 12) no less than those of the wartime coalition[39]. Just as with foreign and defence policy, so with Whitehall discussions of aircraft manufacture the word 'prestige' crops up often in 1945–50 as a reason for clinging obstinately in defiance of the facts to futile but costly commitments, such as the Brabazon and the Tudor airliners (see below, Chapter 12).[40] In this further pursuit of grandiose delusion Britain in 1949 invested £19.3 million in the civil aircraft industry, as against only £15 million in a field so essential to a modern economy as new long-distance telephone cabling and new exchanges.[41]

In the fields of defence electronics, guided weapons and rocket propulsion too this attempt to be self-sufficient severely strained Britain's slender human and material resources in high technology and R and D. Moreover, it led to damaging competition for these resources with civil programmes and with exports. Back in February 1949 the Minister of Supply was complaining that one of the main difficulties in providing new wind tunnels and other experimental kit 'is the time taken to obtain factory-made plant and equipment (electrical generators, switch-gear, compressors, fans etc.). The requirements, of course, compete with other important demands on the engineering industry.'[42] A month later the Defence Production Committee had reported that it was 'obviously important to guard against the danger of designing weapons and equipment which it will prove to be beyond the economic and industrial capacity of this country to produce or maintain and operate on any useful scale even in war'.[43]

Thus it was that, thanks to the triumph of the world-power fantasists in Whitehall over the doubting realists, Britain's strength at the beginning of 1950 remained in a state of overstretch across the whole spectrum of total strategy, from technological and financial resources to military 'world zones' in the Middle East and Far East.

Then, in March, the Chiefs of Staff – just like their predecessors almost exactly eleven years earlier – awoke with a start to the strategic importance of Western Europe to Britain's own survival, reporting to the Government that:

> we have been increasingly impressed by the fact that, in the event of war, the defence of a line at least as far East as the Rhine is vital to the security of these islands. Politically, Western civilisation is unlikely to survive even a temporary Russian occupation of all Continental Europe. Militarily, it would in that event be extremely difficult to defend the United Kingdom.[44]

Went on the COS: 'It must seem to our Allies, that we have employed every device to avoid giving any answer [about the British continental commitment in case of war]. We cannot hold back much longer. . . .' They therefore recommended 'that His Majesty's Government should now enter into a firm commitment to provide a Corps of two Infantry Divisions as a reinforcement to B.A.O.R. in the event of war'. This, they comfortably assured the Defence Committee, 'will in no way commit us to the build-up of a great Continental army . . .'. Moreover, in their judgement it did not mean 'any fundamental change in our accepted policy of the three pillars of British strategy – the defence of the United Kingdom, the protection of our sea communications and the holding of the Middle East . . .'.

Nonetheless, 'while the Middle East is crucially important to Allied strategy and must be held if humanly possible, the allocation of resources to it must not be allowed fatally to compromise our ability to sustain the first pillar . . .'.

Yet, despite this belated commitment to Western Europe as the vital outer defence of Britain, the Defence Committee and its military advisers are found happily talking at the end of May 1950 about such topics as an invitation to Australia, New Zealand and possibly South Africa to meet and discuss defence policy, especially in regard to the Middle East; the need to find forces for garrisons in Europe, the Middle East and Far East; and how a United Kingdom share in the defence of the Egyptian base was 'a priority to be met if humanly possible'.[45] Indeed, just how completely Attlee had wasted his breath back in 1946 in questioning the future utility of Britain's traditional axis of Empire eastwards through the Mediterranean and Middle East is shown by the brief given to the Chief of the Imperial General Staff on 19 May 1950 before his visit to Egypt, which stated that that country 'is the strategic key to the Middle East. Not only is she the gateway to Africa, whose penetration by Communism would be a disaster for Western civilisation, but she forms a vital link in the communications between the Atlantic Powers and their allies [that is, dependents] in the Indian and Pacific Oceans. . . .'[46]

It followed from this belief that only the Suez Canal Zone could provide the necessary base area (Bevin's dream of a new Middle East base in East Africa having been aborted after thirty-six out of seventy vast and costly corrugated-iron storage sheds had been built).[47] Moreover, according to the Foreign Secretary in December 1949, 'it is still regarded as essential to our defence plans for the Middle East that we should secure the right to station forces in Cyrenaica . . . for a period of 20 or 25 years'.

So just as in the 1930s a British government and its military advisers shirked the choice between world deployments and the defence of Europe, and instead opted to try to fulfil both competing roles. In May 1950 the COS were proposing a future British peacetime commitment of land forces to the Middle East of almost 32,000 soldiers.[48] When the British Army's Far East entanglements (including Hong Kong) are added to those in the Middle East the combined total of infantry and artillery in those theatres in July 1950 broadly equals that deployed in the combined defence of Europe and the United Kingdom. Likewise, 40 per cent of the Royal Air Force's frontline strength was deployed outside the United Kingdom and Western Europe.[49] Moreover, as the 1949 *Statement on Defence* remarked about these forces located far overseas, 'their being to an important extent dispersed in comparatively small groups over very wide areas . . . and the added overheads associated with them have contributed heavily to the size of the Defence Budget . . .'.[50] In fact, *direct* disbursements in sterling on forces currently overseas had been running at about £100 million annually in 1948 and 1949,[51] with consequent impact on a British balance of payments which wobbled precariously from a current account deficit of £30 million in 1948 to a narrow surplus of £5 million in 1949.[52]

No wonder, then, that the total British defence budget proposed in March 1950 for 1950–1 amounted to 23 per cent of the entire national budget (or 7.7 per cent of GNP). By comparison Australia was spending just over 10 per cent of her national budget on defence (or 3.3 per cent of GNP); New Zealand under 9 per cent (2.5 per cent of GNP);[53] and Britain's fast re-emerging trade rivals, West Germany and Japan, absolutely nothing at all.

In the absence of exact breakdowns of costs between different theatres, how much of the British 7.7 per cent of GDP may be ascribed to the world and Commonwealth role, and how much to the necessary defence of Western Europe (including the United Kingdom)?

The answer must be about half and half. To give a measure of the cost of making a major contribution to European defence only, West Germany in 1960 would spend on defence 4 per cent of a GDP which was then about the same as that of the United Kingdom.[54] To look at it from the opposite angle, getting on for half the strength of the British armed forces was deployed outside Europe in the spring of 1950. When the disproportionately high logistic overheads of such distant deployments are taken into account, it is a fair guess that these deployments (coupled with their administrative, logistic and industrial back-up, plus reserves for rotation held in the United Kingdom) must have accounted for at least half the 7.7 per cent of GDP being spent by Britain on defence. This broadly tallies with the figure discussed above of 4 per cent of GDP for a European defence role only.

In other words, the simple financial cost alone in 1946–50 of the size of armed forces demanded by the world role (as distinct from Britain's own security in Europe) amounted to something like £300–400 million a year. This is equivalent to the total annual capital investment in those years in manufacturing industry other than iron and steel.[55]

The burden piled on Britain's sagging back by the world and Commonwealth role was not, however, limited to the defence budget alone or even to the pre-empting of scarce technological and industrial resources by the requirements of the armed forces. For Britain had also chosen to play the parts of Commonwealth banker and benefactor.

CHAPTER SIX

'A Never-to-be-Repeated Opportunity'

T
HE COLONIAL EMPIRE, described by a Colonial Office report in November 1948 as being mostly inhabited by producers 'on the margin of subsistence'[1] and by Hugh Dalton in his diary in February 1950 as being composed of 'pullulating, poverty-stricken, diseased nigger communities',[2] constituted a wide-open mouth into which (under the Colonial Development and Welfare Act of 1945) a benevolent Labour Government chose to stuff annually up to £17.5 million (increased in 1949 to £20 million) of capital investment resources so urgently needed to modernise Britain herself. Moreover, for the purpose of doling out largesse, Britain numbered the Burmese too among colonial peoples on the margin of subsistence, and so Burma received from Britain interest-free loans of £45 million between 1945 and June 1947, when she left the Commonwealth on gaining her independence, an event celebrated by the British Government by turning £15 million of the loans into a free gift.[3] In November 1949 the Cabinet Economic Policy Committee approved a proposal to make a further loan of £7.5 million, and solely for political reasons, the Chancellor of the Exchequer having remarked that there were 'no commercial grounds on which it could be justified'.[4]

In its attitude to the colonial Empire as in other aspects of total strategy, this was a government of Edwardian 'social imperialists' advised by civil servants imbued with a no less Edwardian public-school prefect's sense of altruistic responsibility. The energetic Colonial Secretary from late 1946 to 1950, Arthur Creech Jones, was himself a former leading member of the Fabian Colonial Research Group (founded in 1940), and as such had helped to draft visionary blueprints for building New Jerusalems in the lands of the pullulating, poverty-stricken and disease-ridden. Hence, in the words of the report of the Colonial Development Working Party to the Government in November 1948, 'the promotion of the utmost social, economic and political advancement of the Colonial peoples is a goal to which His Majesty's Government is pledged. . . . The honouring of these pledges implies a long-term programme of Colonial development aimed at maintaining and improving the standards of living of the Colonial peoples.'[5]

Yet the report had to acknowledge that this programme would demand much capital investment, especially in infrastructure. Without major improvements in farming, transport and flood control the colonial producers 'will remain, as they have always been, on the margin of subsistence . . . but the margin of saving in the Colonies themselves is as yet too narrow to provide more than a small fraction of the capital investment required . . .'. It followed that the major fraction would have to be found by the United Kingdom, meaning (in the words of an earlier study in July 1948) 'heavy demands on the capital goods available in the United Kingdom' at a time of 'great pressure' on those supplies.[6] Nonetheless, in the true spirit of social imperialism Creech Jones saw the colonies not only as the object of a kind of overseas Toynbee Hall mission but also as future buttresses of British prosperity – markets for British goods, sources of minerals for British industry, providers of margarine for British breakfasts and cocoa for British nightcaps.[7] Such a vision might have made sense in the 1920s or the 1900s, when the colonial Empire was a neglected asset and the United Kingdom was still a rich country with abundant funds to invest,[8] but in the late 1940s it hardly promised the most cost-effective way to employ overstretched British resources of money and capital goods, or, for that matter, overstretched British resources of well-educated young people. Between June 1945 and September 1948 the Colonial Service attracted no fewer than 4100 new recruits, inevitably at the expense of the United Kingdom herself as an industrial society.[9]

What then was the balance sheet of colonial Empire? Firstly, Britain ran a payments deficit with all the colonies together of £195 million in 1947 and £57 million in 1948, due to 'heavy Government expenditure, civil and military, which includes expenditure on development schemes'.[10] To reduce this deficit would mean exporting to the colonies industrial goods which might otherwise go to re-equip British industry or be exported to more profitable and faster-growing markets.[11] In return the colonial Empire supplied Britain with some 10 per cent of her imports[12] and earned a modest surplus on its trade with the dollar countries (£50 million in 1948).[13] Nevertheless, since it was only Malayan tin and rubber and West African cocoa that made the dollar profits, while the rest of the colonies ran up deficits,[14] the colonial Empire all in all hardly warranted Creech Jones's social-imperialist enthusiasm or its cost to the British Exchequer. Yet in 1950 Britain was to shoulder further and even heavier development costs on behalf of the pululating and poverty-stricken.

For just as the deepening Cold War had provided a fresh justification for the United Kingdom's military and political attempt to play the world power, so did it also in regard to handouts to the backward countries of the Commonwealth, especially in Asia after the Communist triumph in China in 1949. Bevin in particular successfully urged that the best means of saving the Indian sub-continent, Burma, Malaya and British North Borneo from succumbing to Communist penetration lay in promoting their prosperity through a colossal development programme. At the Colombo Conference in January 1950 he had his way: a six-year scheme costing £1868 million, of which Britain and the 'white' Dominions undertook to find more than half (and that was not counting the release of sterling balances).[15] No one asked why poverty-stricken countries thus proving a financial liability to the United Kingdom would magically become an asset to the Soviet Union if they were to go Communist.

The majority of the sterling Dominions – Australia, South Africa, India and Pakistan – likewise sucked hungrily on the teat of Britain's withered resources. In the six years from 1946 to 1951 they ran up a combined balance of payments deficit of £700 million, of which nearly £600 million had to be financed by the United Kingdom. Only New Zealand and Ceylon earned small surpluses over the period.[16] The new Dominions of India and Pakistan in particular enjoyed a pre-emptive claim on the teat because of the debt of over £1300 million (the so-called 'sterling balances') which Britain had incurred in wartime for the privilege of defending the Indian sub-continent against the Japanese (see above, pp. 27–8, and below, pp. 109–12). For when India and Pakistan used their sterling balances to buy British goods it meant effectively that Britain was exporting these goods for nothing, or, to put it more baldly, giving them away. Britain was thus paying twice over for her refusal, out of a sense of moral responsibility, to dump India before the Second World War when urged to do so by Indian leaders.

Yet these balances constitute only one aspect of a phenomenon no less important than the pink-on-the-map Empire in causing the United Kingdom's postwar total-strategic overstretch – the invisible empire of the Sterling Area.

Like the pink-on-the-map Empire, the Sterling Area derived from no deliberate and coherent design, but represented the detritus of successive episodes of history, in this case financial and economic.[17] Its origins lay back in the mid-nineteenth century when Britain enjoyed unchallenged supremacy in export markets as the world's first and only industrial nation, and after the adoption of free trade became by far the biggest importer in the world – of cheap food (it kept down labour costs) for her multiplying urban population, and of raw materials for her smoke-palled factories. At the same time, as the world's biggest creditor, Britain massively invested capital abroad in order to balance her trade, the loans being raised in sterling in London. It followed from this unique financial and economic predominance that London became the world's banking centre, and sterling the world's international currency. While up to the Georgian age Britain had remained a basically self-contained and self-sufficient economy (especially in food), she had become by the late-Victorian era geared into a global economic system to an extent unparalleled then or since by any other industrial country. In the temporarily favourable circumstances of the time it seemed the recipe for Britain's envied prosperity. But those temporary circumstances disappeared in the Great War and the world slump of 1929–32, when the complex Victorian web of multilateral world trade and finance centred on London was first of all dislocated, and thereafter replaced by protectionist trading blocs. In any case, British industry, whose domination of world markets had supplied the very engine of sterling's rise to supremacy, had been growing more and more out of date and uncompetitive from the 1870s onwards, and in the 1920s lay stalled in deep recession (see above, pp. 11–17). It remained only for the world slump to reduce Britain's invisible earnings from financial services, shipping and overseas investments by half, and what was left of her Victorian commercial domination was destroyed. In the financial panic of 1931, and for the first time during a peace, sterling ceased to be pegged to the price of gold.

This event brought about the creation of a 'sterling bloc' – a group of countries which chose to peg their own currencies to sterling rather than gold. Many of them were primary producers, especially of foodstuffs, dependent on exporting to the British home market; they included all parts of the British Commonwealth except for Canada, a dollar country. So what had once been a global network spontaneously evolved from British commercial and industrial expansion had now shrunk and congealed into a defensive economic bloc.

The outbreak of the Second World War saw this bloc turned by the Exchange Control Act into a legal entity, with a ring-fence of exchange control round what now became known as the Sterling Area, with the object of conserving and managing for war purposes the area's gold and dollar reserves. On this diminished stage Britain continued to strut her Victorian role of central banker even though by the end of the war she had sold most of her overseas investments and her vaults had been emptied of gold and dollars,[18] – and, what was more, of sterling too. For in 1945 the United Kingdom's sterling debts (or 'balances') had risen to £2969 million.[19] In the case of India (as has already been described) and Middle Eastern countries like Egypt, Palestine and Iraq the debts had been run up by buying local supplies and services (and local currency for paying British armed forces stationed there) in the course of Britain's imperial campaigns against the Axis in the Mediterranean and the Japanese in South-east Asia. In the case of Australia, New Zealand, South Africa, the colonial Empire and some non-Sterling Area countries such as the Argentine, Britain had obtained large quantities of food on tick, a process which continued in 1945–6 while British exports were still a fraction of pre-war, and far too small to pay for essential imported foodstuffs.[20]

For in the Second World War, as in the Great War, Britain had belatedly paid a grim penalty for her Victorian adoption of free trade, which had ended the tariff protection of British agriculture and rendered her dependent for life itself on food shipped in from the far reaches of the globe. In the first place this dependence on seaborne supplies had twice brought her to the verge of starvation and defeat at the hands of the U-boat. Secondly, in 1939–45 her total industrial mobilisation for war meant that she could no longer manufacture and export the goods to pay for the food – a plight unimaginable to

Victorian free-traders such as Cobden in their boundless optimistic certainty. And in the postwar era Britain continued to remain critically dependent on imports of grain, meat and dairy products despite a determined effort to revive her own agriculture and despite rationing even stricter than in wartime. This dependence constituted the major debit item (sterling as well as dollar) in her balance of payments; it therefore imparted its own particular urgency to the postwar drive for exports; and from 1948 onwards it greedily ate into Britain's share of Marshall Aid (see below, Chapter 19). Here was overstretch in a fundamental requirement of total strategy – the nourishing of the nation.

By the end of the Second World War the Sterling Area constituted, just like the Commonwealth, a legacy of history now too burdensome for the United Kingdom to carry except at the expense of damage to her own progress as an industrial society. Whereas in the Victorian age sterling had grown naturally into an international trading currency because of Britain's unrivalled wealth and commercial power, now the reverse was the case, for Britain was contriving artificially to preserve sterling's role and the Sterling Area as an institution (with the sterling members of the Commonwealth as its core) even though she was now poor, commercially struggling and massively in debt to other Sterling Area states. In the words of a Cabinet Office study in July 1948:

> It is obviously necessary for the support of such a system of multilateral trading to carry a considerable volume of reserves in order to allow of the seasonal and other fluctuations that must take place in the trade of the world, including changes in the price of primary products on which the economy of much of the Sterling Area depends. It is for this purpose that the reserves of gold and foreign exchange are required to service the need of the whole Sterling Group; without adequate reserves the Group could not continue to function. . . .[21]

In point of fact Sterling Area reserves in mid-1948 stood at only about a third (in real terms) of what they had been in mid-1939.[22] Needless to say, the consequent task of building up these reserves fell overwhelmingly on the United Kingdom. As a distinguished Treasury economist was to write in 1951:

the U.K. cannot live up to its responsibilities as the centre and mainspring of the Sterling Area unless it puts its house in order to the extent of achieving a surplus on its overall balance of payments. This conclusion is indeed inescapable on any realistic view of the position of the U.K. The existence of the Sterling Area and the widespread use of sterling carry obvious risks for the U.K. In the last resort every expenditure of sterling by an overseas country (and every credit or loan extended to such a country) involves a call either on the physical resources of the U.K. or on the gold and dollar reserves. . . .[23]

The 'risks' were indeed obvious: they sprang yet again from the vulnerability and fragility that come from overstretch. Less obvious is this economist's implication that Britain must achieve a large surplus on her balance of payments not so much in order to invest in her industries or infrastructure, or to build schools and hospitals, or even to fill British shops at long last with food and household goods, but first and foremost in order to keep the Sterling Area afloat.[24]

Given the importance attached to achieving reserves big enough for this purpose, it is not surprising that when in 1948 Whitehall had to decide Britain's priorities under the European Recovery Programme (Marshall Aid) its 'sheet-anchor', in the words of a Cabinet Office memorandum, was 'that our reserves must not fall in the E.R.P. [European Recovery Programme] period. . . . we must emerge from the E.R.P. period with strong reserves and unquestionable financial strength. . . . we cannot allow a seeping of reserves [which] is demoralising in itself and destroys confidence in sterling . . .'.[25] In fact, the same memorandum openly acknowledged that in order so to maintain the reserves Marshall Aid would, as far as permissible, be used (in effect) to finance all the Sterling Area's gold and dollar payments,[26] including, of course, payments for American foodstuffs. This was an order of priority very different from that of continental recipients of Marshall Aid, who used it first and foremost to reconstruct their industrial economies (see below, Chapter 19).

The overstretch caused by the Sterling Area and by the maintenance of sterling as an international trading currency was immensely worsened by the so-called 'sterling balances', that problem within a problem. A report in March 1950 to the Cabinet Economic Policy Committee bleakly summed it up:

The existence of large sterling balances, available for spending outside our control, is an ever-present threat to sterling. The balances played a large part in the events of 1949 in that their existence contributed heavily – and still contributes – to the lack of confidence in sterling. While our affairs are going well, this is not directly damaging, but as soon as we suffer a set-back our weakness is at once intensified. Our vulnerability to fluctuations in the world economy – resulting from our wholly inadequate reserves – is our worst weakness, and the sterling balances greatly intensify it.[27]

Nor was this the full extent of the damage:

The existence of large sterling balances represents a potential direct drain on our economic resources – so-called 'unrequited exports'. If e.g. India is able to run a deficit on her balance of payments by drawing on her sterling balances, this is a charge on our economy, and contributes to our present inflationary difficulties. In 1948–49, the rest of the sterling area [that is, except for the United Kingdom] ran an overall deficit of £320 million, and in 1949–50 the deficit will be well over £200 million. *It is only because we are receiving Marshall Aid that we can support such a burden* [emphasis added].[28]

Why then had the United Kingdom continued since 1945 to carry the double burden of the Sterling Area and the sterling balances? As far back as January 1944 Lord Keynes had concluded an analysis of a necessarily complex subject by warning that:

the maintenance of the sterling area system during the transition period [from war to peace] is not a means of solving our financial problem during that period. On the contrary, it will probably add to our liabilities on a substantial scale; it will certainly put us at greater risk and add to the sum of liabilities which we must prepare ourselves to meet.[29]

Nevertheless, in his detailed proposals for lessening these liabilities he shrank from suggesting that Britain should simply repudiate her sterling debts (especially the bulk of them owed to India and Middle Eastern countries), the core of the whole problem. Instead he recommended that they should be gradually paid off after the war by what would later be dubbed 'unrequited exports', although to do this would still lay a weighty burden on the British economy (as in the event it did).[30] Indeed when in November 1949 (following the summer sterling crisis) the repudiation of the sterling debts was formally discussed by the Labour Cabinet's Economic Policy Committee, it was quickly rejected.[31] Back in 1944, after hearing arguments in favour of a postwar leading role for sterling, Keynes had written that 'All our reflex actions are those of a rich man. . . .'[32] They were certainly those of the Edwardian upper-middle-class public-school-and-Oxbridge-educated governing class to which Keynes himself belonged and which was so well portrayed (and unwittingly impaled) by Noël Annan in his book *Our Age*.[33] In the case of the sterling debts the reflex action took the form of recoiling from so ruthless a stroke of self-interest as repudiation, and instead yielding to an altruistic sense of duty to others. As a Whitehall paper on the topic expressed it in 1948:

> Owing to the free operation of the Sterling Area system and the fact that Great Britain bears the ultimate responsibility for the support of Sterling, that obligation to assist in the maintenance of these great populations has in fact fallen on us and we have had to allow these drawings [of dollars] not to encourage or assist our own trade, but in most cases in order to keep the people of these regions and their economy alive. . . .[34]

In any event, the Bank of England strove from 1944 onwards to perpetuate the traditional role of sterling out of much the same kind of nostalgic illusion as inspired the Chiefs of Staff and the Foreign Office to cling on to the world role. When the Paymaster-General, Lord Cherwell, had asked during the Whitehall debate in 1944 on the postwar role of sterling 'whether the maintenance of the sterling area was an essential condition for the re-establishment of our export trade', the Deputy Governor of the Bank of England had answered that 'he thought that, in order to get maximum trade, we ought not to upset longstanding practices, nor to risk having new exchange controls inside the area'.[35] He and Lord Cobbold (an executive director) insisted that they wanted sterling to be used as a reserve currency by all members of the area. In Cobbold's own words, 'The Bank aimed at making sterling widely acceptable and widely used.' This all too characteristic Establishment view of Britain's future as taking the form of a restoration of her past prevailed over Keynes's and Cherwell's scepticism. According to a report by a special Cabinet Committee on Anglo-American financial discussions later that same month of February 1944, 'it is common ground that it should be our constant aim to preserve indefinitely the main features of the sterling area in full force in the form in which it has been known'.[36]

It is true that for Britain to repudiate the sterling debts (perhaps by counter-invoicing India, Pakistan and Middle Eastern countries for the cost of defending them during the war?) or to pursue some scheme of escape from the overstretch imposed by the Sterling Area itself would almost certainly have led to the break-up of the Commonwealth. Such a break-up would of course have vouchsafed the United Kingdom a double relief, grand strategic as well as financial. However, this was not a reading of the situation likely to occur, let alone appeal, to those who saw sterling as one of the twin pillars (along with the Commonwealth) of Britain's supposed status as a world power. As Bevin put it to the Economic Policy Committee on 1 July 1949 during a discussion of the current balance of payments crisis: 'The Sterling Area, and the countries which were linked with it, included about 1,000 million people and could therefore be associated with the United States and the dollar area on a basis of equality.'[37]

And so yet again the Labour Government chose to interpret a British liability as an asset, and believe that what overstretched the United Kingdom made her stronger.

In its cherishing of the Sterling Area and Britain's economic, political and strategic links with the British Commonwealth the Labour Government resembled nothing so much as the board of a long-established company which smugly clings to a comfortably familiar pattern of trading that has proved profitable enough in the past – what might be termed the 'Founder's Whiskers syndrome'.

And just as such a company is so blinkered by the comfortably familiar that it fails to foresee the markets of the future, so the Government was blinkered by the existence of the Commonwealth from grasping the political and economic potential of Europe. With a patronising arrogance,[38] it looked down on the temporarily war-ruined Europeans, and ignored Europe's astonishing rise in wealth and industrial might in the hundred years before the catastrophe of 1939–45. After all, had not Britain emerged triumphant from the Second

World War, whereas all the countries of continental Europe had suffered defeat and occupation? Was she not a great power with worldwide responsibilities and a 'special relationship' with the United States rather than a mere state of the second rank like France?

The Government therefore publicly lauded in principle the concept of closer European union[39] (just as did Winston Churchill and the Conservative Opposition) while shrinking from it in practice (just as the Conservatives were to do in office after 1951). This had proved true even in the military field: whereas Britain in the person of Ernest Bevin had been instrumental in creating Western Union (a paper military organisation for the defence of Europe) in March 1948, it was not until two years later that she decided to back the gesture with a commitment of reinforcements in the event of war (see above, p. 99). When it came to political or economic integration the gulf between gesture and commitment proved even wider. This was first demonstrated after Britain agreed in September 1947 to join with other states in the Organisation for European Economic Co-operation (OEEC) in a study group on a possible European customs union. That same autumn the Cabinet agreed to Bevin's suggestion that the alternative notion of a British–Commonwealth customs union should be investigated. However, the interdepartmental study group charged with this task found that such a union was no more a runner now than forty years earlier in the heyday of imperialism.[40] In particular, according to the Commonwealth Relations Office,

> While Mr Bevin's suggestion for a Commonwealth Customs Union was enthusiastically welcomed in certain quarters in this country, this welcome has nowhere been echoed in other parts of the Commonwealth. In general, commentators in the rest of the Commonwealth either have been hostile or at best have adopted an attitude of cautious enquiry. . . . Emphasis has everywhere been laid on the paramount importance of protecting the development of secondary industries against the competition from the United Kingdom which would result from a Customs Union.[41]

Here was plain evidence that the Commonwealth could not offer Britain a practicable alternative to a European economic union – indeed that it possessed no economic coherence at all, its principal members actually perceiving British industry as a threat. Some present and future partners! And yet, defying such realities, the British Government continued to put the Commonwealth before Europe. In September 1948 the Cabinet Committee on European Economic Co-operation reported that to join a European customs union would come as a 'shock' to other members of the British Commonwealth: 'in many quarters it will be felt, however unfairly, that we regard our ties with Europe as more important than our ties with the Common-wealth . . .'.[42] Moreover, 'The system of Imperial Preference would, to some extent at any rate, be weakened. . . .' Therefore agreement would have to be reached with Commonwealth countries about mutually acceptable terms before the United Kingdom committed herself to joining such a union.[43] Hence the instructions given to the British delegation to the Customs Union Study Group meeting in Brussels in December 1948 embodied the mandarin's classic tactics of procrastination and intellectual sabotage:

> If pressed on its general attitude towards a Customs Union the Delegation should say that there does not appear to be any immediate prospect of a Customs Union and that in any case the United Kingdom would be unable to commit itself on the subject without further study . . . on a realistic basis. . . .[44]

Come January 1949, and the Foreign Secretary and the Chancellor in a joint memorandum about the future structure of the Organisation for European Economic Co-operation were remarking that the customs-union project 'is, as expected, turning out to be no talisman or open sesame but an unusually difficult and complex affair which would take many years to bring about . . .'.[45] There followed comments on the OEEC itself which epitomise the ambivalence of British attitudes to the fate of Europe. Having warned that the OEEC and with it the European Recovery Programme could break down without some new impetus, the Chancellor and the Foreign Secretary averred that Britain 'alone of the countries of Western Europe has the necessary standing and technical capacity to work out a scheme which can give new life to the O.E.E.C. conception'. But then came the cautious cavil:

> We must not, however, lose sight of the risk that, in taking this lead, and attempting to put Western Europe on its legs, we may be led

into courses which would make this country no longer a viable unit
apart from the rest of Western Europe; and that should the attempt
fail we should then find that we had deprived ourselves of things
necessary to our economic survival. . . .

And so the British Government 'must do nothing to damage
irretrievably the economic structure of this country . . . [for if] the
attempt to restore Western Europe should fail, this country could still
hope to restore its position in co-operation with the rest of the
Commonwealth and the United States . . .'.

The Government did not finally abandon procrastination for
decision – negative of course – over the scheme for a European customs
union until October 1950, when the Foreign Secretary was invited 'to
consider the timing of an explicit statement of our unwillingness to
participate in a European Customs Union'.[46] By this time, however,
the customs-union proposal had been overtaken by two other schemes
no less bound to arouse the fearfulness of the semi-detached British
about too close an involvement with their European next-door
neighbours – a Dutch 'Plan for Action for European Integration' and a
French scheme for a European Coal and Steel Authority.

On the Dutch plan (which proposed the step-by-step creation of a
single European market) the Chancellor of the Exchequer, Sir Stafford
Cripps, commented in July 1950 that 'we could not agree to these
proposals, the acceptance of which would inevitably lead to close
economic integration, and the establishment of something like a
Customs Union, in Western Europe'.[47] The Cabinet's European
Economic Co-operation Committee, for its part, recommended that
in discussions of the plan in Paris, 'we should make it clear that we
were willing to examine the proposals and their implications carefully,
but that we were not prepared to take action which would prejudice
our economic relations with the Commonwealth and other countries
outside Europe'.[48] In the event, however, the plan came to nothing,
even though its basic idea was eventually to bloom in the Single
European Market of 1993.

Much more menacing an immediate problem for the British, as
they sought to reconcile their pretensions to European leadership with
their other pretensions to an independent world role, was the proposal
by the French Foreign Minister, Maurice Schuman, for a European
Coal and Steel Authority vested with supra-national powers.[49]

The French were motivated by a blend of fear and genuine constructive purpose – fear of German industrial strength, now already fast reviving under the new (1949) Federal German Republic; constructive purpose because three wars with Germany (including two total defeats coupled with enemy occupations) in less than a century had taught them that the nation-state alike caused war and then, in their own case, failed in its prime function of defending national independence. They wished therefore to take the basic sinews of German industrial and military power out of sovereign German control for ever by placing them under a supra-national European coal and steel authority along with the coal and steel industries of France, Italy, Britain and the Benelux countries. At the same time the French saw this authority as just the first stage in gradually creating a European economic community and ultimately a federal Europe which would supersede the untrammelled sovereignty of nation-states. Central to all this was the French hope that the new framework would enable France and Germany to bury the suicidal rivalry of the past and work together to build this new Europe. As the Foreign Office correctly divined, 'the primary significance of the Schuman proposals is in fact political rather than economic'.[50]

For the French, therefore, integration was the essential key to the whole process of European development. This was why the Schuman Plan proposed that the new coal and steel authority should have executive powers, rather than be restricted to mere advice and persuasion; that it should, above all, be vested with supra-national authority. But of course for these very same reasons the French proposals were fundamentally unacceptable to the British Government, whose feelings about yielding up any particle of sovereignty to any kind of European institution remained akin to those of a British spinster asked to forsake her kinsfolk and her respectable American gentleman-friend and get into a bed full of garlic-eating Frenchmen, Germans, Italians and what-not.[51] As Jean Monnet, the General Commissioner for the Modernisation and Re-equipment of France, shrewdly pointed out in his memoirs: 'Britain had not been conquered or invaded; she felt no need to exorcise history.'[52]

Here indeed lay the fundamental divide between the European attitude and the British. Defeat and occupation had served the continental countries in the function of bankruptcy to a business, placing a bottom line under the past, liquidating all debts and obligations, signifying that what they had hitherto lived by had failed them, and that they must start all over again along some new path. They did not have to wait for a sense of realism about their present and future gradually to dawn on them; it had been bludgeoned into them by the events of the war. The British on the other hand had never seen enemy soldiers parading in triumph through their streets or enemy flags flying above British palaces. Theirs was the psychology of the victor even though their real postwar circumstances were far more akin to those of the vanquished. They readily forgot that Britain had not been so much a victor in her own right as simply on the winning side – the German Army having been gutted by the Soviet Union and Britain herself as a wartime industrial economy having been towed home by the United States.

So although a few enlightened civil servants and members of the Foreign Office welcomed the Schuman Plan as, in the words of Sir Oliver Harvey, the Ambassador in Paris, 'a turning point in European and indeed world affairs' and 'a never-to-be-repeated opportunity',[53] the Labour Cabinet, together with the Labour movement as a whole, was totally hostile to the idea that Britain should join any kind of integrated European structure vested with supra-national powers. In regard to negotiations on the Schuman Plan the Cabinet therefore hoped to repeat its tactic of participating only in order to delay and preferably sabotage the achievement of the objective. As Bevin informed the French in May,

> we were willing to join with France and Germany in examining the proposal for an integration of the French and German coal and steel industries and . . . we should do so in the hope that we should find it possible to join such a scheme ourselves when it was known more clearly how it would work. . . .[54]

A working party of civil servants therefore proceeded to examine through a magnifying glass the small print of every aspect of the coal and steel industries in Britain and continental Europe (not omitting Imperial Preferences), finally turning in a 37-page report on 16 June 1950 which out of the mass of tactical detail drew the unsurprising strategic conclusions:

> we do not think that the Authority need be supra-national in order

to ensure the effective discharge of its responsibilities. Nor need the Authority be given any outward form which marks it as a prototype of federal institution for Europe nor carry any implications for the future political unity of Europe.[55]

By the end of July this working group had developed these conclusions into a draft proposal for a toothless alternative to the Schuman Plan's supra-national authority which would be limited merely to promoting and encouraging the co-ordinated development of European coal and steel industries, all decisions being reserved to the unanimous vote of nation-state representatives on a council of ministers.[56]

The French, however, had pre-empted such British attempts at sabotage with the speed and ruthlessness of a Gallic driver overtaking and cutting up a car-load of British tourists trundling obstructively in the middle of the road. Before Schuman even first informed the British Government about his plan on 10 May 1950, he had secretly obtained American and German support for it. Dean Acheson, the US Secretary of State, being strongly in favour of closer European integration and also bored and irritated by British pretensions to share – as between two world powers – a 'special relationship' with the United States, enthusiastically backed the Schuman Plan. Konrad Adenauer, Chancellor of the German Federal Republic, agreed to the plan without hesitation, seeing it as a marvellous opportunity for Germany to enjoy equal status with France as a founder member of the new authority. The British found themselves thus already left behind at the traffic lights, to Bevin's intense chagrin.[57] In Monnet's words: 'The essential prize had been won, irrevocably. Europe was on the move. Whatever the British decided would be their own affair.'[58] But, by way of making it even more irrevocably irrevocable, Monnet secretly obtained Adenauer's agreement to accept the basic principles of the plan (that is, a supra-national authority) before negotiations even began. The French Government thereupon formally asked all seven states invited to take part in the negotiations (including, most particularly, Britain) similarly to commit themselves. This, after nearly two weeks of toing and froing, the British Cabinet finally refused to do.[59]

And so Britain condemned herself to lurking outside in the street, while within the conference chamber six European states (France,

Germany, Italy, Belgium, The Netherlands and Luxembourg) embarked on the first stage of constructing a new European order. Yet the British Government by no means gave up hope of influencing the outcome of the negotiations, preferably by selling to the Europeans its proposal for a toothless alternative to a supra-national authority. However, by the time a draft of this was set before British ministers on 24 July, the ungentlemanly Europeans were already on the point of signing a treaty embodying the undiluted Schuman Plan. As the Chancellor of the Exchequer remarked to the Cabinet Economic Policy Committee when it met to consider the British draft,

> in view of the progress of the discussions in Paris on the Schuman Plan it was now less likely that we should have an opportunity to put forward proposals on an alternative plan than that we should be invited to associate ourselves in some degree with a plan on the lines of the Schuman Plan, which had been agreed by the other countries of Western Europe. Studies were now being made accordingly of the form of any such association that would be acceptable to us. . . .[60]

As one such study by civil servants acknowledged at the end of July, the previous British assumption 'that the United Kingdom would be able to play a decisive part in shaping both the form and content of the Authority' was defunct, and 'the situation which we now face is completely new'.[61] The best that Britain could now do, therefore, was to seek 'some kind of an association with an Authority which is acquiring a form and momentum of its own . . .'. Nonetheless, the study endeavoured to comfort ministers by pointing to at least one compensation: 'the Commonwealth countries may be less ready to see political objections to an association with the European industries than to a full participation in an Authority, and the economic problem connected with Imperial Preference may be consequently more easily disposed of'.

In a House of Commons debate at the end of June Churchill and Eden led the Conservative Party in a fierce attack on the Government for choosing not to take part in the negotiations – but then, as an Opposition, they could utter pro-European rhetoric without risk of having to turn it into policy. It can hardly be doubted, however, that the true sentiments of the rank-and-file of both main political parties in Britain and also of the man in the demob suit and his wife in the fish queue were accurately reflected in a tract issued by the Labour Party Executive in May 1950 entitled *European Unity*:

> In every respect except distance we in Britain are closer to our kinsmen in Australia and New Zealand on the far side of the world than we are to Europe. We are closer in language and in origins, in social habits and institutions, in political outlook and in economic interest. The economies of the Commonwealth countries are complementary to that of Britain to a degree which those of Western Europe could never equal.[62]

But sentiment, however deeply felt, is a poor guide to total strategy. The Labour Cabinet had thrown away what Oliver Harvey and others perceived at the time to constitute 'a never-to-be-repeated opportunity': that is, the opportunity of taking a leading role in what Harvey likewise saw at the time as 'a turning point in European and indeed world affairs'. The episode starkly demonstrated that five years after Victory-Europe Day Britain still remained lost in the illusion of a continuing destiny as a world and imperial power – that illusion which was costing her so dear in terms of economic and military overstretch.

On 22 June 1950, while negotiations over the Schuman Plan were still in progress, the armed forces of Communist North Korea invaded South Korea and abruptly turned the Cold War hot. Now it was no longer a question of Britain trimming back her defence budget by salami-slicing the armed forces, let alone savagely chopping it in accordance with some drastic abandonment of overseas commitments. Instead it was a question of full-scale rearmament. This massive new burden must fall on an industrial economy which had borne for five years the cost not only of the world-power illusion, but also of fulfilling the Labour Party's dream of New Jerusalem.

PART TWO

The Dream of New Jerusalem

The people will have won both struggles. . . . They deserve and must be assured a happier future than faced so many of them after the last war.

(LABOUR PARTY MANIFESTO, 1945)

the time for declaring a dividend on the profits of the Golden Age is the time when those profits have been realised in fact, not merely in the imagination.

(SIR KINGSLEY WOOD, CHANCELLOR OF THE EXCHEQUER, 1942)

The rush for spectacles, as for dental treatment, has exceeded all expectations. . . . Part of what has happened has been a natural first flush of the new scheme, with the feeling that everything is free now and it does not matter what is charged up to the Exchequer. . . .

(ANEURIN BEVAN, MINISTER OF HEALTH, 1948)

Any expansion in one part of the [National Health] Service must in future be met by economies or, if necessary, by contraction in others.

(SIR STAFFORD CRIPPS, CHANCELLOR OF THE EXCHEQUER, 1950)

CHAPTER SEVEN

The Brave New World and the Cruel Real World

L IKE SO MUCH of the industrial, institutional and mental furniture of postwar Britain, the dream of New Jerusalem was essentially a late-Victorian survival, even though it had taken the Second World War to inspire its final vivid immediacy. It had begun in an idealistic response to the reality that, although Britain at the end of the nineteenth century was still the richest country in the world, her industrial masses were living out their lives in (to cite the words of a 1905 case study) 'dreadful squalor and surpassing misery'.[1] Should not this immoral contrast between the swaggering wealth of the few and the griping poverty of the many give way to a just sharing out of the national income so that all could live the good life? Should not the dark industrial towns, grim barracks even when not actually slums, be replaced by garden cities of cottages amid the greenery of grass and tree? Should not a sickly and stunted proletariat be succeeded by a brave new race of radiantly healthy Britons? And should not the chaos and greed of capitalist competition yield to co-operation for the common good? Such was the nature of the questioning that sprang from the troubled consciences and outraged aesthetic sensibilities of varied social (and in many cases socialist) reformers in the 1890s and 1900s, from William Morris and Robert Blatchford, with their visions of a 'merrie England' restored, to intellectuals like Bernard Shaw and Sidney Webb who contributed to the 'Fabian Essays' of 1889 on how peacefully to bring about a socialist society.

For the British governing elite and opinion-forming intelligentsia had fallen victim during the Victorian age to a romantic idealism, convincing them that morality and reason could prevail over ruthless pursuit of material interest, that faith and dedication could build an ideal society at home and a new world order abroad, and so usher in an era of harmony among men. Into the brewing of this romantic idealism had gone some highly aromatic ingredients – the early-nineteenth-century religious revival, all guilt, redemption and moral purpose; an accompanying literary and artistic nostalgia for a supposed medieval age of Christian chivalry and community; a nostalgia likewise for rural life and its imagined moral and social beauties; a cult of the knightly 'gentleman' dedicated to the service of others; a belief in the British Empire as a civilising mission in the Greek and Roman mould; and a high-minded 'liberal education' inspired by classical literature and philosophy. The fermenting medium of the brew was provided by a wash of emotion, that basic constituent of romanticism.[2]

The public schools and the universities of Oxford and Cambridge, with their chapels and their games and their codes of manners, constituted not only brewing vats for this heady stuff but also the jugs by which it was slopped out to successive generations of youth, emasculating the sons of manufacturers and merchants into 'gentlemen'.

The lower-middle class and the 'respectable' working class, for their part, had taken their potent drams of idealism in the Victorian era from the non-conformist chapel, moving on later from concern with personal reformation and salvation to the reformation and salvation of British society at large. In the second half of the nineteenth century non-conformists of various sects thronged into the Liberal Party and later, at the end of the century and the beginning of the next, into the Labour Party, dominating both of them by force of moral conviction, earnestness of purpose and aptness for the drudgery of organisation, and making of them missions for evangelising New Jerusalem.[3] The Labour Party in particular possessed all the characteristics of a pseudo-religion from its earliest years in the 1890s, thanks to its spiritual borrowings from real evangelical faith. There was even a Socialist Sunday School movement with heartfelt socialist songs instead of hymns, and a declaration of socialist precepts based on 'Justice and Love' and modelled on the Ten Commandments.[4]

> We desire [proclaimed one of the precepts] to be just and loving to all fellow men and women, to work together as brothers and sisters, to be kind to every living creature and so help form a New Society with Justice as its foundation and Love as its law.[5]

Or as Clement Attlee, Leader of the Labour Party, was to write in 1935: 'Socialism . . . is something more than a political creed or an economic system. It is a philosophy of society. . . .'[6]

After the Great War even the Conservative Party had succumbed to the spirit of secularised religious idealism, for Stanley Baldwin, Neville Chamberlain and their closest colleagues (all public-school and Oxbridge men) were true Victorian moralists seeking to do good at home and abroad by the exercise of the Christian virtues, not least by forgiving those who trespassed against them, such as Adolf Hitler. In several cases their backgrounds showed a former personal or family connection with Liberalism and/or non-conformism. The younger generation of Conservative reformers in the 1930s and 1940s, men such as Quintin Hogg and R. A. Butler, represented the chivalric and Christian tradition of concern for the underdog first established in the party by Lord Shaftesbury, an outstanding Victorian exponent of the application of Christian conscience to social questions.

Thus a century of cross-breeding between the religious, educational, aesthetic and literary strains in romanticism came to make the British small-'l' liberal Establishment of the 1940s what it was: tender-hearted and highminded, in that order. As one of its most distinguished intellectual mandarins, Noël Annan, bears witness, its cardinal virtue – from civil servants to 'quality' journalists, architects to authors, bishops to economists, politicians to dons – consisted in 'compassion'.[7] In his words, 'Compassion for the poor and disadvantaged became the most powerful moral principle for Our Age.'[8] So, in the midst of a world war and with Britain's own survival in question, this liberal Establishment, latter-day White Knights, rode out to combat social evils with the flashing sword of moral indignation, and quested in simple faith for the grail of human harmony and happiness.[9] And, hardly surprisingly, the churches and the religious were as prominent in the muster rolls of the crusade to win a New Jerusalem after the war as they had been in pre-war support of the League of Nations and disarmament.[10]

The 1941 New Year issue of the mass-circulation magazine *Picture Post*, devoted entirely to 'A Plan for Britain', may be taken as the occasion of the successful wartime launch of New Jerusalem. Whether by coincidence or not, the coalition Government had set up a new Cabinet Committee on Reconstruction Problems within six weeks of its publication. While the articles themselves provide a comprehensive vision of the sunlit Britain of the future, their authorship marvellously evokes the nature of the 'enlightened' Establishment ('Our Age', in Noël Annan's phrase) from whose romantic imaginations the vision had sprung. It was in October 1940 that Kenneth Clark, the eminent aesthete, art historian and Wykehamist employed (like so many members of the intelligentsia) in the Ministry of Information, had convinced the proprietor of *Picture Post*, Edward Hulton (Harrow and Brasenose College, Oxford), that he should run a special issue on postwar Britain. Hulton agreed; and his editor, Tom Hopkinson, set to with an enthusiasm all the greater because he himself was a classic product of British romantic idealism – son of an archdeacon, a former assistant editor of the *Clarion*, and a passionate and lifelong chivalric champion of underdogs and noble causes. The cover of the issue bore the title 'A Plan for Britain' across the top of a photograph of six happy naked children on a playground slide; and the entire contents similarly milked the reader's emotions with a skilled journalistic hand. Pre-war pictures of the unemployed slouching on street corners and of idle industrial works, labelled 'The Tragic Tale', provided the object lesson in what must never happen again, and an Oxford economist, Thomas Balogh, explained how management of the economy by the state could instead secure 'Work for All'. Grim old institutional schools were contrasted with cheerful new ones; an aerial view of an existing town with its streets of little terrace houses on one page faced on the next an architect's sketch of tomorrow's city of glass and concrete laid out in wide grassy spaces. The related article by Maxwell Fry, the distinguished modern architect, proclaimed that 'the new Britain must be PLANNED'. A. D. Lindsay, the Master of Balliol (and a 'First' in Classics), a much respected humanist mandarin of the time, sketched 'A Plan for Education'; Julian Huxley, the scientist and broadcaster (Eton and Balliol), showed how to achieve 'Health for All'; and J. B. Priestley, novelist, broadcaster and 'a moralist of a very English kind' with 'a temperament innately romantic',[11] painted the rich life of culture and recreation in the new Britain 'When Work Is Over'.

But it was Hopkinson's editorial foreword which caught the essence of New Jerusalemism: the emotion and the romance. It recalled that, after the Great War, 'We got no new Britain, and we got no new Europe' because peace came so suddenly in the end that it took the nation by surprise, and there was lacking 'imagination, planning, and an idea of the country we wanted to make, and a passionate – actually passionate – determination to make it'.[12]

> This time we can be better prepared if we think now. This is not the time for putting off thinking 'till we see how things are'. . . . More than that, our plan for a new Britain is not something outside the war, or something after the war. It is an essential part of our war aims. It is, indeed, our most positive war aim. The new Britain is the country we are fighting for.

A similarly romantic moral fervour characterised the report of the Beveridge Committee on social security, published as a Government White Paper in November 1942, and the most decisive single factor in bringing about a national commitment to building New Jerusalem after the war. The report's final paragraph, drafted by Sir William Beveridge himself (Classics and Hebrew at Charterhouse and Balliol; a Liberal with non-conformist grandparents), was a masterpiece of uplift:

> Freedom from want cannot be forced on a democracy or given to a democracy. It must be won by them. Winning it needs courage and faith and a sense of national unity; courage to face facts and difficulties and overcome them; faith in our future and in the ideals of fair play and freedom for which century after century our forefathers were prepared to die. . . . The Plan for Social Security in this Report is submitted by one [sic] who believes that in this supreme crisis the British people will not be found wanting in courage and faith and national unity, in material and spiritual power to play their part in achieving both social security and the victory of justice among nations upon which security depends.[13]

The secularised religious emotion of New Jerusalemism came to a wartime climax when after publication of his bestselling report Beveridge toured the country preaching on the theme of the 'New Britain':

> I believe those two words are as good and short a motto as one can find for all that one wants to do in post-war reconstruction. Most people want something new after the war. . . . New Britain should

be free, as free as humanly possible, of the five giant evils, of Want, [of] Disease, of Ignorance, of Squalor and of Idleness. . . .[14]

Noble though the wartime aspirations of the liberal Establishment might be, New Jerusalem nevertheless constituted – just like the postwar illusion of Britain as a present and future world and Commonwealth power, or the pre-war faith in the League of Nations as a preserver of world law and order – a piece of romantic fantasising, rather like some gigantic palace in an engraving by Piranesi. And just as Piranesi's imagination defied the laws of physics and geometry, so did the dreamers of New Jerusalem disregard the real-life problem of funding its construction out of what was now a bankrupt and backward industrial economy instead of the richest in the world that it had been in their youth.

For in all the eager evangelising from 1941 until the Labour victory in the general election of 1945 – by politicians, by men of the cloth, by progressive journals like *Picture Post*, by the BBC and the Army Bureau of Current Affairs (two pulpits favoured by the liberal Establishment for preaching to their benighted inferiors in the ranks), and by Sir William Beveridge himself – there is relatively little discussion about costs in relation to Britain's likely postwar resources.[15] Either so sordid a consideration is brushed aside on the score that to accomplish New Jerusalem merely required (to quote *Picture Post* again) 'passionate – actually passionate – determination',[16] or a fallacious assumption is made (not least by Beveridge) that, if Britain could afford and implement enormous munitions programmes in wartime, she could do the same for New Jerusalem in peacetime, thus neatly ignoring the fact that wartime Britain relied for her existence on an American life-support machine in the form of Lend–Lease.[17] As Keynes in a Treasury memorandum aptly put it in 1944, 'the time and energy and thought which we are all giving to the Brave New World is wildly disproportionate to what is being given to the Cruel Real World'.[18] In sum, the New Jerusalemers chose to proceed on the best romantic principle that sense must bend to feeling, and facts to faith.

Although they envisaged New Jerusalem as a city of many splendours – fine housing for all, work for all, education for all, new life for old industrial areas, the wise planning of development in town and countryside – the proudest tower in the entire shining vision was the welfare state itself. This would provide the citizen with security from want from the crèche to the coffin, together with a completely free national health service, so abolishing those greatest of social evils, poverty and ill-health. It was therefore entirely appropriate that this proudest tower should have been designed by Sir William Beveridge, the very personification of the liberal Establishment, not least in that, though his heart was big, his head was even bigger. A Liberal and a high Victorian born in 1879, he was the son of a judge in the Indian Civil Service, grandson of a Congregationalist bookseller, and with a maternal grandfather who was a self-made businessman Liberal in politics and Unitarian in religion. At Balliol (where he read Greats, or Classics) he was, according to his daughter and biographer, 'deeply influenced' by the then Master, who 'preached lay sermons to the Balliol men about the Christian ethic'.[19] In 1922 he had become Director of the London School of Economics and in 1937 Master of University College, Oxford. Being a prophet and a brilliant Oxford intellect, Beveridge thought a lot of himself (it was not an uncommon characteristic among the small-'l' liberal Establishment),[20] so that righteousness went hand in hand with authoritarian arrogance and skill in manipulating the press to make him the Field Marshal Montgomery of social welfare.

This prize mandarin used his chairmanship of the Interdepartmental Committee on Social Insurance and Allied Services in 1941–2 to turn it into a vehicle for his own preconceptions, so that it was no mere piece of convenient nomenclature to dub the resulting White Paper the Beveridge Report, but an all too accurate description, not least because his was the master-hand in the writing of the final draft.[21] The records of this committee make absolutely plain that, for Beveridge, designing an ideal welfare state came first and considering the burden on the economy – a war-ruined economy – came a long way second. Thus an appendix to the final draft compares his scheme with the social security systems of eleven other countries and smugly concludes that it was, overall, equal or superior to any of them.[22] But out of his committee's total of forty-four meetings and 248 memoranda the basic issue of national resources to fund the scheme came up in only three meetings and eight memoranda.[23] Even when Beveridge did in fact himself raise the question of the 'heavy new costs' on the Exchequer resulting from his proposals for children's allowances, higher old-age pensions and a national health service, he marched grandly on without providing an answer.[24] Yet the Government Actuary calculated that the extra burden on the Exchequer of his draft proposals (excluding a national health service) over existing welfare provisions would be £160 million in 1945; and that the total cost to the Exchequer of the complete Beveridge package, including a free health service, would be £367 million in 1945 and £541 million in 1965.[25]

In November 1942, when the War Cabinet was making up its mind whether or not to allow publication of the Beveridge Report as a White Paper, the then Chancellor of the Exchequer, Sir Kingsley Wood, had exposed the incalculable and open-ended nature of the cost of the package. In a personal note to the War Premier on 17 November 1942, he pointed out: 'The scheme is presented as contributory but like the existing system depends on a deficiency grant, which will grow in the course of time to immense proportions, from the general taxpayer. . . . Is this the time to assume that the general taxpayer has a bottomless purse?'[26] Urging that the Beveridge Report should not be published at that time, Wood told the Prime Minister that the scheme 'is ambitious and involves an impracticable financial commitment':

Whether the report is valuable will be the subject of much argument. But it is certainly premature. . . . Many in this country have persuaded themselves that the cessation of hostilities will mark the opening of the Golden Age (many were so persuaded last time also). However this may be, the time for declaring a dividend on the profits of the Golden Age is the time when those profits have been realised in fact, not merely in the imagination.[27]

Nonetheless, thanks to Beveridge's manipulation of the press and the force of public expectation, the Cabinet consented to the report being published, an event which took place to tremendous national acclaim. But this was not the end of the debate within the coalition Government over the cost of 'Beveridge' in relation to Britain's postwar resources. A memorandum from Kingsley Wood to Churchill ('Secret PM Only') on 6 January 1943 yet again pointed out the rotten real-life financial foundations of the proudest tower in New Jerusalem: 'Acceptance of the complete plan involves a contract with many

'It may be we shall have to consider the British Isles more as an easterly extension of a strategic area the centre of which is the American Continent than as a power looking eastwards through the Mediterranean and the East.' Memorandum by the Prime Minister, Clement Attlee, March 1946.

'. . . the Chiefs of Staff believed that the Middle East was vital on both strategic and political grounds . . .' British troops on a stop-and-search operation in Palestine, 1947, a country then reckoned to be essential to the defence of Britain's Middle East base. Palestine was finally evacuated in March 1948.

Above: '. . . our presence in the Mediterranean served a purpose other than military, which was very important to our position as a great power . . .' Ernest Bevin, the Foreign secretary, justifying in 1946 the heavy cost of Britain's global deployments.

Right: 'The whole picture of defence manpower and expenditure appears out of scale, and if there is no quick drop, particularly abroad . . . he could not promise anything but economic disaster . . .' The Chancellor of the Exchequer, Hugh Dalton, to his ministerial colleagues, January 1946.

'All the institutional, ceremonial and architectural symbols of past greatness were still in place, giving the illusion that nothing had changed, when the reality was of shrinking power . . .'
The Victorian 'Grand Staircase' of the Foreign Office.

'. . . the nemesis of Free Trade when Britain could no longer pay for all the foreign food on which she had come to depend . . .'
Ration-books in peacetime, even for their daily bread.

'Theirs was the psychology of a victor although their circumstances approximated more to those of a loser . . .' The British people celebrate Victory-Japan Day, London, August 1945.

'. . . the monarchy, whose imperial pomp (invented in the late Victorian age to replace an earlier more domestic style) was freshly celebrated in 1947 in the wedding of Princess Elizabeth to Philip Mountbatten.' The official family photograph.

'. . . the problem of whether, after the economic exhaustion of the war years, we have the power and the resources to permit us to play the role of a Great Power . . .' Memorandum by the Minister of Defence, A. V. Alexander, 1949.

'. . . the occasion of the successful wartime launch of New Jerusalem . . .' Cover of the 1941 New Year issue of *Picture Post*, devoted to a vision of a postwar utopia promising work, new houses, education and free health provision 'for all'.

'. . . righteousness went hand in hand with authoritarian arrogance and skill in manipulating the press to make him the Field Marshal Montgomery of social welfare . . .' Sir William Beveridge, author of the *Beveridge Report*, the 1942 blue-print for the postwar Welfare State.

Sir Kingsley Wood, the wartime Chancellor of the Exchequer, who prophetically warned in 1942: 'The Beveridge scheme is presented as contributory but . . . depends on a deficiency grant from the general taxpayer, which will grow in the course of time to immense proportions.'

Right: 'The stigma of the Means Test was to be removed by the simple method of handing out benefits to all, rich or poor or comfortably off, without discrimination as to individual circumstances . . .' James Griffiths, Minister of National Insurance, and author of the Labour Government's 'super-Beveridge' crib-to-coffin insurance scheme.

Below: 'In the person of Aneurin Bevan New Jerusalem had found its true romantic hero . . . whose rhetoric flamed with passion, not to say volcanic anger, at social injustice.' Here Bevan, founder of the National Health Service, examines the model of a new housing estate in 1949. As Minister of Health he was also responsible for the Labour Government's ambitious housing programme.

Above: '. . . beds must be closed, staff dismissed, and waiting lists already appallingly long grow even longer . . .' Aneurin Bevan's plea to his Cabinet colleagues on the consequences of the Chancellor's request in 1949 to hold down rising expenditure on the Health Service.

Left: 'Any expansion in one part of the National Health Service must in future be met by economies or, if necessary, by contraction in others.' Budget statement by the Labour Chancellor of the Exchequer, Sir Stafford Cripps, in March 1950, limiting expenditure on the Service in 1950–51 to a total three times higher than Bevan's original estimate of the annual cost.

millions of beneficiaries, the continued fulfilment of which would properly have to be, in good or bad times alike, a prior charge upon the national resources. . . .'[28]

> The broad impression left by the report on the ordinary reader is that in the author's view the general finance of the scheme can be carried out without undue difficulty. There are, however, lying in the future, so far as it can be discerned, doubts and uncertainties suggesting that large financial commitments cannot be undertaken without misgivings.

Wood again made the point that 'any excess or short-fall of cost of the plan as a whole falls on the taxpayer . . .'. Furthermore the scheme would compete with other charges on the public purse. All this was to prove gruesomely accurate prophecy.

However, such was now the enthusiasm of the public for 'Beveridge' that even Conservative members of the wartime coalition came to accept an economy version of New Jerusalem as agreed government policy. This was announced by Churchill in a radio broadcast in March 1943, and embodied in 1943–5 in a series of White Papers on national insurance, a national health service, education, employment policy and housing.[29] In such fashion did New Jerusalem become the new domestic political consensus.

Yet the Labour Party remained ill-satisfied with the coalition Government's cut-price version. In the 1945 general election, the party, free of its coalition shackles and brushing aside the earlier shrewd misgivings of sceptics like Kingsley Wood, embraced Beveridge's proposals for social security and a free national health service in their lavish entirety, even enlarging various handouts over Beveridge's figures. Here was an offer of a reward for victory hard for the electorate to turn down: an offer to the high-minded voter in the shape of an ideal society, and to the humbler citizen in the shape of free welfare and a secure job. So it came to pass that New Jerusalem at last found incarnation in the committed programme of a British government with a crushing majority in Parliament.

Yet within two months of victory in the general election, the new Labour Cabinet had found out that Kingsley Wood had been right after all, and that the construction of New Jerusalem, and especially its costliest edifice, Beveridge's welfare state (for which work on legislation was already in hand), was far beyond the means of a war-ruined British economy.

What so abruptly and painfully awoke them from their warm romantic dream and plunged them into the coldest of cold realities was of course the ending of Lend–Lease after the surrender of Japan (see above, p. 2). As Lord Keynes bluntly told the Cabinet, without American handouts 'the economic basis for the hopes of the public' was 'non-existent', signifying, he wrote, that 'there would have to be an indefinite postponement of the realisation of the best hopes of the Government [that is, New Jerusalem] . . .'.[30]

Should it be now accepted that Britain ought to live within her means and that therefore plans for New Jerusalem must be jettisoned along with pretensions to be a world power? For the Labour Government this was psychologically and politically impossible. Instead, further American handouts to replace Lend–Lease it must be (see above, pp. 41–4). And so, with the successful cadging in Washington of the $3.75 billion loan, the construction of New Jerusalem could go ahead after all, or, to paraphrase Kingsley Wood, a dividend could be declared on the profits of the Golden Age long before there was any prospect of the profits being realised in fact rather than merely in the imagination. Nevertheless, the fact that the Labour Government was now temporarily flush with dollars did not alter the fundamental truth pointed out by Wood in 1942 that the long-term future cost of the welfare state was incalculable, open-ended in its potential increase, and 'in good or bad times alike, a prior charge upon the national resources.' It remained only for the Government to find this out for itself over the next five years.

In charge of the legislation for the welfare state were James Griffiths and Aneurin Bevan – both of them products, although individually very different, of Victorian romantic idealism as transmitted down the generations by the non-conformist chapel; both of them Welsh, a race itself notoriously romantic, not to say emotional; both of them born into a miner's family.

James Griffiths, the Minister of National Insurance, eleven years old when Queen Victoria died, twenty when Edward VII died, grew up in the hopeful springtime of the Labour movement when men first dreamed of sweeping away raw capitalist exploitation (the raw-ness nowhere more brutally evident than in the mining valleys of

South Wales) in favour of a socialist utopia. All his life he remained 'the soul of gentleness, moderation and conciliation, a chapel-going, Welsh-speaking Welshman whose socialism was ethical and compassionate . . .'.[31] Now, in his mid-fifties, it fell to Griffiths at long last to fulfil the aspirations of a political lifetime, but in circumstances of national indebtedness such as he could never have imagined in his younger days. Of these changed circumstances neither he nor the Cabinet Social Security Committee took any notice.[32] In fact, wherever the coalition Government's 1944 White Paper on Social Insurance had sought to trim back the size of benefits in the Beveridge Plan in order to reduce the overall burden on the Exchequer, Griffiths and his colleagues made haste to restore them or even make them more generous still.[33] For Griffiths's simple intention was to carry out the Beveridge Plan of 1942 in full, and more than full,[34] including the entire, vastly widened range of handouts proposed by Beveridge, such as the new family allowances, estimated in 1945 to cost £64 million as against £4 million under present schemes.[35]

Indeed, fundamental to Griffiths's whole design was Beveridge's principle of 'universality'. In other words, instead of targeting the necessitous of one kind or another (as under existing provisions) it was to be made compulsory for every citizen, whether or not he or she needed state unemployment pay, a state old-age pension, state family allowances and a state-subsidised funeral, to become a participant in the generous new system of out-door relief.[36] The stigma of the Poor Law was thus to be abolished by the simple method of bringing every citizen within the provisions of the Poor Law's successor, and making him or her compulsorily dependent on state charity. The stigma of the means test was similarly to be removed by the simple method of handing out benefits to all, rich or poor or comfortably off, without discrimination as to individual circumstances. Moreover, unlike the existing arrangements for social insurance in which the 'friendly societies' had a key role, and unlike European systems where the state provided financial and administrative back-up to funds jointly run by employers and employees, by trade unions or by benefit societies on the mutual aid principle,[37] the entire system was to be a state monopoly, so demanding an immediate increase of 2000 tax-eating bureaucrats at the Ministry of National Insurance's main headquarters in Newcastle.[38]

It fell to the Government Actuary to cost this proudest tower in

New Jerusalem. In November 1945 he reported that expenditure on national insurance payouts, national assistance, family allowances and industrial injuries benefit (but excluding the cost of the new national health service) would soar from the present £385 million under existing schemes to an estimated £590 million in 1948, the first year of the new welfare state's full operation.[39] The sum to be found out of public funds would rise by over a quarter from the present £293 million to £369 million.[40] But this was by no means all. For now came the catch: the same catch so percipiently noted by Kingsley Wood in regard to the Beveridge proposals. Griffiths's scheme, like Beveridge's, was not a true insurance scheme, where contributions from the insured cover the total cost of the payouts (as was largely the case with the social insurance systems of Western European countries,[41] which were intended to support individual and collective self-reliance). Instead, although the scheme was presented as contributory, it relied largely on a deficiency grant from the Exchequer, which, as Kingsley Wood shrewdly remarked in 1942 in respect of the similar Beveridge plan, would 'grow in the course of time to immense proportions'. The Government Actuary's forecasts (based on 1945 price levels) tell it all: by 1958 total expenditure on the welfare state (again excluding the cost of the national health service) would have climbed to £630 million and by 1968 to £732 million, but income from contributions would remain static throughout, leaving the Exchequer to find the ever swelling remainder.[42]

Nonetheless, Griffiths and his colleagues in government were no more daunted by the future burden on the productive economy represented by the Government Actuary's figures than had been Beveridge three years earlier. In fifteen meetings of the Cabinet Social Security Committee in 1945 and thirteen in 1946, the question of basic cost came up only once; in thirty-four memoranda in 1945 and twenty-two in 1946 it came up only three times (in each case in regard to the Government Actuary's figures).[43] The only battle over the limitation of costs – really a skirmish – in the committee and the Cabinet took place over the incidental question of whether unemployment benefit should be automatically stopped after a certain number of weeks (as under the current Unemployment Insurance Scheme and the coalition Government's White Paper) or paid out for an unlimited duration. Civil servants in reporting on possible safeguards against abuse in the latter case warned that:

it would be possible, once having gained admission to benefit by the payment of 26 contributions, to continue in benefit indefinitely if no automatic limit existed. This means that in the long run numbers of persons with very poor industrial records might become virtually pensioners on the unemployment fund and that applicants for benefit are likely to include not only the steady going worker but that residue of the population, particularly in large cities, which lives on its wits or has concealed sources of livelihood. It is against this residue . . . that special safeguards are required.[44]

They suggested either that it could be a condition of continuing payouts that the recipient had to attend a training centre, or that the persistent scrounger, once identified, could be barred from benefit. Not surprisingly the Minister of Labour, George Isaacs, vigorously opposed the suggestion that his training centres should partly become correction centres for the industrially 'flabby' (his word).[45] The Social Services Committee's discussions of the problem on 26 and 29 November 1945 manifest the romantic optimism, not least about human nature, which inspired the dream of New Jerusalem. The Lord Chancellor, Lord Jowitt (born 1885, son of a rector, educated at Marlborough and New College, with a first in Jurisprudence, Chairman of the wartime Cabinet Committee on Reconstruction Problems, perhaps better called the New Jerusalem Committee), urged that, if there were to be no time limit on unemployment benefit, it was 'essential' that the Minister of National Insurance 'should make an appeal to the public not to abuse the rights of the scheme'.[46] Nevertheless, even though the committee agreed that unemployment pay should be doled out for an unlimited period, it decided against such an appeal because, as James Griffiths naïvely put it, 'the whole scheme depended on the co-operation of the public and . . . a reference to co-operation in this particular field was unnecessary'.[47]

In December 1945 the Cabinet itself took a harder line, deciding that under the National Insurance Bill a limit of thirty weeks should be imposed, except in the case of those with good insurance contribution records.[48] However, when the Social Services Committee came in January 1946 to discuss what should happen after the thirty weeks, the Minister of National Insurance urged that those with good contribution records should enjoy a further twenty-six weeks of benefit, the cost to be borne by the present Unemployment Insurance

Fund. This immediately provoked a split between the Financial
Secretary to the Treasury (speaking for the Chancellor) and such
outright New Jerusalemers as the Ministers of Health and Education,
Aneurin Bevan and Ellen Wilkinson, their compassion at the high
port. The Financial Secretary argued that the suggested further period
of payments would 'involve a serious drain on the Fund [and] could
not be justified'.[49] The Minister of Health, feeling that 'too much
stress had been laid on the possibility of abuse', was all in favour of
raiding the fund, especially for the benefit of the unemployed in the
'Development Areas'.[50] The Minister of Education 'still favoured
the payment of unlimited benefit', which she contended would in
the long run be 'an economy'. Griffiths – along with these other
compassionate trusters of their fellow men – in the end carried the day
over the Treasury hard-hearts, and the committee asked the Cabinet to
reconsider its decision. When it did so, on 17 January 1946, the
Chancellor deftly argued:

> The Government would appear to have little confidence in their
> power to carry through their policy of full employment if, at a time
> of great labour shortage, they put forward proposals which would
> make it possible for people to draw continuous unemployment
> benefit for as much as 2½ years.[51]

He also pointed out that once such a concession had been given, it
could never be withdrawn. It was the Foreign Secretary, Bevin, a man
so experienced in matters concerning workers, who put forward a
compromise now happily bought by the Cabinet – that the Minister of
National Insurance should have discretion to extend benefit beyond
thirty weeks at the recommendation of the Court of Referees.[52]

Back in February 1943 the British Employers' Confederation had
written in regard to the original Beveridge Report that, while they
were in favour of abolishing want, they were not in favour of handing
out public funds to those *not* in want, which they regarded as
inessential and calling for 'consideration from the standpoint of its
desirability in relation to the country's post-war obligations generally
and its available resources . . .'.[53] How much more relevant is this
criticism to the 'super-Beveridge' social security system created by the
National Insurance Act of 1946 (royal assent, 1 August), not least
because the fathers of that Act *did* know exactly how great were the

country's postwar obligations and exactly how scant were its available resources, other than American tick.

Meanwhile Aneurin Bevan had been designing the gilded cupola on top of this proudest tower of New Jerusalem, in the form of a free and comprehensive national health service. This too had formed part of the Beveridge Report, although the broad idea can be traced back to the Webbs, those tireless drafters of blueprints during the pre-Great War era of socialist vision-mongering. Moreover, in 1934 the Socialist Medical Association had persuaded the Labour Party to adopt the idea as part of its programme.[54] The proposed National Health Service differed radically from the existing British health insurance scheme (dating from 1911) and all European health schemes, which were largely self-financed through insurance contributions and the scope of which was restricted in terms either of treatment provided or of types of beneficiary. In the first place, the national insurance contribution towards the funding of the service, as proposed by Beveridge and adopted by Bevan, amounted to only a fraction of the estimated total cost, and constituted hardly more than camouflage of the reality that the taxpayer was going to pick up most of the bill. Secondly, this bill would be potentially limitless because the new service was to provide free and comprehensive medical treatment without stint to all citizens on demand.

In the person of Aneurin Bevan New Jerusalem had found its true romantic hero, a Werther in revolt against a corrupt and conformist society, a brilliant individualist convinced like a Nietzschean superman that his personal powers placed him among a natural elite, an idealist whose self-educated mind loved to play with pretentiously high-flown intellectual concepts, and whose rhetoric flamed with passion, not to say volcanic anger, at social injustice.[55] His family background was typical enough of the descent of New Jerusalemism from Victorian evangelical religion, for his father David, very much 'respectable' working class, was a chapel-goer who loved to sing hymns round the organ, a Liberal supporter who turned to the new Labour Party in the general election of 1906, and who under the influence of Robert Blatchford became 'in the warm-hearted and utopian fashion of the time'[56] a socialist. Aneurin too grew up a man of faith, although in his case the faith was in atheism and that neo-religion, Marxism. For, having swallowed many of the speculations of Karl Marx about the 'class struggle' and the historically inevitable replacement of 'capitalism' (with its exploitation of the 'proletariat' by the 'ruling class') by 'socialism', he believed himself to be a 'scientific socialist', which was about as remote from science as being a Christian Scientist. His other great formative influence consisted in a Uruguayan philosopher by the name of Rodo, the main theme of whose book *Ariel* is, in the words of Bevan's biographer, 'the need to elevate the lofty idealism of the spirit above the sordid reality of the workaday world . . .'.[57]

As was the case with so many progressives since the Edwardian age, Bevan's utopianism embraced the creation not only of New Jerusalem at home but also of a new world order abroad. A pronouncement to the House of Commons in August 1944 on this latter topic gives proof of his broader credentials as a wishful thinker in the romantic British tradition:

> We can win the war militarily but lose it morally unless we succeed in raising before the eyes of mankind . . . a vision of world organisation which sets aside all this talk of big armies, navies and air forces, and tries to establish co-operative principles among the nations of the world so that we can keep our national pride and patriotism and weave it into a pattern of world organisation.[58]

Although the Beveridge Report was concocted by a Liberal while Bevan believed himself a Marxist, he greeted the Report in November 1942 with keen enthusiasm:

> With Liberal fervour [sic] and even a trace of Liberal innocence [sic] . . . Sir William has described the conditions in which the tears might be taken out of capitalism. We should not be surprised, therefore, if all unconsciously by doing so he threatens capitalism itself.[59]

In urging the Labour Party in January 1943 'to go for the Report in its entirety', Bevan distilled the spiritual essence of New Jerusalemism:

> If Britain shows that she has the courage, imagination and resilience to embark on a social experiment of such magnitude in the midst of a war, then she may once more assert a moral leadership which will have consequences in every sphere of her activities.[60]

And to the Labour Party Conference held just before the general election campaign of 1945, he proclaimed:

> we are the memories of those bitter years [before the war]; we are
> the voice of the British people; we are the natural custodians of the
> interests of those young men and women in the Services abroad. We
> have been the dreamers, we have been the sufferers, and we are the
> builders. . . .[61]

In July 1945, in such a mood of hope and resolve, with his powers of will, intellect and self-belief at their crest, Bevan at the age of forty-seven became Minister of Health with the double task of rehousing the nation (see below, Chapter 8) and designing and erecting a national health service.[62] On 13 December, after prolonged wrangles with his colleagues about the administrative structures for the new service,[63] he submitted his perfected proposals for the NHS (intended to serve as the basis of a Parliamentary Bill) to the Cabinet Social Services Committee.[64] In clarity and comprehensiveness they resembled nothing so much as a plan of military organisation produced by a general staff for a great offensive, commencing with the role of the supreme commander: 'General responsibility for the service will rest with the Minister of Health. . . .' For those parts of the service best organised nationally, such as hospitals, 'he will assume direct responsibility'; for those parts best organised locally 'direct responsibility will rest on local government, acting in its ordinary relationship with the Minister'. For the new family practitioner services supplied by doctor and dentist, new local executive machinery would be set up to act 'within national regulations made by the Minister', while the deployment of such practitioners across the kingdom would be decided by a new Central Committee appointed by the Minister. The Minister, as supreme commander, would have his general staff in the form of 'a new Central Health Services Council . . . a statutory advisory body . . . appointed by the Minister'. The existing ragbag of voluntary and local government hospitals would be nationalised and organised into twenty regions under Regional Hospital Boards, with which the Minister would jointly 'determine . . . the best reorganisation of all available hospital and specialist resources in their region'. Beneath these would be smaller Local Hospital Management Committees each running from day to day 'a natural hospital unit in a planned service'. As well as describing detailed arrangements for administering various aspects of the new service, Bevan's paper also comprehensively covered bureaucratic minutiae ranging from the supply of drugs and surgical appliances to home nursing, vaccination and the care of mental patients – not forgetting the remuneration of doctors and dentists.

However, this admirably Napoleonic exercise left out of account one factor of fundamental importance – the likely scale of demand for the free services to be on offer, from hospital treatment to dentures and spectacles. Bevan's scheme resembled a military plan for, say, the Normandy invasion which simply left out such calculations as the number of divisions needed to overcome the enemy defences, the number of vessels needed to transport those divisions to the French shore, the likely rate of casualties and the likely rate of consumption of ammunition and other stores during the ensuing battle. For – unbelievably as it must seem – Bevan, his senior civil servants and his medical advisers had neglected to gather and analyse operational intelligence from available health statistics and thence calculate the probable number of the edentulous or short-sighted or bronchitic or other sickly people at present untreated or inadequately treated who would hasten to avail themselves of treatment and appliances offered free and without limit. They therefore had framed no realistic estimates of the numbers of doctors, dentists, dentures, spectacles and hospital beds, not to say potions and pills of various kinds, required by the new National Health Service. And hence they had not the faintest idea of the cost to public funds of the new service even in its first year, let alone hazarding some guess about the future rate of increase of what must be an open-ended commitment. The annual figure of £145 million (of which only £35.7 million would be met by national insurance contributions) mentioned in Bevan's plan for the early years of the service represented no more than a random guess, as indeed had Beveridge's figure of £130 million in 1942.[65] Here was cigar-butt strategy indeed.

It is significant, therefore, that in Bevan's memorandum to the Cabinet Social Services Committee the topic entitled 'Finance of the Service' is accorded just two paragraphs out of a total of fifty-four, and that those two, in contrast to the black-and-white certainties of the rest, display an evasive woolliness:

Only very approximate estimates are possible of the cost to public funds of the comprehensive health service proposed in this paper. It will be much greater because the service is comprehensive instead of partial; because no charges will normally be made to patients. . . . In the early years of the service the annual expenditure *might be* [emphasis added] £145 million, of which hospital and specialist services would account for £87 million, local authority services for £12 million, general practitioner, dental and eye services for £41 million, and compensation and superannuation for £5 million. . . .[66]

Yet the legacy of ill-health and poor physique bequeathed by the industrial revolution to the British proletariat was well known, not to say notorious, and was abundantly documented in reports and statistics.[67] After all, it was this very legacy which had provided the motivation to create the new health service. Equally well known, because revealed by the demands of war as well as by pre-war surveys, was the decrepitude of Britain's largely Victorian hospitals and their facilities, especially in the old industrial areas where the heaviest demand for 'free' treatment might be expected to fall – a decrepitude that would require £500 million worth of capital investment to remedy.[68]

Unlike Bevan and his advisers, other (if unofficial) bodies had carefully and realistically calculated the probable running costs of a 'free' national health service. In 1937 a PEP report put the combined cost of existing health services at £161 million per annum (1937 prices). A report by Medical Planning Research, described by the official historian of postwar health services as 'perhaps the most scientific estimate', reckoned the cost of a comprehensive service at £230 million per annum.[69] Why then did Bevan, abetted by his advisers, so completely neglect to carry out an operational analysis of likely scales and types of demand, coupled with a calculation of the logistical resources consequently needed? Bevan's biographer, John Campbell, has no direct answer.[70] Could it be that, given Britain's precarious finances, even a Cabinet dedicated to New Jerusalem might have baulked if presented with a realistic estimate of the cost of the NHS? Or was it simply that Bevan, being a true romantic, simply shut his eyes to the Cruel Real World in pursuit of his personal vision of a Brave New World? It is interesting that his biographer acknowledges that Bevan's failure to foresee the future survival and expansion of private medical practice was due to:

> inability to imagine the financial constraints under which the NHS would increasingly have to operate. This in turn reflected the confidence which lay at the heart of Bevan's socialism that in all spheres – in health and housing as in industry – collective organisation must inevitably by the natural process of evolution come to predominate over individualism.[71]

However, in fairness to Bevan and his innocent faith in socialism, the Cabinet Social Services Committee, New Jerusalemers all, accepted his proposals despite having first noted that they 'involved a very large increase in the financial burden on the taxpayer compared with the proposals in the [coalition Government's] White Paper';[72] and the Cabinet (including the Chancellor) tamely followed suit. Indeed, although negotiations for the American loan had been dragging on in uncertainty during exactly those months when Bevan was designing his NHS (the Cabinet accepted the American terms just a week before Bevan put in his final proposals to the Social Services Committee), the question of the overall cost of the new service in relation to Britain's financial and economic plight was never really discussed. Instead the Cabinet merely recognised and accepted that it would be hard to rein back expenditure by the proposed Regional Hospital Boards.[73] Nor did the Opposition, pallidly pink New Jerusalemers themselves and all too aware of public expectations, raise this issue during the Parliamentary debates on the National Health Service Bill in the spring of 1946.[74]

The National Health Service therefore amounted to an even worse case of declaring a dividend on the Golden Age before it had been earned in fact than the new universal and compulsory social security system. For at the least the *initial* cost of the latter was a known quantity, even if its future potential increase was as open-ended as that of the health service.

The 'Appointed Day' for the inauguration of the NHS was fixed for 5 July 1948. By that time, however, the great convertibility crisis had come and gone, along with the bulk of the dollar loan (see above, pp. 77–8) which alone had enabled the Government to embark on the construction of New Jerusalem. Moreover, by that time too the estimated costs of the new health service had already begun to climb like a jet fighter. As against the £145 million per annum in Bevan's original proposals to his colleagues in December 1945 (plus another £17 million for the Scottish health service)[75] the estimates laid before Parliament in February 1948 for the first nine months of operation alone stood at £198 million (including Scotland), and even that figure had been cut by £22.5 million at the urging of a Chancellor also much bothered about the cost of Britain playing the world power.[76] By the last months of 1948 it had become clear that expenditure was well overrunning the increased estimate too, whereupon Bevan sought to pre-empt Cabinet misgivings by putting in what he called a 'Progress Report'. This justified the overrun of nearly £50 million on the score of the service's success. Yet his gushing survey in fact serves as an indictment of his own original failure to make realistic operational and logistical calculations:

> The rush for spectacles, as for dental treatment, has exceeded all expectations. . . . Part of what has happened has been a natural first flush of the new scheme, with the feeling that everything is free now and it does not matter what is charged up to the Exchequer. . . . There is also, without doubt, a sheer increase due to people getting things they need but could not afford before, and this the scheme intended.[77]

He had to acknowledge, however, that 'the whole position in regard to prescribing and appliances cannot help being fraught with risk in a scheme of this kind, and will demand constant vigilance . . .'. Pointing out the 'myriad problems of so vast a service' he further admitted: 'In all this there is bound to be some abuse of the scheme. . . .' But then followed a bugle call of unrepentant New Jerusalemism: 'It has done what we promised it would do and given a new freedom from anxiety in sickness which is worth quite a large monetary burden.'[78] Idealistic pride and passion aside, Bevan had to tell his colleagues that for 1949–50, the second year of the NHS, 'the quite large monetary burden' was estimated at £330 million gross – more than twice the annual figure so airily mentioned in his memorandum of 13 December 1945.[79] Moreover, this figure was mostly made up of running costs, for large-scale capital investment to replace Victorian hulks of hospitals was already deemed out of the question.[80]

From now on the cost of the National Health Service joined the military cost of the world role as a major objective of recurrent Treasury attack. In response to a request from the Chancellor of the Exchequer (Sir Stafford Cripps) in January 1949 to cut the net estimates for 1949–50 by £100 million (£12.5 million for the Scottish health service), Bevan submitted seventeen pages of shuffling explanations and excuses, but at least offered a cut of £27.75 million, mostly in capital expenditure.[81] He rejected any compromising of the sacred New Jerusalem principle of a totally 'free' service by the introduction of charges to patients, which he saw as marking a step back towards the means test and the Poor Law, those humiliating horrors of the proletarian folk-memory. He even urged that yet more money should be spent on the health service, otherwise it would become 'so niggardly and unattractive that it will be considered by many to be a cheat'.

Yet at the same time, in another compartment of his mind, he was fully aware that Britain was hard-up, economically struggling and living off Marshall Aid, for he told health service managers: 'The American Nation was entitled to ask us whether we were spending American money to raise the standard of living beyond that obtaining in America.'[82]

At a Cabinet meeting on 23 May 1949, Bevan and the Secretary of State for Scotland asked for a combined supplementary estimate for 1949–50 of £57 million,[83] otherwise, in the harrowing words of a memorandum to the Cabinet from Bevan, services must be withheld 'which the community has proved it urgently needs – dental treatment and spectacles must be refused, beds must be closed, staff dismissed, and waiting lists already appallingly long grow even longer'.[84] In his view, the rush of demand meant that 'unless we are to deprive people of services they genuinely require we cannot expect the cost of the Service to be as low as we hoped'. Bevan again stood firm against the introduction of charges for health services, his sword upraised as if New Jerusalem itself were under siege. However, Cripps flinched from an all-out assault, finally and glumly agreeing in July to supplementary estimates for 1949–50 of £57 million, which as recently as May he 'could not see his way to accept'.[85] Furthermore, the Cabinet Economic Policy Committee likewise swallowed provisional estimates of £356 million for 1950–1 and £387 million for 1951–2 [86] – each well over double Bevan's original guesstimate of the annual cost during the 'early years' of the service.

When in the wake of devaluation in September 1949 the Prime Minister called for cuts of £280 million in Government current expenditure and capital investment in order to combat inflation, Bevan proved the only Minister not to submit an initial offer of cuts, however inadequate, in his own budget.[87] In answer to the Chancellor's proposals in October to increase the national insurance contribution to the health service by one shilling and make charges to patients for medical services, Bevan again rode out, sword flashing, in defence of his personal socialist version of New Jerusalem: 'in his view the introduction of charges would involve drastic modification of the basic principles of the Health Service. He was therefore opposed to any increase in the National Insurance contribution or any general introduction of charges . . .', although he was prepared to accept a charge of one shilling for each prescription, which would save £10 million in a full year.[88] In the same meeting of the Economic Policy Committee the anxious questioning of his colleagues about the predicted rise in the health service's gross cost over the next two years to £387 million in 1951–2 elicited a defence both specious and emotional:

> much of the increased expenditure represented the cost of bringing additional hospital beds into operation, and the capital cost of building new mental hospitals and health centres; the cost of staff had also greatly increased as the result of recent awards. These figures took no account of the national benefits to be secured by the Health Service, through improved health and the consequent increase in industrial production, since these effects were not precisely calculable. . . .[89]

But Bevan's colleagues were not convinced, recording their desire to see 'some reduction' in the cost of the service. It was pointed out that:

> the public might think it strange that a charge should be made for prescriptions for medicines, but that prescriptions for spectacles (though the spectacles were much more costly than the medicines) would be free of charge. Moreover, a charge amounting to one-third of the cost of appliances might yield the substantial sum of £10 millions a year.[90]

Bevan, blood up, his deepest beliefs under threat, answered that a charge for appliances:

> would be regarded as a retrograde step. Supporters of the Government throughout the country had taken pride in the manner in which the essential needs of the poorer classes of the community had for the first time been adequately met under the National Health Service, and all this good-will was to be thrown away if a general system of charges were now introduced. . . .

A week later the Lord President of the Council, Herbert Morrison, tried again to switch Bevan's mind from the ideals of New Jerusalem to the country's current financial plight:

> the proposal to make a charge for appliances such as spectacles and dentures . . . should be carefully considered. The steady increase in the cost of the Health Service was a matter for anxiety and there was a danger that its heavy cost might bring the scheme into disrepute. It was a matter of common knowledge that the scheme was being abused in some respects. . . .[91]

But Bevan remained 'strongly opposed to the imposition of a charge for appliances. . . . In his view, this would involve a far-reaching departure from the basic principles of the scheme.' Intimidated by Bevan's defiant sword, his critics retired disconsolate from the fray, and the Economic Policy Committee decided not to recommend to the Cabinet charges for dentures and spectacles. It is, however, noteworthy that in this same meeting the committee *did* agree to reduce the defence burden arising from the world role by £12.5 million in the current financial year. In fact, the health service proved the one major area of public expenditure not to suffer at all in the current round of cuts, even though the principle of charges for prescriptions became enshrined in a new National Health Service Act in December 1949 – a principle the implementation of which in practice Bevan thereafter stubbornly resisted.

In 1950 the Chancellor, abetted by the new Minister of State for Economic Affairs, Hugh Gaitskell, at last mounted a sustained attempt to regain control over the service's runaway costs. In his budget statement to Parliament Cripps lashed himself to the mast of £392 million for 1950–1, saying that no overall increase in expenditure on the health service was permissible in the next twelve months: 'Any expansion in one part of the Service must in future be met by economies or, if necessary, by contraction in others.'[92] But almost immediately a pay award to health service personnel by the Whitley Council (which was not obliged to take note of the broad interests of the national economy) threatened to torpedo Cripps's £392 million under him. Amid general alarm a Cabinet committee chaired by the Prime Minister was set up in April 1950 'to fix limits for the total cost of the National Health Service in the financial year 1951/52 and succeeding years', and 'to assist the Health Ministers in securing due economy in the administration of the service'.[93]

The records of this committee show Bevan still clinging to his dream even though he was being nudged more and more insistently by reality. He groaned that it was necessary in the present financial year 'to refuse sanction to developments – many of them desirable – which had been anticipated in the approved estimates'.[94] He refused to recognise that it was the New Jerusalem ideal itself of free healthcare on demand (and hence potentially limitless in scope, scale and cost) that constituted the fundamental cause of the present crisis. Instead he tried to fight off his critics by reporting all kinds of incidental reforms aimed at tightening cost control throughout the service. 'I have, as from 1 May,' he wrote in a preliminary memorandum, 'reduced from 10 to 4 variants the types of spectacles supplied free,' so saving £500,000 in the current year.[95]

At the committee's first meeting he announced that standardised cost-accounting was being introduced. A Treasury team of experts was to determine all hospital establishments, since pay constituted 60 per cent of all costs. Regional Hospital Boards, Boards of Governors of teaching hospitals and Hospital Management Committees were to submit monthly statements of expenditure and commitments, even though, in Bevan's words, 'A laborious check of this kind could not be a permanent feature of the system, but it would have to be maintained sufficiently long to get a grip on expenditure.'[96] His colleagues were not impressed. In their view checks after commitments had been entered into were not enough. Under the old local-authority system hospital expenditure had always been cleared first with the authority's finance committee, but 'it was difficult to see where a comparable financial check existed under the present organisation', since the Treasury could hardly scrutinise the details of every estimate. The critics pointed out that the general function of the Hospital Boards as designed by Bevan was to 'secure an adequate hospital service rather than to ensure that the service was run in the most economical manner possible . . .'.[97] There was risk of 'extravagant use' of drugs and dressings.

But Bevan's reply showed that the dreamer had certainly not yet awakened: 'The Health Minister regarded some of these difficulties as inherent in the organisation which had been adopted, after careful consideration, in the National Health Service Acts. . . .'[98]

At this inaugural meeting the new committee agreed only that patients' travel expenses should in future be paid solely in the case of the needy. It was nevertheless another tiny chip in the walls of New Jerusalem.

At their next encounter the committee turned to the key question of the Chancellor's ceiling on expenditure on the health service, which was clearly quite incompatible with the principle of an open-ended commitment to provide, for free, however much healthcare the public demanded. Bevan sought to make the ceiling one of rubber rather than concrete by arguing in a prior memorandum that, where it was not possible to make good unforeseen overruns by economies elsewhere, 'any resulting excess expenditure due to this kind of item [such as wage awards or breakdown of hospital plant] will be regarded as justifiable ground for a supplementary estimate'.[99] In committee he sought to twang his colleagues' humanitarian consciences by saying that some rejections of proposed development 'would be very unpalatable – e.g. a refusal to provide badly needed beds for tubercular cases. He would endeavour to base his defence of the Government's policy rather on the ground that the physical resources for development were not available than on strictly financial grounds.'[100]

At the third meeting of the committee on 28 May Bevan again raised the banner of New Jerusalem in defiance of such squalid considerations as money:

he could not give any undertaking that under existing conditions it would be practicable to give effect to the statement made by the Chancellor of the Exchequer in introducing his budget that any over-all increase in the expenditure on the Health Service could not be allowed. The hospitals, and other health services, were living organisms and it was difficult to keep within conventional financial limits. . . . apart from Whitley awards, other excess expenditure might have to be incurred. . . .[101]

In fact, what Bevan as a true romantic really wanted was that reality should bow to the ideal, and that whatever resources might be needed by the health service must simply be plucked off the pound-note tree in the Treasury courtyard. He said as much in a June memorandum on the 'Use of Hospital Beds' (the hospital service being the largest and fastest-growing sector of expense within the health service). Acknowledging that there was 'no doubt that the introduction of the National Health Service has been accompanied by increased pressure on hospital facilities – the numbers of in-patients and out-patients have risen appreciably', he claimed that it was 'very doubtful, however, whether the pressure is any greater than might naturally be expected to follow from the removal of financial barriers to treatment'.[102] For him, therefore, the problem lay not in the demand but in the supply.

> The overall picture is therefore one of increased pressure on a service which, owing to limitations on capital investment and general expenditure, cannot expand sufficiently to bear the load. The results are gross-overcrowding . . . early discharge . . . long waiting lists which tend to grow rather than fall . . . and congested out-patient departments. . . .
>
> It must be recognised that, so long as the present wide gap exists between the justifiable demand for hospital facilities and their availability, no improvement in the efficient use of beds can be counted on to produce overall economy. . . .[103]

Five decades later, and despite all intervening experience of the finite nature of the resources of a lame industrial economy, the spiritual heirs of the New Jerusalem movement would still be employing the same kind of argument.

In starkest contrast with Bevan's cast of mind was that of the man who now emerged as his long-term foe, Hugh Gaitskell, then Minister of State for Economic Affairs. A financial realist as well as a social improver from the small-'l' liberal Establishment (Winchester and New College, Oxford; first in Philosophy, Politics and Economics), Gaitskell complained strongly in a paper of 23 June 1950 about the lack of up-to-date 'cash-flow' information provided to the committee by Bevan, which made it difficult to devise remedies if current expenditure were indeed overrunning estimates. He then did the sort of sums which enraged a man of passionate faith like Bevan, and reckoned that the health service ceiling for the financial year was already being exceeded by some £10 million.[104] But, from Bevan's point of view, far worse was to come.

At its meeting on 28 June (out of which Bevan stalked in dudgeon, to be persuaded back later by Attlee)[105] the Health Service Committee decided that a 29-page report (due next day) of an Enquiry into the Financial Workings of the Service by a retired member of the Indian Civil Service, Sir Cyril Jones, should be circulated to its members. Next day Bevan, angry at Treasury ministers' reiteration of the need to relieve the public purse by charging patients a portion of the cost of their treatment, brandished the ultimate political sword, writing to Cripps: 'I have made it clear to you, the Prime Minister and Gaitskell, that I consider the imposition of charges on any part of the Health Service raises issues of such seriousness and importance that I could never agree to it. If it were decided by the Government to impose them, my resignation would immediately follow. . . .'[106]

Sir Cyril Jones's report began with figures which, in his own words, 'gave quantitative expression to the well-known fact of the rapid onrush of the cost in the initial years of the newly inaugurated health service on a nation-wide scale, which was both comprehensive and free'.[107] In 1948–9 the total gross cost (the twelve-month equivalent of the actual nine months) of the service came to £295,961,721, of which £211,299,940 fell on the taxpayer. For 1949–50 the original budget estimate of the gross cost came to £310,822,782; the revised estimate to £396,091,432, of which £320,281,250 fell on the taxpayer. For 1950–1 the budget estimate of gross cost was £426,709,400, of which £349,650,000 was to fall on the taxpayer.[108]

Although Jones acknowledged such reasons for the onrush as backlogs in treatment or pay rises, he went on to provide a shattering indictment of the consequences of trying to fulfil a romantic vision in real life:

It is quite certain, however, that legitimate grounds have been accentuated by the new mentality created by a new free Health

Service paid for out of the general resources of the State. This applies to the hospital administering authorities no less than to the general public and has led, at the best, to subordination of financial considerations and an impatience at financial control, and at the worst to positive but definite abuse. An incidental effect is an almost total disregard of relative priorities at all levels which can hardly be allowed to continue when the financial burden of the Service has about reached the limit of what the country's economy can bear.[109]

The remainder of Jones's report was taken up with a detailed dissection of the health service's faulty administrative structures and pervasive financial unrealism, together with proposed remedies, some drastic. Wrote Bevan (the grinding of his teeth can almost be heard), the report was 'a useful account by an independent observer, and his conclusions obviously merit close study'.[110] At the next meeting of the Health Service Committee on 28 July he contended that hospital expenditure was now 'under control, but underlined the fact that other services, which depended on the extent of public demand, had to be predicted [sic] and could not be closely controlled . . .'.[111] However, he supported Jones's proposals for tightening up hospital administration, and the committee duly decided to recommend to the Cabinet that legislation should be passed to make Regional Hospital Boards advisory rather than executive bodies, and so permit closer control by the Ministry of Health.

But that was virtually all that resulted from the agonising over the cost of Bevan's grand edifice of 'socialism' which had gone on throughout this crisis summer of 1950 when the outbreak of the Korean War blew away the assumptions on which British economic strategy had been founded. For the basic fallacy and folly of a 'free' national health service lacking any automatic limit on expenditure could not now be undone – perhaps could never be undone. The present and future attempts to hold down the inexorably rising costs of the service by tinkering resembled nothing so much as endeavouring to fit brakes on a toboggan already committed to the Cresta Run.

CHAPTER EIGHT

Parlours Before Plant

T O BEVAN IN 1945 had also been entrusted the principal
responsibility for redeeming the most extravagant promise of
all in the Labour Party's prospectus for New Jerusalem – to
provide every family with its own separate commodious dwelling. For
New Jerusalem had always been envisaged from the late-Victorian era
onwards as a smiling land of garden cities, in contrast to the foul and
overcrowded urban slums described by such contemporary social
investigators as Seebohm Rowntree.[1] Slum-clearance schemes
between the wars had only chipped at this legacy of the first industrial
revolution, leaving the bulk of the working class to live out their lives in
the squalid brick 'camps' first run up to house their great-grandparents.[2]
In the studiedly cool language of the report of the Barlow Royal
Commission on the Distribution of the Industrial Population in 1940,
the inhabitants of Britain's 'densely built inner areas of badly
constructed and unplanned housing' suffered 'certain disadvantages'
such as 'lack of space for recreation, difficulties of transport, congestion,
smoke and noise'.[3] It is therefore easy enough to understand why the
dream of a decent home for every family shone forth with a fresh
brilliance during the Second World War. The dream inspired a double-
page spread in that 1941 New Year issue of *Picture Post* on 'A Plan for
Britain' which marked the public launch of the wartime New Jerusalem
movement. It provided a major topic in the coalition Government's
discussions in 1943–5 about postwar reconstruction. The realisation of
this dream by a vast programme of house-building was rated by both
electorate and politicians in the 1945 general election as the most
important single issue before the country.[4] But just how many houses
should – and, more to the point, *could* – be built in the postwar era?

In March 1945 a White Paper had nailed all three political parties in the coalition Government to a minimum target of 3–4 million new houses in the first ten or twelve years of peace.[5] But even this figure proved too mean and modest for the Labour Party, surfing its way to victory in the general election on the sweeping wave of New Jerusalemism, and it raised the bidding to 4–5 million.[6] Given the priority accorded to housing in the minds of the voters, this promise proved electorally shrewd as well as grandiose. Yet grandiose though the promise was, Aneurin Bevan came to office as Minister of Health passionately committed to fulfilling it. He had publicly scorned the coalition Government's plan to build 100,000 houses in the first year of peace and to put in hand 200,000 in the second year, sneering: 'Not much of a blitzkrieg, is it?'[7]

But once he had forsaken the rhetoric of the backbencher for the responsibilities of a minister he quickly learned that the sheer physical scale of the problem measured against the resources of a war-weakened economy rendered a blitzkrieg quite out of the question. For, whereas bombing had destroyed some 200,000 houses and damaged another 3.5 million, the British population had grown by more than a million since 1939. The Conservative caretaker Government had reckoned in May 1945 that 750,000 new houses were needed to provide each family with a home of their own, and then another 500,000 to replace the worst of the slums.[8] As against these needs, there existed crippling shortages of building labour, especially in skilled trades like bricklaying, and of just about every kind of material and appliance that went to make a house and equip it.[9] In his first monthly progress report to the Cabinet on 8 November 1945, Bevan could lay out only a modest initial plan: 15,000 permanent houses to be completed by the end of the Government's first year in office (June 1946), and 150,000 a year later.[10]

Yet the Government still stood committed by its electoral pledge to solve the housing problem. Its own supporters in and out of Parliament nourished a fervent expectation that it would succeed in so doing. The general public, especially those living in slums or packed into small houses with relatives or in-laws, looked to the Government to provide the homes which it had been so ready to promise. And everyone remembered how Lloyd George's coalition Government after the Great War had promised to build 'houses fit for heroes to live in', and had then failed to do so, with calamitous political consequences. The Conservative Opposition therefore ruthlessly made of housing a bludgeon with which to thump an administration stumbling through the aftermath of war. The credit of the Labour Government thus depended more on the number of houses it constructed than on any other aspect of its programme for New Jerusalem. Consequently the moral and political pressure on the Government to pour capital investment into house-building was enormous – quite apart from its own zeal in the cause, as so well personified by the Minister of Health.

And yet here was another and peculiarly damaging example of trying to fulfil the long-cherished dream of New Jerusalem in national circumstances such as the original dreamers could never have imagined. For, whereas the new welfare state and NHS meant paying out a dividend on the Golden Age not yet earned, the house-building programme meant diverting actual labour and materials from that modernisation of Britain's industrial machine which was essential if the dividend were to be earned in fact in the future. Moreover, because of its greedy demand for timber bought with dollars the programme also contributed a major debit item in the precarious balance of payments.[11]

It took until the end of 1946 for Bevan's programme to gather momentum at last, with 251,000 new houses approved and 188,000 of them under construction.[12] For 1947 he ambitiously fixed his target at 240,000 completions, to achieve which as well as carry out house repairs and conversions would demand as much as 60 per cent of the country's total building labour-force.[13] Moreover, out of the Government's planned total capital investment of £825 million in all kinds of new construction in 1947, new housing was allotted no less than £303 million as against only £61 million for new industrial building.[14]

This pattern of deployment had of course been decided on by the Government when it was still confidently proceeding with the general creation of New Jerusalem on the back of the 1945 dollar loan. But this happy time came to an end in the summer of 1947 with the onset of the sterling-convertibility crisis, compelling the Government to trim back public expenditure across the board, including £200 million worth of capital investment. Henceforward, housing investment joined the defence budget and the health services as a desirable object of the Chancellor of the Exchequer's repeated attempts at financial surgery. Henceforward, too, the Government, shaken into a new awareness of the need for economic success, would struggle to reconcile investment in homes with investment in factories and plant and in infrastructure. But, needless to say, Bevan was to fight as tenaciously for his housing programme as for his 'free' National Health Service.

At a meeting on 1 August 1947 the Cabinet entrusted the Central Planning Staff with the tasks of reviewing current programmes of capital investment and 'curtailing those projects which do not contribute to export or import saving . . .'.[15] Officials were briefed by the Chief Planning Officer, Sir Edwin Plowden, in Jeeves-like prose that 'it is desirable that reductions should fall wherever possible on elements in the programme which contribute to amenities or to the domestic standard of life, rather than on productive industry . . .'.[16] Translated into plain English, this meant that what helped the country to make a living must take priority when it came to capital investment, and New Jerusalem second. Here was heresy indeed, and particularly so in regard to the housing programme, for nothing could contribute more to amenities and the domestic standard of life than building new houses, or contribute less to productive industry (except in the case of housing specifically linked to industrial expansion).[17]

According to existing plans, the ceiling for the workforce on construction work for the whole of British industry as at June 1947 stood at 127,660 men, with a projected increase to 149,038 as at March 1948, while the ceiling for housing (new, maintenance and repair) stood at 582,000 men at both dates. Under the cuts now mooted by civil servants, industry's share of the building labour-force would drop to 118,000 as at June 1948, and housing's share to 490,000. The share allotted to construction work on Britain's obsolescent and war-worn transport and communications systems, standing at under 28,000 men in June 1947, was to drop to 16,000 as at June 1948;[18] that allotted to construction work in the energy industries to drop from 53,588 in June 1948 under existing plans to only 40,000.[19] Taking ceilings for labour-forces engaged in construction work across the whole national scene, housing as at June 1947 sucked in 582,000 men out of a grand total of 971,000; would suck in as at June 1948 under existing plans a slightly lower share of 582,000 out of 1,010,000; and under proposed cuts an actually higher relative share of 490,000 out of a grand total of 820,000 (59 per cent as against 57.6 per cent).[20]

These figures starkly demonstrate not only how strongly New Jerusalem had influenced the balance of the Labour Government's deployment of resources for investment in construction, but also how difficult the necessary redeployment was now going to be. After all, 240,000 houses were at present under construction, while contracts had already been placed for another 110,000,[21] and to cancel existing contracts or even stop work on half-built houses would be wasteful.[22] Though more houses could be built with the same labour-force if their size and specification were reduced, Bevan adamantly opposed this, believing that even in the country's present plight the ideal homes of New Jerusalem must not be compromised.[23] But in any case such a reduction would not save labour or materials until late 1948 – no help in the present crisis.

In the event, however, housing still came off best in the proposals framed by the Investment Programmes Committee to meet the Chancellor's target of a £200 million cut in capital investment (of which half was being met by cuts in investment in plant), and industry came off worst. In the words of the committee's report, 'for a period of at least six months only factories of most exceptional importance should be started . . .'. Instead resources must be concentrated 'on completing projects relevant to the export drive'.[24] As for housing, the rate of new starts should be dropped from 15,000 a month to 5000 for at least a year, which would also serve to reduce the 'vast and growing stock' of unfinished houses. The committee therefore proposed the following ceilings for labour-forces in construction work: 123,378 in industry as at March 1948, and 81,050 as at June that year; 43,033 in all the energy industries as at March 1948, and 38,300 in June; 582,000 in housing as at March 1948, and 490,000 in June. In sum, labour on construction work in industry was to be cut by 23 per cent by June 1948, in transport by nearly 46 per cent, and in housing by only 15.8 per cent.[25]

When ministers came to battle over these proposed cuts in capital investment, Bevan strove to keep housing completely immune, partly by speciously arguing that the programme could be redirected towards miners and farmworkers (so important for exports and for import-saving), and partly on the straight New Jerusalem grounds of social need. But Cripps, who became Chancellor in November, would have none of it, telling Bevan that 'control of capital investment was meaningless without some reduction in the housing programme'.[26]

However, 'some reduction', as decided by the Cabinet in November 1947, amounted to a cut in the labour-force to 525,000 by June 1948, as against the civil servants' proposal of 490,000.[27] Furthermore the cut proved completely ineffective in practice, because the labour-force was actually to rise to 606,000 by April 1948.[28] And, whereas the Cabinet decided in November 1947 merely to reduce the 1948 programme for completed houses to 140,000, it suspended new starts in industrial building 'except in cases of real urgency by reason of the contribution of the project to export or import saving'.[29]

Thus even in the aftermath of the convertibility crisis and although now fully alive to the perilousness of Britain's economic prospects, the Labour Government continued to opt for the investment strategy first adumbrated in 1944 in the wartime coalition's planning for postwar reconstruction − one of parlours before plant.[30]

In 1948, the year when yet more dollars came to Britain's rescue in the form of Marshall Aid, Bevan and his colleague the Secretary of State for Scotland were planning to complete 200,000 houses and to do the same again in 1949.[31] In the words of the report in July 1948 by the Investment Programmes Committee on capital investment in 1949, 'The immediate aim of the housing programme continues to be the provision of a separate home for every family in the country. . . .'[32] The committee nonetheless recommended that the target for 1949 be lowered to 175,000 completions, and that the total cost of all capital investment in housing (including maintenance and repair) should be cut from an expected £458 million in 1948 to £438 million in 1949, before rising again to £464 million in 1950.[33] These figures may be compared with a total recommended investment in construction work in manufacturing industry of £70 million in 1948, £93 million in 1949 and £95 million in 1950.[34]

The Whitehall struggle between Bevan, fighting with passionate conviction for his vision of a house for every family, and realists such as the Chancellor and Sir Edwin Plowden, the Government's Chief Economic Planner, continued on through 1948 in the new context provided by Marshall Aid. For the Americans were handing out billions of dollars to the Europeans in order that they might reconstruct and modernise their economies, not in order that they might award themselves amenities like a house for every family built with American timber. At the end of October Plowden wrote sternly to the permanent under-secretaries (top civil servants) of all ministries with regard to the 'Long-Term Programme' submitted by the United Kingdom to the Organisation for European Economic Co-operation (in other words, its bid for a goodly share of Marshall Aid dollars):

> Until the equipment of the export industries and of the basic industries serving industrial production as a whole has been adequately restored and modernised, investment for these purposes must take precedence over investment designed solely or mainly to increase consumption standards. . . .[35]

Therefore, Plowden went on, the level of social service investment should not rise above the present level. But he was only repeating what the Chancellor, Sir Stafford Cripps, had written even more forcefully back in July: 'The overriding need to achieve national economic independence as soon as possible demands that the available resources should be concentrated first and foremost on industrial investment.'[36]

In November 1948 the Investment Programmes Committee freshly estimated that out of a grand total for gross fixed investment in 1948 of £2022 million, housing's share would come to £480 million (including £310 million on new houses). Yet manufacturing industry's share (comprising new plant and machines as well as building work) would come to barely a tenth more than this at £531 million; transport and communications (also including equipment as well as building) would get £304 million; and energy industries £201 million.[37] For the following year, 1949, the IPC therefore proposed that housing's share should be cut to a total of £420 million (of which £250 million would be allotted to new houses), as against cuts in the shares of manufacturing industry to £509 million and of transport and communications to £276 million, and of a rise in the share of the energy industries to £225 million.[38] But the strategic plan for investment for 1949 as eventually approved by the Cabinet nevertheless again favoured housing as against the productive economy. The building of new houses was allotted £253 million, £3 million up on the IPC's figure, while manufacturing industry's share was cut to £480 million (nearly £30 million down on the IPC's figure), and that of the energy industries to £220 million (down £5 million on the IPC's figure). Of the various spheres of the productive economy only transport and communications did better under the Cabinet's decisions, rising to £297 million (up £21 million on the IPC's figure).[39]

However, all these predictions and choices rested on statistical information so unreliable that the planners did not even know whether investment was actually rising or falling.[40] In the event, their hopeful decisions were betrayed by a kind of spending drift; and this drift had the effect of altering the balance of investment even further to the benefit of housing. According to up-to-date figures presented in May 1949 by the Investment Programmes Committee, manufacturing industry's share of capital investment in 1948 had amounted to only £434 million (nearly £100 million less than recommended); that of the energy industries to only £164 million (£37 million less than recommended), and of transport and communications to only £287 million (£17 million less than recommended), while new house-building's share had come out at £322 million (£12 million more than recommended).[41]

The IPC's recommendations for 1950 in the same report ('Capital Investment in 1950–52') therefore marked an admirably strenuous attempt to redeploy investment from housing to the productive economy at long last. Compared with the actual figures for 1948, manufacturing's share was to go up by £43 million to £477 million; that of transport and communications by £14 million to £301 million; that of the energy industries by £73 million to £237 million.[42] On the other hand, the committee concluded that spending on new houses should be stabilised at £253 million a year. This marked a drop of £69 million on the 1948 figure, even though the report acknowledged that the 880,000 homes newly built or converted out of existing dwellings from the end of the war to December 1948 were not enough to 'satisfy the ideal of a separate home for every family . . .'.[43]

Within two months all this work of hopeful strategic calculation was already becoming mere shelf-fodder because of (in the Chancellor's dismal words on 11 July 1949) 'the steady deterioration in our dollar balance of payments'. He opined that, far from it being useful to look ahead as far as 1952, 'even for 1950 it was difficult to settle a programme with any certainty . . .'. And he warned: 'Departments should, therefore, bear in mind that it might be necessary to re-examine the 1950 programmes again in the autumn and should not enter into commitments which would preclude a downward revision of the programmes, if this should be found necessary.'[44]

This proved all too sound advice. After the immediate sterling crisis had been resolved by devaluation in September the grey tide of economic reality swept in again to crumble away yet more of New Jerusalem. For the Cabinet decided that gross fixed capital investment must be cut by £140 million.[45] The Prime Minister himself laid down the broad strategic pattern, which included cuts in manufacturing investment by £15 million, in transport and communications by £10 million, in energy industries by £25 million and in new housing by £35 million.[46]

Bevan therefore now found himself embattled on two fronts: current expenditure on his health service (see above, pp. 145–6) and capital investment in his housing programme. True to his Marxist faith he now proposed to effect the housing cuts by issuing no more licences to builders of private dwellings. This exercise in class warfare was ruled out on pragmatic grounds by the Investment Programmes Committee, which had been entrusted by the Cabinet with drawing up detailed proposals for reducing investment. 'We do not feel satisfied', its members wrote in their report, 'that the policy suggested by the Ministry of Health will achieve the necessary saving in time. At present it looks as if there will be no big savings until 1951. . . .'[47]

In the end, Bevan, though successful in brandishing his sword over the imposition of charges on health service patients, was unhorsed over housing investment, for a figure of £218 million a year was finally agreed by the ministerial Economic Policy Committee on 14 October 1949.[48]

Yet even now he would not abandon his dream of a house for every family, and appealed personally to Attlee, though to no avail. Their exchange of letters wonderfully encapsulates the entire issue of the competing burdens laid on the British economy by the double pursuit of the dream of New Jerusalem and the illusion of world power. When Bevan complained of 'already swollen and engorged defence estimates', Attlee retorted: 'It really does not advance matters to talk about gorged and swollen defence estimates any more than it does to talk about grossly extravagant Health services. . . .'[49]

After the Labour Government had been returned in the general election of February 1950 with an overall majority shrunk from 145 to only 5 and a fresh election therefore probable in a year or so, the political and moral pressures mounted again to build more new houses at the expense of modernising the British industrial economy. In a Cabinet meeting on 17 March Bevan pleaded for enough money to make an allocation of 140,000 houses for 1951 in view of 'widespread public dissatisfaction with housing conditions'.[50] The Chancellor of the Exchequer himself recommended that the housing programme should be stabilised at 200,000 houses a year in 1950, 1951 and 1952, a proposal to which the Cabinet hastened to agree, on the score that it would 'ease the political difficulties which were arising from the public dissatisfaction at the current rate of housebuilding'.[51] The Cabinet therefore issued instructions to the Investment Programmes Committee (civil servants) that 'adjustments would have to be made to other sectors of the investment programme in order to permit the increased expenditure on housing . . .'.[52]

This provoked the Whitehall mandarins on the Investment Programmes Committee bluntly to confront the politicians with the fundamental issue at stake, writing in their report of 24 April 1950 on capital investment in 1951 and 1952:

> We were specially instructed by Ministers to consider whether, within the total of resources available, adjustment could be made which would make possible an increase in the housing programme in 1951. . . . in our view it is necessary to choose between further investment in housing and in some of the highly desirable industrial investment in respect of which we have proposed increases. . . .[53]

The committee pointed out:

> Housing is the largest single field of investment which is effectively under the control of the Government. The proposals put forward by the two Health Departments as desirable in 1951 and 1952 would cost an increase of £35 million a year in investment in housing above the rate to which it was decided to reduce it in October last. . . .[54]

Having noted that in any case there had been delays in achieving this reduction, the committee now uncompromisingly recommended an investment strategy of plant before parlours:

> To achieve the reduced rate of investment required by financial considerations, we see no alternative but to propose a further reduction in the housing programme below the level to which it would otherwise be reduced by the spring of 1951. We fully

161

recognise the political objections to this and the social and economic arguments which will weigh against it. But the lower programme [of two possible capital investment programmes] has to achieve a level overall which is £80 millions below actual total investment in 1949, and even in the lower programme there are some programmes which will during 1950 and must, in our view, be allowed to rise . . . notably petroleum, coal and electricity. We see no other [field] where a reduction can be secured which would be sufficient to enable the programme as a whole to be reduced to the level required. . . .[55]

The committee therefore recommended that gross fixed investment in the energy industries should rise from £200 million (actual) in 1949 to £236 million in 1950; in transport and communications from £266 million to £295 million; in manufacturing industry (including iron and steel) from £449 million to £453 million – and that gross capital investment in new housing should fall from £284 million (actual) in 1949 to £281 million.[56] The committee further recommended that the totals for new housing should drop even lower to £255 million in 1951 before rising modestly again to £273 million in 1952.[57]

However, a final decision as to the scale of future national investment programmes depended on guesstimating the rate at which national productivity might increase – whether as much as 4 per cent or as little as 2.5 per cent. After the usual ramble through a thicket of conflicting considerations, ministers on the Economic Policy Committee decided on 12 May 1950[58] to accept the Chancellor's advice that the planning of capital investment in 1951 and 1952 should be based on the more sanguine of the two assumptions, i.e., a 4 per cent productivity growth.[59]

It is hardly surprising that politicians chose to make this optimistic assumption, since on the basis of only 2.5 per cent growth their wished-for plans clearly could not be afforded, such as the housing programme previously agreed by the Cabinet earlier of 200,000 new dwellings a year, at a cost of £30 million more capital investment in 1951 and £15 million more in 1952.[60] Now ministers could happily resolve to abide by that decision – even though the Chancellor emphasised that other capital investment programmes would still have to shrink by equivalent amounts.[61]

Barely six weeks after the Government had thus freshly given priority to parlours before plant, the outbreak of the Korean War demolished its wishful calculations like a bomb on one of Aneurin Bevan's new council houses.

Over the three full years of the housing programme, 1947, 1948 and 1949, nearly £1400 million of capital investment had been poured into new house-building and into repairs and maintenance of existing stock. But construction in manufacturing industry over the three years totalled a mere £300–320 million; in transport and communications some £262 million; in energy industries perhaps £160 million; £85 million into agriculture and fisheries – some £830 million in all of construction into the productive economy, or little over half that in housing.[62]

Given that Britain began the postwar era with some 3.5 million war-damaged dwellings, it may be taken that the investment in repair and maintenance was essential and unavoidable. On this, indeed, West Germany chose to concentrate her own housing investment, as her long-term programme for Marshall Aid stated: 'For the next four years priority will be given to repair and reconstruction in preference to new construction, the object being to produce the greatest volume of dwelling space with the minimum cost, materials and labour.'[63] But the British investment in *new* housing – that is, in fulfilling perhaps the loveliest dream in all the dreaming about New Jerusalem – alone came to about £950 million in the three years 1947–9, £130 million more than the combined total of investment in new construction in all industries and in the country's decrepit, obsolete transport and communications systems. Measured against the harsh reality of Britain's economic plight, such a deployment of resources amounts to self-indulgent folly.

When capital investment in new housing is added to the current expenditure demanded by the National Health Service and the new social security system over and above previous provisions, the total burden piled on the British economy by New Jerusalem in the two years 1948 (when the NHS came into operation) and 1949 amounted to nearly £1400 million.[64] To this must be added another enormously expensive form of handout at the Exchequer's expense, although in this case a legacy of the war rather than part of New Jerusalem itself –

food subsidies of well over £1 million a day[65] to cushion the citizen, no matter whether rich or poor, from the true cost of nourishment, thus leaving him or her with more money to spend on tobacco, beer (or, as it might be, champagne) and the pictures (or, as it might be, the theatre and the opera), and thereby dissuading him or her from asking for an inflationary rise in wages. In 1948 food subsidies amounted to £520 million.[66] In his April 1949 budget Cripps sought to peg them at £465 million, with the result that in the event they amounted to about £500 million that year.[67] When the combined figure for 1948 and 1949 of food subsidies at around £1000 million is added to the other costs of New Jerusalem in those two years, the grand total of the load heaped on the productive economy (or, to put it another way, the grand total of the resources *pre-empted* from that economy) by New Jerusalem comes to some £2400 million. This amounts to around 11 per cent of total GNP over the same two years.[68] Perhaps more telling still, it amounts to nearly 13 per cent of the output of the wealth-producing part of the economy (that is, leaving out items like Government services).[69]

Such then was the handicap which the British in their social idealism imposed on themselves by their own free choice in the late 1940s, at a time when their military spending in pursuit of the illusion of world power (as against the necessary defence of Western Europe and the United Kingdom) amounted to about 4 per cent of GNP (see above, pp. 101–02). Thus the double pursuit of British dreams and British illusions was costing a total of some 15 per cent of GNP. To this massive burden on a war-ruined economy must be added the direct drain on the balance of payments caused by overseas military deployments (see above, p. 101), as well as the strain imposed by the role of central banker to the Sterling Area (see above, pp. 106–10).

All in all, total-strategic overstretch could hardly have been taken further. It rendered more desperately urgent and at the same time immensely more difficult the fundamental task of remaking Britain as an industrial society exporting to the world.

PART THREE

A Real and Grave Crisis in Economic Affairs

It occurs to me that the Germans are a menacing race by reason of their docility and their ability to toil. No man ought to love work as they do – it's indecent, certainly uncivilised. We English don't love work in this slavelike way, and thank God for it.

(BRITISH JOURNALIST IN GERMANY, 1945)

A Labour Government will plan from the ground up, giving an appropriate place to constructive enterprise and private endeavour in the national plan. . . .

(LABOUR PARTY MANIFESTO, 1945)

Most important of the reasons for higher productivity in the U.S.A. is the general atmosphere there that nothing is impossible and most things are worth trying. In contrast, the attitude here seems to me to be that most things are impossible and not worth trying.

(BRITISH ENGINEER ON RETURN FROM AMERICA, 1952)

CHAPTER NINE

The Character of the Nation

> The solution of the problem of the balance of payments is a first
> condition of the restoration of a measure of balance and independence
> in the national economy. A relatively small deficiency in our
> international trade balance may cause a wholly disproportionate
> dislocation in our whole internal position before it can be remedied.
>   . . . [For] few countries depend in any comparable degree [to the
> United Kingdom] on foreign trade for the essential food and raw
> material supplies without which the nation cannot continue to live and
> work. . . .[1]

Thus in July 1948 did the Central Economic Planning Staff sum up for
the benefit of Labour ministers the economic precariousness ultimately
bequeathed by the mid-Victorian espousal of free trade. Such
dependence on imports meant of course that the nation's life and
work must equally depend on the United Kingdom's ability to export
– a double precariousness therefore. Worse, as the CEPS went on to
point out,

> the insecurity of our trading position has been progressively
> increased by the recent trends in the character of our foreign trade.
> To an increasing extent we have come to live by exchanging for our
> daily necessities the capital goods, the durable consumption goods,
> and certain relatively inessential manufactures in which we have
> specialised.

This, remarked the CEPS, 'has been at once the strength and
weakness of our position' . . .

It was throughout the nineteenth century and in certain periods of the twentieth century an undoubted source of strength. We were enabled to concentrate our industrial efforts on those industries in which the work of our skilled craftsmen could command a greater return, and depend on others to supply us with the goods in which we . . . had less comparative advantage. This policy of specialisation undoubtedly brought rich gains to us in the period of our industrial leadership during the nineteenth century.

But at the same time that policy constituted:

a source of weakness because the specialisation in the production of capital equipment, combined with the high degree of dependence on a specialised foreign trade, exposed the nation very greatly to the risks and uncertainties both of the trade cycle and of the slower secular changes in industrial development in the world outside. Our industrial population and our industrial structure had become too rigidly adjusted to a world in which we no longer held the industrial leadership which we had enjoyed in the nineteenth century.[2]

In 1937, the best trading year for Britain between the world wars, the volume of her visible exports amounted to only two-thirds of the 1913 figure. The British share of world trade in manufactures fell from nearly 24 per cent in 1921–5 to 18.6 per cent in 1936–8, whereas Germany's share actually rose from 17.4 per cent to 19.8 per cent, and Japan's from 3.4 per cent to 7 per cent.[3] As a consequence of this slow defeat and retreat in world markets for manufactures Britain was compelled to look more and more to her invisible exports (banking, insurance and shipping services, plus the income from the vast overseas investments built up during the Victorian age) in order to pay for the imports essential to the nation's life and work. Even at the height of her nineteenth-century dominance as a manufacturing country Britain had relied on such invisible exports to keep her balance of payments in equilibrium – indeed to enable her to earn the surpluses to invest overseas. But the percentage of imports that had to be covered by invisible earnings rose from 19.2 per cent in 1870–4 to 44.4 per cent in 1935–9.[4] Even so, Britain by these latter years was incurring an overall balance of payments deficit. Like some ageing industrialist who finds that the shrunken profits from the family firm are no longer enough to pay for his accustomed way of life, Britain had to resort to spending capital. In other words, in the run-up to the Second World War Britain was gradually selling off her foreign investments and using up her gold reserves.[5]

It remained only for Britain during the war to pour out the rest of the investments and the gold on the purchase of war supplies from the United States, while at the same time cutting visible exports to a third of the 1938 level for the sake of war production, and the basis of Britain's economic existence for the last hundred years had been comprehensively destroyed.

In 1945 Britain was therefore left by this nemesis of free trade with none of the advantages of being highly dependent on foreign trade, and all the vulnerability. In the immediate postwar era, and for the first time since the beginning of the industrial revolution, she would have to depend almost entirely on visible exports in order to secure the life and work of the nation and to rebuild her old prosperity. But this was not all. She would similarly have to depend on such exports for generating the wealth to defray the double costs of the world role and New Jerusalem. Thus the fundamental factor in British total strategy from 1945 onwards must be, ought to be, the competitive prowess of British industry.

But at least Britain would not straightaway have to face a threat from her most formidable pre-war trade rivals, Germany and Japan, for the Second World War had for the time being ousted them from world markets altogether. The Central Economic Planning Staff comfortingly noted in its paper of July 1948 (see above, p. 167) that whereas in 1936–8 Germany had enjoyed a share of nearly 20 per cent of world trade in manufactures, her share in 1947 amounted to a mere 0.5 per cent, while Japan's share had sunk from 7 per cent to virtually nil.[6] To prevent German competition ever again becoming a menace to British exporters therefore became a key objective of British policy in regard to the dismantling of Germany's industrial capacity by the victors.[7] In February 1945 a detailed study by the Economic and Industrial Policy Staff for the wartime coalition Government listed fifteen industries from ball-bearings and machine-tools to steel and textiles where it recommended that German production should be held down in the postwar era for the sake of British commercial interests.[8] In July 1946 a Whitehall study on 'The Long Term Demand for British Exports of Manufactures' examined eighteen different technologies from telecommunications to steam-boilers, and assumed that, thanks to the restrictions imposed by allied reparations policy, German exports in 1951 in all these fields would vary from nil to only 30 per cent of pre-war.[9]

With her main pre-war rivals on their backs and a world hungry for goods after six years of war, Britain as an industrial society was thus presented with a unique opportunity, but likewise a unique challenge – like an army committed to launching an offensive on a gigantic scale, on the results of which hung nothing less than the national future.

Yet, as Britain's wartime record demonstrates and the contemporaneous surveys of postwar export prospects grimly concluded,[10] here was no industrial equivalent of a panzer striking force, superbly equipped with the best of modern technology, its troops brought to a high pitch of morale and tactical training, and blessed with dynamic leadership from the high command down to junior officers and NCOs. Rather, Britain as an industrial society in 1945 more resembled the French Army of 1940 – its equipment (including infrastructure such as ports, roads and railways) largely old and outmoded;[11] its tactical doctrines out of date; the standard of training of its regimental officers (in other words, line and shop-floor managers) often lamentable;[12] its NCO corps (trade union conveners and shop-stewards) more devoted to thwarting the officers than obeying them; the morale and motivation of its ill-educated rank and file low, even to the point of recurrent local mutiny;[13] and its generals (boards and top management) largely too timid, too torpid, too set in the ways of the past to measure up to the exacting role of planning and conducting a war of conquest for world markets.[14]

To the wartime Board of Trade, gloomily studying postwar export prospects, Britain's primary weakness was apparent enough – too much of her industrial strength was deployed in the old Victorian staples like textiles, shipbuilding, steel and coal; too little in new technologies with fast-growing markets. According to a Board of Trade report in 1943 on the 'Recovery of Export Markets', only 4 per cent of British goods entering the United States in 1937 were dependent on modern invention and design. Moreover the value of American goods based on modern invention imported into the United Kingdom in that year was no less than eleven times the value of such British goods exported to the US.[15] In the already booming field of office systems, to cite one example of such neglect of markets for new technologies,[16] Britain only had a few little firms hand-building primitive adding machines at a rate of about fifteen a week. As yet another Board of Trade report noted early in 1945:

> Almost all machines in this group were imported, mainly from the United States, though there is some German and Swedish production. During the war we have been entirely dependent on United States manufacture for accounting machine supplies, and mainly for adding and calculating machines. We have been importing about 7,000 machines p.a. [sic] from the US, mostly on Lend–Lease. . . .[17]

The obvious remedy for this British imbalance between Victorian staples and modern technologies had been spelt out in dry Whitehallese in 1943 by the BOT study on the 'Recovery of Export Markets': 'The development of new types of products will be necessary to compensate for diminution of exports in former staple lines. . . .'[18] Quite so, but before the war such development had been crippled by lack of investment in research, which in turn reflected industry's widespread distaste for innovation and change. 'The extent of our technical research compares unfavourably with the United States, which has established a reputation for the newer types of goods,' remarked the same 1943 BOT report. In 1938, it went on, the US government spent $108 million, as against the British Department of Scientific and Industrial Research's budget of £740,000. American industry's research effort had likewise far outstripped the meagre overall effort of British industry, where only a handful of world-class companies such as ICI and Shell thought it was worth spending much money on R and D. The report noted in passing that pre-war German industrial research 'was conducted mainly by large firms with Government assistance and in collaboration with State institutions'.

But in any case Britain's old staple industries themselves stood in dire need of modernising, as this same report also pointed out:

> Some of our older industries are, for historical reasons, ill-equipped with modern machinery and plant. Up-to-date machinery is essential to low-cost production; many of our factories are unsuited to modern equipment. We compare very badly with the US in regard to the use of up-to-date machinery. . . .[19]

In fact, the average pre-war life of a machine-tool in Britain was twenty years; in the United States, three to four years.[20]

Nonetheless, the problem did not only lie in over-commitment to outdated technologies or the cherishing of worn-out kit. For – again like the French Army of 1940 – British industry in 1945 suffered from a Maginot Line mentality, which in its case stemmed from the previous fifty years of defeat at the hands of its foreign rivals. Far from relishing the prospect of offensive campaigning in the open field of export competition, its boards of directors and its managers thought above all of defence – of existing markets, home or imperial, and preferably from behind protective tariffs; of existing products and production methods. In the words of the 1943 BOT report already cited,

> It is, no doubt, partly due to uncertainty about future policy that industry tends to plan on very conservative lines: some industries recognise the need of bold and constructive plans, but still lack the drive, cohesion or powers to put them into effect. The automobile industry, for example, whilst ready to concede the necessity of some closer but as yet undefined co-operation for export, rules out the idea of a radical alteration of the structure of the industry. . . .[21]

Trade unions likewise, embittered by the memory of pre-war unemployment, were obdurate in their resolve not to abandon the security of their own Maginot Line deep bunkers of outdated crafts and craft demarcations or traditional overmanning agreements[22] – their resolve being all the more effective because they enjoyed a 'uniquely close relationship'[23] with the political leadership of the Labour Party, local and national.

Thus whereas it was vital that Britain's industrial system be transformed if she were once again to win technological leadership in world markets, the system itself was (like the French Army in the years leading to the débâcle of 1940) overwhelmingly resistant to such a transformation, painful as that must be to all its vested interests, psychological as well as institutional. The necessary driving force, the reforming vision, would have to come from outside the system itself. And 'from outside' must mean from government. For the leadership and the authority equal to so grand a task as remaking Britain as an industrial society could hardly be furnished by any lesser agency.

172

Yet politics in a democracy is the art of the possible (as R. A. Butler memorably observed to a colleague during the war), and the extent of the possible is determined by public opinion, that amalgam of collective values, aspirations, myths and illusions – and of the individual's conception of his or her personal advantage.

Here lay the snag. For public opinion in the early postwar era was no more keen on remaking British society for the sake of success in world markets than it had been on rearming against Nazi Germany in 1933–5.

In the first place, the white-collared and cloth-capped masses who daily attended places of employment were themselves flesh and sinew of the existing industrial and commercial system. Under some ruthless regime of reform they might suffer hurtful disturbance to their familiar and not always exacting routines, as fixed in the case of the cloth-capped majority by union deals with employers and by the maze of demarcations between trades, and in the case of the white-collared minority by hardly less rigid administrative precedents and by hierarchies minutely graded by salary. Moreover, in big and old-established concerns such as banks, insurance companies and public utilities, there existed an unacknowledged bargain whereby in compensation for Scroogish pay the employees were offered security for life, first in half-speed jobs on the staffs of grossly overmanned operations, and thereafter as pensioners.[24] What could have been more unwelcome to most inmates of such institutions (and their families) than to have the Government foster a change to a system of high performance, high pay and low manning?

Moreover, broad national sentiment accorded all too well with such individual vested interest.[25] It too favoured the current industrial status quo, whereby, thanks to the abnormal needs of war, obsolete plants long shut down had been unpadlocked and restored to full production, and their workers rescued by the million from the street corners to practise once more their time-hallowed crafts. After all, this was really why the promise of future 'full employment' had gone down so well with the voters before and during the General Election of 1945.

Then again, the Labour Government and the white-collared and the cloth-capped (together with the head-scarved or be-snooded, for that matter) all believed that the wartime policy of 'fair shares' should continue into the postwar era. So too did the New Jerusalemers of the intelligentsia and the civil-service mandarinate, those high-minded, so well-meaning espousers of the ideals of social justice and harmony (see below, pp. 182–5). Yet 'fair shares' coupled with acute shortages necessarily meant a national straitjacket of rationing and allocations – a straitjacket strapping down the material ambition of the able and energetic, that powerful force for change in the Britain of the first industrial revolution, and in the America of the 1940s.[26] No British citizen in the early postwar years could expect to be rewarded for zeal at work, for acceptance of greater responsibility, for willingness to embrace new technologies, or for taking business risk – either by a better and more stylishly furnished house, or by a new car, or by a wardrobe full of new clothes, or even by extra beef, bacon, eggs and butter on the table. The more a man earned the more savagely he was punished by steeply rising income-tax designed partly to redistribute the money via the welfare state and food subsidies to those with smaller pay-packets, and partly to combat inflation by preventing the money being spent at all.[27]

Anyway, what could mere extra cash buy in the Britain of 1946 and after? Under Bevan's 'class-war' regime at the Ministry of Health (see above, Chapter 8), the great bulk of new houses were being built by local authorities for allocation according to priority of social need. Only a trickle of new cars were coming on to the home market, because most were necessarily going for export. Furnishings, clothing and most foods were 'on coupon', and precious little of any of them. By 1948, in the nemesis of free trade when Britain could no longer pay for all the foreign imports of food on which she had come to depend, the weekly food ration amounted to less than a pound of meat, one and half – one and a half – ounces of cheese, six ounces of butter and margarine, one ounce of cooking fat, half a pound of sugar, two pints of milk and one solitary egg. From July 1946 onwards even bread was rationed.[28] Thus it was only by means of 'fiddling' and black-market 'spivvery' that the enterprising (if unscrupulous) could find their reward.[29] In this as in the emptiness of its shops and the length of its queues (including, on town-hall lists, for housing) Britain in the late 1940s much resembled Russia in the 1990s.

Nonetheless, to the white-collared and cloth-capped this rationing out of dearth offered the immense psychological compensation that the able could not 'get above themselves' and 'give themselves airs'.[30] For the British man on the tram and his wife in the fish queue were not in any case conspicuous for thrusting ambition, and little admired it in others.[31] They did not set much store on achievement unless it took the form of goals scored on soccer fields or wins on the 'pools'. No mythical hope of 'making it' inspired them as it did their American equivalents. Given their cut-price and cut-short education and their widespread lack of training,[32] such bovine acceptance of their social lot is hardly remarkable. The author Richard Hoggart, himself from a working-class background, defines working-class consciousness as a 'sense of being in a group of their own, and this without there being necessarily implied any feeling of inferiority or pride; they feel rather that they are "working-class" in the things they admire and dislike, in "belonging" '.[33] And working class they wished to remain. In Hoggart's judgement in 1957, 'Most working-class people are not climbing; they do not quarrel with their general level; they only want the little more that allows a few frills.'[34] But much the same could have been said of lower-middle-class people, whose 'breadwinners' walked out of the front gate of their semi-detached houses each at his same time every morning and headed for the bus stop, tram stop or the station en route to 'business', and every evening each at his same time walked in again through the gate to regale his wife with the day's tidings from 'Town'.[35]

Nor, except in the garden or allotment or on the sports field, did Britons generally evince an eagerness for strenuous effort.[36] A journalist with the British Army advancing into the heart of Germany in April 1945 noted: 'It occurs to me that the Germans are a menacing race by reason of their docility and their ability to toil. No man ought to love work as they do – it's indecent, certainly uncivilised. We English don't love work in this slavelike way, and thank God for it.'[37] And a week later the same journalist, J. L. Hodson, confided to his notebook that the reason why the British were unable to maintain hatred for long was that their temperament was 'too lazy, too indifferent, too good-natured'.[38]

The judgements of Hodson and Hoggart were to be borne out by later probers into the national character. According to Michael Shanks, the distinguished industrial and economic journalist, in 1963:

> The issues that really arouse the British people are not issues of national efficiency, but issues of fair play and social justice. We are unwilling to advance if it means that anybody is going to get

175

hurt. . . . The very niceness of the British, the national desire to do the decent thing, uninformed by any rational calculus of what constitutes the common interest, has become an enormous force for *immobilisme*. . . .[39]

Seventeen years later, in January 1980, William Rees-Mogg, writing in *The Times*, was to come to much the same conclusion:

The British are not much moved by economics, or economies, or by technology, and only a little by science. They no longer, as a nation, set themselves to achieve high economic objectives, and they are bored and resentful when it is suggested that they ought to do so. Some individuals seek high economic objectives, usually of personal wealth but often also of more general development. These individuals tend to be regarded with curiosity, sometimes with suspicion, often with jealousy.

Many of the British do have an economic ambition, but it is to be comfortable, not to be rich. Nor do the British wish to change to new technology; gradually over the centuries they have adapted to the discoveries of science, but only for brief periods have they done so with enthusiasm, and the last time was more than a century ago, under the influence of a foreign prince. . . .[40]

In June that year Rees-Mogg's diagnosis was confirmed by a Times/ORC survey on the attitudes and opinions of the British citizenry. Fifty per cent of the sample 'would not work harder than they do now even if paid a lot more'. Forty-four per cent would 'buy' leisure for cash by taking a shorter working week for the same pay. Fifty-one per cent would not work longer hours even if they could get more money. Forty-three per cent 'would settle for a comfortable life, not much hard work and a low wage'. Forty-five per cent regarded themselves as 'unambitious'. And 56 per cent said that 'they do not have any personal drive to be rich'.[41]

In his 1982 book *On Britain*, that Anglophile German, Ralf Dahrendorf, was to opine that Britons lacked that urge for material achievement which drove his fellow countrymen:

A nice home, a few glasses of beer with friends in the evenings, watching a football match on Saturdays, a Mercedes or at least a

Volkswagen to move about in, holidays in Fuerteventura and the like, are not unknown in Britain. But to add a garage first, then a sauna, then a swimming pool to one's home, or to go to Fuerteventura one year, but to Mombasa the next, and to Penang the third, or rather to have to do these things in order to keep up with the Joneses; in this, Germany is different. If by 'middle-class' values is meant dynamic values, the need to do better all the time, then Germany is middle-class and Britain is not.[42]

The consumer boom of the mid-1980s, when the British were to rush to the household super-stores to stuff their houses with new furnishings and electrical kit of every kind (most of it imported), might seem to prove Dahrendorf wrong. Yet in fact this spending was to be mostly done with borrowed money, thanks to the ballooning, soon punctured, of property values. It did not represent the fruits of extra effort and careful saving,[43] as had the German 'middle-class' lifestyle to which Dahrendorf referred and which constituted the outward manifestation of a genuine economic miracle. Even after undergoing Margaret Thatcher's strident sermons on the 'enterprise culture' in the 1980s, most Britons (according to opinion polls)[44] still aspired to be comfortable rather than rich – an aspiration which, even if morally admirable, hardly compares with greed as a psychological motor of economic growth.

Thus the British lack of personal dynamism in the early postwar years was no mere symptom of temporary lassitude after a long conflict, but part of the enduring national character in the twentieth century.[45] What is more, British society as a whole in the late 1940s hardly made for dynamism, being stiffly corseted by convention and hierarchy, costive with congealed habit in spite of the passing upheavals of war[46] – characteristics outwardly and all too aptly manifested by the tribal flat-caps of the working class, the 'respectable' homburgs of the middle class, and the drab frocks and dowdy coats of all the womenfolk. Moreover, the dominant style of this society was of genteel middle-age, heard or seen at its most obvious in BBC wireless and television announcers, and in newsreel commentators. It even inspired British *haute couture*, where young mannequins were 'girdled' and gowned into a staid dignity more suitable for ageing duchesses at a charity ball. Hard to discern in this stuffy, stodgy society is any trace of the ferment and forward momentum of the era of the first industrial revolution.[47]

Yet in the course of that long-past revolution the British people had had their fill of turbulent change – their fill of being uprooted, of being relentlessly driven (or driving themselves) in workshop and counting-house. It can be understood, therefore, that a century later the descendants of those who made the industrial revolution should just wish to jog along amid all that was familiar and comfortable, while hoping, or striking, for that 'little bit more that allows for a few frills'. The 'little bit more' of course now included free teeth and spectacles and bigger pensions under the new welfare state, the only form of radical innovation in British society for which the British any longer displayed appetite.

Calamitously, however, such hankering for the sedate life of the middle-aged went hand in hand with a national complacency stemming from the Second World War. For instead of the sharp spur jabbed into the Germans by defeat, occupation and the complete demolition of the state and all its institutions, the British received only a pat on the back, self-administered, for their role in the allied triumph. Theirs was the psychology of a victor although their material circumstances approximated more to those of a loser. Was not Britain one of the 'Big Three' along with the United States and the Soviet Union? Was she not the only one of the pre-war European great powers never to be defeated and occupied? Did she not stand at the head of a worldwide Empire and Commonwealth? And then there was her prodigious war effort, its achievements apparently attested by the amazing statistics of the production of ships, aircraft, tanks, guns and vehicles.[48] There was her continuing technological pre-eminence, as demonstrated by the Spitfire, radar and the jet aircraft. Amid the euphoria of victory in 1945 politicians, industrialists and the press, to say nothing of the Ministry of Information, all flattered a receptive public that in Britain's war record lay assurance that in every way she was, and would remain, a first-class world power. In such fashion did the British mind become swaddled in smugness.[49]

Smugness, or at least a lulling sense that things were as they had always been and as they always would be, was further fostered by the very continuity of British life and institutions through the convulsion of total war, in striking contrast to the European experience of exiled monarchies, collapsed republics and destroyed dictatorships, or the Japanese experience of a once divine Emperor taking orders from a foreign proconsul. For in postwar Britain, just as in eighteenth-century

Venice during her decline towards final oblivion, all the institutional, ceremonial and architectural symbols of past greatness were still in place, giving the illusion that nothing had changed, when the reality was of shrinking power and waning vigour. Foremost among these symbols gleamed the monarchy, whose imperial pomp (invented in the late-Victorian age to replace an earlier much more domestic style)[50] was freshly celebrated in 1947 in the wedding of Princess Elizabeth to Philip Mountbatten (the Princess was allowed 100 clothing coupons for the occasion). Then there was Parliament still cherishing its peculiar customs and costumes within the Victorian splendour of the Palace of Westminster (the chamber of the House of Commons, destroyed by a German bomb, was to be rebuilt exactly as if it were still 1846 rather than 1946). There were the mandarins of the civil service still importantly ensconced in their grand Victorian palaces in Whitehall; His Majesty's judges, their common humanity disguised in Georgian fancy-dress, still on their benches in the Victorian Royal Courts of Justice; the Household Troops, soon resplendent again in their peacetime Victorian uniforms of scarlet and bearskin or breastplate and plumed helmet; gold-chained lord mayors continuing to preside over their corporations in proud Victorian city halls built in a now departed era of commercial triumph; the universities of Oxford and Cambridge and the public schools, their education and their rituals still breathing the last enchantments of the nineteenth century; and far off in the sweaty tropics, the traditional flummery of Empire, with the Royal Navy disembarking colonial governors in Victorian rig of cocked-hat or pith-helmet aflutter with feathers to inspect guards of honour and thereafter from Government House to rule various lesser breeds. In 1947, as it might have been 1927 or 1907, the King and Queen themselves embarked in HMS *Vanguard* for a royal tour of South Africa, the *Vanguard* being all too appropriately a newly completed vessel of an already obsolete type, the battleship. That her 15-inch guns were leftovers from a battlecruiser the construction of which had been abandoned back in 1918 made her an even better symbol of anachronism.

And then there was all the rest of the reassuringly familiar furniture of British life that had either survived the war scatheless or was soon restored to place – trade union rallies beneath banners bearing the battle honours of past industrial struggles; test matches at Lords; the cup final at Wembley; Henry Wood promenade concerts at the Albert

Hall; the London 'Season'; Bank Holidays at the seaside; the BBC, Victorian in values if not in technology.

Too much at ease with themselves amid all these cherished institutional mementoes and arrogant with victory, the British populace therefore felt no adrenalin-spurting pang of fear in regard to Britain's postwar plight as might have inspired them to a new industrial revolution despite their lack of native individual drive. Far from it, as a new expert committee on research and productivity discovered in the autumn of 1947:

> There is still a real and very widespread lack of appreciation amongst the actual producers in industry, including management, of the magnitude and real causes of the crisis facing the country. This creates a negative psychological factor militating against greater efficiency. . . . [51]

This diagnosis was to be reaffirmed a year later in the British tender for Marshall Aid:

> The difficulties of the present economic position do not present themselves in an obvious form to the British public. Unemployment is barely noticeable; jobs are apparently secure; industry is finding it easy to earn profits; wages are relatively high; the necessities of life are fairly distributed; and because they cannot buy many necessaries, many people have money which they can spend on things which they would otherwise regard almost as luxuries. . . . [52]

In consequence, 'a real and grave crisis in economic affairs seems remote . . .'.

Not only did the national mood and the national character in the aftermath of the Second World War thus rule out all prospect of a spontaneous industrial revolution, but they also set the limits of the politically possible – the limits within which the Government, supported by its overwhelming majority in the House of Commons, would have to engineer that revolution, if it were to be engineered at all.

It would be regarded as absurd if thirteen out of the twenty members of the new main board of a great industrial combine in need of drastic overhaul were amateurs without direct experience in industry. Yet such was the case with the Labour Cabinet of 1945. Of the seven members with some kind of industrial experience, only one, Sir Stafford Cripps (now President of the Board of Trade), had ever served as a manager, the other six having been trade unionists engaged in struggle against the 'bosses' – not the best way to a sympathetic understanding of technological change and competitive success in world markets.[53] Moreover, seven members of the Cabinet, including three of the 'big five' in the inner circle, belonged to that upper-middle-class progressive Establishment which during the war had successfully peddled the dream of New Jerusalem[54] – products of the 'liberal education' designed a century earlier by such romantic idealists as Dr Arnold and Cardinal Newman for the purpose of creating a governing elite of Christian gentlemen apt for politics, the public service and the professions.[55] None of them had ever studied anything so rudely vocational as, say, engineering, while only one (Cripps again) had ever stooped so low as to work in a factory. During their chosen careers as political evangelists they had perceived industrial Britain not in operational terms of the design, development, manufacture and marketing of products, but instead, via the distorting lens of Christian conscience and middle-class guilt, in terms of the immorality of a capitalism that ruthlessly exploited the working masses for the sake of profit.

The 'chairman of the board', Clement Attlee, personified the virtues and limitations of the governing class produced by the late-Victorian public school and Oxbridge. Born in 1883, educated at Haileybury and University College, Oxford (where he read History), his socialism inspired by his experience of East End slums while secretary of the Toynbee Hall mission before the Great War, Attlee had devoted his political life to improving the lot of those less fortunate than himself. For him socialism was 'something more than a political creed or an economic system. It is a philosophy of society. . . .'[56] Despite such idealistic sentiments, Attlee's was a deeply conventional and matter-of-fact mind, happier in the efficient transaction of current business than in thinking strategically about Britain's long-term future, industrial or otherwise. He himself lacked any direct experience of industry.

The Chancellor of the Exchequer from 1945 to 1947, Hugh Dalton (son of a canon, educated at Eton and King's College,

Cambridge, 'a somewhat romantic socialist through his strong adolescent dislike of privilege'),[57] had certainly perused as wartime President of the Board of Trade the analyses of Britain's technological deficiencies and bleak export prospects, but again lacked first-hand industrial experience. He suffered from what one historian describes as 'a powerful academic mind',[58] that peculiar pride of an Oxbridge 'liberal arts' education. This had earned him a reputation in the Labour Party as a political theoretician, as well as rendering him one of nature's accountants in his role of Chancellor, much at home in the ancient complexities of the British 'system' of public finances.[59]

In the third of the three 'liberal-Establishment' members of the Cabinet inner circle, Sir Stafford Cripps, the President of the Board of Trade (Winchester and University College, London; a barrister of the Inner Temple), the Cabinet possessed its single technocrat, as that term would be understood in France or Germany, for Cripps had served as assistant superintendent of a munitions factory during the Great War and as Minister of Aircraft Production in the Second World War, responsible for the largest British agglomeration of advanced-technology industries. Austere as a prayer in a cold church, formidable of mind, will and personal presence, he unusually combined technocratic ability with Christian and socialist idealism of the purest late-Victorian kind.

That idealism was of course shared by the whole Cabinet, including its chapel-bred working-class members. All their adult lives the vision of New Jerusalem had inspired them to struggle through the sloughs of committee work and along the stony paths of electioneering. However, in the expectation of coming to power in a rich imperial Britain, they had always assumed that they would build New Jerusalem by the simple method of redistributing wealth from the *rentier* class to the working masses. Now, in Government, they found themselves in a plight to which a lifetime's assumptions were quite inappropriate, for instead of redistributing wealth they were faced with the urgent and immensely more difficult task of creating it. Their problem in adjusting their minds to this sordid need was shared by the small-'l' liberal Establishment as a whole, especially the opinion-forming intelligentsia, as Lord Annan acknowledges in his book *Our Age*: 'Unfortunately we were more concerned with how wealth should be shared than produced.'[60]

Nor could this Cabinet of mentally unprepared amateurs call on an industrial general staff of professionals to plan and execute the remaking of British industry, in the way that the War Cabinet had looked to the general staffs and commanders-in-chief of the armed services to organise and carry out complex military operations like D-Day. None such existed. Instead, there was only the civil service, headed by the departmental permanent under-secretaries: men who, unlike the military, carried responsibility for nothing and commanded nothing. For their role lay in playing Jeeves to their ministers' Bertie Wooster – in other words, offering advice and guidance, often as not political. It was the minister who took the executive responsibility before and after a decision, and the minister who paid in public obloquy and perhaps resignation if the decision turned out to be a blunder. Thus British senior civil servants enjoyed what Stanley Baldwin had attributed to the press barons: power without responsibility, the prerogative of the harlot down the ages.[61]

Like so much of Britain's equipment as an industrial country in 1945, the civil-service elite was in the method of its selection, in its concept of its role and in its way of working a Victorian survival overdue for root-and-branch modernisation.[62] This elite being a stem of the liberal Establishment, its members were mostly the fairest blooms of an arts education at public school and Oxbridge, having been originally selected for the administrative grade of the service because of their ability to repeat in the entrance examination the intellectual dexterity on paper which they had already displayed in getting first-class honours degrees. Unsurprisingly, they had since risen to the top by shining as committee-men and writers of memoranda (a continuation of the Oxbridge essay by other means) rather than as executive problem-solvers – their minds judicious, balanced and cautious rather than operational and engaged; their temperaments akin to the academic rather than the man of action; their culture profoundly literary.[63]

Moreover, their working lives had been spent inside the sheltered habitat of the offices and committee rooms of Whitehall and Westminster and the duller clubs of Pall Mall – a kind of extended 'Führer-bunker' the isolating nature of which was disguised by grand historical trappings. While the mandarins operated with a knowing subtlety amid the intricate politics and power relationships of this self-regarding little world, their knowledge of the outside was largely restricted to the City, Oxbridge senior common rooms and what they read in *The Times*.[64] Not one of the permanent under-secretaries of departments in 1945 concerned with Britain's industrial performance had ever had experience of running any kind of commercial operation. Such experience came after retirement, if at all, and then only in the boardroom. Sir Edward Bridges, the Cabinet Secretary from 1938 to 1946 and from 1946 to 1956 Permanent Under-Secretary at the Treasury, was the son of the Poet Laureate Robert Bridges, and had been educated at Eton and Magdalen (first-class honours in classics) in that heyday of Edwardian and Georgian romantic idealism before the Great War. He had joined the Treasury in 1919 after war service, and that was where he had stayed for the next two decades until promoted Cabinet Secretary. The nearest that his successor in 1946 in that post, Sir Norman Brooke (Wolverhampton School and Wadham), had ever got to industry and technology was as Permanent Secretary to the Ministry of Reconstruction from 1943 to 1945.

The Permanent Under-Secretary at the Treasury in 1942–5, Sir Richard Hopkins (King Edward's School, Birmingham, and Emmanuel: first class, Part 1 of the Classical tripos, and Part 2, History tripos), had spent the first quarter-century of his career in the Inland Revenue, and the remaining eighteen years in the Treasury. The Assistant Secretary at the Treasury in 1945 and a forceful voice in economic and industrial policy both then and later, Richard Clarke (Christ's Hospital and Clare), was himself a New Jerusalemer, indeed a former writer of Fabian Society pamphlets. Although he had had to do with industry at second hand while in the ministries of Economic Warfare, Supply and Production during the Second World War, his direct experience was limited to one year working for the British Electrical and Allied Manufacturers Association after coming down from Cambridge.

At the Board of Trade, the Whitehall department most concerned with exports, the PUS in 1945 was Sir Arnold Overton (son of a canon; Winchester and New College) who had served there almost continuously since commencing his career in 1919. In 1947, in accordance with the civil service tradition of the gentlemanly amateur all-round player, he was to become PUS at the Ministry of Civil Aviation. Here he succeeded Sir Henry Self, whose numerous degrees were all in Classics or branches of philosophy even though he had been educated at Bancroft's School and London University rather than at public school and Oxbridge. His long administrative experience included the post of PUS at the Ministry of Production in 1942–3 and thereafter acting as the Minister's deputy on the Anglo–US Combined Production and Resources Board in Washington. In retirement he was to be President of the Modern Churchmen's Union.

At the Ministry of Supply, another Whitehall department dealing specifically with industry and technology, the PUS from 1946 to 1953 was Sir Archibald Rowlands (Penarth county school; University of Wales, with a first-class degree in Modern Languages; Jesus College, Oxford), the leitmotiv of his previous civil service career lying in finance, especially in regard to the government of India. At the Ministry of Fuel and Power from 1945 to 1952 was another lifetime civil servant of the conventional administrative stamp, Sir Donald Fergusson (Berkhamsted School and Magdalen College, Oxford; first-class honours in Modern History). The Director-General of War Transport, concerned therefore with the arteries of industrial success – the national communications network – was Sir Cyril Hurcombe (Oxford High School and St John's College, Oxford), again a man with no experience outside Whitehall.

If in relation to framing and conducting industrial policy these cloistered men of paper constituted the equivalents of the chiefs of military general staffs, what about the staffs themselves? Apart from departmental civil servants, there existed in 1945 two staffs in rivalry with each other: the Economic Section of the Cabinet Office (led by a passionate New Jerusalemer, James Meade, a classicist before turning to Philosophy, Politics and Economics and becoming a don at Hertford College, Oxford), and the economists within the Treasury.[65] In feeble imitation of a military general staff the government in 1947 created a Central Economic Planning Staff to serve a new Economic Planning Board under a Chief Planning Officer, Sir Edwin Plowden. These new bodies lacked the executive powers of a true general staff, and were to serve only as yet another Whitehall seminar, yet another supplier of advice and information, yet another churner-out of paper. Plowden himself was yet another blossom of the liberal Establishment untainted by any technological qualification, having taken a third-class degree in Economics at Pembroke College, Cambridge. However, he had at least enjoyed some experience of industry in junior posts with the American International Standard Electric Corporation and their British subsidiary Standard Telephone and Cables, before joining a firm of sales agents, where he remained until the outbreak of war.[66] As a temporary wartime civil servant he had served with the Ministries of Economic Warfare, Aircraft Production and Supply.

None of the rank-and-file members of the new CEPS or of the existing rival sects of economic advisers was blessed with technological credentials or direct managerial experience in the real world of industry and commerce. Here were not merely academics *manqués* just like the permanent secretaries, but actual academics who in wartime had patriotically abandoned their universities to trail a pike in Whitehall. Of the thirty-four people who served in the Economic Section in 1945–50, for example, no fewer than fourteen later went back to university teaching.[67] It was as if in 1939–45 the War Cabinet had co-opted professors of military history or strategic studies to advise on Britain's grand strategy and devise plans for implementing it.[68] As it happened, the judgements of these rival economic staffs proved often at odds, and there was mutual dispute and jockeying over their respective roles. All in all, their contributions in the postwar era resembled not so much the operational schemes, complete with logistic nuts-and-bolts, produced by military staffs, as a continuing theoretical debate about the 'economy' and how best to 'manage' it. This was coupled with voluminous amassing of information, much speculative statistical calculation and unreliable forecasting,[69] and on occasion even sage advice. But, as Noël Annan points out with regard to the role of academics in public life in general, it was 'one of the misjudgements of dons to imagine that one had but to analyse a problem and come to conclusions and the problem was solved. The implementation of policy did not concern them. . . . They were strong on what, weak on how.'[70]

It is little wonder that when (in the course of protracted discussion in a sprawl of committees) the ministers, civil servants and economists collectively tried to frame industrial strategies, such as in the bulky annual *Economic Surveys* or the British tenders for Marshall Aid, the result tended to be an academic essay magisterially assembling all the available information and judiciously weighing all the factors before proceeding to state desirable, if obvious, broad objectives for the future. What such essays conspicuously lacked were operational plans for attaining those objectives.[71] Indeed, the American representatives in London of the European Recovery Administration (Marshall Aid) in 1948–9 were moved to prod the British about dropping generalities in favour of 'more information about plans and specific projects for the development of production facilities and capacity' – requests evaded by their British opposite numbers with the deftness of long practice.[72] But of course the Americans were being absurdly inept in expecting plans for 'specific projects for the development of production facilities' from a Whitehall whose whole culture was so profoundly untechnocratic.

And yet 'planning' was a great catchphrase of the time, an important aspect of New Jerusalem as evangelised by such as Beveridge during the war. 'Planning' would repeat in peacetime the triumphs of the wartime command economy with regard to industrial programmes and the allocation of resources, replacing the wasteful inefficiency of pre-war capitalist competition with rational decision and control. After all, this is what the Labour Party had always believed in, at least in rhetoric. It was the industrial face of socialism – much admired during the war in its Stalinist form in the Soviet Union. Had not the Labour Party manifesto in the 1945 general election promised that a Labour government would 'plan from the ground up, giving an appropriate place to constructive enterprise and private endeavour in the national plan . . .'? Had it not promised 'a firm constructive hand on our whole productive machinery'?

There was even a pre-war British peacetime precedent for hands-on state development of industry, paradoxically set by a Conservative-dominated Cabinet. For the rearmament programme in 1936–9 under the aegis of the Cabinet's Defence Policy and Requirements Committee had consisted of carefully directed capital investment in new factories and plant to manufacture specific advanced-technology products for which capacity had previously been wholly or partly lacking. A prominent industrialist, Lord Weir, had acted as the committee's expert adviser, in working out the original programme and thereafter in supplying the committee with expert guidance. The whole approach was not dissimilar from postwar French industrial development under 'Le Plan', or the later Japanese creation of new market-conquering technologies under the leadership of the Ministry of International Trade and Industry.

This model of the pre-war rearmament programme might have been adopted by the Labour Government after 1945 in order to develop those new technologies in which, as wartime reports had made clear, Britain was so weak, such as office machines and systems; or to force through the restructuring of ramshackle existing industries, such as motor-vehicles and textiles. But except in the cases of nuclear power, civil aircraft and defence procurement[73] the Labour Government shrank from such direct intervention,[74] thereby throwing away the strongest lever available to a command economy, in which it pretended to believe. Instead it chose to rely on the stunted carrots of meagre financial inducements and on persuasion's feeble goads (see below, pp. 204–06), just as adumbrated in the coalition Government's proposals for postwar industrial policy.[75]

This abdication is the more unexpected in view of the wartime success of state-directed programmes, mobilising the best of scientific, engineering and industrial talent, such as for the production of high-technology kit like radar or the emergency re-equipment of old shipyards.[76] The abdication is explained by the interaction of two factors: the massive inertial resistance to change offered by the vested interests of industry (including, conspicuously, the trade unions); and the British governing elite's deep instinct for appeasement.

*

The will was suspect. Had not two of the sages we read, Shaw and E. M. Forster, told us that imposing one's will has disastrous effects? . . . Yes, leadership was needed but it should be exercised through persuasion and example. We did not neglect power. But we made the mistake of thinking that it could always be tamed: surely reconciliation was always possible through trade-offs. . . .[77]

So writes Noël Annan in *Our Age*, his celebration (some might read it as an indictment) of the liberal Establishment which by 1945 had come to dominate British political and intellectual life, and provide the governing elite. That conflicts of interest between human groups did undeniably exist only confirmed Annan's contemporaries in their belief that 'men of good will must sit down together and work out sensible solutions to their problems . . .'.[78] In the inter-war period the same sentiment had inspired internationalists (many of whom were later to become wartime New Jerusalemers and postwar members of 'Our Age') to shun the balance of power and armed alliances as an answer to aggression, and turn instead to the League of Nations, disarmament and pious treaties abjuring war. This belief in reason, conciliation and compromise had no less inspired Neville Chamberlain, a liberal by family tradition, in his efforts to persuade that noted man of goodwill, Adolf Hitler, to sit down with him and work out a sensible solution to Europe's problems. This was a process that necessarily entailed the 'appeasement' of Hitler's allegedly legitimate grievances – in other words, giving him by due international agreement what he wanted before he had time to grab it by military force. Now, in the postwar era, the same idealistic liberal fallacy that conflicts of interest should be – and, what was more, could be – resolved by conciliation rather than by victory in a struggle of wills was to be applied to Britain as an industrial society, that battlefield where the opposing sides had been entrenching themselves deeper in dour enmity for more than a century. In the hands of the upper-middle-class members of the liberal Establishment across the political spectrum – cowards of social conscience all – conciliation in such circumstances was inevitably to mean a Chamberlain-style appeasement by concession, especially concession to those masters of the power game, the trade unions. Annan indeed even goes so far as to admit that Britain's relative decline in the postwar era actually sprang from 'our desire to bring harmony to society. It sprang from our desire to conciliate the working class and bring the trade unions into partnership. . . .'[79]

It was that same temperamental aversion to the exercise of will, especially if it might lead to ugly scenes of confrontation, which inhibited the liberal Establishment in Westminster and Whitehall from embarking on the compulsory restructuring of ramshackle industries or directly developing new technologies (other than military, aeronautical or nuclear). Except in respect of nationalisation, which anyway had little to do with productive efficiency (see below, Chapter 11), the Labour Government's approach to the operations of civil industry 'in the field' remained classically liberal, as was spelled out in the first annual *Economic Survey* in February 1947:

There is an essential difference between totalitarian and democratic planning. The former subordinates all individual desires and preferences to the demands of the State. For this purpose, it uses various methods of compulsion upon the individual which deprive him of the freedom of choice. Such methods may be necessary even in a democratic country during the extreme emergency of a great war. Thus the British people gave their wartime Government the power to direct labour. But, in normal times, the people of a democratic country will not give up their freedom of choice to their Government. A democratic Government must therefore conduct its economic planning in a manner which preserves the maximum possible freedom of choice to the individual citizen. . . .[80]

'Planning' was therefore a matter of the broad deployment of national resources, using an apparatus of Government controls 'to guide the economy in the direction which is indicated by the plan . . .'.[81] But, warned the *Survey*, 'the controls cannot by themselves bring about very rapid changes or make very fine adjustments in the economic structure. To do this, they would have to be much more detailed in their application and more drastic in their scope. . . .'[82]

It followed from such a timid reading of the 'politically possible', or even politically desirable, that the Labour Government set up no powerful executive agency for remaking Britain as an industrial society comparable to the French *Commissariat du Plan* or (in military terms) to the Supreme Headquarters Allied Expeditionary Force which had planned, organised and directed the invasion of Normandy. Instead, it looked to an institution that was at once a British pride and a British curse, the committee.

To cover every field of government the Labour Cabinet eventually deployed no fewer than 148 standing Cabinet committees and 306 *ad hoc* ones, a case of administrative elephantiasis never to be surpassed.[83] In 1946–7, economic policy fell to the Lord President's Committee, chaired by Herbert Morrison as Lord President of the Council, a man with much experience in local government and none in industry. This was supplemented by a Ministerial Committee on Economic Planning set up in January 1946, also chaired by Morrison and consisting of the Chancellor of the Exchequer (Dalton), the President of the Board of Trade (Cripps) and the Minister of Labour and National Service (Isaacs). At its first meeting Cripps discouragingly pointed out that, contrary to Labour Party rhetoric, 'the Government had not yet formulated a plan for the employment of the national resources and could not hope to do so for several months to come . . .'.[84] It hardly surprises that in 1946 this committee mostly limited itself to that favourite British occupation, discussion of the *ad hoc*. At the beginning of 1947, guided by an Official Steering Committee on Economic Development, it got round to the grand topic of the 'Economic Survey for 1947',[85] the first such intended for publication as a White Paper. In October 1947 it was superseded (together with the Lord President's Committee) by a new Cabinet Economic Policy Committee, which was long to endure as the principal Whitehall political brains-trust on industrial strategy.

But this committee formed only the crown pinion of a machine the cogs, chains, pulleys and counter-balances of which were complicated enough to have been contrived by the cartoonists Heath Robinson or Emett. For there were eventually created upwards of fifty ministerial and official (civil servants) committees, standing or temporary, to deal with some aspect or other of economic and industrial affairs, including policy towards Europe and the Commonwealth. On these were represented every department with any conceivable vested interest in the matter in hand.[86]

The memoranda and minutes of meetings of the most important among these bodies, such as the ministerial Economic Policy Committee itself or the Investment Programmes Committee (of civil servants), eventually filled many a fat foolscap volume,[87] the gold-plated Treasury tag for best performance in this regard going to the ministerial Production Committee with eighteen such volumes.[88] With the subtle variations of a Bach fugue the same core of senior ministers, but with changing extras, would turn up one day as the Economic Policy Committee and on another as the Production Committee, or it might be the Civil Aviation Committee. The number and duration of any standing committee's meetings suggest some claustrophobic hell of boredom imagined by Jean-Paul Sartre, the Investment Programmes Committee alone convening seventy-two times in 1948.[89] In case the system ran short of ministerial and official committees, there were also 'working parties' to ponder and report on particular issues. Beyond this galaxy of Cabinet committees lay further galaxies of departmental committees just as large and sprawling, all emitting their own agendas, minutes and memoranda; all meeting over and over again to debate, but all too rarely to decide.[90]

Since the Government flinched from embarking on a grand industry-by-industry modernisation and development programme, what were all these committees doing? The answer lies in the peculiar version of a command economy cherished in the early postwar years by the Labour Government and its economic advisers, and first publicly described in the *Economic Survey for 1947*. This took the form of comprehensive restrictive controls over the entire economy[91] – controls over the quantity and make-up of imports, on the rationing out of raw materials or basic products like steel; on the location of new factories or extensions; on investment in various industries or parts of the infrastructure. The exercise of these restrictive controls entailed in most cases laborious discussion and much writing of memoranda, not merely in one committee but possibly in several, as reports were referred back and forth, up and down, until at long last a committee with actual powers to make a decision made one. That really meant a committee composed of Cabinet ministers, because this entire monstrous, incoherent sprawl contradicted the basic principle of a good command and control system, whereby the top level concerns itself with broad strategy and general directives, and devolves operational decisions as far downwards as possible.

The Investment Programmes Committee (of officials) offers a classic example of the centralising of even minor matters. It was set up in 1947 with the admirable aim of advising ministers on investment priorities and evolving means of exercising economic leverage: that is, to concern itself with grand strategy. Yet from the beginning it also pondered questions of tactical detail, such as investment in Southern Railway signalling or agricultural machinery or railway coaches.[92] The Cabinet Production Committee, set up in 1947 to 'supervise the production programmes (both for export and the home market) required to give effect to the general economic plan',[93] also allowed itself to waste time on such trivia as whether (in 1949) Rotary Hoes Ltd should be allowed an Industrial Development Certificate to expand their works at East Horndon in Essex, or be induced to go to Basildon. The military equivalent of such a local matter would fall at most to a brigade commander to decide. Nevertheless, in this particular case the ministers of the Crown on the Production Committee still felt unable to take a decision, and resorted to that familiar Whitehall device of referring the matter for further investigation and report.[94] What made the prolonged chewing of this particular very small cud even more ludicrous was that the matter had already been bootlessly discussed by the Cabinet Economic Policy Committee, no less. But such bumbling procrastination pervaded the whole system.

For wholly alien to the mind of politicians and civil servants alike would have been clear-cut chains of command and divisions of executive responsibility, let alone the delegating of such responsibility neat and undiluted to subordinate managers, in the fashion of an army or a world-class business like Shell. It was of Whitehall's very nature to centralise decision, and then, worse still, to befuddle it by subjection to the many-headed lowest common denominator of collective responsibility.

Such, then, was the government apparatus, more redolent of the striped trouser or even the Victorian frock-coat than the rolled-up sleeve or the white coat, to which after 1945 fell the double challenge of winning a desperate balance of payments battle and at the same time modernising Britain as an industrial society.

CHAPTER TEN

'The Ebbing of the Tide of the Sellers' Market'

I N 1946 THE CAMPAIGN to restore the balance of payments
before the exhaustion of the American loan seemed to be going
well enough. From modern factories newly converted from war
production and gaunt red-brick Edwardian mills, from world-class
chemical plants and potteries straight out of an Arnold Bennett novel,
from whisky distilleries and back-street brass-foundries, the goods
were being trundled to the ports in diminutive four-wheeled ten-ton
railway wagons (such as Robert Stephenson would have recognised)
behind ill-kempt steam-engines burning poor-quality coal, or in little
lorries (restricted in width and length by law) at 20 miles per hour (as
also limited by law) along the narrow, winding Saxon cowpaths, now
asphalted, which for the most part constituted the national road
network. In the ports, nineteenth-century in their layouts and short of
modern cranes and other mechanical handling gear,[1] swarms of flat-
capped dockers were muscling the goods into ships strictly in
accordance with traditional union restrictive practices and demarcation
lines.[2] Once these goods – including twentieth-century products like
cars and machine-tools – had been dumped on foreign or
Commonwealth docksides, three-quarters of them (by value) were
being carted off and marketed by local agents or merchants in white
ducks, dhotis or galabiehs according to century-old British trading
custom, only one-quarter being handled by British manufacturers'
own overseas sales and service organisations.[3]

In essence, and despite some notable anachronistic exceptions such
as motor-vehicles, this whole exporting scene resembled a sepia
photograph of Victorian industrial and commercial Britain brought to
life – and not least because in 1946, and thanks to the Second World

War, Britain found herself once again without serious competitors in a world eager for her products. By March the volume of British exports had already reached 88 per cent of 1938.[4] For the year as a whole it reached over 99 per cent of 1938.[5] With imports held down by Government control to less than 68 per cent of 1938 (hence the dreary smidgeon of a food ration), the overall balance of payments deficit that had to be covered by spending money cadged from America and Canada amounted to only £450 million as against an estimate in 1945 of £750 million.[6] 'We shall enter 1947', noted the Treasury in October, 'stronger than we expected.'[7]

With the immediate battle on the export front-line apparently making such good progress, the château generals of Downing Street and Whitehall might have chosen to bend their minds to devising long-term programmes for reconstructing British industry, especially for developing profitable new technologies, new products, to replace the old. As it was, far more exciting topics absorbed them. This was the year when in the course of hot ministerial debate Britain committed herself to perpetuating the world and Commonwealth role (see above, Chapter 3), with consequent overseas expenditure, mostly military, equal to nearly a third of the year's total import bill;[8] the year also when the foundation stones of New Jerusalem were being ponderously laid in the National Insurance Act and National Health Service Act (see above, Chapters 7 and 8). In regard to economic planning, therefore, the Cabinet and the ministerial Economic Policy Committee (under the guidance of the Whitehall academic economists) chose to limit themselves to grand strategy at its broadest, allotting investment and materials between different industrial sectors; deciding what proportion of output should go for export and what for home investment and consumption; fixing affordable levels of imports; setting desirable targets for exports.[9] Even so, as the *Economic Survey for 1947* acknowledged in February of that year, 'the main emphasis so far has been relatively short-term planning – planning for the year ahead'.[10]

Meanwhile, the organ supposed to be concerned with long-term economic development, the Lord President's Committee, lapsed instead into haphazard ad-hockery. The Board of Trade and the Ministry of Supply, for their parts, certainly enjoyed close relations with the industries under their sponsorship, but the relationships were, however, largely consultative, the exception being procurement of defence equipment and civil aircraft by the Ministry of Supply.

Between September 1945 and 1947 Sir Stafford Cripps as President of the Board of Trade went no further towards modernising backward industries by direct intervention in the fashion of *Le Plan* than the setting up of 'working parties' (composed of four representatives each from employers, trade unions and the Board of Trade) in seventeen industries to examine ways of improving their efficiency. However, these were simply seminars without executive authority.[11]

In any case, other bureaucratic fingers were also poking around in the industrial pie, especially with regard to exporting. For instance, in the case of telecommunications equipment, which faced stiff American competition, an official of the Telecommunications Department of the General Post Office wrote to a colleague in the Board of Trade in January 1946 to complain about the 'extremely complicated' system with regard to sponsoring exports, with 'diffusion of responsibility between the Foreign Office, the Board of Trade, the Department of Overseas Trade, the Ministry of Supply, not to mention the Post Office . . .'.[12]

While the château generals and their staffs bumbled, the current battle for the balance of payments was already beginning to run into trouble. In October 1946 the Chancellor of the Exchequer reported:

> We are using up the United States and Canadian Loans, and our other prospective external financial resources for 1947 and 1948, much too fast. This results from . . . the rise in American prices and from the heavy and continuing drain due to military and political expenditure outside this country. . . .[13]

Yet, as an accompanying note by the Treasury pointed out, 1947 was to be the year when, under the original American loan agreement, sterling must become convertible, with inevitably grievous consequences:

> if we have an adverse balance with any other country, we pay it in gold or United States dollars or their equivalent. But if we have a surplus with another country, we get gold or United States dollars only if that country's currency is convertible; if it is not, the surplus will only extinguish sterling debt or accumulate a credit. Thus we pour out gold and dollars to countries with which we have deficits and receive paper from countries with which we have surpluses. . . .

Until those surpluses can be translated into gold and dollars to match
our deficits, we can experience a large draft on our reserves while
our overall balance of payments may look quite favourable. . . .[14]

Since essential imports – basic food, raw materials, tobacco (for that
too was reckoned to be 'essential'), machinery and other industrial
goods, petroleum, seeds and animals – had already been cut to the
bone, the only way out of what Dalton called 'these grim conditions'
was to raise the export target for the second half of 1947 to 150 per
cent of the 1938 volume.[15] But by now production for export was
beginning to be braked by truly fundamental weaknesses of the British
industrial base – in the supply of energy and of steel.

'There is a prospective shortage of finished steel, over 1947 as a
whole, of the order of one-fifth or one-sixth of requirements, or
2,000,000 tons,' the Economic Survey Working Party reported to
ministers in December 1946. 'The consequences of these shortages
will be felt in most sections of industry, but particularly in the motor
industry, in structural steel for building, in electrical engineering and in
the manufacture of industrial machinery'[16] – in other words, the very
spearheads of the export drive and of the re-equipment of British
industry itself. Part of the problem lay in the difficulty of obtaining
imports of steel to supplement inadequate British output; part,
however, in what the working party called 'the prior bottleneck in
coal'.[17]

For coal and energy were synonymous in the Britain of 1946. The
furnaces, foundries and rolling-mills of the iron and steel industries
depended on coal for white heat. The still largely steam-hauled
railways shovelled it into the fireboxes of their locomotives. The
citizenry warmed itself in winter by burning it in thermally inefficient
open grates in homes and offices. The gasworks malodorously baked it
in retorts to make the 'town's gas' which cooked the nation's rations,
heated its bathwater in German-invented 'geysers', and fuelled heat-
treatment processes in industry. The power stations burned it to raise
steam to drive the turbines that spun the dynamos that generated
electric current to light the nation's homes, streets and public
buildings, to drive its trams and underground or suburban trains, and
to give life to most of the machines, big and small, in the factories,
mines and shipyards. Yet in December 1946 a Whitehall committee
was estimating a total production of deep-mined and open-cast coal in

1947 of 192 million tons 'against estimated minimum requirements (i.e., with present restrictions and no increase in exports, but a small building up of stocks) of 200 million tons'.[18] After discussing various ways of building up the labour-force, and urging that 'first priority should be given to everything needed to improve the capital equipment of the mines', this committee glumly prophesied:

> It is clear that, whatever we do, shortage of coal is going to be a drag on the total production of the country for 3 or 4 years at least. Everything that will in any way contribute to increasing the production of coal must be pressed forward with all possible energy.[19]

And 'anything' included speeding up the conversion of industrial plant to oil-burning.

Yet even if there had been more coal it could not have been turned into extra electric power, because, in the words of the same report, 'there is at present a shortage of generating plant at the power stations which shows itself in shedding of the load almost every day . . .'. Although the Central Electricity Board had hoped to add nearly 1 million kilowatts of capacity in 1946, 'delays in manufacture have been such they have not got more than 220,000 kilowatts of this plant'.[20]

> Maximum demand this winter was estimated last May at about 10 million kilowatts. The demand has been rising so rapidly that this estimate will be exceeded. To supply this demand the Central Electricity Board have available less than 9 million kilowatts of plant, and their deficit this winter is about 1.3 million kilowatts. A substantial proportion of their plant is over 20 years of age and should be scrapped because it is liable to frequent breakdowns and is extravagant in its use of coal. Almost certainly in January and February the cuts in electricity supply will be nation-wide and will affect production seriously.[21]

This forecast would have admirably served for a normal winter. But that of 1946–7 was not normal or average; it was the most ferociously cold for over fifty years, engulfing Britain's fragile economy and her overstretched energy resources in a catastrophe of ice and snow akin to that which overtook the Grande Armée during the retreat from Moscow in 1812 or the German Army at the gates of Moscow in 1941. The winter began early and lasted long. Even in December coal stocks were being burned up at the rate of 607,000 tons a week as against the Ministry of Fuel and Power's forecast of 514,000 tons. By the beginning of January the situation was already critical enough to merit anxious Cabinet discussion.[22] In the middle of the month transport workers helped things along by going on strike for a week. Then on 20 January, driven by a savage east wind that cut through every cranny in British houses and froze all within, the blizzards began to sweep in across the country again and again through the rest of January and on through the coldest February for 300 years. In the hills nearly a third of the sheep perished. In East Anglia the snowdrifts piled and piled to a height of fourteen feet. Off the Norfolk coast ice-floes eerily transformed the North Sea into a semblance of the Arctic. London cowered in 16 degrees Fahrenheit of frost. With the railway system iced and snowed into near paralysis, coal could not be moved from the pitheads. Stocks at the power stations dwindled and disappeared, leading to colossal power cuts which brought industry to a standstill. By February 2.5 million workers were idle.

When winter finally relented late in March it had directly cost Britain something like £200 million worth of lost exports[23] as well as upsetting the whole rhythm of production for some time to come. By the fourth quarter of 1947 the volume of exports had risen to only 117 per cent of 1938 instead of the 150 per cent laid down as a target in the *Economic Survey for 1947*.[24] At the same time Britain was once again paying the penalty for her dependence on imported foodstuffs as a result of the Victorian adoption of free trade, for in 1947 the price of such imports, many of them from the dollar area, rose to nearly a third higher than in 1945.[25] As a consequence of this double misfortune, plus the continued £140 million direct dead-weight cost of the world role, Britain was no longer gaining ground in the struggle to close the balance of payments gap, but losing it. In the first six months of 1947 more than half the original 1945 US loan of $3.75 billion was poured away to buy the dollar goods and foodstuffs that Britain could not herself afford.

On 15 July, in accordance with that loan agreement, Britain was compelled to render sterling freely convertible into dollars. The outflow of borrowed dollars became a flood, scouring out the foundations of Britain's pretensions as a first-rank power and threatening her economy with fresh catastrophe. By mid-August only $400 million of the US loan remained – a loan that was originally intended to last until 1951. Yet again Britain confronted imminent national bankruptcy: the appalling prospect of being unable to feed the people or supply industry with raw materials. On 20 August sterling convertibility was suspended, marking the climactic moment of defeat in the 1947 campaign for the balance of payments.

Yet this defeat had not simply been caused by the natural catastrophe of the previous winter and the ill-luck of a steep rise in world prices for foodstuffs. For already the industrial and commercial failings documented by the wartime Board of Trade reports were beginning to affect British sales in overseas markets – as was cruelly highlighted by the convertibility crisis itself, when foreign and Commonwealth holders of sterling who had been previously compelled to buy flimsy, under-powered little British cars designed to potter a clerk and his family from suburb to seaside now made haste to exchange sterling for dollars and buy big, powerful, comfortable, robust American cars at similar or even lower prices.[26] Nuffield alone lost £1 million worth of export orders at this time.[27] But the failings were by no means limited to the motor industry. According to a Whitehall report in February 1948 on exports to Canada, a dollar country, 'the long deliveries offered by British manufacturers, especially for capital goods and engineering products generally, and in particular for goods special to Canadian requirements, e.g., electrical equipment, have made Canadian importers unwilling to place orders with them . . .'.[28] In the following month a similar report on exports to the United States, the key market for solving the overriding problem of Britain's dollar deficit, was warning: 'United States buyers are no longer willing to wait an unspecified time for goods from this country and our delivery dates will in future have to be competitive as well as our prices. . . .'[29] The report pointed out:

> In 1947, this country's exports to the United States of manufactured and semi-manufactured goods represented only 7%–8% of total imports by the United States of these two classes of goods, which suggests that there is an opportunity for the United Kingdom to increase its exports. Moreover, for many consumer goods, there is a

definite American type, and foreign versions of the same goods do not sell readily.[30]

Then again: 'Our prices in the United States are generally considered to be too high . . .'.[31]

Indeed, competitive pricing from foreign rivals such as Italy, America, Switzerland, The Netherlands, Austria and Sweden (as well as from local firms indigenous to a particular market) was adduced in December 1947 by some 1100 firms replying to a National Union of Manufacturers questionnaire as a major reason for their difficulties in selling in world markets.[32] The National Union of Manufacturers remarked in its covering summary that 'the formidable list of goods and markets [in an appendix][33] should provide material for anxious and careful consideration'. That list covered nearly 100 different countries and comprised a vast range of industrial and consumer goods, including light fittings, automatic controls, electrical equipment of every kind, cars, motorcycles, radios, refrigerators, outboard engines, foundry and furnace equipment, pumps, calculating machines, machine-tools, medical and pharmaceutical products, fine chemicals and plastics.

Nonetheless, the failings did not lie in the exporters alone, for they were handicapped by shortages of essential supplies (including energy) and delays in delivery of components. 'The replies [to this questionnaire]', wrote the National Union of Manufacturers, 'bring out prominently that shortage of materials is the general controlling factor in British production to-day. . . . Prominent in the lists is steel . . . for practically all its forms and qualities, but particularly for wire, strip and for certain thicknesses of sheet and plate. . . .'[34] Nor was the sheer shortage of materials in itself the whole of the problem. The National Union of Manufacturers' summary pointed to:

the lack of continuity of production through irregularities and uncertainties in the supplies of raw materials, through power cuts and fuel shortages, all of which add to the incidence of overhead costs and adversely affect the efficiency of labour. Introduction of the 44 hour week has also had the obvious effect of reducing output and therefore of increasing overhead charges.[35]

Moroever, exporters or would-be exporters also found themselves entangled in the bureaucratic web of government controls and allocations. In regard to steel, according to this summary,

> there is evidence of extraordinary confusion and distress arising from the operation of the scheme for allocating steel. Whilst allocations frequently bear little or no relationship to actual requirements or production capacity, for the smaller manufacturer the delays and difficulties in getting his case for an improved allocation considered are particularly serious. . . .

And worse still:

> The prospect of an extension of existing systems of allocation to other materials with consequent delays, frustration and paper work is spreading alarm and despondency among the smaller manufacturers, a large part of whose daily working lives is already being spent in attending to this side of the business.[36]

Then again, manufacturers were encountering 'particular delays and difficulties in obtaining permission to repair, re-build or expand [their] premises'.[37]

Yet these difficulties of British exporting firms were naturally of no concern to overseas buyers, who were solely interested in the early and punctual delivery of well-designed, well-made and competitively priced wares, no matter from what country of origin.

Thus the brief happy time for British exports was already over. As the National Union of Manufacturers commented, the remarks in answers to its questionnaire about the strength of foreign competition might be read:

> as evidence of a buyer's market, to a greater or lesser extent, in those goods [listed]. If it be argued that all firms in that trade do not have a similar experience and therefore that the real cause is the low efficiency of a particular manufacturer, then it must be pointed out that it is only in a buyers' market that this discrimination will be felt. It is the marginal firm which like flotsam on the ocean shows the ebbing of the tide of the sellers' market. . . .[38]

*

The convertibility crisis of July–August 1947 marked the Labour Government's economic Stalingrad, destroying its facile confidence that thanks to 'planning' it was successfully leading Britain in an advance towards a fairly shared prosperity. In the aftermath of the panic a shaken Cabinet reconsidered all aspects of total strategy, from public expenditure across the board – including the cost of the defence policy and overseas deployments demanded by the world role (see above, pp. 77–9) – to the performance of exports.

In the field of economic and industrial policy, it began by reorganising the Whitehall supreme headquarters. This was the time when the lackadaisical Lord President's Committee and the ministerial Committee on Economic Policy lost their responsibilities to a new Cabinet Economic Policy Committee charged with 'a general oversight' on behalf of the Cabinet 'over the work of economic planning, in relation to both external and internal economic questions . . .'.[39] The committee met for the first time on 10 October 1947. Its work was underpinned by the equally new Investment Programmes Committee and Production Committee (see above, pp. 190–92) – the latter entrusted with supervising 'the production programmes (both for export and the home market) required to give effect to the general economic plan'.[40] The Investment Programmes Committee, composed of senior departmental bureaucrats and Whitehall economists, now held the responsibility for advising ministers on how capital investment should be deployed between different sectors of the national life. Sir Stafford Cripps, the Cabinet's only technocrat, was appointed to head a new Ministry of Economic Affairs. This was also the time when novel bureaucratic bodies such as the Economic Planning Board (purely advisory and without executive powers), served by a Central Economic Planning Staff, and an (official) Committee on Exports (which actually included a single businessman among its twenty-nine members)[41] took their place in the line.

Thus did the Labour Government at last set out to grip its economic and industrial battle. In the closing months of 1947 and on into 1948 a new urgency set Whitehall a-bustle. The civil servants and academic economists gallantly steered their desks into action, firing off broadsides of paper and talk unprecedented in scale and at an amazing variety of targets.[42]

Yet for all its ultimate elaboration (see above, pp. 190–91), this new government apparatus was like a powerful-looking motor-car which in fact had neither linkage between the steering wheel and the front wheels, nor a transmission between the engine and the axles – the owner of which nonetheless busily twiddled the steering wheel, changed the gears and trod on the accelerator in the happy delusion that he was directing the vehicle's progress. For even now, and apart from 'socialisation' (see below, Chapter 11), the Labour Government renounced the one advantage of a command economy – direct intervention in the cause of remaking Britain as an industrial society. Except in the fields of defence, nuclear power and civil aircraft manufacture, there were still to be no imposed plans of development – even in regard to industries where the need had been long apparent, such as shipbuilding, steel and textiles.

As for the ramshackle motor-vehicle industry, now the vanguard of the export offensive, there was still to be no state enforcement of amalgamations, nor of revolutions in management, nor of developments of 'world cars' in order to cure the profound weaknesses analysed by a March 1945 Whitehall report on the industry ('too many, often small-scale units, each producing too many models'). Yet a splendidly clear-headed blueprint for such reconstruction existed in Whitehall. It was the British 1944 report (commissioned by the Economic and Industrial Planning Staff from the Motor Vehicle Study Group), on *Germany*'s pre-war plan (published in 1939) for developing *her* motor industry. The plan's broad strategy coupled the building of an autobahn network with the mass-production of the *KdF* ('Kraft durch Freude', later the Volkswagen) car, and the reduction in the types of car and components to be manufactured by the rest of the industry. In the words of this British report, the plan defined:

> the types of motor vehicle, and which firms were to be the manufacturers of each type. . . . The manufacturers of components and accessories were also controlled by the programme which dramatically reduced the number of types of any given component allowed to be manufactured. All research and development work, largely under the guidance of Dr Porsche, was to be coordinated for the benefit of the industry.

> All these great national developments were stated to be for the purpose of improving German trade and making Germany a great motoring country. A remarkable single-mindedness of purpose was

evident, both in road building and in the expansion of production facilities.[43]

Remarkable single-mindedness of industrial purpose hardly being a characteristic of the Whitehall of 1947, no state-sponsored programmes were contemplated to develop new other twentieth-century technologies such as electronics and office systems, in order to remedy Britain's over-commitment to the old Victorian heavies.

And no attempt was to be made to smash open the shackles of restrictive practices, whether price-fixing and market-rigging by business, or, more notoriously, the labyrinthine demarcations, over-manning and 'closed-shop' monopolies inflicted by trade unions. The War Cabinet's Reconstruction Committee had at least discussed the heads of a draft Parliamentary Bill to set up a Restrictive Practices Commission, even agreeing that 'before authority was given to introduce a Bill dealing with restrictive practices by employers, the Government would have to consider what should be said about restrictive practices by labour'.[44] But the Labour Government got no further than creating a Monopolies Commission in 1948 to deal with situations where one company supplied 25 per cent or more of a market, though not of course dealing with the 'closed shop', the trade union equivalent. It shrank from tampering with all the other ramifying shackles – whether company or union – on competition and production, and instead (also in 1948) merely appointed a Committee on Industrial Productivity, which plodded on for two years elaborately examining and reporting on every conceivable factor affecting its stock-in-trade except for the key but flammable one of restrictive practices by both sides of industry (see below, pp. 354–5).[45]

Thus the Government's cautious sense of the 'politically possible', reinforced by the distaste of the civil servants and economists of the liberal Establishment (or 'Our Age') for confrontation and the exercise of will, forbade ruthless and wide-ranging intervention in British industry. All was still to be done by advice, persuasion, consultation, fiscal encouragement (the 1945 Income Tax Act provided for tax relief on profits ploughed back into a business rather than distributed to shareholders), and the hopeful fixing of agreed targets for production and exports. As the introduction to the British tender for Marshall Aid in 1948 put it, 'recovery must not be bought at the price of arbitrary and excessive interference with the rights of the individual. The

United Kingdom intends to make resolute [*sic*] use of its traditional techniques of financial policy and the direct public control of certain basic industries. . . .'[46]

Nevertheless, in November 1947 Cripps in a memorandum on 'The Framework of Economic Planning' acknowledged:

> It is not sufficient for realistic planning to determine that certain levels of output, etc. are desirable. It is essential to be able to influence those levels by direct and/or indirect means. Otherwise planning is reduced to mere guesswork or wishful thinking. . . .'[47]

His own suggested means, however, fell far short of the direct – in fact, could hardly have been more remotely *indirect*, consisting as they did of controlling the level of imports while fixing export targets ('mere guesswork or wishful thinking'?), deciding the deployment of national investment, and controlling personal consumption by rationing and taxation.[48]

The Industrial Organisation and Development Act of 1947 marked the limits of the Labour Government's vision and resolve when it came to reconstructing private industry, marking as it did a final emasculation of the wartime Board of Trade's proposals for Industry Boards under an Industrial Commission 'responsible for a range of closely inter-related projects . . . all concerned with various aspects of industrial efficiency in the widest sense – re-equipment, re-organisation, development of new ideas . . .', and armed with the ultimate sanction of compulsory purchase.[49] For the Act only provided for the setting up of development councils for various industries, to be composed equally of employers and trade unionists, but lacking any powers of compulsion and intended to serve merely as forums for discussing problems and focuses for voluntary co-operation over research or export marketing. They therefore, in the words of the President of the Board of Trade in July 1950 (Harold Wilson), 'largely depended for the success of their efforts on securing the agreement and co-operation of the individual undertakings in an industry'.[50] Given that the British industrial system was deeply, doggedly resistant to change, and no parts more so than those most hidebound and therefore most in need of reform, such agreement and co-operation proved hard to find. By the summer of 1950 only four development councils had been set up, one of them against the opposition of the majority of employers in the industry (clothing).[51] Thus died on the wire the first, but by no means the last, foredoomed hope that by means of consensus could the structure of British industry be remade.

Nonetheless the Government considered the question of technological efficiency and change to be so important that on 18 December 1947 it resorted to the British cure-all, a committee.[52] Soon this new Committee on Industrial Productivity spawned 'panels' on 'Human Factors',[53] 'Technology and Operational Research',[54] 'Import Substitution'[55], and 'Technical Information Services',[56] plus a 'working party' of civil servants. The Panel on Human Factors then proceeded to set up its own Research Advisory group. In turn each of the panels sponsored a clutch of research projects. A motley regiment of scientists, social scientists, research institutes, industrialists, civil servants and even the odd trade unionist was mustered and put to work. The first annual report of the Committee on Industrial Productivity in spring 1949[57] came up with such amazingly useful insights as: 'Production is the result of human skill and effort applied to raw materials (men and management – machines and raw materials). . . .'[58] The Panel on Technology and Operational Research had reached a no less astonishing conclusion in regard to the cotton industry:

> Although the immediate need in the cotton textile industry is for a more efficient use of the existing labour force rather than for extensive re-equipment, we are convinced that in the long run greater efficiency and improved productivity can only be achieved by a substantial programme of re-equipment with up-to-date machinery.[59]

Until wound up in summer 1950 the committee and its panels were to slog on amassing vast quantities of information (for the historian an invaluable dossier on current British failings) on every conceivable topic from standardisation,[60] time-and-motion studies in engineering[61] and 'the Human Factor in the Docks',[62] to, of all things, 'Rabbits and the Balance of Payments'.[63] In 1948 the Panel on Human Factors alone produced a file as thick as the operation orders for moving 2700 vessels to the Normandy shore on D-Day[64] – largely research projects proposed by academics keen to get a muzzle into the nosebag. One CIP report in 1950, on the Royal Ordnance Factories, alone ran to 163 pages.[65]

For once again these were no general-staff analyses of urgent operational problems, together with plans of action for solving them (like the pre-war German plan for the motor industry), but yet another protracted unloading of long-worded academic fustian by the Whitehall Establishment and its sub-contractors in the intelligentsia. A military staff would, after all, hardly have wasted time on such topics as 'Discussion of Methodology' and 'Clarification of Hypotheses'.[66] As the Treasury member of the CIP unkindly wrote of the Human Factors Panel in October 1949, its stock-in-trade was, 'in the main, long-term, and more comfortably related to general sociological research than to quick results on the productivity of industry . . .'.[67]

In any case, as the man from the Treasury also noted, a whole new array of study-groups and talking-shops – governmental or industrial – had taken the field since the CIP was first set up, such as the National Research Development Corporation (to act, according to its first annual report in November 1950, as 'a go-between linking the research worker to the industrialist'),[68] the British Institute of Management, a committee of industrialists on standardisation, and some twenty trade associations in the engineering industry, some of which had in turn set up their own production efficiency committees which could meet from time to time and have a nice chat about things.[69] Most notably, an Anglo-American Productivity Committee had been created at the suggestion of Paul Hoffman, the Marshall Aid administrator in Washington, who divined that 'the essential problem for the United Kingdom was an increase in productivity'.[70] Under this committee's sponsorship British teams from some seventy industries were to visit their American opposite numbers at American expense in order to compare and to learn. The exercise eventually resulted, however, in just another of those comprehensive but barren indictments of the widespread old-fashionedness, material and mental, of British industry compared with foreign (in the present case, American) that had been piling up since the 1880s.[71]

This entire hotchpotch of research into productivity suffered from the drawback that it was all purely educational.[72] Even British Standards were not rendered mandatory. Only in the case of the Ministry of Supply, which did impose standardisation on its suppliers, was there direct action.[73] Otherwise enlightenment was supposed to permeate through the stone skulls of British managers and workpeople like rain down into an aquifer, thanks to the voluminous reports on their own industries which they would obviously read with fascination and the subsequent creative discussions which they would hold in committee, canteen and club-house.

It is hardly astonishing that these various well-meant efforts at persuasion had resulted, according to the judgement of the Chancellor of the Exchequer in July 1949, in 'comparatively little' progress towards the productivity 'necessary to make us more competitive with North America'.[74]

And nowhere is this 'comparatively little' progress, and with it the ineffectualness of the Labour Government's industrial measures, more evident than in the case of cotton, whose 'dark, Satanic mills' (in Blake's phrase) had once been the manufacturing heart of the first industrial revolution and the glory of Britain's technological leadership, but were now not so much satanic as senile.

It was a mark of how profoundly twentieth-century industrial Britain had remained stuck in an early-nineteenth-century rut that even in 1937 exports of cotton (despite having collapsed by three-quarters since 1913) still remained a third more valuable than exports of machinery and two-and-a-half times more than exports of chemicals.[75] Moreover, the cotton industry, with its 'obsolescent machinery and an out-of-date form of industrial organisation' (according to the President of the Board of Trade, Dalton, in 1943),[76] by now epitomised everything that was defective about older British technologies. Wrote Dalton: 'Between 60 and 70 per cent of its buildings had been put up before 1900! Much of the machinery is older still. . . .'[77] By the end of the Second World War its efficiency had fallen still further, well below that of its competitors.[78] A study in 1944 found that 95 per cent of the looms in America were automatic, as against only 5 per cent in Britain.[79] Although it had been as long ago as 1929 that a government committee had vainly recommended amalgamating the industry into larger units and re-equipping it for mass production and long runs,[80] there was little hope of such a reorganisation ever spontaneously occurring because, as Dalton put it in 1944, 'this industry, more than most, is in the hands of old men, prone to take short views . . .'.[81]

These pessimistic wartime diagnoses were repeated in the reports of the Cotton Industry Working Party in 1946 ('a substantial proportion of the machinery now in place is . . . not only old in type but beyond its efficient working life'),[82] and of the Committee of Investigation into the Cotton Textile Machine Industry in 1947.[83]

Dalton as wartime President of the Board of Trade had proposed to cure this sad case of senile decay by setting up a statutory board to reshape the industry, compulsorily if need be. But there only materialised in 1947 a purely consultative, and therefore toothless, Cotton Board (later redubbed Development Council). Whitehall fell back on such familiar but hopeless nostrums as an 'educational crusade'[84] to convince this most dinosaurian of industries of the need to transform itself and its entire operational outlook.

However, although the Labour Government shrank from compulsion, it was willing to try bribery, and in 1948 passed the Cotton Spinning Re-Equipment Subsidy Act of 1948, a well-meant attempt to accelerate change by handing out taxpayers' money to approved groups of textile companies which submitted schemes of modernisation. But so supine, so set in their comfy familiar ways, proved most of the firms in the industry that they could not even be bothered to stretch out an open palm. As Harold Wilson, President of the Board of Trade, acknowledged in 1950, there 'has been considerable disappointment about the use of this Act, and about what has been considered to be the slow rate both of grouping and re-equipment . . .'[85]

It little helped to solve the problem of modernising the cotton industry that most of the makers of its machinery were equally supine and out of date, and equally deaf to governmental persuasion by means of reports, seminars and conferences. Whereas one important manufacturer of winding machines went into receivership, by far the largest supplier of automatic looms, the British Northrop Loom Company, was making a product already rendered obsolescent by the latest American designs.[86] This was hardly surprising in view of Northrop's neglect of research and development, glumly noted by the Cabinet Production Committee as late as July 1950.[87] But Northrop was no exception: the textile machinery industry as a whole lacked any comprehension of R and D as practised by its American opposite number or, for that matter, by a British company like ICI. It remained smugly content with traditional designs 'developed', as one report put it in July 1949, 'over many years by skilled craftsmen',[88] or with importing new developments from abroad.[89] Another study a year later contrasted the industry's neglect of R and D with its foreign rivals' commitment to it. For instance, the Swiss firm of Ruti, though smaller than Northrop, had a staff of graduates 'engaged solely in development work'.[90] Just one British textile company (in the spinning sector) had so far founded a research centre.[91]

Although in November 1950 Harold Wilson, in a greasily flattering address as President of the Board of Trade to a Cotton Board conference, averred that in the five years since the war 'a great deal had been done' to make good the neglect of the past,[92] he nonetheless went on to ask his audience: 'Yet who in the industry can say that it is yet in a position to meet the full blast of foreign competition when it develops . . .?'[93]

Presumably no one could say, since even now most of the machinery in textile industries as a whole (with the exception of the spinning in the jute industry) was 'about 40 years old and some is as much as 80 years old . . .',[94] while the cotton industry in particular had only managed to achieve by 1950 cloth production at an annual rate of less than three-quarters of the 1938 total, and exports of woven piece-goods at an annual rate of 56 per cent of 1938.[95] The impotence of the Labour Government's industrial policies could hardly be more clearly demonstrated.

Yet the Government did equip itself with one tool at least for directly compelling technological change – nationalisation. However, the effectiveness of that tool depended, like that of all tools, on the fitness of its design for its purpose.

Chapter Eleven

'The Remedy Is Public Ownership'

FOR A CENTURY the vision of 'public ownership' had beguiled the romantic idealists of the left, for here lay the means by which one day a new socialist commonwealth would replace capitalism, and what Robert Blatchford stigmatised as 'the incentive of gain' would give way to what Ramsay MacDonald lauded as 'a willing gift of service'.[1] In 1893 the Independent Labour Party at its inaugural conference had defined the party's purpose as 'the collective ownership of all the means of production, distribution and exchange'.[2] The Labour Party itself in its 1918 constitution (as amended in 1929) pledged in almost identical terms to secure to the workers by hand and brain the 'full fruits of their industry . . . upon the basis of the common ownership of the means of production, distribution and exchange'.[3] In its manifesto for the 1945 general election, *Let Us Face the Future*, the party trumpeted that it was 'a Socialist Party, and proud of it. Its ultimate purpose at home is the establishment of the Socialist Commonwealth of Great Britain';[4] and promised to nationalise (by way of a start) the Bank of England, the fuel and power industries, iron and steel, civil aviation, and the canals, railways and road haulage.

However, it followed from the character of the Labour movement as a pseudo-religion tracing its spiritual descent from the religious revivalism of the early nineteenth century[5] that it had always thought of public ownership too much in terms of moral ends and too little in terms of practical ways and means. As Ernest Bevin had ringingly preached in 1909 when campaigning for election to the Bristol City Council, 'you will realise the chaos, misery and degradation brought upon us by the private ownership of the means of life. I claim that Socialism, which is the common ownership of these means, is the

ONLY SOLUTION OF SUCH EVILS.'[6] Eighteen years later Clement Attlee, now Leader of the Labour Party, was still delivering much the same sermon: 'The evils that Capitalism brings differ in intensity in different countries but the root cause of the trouble once discerned, the remedy is seen to be the same by thoughtful men and women. The cause is private property; the remedy is public ownership.'[7]

Even though in 1945 *Let Us Face the Future* claimed that one purpose of nationalisation was to reconstruct 'industries which have failed the nation', the whole concept still owed as much to pious sentiment as to industrial strategy – as was demonstrated by the total neglect even as late as 1945 to work out plans for the ragbag of industries listed in the manifesto. And ragbag they were in their lack of strategic coherence. To take the sources of energy – coal, gas and electricity – into public ownership made some sense; and anyway the coalminers figured so large in working-class myth and were so powerful a force within the Labour movement that to hand the mines over to the 'people' was to fulfil a moral and political bond. There was a case too for iron and steel, another old Victorian heavy and now a high-cost mixture of some big modern plants dating from post-1936 rearmament and a rabble of the small and out of date.[8] To nationalise the Bank of England, whence in Labour myth the top-hatted and fat-bellied had masterminded bankers' ramps against the working class, amounted to no more than a self-gratifying gesture. But why were old and partly decrepit industries (including the railways and canals) mostly selected for nationalisation, and (except for civil airlines, very much the odd one out) no new technologies like chemicals or aircraft or electronics? Why were there no proposals to set up new public enterprises to exploit at present neglected fields like office systems and machines? Was it because the Labour Party, like so many British institutions, was carrying history on its back?

From the very start, therefore, fundamental ambiguities compromised the design process for nationalisation, the Labour Government's one and only tool of direct industrial change. Worse, in 1945 that design process fell not to technocratic professionals but to the humanist amateurs of Whitehall, political or bureaucratic. The Cabinet Socialisation of Industries Committee, which met for the first time on 9 November 1945, was chaired by Herbert Morrison, the Lord President, and included Dalton, the Chancellor of the Exchequer, and

Cripps, the President of the Board of Trade and also the Cabinet's only approximation to a technocrat. The other members comprised Emmanuel Shinwell, the Minister of Fuel and Power (formerly a ferocious Clydeside left-winger); Alfred Barnes, the Minister of War Transport (a one-time arts-and-crafts designer and later a leading figure in the Co-operative movement); John Wilmot, Minister of Supply and Aircraft Production (a banker before becoming a politician); Lord Winster, the Minister of Civil Aviation (a former naval officer). With the exception of Cripps, not one of them had therefore enjoyed direct industrial experience of any kind, let alone in senior management jobs. With the exception of 'arts-and-crafts' Barnes, not one had ever received anything that could be called a technocratic education.

The Whitehall men of paper who attended the meeting could hardly make up for these lacks. Sir Cyril Hurcombe, the Director-General, Ministry of War Transport (St John's College, Oxford), had been a career bureaucrat since 1906. Sir John Woods, Permanent Under-Secretary at the Board of Trade and latterly PUS at the Ministry of Production (Christ's Hospital and Balliol College, Oxford), was likewise a career bureaucrat; and so too was the PUS at the Ministry of Fuel and Power, C. H. S. de Peyer (Cheltenham and Magdalen College, Oxford; honours degree in Philosophy, Politics and Economics). Two Whitehall economists made up the weight: James Meade, the committed New Jerusalemer in the Economic Section of the Cabinet Office, and R. F. Kahn, of the Board of Trade (St Paul's School and Magdalen College, Oxford; honours in PPE). Absent from this array was any equivalent of Jean Monnet (deviser of, and later General Commissioner of, the Plan for the Modernisation and Equipment of France), with his long and direct industrial experience; or Louis Armand, Director-General of the nationalised French railways (*Ecole Polytechnique*; mining and railway engineer); or, in terms of sheer executive drive and resourcefulness, Albert Speer.

It was Morrison who set the agenda for the forthcoming Whitehall attempt to work out plans for nationalising the industries on the Labour Party's shopping list, and he did so by despatching to the relevant ministries a list of eight questions on the problems to be solved – as he saw them. Morrison was as much an administrator as a politician, and if asked to describe his soul would probably have described a local-government minute-book. As Chairman of the London County Council in 1932 he had been responsible for creating the London Transport Board, charged with running all bus, tram, coach and underground services in the capital. His questionnaire reveals a characteristic order of priorities. First come questions relating to compensation to the existing owners of undertakings to be 'socialised', whether local authorities or shareholders of companies: how to calculate the compensation, and what form it should take. Then follow questions with regard to the administrative structures of 'socialised' industries and to their pricing policies, in particular whether prices should be nationally averaged or reflect local conditions; questions in regard to wage rates, and again whether these should be fixed nationally or reflect local conditions and productivity; a question in regard to 'arrangements' for the timing and planning of investment; and finally a question asking what principles should govern the export trade of 'socialised' industries.

Left out altogether is any enquiry about what should be the overall strategic objective of 'socialisation', such as to create highly productive, highly profitable modern enterprises, or, alternatively, to bring about that democratic fellowship within industry dreamed of by the socialist pioneers (these things being by no means incompatible, as the Germans were to prove). In consequence was also left out any question relating to the conduct of industrial operations in the field.[9]

Thus confined by Morrison to the administrative-cum-political issues with which they anyway felt most comfortable, the departmental ministers and bureaucrats duly returned answers to the questionnaire long on such matters as compensation and administrative structures, and short on strategic objectives and operational means, especially the key issues of investment and exports. To these issues, for instance, the memorandum on fuel and power (but mostly on coal) by the Minister thereof devoted less than one page out of seven and a half.[10] A brief overview by the Chancellor of the Exchequer did no better, offering out of eight paragraphs a short one on investment ('Socialised industries would be expected to arrange their capital projects in harmony with national investment policy') and another, equally short, on exports.[11]

Morrison also asked the Economic Section of the Cabinet Office (but, of course, no team of production engineers or industrial managers) to answer his questionnaire. Their academic minds came up with such challenging thoughts as, for one, that industries 'may be socialised for a variety of reasons, political, strategical, social or economic. We are here [that is, in their memorandum] concerned exclusively with the economic objectives . . .', and, for another, that it was 'not possible for the economist as such to say whether any particular industry is likely to be run more efficiently under private or public operation. This will depend on a great many circumstances of a political, psychological and administrative character. . . .'[12] Nonetheless, their memorandum assumed that the economic objectives of socialisation were 'to be sought in the sphere of productive efficiency'.

It turned out that this was something very different from the technological efficiency resulting from huge long-term investment in R and D and new equipment, coupled with high productivity, on which the Germans and Japanese were later to base their 'economic miracles'. For example, in regard to the electrification of the railways a later report by the Economic Section argued that 'the new capital installation must be one for which the new capital costs are less than the old operating costs it economises. The natural enthusiasm of the engineers for the most up-to-date technical discovery must not be allowed to overrule these economic considerations.'[13] With this kind of 'expert' advice, it is no wonder that decades after European and Japanese travellers had been electrically hauled at start-to-stop speeds of 90 m.p.h. and higher yet, British rail travellers would still be getting smuts in their eyes while travelling at a mere 60 m.p.h.

Productive efficiency [lectured the Economic Section in answer to Morrison's questionnaire] is not attained merely by applying the most up-to-date engineering, chemical or other technical methods of production to the socialised industry. It also depends on securing a proper balance in the allocation of resources between the various plans and industries, whether publicly or privately owned. It is, therefore, a necessary part of the efficiency of any industry that, in determining the scale and methods of production, due regard should be had to the criteria of costs and prices.

In general, output should be produced by whichever methods are, *at currently prevailing prices and costs* [emphasis added], the cheapest, and production methods should continue to be expanded as long as the cost of additional output does not exceed the price which consumers are willing to pay for it.[14]

216

Although this kind of academic economists' rule-of-thumb coloured the Government's whole approach to economic policy, it was particularly stultifying when as in this instance it took the form of advice to a Cabinet committee specifically charged with industrial change.

But in any case nationalisation as a tool of such change or of technological efficiency in itself was from the start relegated to a mere secondary or even tertiary importance in ministerial discussions. For Morrison's questionnaire and the answers to it effectively set the pattern for all that was to follow. At the very first meeting of the Committee on the Socialisation of Industries, Morrison as chairman limited debate to the favoured topics of compensation and administrative structures, suggesting that if agreement could be reached 'on broad lines of policy [sic] then the details could be left to the departments concerned'.[15] But the meeting in fact only agreed that socialised industries should 'normally be run by Boards', that is, autonomous public boards on the model of Morrison's own pre-war London Transport Board. All other matters were referred in the usual Whitehall way for further examination either by departments or by the Official Committee on the Socialisation of Industries. This body, the customary collection of humanist mandarins and academic economists,[16] reported back after only three and a half months (an amazingly short delay in Whitehall terms) with its views on compensation and on suitable procedures for acquiring the assets of industries to be nationalised.[17] The ministerial committee itself met sixteen times in 1946 and discussed a total of thirty-one agenda items, but only four of these items dealt with future commercial and industrial efficiency or long-term reconstruction and development, as did only two of the thirty-nine memoranda submitted to the committee. All the rest of the agenda items and the memoranda were concerned with such congenial but incidental topics as administrative structures, compensation of various kinds, salary rates for board members and workers' participation.[18] Here is unwittingly revealed what mattered most to the committee and what least.

In 1947 only three out of thirty-three items discussed by the committee and six out of fifty memoranda touched on operational efficiency and long-term development, the rest chewing over the customary favourites, including the drafting of Parliamentary Bills.[19] In

1948, the proportion was five out of sixty-one agenda items and fourteen out of sixty-seven memoranda.[20] The agenda items and memoranda of the official committee in 1946–8 reveal a similar choice of priorities.[21]

In any case, the whole drift of the ministerial committee's discussions confirmed that the nationalised sector would be given no *Schwerpunkt* (to use the German military term signifying the point of maximum effort, or main thrustline) of bringing about radical change in technology, management methods and working practices, nor an overriding objective of maximum performance and profitability. Instead in the minds of the committee from the start was a model of a 'steady-state' public utility to be 'administered' rather than dynamically managed. The Minister of Civil Aviation, Lord Winster, acknowledged this in plain terms when he wrote that the 'ultimate aim' of nationalising air transport services was to make them 'self-supporting *on public utility* lines [emphasis added]'.[22] In the case of the railways, road haulage and inland waterways, the Minister of Transport was retrospectively to acknowledge in 1949 that the objective had been to create a single whole 'which would operate as a non-profit-making utility service . . .'.[23]

It followed that ministerial designs for the nationalised industries were to be shaped by social-cum-political factors as much as by technological or commercial, if not more so. In the first place, the Socialisation of Industries Committee agreed in November 1945 that, in general, prices and wage rates should be averaged nationally, rather than related to local costs and productivity, as the Economic Section, to its credit, had vainly recommended.[24] In the case of iron and steel, where uniform national prices had been fixed before the war and statutorily controlled during it, the Minister of Supply reckoned that 'it is desirable they should be retained'. He further reckoned that 'owing to widely different conditions it is doubtful if wage rates should be related to productivity . . .'.[25] In regard to coal, the country's basic source of energy and the first industry to be nationalised, the Minister of Fuel and Power shrank from an idea so cruel as that prices should be related to local costs, which would have inevitably subjected inefficient, ill-equipped or geologically difficult pits to euthanasia. Instead prices should be averaged so that, 'in effect, the lower cost undertakings subsidise those with higher costs . . .':

Until the backward technical state of the industry can be remedied by a thorough reorganisation, which will take time before its effects are seen in reduced costs, many of our important export industries will continue to be seriously hampered by high coal prices. I should therefore be in favour of fixing coal prices at the lowest level at which they cover costs, including interest and amortisation and allowing due provision for research, development and the accumulation of reserves. In other words, I am satisfied we should aim at making average prices equal to average costs.[26]

It followed from this that wages in the coal industry must not be related to local costs either. The Minister happily remarked that the national minimum-wage awards introduced during the war, combined with the Coal Charges Account (by which low-cost districts supported the high-cost via a central fund), 'have gone a long way towards shifting the burden of subsidising the high cost fields from the shoulders of the mineworkers in those districts [through lower wages proportionate to their lower productivity] on to the undertakings in the more productive districts . . .'. Since this process was not complete, the Minister felt that 'a nation-wide basis for wage rates is certainly the ideal to be aimed at; this means trying to secure that workers receive the same remuneration for similar work in whatever part of the country the work is done'.[27]

The Minister had of course to take into account both the current national coal shortage and the muscle of the strike-prone miners alike in the coalfields and in the Labour movement. As he wrote, 'Moreover, in an old-established industry like coal, we cannot ignore altogether the existing wage structure, which has grown up as a result of a long and bitter struggle, and of which some features would not be lightly given up by those who fought for them.'[28]

In the case of transport, especially the railways – positively Victorian in their present pricing, which was based not on what the market could bear or even on the cost of providing the service, but on the value of the goods carried[29] – the Minister of War Transport hedged, calling for 'special investigation' of the problems.[30] However, he did make one remarkably defeatist assertion: 'It is not practicable to ascertain the true cost of dealing by rail with a particular unit of traffic or even with particular classes of traffic. . . .' However, 'if Railway charges were in future to be based on the principle of cost the rates for

coal and other low-grade traffic might be substantially increased'.[31] In
the end the Minister followed his colleagues in suggesting an all-in
national fudge for both prices and wages:

> The quantum of charges made should be so fixed as to provide the
> amount of gross receipts needed to ensure, with efficient and
> economic management, the financial stability of the [railways]
> undertaking and to support a policy of progressive capital develop-
> ment. Provided this object is achieved, it would be a matter of policy
> whether the charges for any given service or commodity or in any
> given area should be so fixed as to yield a profit or should be
> supported by profits earned on other services or traffic.[32]

And: 'It seems inevitable that in any unified undertaking base rates for
comparable work will tend to approximate to one another and be
governed by national agreements.'[33]

It would be hard to imagine a more disastrous choice of
fundamental strategy than to mask in this way the realities of varying
costs and productivity within key basic industries like coal, iron and
steel and the railways, and opt instead for national averaging of prices
and wages. All three industries stood in urgent need of the most
ruthless and radical adaptation. Yet far from spurring on such
adaptation, the strategy chosen could serve only to perpetuate the
status quo by acting as a form of invalidity benefit for the industrially
halt and lame.

But in any case ministers proved generally squeamish in regard to
anything so vulgarly commercial as profitability and pricing. As early as
November 1945 the Chief Economic Adviser to the Board of Trade,
Austin Robinson, was writing to a colleague to complain that the Coal
Industry Nationalisation Bill 'is extraordinarily vague about the
marketing of coal . . .':

> Our main interest, I think . . . lies in securing cheap coal. . . . You
> will notice however that there is no clause in the Bill . . . laying down
> the principles by which the National Coal Board should be guided in
> determining its prices. The only relevant clause is I(1b), which says
> that they shall make coal available . . . at such prices as may seem to
> them best calculated to further the public interest. There is nothing
> that I have found that requires them to aim to cover their costs. . . .[34]

Even in regard to so modern a business as civil aviation, it was with an apparent sniff of distaste that the Minister (Lord Winster) had to acknowledge that 'overseas air services are an invisible export and we cannot afford, therefore, to disregard exploiting this source of foreign trade on a profit-making basis . . .'.[35] The official committee in defining the role of profit in the entire nationalised sector took a similarly grudging view:

> it was very unlikely on the one hand that any socialized industry would be permitted, over any long period, to earn extravagant profits, and that on the other there were great practical objections from the point of view of management in relieving Boards of the responsibility of *earning a certain minimum of profit* [emphasis added].[36]

The official committee therefore recommended that 'the aim of a Board should be to cover the service of the stock over a reasonably short period, with an adequate margin of earnings in good years to meet deficiencies in bad years . . .'.[37] According to the minutes,

> It was also agreed that in certain circumstances . . . the Board of a particular industry might have no chance of achieving this object. . . . In such cases the capital would have to be regarded as lost and the Government, which in effect owned the equity of the business, would have to write it off. There was little support for the suggestion that in such circumstances the losses of one socialised industry could be made good by the profits of another, and it was felt that the service of the stock would rather have to be met out of the general revenues of the Exchequer.[38]

But the ministerial committee proved equally undemanding over pricing and profits. In May 1946 it decided, in terms that echoed the civil servants' recommendations, that 'the controlling board of each socialised industry should normally be under obligation to fix its price at a level which, taking an average of good years with bad, would cover its costs and leave a reasonable margin for contingencies'.[39]

Thus no tight discipline of minimising costs and prices and maximising added-value was to be laid on the nationalised industries; no discipline as might have whipped them into reorganising their operations, closing high-cost plant and shedding redundant personnel. It further confirmed the future character of nationalised industries as 'steady-state' utilities rather than dynamic enterprises. Already by July 1946 Austin Robinson, the Economic Adviser to the Board of Trade, was fearing that the industries and their ministry godfathers would be too much oriented towards the interests of producers, too little towards those of consumers. This, he warned,

> may ultimately have very grave repercussions on real income and on general industrial efficiency in costs in this country. For the industries we have been nationalising are in almost all cases the key basic industries upon which our manufacturing system is built up. If their costs and prices are unduly high the whole system of our costs and prices will be inflated.[40]

By July 1947 Morrison himself was admitting in a paper called 'Taking Stock': 'We have taken no steps to ensure that the Boards have before them a standard of efficiency and costs which they should endeavour to achieve; and prices and charges to the public are important. . . .'[41] By the early months of 1948, with coal, electricity supply, transport, the Bank of England and the airlines all now in state ownership, ministerial minds had become darkened still further by doubt. On 9 April another report on 'Taking Stock', this time by the Socialisation of Industries Committee, conceded:

> War experience in most of the industries which have been subsequently socialised tended to reduce the incentive to secure greater efficiency by a lowering of costs. This was true of the coal industry under war-time control and under the system of the Coal Charges Account. It was also true of the Airways Corporations.

Moreover:

> Although socialised industries have to pay their way, the monopoly position which many of them occupy would make it possible for them to extract from the consumer the cost of excessive office staffs, unnecessary ancillary services and other manifestations of extravagant administration. Overheads and the number of non-productive personnel require to be scanned vigorously. . . .[42]

But how could these defects be remedied, given the cosy protected operational environment that had been provided by the Government in its design for nationalisation? The committee could only wave its hand hopefully at 'efficiency audits' by some team of experts. Even then, it would be 'undesirable to do anything which might undermine the sense of responsibility of each board for the efficient running of its undertaking'.[43] Meanwhile, and again rather late in the day, ministers had been studying the organisations of successful large-scale private companies (ICI and Unilever in Britain, and General Motors and Standard Telephones and Cables in America)[44] – an irrelevant exercise because unlike the nationalised industries, which were subject to no goads to efficiency, these companies were competing in world markets, were answerable to their shareholders and could not look to governments to bail out their losses if their managements proved inept.

The very appointments to the nationalised boards underlined how Whitehall – politicians and mandarins alike – were treating these industries as 'steady-state' utilities, for they chose administrators of their own kidney, sound chaps unlikely to rock boats, rather than innovative leaders strong in will and personality. To run the coal industry, so much of it a museum of Victorian industrial attitudes and working practices, Whitehall appointed the first Viscount Hyndley, a sixty-three-year-old veteran of the industry whose experience had lain almost entirely in marketing and distribution. Having served during the war as Controller-General of the Ministry of Fuel and Power, he was also well tarnished by exposure to Whitehall. Such a man with such experience could hardly bring the fresh and dynamic leadership that the coal industry needed more than any other. To the British Transport Commission (responsible for the railways, canals and road haulage) was appointed that other safely bureaucratic mediocrity, Sir Cyril Hurcombe, formerly Director-General of the Ministry of War Transport, and a man whose entrepreneurial experience and knowledge of engineering were nil. The gas boards drew the heads of former large gas companies, such as Sir Michael Milne-Watson (Eton and Balliol), once Governor of the Gas Light and Coke Company and now Chairman of the North Thames Gas Board[45] – so no chance of new minds and ruthless reforming zeal here either.

The membership of nationalised boards followed the pattern of the safe but mediocre set by the chairmen. In Morrison's words in

October 1947, 'There has been a natural tendency to confine the field of choice to men and women of established reputations and long experience; and, while such members are essential, freshness of vision, initiative and readiness for change are also needed.'[46] Writing to his colleagues on the Committee for the Socialisation of Industries the Lord President confided that 'he was sure every minister responsible for making these appointments has felt somewhat uneasy about the lack of available information about possible candidates . . .'.

In fact Whitehall simply chose from its standard list of worthies thought suitable to serve on various public bodies. According to a report by the Official Committee on the Socialisation of Industries in May 1948,

> This list has, since the war, been expanded to include persons known to have given outstanding service to Government departments during the war, particularly in the fields of Industry, Finance and Commerce. Many of them were temporary Civil Servants or were otherwise closely connected with wartime administration. Most of the famous names included were obtained as a result of recommendations elicited from Heads and Departments, particularly the Ministry of Supply, Board of Trade and Ministry of Labour, and not by any direct approach to financial and industrial circles. Also, attention was directed mainly to all-round usefulness and experience, rather than to eminence in specialised or technical fields. . . .[47]

As a consequence, Morrison acknowledged in October 1947,

> It has been a case of thinking of possible names and consulting one's colleagues, with the feeling that there were reserves of talent which we were not touching. For example, there are lively and able industrialists in the provinces, Scotland and Wales who may not have national reputations but who are good. Some of them may be on Regional Boards or known to the regional organisations. They should not be forgotten. . . .[48]

He therefore suggested that 'we ought to arrange for the central compilation of a list of persons suitable for appointment to public boards . . .'.

Six months later the Official Committee on the Socialisation of Industries was repeating the same message, recommending that the Treasury (that turbine house of industrial progress) should be charged with drawing up a special list, based on its present address-book of worthies but not overlooking 'younger men of ability and promise'.[49]

The problem of poor calibre of leadership extended to the senior and line managers of nationalised industries too, so often the very same poorly educated and self-trained 'practical man' who had proved inadequate under private ownership. In the cases of some industries, however, Whitehall proved all too complacent about the existing standards of management. Of the railways, which in terms of their steam-age culture and engineering philosophy were actually among the most stubbornly backward-looking businesses in the country, the Minister of Fuel and Power wrote in November 1947 that there had been:

> a century of development towards large scale organisation, and the managerial and supervisory staff and indeed the general body of railway men are trained and accustomed to its problems and methods. . . . Nationalisation of the railways will presumably involve no great change in organisation or in methods and outlook of the managerial staff. . . .[50]

While the Minister observed more justly that 'in electricity there is at least the nucleus of persons accustomed to the problems and methods of large scale organisation', his description of the mining engineers appointed to the National Coal Board as 'the best . . . that could be found in the country'[51] has to be weighed in the context of, in his own words, 'the almost total lack of men [that is, managers] . . . with any experience or idea of working in a vast nation-wide industry . . .'.[52]

> The [private] coal industry [he wrote] . . . consisted of a large number of comparatively small and highly individualistic under-takings and there was no one (apart from a few chairmen of companies who for various reasons could not be included in the management of the nationalised industry) who had any experience of running a really large organisation. Very few people in the industry had any conception of what is involved in being on the staff

of one. The Managing Director of even a comparatively large and successful colliery company was accustomed to only the simplest type of organisation. He had everything under his own eye and hand and could exercise personal and direct management like the manager of a single factory. . . .[53]

Yet no drastic culling of those who Field Marshal Montgomery would have called 'useless' was carried out in the nationalised industries at any level of management; no wholesale replacing with the best who could be hired from anywhere in the world.[54]

In the case of old technologies, therefore, nationalisation turned out in all respects to be not so much a revolution as a prolonging of the industrial *ancien régime* by bureaucratic means. Worse still, nationalisation, far from serving to whip progress forward, enabled Whitehall the better to rein it back. To give one gruesome example, instead of sponsoring the modernisation of the out-of-date and war-worn railway system like their French and Dutch opposite numbers, the Government actually prevented it by refusing year after year to provide the necessary capital investment (see Chapter 14). Again, those sections of an industry that had been profitable and efficient before nationalisation were now no longer free to raise capital in the market to invest in new development, but instead were shackled by dependence on government money and the vagaries of government investment policy.[55] Nor, thanks to their tightly restrictive remits under the relevant Acts of Parliament, could nationalised industries venture into new and potentially profitable fields of service or manufacture. The leitmotiv of the whole programme thus lay in constraining enterprise rather than spurring it on.

On the Government's confusions of purpose a particularly glaring light is shone by the case of the three nationalised airlines: the British Overseas Airways Corporation (BOAC), British European Airways (BEA) and British South American Airways (BSAA). For these, in contrast to their fellow 'socialised' industries, belonged to twentieth-century technology rather than nineteenth-century technology, and were struggling in a competitive international market rather than reclining comfortably on a domestic monopoly. Moreover, they were yoked by government to the privately owned British aircraft industry in a combined national policy for civil aviation masterminded by a special Cabinet committee (normally composed of ministers and civil servants undiluted by aeronautical expertise). This policy constituted the one large-scale attempt (apart from defence procurement and nuclear power) to develop a major industry based on advanced technology. Yet the policy was not founded on industrial and commercial realism but was instead inspired by that same delusion which underlay postwar British total strategy as a whole – the delusion that Britain with the Commonwealth was, and would remain, a power in the same league as the United States.

CHAPTER TWELVE

'The Prestige of the Aircraft Industry'

To MAKE a profitable return on investment was from the beginning only a secondary function of the nationalised airlines – merely something that, as the Minister of Civil Aviation put it in 1946, 'could not be disregarded'. The financial record made its own retrospective comment on the Minister's remark, for in actual fact the three airlines lost £10.2 million in 1946, £11.1 million in 1947–8, £9.7 million in 1948–9 and (it was estimated in January 1950) about the same in 1949–50.[1]

What then were the primary functions of the 'socialised' airlines? One such, first formulated under the wartime coalition,[2] lay in helping to realise the neo-Edwardian dream that the global scatter of the Commonwealth might yet be linked together into a political and economic entity. According to the wartime coalition's White Paper proposals in March 1945, subsidies might be paid to the British Overseas Airways Corporation (BOAC) for certain Empire routes 'essential in the interests of Commonwealth communications'.[3] Indeed, BOAC was specifically set up 'to provide Imperial communications' to Africa, the Middle East, India, South-east Asia, the Far East, and Australia and New Zealand. The future of these imperial routes and the choice of the right aircraft to fly them dominated discussion in the Cabinet Civil Aviation Committee in the years 1946–50.[4] Even the revolutionary jet-propelled de Havilland Comet, due to enter service in 1953, was being designed for the stopping route between Britain and Australia via Cairo and India, not for the long non-stop haul across the North Atlantic.[5]

Although in the late 1940s the imperial routes were operating at a loss of some £2.5 million a year,[6] neither the Minister of Civil

Aviation nor the committee ever suggested closing any of them down, but only cutting losses by replacing British airliners with American. However, the frequent and painful discussions of this latter proposal simply served to emphasise what was truly the most important function, indeed the overriding function, of the nationalised airlines. And that was to 'Fly British' in order to justify the existence of British civil aircraft manufacture, and so preserve its future.[7] In the words of the Minister of Civil Aviation in January 1950 in surveying the record since the war,

> as a matter of agreed national policy our nationalised Corporations have been heavily handicapped in the interests of the all-important aircraft manufacturing industry whose prosperity has understandably been considered to be so vital to our national survival.[8]

It was again the wartime coalition which had taken the original decision that after the war Britain should not only supply all types of aircraft needed by her armed forces, but also compete with the United States in manufacturing and selling civil air-transports. If this were not technological overstretch enough, the coalition Government further decided that British constructors should not limit themselves to smaller short-haul passenger aircraft, even though this 'niche' market was recognised as offering the better prospects of foreign sales, but should challenge the Americans head-on in the most competitive market of all, that for large long-distance air-transports.[9] In December 1943 the Government gave authority for work to begin on the project of designing and constructing a huge airliner to fly the Atlantic non-stop, later named the 'Brabazon' in honour of Lord Brabazon, a famous pioneer pilot and the Minister of Aircraft Production in 1941–2. This decision appears the more wayward since the British aircraft industry and specifically the Bristol Aeroplane Company, the designated contractor, had no previous experience of building an aircraft of the Brabazon's size and technical complexity. To put so much hope and money into one inherently risky project hardly constituted a sound investment strategy.

Nor is there evidence that the basic policy decision to pour scarce resources (including scarce high-grade scientific and technical personnel) into the civil-aircraft industry resulted from favourable comparisons with other technologies in terms of potential cost-benefit, return on investment and future market growth. Rather, the wartime coalition simply took it for granted that to be a world leader in civil aviation rightfully belonged to Britain's status as a first-class power.

From this first and basic misjudgement were to stem all the unrealistic decisions, all the costly disappointments and disasters, that were to beset postwar British aviation policy. Nonetheless, in one sense the misjudgement is understandable. It was made, after all, at a time when the British aircraft industry stood at the apogee of its wartime expansion, when British airpower was still more or less on a par with American, when the fame of such aircraft as the Hurricane, Spitfire, Lancaster and Mosquito seemed to admit of no doubt about Britain's pre-eminence in aeronautical design. In such a climate of pride it was all too easy for a War Cabinet of patriots to decide that Britain must remain in the forefront of this, the most glamorous of modern technologies.

And yet the War Cabinet came to this crucial misjudgement in the face of the objective evidence available to it that the British aircraft industry was by now lagging far behind the American in every kind of resource, and especially R and D facilities and personnel[10] – too far behind to have a realistic chance of ever catching America up and beating her in the market for civil air-transports on top of building every kind of military aircraft. Moreover, Britain would be starting from scratch with blank sheets on the drawing board at a time when the Americans had already got prototypes of postwar airliners to the stage of taxiing trials.[11]

The 1943 report of a British aircraft-industry mission to the United States led by Sir Roy Fedden made all this bleakly clear.[12] The technical and engineering staffs of American firms were, he wrote, five to seven times larger than in British firms. The American firms' instrumentation and testing techniques were superior. Their R and D was on a scale impossible for Britain to equal. They were spending huge sums on the development of transport aircraft, with no fewer than 260 Lockheed Constellations on order. Wrote Fedden: 'It is out of the question for Great Britain to compete in civil aircraft for at least five years after the war . . .',[13] during which period she would have to buy American. However, it says much about the mood of the time that Fedden should nevertheless then go on to contradict his own evidence by recommending that Britain should adopt without delay a policy for civil aircraft production – on the basis of developing R and D resources a quarter the size of America's!

Even after the wartime coalition had committed Britain to the immense task of eventually overtaking America in the manufacture of airliners, lips were still occasionally plucked in Whitehall. In July 1944 the Minister for Aircraft Production (Cripps) was writing:

> the prospects of our aircraft industry securing their fair share of the world market for civil aircraft will be poor enough in the immediate post-war years, having regard to its concentration on war types, and the time entailed in bringing most of the Brabazon types [that is, recommended by the Brabazon Committee], of which we have commenced design, to the stage of commercial production.[14]

Nonetheless, the Labour Government after coming into office reaffirmed the 'Fly British' policy, which was henceforward to be imposed on the airlines by direction of the Minister of Civil Aviation. It also endorsed the existing production programmes. According to a memorandum in September 1945 by the Minister of Civil Aviation (Lord Winster), the supply of long-haul aircraft had been planned in three stages:

> (i) conversion of bomber types for immediate 'stop-gap' use as transports, revenue earning capacity being necessarily of secondary importance;
> (ii) production of interim types. These represent re-designed bomber types and are competitive with current American transport aircraft in performance and comfort and are almost competitive in economy of operation;
> (iii) new civil types designed *ab initio* in accordance with the recommendations of the Brabazon Committee.[15]

But by the time of nationalisation of the airlines in 1946 the 'Fly British' policy had led to a recurrent and at times bitter conflict between the operators (backed by the Ministry of Civil Aviation), who wished to buy American aircraft in order not to fly at crippling losses both of money and customers, and the aircraft firms (backed by the Ministry of Supply, successor to the Ministry of Aircraft Production), who wanted captive purchasers for the turkeys coming out of their factories – at first wartime Lancaster bombers newly fitted with seats; then interim types like the Tudor Marks I and II, based on the four-engined Avro Lincoln bomber but with new fuselages; and finally the biggest turkeys of all, and the last to be hatched (if ever), the Bristol Brabazon and the Saunders-Roe SR-45 flying-boat (see below, pp. 239–43 for an account of the programme's production problems).

As early as January 1946 the Minister of Supply (John Wilmot) was opposing (vainly as it turned out) the purchase of five Constellations as a stop-gap until the Tudors were delivered. He averred that, apart from the bad publicity, 'once BOAC had got American types there would be a tendency for them to wish to continue to use them . . .'.[16] Hence there was 'a danger that we might be driven out of the civil aircraft manufacturing field and be forced to all kinds of undesirable devices to maintain the necessary war potential'. Nevertheless, in August the Cabinet had willy-nilly to authorise the purchase of six Boeing Stratocruisers for the North Atlantic in default of a suitable British aircraft. Yet the Dominions Secretary (Lord Addison), reporting to the Prime Minister on the current state of the civil aircraft programme, still reaffirmed that 'it is essential that we should continue to plan for the development of British aircraft manufacture so that it will have a secure leading position at least by 1950 . . .'.[17]

It was in spring 1947 that the battle between the airlines and the British aircraft industry, together with their ministerial sponsors, over long-haul airliners really began. The *casus belli* lay in the Tudor Marks I and II. The Tudor I was suffering from 'operational difficulties' which, even if cured in part, would limit it to medium ranges. That ruled it out for its designated route, the North Atlantic.[18] The Tudor II, of which fifty were on order, was late in delivery, and 'heavier, slower and has less range than expected. In consequence it cannot compete with the Constellation. . . .'[19] It would not be technically able to operate with an economic payload on Empire routes south of Nairobi or east of Calcutta. The national airlines of Australia and South Africa had by now put aside Commonwealth solidarity for the sake of aeronautical realism, and cancelled their own orders for the Tudor II in favour of buying Constellations and Skymasters – aircraft also to be operated by Air France and KLM on routes to South Africa and Australia.[20] While waiting and waiting for the Tudor II the unfortunate BOAC was compelled to run its Australian services with nine-passenger Lancastrians (converted Lancaster bombers) and Hythe flying-boats at a loss of some £1.4 million a year, and its South African service with Yorks (another converted bomber) at an annual loss of £400,000.[21]

Moreover, the nationalised airlines were going to have to wait for about five years at least before they could 'Fly British' with aircraft profitable to operate – supposedly. The Tudor II's successor, the Hermes IV, could not come into service before early 1950 and even then would not be competitive with the Constellation. The Brabazon I, the Saunders-Roe SR-45 and the jet-propelled DH 106 (Comet) were unlikely to be in service before 1953.[22]

What then to do in the meantime? The Minister of Civil Aviation argued strongly against keeping Commonwealth services going with a mixture of available but unsuitable British aircraft at an estimated loss of £11 million over five years.[23] He saw great promise in current discussions with the Lockheed Corporation about a Constellation powered by Bristol Centaurus engines, for nine of these would suffice for BOAC's South African and Australian services, eliminating the expected operating loss.[24]

The Minister of Supply, loyal mouthpiece of the aircraft manufacturers, 'confidently expected that the British industry will, in a few years' time, be producing civil types which are at least equal to any foreign competitor, but the process of *obtaining supremacy* [emphasis added] will be neither short nor easy. . . . In the meantime, however, we must do the best we can with our interim types.' He contended that the current operational problems of the airlines:

> should not, I submit, be allowed to obscure the wider reasons of policy in favour of the principle that the British Corporations should operate aircraft produced by our own industry and any departure from this principle should be allowed only in the most exceptional circumstances.[25]

He proceeded to give his reasons – neither of them related to the earning of a profitable return on investment by the airlines or the aircraft industry:

> (a) The Aircraft Industry is of fundamental importance to the nation's security. Every order that is taken from a British constructor

and given to a foreign constructor is a step in the direction of weakening British war potential. . . .

(b) Aircraft are of great importance to the export trade and are likely to become more so as air transport and flying generally become more established and widespread. Moreover, export orders contribute to the maintenance of war potential without cost to the taxpayer. The normal principles of international trade should, therefore, be applied only in a limited sense to the aircraft industry.[26]

In the Minister of Supply's view it all came down to a question of Britain's place in the world and a patriot's duty to uphold it:

If our own public Corporations buy American one cannot expect the rest of the world to buy British. There is therefore a need for reaffirmation by the Cabinet of the general policy . . . that the Corporations would be required to use British types; if need be at the cost of increasing subsidies.

He complained that there was 'an increasing tendency to claim that the British Corporations should be equipped with the best aircraft available at a particular time regardless of their country of origin . . .'.

. . . I suggest that the word 'British' in the titles of the Corporations should mean that their services are invariably operated with aircraft of British design and manufacture, unless it is agreed by the Ministers concerned that there are overwhelming reasons to justify an exception being made.

And so: 'If we have faith in the competence of the British aircraft industry to produce the goods, it is fair to ask the public Air Line Corporations to tolerate for a while the shortcomings inevitable during the aftermath of war. . . .'

There now slid into the debate that seductive word which figured so much in the discourses of the Foreign Secretary, the Defence Secretary and the Chiefs of Staff about Britain's global strategic role – 'prestige'. The United States and, in the present case, the American aircraft industry did not of course have to concern themselves with 'prestige' because they enjoyed it as an inevitable by-product of their power and success. For Britain and the British aircraft industry, neither of them powerful or successful, 'prestige' meant consciously keeping up appearances, like a businessman in financial trouble hanging on to his Rolls-Royce. Round this touchy question of 'prestige' now revolved the decision whether or not to buy nine Constellations for use on the Empire [sic] services and the North Atlantic.

On the one hand, according to a joint statement on 19 April 1947 by the Ministers of Civil Aviation and of Supply,

> the prestige of the British aircraft industry as a whole would be bound to suffer gravely from the decision to operate the main Empire routes with American aircraft (even if later to be powered with British engines); this would particularly tend to discredit the British interim types themselves, but the repercussions would be felt throughout the industry and earnings from exports . . . would be affected. . . .[27]

But on the other hand:

> there is a serious danger that the prestige and efficiency of our operators will suffer gravely if they have for long to compete on the Empire routes with planes which are slower and less economic than the Constellations flown by our American, Dutch, French and Australian competitors.[28]

When the Cabinet Civil Aviation Committee met to resolve this dilemma, the Minister of Civil Aviation was indelicate enough to display a sense of realism:

> What it came to was that if the Constellations were not purchased there would be no new aircraft, except the Tudors, likely to become available before the Brabazon I on the North Atlantic route and very little apart from the Tudors on the Empire routes, until the new types came into operation. *As a purely business proposition* [emphasis added] this complete lack of insurance against the possibility of failure of what were admittedly experimental types seemed to him most dangerous.[29]

The Minister of Supply, for his part, shrewdly chose to milk his colleagues' patriotic emotion:

in his view the proposal to purchase Constellations had nothing to commend it. It would mean a grave loss of prestige to the British aircraft industry as a whole and the effect of this on our export prospects and war potential could not fail to be extremely serious. It was no recompense for this loss of prestige to fit British engines in the Constellations. . . .

In his view the right course was to carry on our services with our own types of aircraft. The Tudor aircraft were by no means failures. These interim aircraft would bridge the gap until the Brabazon I and the other new types came into production and on every ground it seemed to be better to carry any loss which might result from their use, rather than to buy further Constellation aircraft and make it plain to the world that we had no confidence in our own industry, with all that that entailed.[30]

Roused by this patriotic bugle-call the committee duly recommended to the Cabinet that the Constellations should not be bought, and that the airlines should be required to make do with the British aircraft industry's stop-gaps until the delivery of its new types.[31]

This piece of ad-hockery did not resolve the fundamental conflict of interest between the nationalised airlines (and the Ministry of Civil Aviation) and the aircraft manufacturers (backed by the Ministry of Supply). In January 1948 the very procedure for ordering new airliners became a matter of dispute. Under the existing procedure, laid down by the Prime Minister in September 1946,[32] the Ministry of Supply bought aircraft on behalf of the airlines, although supposedly in close consultation with them about their requirements, and supposedly also on the basis of guarantees by the plane-makers about delivery dates and performance. This procedure had flown no better than the Tudor. The manufacturers had not been prepared to give guarantees – understandably enough. The airlines resented having to use the Ministry of Supply as a purchasing agent, and conducted a propaganda campaign against it.[33]

The Minister of Supply (now George Strauss) therefore proposed to the Cabinet Socialisation of Industries Committee that all say in the forward planning of aircraft requirements should be taken away from the airlines and vested in a new Civil Aviation Authority, while his ministry would continue to be responsible for actual development and production. The airlines' role would be restricted simply to operating services with whatever kind of aircraft they were given.[34]

But the Minister's arguments in support of this proposal only served unwittingly to confirm how little Britain's national aviation policy had to do with calculations of return on investment as compared with, say, investment in office machines and systems, or, for that matter, garden gnomes; little to do with coolly assessing whether the industry possessed the technical capability to beat its American rivals; in fact, little to do with any aspect of commercial reality:

> The cost of development of modern aircraft, particularly the medium and larger types, is very high and the development period protracted. The sums at risk are normally beyond the resources of the aircraft manufacturer, and the cost cannot be borne by the Corporations which have to aim at reducing their dependence on Government subsidy as soon as possible. . . .[35]

Then again:

> Because we are passing through a phase of rapid technical development work, the volume of aeronautical development work at the present time is high and every firm's design team has plenty of work. In such circumstances some form of central planning is necessary to ensure that all users of aircraft get their fair share of the design resources of the country, not only in quantity but in quality also, for the various teams are not of equal merit. . . .

If then the required investment was so enormous and the return so distant (and by implication so risky), and if the industry's R and D resources were so stretched, why was Britain pursuing the present policy? The Minister gave the answer:

> considerations affecting wider national interests than those of particular Corporations are involved in aircraft development and production. The maintenance of a healthy aircraft industry in peacetime on as big a scale as the demands on the public purse permit is of vital importance to national security, as is also the general advancement of aeronautical knowledge.[36]

Yet neither he nor any other supporter of Britain's aeronautical ambitions in this period cared to explain why it helped national security to load the development and large-scale manufacture of airliners on to an industry already overstretched by military orders.

Unsurprisingly the Minister of Civil Aviation found himself 'in complete disagreement' with his colleague's proposal.[37] As he told the Civil Aviation Committee, the question was 'essentially a commercial one. It was fundamental that the user should be free to obtain the type of aircraft that he required for the efficient conduct of his commercial operations, in competition with foreign airlines pursuing the same commercial objectives.'[38]

After much argument the committee recommended no change in the present procedure.[39] This decision hardly cured the basic drawbacks of the 'Fly British' policy in regard to the long-haul routes, which lay in the late delivery of 'interim' aircraft which were then found not to be commercially up to the job, and in rising doubts and receding delivery dates in respect of the models like the Brabazon supposed eventually to 'obtain supremacy'. In the meantime, it was now a year since BOAC had been condemned to operate its Empire routes with Lancastrians and Yorks, with the ludicrous consequence that in the four months ended December 1947 the airline had conveyed just 26 out of the 610 passengers travelling from South Africa to Britain – about one per aircraft. South African Airways had carried the rest in Skymasters.[40]

In spring and summer 1948 a 'battle of the air' therefore took place in Whitehall over 'The British Civil Aircraft Position' – future policy in general, but in particular whether or not to cancel some now highly dubious projects. The first prototype of the 'interim' Tudor II, for instance, had been completely destroyed in a crash, killing its designer.[41] With little prospect of Tudor IIs being delivered to BOAC in 1948, the Minister of Civil Aviation recommended on 11 March that the forty-three aircraft on order should be cancelled, at a cost of £3 million. The huge Saunders-Roe SR-45 flying-boat would be heavier than expected, requiring no fewer than ten engines. The estimated cost of three boats had risen from the original £2.8 million to between £4.5 and £5 million.[42] The SR-45 would also demand costly marine airports along its routes. Wrote the Minister of Civil Aviation, 'it now appears certain that the SR-45 could not be flown at a profit'.[43] He therefore recommended that the project should be cancelled, writing off the £850,000 already spent.

The Brabazon I, 'the only new British type under construction which is likely to be capable of North Atlantic operations',[44] had 'many specialised problems of its own', but had 'reached an advanced state of construction and should be flying this year'. So far some £6 million had been spent out of an estimated total for four aircraft of £17 million. 'The abandonment of the project at this stage', wrote the Minister, 'would thus mean writing off a very considerable sum when success may be within our grasp.' He reckoned that on balance the aircraft 'does hold out promise of both technical and commercial success', and that therefore work on the prototypes should go forward 'with all speed', with a production order for a further three aircraft if trials proved successful. 'In aiming high,' said he, 'risks must be taken.'

But were they justifiable risks, or yet more of the wishful-thinking, the delusions of aeronautical grandeur, that had misled British policy on civil aviation ever since the middle of the war? There were doubts about the Brabazon's range in the face of westerly winds, evoking speculation about in-flight refuelling by tanker aircraft, a novelty in regard to airliners. It was not even absolutely certain that the aircraft could operate economically at a competitive fare.[45] But it was the sheer technical problems that cast the gravest doubts over the Brabazon project:

(a) The systems for the power operated controls and the gust alleviating devices, on both of which the aircraft must depend, are as yet completely untried and break ground hitherto unexplored.

(b) The machine is many times bigger than anything the Bristol Aeroplane Company has undertaken before. The structural and aerodynamic problems, which have proved so much of a trial on smaller civil projects of more conventional aspect, may therefore be found to be greatly magnified in the Brabazon I.

(c) For commercial operation the aeroplane is to be powered with eight propeller turbine engines coupled in pairs. These engines have not yet flown in any aeroplane. Their fuel consumption, their reliability, their service life and their maintenance costs are therefore largely unknown factors.

(d) The pressurisation of so large a fuselage has not been achieved in this country up to the present.[46]

Despite such problems the Minister of Supply was, for his part, all in favour of continuing with the Brabazon project, 'having great confidence that it will turn out a success'.[47] He even put in a plea for the SR-45 flying-boat, not least on the score that 'abandonment of the enterprise after more than two years' work on it will certainly come as a shock to public opinion . . .'. As for the Tudor II, 'the effect of complete cancellation on the reputation of British aircraft (including the Tudor IVs and Vs remaining in operation) would undoubtedly be serious'. Could not a study be made of the question whether the problem of operating the aircraft on the South African and Australian routes might be solved by in-flight refuelling?

When the Civil Aviation Committee came to consider these topics on 8 April 1948, it had to face the fact that the 'Fly British' policy had fallen into a tail-spin. The Lord Privy Seal (Addison) observed that 'it was clear that we must continue to expect large deficits on the operations of the Corporations and the Cabinet should be furnished with an estimate of the losses entailed by the proposed aircraft programme'.[48] The Minister of Civil Aviation agreed that 'the outlook was a gloomy one, in some respects even gloomier than that outlined in his memorandum . . .'.

> Thus, it was already doubtful whether the Corporations would be able to maintain their present services within the maximum subsidy of £8m. payable in the current year.
>
> Fundamentally the trouble was that there was no single dependable British aircraft in sight for the Corporations. Even the success of the Brabazon I and the Comet was by no means assured, and he felt that we must expect serious public criticism in the next few years. In particular it would be difficult to escape criticism that we were continuing to produce types of aircraft which we knew from the outset could not even meet their direct costs of operation, let alone make a profit.[49]

Although the Minister of Supply for his part acknowledged that the situation over the next three to four years would be 'a difficult one', he nevertheless remained 'confident that once we were out of the interim stage of civil aircraft development we should be able more than to hold our own against foreign competition'.

The committee got no further than agreeing to draw the Cabinet's attention to 'the very serious situation', and calling for further studies.[50]

At the committee's next meeting on 17 June 1948 George Strauss, the new Minister of Civil Aviation, actually got to the point of recommending that the Cabinet should bail out of the 'Fly British' policy before it hit the ground. Even the Hermes IV on order was 'still an untried type' and had yet to make its first flight. To be successful the engines would have to deliver 20 per cent more power than the Hercules engine had so far achieved. 'In addition, stability and other problems revealed in the Hermes II prototype are not yet solved,' while the cabin air-conditioning system might be delayed.[51] He therefore urged that either twenty-two Canadairs (Canadian-built, Merlin-engined Douglas DC4s) or seventeen Constellations should be bought, and that a final decision be made to cancel the Tudor II.

Yet even now the Minister of Supply tried to save this dismal aircraft, reminding the Civil Aviation Committee that cancellation would entail writing off some £4 million, and would 'seriously damage the prestige and export prospects of the aircraft industry'.[52] Meanwhile the air correspondent of *The Times*, lost in the dream of a new British Empire of the air, was raving away on behalf of the British aircraft industry. He wrote that 'given the maximum drive and encouragement, and I mean maximum', the Brabazon and the SR-45 'will revolutionise civil aviation. There will be nothing in the world to approach them either in size, or comfort, or in advanced design. There will be no competition from the Americans, because they have nothing comparable on the stocks. . . .' With a gas-turbine Brabazon flying the Atlantic 'every country in the world, and certainly every airline operator, would want to fly British. . . . our prestige would soar.'[53] He therefore urged the Government: 'be British, think British, and stand up for British civil aviation. There is nothing we have to learn from other countries. We have the tools, the skill, the courage and "know how" to lead the world. . . .' No doubt these swelling emotions were shared by the man in pub or club at large.

Within Whitehall the debate also turned once more on the question of 'prestige'. The Minister of Supply told the Civil Aviation Committee that 'he would feel it necessary to contest as strongly as possible any departure from the "Fly British" policy . . .'.

He fully understood the desires of the Corporations to use the best and most economic aircraft which admittedly at present were mainly American in origin, but it was plain that the purchase of United States or Canadian machines would have a most serious effect on the prestige and prospects of the British aircraft industry.[54]

Therefore:

Having regard to the total outlay being incurred on behalf of civil aviation, which was of the order of £50m. per annum, it was his submission that an increase of 2% in the total in order to maintain the 'Fly British' policy was not excessive, and for the advantages it would give it was a very small price to pay.

But, as the Minister of State (Hector McNeil) pointed out,

the argument of prestige was not entirely on the side of maintaining the 'Fly British' policy without modification. There was evidence in the form of traffic statistics and of specific incidents that the continued use of interim British types was doing harm to the goodwill and the reputation of British manufacturers. . . .[55]

The Lord Privy Seal agreed: 'it must be borne in mind that the Corporations were losing money and traffic at a rate which was bringing British civil aviation into discredit'.[56]

Although the committee in the end duly agreed to recommend to the Cabinet that the Tudor II be cancelled and Canadairs be bought, the Minister of Supply continued to wrestle with the controls of the 'Fly British' policy, striving to keep it aloft. There was little to choose, he wrote, between Canadairs and Tudors and Hermes in speed and safety, and the British types were 'just as likely to attract passengers. The prestige argument is in favour of using them, not only from the point of view of the British aircraft industry but also of the British airlines themselves.'[57] He called for the 'Fly British' policy to be publicly reaffirmed, even if this meant bigger subsidies:

A case based not merely on patriotism but on convincing arguments of security, employment for our own workpeople, encouragement of British trade, and the maintenance of national prestige would place Civil Aviation in a better light in the public eye, while the benefits of a Socialist form of organisation which had enabled wider national interests than the profits of individual operators to be taken into account would be demonstrated.[58]

It was to no avail. On 30 June 1948 the committee decided to recommend that the Tudor order for BOAC should be cancelled in favour of Canadairs.[59]

However, British South American Airways continued to be handicapped by Tudors, in their case the Tudor IV. After one of them (the Star Tiger) vanished in flight on 31 January 1948, the type was withdrawn for exhaustive tests and not returned to service until August that year. But the disappearance of yet another Tudor IV in January 1949 led to its final abandonment, all outstanding orders being cancelled.

Nevertheless, the closing of this depressing chapter in the history of British aviation led only to further problems. How was the Tudor to be replaced? The only possible British contender was the untried Handley Page Hermes IV, of which twenty-five were on order for BOAC for Empire routes, although BOAC did not really want to fly it even on these services. The corporation (which took over British South American Airways after the Tudor débâcle) were even more reluctant to accept it for operation across the Atlantic. They doubted whether it would prove economic and they doubted whether Handley Page would live up to their promised delivery dates.[60] They wanted Boeing Stratocruisers. And Stratocruisers for the Atlantic routes they got.[61]

Henceforward the argument about 'prestige' and the 'Fly British' policy focused on the hoped-for world-beaters that were to replace the 'interim' types of airliner from 1950 onwards. Most prominent among these world-beaters was the Brabazon, although BOAC had long come to the conclusion that it would in fact prove a loss-making turkey. According to the Minister of Civil Aviation in January 1950,

they [BOAC] indicated some two years ago that they would be prepared to operate the Brabazon if required to do so, but would do so specifically on grounds of national interest, and would wish to be remunerated for doing so on a special basis which made it clear that the operation of the Brabazon should not be regarded as part of their normal commercial activities.[62]

Now BOAC's chairman, Sir Miles Thomas, could see a future for the Brabazon only as 'an experiment which must be pursued in the national interest . . .'.[63] In July the Minister of Supply had to report that, if a second prototype was to be completed, then the original estimates for two (£5.836 million) was likely to be exceeded by £2.264 million, making a total of £8.1 million in all. Over £2 million had already been spent on the design and construction so far of the second prototype.[64] 'The only choice', he wrote, 'is in fact between approving the extra expenditure and cancelling the project. . . .'

> To my mind it is unthinkable that we should drop the project now. So far the experiment has gone well. . . . The whole project has fired the imagination of the public and, along with the success of the Comet, the Viscount and our other new civil aircraft types, has increased our prestige abroad and cannot have been without its effect on morale at home.[65]

So the Brabazon project, powered by prestige and lifted by the imagination of the public, flew cumbersomely on. So too did the Saunders-Roe SR-45 project, which the Government had shrunk from killing in 1948.

It was in December 1950 that the postwar 'Fly British' programme finally crashed in a collision with reality. According to a joint report by the Ministers of Supply and Civil Aviation, the latest estimates of the joint costs of developing two Brabazon prototypes and three SR-45s stood at £19 million, of which £13.4 million had already been spent.[66] It was now clear that the SR-45 could not be economically operated on any route, while the Brabazon would lose about £1.47 million a year. Moreover, it appeared that the Comet with Rolls-Royce Avon jet engines would have the range to fly the North Atlantic, and do so more economically than either of the other two types.[67] The two ministers considered, therefore, 'that B.O.A.C. ought not to be required to operate either the Brabazon or the S.R.45 and we recommend that they should be relieved of any obligation to do so'.[68]

Yet this 'does not mean, however, that in our view either of these projects should be abandoned. On the contrary, we think, for a number of reasons, that they should continue. . . .' But, true to the original character of the 'Fly British' policy, not one of these reasons had to do with cost-effective investment. There was, for instance, the alleged value to aeronautical research in pressing on with two Brabazon and two SR-45 prototypes. Then again: 'Cancellation would have a serious effect on the Bristol Aeroplane Company, which are not only the constructors of the Brabazon, but the manufacturers of the Proteus engines required for the flying boats. . . .' Moreover: 'Cancellation would be damaging to our prestige. . . .'[69]

In a painful meeting that December the Civil Aviation Committee accepted the Minister's recommendations in regard to the Brabazon, but still deferred a decision about the SR-45 until the three service ministries and the Treasury should have pondered whether the flying-boat could have military value in the six-month-old context of the Korean War.[70]

Back in January 1950, and a week after the Prime Minister had announced that a general election would be held on 23 February, the Minister of Civil Aviation had provided for the benefit of his electioneering colleagues a survey of the progress of civil aviation while they had been in office. Although written at a time when 'Fly British' was already spiralling out of the sky, the survey failed coolly to reappraise civil-aviation policy on the basis of opportunity-costs and likely returns on investment. Instead the Minister clung on to the patriotic illusions which had originally inspired the wartime coalition's resolve to 'Fly British' after the war:

> the British aircraft manufacturing industry – essential in war and an important contributor to the export trade in peace – finds itself in a position of strength and promise which would not have been possible if our Corporations had been allowed to compete on equal terms with their competitors in the purchase of foreign aircraft. . . .
> The de Havilland Comet, the world's first four-engined jet airliner, has no rival in its striking advance on contemporary types. This aircraft has already considerably enhanced the prestige of the British aircraft industry and should place it in a position of undeniable leadership. [71]

Yet six months later, in a memorandum to the Cabinet Defence Committee on the 'Size and Shape of the Aircraft Industry – Need for Planning to Preserve War Potential',[72] the same Minister gave the lie to this pre-election bombast and indeed to the long-standing case that the airlines must fly British in order to preserve an industry vital to Britain's national security:

> The livelihood of the industry is obtained from three sources — orders for military aircraft required by the Services, export orders, both military and civil, and civil aircraft required by the Airways Corporations. Of these, orders for aircraft required by the Services are by far the most important, both in total value and in the degree of forward planning which they render possible. In the long run, the size and shape of the aircraft industry are determined by the nature and volume of Service requirements.

In fact, reported the Minister, out of the total annual value of the industry's production and repair work of £60 million, military contracts accounted for £49 million.[73] He went on to acknowledge, moreover, that the industry had been overstretched by the sheer number of separate projects loaded on to it; equally that the industry's resources were at present fragmented among too many firms (no fewer than nineteen).

Thus it had been in vain that the airlines' commercial interests had been sacrificed to the 'prestige' of the aircraft industry and the dream that the industry could 'obtain supremacy' over Douglas, Lockheed and Boeing. The fate of the airlines stands as a crowning example of the botch the Labour Government had made of nationalisation, its only tool for directly reconstructing industry.

And so whereas the Labour Government certainly *wished* to speed up technological change, it had nonetheless failed to create an effective accelerator and tread hard on it. Worse, it was at the same time applying powerfully effective brakes on such change.

PART FOUR

The Brakes on Industrial Change

the failure to press on with major schemes of industrial development is doing irreparable damage to the national economy, to our export prospects, and to production. . . .

(THE PRESIDENT OF THE BOARD OF TRADE,
MARCH 1948)

an excessive proportion of our resources were being devoted to exports at the expense of the vital re-equipment of the basic industries. . . .

(CABINET PRODUCTION COMMITTEE, JULY 1948)

It is clear that a very difficult problem faces a country such as ours, which wishes to maintain full employment and yet avoid the undoubted evils of rising prices at home and balance of payments difficulties abroad.

(THE CHANCELLOR OF THE EXCHEQUER,
DECEMBER 1950)

CHAPTER THIRTEEN

A Disastrous Choice of Priorities

FOR JAPAN under General MacArthur's viceregal rule and for West Germany under allied military government, economic recovery and total strategy came to one and the same thing, firstly because these countries were lucky enough to be forbidden foreign policy and armed forces by their conquerors in the Second World War, and secondly because any dreams of building some ideal society after the war had been brutally dispelled by national defeat.

It was otherwise with British total strategy, wherein economic recovery had to compete for priority with the double pursuit of the illusion of global power and the dream of New Jerusalem. This competition grew especially fierce in the wake of the sterling crises of 1947 and 1949, when the Government had to make drastic cuts in national expenditure. In consequence economic recovery never during the first five years after the war formed the *Schwerpunkt* of British total strategy, despite all the Cabinet's apparent anxiety to achieve that recovery and all the volumes of talk and paper devoted to it in Whitehall.

Moreover, the key to it, modernisation of Britain's equipment as an industrial country, had directly suffered from the pursuit of the world role. Thus in the autumn of 1948 the Cabinet Production Committee, in allotting the next year's rations of the inadequate national output of steel, agreed that:

> defence requirements should be met partly by a cut in the steel allotted for the domestic production of capital goods equivalent to the switch of man-power from the production of such goods to defence production and partly by a percentage cut applied equally to

all steel allocations, except . . . for direct exports of finished and semi-finished steel.[1]

Moreover, Whitehall was compelled to compensate for the strain laid by the world role on the precarious balance of payments by means of throttling back imports of foreign (especially dollar) machinery, steel and timber. According to the 1947 *Economic Survey*, for instance, import of a machine was permitted 'normally' only in cases where it was 'of essential importance and cannot be supplied in comparable conditions from United Kingdom production . . .'.[2] For similar reasons it was likewise standard policy to divert into exports British-made machinery which might have gone to modernise industry or infrastructure at home. In December 1947 a Whitehall report on the forthcoming British application for Marshall Aid urged: 'Insofar as there is a choice between exporting capital goods and using them for home investment, the need to achieve viability [that is equilibrium in the balance of payments] quickly will continue to make us lean towards exporting them as at present. . . .'[3] Pronounced the draft version of the 1948 *Economic Survey*:

> While there are undoubtedly cases, e.g., of certain capital goods such as mining machinery or railway wagons, where home requirements deserve precedence over exports, the onus of proof ought to lie with those who would claim that home demand is more essential than the demand for the imports for which the exports could pay. . . .[4]

From time to time ministers were vainly to vent their disquiet about such sacrifices. For instance, when in July 1948 the Production Committee was pondering recommendations for capital investment in 1949, some members expressed the view that 'an excessive proportion of our resources were being devoted to exports at the expense of the vital re-equipment of the basic industries . . .'.[5]

Yet the sharpest contrast between the place of economic recovery within British total strategy and its place within German or Japanese lay in the relative priority given to capital investment. Germany and Japan treated such investment as the *Schwerpunkt* not only of economic recovery, but even of total strategy itself. Britain treated such investment as the *Schwerpunkt* of neither. Whereas in 1948 the Government poured out some 15–16 per cent of gross national product on the double pursuit of the world role and New Jerusalem (see above, p. 164), it spared only some 13–14 per cent of GNP for gross fixed investment of all kinds (including housing). Despite the need to make good all the war damage and arrears of maintenance as well as modernise industry and infrastructure, this latter percentage was certainly no higher, and may well have been actually lower, than in 1938, when 14.5 per cent of GNP is recorded as having been devoted to gross fixed investment. It was also a miserably smaller percentage than the West German 1950 figure of 24 per cent of GNP.[6] In 1950 Britain invested a mere 9 per cent of GNP in new industrial plant and buildings – less than half the then German percentage of 19.04.[7] Yet the Labour Government persisted year after year in this disastrous choice of priorities even though ministers knew all too well how ramshackle and old-fashioned was so much of Britain's national equipment, beginning with infrastructure itself.

CHAPTER FOURTEEN

'Ludicrously Inadequate' – Investment in Infrastructure

THE SUCCESS of an industrial country competing for exports, like that of a campaigning army, depends first and foremost on logistics – that is, the capacity and efficiency of its ports and base depots, and of its lines of communication. In the latter case this means both vehicles and such fixed assets as roads, railways, bridges and telephone and teleprinter nets. In postwar Britain all these logistic resources were out of date and in poor repair, partly because of neglect inevitable during the war, partly because of previous decades of under-investment. Yet even modest programmes of maintenance, repair and modernisation were to be scrutinised to death year after year during the late 1940s in the name of rigid limits on public expenditure laid down by the Cabinet in its attempts to mitigate the financial overstretch caused by the world role and New Jerusalem. The result was a melancholy record of contrasts between what needed to be done and what was sanctioned to be done.

The roads, a primary logistic asset, serve as a particular case in point. Before the war Britain had failed to construct a single mile of motorway, preferring patchy improvements like bypasses to a network which essentially dated in configuration from the horse-drawn or even ox-drawn era.[1] When the trunk routes were surveyed in 1937, it had been found that on 85 per cent of their length the overall width was no more than 60 feet.[2] Nonetheless, the Ministry of War Transport had pronounced in 1943 against constructing an integrated motorway system after the war, even though a consulting engineer's report made clear that it cost no more to build a given length of motorway than to improve an existing arterial road, and that trucks could travel faster and at lower running costs on a motorway. In any case, in December

1943 a Treasury forecast of capital expenditure in the early postwar years allotted less to highways and bridges than had been spent in 1938.[3]

After coming into office in 1945 the Labour Government carried on this grudgingly cautious policy, with consequences spelt out in September 1947 to the new Investment Programmes Committee (of civil servants, set up in the wake of the sterling convertibility crisis to recommend cuts in investment). Although the trunk roads 'might appear to be in good condition', reported the man from the Ministry of Transport,

> owing to years of under-maintenance the 'crust' was extremely thin and in many cases there were cracks permitting rain to penetrate into the road bed. If there was another serious winter like the last there was a serious danger of many of the road surfaces giving way completely under heavy traffic. . . .[4]

Nevertheless, current spending on road maintenance stood at only 75 per cent of pre-war. As for new construction, the ministry had already decided to postpone fourteen projects ranging from bypasses to a Severn Bridge and a tunnel under the Thames at Dartford. Its present plans went no further than a handful of local improvements such as an extension to the Great West Road in London (the route to London Airport) and a new bridge to link Widnes and Runcorn, essential because the existing bridge was 'in such a bad state of repair'.[5] Essential or not, the Investment Programmes Committee decided to recommend to ministers that its construction be postponed.[6] Even a new tunnel at Jarrow 'to serve very important traffic to and from the shipyards on each side of the river [Tyne]' should, the committee decided, be constructed for cyclists and pedestrians only.[7] And the committee agreed that the general maintenance programme for the nation's roads should be cut from 75 per cent of pre-war to only 60 per cent,[8] for in their amateur opinion 'the dangers of postponing repairs or replacements can be exaggerated . . .'.[9]

The practical effects of thus paring down work on roads and bridges were spelt out to the IPC eight months later by the Ministry of Transport when it submitted its Road Investment Programme for the years 1948–52:[10]

there were heavy arrears to make up, and the surface of many roads was wearing so thin that unless some work could be done on them in the near future damage to the foundations was likely to result. Very much heavier expenditure would be required to make this good, than to carry out the maintenance necessary to prevent it. As it was, many of the main roads were not in a fit state of repair to take the vastly increased volume of traffic now using them, and the wear and tear caused by these vehicles was serious.[11]

The ministry had now put back construction of the new Widnes–Runcorn bridge as well as a Severn bridge to 1951–2. But no such delay was thought possible with the rebuilding of the bridge that carried the main road between Portsmouth and Southampton since it was 'in such a deplorable state'.[12] For the rest, the ministry's proposed programme for 1948–52 consisted of the familiar chopped *tagliatelle* of local trunk-road improvements, such as a bypass round Neath in Glamorgan. However, the IPC, while endorsing the Ministry of Transport's commendable sacrifice of major new projects, doubted whether the Widnes–Runcorn and Severn bridges could even be started by 1952; and it reckoned that maintenance of the roads in 1949 should be limited to the same quantity of materials as in 1948.[13]

It is therefore little wonder that when in July 1948 the IPC's recommendations came before the Cabinet ministers on the Production Committee, the Minister of Transport (Alfred Barnes) protested that the sums proposed for roads (and railways: see below, p. 260) were 'ludicrously inadequate'.[14] The allocation for roads 'was only sufficient for unavoidable work on strengthening road bridges and no new development would be possible'. In the face of this and other objections the Production Committee asked the IPC to think again. This it did next month within the context of rationing out the country's inadequate output of steel between all users. The Ministry of Transport wanted 21,000 tons for roads and bridges in 1949; the Investment Programmes Committee proposed 13,000. Groaned one Ministry of Transport representative to the committee:

A reduction of this order would, in the Ministry's view, have serious consequences – particularly in regard to bridges. Certain bridges in need of urgent attention carried essential traffic, e.g. heavy electrical gear, coal and export goods, and any breakdown would cause major difficulties. . . .[15]

A colleague emphasised:

the seriousness of the position regarding bridges and said that disquieting risks were being taken in certain instances – particularly where heavy and indivisible loads for the docks were subjecting road bridges to stresses which they were not designed to take. . . .[16]

The committee eventually settled for an extra 10,000 tons – to be shared, however, by ports (for which 5000 tons extra had originally been asked) as well as roads: in other words, 10,000 tons to meet a combined need of 13,000 tons.[17]

In December 1948 the Ministry of Transport was again pleading for more money for maintenance lest the road network should wear out, even proposing that in 1949 the volume of work should rise to 75 per cent of 1938–9, to 90 per cent in 1950 and 100 per cent in 1951 and thereafter.[18] Nonetheless, the ministry accepted that new construction would have to be limited to 'urgent public safety needs, restoration of essential communications (e.g. over a collapsed bridge), roads directly assisting production . . .'. There were, however, exceptions – related not to any major strategic route, but to the Government's attempt by means of regional policy to resuscitate the moribund Victorian industrial areas (see below, Chapter 17). In these areas of 'high unemployment' [sic] the ministry adopted 'less stringent criteria'.[19]

Plead as they might for more money to enable better maintenance as well as some modest new construction, the men from the Ministry of Transport proved once more out of luck. Whereas they had estimated the minimum necessary total investment for 1949 on roads and bridges at £67 million, the IPC now decided that a figure of £66 million already approved by ministers must stand.[20]

However, the worst was yet to come. In May 1949 the Ministry of Transport was reckoning actual expenditure that year at only £51.7 million, of which only £2.3 million was to be spent on improving strategic routes.[21] It asked for the budget to be increased to £65.3 million in 1950, £72.4 million in 1951, and even £76 million in 1952. But the IPC 'were unable to recommend an expenditure of more than £50 million in 1950. We do not expect that any increase will be possible either in 1951 or 1952. . . .' They accepted the inevitable consequence: 'It is clear that the list of projects for road improvements will have to be drastically cut.'[22]

In the autumn of 1949, in compliance with the cuts in public expenditure laid down by the Prime Minister in the aftermath of the balance of payments panic and the devaluation of sterling, the IPC still clung to its figure of £50 million for 1950, as against the £52.8 million asked for by the Ministry of Transport.[23] The ministry protested that in order to provide (within this reduced budget) a margin for 'vitally urgent' work in the interests of public safety it would either have to curtail general maintenance or cancel new projects already in hand.[24] When in November 1949 the matter (along with recommendations for cuts in future capital investment across the board)[25] floated up from the bureaucratic leg-men on the IPC to the Cabinet Economic Policy Committee, chaired by the Prime Minister himself, the Minister of Transport told his colleagues that 'he was advised that there was an imminent risk of widespread disintegration of the roads . . .'.[26] To no avail: the committee agreed that the IPC recommendations should be accepted, on the score that 'the roads seemed in general to be in a good state of repair, and it was often hard to see the justification, under present economic conditions, for some of the minor improvements carried out . . .'.[27]

It serves as a measure of the consequences of such relentless parsimony that at the beginning of 1950, nearly five years now after the end of hostilities in Europe, not even all the war damage to the road network had yet been repaired.[28] A representative of the Ministry of Transport reminded the IPC in January that if total investment on roads in 1950 'were kept at the level of £48.5 million already approved by Ministers, the standard of maintenance would be . . . equal to about 61.5 per cent of pre-war'.[29]

As for new construction, the ministry asked for the very modest sums of £4 million in 1951 and £9.5 million in 1952. These were amounts dwarfed by the £17 million spent in 1949 by local authorities on maintaining rural by-roads or suburban streets. Yet the divided structure of British government meant that no portion of the £17 million could be redeployed on strategically important routes; nor could this wasteful expenditure be easily curbed by Whitehall.[30]

In pleading for the £4 million and £9.5 million the Ministry of

Transport argued that these sums would make it possible to proceed (along with some other important local projects) . . .

> with work on the Dartford–Purfleet tunnel scheme, which was started about 12 years ago. There was at present equipment valued at £450,000 on the site, and this cost about £8,000 per year to maintain. Moreover, the shields to be used in this scheme were also needed for the Tyne and Blackwall tunnel schemes, and as they were expensive (£100,000 each) it was important to proceed with the work at Dartford as quickly as possible, thus releasing the equipment for the other projects. The Dartford–Purfleet tunnel scheme would cost about £5 million, spread over five years. . . .[31]

In the event, the first (single-carriageway only) bore of the Dartford Tunnel was not to be opened until November 1963.

When – a month before the outbreak of war in Korea, as it turned out – Cabinet ministers finally decided on capital investment programmes for 1951 and 1952, with priority to housing (see above, Chapter 8), the road network was allotted totals for all purposes of £49.9 million and £54 million for the two years respectively: in other words, only £1.4 million and £5.5 million more than approved for 1950, but some £5 million and £10 million less than the Ministry of Transport had requested.[32] In reluctantly accepting this decision the Minister of Transport delivered an epilogue on five years of a policy more make-do than mend:

> at the present time maintenance work on the roads was only 64 per cent of the pre-war rate, and if this policy were continued the foundations of the roads would deteriorate and higher capital investment would have to be undertaken in future years. Many bridges were in a poor state of repair and, if these collapsed, industrial transport would be seriously dislocated. . . .[33]

*

The railways, still the principal carriers of people and goods over long distances, still the principal means of moving bulk commodities such as coal and raw materials, had fared no better. Yet with a route layout and most of their fixed assets dating from the mid-Victorian age they stood in direst need of radical modernisation.

Before the war they had been starved of investment by the four private railway companies, their technological stagnation concealed but unredeemed by a handful of 'streamlined' expresses breaking records along specially cleared tracks. In 1939 Britain was equipped with neither electrified main lines like Switzerland and France[34] nor long-distance diesel traction like America and Germany. During the war the railways had nonetheless coped commendably with the massive overloading consequent upon Britain's total mobilisation and her development into a main base for a great American army and air force as well as British and Commonwealth forces. But the price had been paid in time-expired motive-power, coaches and wagons, and ill-maintained permanent way. Thus Britain entered peacetime with a railway system both obsolete and largely worn out.

However, postwar plans for the railways, as reviewed by the new Investment Programmes Committee in September 1947, focused exclusively on short-term needs such as making good arrears of maintenance or piecemeal improvements, to the neglect of any long-term strategy for modernising the system. No electrification of any main line was contemplated, but only of the route between Sheffield and Manchester, saving 100,000 tons of coal a year, and of the suburban line between London (Liverpool Street) and Shenfield, where the existing steam-hauled stock 'was in a shocking condition'.[35] On the Sheffield–Manchester route the existing Woodhead tunnels under the Pennines (built in 1845) would have to be replaced because they were 'so old they were in serious danger of collapsing . . .'.[36] On the busiest section of the electrified line between London and Brighton, the present mechanical signalling was fifty years old and unless it was replaced with colour-light signals, there would be 'a grave risk of accidents'.[37] These projects were approved by the IPC, but with the proviso that the installation of this new signalling was to be dragged out over six years, and the electrification of the Manchester–Sheffield line over five years instead of the planned four.[38]

The IPC proved just as restrictive with regard to engines and rolling stock. The railways needed 780 new locomotives a year in order to retire the aged and worn-out and catch up with wartime arrears of replacement: they were allowed 600 a year. They needed 4000 new coaches a year: they were allowed 1000. They needed 62,000 new wagons a year; they were allowed 48,000.[39]

As if the existing speed restrictions consequent upon wartime neglect of the permanent way were not enough, it was now even suggested to the same meeting of the IPC by some unidentified desk-driver fresh from his Whitehall footplate that savings could be made by lowering the standard of maintenance (and hence still further the speed of trains).[40] This, he reckoned, would also enable the railways' steel allocation to be cut. The Ministry of Transport representative successfully protested that to diminish maintenance standards would 'have a very serious effect on the freight capacity of the railways' by reducing the speed of all trains (thus increasing the time they occupied the line), quite apart from the danger of 'more frequent de-railments and accidents'. As for cutting the steel allocation, 'the effect on the railways' efficiency would be disastrous'.[41] The exchange serves to illuminate the gulf that existed between a hostile and technologically ignorant Whitehall establishment and those departments directly concerned with the dilapidated state of the country's infrastructure.

Given the IPC's refusal to sanction in full even essential repair and replacement programmes, it is hardly surprising that the railways still remained in deplorable shape when in the summer of the following year (1948) future investment programmes for 1948–52 came under discussion. No less than 40 per cent of the locomotives, 24 per cent of the wagons and 28 per cent of the coaches were more than thirty-five years old,[42] while poor maintenance of the track was in many places slowing trains to a cautious crawl. In the four weeks ending 12 June 1948 as many as 1000 expresses ran more than half an hour late.[43] The Ministry of Transport's suggested five-year programme of capital investment in the railways therefore allotted what it called 'the minimum essential expenditure' to the permanent way, arguing that 'in no circumstances could this be cut without increasing still further the delays on the railways, through the imposition of more speed restrictions, which were already causing enough trouble . . .'.[44]

It now turned out that one immediate effect of nationalising transport had been to derail the railways' forward thinking, for according to the ministry it was 'impossible at this stage to submit a detailed programme because the [Railway] Executive had not yet had time to formulate one'.[45] With perhaps unintended irony the IPC reported later to ministers: 'The programme of the British Railways is not closely related to possible changes in the volume of traffic to be handled or in the lengths of hauls and . . . still less to any long-term plan for the reorganisation of the transport system.'[46]

And so apart from 'major works' [sic] in connection with the new London satellite towns of Harlow and Stevenage, the Railways Executive (as the high command of the nationalised system had been inspiringly named) had in mind only local projects, such as finishing half-built carriage sheds and sidings at Willesden 'connected with the modernisation of Euston, for which no definite plan had yet been settled . . .'.[47]

When in June 1948 the IPC came to discuss the railways' programme,[48] it learned that it had proved impossible for the Ministry of Transport to arrive at a satisfactory draft 'owing to the inadequacy of the figures supplied by the British Transport Commission'. The IPC simply proceeded to throttle down future investment – 400 new locomotives in 1949 instead of the 500 requested; 1200 new carriages instead of 2000; 13,000 fewer new wagons than in 1948; no more steel and timber for track renewal than in 1948. As for building works and repairs in general 'austerity standards should be considered for another year . . .'[49]

These were the recommendations which along with the committee's road proposals earned the condemnation of the Minister of Transport in the Production Committee as 'ludicrously inadequate':

> the allocations proposed represented replacement rates of 2½ per cent for locomotives, 4 per cent for carriages and 3 per cent for wagons. The margin of safety for the railways was already dangerously narrow, and there was little reserve from which to meet a national emergency or the situation created by unduly adverse weather conditions. . . .[50]

Referred back to the IPC for further debate, the proposals raised a powerful head of steam in the representative of the British Transport Commission.[51] The railways, said he, were being asked to accept reduced output of coaches and wagons even though passenger traffic was expected to increase in 1950 by 10 per cent and freight traffic by 15 per cent. Any reduction in the planned requirement of carriages would be 'a particularly serious matter', given that there was a shortage of 6000 compared with pre-war. It would be likewise impossible to increase the number of locomotives 'to the level required for satisfactory operation'. The suggested rations of material for maintenance would make it impossible to overtake arrears on the permanent way, with 'indefinite continuance of speed restrictions imposed on safety grounds'. It would also be impossible to keep up the general programme of building and maintenance of buildings, or to carry out 'new signalling and communications projects which were vitally necessary on grounds of safety'.

His plea eventually won an extra 40,000 tons of steel for the railways in order to 'avoid drastic cuts in the building and maintenance programme'.[52] But this still left them 60,000 tons short of their needs. So when in February 1949 investment for 1950–2 came up once again before the IPC, the railways continued to offer a picture of decay palliated by the makeshift. According to the spokesman of the Railways Executive, the cuts in steel had meant that 'old wagons had been patched up uneconomically in money and materials and this would result in a delay in the efforts to get a more reliable and economical wagon stock'.[53] The number of speed restrictions was 'still about 25 per cent higher than pre-war', owing to shortage of steel for the permanent way. 'The signalling position was still serious . . .':

Apart from renewals, required on a large scale in many places, there was a good deal to be done in modernising the signalling system, e.g. by substituting coloured lights for semaphores, which were better for safety, particularly in fog. . . . As far as structures were concerned many of the stations required a lot of attention. . . .

As for the one major project of main-line modernisation, the Manchester–Sheffield–Wath electrification scheme, work 'had not been going ahead very quickly, but it could be accelerated when the skilled labour was released from the Shenfield scheme in the autumn of 1949 . . .'.[54]

In submitting to ministers in May 1949 its recommendations for national capital investment in 1950–2, the IPC acknowledged:

Heavy investment is needed by the railways partly to maintain and renew the very large amount of existing equipment; partly to take advantage of new developments and reduce operating costs; and partly to make up for arrears incurred during the war. . . . A long-term programme is essential if investment and re-organisation are to yield the greatest benefit. . . .

But this seeming enlightenment was swiftly betrayed when the committee proceeded to cut the British Transport Commission's proposals for capital investment in 1952 by a quarter.[55] The BTC had actually had the temerity to propose investing about the same as had the railways in the best of pre-war years. As the IPC sagely pointed out: 'The maintenance of such a level of investment would go far beyond merely preserving the present equipment of the railways, which, despite difficulties, is more than adequate to carry the traffic coming forward.'[56]

On this present scene of slow, late, dirty and overcrowded passenger trains, of freight trains often still made up of individually hand-braked four-wheeled wagons, and of antique local goods-yards and crumbling engine-sheds and stations, there descended in the autumn of 1949 the new curse of the Government's drastic cuts in capital investment in the wake of the devaluation of sterling. In the case of the railways the cut amounted to 10 per cent in money terms, but, taking into account rising costs, 18 per cent in real terms.[57] Given that there was, according to the oral evidence given to the IPC in October 1949 by the Railways Executive, 'practically no inessential work' in the existing programme, what could be cut? Not coaching stock, which 'fell below the minimum requirements of ordinary travel'.[58] Not wagons, for large numbers of 'very old wagons had been taken over from private owners and they were so old that they should be scrapped.' There were at present 168,000 wagons over forty years old and 'resources would either have to be put into maintenance of these or into new wagons . . .'.

The cuts must therefore fall partly on the programme for new locomotives, but 'chiefly upon plant and machinery and new physical works' such as the completion of the new carriage shed and sidings at Willesden. Postponements could include:

> the reconstruction and widening [of the main east-coast line] at Potters Bar, the introduction of colour signalling at York and the resignalling at Newcastle, as could also the replacement of glass in station roofs. These and many other pressing needs would have to be postponed if the programme was to be cut.[59]

But in November 1949 the ministers on the Economic Policy Committee, while acknowledging that 'the position of the railways was clearly very difficult . . .', took the general view that the savings proposed on the rail and road programmes (of £3.5 million) 'did not seem disproportionate in relation to the total reduction needed'.[60]

Five months later the IPC, in pondering afresh the general topic of capital investment in 1951 and 1952, took note that much of the railways' present fleet of locomotives was 'out of date and inefficient', and that the state of wagons was 'so poor' that twice as many had to be scrapped in 1948–50 as had been built. The committee therefore generously conceded that there was 'a strong case for an increase in investment on the railways', so that they could better adapt to the changing needs of industry.[61] Yet its recommended totals (to include the London Underground) came only to £86 million in 1951 and £89 million in 1952, which compares miserably enough with the £111 million and £119 million reckoned essential by the Ministry of Transport a year before.[62] Nevertheless, the IPC's recommendations were confirmed when in May 1950 ministers finally opted to sacrifice productive investment to housing in 1951 and 1952.[63]

In what condition, therefore, had government policy left the national railway system, this key logistic asset, five years after the end of the war in Europe? According to a Ministry of Transport representative on the IPC in February 1950,

> There was a great deal of work to be done. A very high proportion of railway bridges and tunnels were between 80 and 100 years old, and the next few years would be a critical period for these structures, and much rebuilding was necessary. A further difficulty . . . in restricting capital investment was that of keeping the staff contented. They were very dissatisfied with the condition of many railway structures, which were probably the worst in any industry. . . .[64]

His colleague from the Railways Executive pointed out:

> Most of the expenditure on . . . stations and buildings was on day-to-day maintenance repairs . . . absolutely necessary to keep premises weather-tight and in fair condition for use by staff and passengers. The remainder, about one-quarter of the total, was on the replacement of roofs and roof structures, where the condition had deteriorated to such an extent that repairs and patching were no longer possible or economical.[65]

This was at a time, it must be remembered, when vast construction works using large quantities of steel had gone ahead on the new British Middle East military base in the Suez Canal Zone and on Bevin's pet scheme for another base in Kenya (see above, Chapter 5).

As for locomotives, although the pre-war replacement life of thirty-three and one-third years had now been extended to forty years, the current annual production of 290 new ones permitted by the investment programme was far short of meeting the need for replacements, since in the opinion of the Railways Executive even 400 a year would not suffice. In the case of wagons, so vital for the movement of fuel, raw materials and export goods, there was now a deficit of 87,000, equal to 10 per cent of the entire fleet – 'an exceedingly serious position'.[66]

In short, in the laconic words of a Ministry of Transport spokesman at that February 1950 IPC meeting: 'There was no doubt that the railways were in poor shape, and a great deal of urgent work ought to be undertaken.'[67]

Much the same could have been said about the national telecommunications net in 1950, which had likewise suffered for five years from Whitehall's grudging of capital investment. In September 1947 the Post Office, faced with the requirement (in the wake of the sterling convertibility crisis) to cut its capital expenditure, had explained to the new IPC 'the magnitude of the Post Office's problems'.[68] In the first place, the total waiting list for telephone lines stood at 450,000 compared with 300,000 a year earlier. Nevertheless, observed the Post Office, investment could be economised by the simple expedient of not providing new lines to would-be subscribers, thus reining back the growth of local traffic. This was, however, no answer to the need for new long-distance cabling: 'unless the whole system was to become completely inefficient the trunk lines had to be kept up with demands . . .'. Then again, telephone exchanges and their equipment in the London area were thirty to forty years old and 'becoming almost impossible to work'. If, as was being mooted in the IPC, expenditure on new kit was held down to £6 million per annum for two years in order to release production for export,

> it would [argued the Post Office representative on the committee] take a further five years afterwards to overtake the arrears of work on

the telephone system and make it equal to the demands upon it. It should be clearly understood that in diverting so large a proportion of telephone equipment to export, the efficiency of the Post Office telephone system was being mortgaged for years ahead.[69]

But the IPC stuck to its limit of £6 million in 1948 for new telecommunications equipment, and with equal severity recommended that the parallel building programme should be limited to £1.5 million, a mere quarter (in real terms) of expenditure in 1937.[70] So when the IPC in the summer of 1948 pondered national investment programmes for 1948–52 the waiting list for telephones still stood at 450,000. Under the Post Office's own modest proposals for future expenditure on new equipment (£5.5 million in 1949–50 and 1950–1, and £7.5 million in 1951–2 and 1952–3) this waiting list was expected to rise to a peak of 520,000 in 1949.[71]

At the same time an increase of 60 per cent in long-distance calls since the war was further straining the capacity of exchanges and trunk cabling. The IPC thereupon approved the Post Office's intention to concentrate on 'relieving the overloaded exchanges in big cities and changing over manual exchanges to the automatic system . . .'.[72] Indeed, the committee endorsed the Post Office programme as a whole because it was 'realistic and will not do much more than maintain necessary communications . . .'.[73] Thus there was little early prospect of Britain being equipped with a first-class modern network. Instead it would remain in terms of telecommunications as it was in 1948, a backward country, with only 8.5 telephones per 100 of the population compared with 22 in the United States, 19 in Sweden, 15.5 in New Zealand and 14 in Denmark.[74]

A year later, when Whitehall was carrying out its second drastic lopping of capital investment (in the aftermath of the devaluation of sterling), the IPC again patted the Post Office on the back for 'making a very real effort to restrict their level of investment . . .'.[75] It was therefore let off with a cut of only £1 million on top of the £1.5 million already lopped off its stated requirement in the previous May. But that 'very real effort', coupled with Whitehall's own clenched fist on spending, would, as the IPC acknowledged in its report to ministers, 'cause serious difficulties and will probably mean that the telephone waiting list lengthens to over 675,000 by the end of the year'.[76] That the telecommunications system was going to fall further and further behind demand, as well as becoming relatively ever more decrepit and out of date, became grimly apparent in January 1950, when the IPC began its discussions of investment in the years 1951 and 1952:

> it was clear that the normal programme of Post Office development would suffer if [its] total capital investment had to be restricted to £44 million (1950 level). The waiting list for telephones was now 550,000 compared with the gross number of new lines installed in 1948/49 of 268,000 and 340,000 in 1949/50. After allowing for cessations, net installations were 116,000 and 155,000 in 1948/49 and 1949/50 respectively. The new annual demand was for 300,000 lines. The pre-war waiting list for telephones was about 5,000, i.e. it took about a week to have a telephone installed. Today, the delay was anything up to 18 months. It was estimated that, after allowing for consequential capital expenditure, it might cost as much as £100 million to wipe out the waiting list completely.[77]

But:

> If the Post Office capital investment were restricted to £44 million in 1951/52 the number of new telephone lines installed would be 55,000 compared with 116,000 in 1948/49, and if this policy were pursued in the following year, the net number of new lines installed would be 13,000; this programme would in view of the large percentage of new applicants for business purposes be unacceptable to the Post Office.[78]

The London Trunk Exchange, the hub of the whole network, would 'shortly reach capacity despite various alleviating devices . . .' because the traffic was growing so fast. It was therefore now necessary 'to mechanise the handling of a large part of trunk traffic'.[79]

Indeed, as the Postmaster–General acknowledged in the House of Commons in April 1950, adequately to develop and modernise the British telecommunications system would require for a period of eight years some £8 million annually over and above the 1950 provision of £44 million.[80] The very minimum for all Post Office investment in 1951 and 1952, the IPC was told, must be programmes of £45.5 million and £48 million respectively. But in May 1950 the Minister of

State for Economic Affairs (Gaitskell), in drafting proposals for national investment across the board in 1951–2, allotted the Post Office no more than £44 million and £47.5 million. When the Cabinet Production Committee met on 25 May to make the final decisions, the Assistant Postmaster-General fought as best he might against these cuts, pointing out to his colleagues that of the 500,000 applicants now on the waiting list for telephones as many as 100,000 represented 'urgent business requirements'. If a 4 per cent cut were imposed, 'there would be a further delay in meeting commercial needs for telephones . . .'.

The Production Committee relented, and upped Gaitskell's suggested figures by no less than, yes, £0.5 million each year.[81] The £44.5 million now to be invested in the national telecommunications and postal network in 1951 may be compared with the £50 million being cast annually into the bonfire of the 'Fly British' policy, partly in subsidies to 'socialised' airlines condemned to use unprofitable British aircraft and partly to the aircraft industry for its development work on such wonders as the Brabazon.

And so five years after the end of the war in Europe those businessmen lucky enough to possess a telephone line would have to continue hanging on patiently while their calls braved the hazards of worn-out 'strowger' electro-mechanical exchanges, hard-pressed operators in unmechanised trunk exchanges, and overloaded long-distance cabling. As for the unfortunate 100,000 businesses on the waiting list, the Production Committee's decision signified an indefinite future of popping out to the nearest call-box with a handful of shillings and pennies, and preferably an umbrella.

To an island industrial economy the ports serve as do gates to a factory: through them are brought in components and raw materials, and through them are sent out finished products to the markets of the world. But if those gates prove too narrow, or are kept partly shut (and sometimes entirely shut) by bloody-minded gatekeepers,[82] so impeding this free flow in and out, then production and cash-flow must suffer. It was therefore a crucial disadvantage for Britain that almost all her major commercial docks dated in layout and construction from the Victorian era; that their machinery was often hardly more modern; and that much the same was true of the mentalities of their management and trade unions.[83] Moreover, the ports of London, Liverpool and

Southampton had suffered badly from bombing (although only to a fraction of the extent that had Hamburg), with up to two-thirds of their sheds and warehouses destroyed or damaged.

Here then was an outstanding case for a programme of radical reconstruction – perhaps even for a new 'green fields' port designed for the future, like Europoort on the Maas near Rotterdam, begun in 1960. The IPC indeed acknowledged in July 1948 how much needed to be done:

> There has been a substantial increase in the size of ships with the result that it is necessary to construct new dock entrances, deeper quays and even new docks to accommodate such vessels adequately. As the trend of shipping design is towards larger cargo vessels there is no doubt that work for these purposes must be undertaken before long.[84]

Yet in the previous September the committee had itself recommended postponing various major projects on the score that 'they would not produce early returns'.[85] Instead they had sanctioned only piecemeal improvements such as new transit sheds at Bristol, Glasgow and London, to a total cost of £3.5 million.[86] Now in the summer of 1948 they advised ministers that investment in the next year must be kept down to a steel allocation of 50,000 tons. This was much the same as in 1948, and amounted to two-thirds of what the Ministry of Transport thought 'essential', and about half of what it thought 'desirable'.[87] Echoing their recommendations of September 1947 the IPC pronounced: 'Resources should be concentrated on those schemes which promise quick and certain returns in the shape of improved turn-round.'[88] Never was the endemic short-termism of postwar British industrial policy more plainly stated.

In November 1948 the Cabinet Production Committee settled for investing £17 million in British ports in 1949 – £11 million on construction and £6 million on plant.[89] According to their guesstimate, this total would amount to £2 million more than in 1948. But five months later, when the IPC came to make recommendations for capital investment across the board in 1950–2, it was reckoned that only £9.5 million had been invested in ports in 1948 instead of £15 million; that only £13.5 million would be spent in 1949 instead of £17 million. Yet the port of Liverpool alone – 'the most congested port in the country'[90] – had suffered war damage amounting to over £13 million.[91] In Hull and Southampton two-thirds of the war damage was still awaiting repair. In addition, the need to modernise the ports was becoming ever more urgent with each year of neglect. According to the IPC in May 1949, as briefed by the Ministry of Transport,

> About 24 per cent of the British merchant fleet now consists of ships of more than 6,000 tons gross as compared with 14 per cent in 1939 and a number of very large tankers (of about 30,000 tons deadweight) are now being built. This trend calls for new dock entrances, deeper quays and even new docks.[92]

To speed up the turn-round of ships in British ports would also require a 'large amount' of mechanised handling equipment to supplement or replace the muscles of the flat-capped. The Ministry of Transport therefore proposed that capital investment should be pushed up to £18.8 million in 1950, £19.8 million in 1951 and £21.3 million in 1952.[93] But the IPC, although acknowledging that the programme 'covers important needs and there is a strong case for carrying it out', sliced a third off the figure for 1950, and a fifth off those for 1951 and 1952.[94]

When only four months later, in September 1949, the IPC was wielding its salami-knife again in the wake of sterling devaluation, it sought to cut the Ministry of Transport's latest request of £16.9 million for 1950 down to £14 million.[95] The Chairman of the nationalised Docks and Inland Waterways Executive (Sir Robert Letch) argued that in the case of many specific schemes for modernising Britain's docks, 'unless approval was given, war damage due to the war [sic] and obsolete equipment would impede trade even at the present level; as regards obsolescence, for example, virtually no capital works had been undertaken by the former owners of Hull Docks for 40 years . . .'.[96]

The argument crawled on from meeting to meeting into 1950, with the IPC actually trying to cut £500,000 off its own previous figure of £14 million for that year.[97] When in April the IPC drew up its recommendations to ministers for capital investment in the later years of 1951 and 1952, it allotted the ports £16 million for each year – some £2 million less annually than asked for by the Ministry of

Transport.[98] The IPC noted that 'a large part of the proposed expenditure . . . would consist of works carried over from previous years', such as an oil terminal on the Manchester Ship Canal, the Canada Dock at Liverpool (the gates of which the IPC had known for two years to be in danger of collapse) and a new Union Castle terminal at Southampton.

Here is a tacit acknowledgement that after five years of peacetime Britain had still failed to equip herself with a single port comprehensively up to date in layout and equipment. Yet in May the Cabinet Production Committee endorsed the recommendation of the Minister for Economic Affairs (Gaitskell) that even the IPC's suggested meagre rations of investment for the ports should be further cut by 4 per cent in 1951 and 1 per cent in 1952.[99]

In the meantime the archaic layouts, tackle and working systems of British ports, their reliance on legs and biceps, continued to provide the perfect habitat for the docker, the stevedore, the tugman, the bargeman, the lighterman and the comporter, and their bizarre, time-hallowed demarcations and restrictive practices. It is sadly certain that even had the Government invested more in modernising the ports, and especially mechanising their operations, the effect on efficiency would have been stultified by the obdurate resistance of the flat-capped to any change in their familiar habitat. This is clear from those cases where employers already had attempted to introduce new machines. When a stacker-truck requiring two operatives was introduced in the London docks to do the work of three existing gangs of seven men each, it led to stoppages until the employer agreed to keep the three gangs on his payroll.[100] For the flat-capped were resolved that if and when they were made redundant by machines they were going to be unemployed in the docks on full pay rather than on the street corner on the dole. In April 1950 the *Financial Times* reported the President of the Glasgow Chamber of Commerce as saying in regard to the handling of ore cargoes on Clydeside: 'They [new ships] have the very finest machinery for the handling of ore, but meantime the dockers insist that the same number of men should be employed as in the old-fashioned ships, which means that in a gang of eight to twelve men only two do the actual work.'[101]

According to the report of a Working Party on Increased Mechanisation in British Ports, published on 26 May 1950, union representatives 'have told us that they are not prepared, except in certain circumstances, to depart from the present arrangements which call for certain numbers of men to be employed on stated tasks'.[102] In regard to cases where men were paid for doing nothing while the machine did the work, the report said: 'We have been informed that this is the only method in which machinery can be used without causing disputes and stoppages.'

Thus with the ports, as with so much of the British industrial system, successful modernisation depended not just on investment in new plant, but on the extinction of a primitive industrial tribe ill-fitted for the technological future. In the meantime, however, the ports remained creaking drawbridges, prone to be closed at the instant caprice of disgruntled guardians, rather than power-operated gates. But in any case, the Britain of the late 1940s was short enough of power, for the energy industries too were victims of the Labour Government's repeated squeezing of investment.

CHAPTER FIFTEEN

'The Spotlight Has Always Been on Coal'

A FTER THE AUDIT of Britain's energy supplies so ruthlessly carried out by the great freeze of 1946–7 – tiny domestic rations of ill-burning coal, barely enough gas pressure to keep air out of the mains, widespread electrical black-outs – the Government hardly needed to be convinced that here was a field demanding investment on the grand scale, and above all in electricity generating plant. For it was the power-cuts, plunging shops and houses into darkness and paralysing factory machines, that had most painfully and publicly demonstrated the nation's shortfall in energy. The failure was the more glaring because electricity supply was no worn-out, time-expired first-industrial-revolution survivor like the railways or the docks, but twentieth-century technology's prime mover.

In the coming years ministers and their bureaucratic advisers were therefore to greet proposals for vast investment in new power stations and transmission lines with a financial sympathy accorded to no other industry except perhaps aircraft manufacture or the nuclear pro-gramme. Rather, their cavils were to be evoked by the sheer size of the demand for steel and by the tangles, delays and shortfalls in the process of constructing and commissioning new power stations, which by the end of 1947 was taking an average of three years.

In the autumn of that year, with the memory of the power-cuts still smarting, the Ministry of Supply (responsible for the electricity industry) planned to install enough new generating capacity by 1951–2 to ensure 'a substantial surplus above demand'.[1] The programme was ambitious: 1150 megawatts extra in 1948, 1600mw in 1949, and 2000mw annually in 1950–2. In October 1947 the Investment Programmes Committee blessed the targets for 1948 and 1949 but judged those for 1950–2 to be unrealistic because of 'the enormous quantity of steel required'.[2] Instead the committee recommended lower, if still ambitious enough, targets of 1500 extra megawatts annually.[3]

However, by the start of 1948 the programme was already being short-circuited by industrial inefficiency. For whereas the manufacturers of the turbines had delivered to schedule, the building side had fallen far in arrears.[4] In consequence it was now reckoned that new capacity in 1948 would amount to less than 1000 megawatts (in fact, it turned out to be only 562mw), and in 1949 to less than 1200mw. Meanwhile there was the problem of what to do with the surplus machinery – should it be stored or could it be diverted to other projects? These options were pondered in vain by a group of Whitehall brains which had been convened specially in April 1948 to discuss how to sort out the generating programme as a whole. A third option was discarded on the score that 'there was little chance of selling any of it [the machinery] abroad, since all production for export was to particular specifications'.[5]

After the Minister of Fuel and Power (Gaitskell) reported to his ministerial colleagues on the Production Committee about this woeful disarray on 2 July 1948,[6] there followed the standard Whitehall expedient – a steering committee, which in turn set up a working party. The latter then examined the generating programme power-station by power-station. Its melancholy conclusions were conveyed to the Production Committee by Gaitskell at the end of November:

> the original estimates of new power station construction were not based on any realistic application of what was possible and were consequently far too high. Until now, no-one has worked out in detail with the various manufacturers and constructors what is likely to be achieved in the year ahead.[7]

However, it appeared that this was not the only reason for the shortfall, and that also responsible was the inadequate output of skilled personnel by the British education and training system, so familiar a factor in Britain's poor wartime industrial record:[8] 'Delays – in some cases considerable – were caused through a shortage of design and drawing office staff and this meant that orders and contracts were not always placed in time to secure proper phasing of the various stages of construction. . . .'[9] Then again, before the nationalised British Electricity Authority was set up, each local undertaking had placed its own contracts, without any central co-ordination or engineering standardisation.[10]

Unfortunately, such direct means of boosting the supply of power-station equipment as importing boilers from Germany and Belgium (a suggestion proffered in the Production Committee)[11] or switching British production from exports was ruled out because of the fragility of the balance of payments. Although about 30 per cent of the generating industry's output was exported, much of it to Common-wealth countries, this was, according to Gaitskell, essential in order 'to secure increased production of dollar earning and dollar saving food and materials'. He therefore reported himself satisfied that 'no reduction in these exports is possible . . .'.[12]

Already, in July 1948, the IPC, in submitting its recommendations to ministers on capital investment in 1949, had had to take note that earlier glowing hopes of a surplus of 890 megawatts over peak demand in 1952 had now dimmed into a darker prospect of a deficit of 295 megawatts:[13]

> Given sufficient steel the generating plant required . . . can be produced, and all the plant required up to the middle of 1951 is already under construction.
>
> But the other parts of the programme are badly out of phase. The building programme has lagged far behind the plant programme, and generating stations will not be ready to house a substantial amount of plant which is due to be completed in 1949–50. . . . Delay in making buildings ready is further increased by the fact that the supply of boilers, which have to be built into the stations, has also fallen behind that of generating plant.[14]

The IPC noted that the newly nationalised British Electricity Authority was planning to boost the programme to 1750 megawatts of new capacity annually by 1952 'in order to make up ground lost in earlier years'. This would call for the huge total of 800,000 tons of steel in 1949 (150,000 tons more than in 1948), and an average total of 650,000 tons a year thereafter.[15] The IPC opined that 'an increase of this order could not be met unless further cuts were imposed on other very important programmes, which have already been severely limited in the recommendations made elsewhere in this report'.[16] It therefore proposed that the programme be held down to 1300 megawatts of new capacity annually. But ministers, still politically wincing at the memory of the 1947 winter, chose to raise this figure to 1500mw.[17]

When in January 1949 the British Electricity Authority, its ambitions unabated, sought approval to invest in 1600 megawatts of new capacity in 1951 and 1800mw in 1954 (as against the 562mw actually installed in 1948), the IPC 'generally agreed that the capacity covered by the programme was, in fact, needed, but there was some doubt as to whether, in practice, the marked increase in capacity for the latter years could be maintained'.[18] However, Sir John Hacking, Deputy Chairman of the British Electricity Authority, glibly assured the committee that there would be no problem in the delivery of turbo-alternators, while Germany could furnish 'good quality supplies of boiler tubes and high-pressure piping' if British industry failed to deliver enough. The one likely bottleneck, he admitted, lay in boilers[19] – as the event was to prove.[20]

In its report to ministers in May 1949 on capital investment in 1950–2[21] the IPC unkindly pointed out that the new generating capacity actually installed in 1948, at 562 megawatts, hardly offered promise that a programme of 1600mw in 1951 and 1800mw in 1952 could be achieved. It reckoned that 1500mw annually was the practicable limit, and even this depended on 'optimistic assumptions about the boiler manufacturers' ability to step up output . . .'.[22] It therefore recommended capital investment in the industry of £113 million in 1950 (enough to provide 1500mw of new capacity) and £140 million in 1952, as against BEA's bids of £125 million and £156.8 million.[23] In the post-devaluation round of cuts in autumn 1949, the electricity programme for 1950 suffered further amputation of £10 million.[24]

It was not merely the sheer scale of BEA's plans that brought on frissons of anxiety in the IPC. For in the committee's own words, it was 'by no means clear that the difficulties of managing so large and complex a programme had yet been mastered . . .'; or, to put it in less Jeevesian language, the committee feared that the non-adjustable muddles already perpetrated were all too likely to be repeated, thanks to the dismal professional calibre of the various responsible managements. The fear was to be borne out in the event: when the committee in April 1950 submitted its recommendations for capital investment in

1951–2 it took note that only 700mw of new capacity had actually been installed in 1949 as against a target of 1100mw.[25]

By now even the British Electricity Authority, under the cumulative shocks of reality, had abated its ambitions, only requesting future capital investment enough to add 1016mw extra capacity in 1951, 1052mw in 1952, and 1349mw in 1953. As the IPC drily observed, 'the new rate of commissioning is based upon the probable capacity of the industries concerned . . .'.[26] What was more, the IPC was relieved to report to ministers,

> We have been informed that the progress of building and civil engineering work is now effectively co-ordinated with that of plant installation and that the two sides of the programme are likely to be kept in balance in the future. Boilers and ancillary equipment are now the main shortage limiting the increase in generating capacity. . . .[27]

Nevertheless, the IPC, now becoming more and more alarmed about the impact of national investment as a whole on inflation already stoked by 'full employment' (see below, Chapter 18) and by high government expenditure on defence and New Jerusalem, blenched at the 'great cost' of the programme submitted by BEA and the Ministry of Supply. It therefore chopped 7.5 per cent and 6.6 per cent off the ministry's figures for 1951 and 1952 respectively,[28] recommending that to the end of 1955 the maximum annual new capacity should not exceed 1400mw. But a penalty would have to be paid – as late as the winter of 1954–5, it was reckoned, Britain would suffer a deficit of 1090mw below peak demand, while the amount of electricity produced by plants more than twenty years old would rise to nearly treble the 1949 figure.[29]

Yet even so the Minister of State for Economic Affairs, Hugh Gaitskell, in making his final recommendations to his ministerial colleagues for capital investment in 1951 and 1952 pared another 4 per cent and 1.4 per cent off the IPC's figures.[30] In vain did the Minister of Fuel and Power (now Philip Noel-Baker) protest to the Cabinet Production Committee that 'increased efficiency in manufacturing industry depended very largely on increased utilisation of electricity . . .'.[31] By way of a valediction on the last five years of shortfalls in equipment supplies and inept management, the Minister wistfully added: 'But unless generating capacity could be expanded, load-spreading and load-shedding would have to continue for a long time to come.'[32]

What to do in the meantime? Perhaps, thought the IPC, the demand for electricity might be relieved and the burden on the electricity programme thereby reduced if more British meat rations could be roasted by gas, more British bodies washed in gas-heated water, and more British living-rooms warmed by gas-fires.[33]

The pride of the British gas industry in 1945 was 'the largest gasworks in Europe' (as proclaimed its then owner, the Gas Light and Coke Company) on the bank of the Thames at Becton in east London. This technological marvel had been laid out in 1874, and much of its basic gas-making equipment was still of that vintage, at least in design, complete with horizontal retorts into which sweating men shovelled coal from the piles on the retort-house floor. At the other end of the scale were numerous tiny small-town works where, myth had it, the duty staff had to sit on the gasholder in order to boost the pressure for the cooking of the locality's Sunday dinners.[34] And, whereas the United States was already exploiting natural gas and piping it over long distances, Britain still relied entirely on 'town's gas' made from coal.

Over the next five years this essentially Victorian scene was to change little, for the meagre amount of permitted capital investment left very little to spare for modernising either the plant or the distribution system. In the October 1947 review of national investment in the wake of the débâcle over sterling convertibility, the gas industry's allocation of steel was axed from 120,000 tons a year to 100,000 tons. The pre-war average annual usage had amounted to 180,000 tons. This steel ration for 1948 meant that 90 per cent of investment would be swallowed by the need to repair and maintain existing plant 'run down severely in the war' and 'now in a bad condition'.[35] In the IPC's July 1948 recommendations for investment in 1949 it was acknowledged that 'a full appraisal' of the needs of the gas industry would have to await the forthcoming nationalisation of the industry. In the meantime, and despite 'large arrears of repairs and replacements', the IPC endorsed the Ministry of Fuel and Power's 'modest' programme 'as the minimum necessary to prevent break-downs and maintain supplies to essential industries'.[36]

Nearly a year later, in May 1949, the IPC turned down a

programme for investment in 1950–2 submitted by the Ministry of Fuel and Power even though it acknowledged that the proposed programme:

> will not enable the full prospective demand to be met and especially in the earlier years is not intended to permit much more than the maintenance of supplies and the extension of the main distribution system. . . . Even at the level proposed it will be necessary to retain old plant beyond the time when it would normally have been scrapped, thus tending to make the cost of production higher than it otherwise would be.[37]

In characteristic sacrifice of long-term efficiency to short-term savings, the IPC now recommended capital investment in the gas industry of £39 million in 1950 (as against the Ministry of Fuel and Power's proposal of £41 million), and £40 million in 1951 and 1952 (as against £47 million and £57 million).[38]

In November 1949, as part of the hangover cure following the devaluation of sterling, the gas industry's ration of £39 million for 1950 was even hacked back to £32 million, so wholly ruling out the creation of a technically modern and well-integrated industry in place of the existing anarchy of gasworks large and – in too many cases – small.[39] And in the Minister for Economic Affairs' recommendations of May 1950 for the years 1951 and 1952, gas production's share of capital investment stood at a measly £32.6 million and £36.6 million respectively: enough for make-do and mend, but little more.[40]

By the eve of the Korean War, therefore, the industry had hardly begun to emulate the American developments described in the report of the Anglo-American Productivity Committee on the Gas Industry – hardly even begun to think about them.[41] No attempt had yet been made to explore for resources of natural gas, nor to examine the possibilities of importing refrigerated methane-gas by ship, although the IPC took grateful note in June 1948 that 'the Ministry of Fuel and Power had the general question of the supply of methane gas under consideration'.[42] At that same time the IPC also observed that a plant had been built at Greenwich to experiment with a method of completely gasifying coal first marketed in 1936 by the German firm of Lurgi: 'The experiment had been successful but much bigger plants were needed to explore the commercial possibilities and no large-scale results could be expected for 5–10 years.'[43] In any event, the small number of specialist firms which supplied gas plant even of the conventional type 'found it difficult', recorded the IPC, 'to recruit the necessary technical staff'.[44]

Yet Britain in 1945–50 faced a problem in regard to the supply of energy more profound than the obsolescence or restricted output of the gasworks and power stations. For these in turn still depended on a single fuel – mined out of the ground by an industry with an abysmal wartime record of widespread technical backwardness, poor management, an embittered, strike-happy labour-force with a penchant for absenteeism – the consequences being low productivity, high costs and torpid output.[45] For what should have been the nation's most valuable economic asset proved a constant liability; what should have served as the rock-solid foundation of British strength in the postwar world proved a buckling prop.

The 1945 Report of the Technical Committee on Coal Mining (the Reid Report, after the Chairman, Sir Charles Reid)[46] recommended a 'vast programme of reconstruction of existing mines and the sinking of new ones', and a concomitant policy of closing down out-of-date low-productivity pits. For there existed an immense gulf in output per manshift and hence cost of coal at the pithead between the relatively few large-scale and technically advanced undertakings and the mass of backward pits, some very small. At the extremes Cumberland coal cost (1943 prices) over two pounds a ton to produce as against Leicestershire's one pound.[47] In 1947 a loss of ten shillings or more per ton was incurred on 23 million tons of coal (more than 10 per cent of total production).[48] The young and rising Labour politician, Harold Wilson, in his book *New Deal for Coal*, already in the press before publication of the Reid Report, likewise called for massive investment, coupled with 'a national plan which would provide for a progressive programme of new sinkings and widespread development, so that more and more of the unproductive mines could be closed'.[49] He hoped that nationalisation would enable such a plan to be framed and carried out.

But, in the event, nationalisation (vesting day, 1 January 1947), taken in conjunction with the Labour Government's general rationing of investment because of the competing costs of the world role and New Jerusalem, actually served to thwart the transformation of the coal industry envisaged by Wilson and the Reid Committee. For, whereas the efficient among the private colliery companies would have been free to plan their own development while the backward ones simply stagnated, the new National Coal Board had to work out from scratch its long-term plans for the entire industry, as well as create, and run in, a new nationwide organisation. In June 1948, now eighteen months after vesting day, the NCB could only submit to the Investment Programmes Committee a mere sketch of investment for 1948–52. The IPC was asked by the Ministry of Fuel and Power to note 'the great difficulties which had been experienced in drawing up a programme in this field'.[50]

> It was generally recognised that what amounted to a technical revolution was required in the coal industry and the National Coal Board were still in the process of making the preparatory survey necessary before a detailed plan for carrying out this re-organisation could be formulated. Local schemes had been drawn up by each area, but these still needed to be integrated by the Board to form a balanced programme. The chief difficulty was in estimating the effect of investment owing to the many uncertainties about output per man-shift. Much of the work necessary, e.g. sinking of new pits, construction of new roads and the erection of preparation plant, was of a long-term nature and could not easily be related to short-term results. . . .[51]

In consequence, the IPC was told, the estimates for 1950–2 in particular 'were little more than guesses by the Ministry of Fuel and Power and not based on the plans of the National Coal Board . . .'. Nonetheless, the IPC somewhat testily recorded that as regards 1949 the board 'must surely have some idea what major projects were to go forward, because major investment intended to be well advanced in 1949 must be started soon. Similarly projects designed to start in 1949 must at least be in the detailed stage now. . . .' The Ministry of Fuel and Power consented to draw up something along these lines in conjunction with the NCB.[52]

Meanwhile, the British economy continued to suffer from the high cost and limping production of its primary fuel. In July 1948 the ministerial Economic Policy Committee was told that the coal bill incurred by the railways would be up to £37.5 million in 1948, compared with £12.5 million in 1938, while the proportion of uncleaned small coal (really unsuitable for locomotive fireboxes) had risen from virtually nil in 1938 to 45 per cent currently.[53] 'Nothing is more calculated to damage the prestige of the nationalised railways', complained the Minister of Transport, 'than bad time-keeping, and nothing is more likely to promote bad time-keeping than inferior coal.'[54] And on the same day the Chancellor of the Exchequer, in passing on to the EPC a report on the prospects for coal exports, commented that 'the state of affairs which this [report] reveals is extremely serious . . .'.[55] Under the European Recovery Programme (Marshall Aid) Britain had committed herself to supply participants with 19.12 million tons of coal in the (American) fiscal year July 1948–June 1949. But the quantity actually likely to be available would fall short by 1.53 million tons. The Ministry of Fuel and Power proposed to meet this deficit with the same 'untreated smalls' foisted on the railways and fatuously marketed to the British domestic consumer as 'Nutty Slack' (complete with a cartoon advertisement character of that name), the unwary buyer then discovering that it malodorously smouldered rather than burned. As for Britain's other overseas coal customers, nothing would be available in 1949 except for 4 million tons of the same rubbish. But according to the Chancellor 'our overseas customers are not willing to make further purchases of this quality . . .'.[56]

This meant that Britain would default on her export commitments to the extent of 4 million tons of coal. 'The gravity of the consequences of the virtual cessation of our coal exports at the end of the year cannot', he wrote, 'be over-stressed':

(a) Our standing in O.E.E.C. and with the Americans would be seriously damaged by so sudden a change in our contribution to Europe's resources. The spotlight has always been on coal.

(b) The virtual disappearance of our coal exports even temporarily would rob us of one of our most effective bargaining counters in bilateral negotiations. . . .

(c) Even a temporary interruption of our coal exports at this point of time would be especially damaging to our future position as a coal exporter, since our overseas customers would inevitably turn to other and more reliable suppliers. . . .[57]

The Chancellor saw only one solution – the British customer, whether industry or the householder, would have to forgo coal to make up the export quota.

On the same day, 8 July 1948, the Minister of Fuel and Power sent to the same committee a memorandum asking that coal prices to British industrial customers – the railways, the iron and steel industry, power stations, gas works and coke ovens – be raised by around two shillings a ton.[58] When the committee met next day, the Minister of Supply and the Parliamentary Secretary to the Ministry of Transport held forth with passion about what the consequences of such increases must be. The railways' coal bill, already standing at £37.5 million compared with £12.5 million in 1938, would rise by another £1.5 million a year, in turn making likely an increase in railway freight rates.[59] The rise in the price of large coal was 'bound to involve an increase in the production cost of steel', and therefore 'it would be impossible to resist the consequential claim for an increase in steel prices . . .'.[60] In short, as the Parliamentary Secretary to the Ministry of Transport put it, 'the cost of the change would fall mainly on the basic industries and services, with the result that the effects would be spread widely throughout the national economy . . .'.[61] But the Economic Policy Committee tamely agreed to leave it to the National Coal Board to fix the prices that covered its inordinate overall costs.[62]

Only a week later the Investment Programmes Committee acknowledged in its recommendations to ministers for capital investment in 1949 that the NCB were still in the preliminaries of carrying out divisional and area surveys, 'and until these are completed and the results are collated and analysed, the Board consider that a major long-term plan cannot even be outlined . . .'.[63] All that could be offered was 'simply a very approximate forecast of the scale of work which the Board think they will wish to do . . .'. Nor did the NCB provide any estimate of the savings in costs or the improvements in output that might result from investment, on the grounds that 'uncertainty about changes in absenteeism and the physical effort of the miners makes any such forecast worthless . . .'.[64]

It was now three years since the Reid Report had called for 'a vast programme of reconstruction' in the coal industry. How far Britain still remained from even starting on such a programme is shown by the record of a meeting between two representatives of the Economic Co-operation Administration (ECA) in London and four bureaucrats in the Ministry of Fuel and Power on 13 October. In answer to a question from the ECA representatives about why increased mechanisation had not resulted in a corresponding increase in effort per manshift, the men from the ministry 'explained that much of the machinery installed was by way of replacement and the total increase in coal cut and conveyed had not been substantial. No very marked increase in productivity at the face could be expected. . . .'[65] Significant increases, they went on, 'could be obtained only after extensive re-organisation of haulage systems. The NCB's production plans provided for such developments, but it was necessarily a slow process. . . .'

Asked whether there was 'not room for extensive rationalisation of the preparation and grading of coal', the men from the ministry replied that the NCB had 'made a start' on standardising coal grades and introducing standard cleaning plants wherever practicable. 'Such plant, however, took a long time to construct and the benefits were not appreciable yet, though they would become so in the next two or three years.'[66]

A report on 2 November 1948 by a joint committee of the NCB and the National Union of Mineworkers (NUM) on 'Coal Production and Manpower in 1949' drew the same depressing conclusion as had reports in wartime[67] – that the main immediate obstacle to higher output lay in a demoralised and unwilling workforce, to whose attitudes nationalisation had made little difference. In fact, although this report forbore to mention it, in the summer of 1947 the Yorkshire miners had celebrated the passing of the industry into the ownership of the 'people' by going on strike. Moreover the grand old British customs of the unofficial strike and absenteeism were lovingly preserved in many coalfields, especially in Wales.[68] According to the joint NCB–NUM report, absenteeism at the coalface during the current year, 1948, 'may average 14 per cent',[69] which in the context of the new five-day week would mean a total deep-mined output of 198 million tons, or some 12 million less than was needed to fuel British industry and the British domestic consumer, and also meet the 1949 target for exports. But if only output per manshift at the coalface could be raised from the present 2.96 tons to 3 tons, pleaded the report, and if only enough miners would consent to work on Saturdays, production in 1949 could reach 210 million.[70]

However, the Minister of Fuel and Power, reporting a fortnight later on coal prospects for 1948, 1949 and 1950, himself reckoned that 210 million deep-mined tons in 1949 would be 'out of reach', and that 204 million 'is all we can safely rely on for planning purposes'.[71] On the other hand, '204 million tons would come as an unpleasant shock to everyone', so better perhaps, he thought, to compromise on a figure of 207 million. In the event the total came to 205.9 million tons.[72]

Here then was an industry incompetent to supply the coal that was vitally needed to fuel the national recovery, not least because of the utter failure even to begin to carry out the recommendations of the Reid Report. It is therefore astonishing that when in November 1948 the ministerial Production Committee finally settled on the national rations of capital investment for 1949, it chose to allot the industry a mere £30 million – just £2 million more than to be invested in government buildings.[73]

Come May 1949 and the IPC's report on capital expenditure in 1950–2, and it turned out that the NCB still could not submit a detailed programme: 'Until the National Coal Board have analysed and co-ordinated all the Divisional and Area Surveys and have drawn up a comprehensive plan of re-organisation and development, *which they hope to do later this year* [emphasis added], they cannot put forward a comprehensive national plan for the next four years. . . .'[74]

In the meantime, a shopping list of piecemeal proposals added up to £2.6 million for short-term development projects, and some £13 million for others 'essential to the Board's long-term plans for the modernisation of the coalfields'.[75] Yet these handfuls of projects, of which only one was for the sinking of a new colliery, still hardly matched the vision of the Reid Report, nor even accorded with the IPC's own comments that this type of scheme 'is clearly necessary, since there have been practically no pits sunk for some ten years; without, it would be impossible to replace old and inefficient pits', and that there is 'certainly much to be done'.[76]

Nonetheless, much to be done or not, the IPC finally recommended a total investment in 1950 in the deep-mined coal industry for all purposes of only £34 million.[77]

Even by October and November 1949, when the Government was slicing expenditure again in the aftermath of its defeat over the dollar value of sterling, the NCB had still not completed its long-term development plan. However, it was decided that the coal industry's share of the new cuts, amounting to £1 million, should fall mostly on new plant for cleaning coal, even though such plant was essential for overseas marketing.[78]

When on 2 February 1950 the Investment Programmes Committee began to discuss the coal industry's share of investment in 1951 and 1952, the National Coal Board's submission proved to be yet another cockshy: the grand national development plan, so long in the gestation, would not be ready until the middle of the year.[79] The Under-Secretary at the Ministry of Fuel and Power, Mr C. H. S. de Peyer (a man well qualified to speak about the technical development of the coal industry, given his education at Cheltenham College and Magdalen College, Oxford, with an honours degree in Politics, Philosophy and Economics), gave the committee a fascinating potted history of how, thanks to five years of sloth and neglect (three of them under nationalisation), the ramshackle and out-of-date coal industry of 1945 still survived almost intact. He did so, no doubt wisely, in language appropriate to addressing a class of ten-year-olds:

> When the assets of the industry had been taken over in 1947, the equipment was often in bad condition and the mines were frequently badly arranged. The coal industry was a basic industry, playing a prominent part both in the home economy and in the export markets. So far, investment had been on a small scale in relation to the needs of the industry, as assets had been in poor condition, which had made it necessary to review the technical plans very carefully, and also as the plans had not been very numerous and there were comparatively few people who had the knowledge or experience to do this type of work. Even now, the industry could not be said to have got into its stride. . . .[80]

This last sentence was hardly an exaggeration: British output per manshift (all employees) in March 1950, at 1.27 tons, remained below that of the German coal industry in 1938, at 1.59 tons.[81]

The IPC, unmoved by the sad little story told by the Under-Secretary at the Ministry of Fuel and Power, chose to carp about the NCB's bid for £43 million of capital investment for 1951, as against the end-1950 rate of £38 million. A representative of the NCB then tried to explain to the assembled civil servants and economists that technical development in the coal industry could not be a matter for this year or next, but had to be considered in terms of an eight-to-ten-year lead-time:

> At present, the industry was in a very grave position, far worse than it had been thought at the time of the previous review. Unless action was taken in the near future, output would be running down very quickly and costs would be rising. An example of the revolution in costs was provided by the fact that, in 1938, the difference in costs per ton between the best and the worst mines was 6/- per ton. The difference was now over 27/- per ton.[82]

He ended with a plea worthy of Sir Marshall Hall addressing a jury:

> Generally, the prospective position was desperate, and unless substantial capital development took place within the next few years, the industry would run into very great difficulties. If the Government was fully seized of the problem, they would make no attempt to cut the programme now submitted, but would exert pressure on the National Coal Board to increase it. . . .[83]

Yet although in April 1950 the IPC chose to paraphrase much of this in its final report to ministers on 'Capital Investment in 1951 and 1952',[84] it still recommended investing only £42 million in 1951 and £48 million in 1952 – a combined total only £8 million greater than allotted to the petroleum industry, which for all its value as an earner or saver of dollars hardly matched coal in national importance.[85] For that matter, the projected annual investments in coal seem the more meagre in the light of the IPC's recommendation that £21.5 million be invested each year in government buildings,[86] or in comparison with the £30 million so far poured on to the sun-hardened soil of East Africa in pursuit of the fantasy of growing enough ground-nuts there to spread every Briton's bread with margarine.[87]

Yet worse was to come in May 1950 when Gaitskell, as Minister of State for Economic Affairs, made his final recommendations to his Cabinet colleagues about future investment, for he cut the coal industry's ration to £40.3 million in 1951 and £47.5 million in 1952.[88]

However, the industry did at least benefit from the last-minute entreaty by the Minister of Fuel and Power to the Production

Committee on behalf of all three sources of energy, which won him an extra, yes, £2 million, to be shared out between them.[89]

The failure to press on with reconstructing the coal industry on the lines of the Reid Report was the more serious because no other comparable sources of energy existed. Commercial generation of electricity by nuclear power remained a mere futuristic talking-point,[90] for it was only in 1946 that Britain set up the Atomic Energy Research Establishment at Harwell near Oxford. In any case, the overriding purpose of this new British nuclear research programme was military,[91] begun because the United States, in poignant demonstration of how close was the 'special relationship', had refused to share with Britain the fruits of wartime development in America to which British scientists had contributed so much.

In regard to oil, the Government certainly embarked early in 1946 on a 'Coal/Oil Conversion Programme' for industry and power stations, the spur being a grave shortage of British coal coupled with an apparent world surplus of oil. The great freeze of 1947 prompted a positive rush to convert from coal, and the original target of 5 million tons of oil consumption a year was raised by another million.[92] Sadly, an oil shortage now ensued, thanks to scarcity of tankers and greedier consumption by the United States. In December 1947 the Government therefore reversed engines, suspending all schemes authorised but not yet in operation.[93] The Federation of British Industry and other bodies complained that Whitehall had made a mistake 'in encouraging so many firms to incur heavy expenditure on oil burning equipment and storage tanks before making sure that the oil would be available . . .'. So recorded the Minister of Fuel and Power in March 1949.[94] By this time, however, the oil dearth had given way to an oil glut, prompting the Minister to recommend that the deferred conversion schemes should now be allowed to go ahead. Nonetheless, because of long-term questions to be settled with the United States over dollar imports of oil and oil-refining equipment, the Minister still did not propose to 'authorise any new schemes of conversion from coal to oil except where they are of exceptional economic merit (e.g. in coal to oil ratio) or where it is extremely difficult to use an alternative fuel . . .'.[95]

Coal, then, it had to be: cheap coal from geologically easy coalfields and efficient modern collieries, but also (because of the desperate short-term pressure for output at all costs, coupled with the failure to reconstruct the industry) expensive coal from geologically difficult fields and primitive pits. It followed that Britain's international competitiveness as an industrial society must continue to suffer from dependence on a high-cost and unreliable primary source of energy, just as it must also suffer from worn-out and obsolete infrastructure.

Yet there was a third essential support service the shortcomings of which further damaged such competitiveness – education and training, which between 1945 and 1950 proved to be another victim of the Labour Government's failure to make investment in modernising Britain the *Schwerpunkt* of its total strategy.

When Whitehall in August 1947 was pondering its first round of cuts in investment following the suspension of sterling's convertibility, the representative of the Ministry of Education pleaded to the IPC that the department's 'austerity' [*sic*] programme should not suffer:

> The programme allowed only for the doing of essential things, namely the raising of the school-leaving age [under the 1944 Education Act] and the provision of new school places required to meet housing developments and the rising birthrate, all of which were statutory requirements, *plus a certain provision for technical education which seemed to be essential in the interests of the country* [emphasis added].[96]

The provision was 'essential' in order:

> to enable the country to retain its competitive position in world markets. British technical education had fallen behind American, and various developments which were planned in industry could not be effectively carried out without additional facilities for training managers, supervisors and workers. There was very little possibility of carrying this technical education in existing employers' premises and even when the school-leaving age was ultimately raised to 16 there was not likely to be any reduction in the volume of demand for technical education. . . .[97]

In fact, in the context of Britain's failure for the last hundred years to keep pace with her rivals in general and technical education at every level (see above, Chapter 1, for a summary), and the crippling shortages of skilled personnel revealed by the war,[98] the programme was ridiculously modest. On new buildings for technical education a mere £500,000 was due to be spent in 1947, £3.5 million in 1948, £7 million in 1949, £10 million in 1950 and £13 million in 1951 – £34 million in all, as against £26 million to be spent on facilities for school meals.[99] No provision was made in the programme for the new buildings required for extra classes when the school-leaving age was raised to sixteen; no provision for compulsory attendance of fifteen-to-eighteen-year-olds at county colleges (in order to repair the long-standing British educational neglect of this age group).[100] This 'austerity' programme would demand a building labour-force of 30,000 by the end of 1948. A ceiling of only 20,000 men 'would mean a cessation of all buildings for technical education'.[101] The IPC recommended a total of 20,000.[102]

When in July 1948 the Ministry of Education hopefully put in its 'minimum'[103] programmes for the years up to 1952, its spokesman 'laid special emphasis on the need to increase facilities for technical education. The provision of this was recognised as vital to the country's economic recovery and the demand for it was virtually unlimited.'[104] He reminded the IPC that although the Government in its White Paper on capital investment in 1948 had promised 'first priority' to technical education after the urgent needs for primary and secondary schools had been met, work actually put in hand (£1 million) had amounted to only a sixth of that planned.[105] The Ministry therefore bid for £3 million for investment in technical education in 1949, £4.5 million in 1950, £9.5 million in 1951 and £15.25 million in 1952. This time the IPC endorsed the ministry's proposals, on the score that clearly 'the provision of adequate facilities is of first class importance to the country if it is to maintain and improve its industrial potential,' and that 'this is a sector which will give a high return in a short time for a comparatively small expenditure [sic] . . .'.[106]

But even now resources which might have been deployed in this task of 'first class importance' instead went into building new schools on Aneurin Bevan's housing estates, at an estimated cost of £11.75 million in 1948, £9.5 million in 1950, £8.5 million in 1951 and £8.75 million in 1952.[107] Nor was this the only harm inflicted by New Jerusalem on technical education. For further resources were swallowed by the need to cope with the extra number of pupils caused

289

by raising the school-leaving age to fifteen in 1947. This, though a fulfilment of the 1944 Education Act, was in Britain's present circumstances just an idealistic gesture, supposedly giving every child a 'secondary education', but in fact merely keeping them in school for another year with no ticket to further education and training at the end of it. Moreover, in the projected total programme for 1948–52, investment in facilities for cooking, dishing out and bolting the mince and rice-pudding of school dinners still rated half that of investment in technical education.[108]

In May 1949 the Ministry of Education submitted to the Investment Programmes Committee fresh programmes for capital investment rising from £38 million in 1949 to £71 million in 1950 and £107 million in 1952, of which technical and further education's share was to be £7 million in 1950 (compared with £3.5 million in 1949) and £17 million in 1952. But the IPC chopped these grand totals down to £45 million in 1950 and £65 million in 1952, with parallel cuts in the Scottish education programme.[109] Without avail the Minister of Education later pointed out to his ministerial colleagues that such cuts would (among other effects) make it 'quite impossible to maintain a technical education programme of the size proposed. . . .'[110]

When in January 1950 the IPC again discussed education in 1951 and 1952 as part of its general review of future investment, it was told that work on further education in England and Wales in 1950 would total £3.5 million (as against the £4.5 million agreed in summer 1948), but that '£50 million would be required to provide the country with the technical colleges needed if the industrial worker was to receive the training he required . . .':[111]

the Ministry had the difficult task of trying to remedy the deficiencies in further education which had existed over the past thirty years. . . . The pressure for new technical colleges was so great that all the technical colleges opened since the war had been over-full on their day of opening. In the present economic situation of the country the need for further technological education to assist in raising productivity was pressing. It was necessary to meet the needs of small firms who in many cases had not even adequate accommodation to provide practical experience for their employees quite apart from theoretical tuition. The present plans were partly due to the continued neglect of technical schools over many years.[112]

Pressing need or not, past neglect or not, investment in technical education took second place in the IPC's April 1950 recommendations for 1951 and 1952 to investment in facilities for school dinners, special schools for the backward or crippled, and teachers' training establishments. In fact, technical education was allotted 'rather less' for these years than in 1950, while these other clearly deserving cases were to get a 'very small increase'.[113] In the hard bargaining between ministers in the Production Committee in May 1950 over the Minister of State for Economic Affairs' final carving-up of investment in 1951–2, the Minister of Education (George Tomlinson) and the Secretary of State for Scotland (Hector McNeil) won an extra £2.45 million for education – but not for technical colleges: only in order to provide more new schools to match the increase in house-building now agreed by ministers.[114]

Thus it was that five years after the end of the war British technical education remained, and would remain, a scene of over-crowded class-rooms and workshops, often poorly equipped, and would-be students condemned for want of places to remain unskilled coolies – hardly the kind of rank and file to enable Britain to win the commercial battles of the future.[115]

As if slowing to a crawl the re-equipment of the country's logistic services were not damaging enough, the investment policies of the Labour Government also served directly to put a brake on the modernisation of manufacturing industry itself, the field army of export markets.

CHAPTER SIXTEEN

'A Policy of Make-Do and Mend': Manufacturing

THE LABOUR GOVERNMENT certainly *wished* to see industry invest in new development. By the 1945 Income Tax Act it exempted from profits tax those profits ploughed back into the business instead of awarded to shareholders, and gave generous depreciation allowances to encourage British industrialists to overcome their horror of replacing ancient machinery that happened still to be working. Unfortunately, however, the Government wished even more to maintain Britain's political and financial status as 'a centre of world influence' and at the same time build New Jerusalem. This is why, in terms of investment in manufacturing, its foot kept slipping from the accelerator on to the brake, especially when a sterling crisis brought about an emergency stop.

However, in seeking to control the progress of industrial investment the Government was fogged in by ignorance. It knew far less about the current and future investment plans of all the myriad of enterprises, big and small, that made up private industry than did the allied command about the plans and deployments of the German armed forces in 1944 thanks to Ultra. In October 1947 the newly created IPC in its first report on capital investment acknowledged that 'there is neither detailed knowledge of the investment which is going on, nor data on which to judge its adequacy, and short of re-introducing a system of individual licences to obtain plant and machinery [as in wartime] there is no possible method of detailed control . . .'.[1] So year after year the guesstimates and hopeful prognostications of the Government and its economic brains-trust went widely astray, with the deceptively detailed figures in Whitehall reports proving frequently subject to amendment by those who had got them wrong, and sometimes to belated apology. The figures can thus only be taken as broadly indicative of the Government's intentions.

At the end of 1946 the *Economic Survey for 1947* reckoned on a sum of £825 million for all new construction, of which housing was allowed £303 million, leaving £61 million for new industrial building. In addition, the *Survey* allotted £300 million for new plant and machinery for industry.[2] In August 1947, after sterling had nearly foundered when its unwilling holders had been briefly free to convert it into hard currencies, Sir Edwin Plowden (the Government's new Chief Economic Adviser) asked all Whitehall departments (including those sponsoring industry) to curtail investment wherever possible.[3] In October the IPC's report on capital investment in 1948 obediently proposed cutting it across the board by about one-third, and gave priority to that 'which will most directly and rapidly assist in solving our balance of payments problem . . .'.[4] There would be required, wrote the IPC, a policy of 'the maximum amount of "make-do and mend"'. With a further slippage from the accelerator to the brakes, the IPC in its anxiety about fiscal measures which at present 'encourage a high rather than a low rate of investment . . .',[5] recommended that the Government modify 'its general policy [under the 1945 Income Tax Act] of encouraging industrial modernisation and investment . . .'.[6]

While the IPC even recommended trimming the housing programme, it proposed 'steps of even greater severity in order to bring industrial building work into order . . .'. For a period of at least six months 'only factories of exceptional importance should be started, and resources should be concentrated on completing those projects now under way which are of most importance to the export drive . . .'.[7] The overall effect of the IPC's recommendations was to cut building labour for manufacturing by some 20 per cent, as against housing's cut of 15.8 per cent.[8] Investment in plant and machinery (including vehicles) was to be slashed from a guesstimated mid-1947 annual rate of £340 million to an annual rate of £291 million by the end of 1948.[9] The IPC further suggested: 'Appeal to be made to industry to refrain from investment except for balance of payments reasons. . . .'[10]

By January 1948 new work licensed for industrial building had tumbled to only a fifth of the January 1947 figure.[11] Two months later the President of the Board of Trade was complaining that as a consequence of the ban on new industrial construction, the current rate of investment was lower than in 1935:[12]

> the failure to press on with major schemes of industrial development is doing irreparable damage to the national economy, to our export prospects, and to production which would permit substantial annual savings in our imports from hard currency countries. . . .[13]

Wrote the President:

> I would direct particular attention to the claims of the group of chemical industries, alkalis, acids, petroleum chemicals, plastic materials, synthetic fibres, dyestuffs, carbon black, pharmaceuticals and fine chemicals. In 1947 imports of these materials into the United Kingdom from U.S.A. alone amounted to $50 millions.[14]

But except for this ban on new industrial building the brakes on investment designed by the IPC and applied by ministers had proved all too spongy. In July 1948 the IPC was reckoning that in April that year the number of workers deployed on housing stood at 625,000 instead of the 525,000 laid down by ministers in the previous September, and even on industrial building (including iron and steel) at 126,000 instead of 110,000.[15] All in all, investment across the board in 1948, the IPC now guessed, was likely to turn out about 5 per cent greater than in 1947 instead of 8 per cent lower as hoped,[16] although the resources specifically put into construction in industry would only be about the same as in 1947.[17] Since 'the chief aim must be to regain national economic independence at the first possible moment',[18] it followed that a short-term scramble for exports (especially of capital goods) for the sake of the balance of payments must take precedence over long-term industrial modernisation.[19] Hence, in the words of the IPC in its July 1948 report on capital investment in 1949 (later endorsed by ministers with some adjustments)[20],

> A policy of make-do and mend, which will be as necessary in 1949 as in 1948, means that extra capital expenditure should be directed to getting more output from existing plant rather than creating fresh

capacity. By keeping old and obsolete plant in use, by working overtime, or double shifting, by reconstruction to boost rated capacity . . . results may be obtained earlier and with less capital expenditure than by more ambitious projects which in other circumstances might be pushed ahead. . . .[21]

What this policy added up to was 'some reduction on present investment rates' in plant and machinery, while industrial building would remain at the same level in 1949 as in 1947 and 1948.[22]

This British stress on simply shovelling goods abroad as fast and as copiously as possible evoked censure in November 1948 from the American ECA (Economic Co-operation Administration) Mission in London, on the score that Britain's ability to meet future foreign rivals 'depended in the final analysis on the unit costs of British goods competing in world markets', which in turn depended on increased productivity. The ECA Mission therefore judged 'that the United Kingdom should provide for even larger investment in the modernizing of its plants so that when E.C.A. aid terminates the country will be in a sounder competitive position . . .'. However, it did 'not believe that a greater investment can be accomplished . . . if too much emphasis is placed upon reducing present payment difficulties between now and 1952 to the detriment of plant modernisation'.[23]

In May 1949 the Investment Programmes Committee in its report on capital investment in 1950–2 acknowledged that investment in manufacturing industry was 'at once of great importance and difficult to estimate'.[24] It no doubt astonished ministers to learn from this report that 'a large proportion' of this investment was carried out 'by numerous individual enterprises about whose intentions very little is known'. Nonetheless, the IPC now guesstimated that total investment in this sector in 1948 had amounted to about £400 million, of which £120 million went to building (£55 million of that on new work) and £280 million to plant and machinery.[25] This compares with the IPC's estimate of £322 million spent on new housing.[26]

The Board of Trade, Ministry of Supply and Ministry of Food (which each sponsored a different group of industries)[27] hopefully proposed that investment by manufacturing industry should rise to £500 million in 1950, £532 million in 1951 and £535 million in

1952.[28] But these expectations were quickly crushed by the IPC, which recommended that the totals 'should not exceed £430 million in 1950, and £450 million in 1952 . . .'.[29] The departmental bids, remarked the IPC severely,

> would mean, for example, nearly doubling the annual rate of new factory building between 1948 and 1952, and an increase of 30 per cent in the rate at which plant and machinery were being installed. Furthermore, the Departmental suggestions would involve taking for manufacturing industry alone about two-thirds of the whole increase in total fixed investment of all kinds which we believe to be possible between 1948 and 1952.[30]

After all, was not total investment in manufacturing in 1948 'already higher than the pre-war peak year of 1937'?

The IPC therefore thought that its own proposed rations of investment up to 1952 (that is, seven years after the end of the war) 'will leave room for nearly all essential needs to be met'.[31]

Yet these meagre rations hardly met the *fundamental* need – that is, the need to transform the British industrial machine as a whole into a high-technology operation fit for the world markets of the future. Back in 1943 the Board of Trade 'Report on the Recovery of Export Markets' had spelt out what had to be done:

> The development of new types of products will be necessary to compensate for diminution of exports in former staple lines. . . . United Kingdom industrialists must widen the scope and capacity of their production, substituting new products [such as, according to the report, consumer durables, typewriters, calculating machines and cash registers] for traditional lines of manufacture for which export demand is likely to continue to decline. . . .

And again:

> Some of our older industries are, for historical reasons, ill-equipped with modern machinery and plant. Up-to-date machinery is essential to low-cost production; many of our factories are unsuited to modern equipment. We compare very unfavourably with the United States in regard to the use of up-to-date machinery.[32]

However, in the light of this need for root-and-branch adaptation even the particular proposals for deploying investment between different industries submitted by sponsoring ministries seem strangely ill-conceived. For example, the suggested investment in new building in 1950 for the manufacture of synthetic fibres such as rayon and nylon amounted to only 70 per cent of that suggested for the traditional textile industries;[33] the suggested investment in new building for the radio industry to hardly more than that for the leather trade; that for ball-bearings to only a quarter of that for pottery and glassware.[34] Business systems, including cash registers, typewriters, punched-card machines and calculating machines, do not even merit a separate mention in this report on future capital investment – nor in any similar document in the period 1945–50, whether annual economic survey or programme submitted to the Organisation for European Economic Co-operation, except, sadly, as a listed import.[35] And it is noteworthy that in the United Kingdom programme for 1949–50 submitted by the Government to the OEEC, the food and drink industries' portion of investment in 1949 amounted to no less than 60 per cent of that of all engineering industries (including motor-vehicles and aircraft), and about the same as that allotted to all branches of the chemical industry, including the new field of plastics.[36]

In November 1949, as part of the Prime Minister's cuts after the financial Stalingrad of devaluation, a further £15 million were lopped off the 1950 programme of investment in all manufacturing,[37] the impact falling 'of necessity . . . with greater severity on new work'.[38] In vain did the Board of Trade and the Ministry of Supply object, the former arguing that to reduce new building to the level now proposed meant rejecting nearly half the applications coming forward in that year.[39] Although the IPC freshly acknowledged that in the absence of accurate and comprehensive operational intelligence it was merely guessing, it finally stuck its pin on £61.75 million for investment in new construction for industry, compared with an estimated £62 million in 1949, £60 million in 1948 and £55 million in 1947 – hardly the stuff of technological transformations, and comparing ill with the £218 million still intended to be ladled out annually to new housing.[40]

In April 1950 the last IPC report on capital investment before the outbreak of the Korean War recommended a meagre increase in manufacturing's ration from £404 million in 1949 (actual) to £435 million in 1951 and 1952, of which new building would account for £80 million in each year.[41] After all, as the IPC admitted, the sponsoring departments had shown industry's needs to be 'pressing'.[42] Yet the Committee also accepted that investment in new housing should rise from the annual rate of £218 million decided in autumn 1949 to £255 million in 1951 and £273 million in 1952.[43] And ministers themselves, it will be remembered, chose to bump up housing's ration by £30 million in 1951 and £15 million in 1952,[44] marking the final triumph of Aneurin Bevan's crusade for parlours before plant. These sums had now to be found at the expense of other programmes. The task of butchery fell to the Minister of State for Economic Affairs, Hugh Gaitskell, who proposed that new building for manufacturing industry should be cut by £7 million in 1951 and £5 million in 1952, with consequent reductions in spending on new equipment. This, he reckoned, would give a total saving of 4 per cent in 1951 on investment in manufacturing industry as a whole, including plant, machinery and maintenance.[45]

This final slamming of the brakes was fiercely criticised when in late May 1950 the Cabinet Production Committee came to discuss Gaitskell's general proposals. The criticisms, though once again unavailing, serve as a depressingly apt summing-up of five years of failure to make industrial modernisation the *Schwerpunkt* of investment policy:

> Some Ministers felt, however, that the proposals . . . were too severe and would be damaging to the industrial economy of the country. At the present level of investment in manufacturing industry, all applications for new industrial building based on considerations of increased efficiency and productivity had to be rejected unless they contributed directly to the earning or saving of dollars. The Government could not continue to press manufacturing industry to increase its efficiency and productivity and at the same time reject applications for industrial building which were entirely justifiable on grounds of increased efficiency.

It was ironical, the critics continued,

> that the Government should reject, on the grounds of insufficient national income, projects which would undoubtedly serve to

increase the national income. . . . These proposals would have the
effect of prejudicing the productive and competitive position of our
manufacturing industry; and the contribution they make to reducing
the risk of inflation in the short term would be more than offset by
the loss of national efficiency and the consequent loss of national
income in the long term.[46]

In the meantime, far from the desks and committee rooms of the
Whitehall GHQ where this investment strategy of make-do and mend
was devised, the 'field army', that is, industries old and new, had borne
the practical consequences.

In the case of cotton, the strategy, far from acting as an
accelerator of change, had helped only to preserve its obdurate
traditionalism. A comparison in May 1949 between the British and
American industries found that production per man-hour was higher
in the USA; that 'most machinery used in the winding processes in
the U.S.A. was automatic, whereas very little automatic machinery
was used in Britain . . .';[47] and that in weaving 'the Americans use
almost exclusively automatic looms, whereas British manufacturers
use mostly non-automatic. *This is largely a matter of capital equipment*
[emphasis added].' As Harold Wilson, then President of the Board of
Trade, rhetorically asked the Cotton Board Conference in October
1950: 'who in the industry can say that it is yet in a position to meet
the full blast of world competition when it develops?' (see above,
p. 211).[48]

That other stalwart of Britain's Victorian industrial supremacy,
shipbuilding, had been ferociously criticised by technical experts
during the war on the score of time-expired equipment and methods
(see above, pp. 35–7). In 1944 it had provoked a warning by the then
First Lord of the Admiralty (A. V. Alexander) about a postwar danger
of 'the fossilisation of inefficiency'. As early as May 1948, in the midst
of a huge world demand for ships in the aftermath of wartime losses,
the First Lord of the Admiralty and the Minister of Transport were
informing their colleagues that 'the high costs of shipbuilding in the
U.K. have already engaged the serious attention both of the
shipbuilders themselves and of their British and foreign clients'.[49] In
January 1949 the Investment Programmes Committee was noting that
capacity 'was at present fully occupied'.[50] In July another hefty
memorandum from the First Lord and the Minister of Transport on

the shipbuilding and shiprepairing industries accepted that the peak of the postwar boom was already past, along with the sellers' market. It saw 'the greatest deterrents to the placing of orders for new ships' as lying in 'high prices and the inability of the builders to keep to fixed and reasonably early delivery dates'.[51] Looking ahead at long-term prospects, the memorandum warned:

> In seeking foreign orders the industry must expect serious and increasing competition from foreign builders. Ex-enemy countries, particularly Japan and Germany, may not for many years reach the same competitive level *vis-à-vis* the United Kingdom industry as they did before the war, but Italy is making considerable progress; on the other hand, many countries which used to rely on the United Kingdom industry for their ships have since developed shipbuilding industries of their own: Canada and Australia are notable examples. Other countries, such as Holland and Denmark, whose shipbuilding facilities suffered damage in the war, are now again emerging as keen competitors. Sweden has greatly expanded her shipbuilding capacity and appears to have abundant supplies of steel. . . . British shipbuilders will have to fight hard for orders. . . .[52]

But far from envisaging major investment to expand the capacity of British yards, and at the same time modernise their operations in order to reduce costs – perhaps even create new yards fit in layout, equipment and manning to defeat the best of foreign rivals – the First Lord and the Minister of Transport merely saw 'no reason why the industry should not continue to secure something like the same general level of foreign orders as it secured before the war . . .'.[53] They therefore tamely accepted that capacity and employment must shrink,[54] a view later endorsed by their ministerial colleagues on the Production Committee.[55] So piecemeal local new works to enhance productivity were as far as investment was to go.

The Government proved equally limp in regard to that other long-standing weakness of British shipyards indicted in wartime expert reports – the grotesque overmanning and labyrinthine demarcations imposed by the trade unions, which unless swept away would in any case vitiate extra investment. In December 1949 during a meeting of the Cabinet Production Committee, attention was drawn to the existence of restrictive practices by the Trade Unions in the shipbuilding and shiprepairing industries. These practices had been devised before the war under conditions of heavy unemployment; they were wholly inappropriate at the present time, and their effect was extremely prejudicial to the efficiency of the industry and to its level of costs. But the existing methods of payment, which roughly approximated to the cost plus profit margin basis, meant that neither side of the industry had any inducement to eliminate these practices.[56]

But when the committee invited the Minister of Labour to make a full report on these restrictive practices, the Minister finally replied four months later to say that '. . . I shall be grateful if I am not pressed for the report. . . .' He explained that this 'is a very delicate question and one on which the unions are particularly sensitive; I am certain that we shall get nowhere without the full co-operation of both sides of industry . . .'.[57]

Meanwhile the failure either to invest enough in modernising the industry, or to compel its reorganisation, or to tackle the unions, had already begun to incur its due penalty. At the beginning of November 1949 the Economic Secretary to the Treasury reported that 'it appears that the foreign ship repairer can often do the job both in a shorter time and at less cost . . .'.[58] Since the Exchange Control Act of 1947, wrote the Economic Secretary, British shipowners had not been allowed to have vessels repaired abroad, a restriction which, he pointed out, had simply removed the competitive spur to efficiency from British yards.

In May 1950 a 29-page report by a working party on the 'Future Level of the Shipbuilding and Shiprepairing Industries' noted that, although the order books might still be full at the moment, new orders for merchant ships had dropped from 193,000 gross registered tons in the last quarter of 1948 to only 84,000 in the last quarter of 1949,[59] while Britain's share of world shipbuilding had fallen from 53.3 per cent in 1946 (a figure last reached in 1929) to 40.7 per cent in 1949.[60] Yet, although this report accepted that British shipbuilding was 'now entering a period of fierce competition', and that 'its success in attracting orders will primarily depend on its ability to offer competitive prices and terms', it went on smugly enough to aver: 'Great technological improvements have been made and will doubtless continue. Shipbuilders are now tending [sic] to offer fixed price contracts with shorter and firm delivery dates.'[61] However, the working party acknowledged that it had 'not considered restrictive practices in the industry and their effect on costs. . .';[62] and that it had 'not found it possible to make a detailed study of the productive efficiency of the industry which would have involved close consultations with the industry itself . . .'. Despite this omission the working party still went on complacently to assert: 'It is evidence of the present competitive efficiency of British shipbuilding that there has so far been no pressure from any section of the British shipping industry to revive the pre-war practice of building abroad part of its requirements for ships.'[63] Nonetheless, the working party's faith in the industry's competitive efficiency did not deter it from drawing the defeatist conclusion that:

> in the not far distant future, a much smaller part of our resources in manpower, equipment and materials will be required in these industries. At present the shipbuilders' order-books are still full but the decline in the demand for ship repairs has already begun. Our main preoccupation is with the major problems of adjustment in the shipyards which will follow the completion of the immediate post-war task. . . .[64]

Of the future of shiprepairing the working party took an even glummer view:

> The industry's ability to compete with foreign repair firms for long-term repairs also affects its prosperity: in this connection recent low German prices for repairs are causing concern and the subject is under separate examination. Time is also an important factor in placing contracts for ship repairs of a major nature. In this respect, the U.K. yards are at a disadvantage compared with their Continental competitors, which have an abundant supply of labour and can, at will, work a two-, or even three-shift system.[65]

This of course dodged the 'very delicate question' of the abundant labour at present uselessly locked up by British overmanning, as also the question of the British trade unions' certain refusal in any case to work a two- or three-shift system either at all or without ruinous extra money. Even in wartime the shipyard mateys had proved inveterate clock-jumpers and dodgers of overtime.[66]

On 30 June 1950 – as it happened, six days after North Korea invaded South Korea – the ministerial Production Committee approved this working party's report. Having done so, they then uneasily discussed its implications for future unemployment in shipyard areas, which had been throughout the period the Government's principal concern in regard to the future of British shipbuilding.[67]

To this failure during half a decade to invest enough to provide Britain, or begin to provide her, with a shipbuilding and shiprepairing industry thoroughly modernised in both human and technical terms, a sourly suitable postscript is provided by a joint memorandum in July by the First Lord and the Minister of Transport on the repair of British ships in Germany:

> In Germany industrial relations are good and there are no records of time lost through strikes or disputes. Interchangeability between trades, while not a recognised practice, is permitted when necessary to progress work that must be completed within a given time. The equipment of the German yards is up to date and adequate.[68]

Yet the effect of the Government's brakes on investment was more serious still in the case of machine-tools, because, in the words of a report by an expert in 1948, this industry was:

> of supreme importance to any country. It is the true home of precision and skill for the whole engineering trades; it is a school where good craftsmen are bred; it acts as a kind of leaven for the engineering trades of a nation. . . . A powerful and well-organised machine tool trade enables a country quickly to switch from one type of engineering product to another by its own resources. No country can wage total war without it, nor can an industrial state hope for a prosperous peace in the absence of its own machine tool trade . . .[69]

In particular:

> The modernisation of our machine tool population and the continuous maintenance of its up-to-datedness is of primary importance to British Industry as a whole. If this country were to

303

replace [pre-war] Germany as the world's principal supplier there would be a potential market for British machine tools seven times our present output. The potential export demand would then be as much as 15 times our actual exports. . . . Both these aims (if accepted) could be fostered by suitable and timely Government action.[70]

Britain's critical dependence on imports of foreign machine-tools during the war and the pre-war rearmament programme[71] had revealed to government how old-fashioned in design were the industry's products and how limited its output. According to this expert in 1948 little had changed. Britain was lagging behind the foreigners in cutting tools utilising tungsten carbide, lagging behind in certain specialised machining tools, lagging behind in automatic tools, lagging behind in electric drives (which in foreign machines were built in functionally, 'whereas in many British machine tools they seem to have been added as an afterthought'),[72] lagging behind in automatic tools. The gulf between unsophisticated British designs, clumsy with cast-iron, and American advanced technology was shown up by 'the differences in the average price per ton of machine tool which British and American machines respectively fetch in foreign markets. . . . at the present time American export machines are worth approximately twice as much per ton as ours. The same applies to Swiss machine tools. . . .'[73]

However, it was the small size of the British industry as well as its backward designs which concerned this expert. In 1948 it employed some 38,000 operatives, just 0.2 per cent of the industrial population, or 1 per cent of all metal workers, or 1.37 per cent of engineering workers or 1.9 per cent of mechanical engineering workers.[74] Switzerland by contrast employed in proportion to all her metal workers seven times as many machine-tool operatives. Germany's 1939 production had been worth (in 1948 prices) six times Britain's 1948 production, and her machine-tool industry's productivity in terms of output per man per annum had then been 50 per cent higher than the British industry's productivity even in 1948.[75] And British exports of machine-tools in 1948 amounted to just 0.6 per cent of Britain's total exports.[76]

To fill the gap in world markets now temporarily opened up by Germany's defeat (as well as to re-equip Britain's own manufacturing industries and satisfy the needs of world-role defence production) would require the machine-tool 'trade' both to revolutionise its designs and to multiply its output many times: in other words, generous long-term investment. Not a hope. Instead the Government's miserliness served only to nourish the dislike of change among managements whose conservatism of mind seemed as cast-iron as their outdated products (for instance, it was only in 1948 that a Machine-Tool Industry Research Association was set up, at the urging of the Department of Scientific and Industrial Research). In consequence, the industry invested in 1948 a mere £1.5 million in machinery and plant, and £415,000 in new buildings;[77] in 1951, just over £3 million in new plant and machinery and £694,000 in new building.[78] These figures for an industry truly vital to an advanced industrial system may be compared with the £13.4 million spent by mid-1950 on developing two prototypes of the Bristol Brabazon and three prototypes of the Saunders-Roe SR-45 flying-boat (see above, p. 244), or the £17.5 million (raised to £20 million in 1949) being allotted annually to capital investment in the colonial Empire (see above, p. 103), or the £30 million a year cost to the Exchequer of free medical appliances like false teeth under the National Health Service (see Chapter 7).

It is little wonder, then, that between 1948 and 1950 the machine-tool industry's blue-collar workforce rose from some 38,000 to only 39,000,[79] while the value of its net output rose from £25 million to £31 million, still only about a fifth of Germany's 1939 output.[80] Had the industry been as strong in 1950 in proportion to national population as its American counterpart in 1947, its net output would have amounted to some £58 million, or about twice what it was.[81]

Mercifully Britain was still benefiting from the 200,000 machine-tools (including 126,000 American) bought by the state in 1939–44 for war production at a cost of £150 million,[82] though these were now near the end of their working lives.

Yet, though modern machine-tools were essential to the growth of other advanced technologies, the current weakness of some of those technologies in Britain contributed in turn to the stunting of the machine-tool industry's own growth. For instance, in February 1948 it was being noted in Whitehall that shortages of electric motors and ball-bearings partly explained why machine-tool production was 'lagging behind', with 'the re-equipment of industry . . . suffering as a result . . .'.[83]

Shortages of such modern technological products were indeed all too commonplace in an industrial system still heavily biased at the end of the war towards the old traditional staples. To remedy these shortages and at the same time redress the present bias of the system called for investment on the grand scale. More, it called for a vision of an industrial society transformed.

This challenge the Labour Government dismally failed to meet. At the end of their rainbow lay New Jerusalem and Britannia on the throne of world influence and power, not the technologically futuristic society of the H. G. Wells film *Things to Come*. By restricting investment in manufactures for the most part to make-do and mend, and in running present industries flat-out for the sake of a quick surge in exports of no matter what products, the Government ensured that in 1950–1 Britain remained essentially Victorian in her industrial anatomy, with mid-twentieth-century technologies simply grafted on.

In the first place, textiles, the original first-industrial-revolution product and in Britain perhaps the most mentally and technically backward industry, still accounted in 1951 for 12 per cent of capital expenditure in manufacturing, some 10 per cent of net output (2 per cent less than in 1938), and 12 per cent of employment.[84] But within this total output the value of the new synthetic materials like rayon and nylon produced in light, bright modern factories was less than a seventh of that produced by the grim, gaunt mills of Lancashire and Yorkshire and their clattering old machines – less than a quarter of that of woollens and worsteds alone, half that of cotton spinning, and three-quarters that of cotton weaving.[85]

It is true that the metal-working industries' share of net output had risen from 7 per cent in 1935 to 8.1 per cent in 1948, and mechanical engineering's share from 7.7 per cent to 10.8 per cent.[86] But this was thanks to major investment by the state during the pre-war rearmament programme and the war itself, such as the spacious new 'shadow' factories for making Spitfires and Hurricanes now handed over to car firms like Austins and Rootes. Even so, the *combined* share of the metal-working industries and mechanical engineering in total British net output in 1948 was still less than double that of textiles, whereas in the United States the combined 'added value' produced by these two groups of industries in 1947 was well over double that of the textile industries (*including* rayon).[87] Yet, although so much needed to be done in Britain to strengthen metal-working and mechanical engineering, capital expenditure in the former industry actually dropped slightly between 1948 and 1951, while in the latter it crept up by only 1 per cent.[88] Hardly surprisingly, metal manufacturing's share of Britain's net output increased in 1948–51 by no more than 0.5 per cent, while that of mechanical engineering rose by just 0.7 per cent – a miserable performance compared with 1935–48.[89]

The broad industrial heartland of 'mechanical engineering' embraced a vast range of disparate products from ponderous first-industrial-revolution assemblies of iron, steel, copper and brass put together by giant nuts and bolts and heavy rivets, such as steam locomotives, to sophisticated twentieth-century equipment such as air-conditioning, office machines and ball-bearings. Characteristically, these twentieth-century products weighed light in the balance of British production in 1948, and, thanks to lack of investment, not much heavier in 1951. For instance, a modern technological society literally runs on ball-bearings and roller-bearings. Yet British net output came to a mere £10.9 million in 1948 and £14.9 million in 1951 – which should not exactly be a cause for astonishment, given that the industry was granted only a quarter of the investment in new building allowed to those earliest of technologies, pottery and glass (see above, p. 297). Net output of air-conditioning, heating and ventilating plant came to £6.8 million in 1948 (1951: £9.4 million); of refrigeration plant to £8.7 million (1951: £13.07 million); of office machines to £8.6 million (1951: £14.9 million) – and of home electric washing machines to the ludicrously tiny figure of £310,000 (1951: £521,000). Net output of agricultural machinery amounted to £11.2 million and in 1951 to £15.2 million[90] (in December 1948 the Chancellor of the Exchequer and the Minister of Agriculture congratulated themselves that in 1949 about two-thirds of UK supplies of combine-harvesters would actually be British-made[91]).

In 1948 the total net output of all such newer engineering technologies amounted in value to less than a fifth of that for mechanical engineering as a whole;[92] and to less than a fifth again in 1951.[93] Again the contrast with the US is striking. Had British production in proportion to population in 1951 equalled American in 1947, output of refrigeration plant would have been about £53 million, not £13 million; of office machines about £86 million instead of £8.6 million; of domestic laundry equipment, about £14 million instead of £521,000.[94]

That Britain before the war had been virtually a non-starter in the field of office machines or business systems, and that in wartime she relied almost entirely on American imports had been documented by the 1943 Board of Trade report on the recovery of exports. In 1948 British output remained that of a cottage industry. Yet this already important world market offered vast future opportunities as businesses became ever larger and their command and control systems ever more complex. Here, then, as the Americans (and the Swedes and Germans) had long recognised, was a field meriting heavy investment in production resources and technological innovation. In postwar Britain it simply did not receive it. Although by 1951 the value of British net output had climbed from £8.6 million to £14.9 million, no native British firm was in sight of competing with the IBMs and the Holleriths and the Remingtons. In 1949, for example, a Whitehall working party was remarking on 'a great shortage of calculating machines for scientific work, as they all had to be imported from hard-currency countries . . .'.[95] Even including the contribution of American outstations in the United Kingdom, British sales of electro-mechanical accounting, adding, calculating and listing machines rose from £4.02 million in 1948 to only £5.6 million in 1951 (proportionate to American production it would have been around £21 million); of typewriters, that universal item of administrative kit, from £1.6 million to £4.2 million (proportionate to American production, it would have been some £11 million); of duplicators from £1.3 million to £1.8 million.[96]

This backwardness held within it the seeds of a possible far, far greater failure in the future, for it was the expertise in business systems based on existing electro-mechanical equipment enjoyed by the big American companies, coupled with their international marketing organisations, which was to launch them into the age of computers in the 1950s and 1960s. In the meantime Britain was not even at the startline of computer research and development. Contrary to comforting British legend, the wartime Colossus machine for deciphering German Enigma signals was *not* a general-purpose digital computer, let alone the first.[97] The first was in fact German, designed by Konrad Zuse in 1934; and by 1941 the Germans had a fully general-purpose programme-controlled calculator in operation.[98] Immediately after the war the lead passed to America, in which connection it is fascinating to read the awed hearsay report to a

Whitehall working party in June 1948 by a British scientist about the Univac computer, the first production model of all those American machines that would in time bring about a paradigm change in the way that all organs of advanced industrial societies, from industry and armies to healthcare, conducted their affairs:

> The Univac . . . stores up code impulses by magnetizing a pattern of spots on a steel tape, these impulses being produced by operating a keyboard like a typewriter whereby any kind of information, preceded by the desired code symbols, can be recorded. Conversely it can be set to pick out any required information so registered on the tape, being 'capable of selecting any code group designated as it is fed in, of sequence-sorting the code groups, and of collating from two to seven simultaneous feeds' at a rate corresponding to 10,000 decimal digits per second. . . .[99]

But in any case British electrical products right across the board, from switchgear to radar, accounted for only 6.3 per cent of Britain's net output in 1948, or half that of textiles.[100] Although this was better than the 1935 figure of 4.9 per cent – another tribute to industrial expansion pushed by the needs of war – only a tiny further increase of 0.2 per cent in share of output was recorded between 1948 and 1951.[101] In fact, electrical engineering's share of capital expenditure in all branches of British industry actually fell in these years from 5.1 per cent to 4.2 per cent.[102]

Furthermore, with the electrical industries (just as with mechanical engineering) it was the older 'heavy' end which outweighed the newer technologies in 1948, with net output of traditional gear such as transformers, dynamos and motors of all kinds amounting to £128.2 million, and of radio and telecommunications equipment and components to £92.5 million.[103] In this field too, therefore, the balance needed to be redressed by investment in the new technologies with fast-growing markets. After all, even the academic economists and bureaucrats on the Investment Programme Committee laid down as their fourth investment priority out of five for the period up to 1952 that of putting money into 'Marked technical advances and new products of importance'.[104] According to the 1951 *Census of Production*, however, sales of radio receivers and radiograms had crept up only very slightly from £16.4 million in 1948 to £16.8 million (proportionate to American production, it would have been about £70 million).[105] More encouragingly, sales of radio-communication and navigation equipment (including radar) had risen by half as much again, from £8.4 million in 1948 to £12.6 million; of television sets eight times, from £3 million to £24.3 million; of cathode-ray tubes nine times, from £444,000 to £3.6 million. Sales of thermionic valves, the glowing heart of all electronics from television to radar, had doubled from £4 million to £9 million.[106] Nonetheless, these 1951 totals, admirable though they were relative to 1948, signified in their actual magnitude not so much a technological revolution in full swing as a modest overture to such a revolution. For example, in 1951 exports of radio-communication and navigation equipment (including radar) were worth a mere £5.3 million out of total British 'visible' exports and re-exports of £2735 million.[107]

The first of all operational obstacles to the development of advanced technologies in Britain, from electronics to jet engines, lay in a national base in research facilities and high-grade staff that was just too small to meet the demands made on it,[108] and the reluctance of the Government, squeezing investment for short-term reasons, to spend enough on enlarging this base. The 1947 convertibility crisis had led to the deferring of many projects in what had been a 'substantial post-war programme' for civil R and D.[109] In autumn 1948 the Board of Trade only dared to put in a modest bid for £1 million for industrial research in 1949, £600,000 of which would go to support approved projects of research associations – 'not a generous provision', it wrote, 'and . . . only just enough to demonstrate to industry that the Government was in earnest in its support of research . . .'.[110] In February 1949 the Investment Programmes Committee took gloomy note that, whereas during the war the Advisory Council on Scientific Policy had recommended a four-year postwar capital programme of £5.5 million, actual investment in 1948 had come to £197,000. Though the plan now was to spend £639,000 in 1950, it already looked as if there would be a shortfall of about £100,000.[111] A year later a representative of the Department of Scientific and Industrial Research was reminding the IPC that 'a number of projects had been postponed in order to keep the total level of investment on this work within the limits set'.[112] Moreover, he said, the 1952 programme would now include projects 'which were not now scheduled to start in 1951 . . .'.[113]

A further brake yet on civilian R and D in advanced technology such as electronics was applied by the competing demands of defence R and D (the 'first-class power' syndrome again) for use of scarce resources of plant and personnel. In September 1948 the Minister of Defence was complaining that the export drive was diverting industry from the Royal Navy's needs 'throughout the whole range of research and development'.[114] In January 1949 the Cabinet Production Committee endorsed his complaint, and agreed to recommend that there should be every effort by administrative means to expedite production of plant and equipment needed for 'high priority' defence R and D.[115] Not long after this the Minister of Supply was reporting to the Cabinet Defence Committee that 'the Research and Development capacity available to Departments and in industry was totally inadequate to meet the urgent and increasing demand of the Services for electronic equipment . . .'.[116]

Yet investment in all fields of defence R and D in the year 1947 alone had amounted to £66.1 million. The defence departments argued that much of this research benefited civil technological development: for example, in regard to radar. However, a net output of radio-communications and navigational aids worth only £12.6 million by 1951 (proportionate to American production, it would have been ten times higher at around £122 million)[117] and exports running at a derisory £5.3 million hardly go to prove their point. Had a sum of some £66 million annually been directly invested in civilian R and D it would unquestionably have bettered Britain's pitiful postwar performance in developing modern business systems and machine-tools as well as all forms of civil electronics production.

Similar neglect befell that key to R and D itself, the supply of scientific instruments (comprising aircraft instrumentation, naval and military fire control, and medical, laboratory, meteorological and telecommunications apparatus).[118] In 1944 a Whitehall report on the industry[119] found that, though it was 'of vital importance to the Nation', its pre-war methods of production were 'in many cases out-of-date', its products 'inferior to those of its competitors' and its prices 'too high'. There existed 'no combination of firms for research and development, and even among the individual firms which claimed to do research, this was sometimes hardly worthy of the name . . .'. The report struck an all-too-familiar British knell of doom by adding that 'much of the business is in the hands of family concerns whose outlook is, to say the least, conservative'.

When these conditions are compared with an organisation like the Zeiss or Goertz concerns in Germany, the difficulty of competing in foreign markets becomes apparent. It is quite evident that unless the Industry is reformed the history of 1919 to 1939 will be repeated or, as is probable, the conditions will be worse.[120]

Like other backward industries, the manufacture of scientific instruments had benefited from wartime expansion – 'the erection of many new buildings financed by and at present owned by the Government, and the provision of many machine tools, also at present owned by the Government . . .'.[121] For the future this committee recommended that 'many of the old and inefficient workshops and much of the antiquated machinery should be scrapped . . .'.

If a better article is to be produced at a cheaper price than that of our competitors, then intensive research is needed so as to ensure novelty and high quality, and up-to-date manufacturing methods so as to ensure cheapness of production. All this calls for ample finance in any industry, and in none is this more true than in the Scientific Instrument Industry. . . .[122]

The bald figures record the postwar fate of such hopes. Whereas between 1935 and 1948 the industry's share in net industrial output had risen from 0.6 per cent to 1 per cent, this stayed stationary between 1948 and 1951, while its share of capital expenditure in manufacturing even fell slightly from 0.7 per cent in 1948 to 0.6 per cent in 1951.[123]

Exempt, however, from the Government's brakes on investment were the two great gambles in developing advanced technology – long-distance air-transports, where all the turkey eggs had been placed in one expensive basket; and nuclear fission, greedy of precious industrial resources and scientific talent,[124] and in the late 1940s principally focused on producing an atomic bomb for the sake of Britain's world-power pretensions.

Meanwhile, far from such glamorous pursuits of technological prestige, the ramshackle British motor industry was actually proving to be the country's largest single earner of foreign currency, exporting £61 million worth of vehicles in 1947 and £101 million worth in 1948,[125] as it enjoyed a temporary 'happy time' while its rivals were recovering from the effects of defeat and occupation. But as the March 1945 Whitehall report on the 'Post-War Resettlement of the Motor Industry' had made plain, the industry needed to be radically redesigned and re-engineered if it were to have a long life on the bumpy road of international competition. Given the baronial arrogance, individualism and personal rivalry of the men who ran the three biggest native British companies, Lord Nuffield, Leonard Lord of Austin and Sir William Rootes (all of them throwbacks to the self-made 'practical man' of the first industrial revolution), it could take decades for a new-model industry based on economies of scale and standardisation, on sophisticated R and D and industrial design, to evolve by natural market selection.

But the Labour Government, rather than acting to accelerate the process of evolution, slowed it down. In the first place, the export quotas imposed on the industry, coupled with a 'fair' rationing out of steel in return for exports, 'supported the weak and outdated manufacturers at the expense of the more efficient . . .'[126] – really much the same pattern of the survival of the unfittest as in coal or cotton, or, to adapt the phrase of the First Lord of the Admiralty about shipbuilding in 1944, that of the fossilising of a structure of inefficiency. Secondly, to create a motor industry capable of triumph in the world markets of the future demanded not only restructuring but also sustained large-scale investment of the kind which in the 1950s the Japanese Ministry of Trade and Industry, in conjunction with the banks and industrial combines like Toyota and Nissan, committed to developing over twenty years a great Japanese car industry from a handful of workshops.

Instead, Whitehall in the late 1940s sought to limit investment largely to such short-term and piecemeal projects as repair of war damage, improvement in the layout of plants and installation of new machinery, with the aim of maintaining production at the existing level 'and nothing more'.[127] Investment in expanding capacity was to be permitted only 'where exports were likely to be greatly increased',[128] and in any case such projects (mostly mooted by the American outstations, Ford and Vauxhall) ran foul of the Government's New Jerusalem policy with regard to the location of industry (see below, Chapter 17). Thus, according to an IPC guesstimate in May 1949, only £2.75 million worth of building work had been authorised in 1948. This was likely, thought the IPC, to rise – wonder upon wonder – to £3 million in 1949, while in 1950 'a level of £3½ million may be desirable . . .'.[129] Looking ahead to what the British mind would then have conceived of as the long term, that is, 1950–5, the IPC guessed that 'projects put forward by firms in the industry might amount to £14½ million for building and a further £16½ million for plant'.[130] These staggering totals of investment together average out at £6.2 million a year, or a fifth of the annual Exchequer outlay on free false teeth – hardly the stuff of technological transformation.

In May 1947 a senior executive of General Motors had told a member of the British Treasury Delegation in Washington that GM 'had often considered putting forward plans to rationalise the British motor industry but had refrained from doing so as they felt that this would be regarded as an unwarrantable intrusion by an alien and powerful group'.[131] But intrusion by an alien and powerful group, backed by a ruthless British Government with abundant investment, was perhaps exactly what Austins and Nuffields and Rootes (to say nothing of the cottagey little firms like Jowett and Singer) and their higgledy-piggledy scatter of plants really needed in the late 1940s, while time still served. As it was, the scornful remarks made in 1947 by this General Motors executive about 'the multiplicity of designs' that characterised Britain's native car industry, 'the fantastic bottle-necks in accessories, and the general high cost of components due to the excessive number of models and designs arising from a desire to turn out an individual car . . .'[132] remained just as true on the eve of the Korean War.

But at least it was not the fault of the motor-vehicle manufacturers that they were short of steel, and that what they received was not always of the best quality.

In 1945–50 every programme of new construction, whether bridges, coalmines and power stations or car factories and aircraft hangars, depended on steel – every programme of new equipment, whether locomotives and rolling-stock or combine-harvesters or machine-tools or radar-sets. In the vexed and voluminous discussions of future capital investment by politicians and mandarins in these years the problem of steel vied in their minds with the problem of money. Of the two, that of steel proved the more intractable. For whereas the Labour Government *could* have found extra financial resources at the expense of the world role and New Jerusalem (had it been thought desirable or politically possible), the supplies of steel – or at least *British* steel – were finite in any given year: finite and too small. Thus what should have been a basic sinew of national strength proved a laming disability. Even the development plans of the chemical industries (Britain's single world-class, science-based industrial cluster, thanks largely to the German-style creation of the ICI combine in 1926)[133] were to suffer, especially in regard to plants for producing new plastic goods, new synthetic fibres, new drugs, new insecticides.[134]

In iron and steel, therefore, the unfortunate Labour Government had inherited one of the grimmest of all its legacies from past industrial neglect and decline, as was spelt out in April 1945, three months before it took office, in a joint memorandum by the Ministry of Supply and the Board of Trade under the 'caretaker' Conservative administration. The average cost of British steel 'was now estimated to be at least £2 a ton *above* that of our competitors and the new increase of 3/6d on the price of coal would raise it by a further 7/- a ton'[135] – an example of the knock-on effect of a similarly high-cost and outdated coal industry. But in any case, the report pointed out, 'American plants need only 60 per cent of the man-hours per ton of output needed in British plants.'[136] Surveying the likely postwar world market, the report gloomed that 'the competitive position of the British industry cannot be regarded as good'. Much depended on whether Germany after her defeat (then one month away) retained a strong steel industry, and, if that were so, 'we will have difficulty in geting export orders . . . .'[137]

The report attributed low average British productivity and concomitant high costs to the fact that half the output came out of small and obsolete plants. In 1936 eighty out of a hundred blast furnaces making pig-iron were out of date, yet supplied 60 per cent of the output, while just twenty-nine modern furnaces supplied the remaining 40 per cent. Only 45 per cent of total production was being made in furnaces bigger than 125,000 tons annual capacity, leading this report to recommend that after the war Britain should build furnaces of 150,000 to 250,000 capacity, an order of magnitude attained in Germany and America back in the 1920s. In regard to steel itself, the report reckoned that 'a significant volume of production is not economic at any probable level of prices and is overdue for replacement by modern plant.'[138] Not more than three steel mills in the country could be regarded as efficient, each turning out half a million tons annually – less than half the total production. Even in a modern British steel works 'it is seldom that every section of the plant is equally up to date and efficient'. Moreover, old plant compromised quality as well as costs, because modern plants made better steel.[139] Although this report forbore to mention it, Britain in wartime had absolutely depended on American supplies of steel because of the limited output of her own industry, particularly in special steels demanded by high technology. Between 1940 and 1944 no fewer than 14.5 million tons made the hazardous North Atlantic passage.[140]

Here then was the latest instalment of yet another version of the familiar British story – past decades of neglect by managements of 'practical men' scorning scientific research[141] and grudging new investment; an anarchic Victorian litter of small firms round a core of bigger companies themselves technically outclassed by huge modern foreign combines. It was, after all, as long ago as 1913 that British steel production per capita had first been overtaken by American, German and Belgian.[142] In fact, such large modern plants as Britain possessed at the end of the Second World War mostly owed their existence to the pre-war rearmament programme, like the American-type continuous strip mill at Ebbw Vale with a capacity of 600,000 tons a year.[143]

The consequent postwar prospects for the industry were summed up by the April 1945 report in one terse sentence: 'Thus in general the industry was in great need of modernisation, had large arrears of maintenance, and its competitive position had greatly deteriorated. . . .'[144]

It now fell to the Labour Government to work out what to do about this inheritance. One obvious doctrinaire cure-all lay in 'socialisation'. Since this proposal was totally irrelevant to the industry's productive efficiency and competitiveness, it is enough to note that between 1945 and 1950 it caused vast and time-wasting dissension both within the Labour Government and between the Government and the British Iron and Steel Federation (representing the existing companies), and also prolonged windy debate in Parliament.[145] Though a Bill was passed into law at the end of 1949, the industry had still not been taken over when the Korean War broke out in June 1950, vesting day having been postponed till after the next general election.[146]

The April 1945 report had made it plain enough that the iron and steel industry stood in urgent need of root-and-branch restructuring coupled with massive investment in new plant. In December 1945 the British Iron and Steel Federation tabled a development plan costing £168 million over seven and a half years to replace about 40 per cent of the industry's plant and expand its capacity to 15 million ingot tons.[147] However, this plan, though apparently admirable enough in view of the industry's previous record, was no plan at all in the sense of an overall strategy framed by the Federation, but simply a totting-up of all the individual plans of the major steel companies.[148] Moreover, it contained no design for a guillotine to dispose of its Victorian and Edwardian relics, only an 'advisory and consultative' Economic Efficiency Committee that was supposed to co-ordinate modernisation throughout the industry. Nor had the Labour Government any design of its own for such a guillotine for the inefficient, any more than it had for other industries such as motor-vehicles. Rather, its desperate short-term scramble for production at all costs for the sake of exports was to have its customary effect of keeping the uncompetitive and out-of-date in business.

What the Government and its Whitehall advisers could do, and did, was year by year to monitor the scale of investment in the iron and steel industry's modernisation plan. In March 1946 the abacus operators in the Economic Section of the Cabinet Office, while flattering the plan as 'comprehensive and imaginative', immediately went on to cavil that:

> it is possible that in its 'bigness' the scheme goes too far. At a time when national resources are being severely strained it is essential to scrutinise the entire basis of the plan and make sure that efforts are concentrated on the sound and not dissipated on the grandiose.[149]

Even though the Economic Section acknowledged that the plan, at £168 million, involved only 2 per cent of gross national investment, it advised ministers that it should be redrawn more modestly and that 'there should be the usual stress (dictated by broad investment policy at the moment) on exports, quick results and breaking of bottle-necks . . .'.[150] In the event, an initial programme of £135 million over the five years 1947–51 was adopted, with an output target of 15 million ingot tons.[151]

In 1947 about £14 million was actually spent on plant and new construction, as against the £19.9 million originally planned.[152] In

May 1948 it was expected that the target of £30.2 million of investment on new equipment that year (itself a reduction on the original target of £37.1 million)[153] would likewise not be achieved.[154] The IPC took note that:

> something had been done to postpone major expenditure by increased emphasis on adaptations as opposed to new works, but the extent to which this could be done was limited by the need to supply better products than those now made by some branches of the industry, e.g. tin plate and wire rod; this could only be done . . . by complete modernisation. . . .[155]

The committee hopefully wondered:

> whether in view of the probable shortage of steel in 1949 it would be possible to increase production as a short term measure by keeping in operation plant which was due under the original programme for replacement. They were informed . . . that much more provision was made in the present programme for the continued use of blast furnaces due for replacement than in the [original] programme . . . notwithstanding that in some cases continued operation was uneconomic.[156]

By this time, May 1948, it had already become clear that the modernisation programme would probably not be completed by 1952 (as latterly hoped), while the likely cost had risen from £168 million to about £240 million,[157] the ultimate output objective for the mid-1950s having been raised to 18 million tons of ingot steel in order to meet expected home and export demand.[158] Nine months later it was apparent that the programme had fallen into general disarray, with construction of new plant now four to six months behindhand[159] and capital expenditure for all purposes in 1948 consequently falling £11.6 million short of the March 1948 estimate of £46.6 million.[160] The culprit was not in this case Whitehall's habitual stinginess, but the same kind of muddles and delays over construction that were besetting the power-station programme. Those responsible for planning new steelworks were sometimes slow to make up their minds about the specification and then prone to change them. It also sometimes proved hard enough even to agree on the appropriate sites, since in New

Jerusalem such matters had to be decided on 'social' as well as operational grounds. Both these factors were responsible for the delays with new mills for Dorman Long and with new coke ovens and melting furnaces for Colville's on the Clyde. Nor did it speed the preparation of sites, once agreed, that while the navvies and their wheelbarrows of Brunel's time had vanished from the British scene, an abundance of heavy earthmovers of the American type had yet to appear. Thus it was 'difficulties' in preparing the site that held up work on a new blast furnace and coke ovens for John Summers on the Dee.[161]

But now the backseat drivers on the Investment Programmes Committee again began to feel for a brake-pedal, on the score that, unless other programmes were to suffer, it would be hard to accommodate the steel industry's plans to expand capacity to 18 million tons by the mid-1950s within the Government's overall limit on national investment. Yet, as a representative of the Iron and Steel Board tried to point out, any attempt to hold up modernisation schemes 'would only mean that old plants would be kept in operation, resulting overall in the long run in lower quality steel being produced at high costs . . .'.[162] Nevertheless, when in May 1949 the IPC put in its recommendations to ministers on capital investment in 1950–2 it accepted that the output target for 1952 could be met only 'if obsolescent plants are kept in operation and better use is made of plant already in existence . . .'.[163] For instance, 'the capacity of the new sheet and tinplate mills will not equal that of existing hand and semi-mechanised mills, most of which will have to be retained in use, although their products are inferior in quality and more expensive than those from modern mills'[164] (in the event, these old mills were not to be closed down until 1957–8).[165] Thus even with iron and steel, that prerequisite of industrial success now and in the future, the balance was steadily shifting from thorough modernisation to make-do and mend.

But at least the industry was spared by the Prime Minister when he carried out his rough surgery on national investment in autumn 1949.[166]

In December the Ministry of Supply and the Iron and Steel Board took general stock of the present state of the development programme, including 'current costs of schemes in hand, amendments to completion dates, and the latest information on projected schemes . . .'.[167] The result did not make cheery reading. Whereas the original plan of 1946 had envisaged that the peak expenditure would occur in 1948 and 1949, then sharply tail off through 1950 and 1951,[168] the peak was now expected to occur in 1950, followed by only a small decline in 1951–2: effectively a delay of some two years.[169] This was because investment in 1949 was estimated to have been only £43.2 million (in fact, it was £40 million),[170] well short of the target of £48.8 million, largely thanks to delays in construction. Therefore an extra £2.9 million above the existing estimate of £45.6 million would have to be spent in 1950 in order to catch up, plus further extras of £2.6 million in 1951 (making that year's total £47.3 million) and £6.7 million in 1952 (making a total of £46.1 million).[171]

Should such extra investment be denied, the IPC was warned in February 1950, the effect would 'broadly' be 'a picture of wasting assets', with steel available but 'no means of rolling it'.[172] The IPC was also reminded that:

> The main objective of the steel development plan was to modernise the industry, rather than to expand its capacity, although, of course, with modernisation, there was bound to be greater efficiency, and therefore larger output. It was the intention of the industry to close the more inefficient plants as the development plan progressed, and many of them were at present only being retained in use because of the high demand for supplies.[173]

However, some members of the committee were still disposed to carp at the extra spending:

> many other industries could show that they would be able to make a substantial reduction in costs if they were permitted to proceed with a higher capital investment programme. . . . It was therefore necessary to consider very carefully the relative advantages from investing in other industries and from investing in the steel industry, in order to replace inefficient mills. . . .[174]

Despite such doubts the committee nevertheless eventually recommended that the Ministry of Supply's proposed totals for 1951 and 1952 be accepted.[175] It was left for the Minister of State for

Economic Affairs in his final carving-up of future investment in May 1950 (later approved by his ministerial colleagues on the Production Committee) to trim these totals back to £45.4 million and £45.6 million.[176]

At this time, exactly five years after the end of the war with Germany, not one of the grand new plants proposed in the Iron and Steel Federation's development plan and blessed by the Labour Government was yet making steel or processing it. The largest project of them all, the Port Talbot (Margam) integrated steel-mill in South Wales, and its associated tinplate plant at Trostre were not expected to come on stream until 1951 (it turned out in the event to be 1952),[177] with the consequence that 71 per cent of output still consisted of the low-quality, high-cost product of hand-mills, the remaining 29 per cent being supplied by the Ebbw Vale continuous strip mill dating from pre-war rearmament. This sluggardliness in construction compares wretchedly with such wartime American examples as the new works at Fontana, Pittsburgh, where the ground was broken in April 1942, the first pig-iron was produced the same December and the first steel the following May, or the Homestead Works, Pittsburgh, where site clearance began in mid-October 1941, the first heat from the open-hearth furnaces was in June 1943, and the slabbing and plate mills came into operation early in 1944.[178]

Meanwhile Britain's existing steel industry had been run flat-out for the sake of supplies at any cost and any quality, so that in the little old works that made up nearly half the national output it was as if 1920 or 1910, or 1890 had never ended. Output of ingot steel rose to 14.9 million tons in 1948, compared with 13 million tons in 1937–8, and to 15.6 million tons in 1949; of finished steel to 11.1 million tons in 1948 and 12.2 million tons in 1949.[179] It was a valiant effort, but not enough. In 1948 a gap existed of nearly 3 million tons of ingot steel between supply and national demand even as suppressed by the Government's strict rationing of investment.[180] Hence shortage of steel continued throughout to bedevil the Government's planning of future capital expenditure.

Yet in the four years 1946–9 Britain exported an average of 2.1 million ingot tons a year, while holding down imports to an average of a mere 630,000 ingot tons a year.[181] Had she instead chosen to export far less and import far more, she could have thereby released one especially powerful brake on all investment programmes in manufacturing industry and infrastructure. However, this expedient was ruled out by such overriding factors as the obligation to furnish steel to the British colonies or to supply it to the holders of sterling balances as part of Britain's 'unrequited exports' to them, to say nothing of the Government's concern with driving up exports (including steel) and at the same time cutting down on imports (also including steel) for the sake of the balance of payments and the role of banker to the Sterling Area. Nor should it be forgotten that dollars saved on American steel could serve to buy American timber for Aneurin Bevan's new council houses.

Thus it was that in 1950, and despite the patching and piecemeal improvement of the last five years, the broad industrial scene remained much the same as in 1945, with most of the country's energy still derived from out-of-date coalmines; with the majority of British export goods still Victorian staples manufactured on time-expired machinery in cramped old 'works'; with these goods still being conveyed to Victorian ports via Victorian goods-yards in primitively braked steam trains chuffing along poorly maintained track equipped for the most part by mechanical semaphore signalling; and with these goods, if moved by road, still being loaded into vehicles barely half the capacity of an American long-distance truck, and trundled at 20 m.p.h along mostly single-carriageway routes through the narrow streets of medieval villages and market towns, and on down to cobbled alleyways and yards beside dockside warehouses largely dating from the first industrial revolution.

But what else could be expected if the Government chose to allot only 9 per cent of GNP to investment in the entire British industrial system?[182]

Nevertheless, this rationing of investment did not by any means constitute the only powerful brake applied by the Labour Government to the wheels of technological change. There were others, the application of each being inspired by the most high-minded of social intentions.

CHAPTER SEVENTEEN

Exports or Social Rescue?

T HE GEOGRAPHY TEXTBOOKS in use in British schools in the late 1940s still described them in Edwardian terms as the heartlands of Britain's industrial strength,[1] whereas in fact they now constituted the so-called 'Distressed' or 'Special' areas – soot-grimed swathes of obsolescence and decay across northern England and the Black Country, and across southern Scotland and South Wales. The problem could be dissected industrially as well as geographically, in which case it appeared to be that of overwhelming dependence on nineteenth-century technologies – coal and iron and textiles, shipbuilding and heavy engineering – now in varying states of dilapidation. It could be dissected in human terms, in which case it appeared to be that of an unhealthy, ill-housed, ill-nourished and ill-educated mass proletariat, or of the 17–25 per cent out of work before the war.[2] It could be dissected in terms of mental attitudes, in which case it appeared to be a matter of obdurate resistance to change. But it still remained the same problem, the most intractable of all Britain's handicaps – in other words, that represented by the entire legacy of the first industrial revolution.

The pattern of natural change had already become clear enough between the world wars, with the 'Distressed' or 'Special' areas more and more evidently species at the end of their evolutionary line, unwilling or unable to adapt, and new species like the radio industry spontaneously evolving in southern England that were better fitted for survival in present and future markets. Attempts by the state and local government in the 1930s to buck this natural evolutionary trend by bribing industry to set up operations in the Special Areas had resulted in the creation of only 35,000 new jobs by 1941.[3] That this exercise should prove so cost-*in*effective is hardly surprising. In the dry language of a Board of Trade report in 1943 on the location of industry:

> Before the war, when remedial measures were applied to the Special Areas, they were already suffering from the handicaps, resulting from unemployment and poverty, of sub-standard social services. The land was cluttered with industrial waste and ruin. Such conditions were forbidding to industrial enterprise. . . .[4]

What then should be done with the Special Areas after the war? The tender twentieth-century British social conscience ruled out one simple solution of the problem, which was not to intervene at all, but instead allow the natural process of decline and extinction (or, under threat of such extinction, maybe even of spontaneous adaptation) to take its course, just as Georgian England had done nothing to arrest the supplanting of hand-loom weaving and the Sussex iron industry by the new mills and furnaces of the north.[5] Otherwise there were at base two possible national strategies for dealing effectively with the handicap of the Special Areas. An attempt could be made to reverse their decline by a comprehensive programme of industrial and social reconstruction at stupendous cost in state resources, as actually proposed in 1944 by Cripps when Minister for Aircraft Production: in his words, 'a new approach in keeping with the great public enterprises of this war',[6] but in truth the equivalent to the military sin of squandering reserves on reinforcing failure. Or the handicap could be outflanked by instead using state resources to speed up the workings of change by paying off obsolete plants and buying out their workers while at the same time promoting a new technological revolution elsewhere in 'green fields' unencumbered by the physical and mental detritus of the past – something like the French strategy of *pôles de croissance*, whereby new urban centres, complete with supporting universities and technical colleges, were developed round clusters of related modern technologies such as aeronautics.[7] For success either of these strategies would have demanded colossal investment.

In the event neither was adopted – not because Whitehall foresaw that a war-ruined Britain could not provide the necessary 'critical mass' of resources, but because such clear-cut strategies were alien to the minds of British politicians and mandarins alike. Instead, the pre-war attempt to arrest the decay of the Distressed Areas by piecemeal implanting of new factories making modern products was to be continued, but this time through outright compulsion as well as bribes.[8] It was in January 1940 that the Royal Commission on the Distribution of the Industrial Population (chaired by Lord Justice Barlow) in a report of far-reaching influence proposed that further industrial development in the south-east should be shackled by means of government licensing. Such control, the report contended, would serve both to buttress inducements to firms to set up new operations in the old Victorian industrial areas and to halt the spontaneous drift of people from these areas to new industries elsewhere.

Yet at the same time the Barlow Report took note that this purpose of resuscitating the old industrial areas could well clash with another purpose, even more important:

> Undoubtedly a principal national consideration is the successful conduct of industry: any control which fatally hampered or handicapped industry would in any Western nation, especially in one so highly industrialised and so dependent on manufactures as Great Britain, deal a blow of the gravest character to the national existence. . . .

On the other hand:

> while making all necessary allowances on that account, when conditions affecting the health or well-being rather than the wealth of the State demand attention, when slums, defective sanitation, noise, air pollution and traffic congestion are found to constitute disadvantages, if not dangers, to the community, when the problem, in fact, becomes social in texture rather than economic, then modern civilisation may well require a regulating authority of some kind to step in and take reasonable measures for the protection of the general and national interests. . . .[9]

Productive efficiency or social rescue? This dilemma, which was later much to perplex the Labour Government, manifested itself from 1943 onwards in Whitehall arguments about the shape of postwar regional policy.[10] New Jerusalemers in the wartime coalition like

Hugh Dalton (then President of the Board of Trade) followed the Barlow Report in wishing to reverse the natural processes of decline and depopulation in the Special Areas and of growth of new technologies and employment in southern England. In October that year the Board of Trade, in consultation with the Ministries of Labour and Town and Country Planning and the Scottish Office, put in a 17-page report (plus appendices) on the 'Location of Industry'.[11] Based on thorough field investigations, it served only to confirm how dim were the long-term postwar prospects of the depressed areas, how guttering the flame of indigenous enterprise, capability and adaptability. The implications were obvious:

> If, however, measures are not taken to induce industrialists to go to
> the depressed areas or to direct production to them, there is danger
> that those areas will be drained of their mobile workers, while
> immobile workers may be left unemployed in them even during a
> time of active trade in the country as a whole. . . .[12]

The Board of Trade (in the spirit of the Barlow Report) therefore proposed a range of fragmentary and uncosted measures for thwarting this course of events: preferential treatment for depressed areas in awarding government contracts; bigger capital grants and other financial inducements to set up shop amid the slagheaps; even a massive programme (à la Cripps) to rehabilitate the entire environment created by the first industrial revolution. But the most drastic proposal – in fact, on the recommendation of the new Ministry of Town and Country Planning – was for a total ban on further industrial development in the London area and the Home Counties and even possibly greater Birmingham as well: that is to say, an attempt by administrative fiat directly to block the evolutionary workings of extinction and survival.

It is noteworthy that in this document of fifty-five mostly long paragraphs only a single short one touched on the paramount question of 'the efficiency of industry as a whole':

> Vital though it is to find a solution for the problems [of the depressed
> areas]. . . *our first consideration must be to raise the efficiency of industry as*
> *a whole, and particularly to stimulate the export industries* [emphasis in
> original]. In other words, if there should be a sharp conflict between

industrial efficiency and export considerations on the one hand and location policy on the other, the decision must go in favour of the former.[13]

The paper then sought to escape this dilemma by all too speciously asserting: 'In general, however, a successful location policy will help to increase industrial efficiency.' However, only two days after this paper had been circulated, the Economic Section of the Cabinet Office questioned whether indeed, in its words, 'the attainment of maximum efficiency coincides with the policy of encouraging industrial development in the depressed areas . . .'.[14]

> It is vitally necessary to be clear on this point. At best, the case for regarding the depressed areas as the most efficient areas for production is not proven; at worst there may be a big margin on the wrong side. There is, indeed, much evidence which leads us to suggest caution here.[15]

In January 1944 the Steering Committee on Post-war Employment pronounced itself in favour of inducements rather than compulsion as a means of promoting new industries in what were now formally renamed the Development Areas.[16] But it also went to the heart of the whole problem of Britain's Victorian legacy in a way shirked by previous studies, and to be shirked by the postwar Labour Government:

> We must know whether the areas are handicapped, for example, by such matters as comparative efficiency in their basic plants, or by unsatisfactory local communications both for workpeople and goods, for these are curable, and in a short time, or whether deeper causes are at work such as a long-term shift of demand or market, or an outworn but obstinate industrial tradition, or instability of labour.[17]

The committee failed, however, to ask itself whether an 'outworn but obstinate industrial tradition' in these areas might render 'inefficiency in their basic plants' not quite so curable in the short term. But it did make absolutely plain that regional policy ought not to be some kind of extension of the welfare state:

The policy of preference and technical nursing which we have in mind can, of course, only be temporary and conditional. Nothing could be more dangerous than to give firms in the Development areas the impression that they will be permanently carried by Government orders irrespective of their competitive position. . . .[18]

This report opened the gap even wider between the corporate strategists of Whitehall, concerned with maximum efficiency, and the New Jerusalemers like Dalton who could not stomach the prospect of ever worsening dereliction and depopulation in the Victorian industrial regions. The Cabinet Committee on Reconstruction therefore agreed that Lord Woolton, the Minister for Reconstruction (and a progressive Tory), should draft a Government statement on policy with regard to the location of industry.

It was his draft, 'The Balanced Distribution of Industry',[19] which served as the blueprint for the postwar Labour Government's policy towards the Development Areas, for, duly approved by the War Cabinet, its provisions were passed into law early in 1945 in the Distribution of Industry Act. Woolton's recommendations broadly echoed the Barlow Report and the 1943 Board of Trade memorandum. Industry in the Development Areas must be diversified in order to relieve the reliance on single or few technologies and export markets. To achieve this diversification, all proposed new factory developments should be notified to the Board of Trade, so that the board could 'exercise substantial influence' over their location, even by means of actually prohibiting construction in some areas (presumably those where firms would most wish to go). There should be special financial inducements to firms to set up amid the blighted surroundings left behind by departed nineteenth-century prosperity. The government should stimulate 'a progessive programme of developing and modernising the capital equipment of these areas',[20] such as communications, docks, harbours, housing, amenities, public services. However, neither Woolton nor any other body put a cost on these broad-front and essentially piecemeal schemes, or suggested how that cost might be funded out of Britain's likely postwar resources along with competing projects of New Jerusalem – let alone how this unquantified but clearly enormous investment could pay a better return on capital than 'green fields' development elsewhere.

Naturally enough, however, the postwar Labour Government

fullheartedly embraced this inherited policy, of which, after all, some of its leading members had acted as co-authors. To rescue the stricken Victorian industrial areas from pre-war decay and unemployment formed for the Government and the Labour Party an essential part of the building of New Jerusalem. It happened too that the densely working-class and highly unionised populations of these areas constituted the Labour movement's power base, electoral and otherwise. Moreover, the party's astonishing triumph in the 1945 general election partly owed itself to winning formerly Conservative seats on the suburban fringes of such areas.

And so after coming to power the Government rigorously applied all possible inducements and sanctions in order to steer new industry into the Development Areas, including the conversion of wartime government factories therein and the building of new ones at taxpayers' expense ready for firms to occupy. But the most effective persuasion lay in the bludgeon of building licences, readily refused if an applicant wished to construct or extend plant *outside* the Development Areas, readily granted if he agreed to construct *inside*. The bludgeon was rendered even more persuasive by the Town and Country Planning Act of 1947, whereby no local planning authority could even consider an application to build a factory of over 5000 square feet unless the Board of Trade had certified 'that the development in question is consistent with the proper distribution of industry'.[21] As a result of these measures, the Development Areas received in the three years 1945–7 an annual average of 51.1 per cent of new industrial building, even though their insured workers amounted to less than 20 per cent of the national total.[22] This being of course the blissful time of constructing New Jerusalem on the back of the American loan, it was little wonder that the Government felt emboldened to give the social objective of regional policy such clear priority over industrial efficiency as a whole. Therefore the conflict between these two aims which had been foreseen by the Barlow Report in 1940 and the Board of Trade report on 'The Location of Industry' in 1943 did not yet arise. But then came the convertibility-cum-balance-of-payments crisis of 1947, frosting the Labour Government's facile economic optimism, and awakening ministers with a shiver to the desperately urgent need to drive up production and exports. Henceforth, applications by successful exporters to expand or build plants in southern England were to present the Government with an anguishing

329

choice between (to cite again the words of the Board of Trade back in 1943) 'industrial efficiency and export considerations on the one hand and location policy on the other'.

Thus in February 1948 the Distribution of Industry Committee (parliamentary secretaries and civil servants) had to advise grander committees (in the first place, the Production Committee, composed of Cabinet ministers) whether GEC should be allowed to build a new assembly shop for turbo-alternators at their premises in Witton, Birmingham, as the firm wished, or be coerced into setting up a detached operation in a Development Area or – no less crumbling and forlorn – Merseyside. According to the Parliamentary Secretary to the Board of Trade, GEC were:

quite emphatic about the impracticability of siting this particular extension away from their main factory at Witton. The new turbo-alternator shop would not be a self-contained unit but would be dependent on other engineering shops and common purpose tools already available at Witton. It would, in fact, be impossible to isolate a small part of their heavy engineering capacity, and the transfer of a complete self-contained unit would take a number of years to complete and would cost the Company several millions.[23]

But, as he now pointed out, there was an even more telling argument to be considered:

The Company's main anxiety was the effect of their refusal of their application on their ability to accept export orders. They had a full order book at present and without the proposed extension they could not quote acceptable delivery dates for further substantial contracts which had been offered to them. . . .[24]

Exports or succour for the Development Areas? Here was the dilemma which, far from being unique to the present case of GEC and its turbo-alternator shop, beset regional policy as a whole. The Joint Parliamentary Secretary to the Ministry of Supply, another department much concerned with industrial performance, argued that it 'was unreasonable of the Government on the one hand to urge industry to increase its output of this vitally necessary equipment and on the other to refuse G.E.C. the necessary facilities of approval to essential modifications in their plant . . .'. But other departments thought that it was more important to promote a better balance of supply and demand for labour as between the decaying and the thriving areas of the country. The Ministry of Labour contended that it would be wrong to allow GEC to go ahead in Birmingham, where labour was already scarce, while the Parliamentary Secretary of the Ministry of Town and Country Planning (which had a vested interest in regional policy) added that 'the plea of economic necessity was one which could be used equally effectively by many other firms in the Birmingham area. Would any useful purpose be served by approving projects for which labour could only be found at the expense of existing industries in the area?' But the Economic Secretary to the Treasury (Douglas Jay), in the chair, let the wind out of these large considerations with a needle of realism: 'it was clear that if G.E.C. were refused permission to build the turbo-alternator shop at Witton they would abandon the project entirely, and in the circumstances he considered that the Committee should approve the proposed location . . .'. This it duly did.[25]

However, the committee wanted GEC as a *quid pro quo* to cut back their workforce at their wartime radio-valve factory in Oldham, which had been converted in 1947 to making fluorescent tubes and starters, because the plant was competing all too successfully with local cotton mills in recruiting women, who, oddly enough, preferred to work in a modern factory making electrical components rather than in the noisy industrial barracks endured by their mothers and grandmothers.[26] Negotiations with GEC and discussions in the committee over this one dragged on into June 1948, when the Parliamentary Secretary to the Board of Trade recommended that the company should be 'left undisturbed' on the understanding that their female workforce was not to increase for at least two years without the agreement of his department.[27] Here was an example of how regional policy could serve not to speed industrial change by promoting a new technology, but actually to slow it down by protecting an old one.

It was the motor-vehicle industry which presented Government with the starkest choices between exports and the resuscitation of the Development Areas. For, with its pre-war European rivals still recovering from the wreck of war and with world markets hungry for any vehicle with an engine and four wheels, the industry was able in 1947 to export half its production, with a Government-set target for

1948 of three-quarters.[28] At Dagenham on the Thames in Essex lay its most modern production plant – indeed its *only* integrated plant combining on one site every process involved in making a car. It belonged – no surprises here – to the British subsidiary of the American Ford Motor Company. In October 1948 the British Ford Motor Company applied to the planning bureaucrats and politicians for permission virtually to double the size of the foundry at Dagenham, and at the same time take over a wartime Hawker aircraft factory at Langley, Buckinghamshire, for the production of spare parts.[29] The company also wanted greatly to extend their machine and assembly shops at Dagenham. But Dagenham and Langley were both in south-eastern England, indeed within the Greater London area, exactly where according to the Barlow Report of 1940, the Distribution of Industry Act of 1945 and the Town and Country Planning Act of 1947 further industrial development must be thwarted by every possible means. Already, in October 1946, ministers had reluctantly given Fords permission to extend the Dagenham works on condition that the workforce did not exceed 14,000 (it now actually stood at 16,100). At that time they had 'stressed the need for putting a stop to any further expansion of the works'.[30] Now here were Fords again. What to do?

In a memorandum to the Cabinet Production Committee on 28 October 1948, George Strauss, the Minister of Supply, neatly laid out the problem. While the Board of Trade was 'pressing for the removal of part of Ford's production to a development area' (either Merseyside or Clydeside), he himself agreed with the company's view that 'they are not prepared to consider accommodation in a development area since the arrangement would be uneconomic . . .'.

> The works at Dagenham include a blast furnace, coke ovens, a by-products plant, foundry and steelworks, machine and assembly shops. The Company has its own power house and bodies are made by Briggs Motor Bodies Ltd. and brakes and wheels by Kelsey Hayes Wheels Ltd. who are both located on the estate. The Dagenham factory was designed, built and equipped to produce for export and is therefore in a unique position to contribute to economic recovery. The advantage of a comprehensive and integrated plant is reflected in the comparatively low cost of the Company's products. These advantages would be lost by dividing the plant. . . .[31]

Moreover:

> To remove part of the Company's production to another area would
> mean a greater expenditure on buildings, plant and equipment for
> the same output. Proportionately more labour, mainly unproduc-
> tive, would be required and administrative costs would be increased.
> Increased costs would be involved in the transport of heavy material
> to the main works at Dagenham. The additional costs would be
> reflected in a rise in the prices of the Company's products. . . .[32]

It would be hard to make a better practical case against the lofty
social aim of redistributing industry for the benefit of the Development
Areas; and on this occasion, backed by Strauss, it carried the day. But
only in part. While ministers kindly gave Fords permission to extend
their foundry at Dagenham, they also asked the company 'to furnish a
full statement on the effects of transferring a part of their production to
a development area',[33] as the Government had been nagging Fords
unavailingly to do since 1946. The new request compelled a busy
management to waste time both on making an elaborate case for
extending plant where it made technological sense and also on
negotiations with the Government teased out to the end of April 1949.
On the Government side, consideration of Fords' 'full statement'
repeatedly spiked the relevant Whitehall committees[34] on the choice
between boosting tomorrow's exports and rehabilitating yesterday's
industrial areas.[35] In the words of the first such body to ponder the
statement, 'while the Company's proposal to extend their machine and
assembly shops at Dagenham was open to many serious objections, the
arguments for the project on grounds of efficiency were undoubtedly
weighty'.[36] The Distribution of Industry Committee proved no less
baffled at its meeting on 14 December 1948:

> The objective was the production of a low cost, high quality model;
> and while the fundamental considerations determining the Govern-
> ment's distribution of industry policy had been kept in mind in
> reviewing the proposals, it was suggested that in the particular
> circumstances the issue turned rather on the practical production
> requirements. . . .[37]

Some members urged that Fords urgently needed extra production resources if they were to launch new models of car, truck and tractor for export in spring 1950, and that to move part of production away from Dagenham would make this impracticable. They agreed with the company that dispersal to Kirkby (an overspill development for urban primitives decanted from Liverpool slums, 200 miles distant from Dagenham over a decrepit rail system and cowpath roads) would add to labour and transport costs. 'There was again the likely difficulty of obtaining a satisfactory labour force in a new area. . . .' And it was therefore their opinion that 'when vital importance attached to the maintenance and expansion of exports, the Company ought to be allowed to proceed with their proposal . . .'.[38]

But other members of the committee saw it as a test case:

to agree to the Company's proposal would strike at the whole basis of the distribution of industry policy. . . . The issue could not be viewed solely as a matter of short-term development in the interests of production efficiency. . . . a decision to allow the Company to proceed would seriously undermine the policy of dispersal and would make it very difficult to resist applications by smaller firms for expansion in the Greater London area. The objections put forward by the Ford Company to dispersal are exactly the same as those used by every other company wishing to expand in congested areas.[39]

Then again, contended these members, a bigger labour-force at Fords at Dagenham meant loss of labour from other essential work thereabouts, 'and the waste of labour now unemployed in areas where the new project might have gone'.[40] Since Fords and their associated companies were known to be planning further large expansion schemes, 'the present seems the best moment for work to start on a new site, particularly as they [the company] have carefully considered Merseyside and Clydeside'.[41]

Unable to resolve their deep differences, the committee passed the problem over to the Production Committee, composed of Cabinet ministers. On 17 December 1948 these no less puzzled gentlemen went over all the same ground and put much the same arguments for and against, the President of the Board of Trade (Harold Wilson) and the Minister of Supply both arguing that production for export 'must be the decisive factor'.[42] Nevertheless the committee eventually came to agree that the company should not be allowed to expand at

Dagenham or Langley, and gave the Chancellor of the Exchequer, supported by the President of the Board of Trade and the Minister of Supply, the jolly task of meeting the Chairman of Fords, Sir Patrick Hennessy, to tell him so in person, which they did on 6 January 1949.[43]

Fords, however, battled on, the Deputy Chairman, Sir Rowland Smith, writing to the Minister of Supply on 29 January to argue:

> It is neither good economic or business judgement for this Company, or the Country, to upset the balance of the only integrated factory in the motor industry by so distant a dispersal that movement of a very large part of the manufacturing processes would be necessary to avoid excessive 'on-cost' due to heavy transportation charges.[44]

Smith insisted: 'If, therefore, the issue is forced upon us, we find it necessary to say that we can only consider the dispersal if the Government will build such a factory, including its permanent installations, and lease it to us.'

By way of impaling the Government once again on the choice between exports and social rescue, Smith went on to mention that so impressed was the American parent company with Ford of Britain's plans and possibilities that it had been about to give its British subsidiary the freedom to sell anywhere in the world:

> Although these negotiations were reaching the final stages, it is clear that the whole position must now be reviewed by our American associates in the light of the restrictions which you impose upon us, and the consequent uncertainty of our ability to meet the demands for our products which we could have anticipated.[45]

An anguish of indecision now once more tormented the Whitehall committees. To build a 500,000 square feet factory at Kirkby for Fords to lease and equip it with basic services would cost £330,000.[46] A foundry and its kit would cost another £750,000 – call it in all a round £1 million of taxpayers' money.[47] Moreover Fords were asking for an option either to quit at the end of a five-year lease or to purchase at 1939 prices, as well as rents throughout the lease at 1939 levels. As the Ministry of Supply reported to the Distribution of Industry Committee:

> This means that if this project does not turn out to be a success Fords
> can withdraw and leave the factory on the Government's hands; if it
> is a success, they can buy the factory and equipment at 1939 values.
> Fords admit that what they are asking for would be unreasonable as
> between a willing buyer and willing seller, but they say they are not
> a willing buyer.[48]

At its meeting on 8 March 1949 the committee conditionally agreed
that the foundry and assembly shop should be erected (though without
basic services as well) for Fords at taxpayers' expense, but rejected all
Fords' other demands.[49]

Three weeks later the Production Committee confirmed that
Fords should at least be allowed to have temporary accommodation in
part of the wartime aircraft factory at Langley in order to make spare
parts. It was now six months since Fords had first put in this particular
application. In the same meeting, however, the committee accepted
the President of the Board of Trade's view that he 'did not consider it
advisable, for the time being, to press further the question whether the
Company should transfer part of their production to a Development
Area . . .'.[50]

So sputtered out this laborious attempt, immensely wasteful of
time and effort for both sides, to frustrate the plans of Britain's most
efficient car-maker greatly to increase the capacity of the only
integrated motor-vehicle plant in the country.

Vauxhall Motors, the British subsidiary of General Motors, had
fared better when in June 1948 their Chairman put a proposal 'in
special circumstances of urgency'[51] to the Joint Parliamentary
Secretary to the Ministry of Supply to build an 800,000 square feet
factory at the company's works at Luton, Bedfordshire, to house a
modern mass-production system for car engines. At a time of serious
dearth of steel in Britain, General Motors were offering their British
subsidiary the necessary constructional steelwork at an advantageous
dollar price. However, as the Parliamentary Secretary explained, 'the
offer is only open for a short time'.[52] He was therefore bypassing the
bureaucratic bodies which in the first place vetted such applications
because they would either have rejected Vauxhall's proposal out of
hand as contravening location policy or have referred it up to ministers
anyway. The Parliamentary Secretary argued: 'Dispersal of the new
building to other areas is impracticable. It would defeat the object of

the scheme through a) greatly increased handling costs, and b) an impossible strain on the firm's limited resources of highly trained technical and production planning staff.'[53] Given Vauxhalls' 'virility in export markets', he urged that the project should go forward.

Even so, the committee plucked its lip. If Vauxhalls were allowed to expand at Luton, might not Fords, who were 'thinking'[54] of moving their tractor production from Dagenham, perhaps to Merseyside, think again? There were other firms at Luton keen to expand, such as Skefko ball-bearings (the British outstation of the Swedish company), whose claim would be hard to resist unless it could be shown that Vauxhalls' new plant would not mean an increase in the labour-force.[55] So it was decided that Whitehall experts must trail out to Luton to make a technical inspection of Vauxhalls' plant and proposals. Only after these experts had turned in a favourable report did the Financial Secretary to the Treasury give his sanction on 25 June – with the proviso that the labour-force at Luton must not exceed the present level of 12,000.[56]

In September 1949, in the aftermath of the sterling crisis and devaluation, it was the turn of Champion Sparking Plugs to compel ministers to choose between 'industrial efficiency and exports on the one hand and location policy on the other'.[57] Champion, located at Feltham, Middlesex, were the largest manufacturers of spark-plugs in Britain, accounting for a third of total production. Like Fords and Vauxhalls they were the subsidiary of an American company. At present only the metal base of the plug was manufactured at Feltham, the porcelain insulator and the electrode being imported from the United States at dollar cost.[58] In order to save this dollar cost the Ministry of Supply had persuaded the American parent company to agree to manufacture these components in Britain, and the ministry therefore gave (in the words of a report to the Distribution of Industry Committee by the Parliamentary Secretary to the Board of Trade) 'their wholehearted support to the project and are most anxious for the scheme to proceed as early as possible'.[59] The President of the American company had made it clear, however, that 'he is not willing to proceed . . . unless he is allowed to do so in works adjoining the plug assembly plant [at Feltham] . . .'.[60] But on the other hand, 'Industrial ceramics is a type of permanent and prosperous industry which would be most useful either in a development area, or in a pottery area to give some diversification to existing industry. . . .'[61]

Commented the Parliamentary Secretary: 'I can think of no compromise or easy way out of the dilemma which this case provides. . . .'

In the event the prospect of saving dollars triumphed over social considerations. The Distribution of Industry Committee swiftly blessed the proposal, but with the caveat that no more than sixty extra workers should be employed.[62]

No such ease and swiftness of decision attended the application of the De Havilland Aircraft Company to build a 176,000 square feet extension, costing £480,000, to their factory at Hatfield, Hertfordshire, in order to house the assembly of a revolutionary new jet-propelled long-haul civil airliner, the DH 106. This aircraft, it was hoped, would win back much of the world market from the Americans, who were believed to have nothing comparable yet under development.[63] The company also planned to build at Hatfield by 1952 a 600,000 square feet research and development centre and another building for production and repairs of 900,000 square feet.[64] In other words, this was a question of the major expansion of a successful high-technology British company in a fiercely competitive world market where delay in developing a product could be disastrous – a question too of a key project in the Government's own cherished 'Fly British' policy (see Chapter 12).

The location-of-industry bureaucracy had laid its restraining hand on De Havilland's shoulder as early as 27 November 1946, when the Board of Trade was asked to report both on the company's proposals and on the Ministry of Supply's own plans for the company.[65] It was on 26 August 1947 that the company's proposals, in particular for the assembly shed for the DH 106 (later famously named Comet), came before the inquisitors of Panel A (the body charged with preliminary vetting of industrialists' proposals), who batted to and fro the familiar kind of pros and cons. On the one hand, they opined, this advanced aircraft 'will overcome our present dependence on American aircraft and would enable Britain to capture part of the world market for large commercial aircraft'; and since it was being 'put into production straight from the drawing board, and involves many novel design features, the work of manufacture and assembly must be done at Hatfield, in close and immediate touch with the design and technical resources of the Company'.[66] But on the other hand the project 'was open to strong objections on both distribution of industry and physical planning grounds . . .'. Despite such objections, Panel A recommended to ministers that the project for the DH 106 assembly shed should kindly be allowed, but that the company's further plans for expansion should be rejected, commenting: 'Any proposal by the Company to decentralise production would be welcomed.'[67]

Four months later, in January 1948, the panel's recommendations finally came before the Distribution of Industry Committee.[68] Although the committee now at last gave De Havilland the go-ahead for the DH 106 assembly shed, their uneasy social consciences goaded its members into asking for a survey of the aircraft industry as a whole and a report on 'long-term plans for its proper location'.[69] Six months then dragged past before the committee came to debate this report, concocted by the Joint Parliamentary Secretary of the Ministry of Supply.[70] According to the minutes, 'Attention was first drawn to the general need to exert pressure upon aircraft firms to move into areas which were more suitable both from the strategical and the distribution of industry point of view.'[71] The committee happily noted in this connection: 'The move of De Havilland to a factory near Chester had been insisted on by the Ministry of Supply in order to limit future proposals at Hatfield and the firm had now agreed to make it.'

But De Havilland were not the only aircraft manufacturer to feel the ministerial grasp on the shoulder. Because the Fairey Company wished to move from Hayes in Middlesex to White Waltham in Berkshire, the Location of Industry Committee agreed 'that the Ministry of Supply should do their utmost to press the Company to move instead to an area where there was a real need for new industry, e.g., a development area'.[72] Handley Page too were to be 'persuaded' to move to 'a more suitable area' than Radlett, Hertfordshire, where they themselves wanted to concentrate their business.

However, the committee had by no means finished its badgering of the aircraft industry, for it now requested the Joint Parliamentary Secretary of the Ministry of Supply to furnish a further report on its location, this time including its components suppliers. Another six months staggered by before the Parliamentary Secretary was ready to put in this document,[73] duly mulled over by the Distribution of Industry Committee.[74]

Meanwhile the De Havilland Company had for long been struggling with the planners over another project. Among the company's proposals for expansion considered and deferred by the Distribution of Industry Committee back in January 1948 had been that of enlarging its engine factory at Leavesden, near Watford. Later that year, with new jet engines needed both for RAF aircraft and for the DH 106, the company applied to close its other engine factories and concentrate all production at Leavesden. This ranged the Ministry of Supply (punching for production efficiency and exports) against the Ministry of Labour and the Ministry of Town and Country Planning (in the regional-policy and distribution-of-employment corner). While the company waited, civil servants of these ministries went on arguing the toss with each other month after month.[75] An informal meeting on 4 July 1949 between representatives of the company, the Board of Trade, Ministry of Labour, Ministry of Supply and Ministry of Town and Country Planning resolved nothing.[76] On 17 September the Parliamentary Secretary to the Board of Trade haplessly dumped the whole matter on his fellow members of the Distribution of Industry Committee, reporting:

A year of negotiation between Departments has failed to produce agreement on this problem, and it seems clear that no compromise can be reached at official level. On balance I consider that the production arguments in favour of this proposal are sufficient to outweigh the objections to it, but I am anxious to seek the advice of my colleagues before the case is decided.[77]

A week later, and in the face of a terminal wringing of hands by the Parliamentary Secretary of the Ministry of Town and Country Planning, the committee at long last agreed after all that 'the De Havilland Engine Company should be permitted to extend their Leavesden factory by 100,000 square feet . . .'.[78]

In the cases just cited – each of a leading firm in a modern technology – the cause of productive efficiency had in the end (and the 'end' could be a long time coming) prevailed over the social aims of regional policy. This no more than reflected the national pattern in the years following the 1947 convertibility crisis, when exports became for Government a supremely urgent consideration. Whereas in the period 1944 to mid-1948 about half of all new approved industrial projects lay in the Development Areas, the proportion dropped in 1948–50 to about one-sixth, with five-sixths in the rest of the country; in other words, a ratio roughly corresponding with the spread of population.[79] However, as well as the paramount need for exports there existed another factor serving to swing the balance of new investment sharply away from the Development Areas in 1948–50. When in July 1948 the Government simplified the bureaucratic procedures whereby firms applied for permission to expand their plants, it unwittingly relaxed the strictness with which such permission had hitherto been freely granted in respect of Development Areas and largely refused elsewhere.[80] With the consequent weakening of the bureaucratic dyke, the pent-up tide of industrial development began to flow again along its natural channels. As the Economic Secretary to the Treasury reported to the Production Committee in May 1949,

> *applications* [emphasis added] for location certificates are distributed, as between the Development Areas and the rest of the country, almost exactly in the proportion of actual industrial building in the 1930s; which means that, in the absence of deliberate steering by the Government, the tendency for concentration on London and Birmingham would set in to exactly the same extent as in pre-war years.[81]

The Government's other schemes for getting firms to move to Development Areas, such as bribing them with Treasury loans or grants, or of tempting them by spec-building factories for them in advance, had likewise shown small profit in return for much taxpayers' money. In the year 1947–8 an expenditure of £12.8 million bought a total of just 30,305 jobs in Development Areas.[82]

The dismal truth was that the fall in unemployment in the Development Areas compared with 1939 owed far less to new factories brought in under regional policy than to the industrial demands of war and postwar world shortages, which for the time being had restored to life the moribund old heavy industries (such as shipbuilding).[83] Even so, in summer 1949 the rate of unemployment in the Development Areas still stood at 3.3 per cent, compared with 0.9 per cent in the rest of the country.[84]

Weighing all the distasteful facts, ministers could only acknowledge to themselves that regional policy had so far failed in its purpose:

The problems of the Development Areas had not been cured [moaned the Production Committee in May 1949]; indeed, even now, there were many thousands unemployed in spite of the very large unsatisfied demand for labour in other parts of the country. Factories had been built which were still unoccupied; many firms in these areas were only subsidiaries and would be the first to feel the effect of any depression of trade. . . .[85]

The committee also conceded that 'a major obstacle to the transfer of industry lay in the reluctance of managers and executives to move to Development Areas; and it was not difficult for a firm to make out a powerful case against such a move . . .'.

It was, of course, beyond the bounds of the politically possible, as well as being psychologically too uncongenial, to accept the cumulative empirical evidence about the force and direction of the natural tide of industrial development, and so simply leave it to flow where it listed. Instead ministers now set themselves to pondering how better either to dam the tide by repairing the present planning dykes or divert it towards the Development Areas by digging new channels at the taxpayers' expense. The Parliamentary Secretary to the Board of Trade suggested (in May 1949 and again in September) that the taxpayers should pay a firm's costs in moving plant to a Development Area and training green labour.[86] In May 1950 the President of the Board of Trade (Harold Wilson), 'being extremely concerned at the present and prospective position in the Development Areas', urged that an extra £8 million should be spent over the next three years on capital investment therein, including fifteen new Government-financed advance factories.[87] Three weeks later (and a month before the outbreak of the Korean War blew away all the Government's assumptions), the Minister of Labour (George Isaacs) was suggesting 'a flat rate for transport of goods irrespective of the length of the journeys' as a bribe to any industrialist 'asked to go a long way from his markets and his sources of raw material'.[88] Isaacs wished to have it examined whether 'the public interest warrants substantial induce-ments over and above those provided in the Distribution of Industry Bill in order to persuade industrialists to move to the areas in which we would like to see them, even though they themselves have no desire to move or expand . . .'.[89] As Dr Johnson observed in another context, here was the triumph of hope over experience.

By mid-summer 1950 regional policy, with all its compulsions and bribes, past or prospective, had thus proved a failure even in terms of its avowed social purpose. It had added nothing to the nation's productive resources, but at best had merely switched some new capacity from where it would have happened in any case to somewhere else.[90] But at the same time the friction of regional policy's cumbersome and tardy bureaucratic procedures had served as an all too effective 'hot box' on the axle of technological advance. For it was not only great companies like Fords or De Havilland which had to go through the protracted palaver of getting their projects approved by bureaucrats or possibly ministers – or not, as the case might be. It was every one of the thousands[91] of firms, big, middle-sized or relatively small, throughout the realm who wished to expand their plant by 5000 square feet or more, perhaps in order to branch into a new technology or a novel range of products. Each of them had to squander time and managerial effort preparing their case, submitting it to a regional committee or Panel A; arguing it; waiting in important instances for weeks or maybe months while the matter was passed up to higher bodies such as the Distribution of Industry Committee or the Production Committee for them to dither and dither before reaching a decision. And this on top of government restrictions on capital investment and all the other entanglements of the time with the bureaucrats over such matters as allocations of raw materials. Compare the happy lot of an American aircraft company or a German car manufacturer (or even a small family engineering firm), free to decide what factory to build, when, in what part of the country, and then to go straight ahead and build it.

The truth is, as the Whitehall arguments over individual cases so clearly demonstrate, that regional policy's real concern lay not with productive efficiency, which it served only to hinder, but with jobs -- with levelling up the disparity between levels of employment in the new technologies of the midlands and south-east and in the mouldering first-industrial-revolution technologies of the north and the Celtic fringes. In other words, regional policy was intended to act as one means towards achieving and maintaining 'full employment'.

For 'full employment' was now seen by all political parties and by public opinion alike as the supreme social good and therefore as properly the supreme goal of government economic policy – no more Jarrow Marchers; no more disconsolate huddles of the flat-capped

343

outside the padlocked gates of silent works; but instead everyone of working age happily a-bustle in all corners of New Jerusalem with spanner, shovel, hammer, lathe and pick.

Yet in the event 'full employment', far from being the supreme social good, was to prove the most pervasively effective brake of all on the pace of technological change, slowing this to a calamitous crawl just when Britain's rivals were working up speed again.

CHAPTER EIGHTEEN

The Pervasive Harm of 'Full Employment'

THAT THE MASS UNEMPLOYMENT of the pre-war era must never be allowed to return had been from the start a fundamental tenet of wartime New Jerusalemism, written by Harold Nicolson (a well-known if effete member of the liberal Establishment) into a paper 'Why are we fighting?' laid before the War Cabinet as early as July 1940.[1] It supplied the theme for a glib article explaining how to secure 'Work for All' in *Picture Post*'s influential special issue 'A Plan for Britain' in January 1941, and for a host of New Jerusalem pressure groups thereafter. 'Idleness' constituted one of the five 'giant evils' from which, Beveridge announced at the end of 1942, 'New Britain' should be free. And at this same period a Ministry of Information survey of public opinion confirmed that the top postwar priority in people's minds was 'guaranteed jobs for all'.[2] The War Premier himself in his broadcast of 21 March 1943 on postwar reconstruction committed the Government to abolishing unemployment by Keynesian demand management. Thus in yet another field of public policy had the wartime New Jerusalem movement succeeded in defining the postwar limits of the politically possible; more, in determining what must be politically inevitable.

When that same month Sir William Beveridge announced that he proposed to embark on another Beveridge Report, this time on full employment, Whitehall was stung into its own studies of the question, naturally setting up a committee.[3] The Whitehall discussions turned on one central issue: whether Keynes was right or not in arguing that full employment *could* be maintained by means of the government feeding money into the economy in order to maintain consumer demand at a level that would require virtually the entire labour-force to satisfy it.

Dalton as President of the Board of Trade argued that boosting aggregate demand would not cure the structural unemployment in the old industrial regions. In October 1943 the Permanent Secretary to the Treasury, Sir Richard Hopkins, distinguished between low overall consumer demand and investment as a cause of unemployment, and specific causes like loss of an export market or the obsolescence of an industry in the face of new technology.[4] The Treasury believed that structural unemployment could not be cured merely by hiking up overall consumer spending, and argued that 'the factor of structural adjustment deserves to be regarded as equally important and equally fundamental . . .'.[5] Moreover, the Treasury expressed itself deeply unhappy about the prospect of inflating demand by pumping in public money at a time when Britain was going to be hard up and yet faced with competing demands for state expenditure. It was strongly against adopting a policy of deficit financing as a means of curing structural unemployment, and it proceeded to couple a warning with a remarkably accurate long-term prophecy:

> If the principles of deficit financing were to be applied in an attempt to solve a problem of unemployment which was basically one of structural readjustment, and were in fact to prove largely ineffective for the purpose, it must not be supposed that no harm would have been done. Our financial solvency might be seriously jeopardised with repercussions on our whole economic stability, on the standard of life, and ultimately on employment itself.[6]

The Economic Section of the War Cabinet Secretariat, Keynesians all, fiercely disagreed: 'we believe that the evils which may follow from deficit financing are capable of being overcome and are in the last resort less serious than those of unemployment'.[7] The Board of Trade took a middle position in this 1943 debate: it agreed with the Treasury that 'chronic structural, or rather local, unemployment' was likely to prove a major postwar problem, hence its support for special measures under a distribution-of-industry policy, which it saw as complementary to, not competitive with, policies aimed at maintaining high aggregate demand.[8]

Thus were the battle lines drawn between the Keynesians and the sceptics. Yet certain crucial fallacies underlay the arguments of the

Keynesians, especially popularising Keynesians like Beveridge in his report on full employment in 1944.

For a start, except during the hurricane of the world slump in 1930–3, unemployment had never constituted a *general* problem in pre-war Britain, but a local and structural one, just as the Board of Trade and the Treasury argued. Demand and investment in south-eastern England in 1938 had sufficed to limit unemployment to 8 per cent of the labour-force – Keynes's and Beveridge's own definitions of *full* employment. It was unemployment in the Victorian industrial regions at around 18 per cent overall (far worse in some places) which had pulled up the national average to an apparently unacceptable 13 per cent. But, as all the evidence makes plain, unemployment in the old heavy industries stemmed from their being out of date and uncompetitive. For instance, in 1938 world shipbuilding output stood at its highest ever tonnage, yet the British share reached only 34 per cent as against 54 per cent in 1929.[9] Such a problem could not be cured, only temporarily masked, by turning up the Keynesian burner under the economy as a whole.

Then again, New Jerusalemers like Beveridge fallaciously looked at the British wartime experience as proof that, in his words, 'unemployment disappears and all men have worth when the State sets up unlimited demand for a common purpose. By the spectacular achievement of its planned economy war shows how great is the waste of unemployment.'[10] Yet wartime 'full employment' was in truth entirely bogus and therefore quite misleading as a guide to future policy. In the first place the British war economy as a whole was artificial, kept going by American aid and Commonwealth credit instead of paying its way by successful exports. Nothing about it bore any relevance to normal peacetime conditions, as was indeed pointed out in 1944 by the Cabinet Committee on Post-War Employment.[11] Secondly, wartime 'full employment' in no sense owed itself to Keynesian across-the-board boosting of demand and investment. On the contrary, while some parts of the economy massively grew, other parts massively shrank. Manpower in coalmining, a pre-war unemployment black spot, actually dwindled during the war.[12] And while for the moment the special needs of war had certainly solved the grievous structural unemployment in the shipbuilding industry, raising the total employed from 134,000 in 1939 to 260,000 in 1943,[13] how could Keynesian demand management serve to secure enough foreign orders in peacetime against ferocious competition to continue this happy revival?

The total manpower (that is, not including women) employed in British manufacturing industry rose by 705,000 between June 1939 and the wartime peak in June 1943 – by no means enough to swallow up the national total of 1,013,000 unemployed males in 1939.[14] By far the biggest share of this increase of 705,000, plus the colossal rise in the number of women employed in manufacturing industry from half a million in 1939 to nearly 2 million in 1943, was gulped by new technologies (machine-tools, light engineering, the aircraft industry above all), not by old. In any case, employment in sectors not vital to the war effort, but highly important to peacetime prosperity – food, drink, clothing, building, civil engineering, commerce and banking – had to be cut back by no fewer than 3.5 million.[15]

In point of fact, total employment in all sectors of the British *productive* economy (that is, other than the armed forces and public services, education, health and so on) did *not* rise during the war, but actually *fell* by some 1,600,000[16] – hardly evidence of a magic cure for general unemployment, let alone structural unemployment, imagined by pundits like Beveridge.

The magic wartime cure was actually provided by the demands of the armed forces of the Crown, civil defence and the swollen bureaucracy – overwhelmingly the armed forces, which rose from half a million men and women in 1939 to just over 5 million in 1943[17] – a figure more than equal to the combined total of the 1939 unemployed plus the manpower shed by non-essential sectors in wartime.

The 'full employment' of wartime could delude in other ways too, for it included the brazier-watchers in shiprepairing and the clock-jumpers in shipbuilding; the strikers and go-slowers; the card-players and cigarette-lighter makers in the aircraft and motor-vehicle industries – the whole gamut of low British productivity tolerated by management and documented in the files of the production ministries.[18] As the Economic Section of the War Cabinet Secretariat drily pointed out in October 1943, 'any connection between productive efficiency and full employment is indirect and, indeed, ambiguous'.[19]

On 10 January 1944 the Steering Committee on Post-War Employment in a 78-page survey of the entire likely postwar economic and industrial scene broadly came down on the side of the Keynesians: 'The essence of the kind of policy here contemplated is this: to plan the controllable items in total national expenditure that the whole is maintained at such a rate as to keep employment as constant as possible at a relatively high level.'[20] The committee pronounced itself as not being against a small creeping inflation in order to achieve this. On the other hand it acknowledged that the maintenance of aggregate demand was not 'a universal panacea', especially with regard to backward industries and their export markets, for, as the report all too accurately forecast,

> An expansion of home demand will not do much in the short run to alleviate the unemployment so created in the export trades. In certain case this development will give rise to an adverse balance of payments which would justify an adaptation of the foreign exchange rate. . . .[21]

When the War Cabinet Reconstruction Committee came to discuss this report later in January 1944, it quickly agreed that the Government should issue a public statement on employment policy without delay. Moreover, this consensus extended to the basic strategy proposed by the report:

> There were general agreements as to the importance of the recognition given in the Report to the principle of maintaining aggregate demand at a high level, with a view to avoiding at least the severest fluctuations in the level of unemployment; and it was felt that this principle should be placed in the fore-front of the proposed White Paper.
>
> At the same time it was recognised that structural unemployment arising in particular industries or particular areas could not be dealt with by this method alone.[22]

Nevertheless, some unidentified realists on the committee are recorded as thinking that the report 'paid insufficient attention to international relations and the problem of the foreign balance'.[23]

The White Paper on employment policy[24] which finally emerged that month therefore pledged that full employment would be maintained after the war by Keynesian manipulation of aggregate demand, while at the same time hedging this promise about with cautious references to this not being a universal cure.

Thus did future postwar governments finally embrace 'full employment' as the factor which must govern their entire economic strategy – not so much a *Schwerpunkt* as a shackle.

*

> Between the wars, the heavy unemployment in Great Britain and keenly competitive conditions abroad were factors which had to be taken into account in wage negotiations. Employers were afraid that higher wages, by adding to their costs, would make it more difficult for them to sell their goods, especially in export markets. If this happened unemployment would increase and workers' representatives had to bear this in mind also. The larger the number of unemployed, also, the more difficult it was to maintain full workers' solidarity, i.e. an employer could resist a strike, and make cuts in wages more easily the more workers were out of work. Thus in the last resort it was the existence of heavy unemployment, at home and abroad, which allowed employers to resist wage claims and discouraged workers from pressing them too far. . . .
>
> Moreover . . . wages were more under pressure in declining industries than in expanding industries. . . .[25]

Thus in December 1950 did the Chancellor of the Exchequer, Hugh Gaitskell, remind his colleagues of how things had worked in the state of nature that existed before the coming of New Jerusalem and the artificial economic habitat of 'full employment'. Mercifully, however, such grim realities as wages being related to productivity or to the market success and profitability of a business were now things of the past, for as Gaitskell pointed out, 'Conditions have greatly changed in Great Britain since the end of the war owing to the existence of full employment. Negotiations about wages between the two sides of industry now take place in entirely different circumstances.'

> There is no reserve of labour to compete for jobs. There is far less danger that an increase in wages will be ruinous to an industry, while at the same time there is some danger that employers may lose their labour force if they try to drive too hard a bargain. If wages rise faster than productivity the increases in cost can usually be passed on in increased selling prices. There is thus in the economic

system very much less check on the upward movement of money wages.[26]

Gaitskell was here backhandedly acknowledging that, even though 'full employment' had provided an enviably secure and comfortable game-park for its proletarian fauna and their pack leaders, the trade unions, it had by no means proved to be all gain. Furthermore, Gaitskell also acknowledged that 'full employment' was indeed serving as an effective brake on industrial adaptation, this being not only calamitous in itself but also causing yet more inflationary over-heating in the labour market:

> The problem of the supply of labour to different industries is also more difficult since there is no reserve pool to draw on. If a particular industry is under-manned it will not be able to expand unless it can attract labour from other industries. This could be done by making it more attractive, by increased wages or shorter hours or improved conditions. But, with full employment, such improvements are made the excuse for demands for similar improvements in other industries. Thus the deficiency will only be met if the under-manned industry keeps ahead of the others and therefore acts as a constant stimulus to the general upward movement.[27]

In this way too, then, was 'full employment' serving to push wages ahead of productivity and contribute to general inflation. Nor, Gaitskell had to admit, was this all:

> There is also the external side. In some circumstances costs elsewhere might rise faster than costs at home. So that despite the rise in cost exports can be maintained. But if wages at home rise unchecked, it is more likely in general that exports will gradually cease to be competitive and there will be balance of payments difficulties. These can only be met, in the end, by devaluation. A succession of devaluations completely undermines confidence in any currency. In the special case of the U.K. the international position of sterling would be destroyed and the general effects on our own position, and, indeed, on much of the trade of the world, which is at present carried on in sterling, might be disastrous.[28]

351

Here was a remarkable indictment for a committed New Jerusalemer like Gaitskell to make. Its import did not escape his first-class-honours Wykehamist intellect. 'It is clear', he wrote, 'that a very difficult problem faces a country such as ours, which wishes to maintain full employment and yet to avoid the undoubted evils of rising prices at home and balance of payments difficulties abroad.'[29]

With this 'very difficult problem' the Labour Government had now been grappling for five years. To begin with, in 1945–6, the problem arose not from full-employment policy as such but from the aftermath of the war. Even after the demobilisation of nearly 7.5 million men and women by autumn 1946, manpower in the armed forces and the defence industries still amounted to 2.35 million – 600,000 more than in mid-1939.[30] Central and local government bureaucracy swallowed 440,000 more than in mid-1939, while manpower in the export industries was nearly 400,000 higher because of the drive to earn foreign exchange from a world long deprived of goods. Far from 'full employment' needing to be artificially maintained, there existed such a general scarcity of labour that in July 1946 nearly 340,000 prisoners of war were helping to make up the shortfall.[31] Nonetheless, it is noteworthy that even in these conditions there was rising unemployment in decrepit Victorian industrial areas such as South Wales, much to the perturbation of the Labour Cabinet and the Party in Parliament.[32]

When 720,000 more pay-packets than in 1939,[33] plus personal savings accumulated during the war, were balanced against a dearth of things to buy (and against production and productivity below pre-war levels) the result was, in the words of a Ministry of Labour report in October 1946, a 'potentially highly inflationary excess of effective demand over physically available supplies . . .'.[34] The Ministry of Labour considered that in the future the crux of this problem of inflation would lie in the rate of increase of wages, which under wartime and current 'full employment' had already risen since 1938 by 64 per cent, as against a mere 30 per cent rise in the cost of living index.[35] Warned the ministry: 'a persistent all-round advance of wage levels, unsupported by increased productivity, directly threatens our power to compete in overseas markets. . .'.[36]

As 1946 turned to 1947, the Labour Government found itself still struggling with a desperate shortage of manpower owing to the military demands of the world role and now the burgeoning Cold

War.[37] In December 1946 the Steering Committee on the draft *Economic Survey for 1947* reckoned that the total claim made by the armed forces and defence industries would amount that year to around 2.8 million, or more than one-eighth of the country's manpower resources.[38] Here lay the true explanation of the current 'full employment' on which New Jerusalemers in and out of government were then priding themselves. Here consequently lay the root cause of current wage inflation and the arthritis in the labour market – yet another way in which the demands of the self-inflicted world role damaged the British economy. However, by March 1948 the *Economic Survey* for that year was estimating that the total demands of defence on manpower would have dropped by the year's end to about 1.3 million[39] – still a higher figure than in 1939, still a burden on the economy, but no longer the principal cause of 'full employment'.[40] Instead, this blessing owed itself more and more to the Government's Keynesian policy of allowing (in Gaitskell's words in January 1950 while still Minister of Fuel and Power) 'money incomes to remain at a level which virtually guarantees sufficient demand to maintain full employment (i.e. unemployment at less than ½ million) . . .',[41] although with the consequence, as Gaitskell acknowledged, of 'continuing excess of demand over this supply . . .'.

The sterling crisis of 1949 gruesomely fulfilled the Ministry of Labour's prophecy three years earlier that 'a persistent all-round advance of wage levels, unsupported by increased productivity, [would] directly threaten our power to compete in overseas markets'. The Chancellor (Cripps) had to admit to his colleagues: 'Though we have achieved considerable success in our policy of increasing production and maintaining full employment, this has been accompanied by constant pressure for higher wages resulting in higher prices. We have not yet found out how we can maintain full employment in combination with stable or decreasing costs and prices. . . .'[42]

Yet in regard to the long term the most damaging consequence of 'full employment' lay in retarding Britain's modernisation as an industrial society – not only because (as Gaitskell acknowledged) it enabled unions and workers to resist technological change, but also because its inflationary impact meant that Britain dared not invest as high a proportion of GNP in industry and infrastructure as her continental neighbours (such capital investment being in itself a potential cause of inflation). As Sir Alexander Cairncross (at that time a member of the Economic Section of the Cabinet Office) acknowledges, 'Had we added to investment in 1945–50 it would have been pure inflation since we had full employment and the continent did not.'[43]

Nevertheless, even under pressure of the sterling crisis of 1949 the Government ruled out a strategy of deflating the economy, although this would have disarmed the unions, freed the labour market and turned down the gas under inflation. They did so on the score that it would be 'inconsistent with policies on such questions as the maintenance of full employment, to which the Government were pledged . . .'.[44] How then could the pervasive harm of full employment be palliated? In January 1947 the Ministerial Committee on Economic Planning was toying with the idea of a wages policy based on tripartite agreement between the state, employers and unions on what the economy could afford. This idea was to beguile the small-'l' liberals in Conservative as well as Labour governments down through the 1970s, because like the pre-war League of Nations it held out a promise – in the event, equally false – that consensus might replace conflict. The MEP got no further in January 1947 than philosophical discussion of how different jobs ought to be valued in a planned socialist economy.[45] It fell to the Lord President (Herbert Morrison) to strike a discordantly practical note by pointing out that the problem lay not only in wages but also in hours of work: the country needed increased production above all else, 'yet, as things were, the trend was still in the direction of reduced hours even when it was accepted that reduced production would follow. In the circumstances, could the Government stand aside?'[46] The committee's idea of not standing aside was to resolve that the Minister of Labour should put the position 'frankly' before the TUC, and that the Lord President should prepare a statement of the objectives of a wages policy.

In the aftermath of the débâcle over sterling convertibility in the summer of 1947, a Whitehall working party of bureaucrats was set up to study the problem of the 'Stabilisation of Wages'.[47] Its interim report in September recommended that 'the Government should make the fullest possible use of subsidies, grants and price fixing arrangements under Government control to discourage undesirable wage increases'[48] – in other words, thicker fudging than ever of the links between the demand for a worker's particular skills, his selling price, his productivity and his own personal standard of living. The working party also thought that some paternalistic moralising from Government, giving 'definite guidance in some cases as to which wage increases are clearly in the national interest', would not come amiss. However, four months later, in January 1948, the Government's Chief Economic Planner, Sir Edwin Plowden, was freshly warning the Chancellor that 'the effect of rising costs on our export prices must lead to continual balance of payments difficulties, with all the menace these hold for our levels of nutrition and of employment . . .'.[49]

But the gauzy hopes of a wages policy were crumpled up by the opposition of the trade unions, who refused to abandon their vested interest in what was ironically called 'free collective bargaining'. Instead, the union grandees in kindness to their struggling 'brothers' in the Labour Government enforced their own wage-freeze from March 1948 to September 1950. In return for this act of rescue, the Government left the unions in enhanced enjoyment of their hallowed corporate privileges; their elaborately divided ownerships of manufacturing processes; and their power to hold down productivity, to insist on overmanning and to obstruct technological change.[50]

Nonetheless, in defiance of the wage-freeze decreed by the trade union bosses, average weekly earnings rose between 1945 and 1950 by 27 per cent, ahead of retail prices at 19 per cent. Both figures compare poorly with the equivalent five-year period after the Great War, when earnings and prices each *fell* by 19 per cent.[51]

And yet 'full employment' was by no means the only inflationary pump at work on the British economy, as was pointed out in April 1949 by a draft report to the Organisation for European Economic Co-operation (OEEC) on the Internal Financial Position of the United Kingdom:

Since the war there has been . . . a heavy need to modernise equipment and rebuild houses and factories. Real consumption, particularly of durable goods, was strictly curtailed during the war; and the war ended with consumers holding an abnormal stock of liquid savings, amounting almost to a year's normal consumption expenditure, and having also many deficiencies of consumption which they have wished to make good. Consumers have therefore wished to spend more and save less than before the war.[52]

Nor did the report omit to mention also how the Government was directly pumping up inflation by means of its own expenditure – above all on defence, housing and the welfare state.[53]

The Labour Cabinet had attempted to contain all these cumulative economic pressures by carrying forward from war into peace a ramifying apparatus of high taxation (40 per cent of GNP),[54] rationing, food subsidies, price controls and other 'controls'.[55] But this had led to much the same industrial stultification as the similar artificial economic habitats maintained by the Soviet Union and its East European satellites until their final collapse in 1990. In other words, it was not just that regional policy and 'full employment' in themselves served as brakes on technological change and efficiency, but rather that the British 'planned economy' as a whole constituted a ubiquitously effective *system* of braking.

This did not go unremarked in Whitehall. As early as 1948 a draft speech written for the Chancellor of the Exchequer by an economist on the Economic Planning Staff said of the rationing out of raw materials to firms:

> I do not defend this method of allocation; in fact, I hate it. It acts as a disincentive to enterprise and efficiency; it holds back the expanding firm and perhaps maintains in being a firm which according to the pure milk of laissez-faire competition ought perhaps to be passing out of production. . . .[56]

In July 1949, with the sterling crisis in full spate, the Chancellor himself acknowledged:

> There can be no doubts . . . that we have reached a degree of rigidity in our internal economy which makes it exceedingly difficult to bring about voluntarily helpful adjustments calculated to assist price movements and to encourage enterprise in the industrial and commercial fields. . . .[57]

Yet, like a bloated woman who dares not shed her steel-reinforced corset and submit to the pain of having her muscles hardened in a gymnasium, Whitehall shrank from the consequences of abandoning 'controls'. According to the already cited 1948 draft speech for the Chancellor:

> To remove the control [on the allocation of raw materials to industry] would lead to an inflationary scramble for materials which might completely defeat the needs of all national purposes and might result in the wholesale closing-down of firms who did not have a special 'pull', i.e., with the materials suppliers. We cannot afford either on a short- or long-term basis to see such wholesale closing, together with the loss of manpower. . . .[58]

But was this debilitating artificial habitat of 'full employment' and the 'planned economy' the inevitably right solution, as British politicians and civil servants took for granted? Fascinating light is cast on this question by the radically different strategy for national recovery adopted by West Germany.

At the beginning of 1948 West Germany (then the so-called Bizone, comprising the British and American occupation zones, created on 1 January 1947) confronted problems of far greater severity than did Britain. Five per cent of her industrial capacity had been removed as reparations.[59] Her industrial output stood at only 47 per cent of 1938.[60] Her traditional markets in central and eastern Europe were lost behind the Iron Curtain. Her current exports of mechanical and electrical engineering goods, machine-tools and instruments amounted to a meagre $45 million, as against the United Kingdom's £1440 million.[61] Her shops were even emptier than those in Britain (except for black-market trading). Her currency, the Reichsmark, had become of less use for making purchases than American cigarettes. She had, moreover, inherited from the Nazi regime an apparatus of rationing, allocations and controls over prices, wages and rents just as cumbersome as those in Britain – its purpose, as in Britain, to act as a corset holding a dropsical and deformed economy together.

Yet West Germany did enjoy certain countervailing advantages, paradoxically springing from defeat and occupation by the allies and from national guilt at the crimes of the Third Reich. For such a plight meant that Germany's leaders and people could no longer cherish costly illusions of a world-power role or even a great-power role, while in any case it was their good fortune to be forbidden any defence expenditure whatsoever by their conquerors and occupiers. No 'Reichsmark Area' existed to cast a nostalgic spell of financial self-importance while actually helping to empty the pocket. Nor could the Germans in their present impoverishment entertain expensive dreams of a New Jerusalem to be constructed without delay. So circumstance dictated that West Germany's total strategy could have only one possible *Schwerpunkt*, and that was to achieve future success as an industrial society.

She enjoyed other advantages as well. Her previous governing elites – political and bureaucratic – had been broken up by defeat, so compelling a new start, often with new men, amid the rubble of habit and tradition. Her old militant trade union movement had been smashed by the Nazi regime, and an entirely new and rational industry-based union system had been set up by the victors. Class distinctions in industry and in society at large had been eroded by Nazi egalitarianism. All these were assets rich in potential compared with a Britain still lumbered with the structures and elites of the past. Nor should be forgotten the factor of national morale and motivation. While the smugness of victory acted on the British like a relaxing drug, 'Day Zero' (8 May 1945, when, like a giant machine switched off, Germany lay stopped and silent amid the rubble) inspired the Germans to reach for their shovels and go to work. It makes an apt parable that twelve days after 'Day Zero' the first underground train ran again in Berlin, followed two days later by the first bus,[62] while in London no buses were running because the crews were on strike.[63]

The first phase of West Germany's campaign for economic revival opened on 20 June 1948 with the replacement of the Reichsmark by a new currency, the Deutschemark, at a conversion rate for bank deposits of only 6.5 DM to 100 RM, 10 DM to 100 RM for mortgages and other private debts – and zero for public debt: that is, cancellation. In exchange for all his Reichsmark notes each citizen was allowed a total of just 40 Deutschemarks (plus another 20 DM shortly afterwards), and no more. Only rents, wages and prices were converted at parity.[64] At once all the distending froth of inflation from too much cash and savings, plus all the accumulated paper of public debt, was blown away. Money and the quantity of available goods – national resources and national obligations too – were brought abruptly back towards balance. A new central bank was created, which – unlike the nationalised Bank of England – was to be independent of politicians who would debauch the currency in order to puff up 'full employment' or to shove more paper money into the voters' pockets before a general election. It was therefore free to discharge its given paramount duty of maintaining the value of the Deutschemark. At a stroke West Germany had largely banished inflation, and, in comparison with most other currencies (including sterling), it would stay largely banished for more than four decades. In Britain by contrast, and despite all the 'controls' and subsidies, the value of the pound dropped from 38 per cent of its 1914 value in 1946 to 31 per cent in 1950.[65]

Currency reform supplied only the opening German attack on the economics of fudge. The elaborate system of rationing and controls on prices and supplies was demolished except – for the time being – in regard to some basic foodstuffs and key supplies like coal and steel. In the autumn the control on wages too was abolished. German companies were free to expand as much as they could in pursuit of profit; German workers were free to earn real money, as much of it as their own talent and effort enabled, and then, as they wished, save it or spend it on the goods that soon began to fill the shops after the currency reform. In the second half of 1948 industrial production soared by 50 per cent.[66] Yet the return to economic and productive reality, coupled with the abolition of controls over prices and wages, temporarily caused the price of goods and also unemployment to rise steeply, alike horrors which the Labour Government desired to avoid in Britain at all cost. Moreover, when the Bizone authorities refused a demand by German trade unions for the restoration of price controls this provoked what in Britain would have seemed worse than a horror, in fact a social nightmare: to wit, a general strike. It achieved nothing. Fuelled by Marshall Aid (though Germany was to receive in all a third less than Britain)[67] and boosted by an undervalued exchange rate for the D-Mark, the march towards a market economy rolled on through 1949, the year when the Bizone became the Federal Republic of Germany. Free of the kind of restrictive control exercised by government in Britain, investment followed where there beckoned prospects of fast growth in productivity and exports, such as motor vehicles, chemicals, machinery, electrical engineering.[68]

For it was in a *blitzkrieg* expansion of such exports – by twenty-five times by 1953–4 to the Western hemisphere alone, according to the target – that there lay the thrustline of West Germany's longer-term strategy for recovery, as embodied in her tender for Marshall Aid in 1948. This expansion was to be coupled with high imports of industrial goods and raw materials to feed the expansion, and of foodstuffs to feed the German worker.[69] Clausewitz would have applauded such a bold strategy of concentrating all effort, all resources, on a single chosen *Schwerpunkt*.

No less fascinating a light is shed on Whitehall's own cast of mind by its reaction to this German strategy. In November 1948 the working party appointed to comment on the German tender for Marshall Aid reported: 'we are impressed by the great size of the task [in regard to exports] which the Germans have set themselves . . .'.[70] Yet the working party reckoned that the German export targets 'were not impossibly high', and spoke quaveringly about how these targets caused 'grave concern' with regard to British exports.[71] It considered the German intention to invest 15 per cent of net domestic savings in 1952, as against Britain's 13 per cent, to be 'a very high proportion and to attain it a large budget surplus would be required if inflation is to be avoided'.[72] Next month a report on the same topic to the Cabinet by the European Economic Co-operation Committee (civil servants) opined that the German export targets were unrealistic unless there was a return to 'unfair trade practices', and even, oh horror, 'cut-throat competition', which could put 'in danger' Britain's own plans for long-term recovery.[73] Disquieted by this report and prompted by the Foreign Office,[74] the Chancellor of the Exchequer considered the possibility of using Britain's position as an occupying power to rein back the German plans, only to decide that it 'would be impolitic' to give General Robertson (the British C-in-C in Germany) instructions 'clearly based solely on consideration of British commercial interests . . .'.[75] In its report the Economic Co-operation Committee also questioned the German intention to lose no time in providing the German worker with 'a more plentiful and varied diet' by way of rewarding and encouraging effort. In its view, the Germans 'cannot afford so big an improvement. As with export plans, a rather slower rate of improvement would be reasonable. . . .'[76]

But it was this committee's summing-up of West Germany's overall situation which so graphically portrays the conventional 'soundness', if not defeatism, of the Whitehall mind:

The Bizone is not a country economically maladjusted by the war. It is an artificial segment of a highly complete economic unit, split on an artificial boundary. This segment cannot expect rapidly to become a viable economic unit by itself. It must either rejoin the rest of Germany and regain access to its economic hinterland . . . or it must begin *a slow and painful process* [emphasis added] of fitting its economy into that of the West. . . .[77]

It might have been an old-fashioned family accountant giving incontrovertible reasons why a future millionaire could not possibly make a quick fortune.

Likewise unconsciously revealing of the doctrinaire 'givens' which determined British policy is a report six months later, in June 1949, by a working party led by the (Keynesian) Economic Section of the Cabinet Office on the current performance of the German economy. The working party noted that the index of German industrial production in March 1949 stood at 89 per cent of 1936 compared with 51 per cent a year before, and acknowledged that this 'rapid increase in output is almost certainly due to the effect of the currency reform in restoring economic incentives . . .'.[78] It accepted that wage increases at a stunning (in British terms) annual rate of 18 per cent nevertheless 'appeared less than the increase in productivity' (amounting to 35 per cent since 1947). It further accepted that despite the rise in wages the cost-of-living index had remained stable for the previous four months.[79] And yet, although these were achievements unequalled by the British economy, the working party typically chose to focus on the level of German unemployment, currently running at about 6 per cent, compared with the British figure of about 1.5 per cent.[80] While it had to acknowledge that this rise in unemployment had been 'accompanied by a very large increase in production' as well as by a rise in the total size of the workforce, it nonetheless fearfully doubted 'whether the "free economy" to which the Germans are moving will be able to solve this problem' of keeping the country fully employed.[81] It even asked whether a dose of Keynesian boosting of demand might not help to bring down German unemployment.[82]

Then again, while the working party accepted that the 'shift to profits' in Germany had 'helped to increase savings', the small-'l' liberal social consciences (and perhaps an underlying puritanism) of its members were troubled by the thought that, 'if investment is financed in this way, it will be at the cost of very unequal distribution of wealth, and at the cost of considerable investment in luxury trades and of ostentatious consumption by a few'.[83] They therefore naturally also disapproved of the German policy of encouraging private savings by 'low taxation of high incomes' because of 'its social disadvantages' and reckoned that the total of the German nation's savings could probably be increased even further by bleeding the successful by progressive tax rates as in Britain.[84]

And as for the German intention swiftly to abolish remaining controls, the working party commented with a sniff: 'The implications of so rapid an abandonment of direct controls are as much political as economic, but the [German] statement that "Decontrol of goods is preferable to maintenance of control" is so absurd a general statement that it might well evoke at least a mild comment.'[85]

In the light of such criticisms it hardly astonishes that Britain's own tender for Marshall Aid[86] is well marinaded in the social and economic values of the 'postwar consensus'. Indeed, in its choice of national priorities the tender marks the very consummation of British total strategy in the five years after the Second World War.

PART FIVE

The Opportunity Slips Away

The French Government has prescribed the setting-up *of a plan* of modernisation and equipment . . . [in order] to achieve as high a rate of productivity as those of the most advanced countries.

(FRENCH TENDER FOR MARSHALL AID, 1948)

New chemical processes, new methods of food processing, new uses for glass, plywood and light metals are a few developments that may need large capital expenditures, give opportunities for establishing new businesses and perhaps entire new industries. . . .

(GERMAN TENDER FOR MARSHALL AID, 1948)

The development and modernisation of industrial and agricultural equipment is one of the explicit objectives of the European Recovery Programme. A careful balance between this and other objectives must be maintained. Excessive home investment might defeat its own ends. . . .

(BRITISH TENDER FOR MARSHALL AID, 1948)

The Mission believes that the United Kingdom should provide for even larger investment in the modernizing of its plants so that when E.C.A. aid terminates the country will be in a sounder competitive position. . . .

(LONDON MISSION OF EUROPEAN RECOVERY ADMINISTRATION, 1948)

CHAPTER NINETEEN

The Wasting of Marshall Aid

IN THE 1960s and 1970s British folk-wisdom cherished (perhaps still cherishes) a comfortable explanation for Britain's relative economic decline since the Second World War, and especially her then all too evident industrial backwardness compared with West Germany. West Germany, so the story goes, had all her industries and transport systems bombed flat during the war, and then, thanks to Marshall Aid, was able completely to rebuild them with the most up-to-date equipment. Meanwhile poor old Britain had to struggle on with worn-out or obsolete kit.

This favourite British 'wooden leg' excuse is pure myth. In the first place, West German industrial capacity in 1948 stood at 90 per cent of 1936 despite wartime bombing and postwar reparations.[1] Secondly, Britain in fact received a third more Marshall Aid than West Germany – $2.7 billion net as against Germany's $1.7 billion. She indeed pocketed the largest share of any European nation.[2]

The truth is that the Labour Government, advised by its resident economic pundits, freely chose *not* to make the re-equipping of Britain as an industrial society the *Schwerpunkt* of her use of Marshall Aid. Instead, the Government saw Marshall Aid (like the American loan of 1945) primarily as a wad of greenbacks stuffed by a kindly Uncle Sam into the breeches pocket of a nearly bankrupt John Bull who, though diligently seeking future solvency, nevertheless still wished in the meantime to go on playing the squire, beneficent to his family and the poor, and grand among the neighbours.[3]

This is made clear in back-handed fashion by the response in July 1947 of a group of Whitehall economists and civil servants to the 'worst possible case' of there being no early prospect of Marshall

Aid.[4] As one of them put it, such a situation would require 'drastic action internally and on import programmes, and a major reversal of engines in the whole field of overseas commercial and financial policy . . .'.[5] It would, moreover, entail a 'review of military and other commitments overseas':[6] an echo here of Keynes's tolling bell of August 1945 (see above, p. 42). Dollar imports would have to be cut by some £250 million, meaning skimpier rations of meat, sugar and dairy produce for the British public, and also, because of lack of North American timber, a harsh curtailment of the New Jerusalem programme to provide every family with its own dwelling. There would have to be 'drastic action, equivalent to national mobilisation, to expand export production (e.g. coal and textiles), stimulate import-saving production (e.g. agricultural), and stop long-term capital projects . . .'.[7] The Chancellor of the Exchequer, Stafford Cripps, took a similar view of life without Marshall Aid, foreseeing in January 1948 that 'a serious drain on our reserves, estimated at between £150 and £255 million, will continue through 1949. This would bring our reserves far below the danger point long before we could have any chance of restoring a balance.'[8] Without United States aid, he continued, there would be no option but further drastic cuts in imports, especially in raw materials, 'even to the point of causing serious unemployment . . .'. This last chilling thought was repeated in the draft *Economic Survey for 1948.*[9]

It followed from such 'worst possible case' analyses that, in the words of the draft *Survey,* 'the chances of receiving American assistance in extent and form adequate to avert these possibilities become of overwhelming importance in any final assessment of economic prospects . . .'.[10] This led the authors of the draft *Survey* to the conclusion that '*the primary purpose* [emphasis added] for which aid of any kind must, therefore, be used (if it were in a form that so allowed) is to enable us to maintain import programmes now financed from vanishing reserves and continue our contribution to European recovery . . .'.[11]

On the same date the Chairman of the London Committee on Marshall Aid (Richard Clarke, Under-Secretary at the Treasury, one of the elect of the liberal Establishment, and a leading back-seat driver of British policy in regard to Marshall Aid) advised ministers that Britain should aim for:

food consumption restored to a level broadly similar to that ruling before the cuts were imposed this summer [in the convertibility crisis]; the present consumption of textiles, tobacco and steel-using consumer goods; restoration of some basic petrol and tourism and a six-page newspaper; *some increase in investment* [emphasis added]; some re-stocking of raw materials. . . .[12]

Such a level of food consumption would, according to the London Committee, 'leave us better off than most of the Western European countries are now or would expect to be during the early years of the European Recovery Programme . . .'.[13] In accordance with this priority Britain in her interim claim for Marshall Aid (in respect of the period April–June 1948) allotted $176 million to dollar imports of food, and $18 million equally to tobacco and machinery.[14] A later report by the London Committee on 19 March 1948 argued that the Americans should give Britain the latitude 'to use the aid to buy the supplies we need most' – such as enough materials to make possible the increases in the housing programme agreed on by the Government.[15] Nevertheless, maintaining import programmes 'now financed from vanishing reserves' in order to sustain 'full employment', the housing programme and the British standard of living did not constitute the sole 'primary purpose' for which Britain proposed to use Marshall Aid. There was another, pithily spelt out by the Chancellor of the Exchequer on 25 March 1948: 'We must . . . so manage our affairs as to have no loss of [gold and dollar] reserves during that period. This is fundamental to our survival after the period of Marshall Aid. . . .'[16] He reiterated this in May 1948, after the passing of the European Recovery Act by Congress:

In particular, we must maintain our reserves at a reasonable level throughout the E.R.P. period so that at the end of this time they will be in a tolerable condition. . . .

It is of first importance to persuade the United States Administration of *the overriding need* [emphasis added] to us of maintaining our reserves. The point has already been put to them, but it appears [from a telegram] from Washington that the administration will be under considerable pressure to force us to draw our reserves down. This would be disastrous to our whole prospect of recovery, and I hope my colleagues will support the strongest possible representations when these are needed.[17]

And he laid down as one requirement for maintaining the reserves: 'minimum [dollar] purchase of machinery and manufactured goods'.[18]

Why was the British Government – unlike the German or French – so worried about conserving its pot of gold and dollars? It was not only because of a prudent concern about Britain's own balance of payments after the end of Marshall Aid, but also, more importantly, because of its resolve to cling on to Britain's role as banker to the Sterling Area, and so perpetuate her historic status as a financial world power. According to the report on 23 December 1947 by the London Committee on the prospects of Marshall Aid, 'The United Kingdom gold and dollar reserves which are threatened are the reserves also of the Colonial Empire and the independent countries, mostly members of the Commonwealth, who are members of the Sterling Area. . . .'[19] The committee judged that the United States Government would not relish a British request directly to stem 'the sterling area dollar drain on our reserves'.[20] It therefore recommended that Commonwealth countries should seek to cover their dollar needs either by themselves approaching the International Monetary Fund, the International Bank or – here it came – by drawing from 'sterling area reserves', that is, Britain's pot of gold and dollars.

In July 1948, at the request of the European Recovery Programme representative in London,[21] the Cabinet Office produced lengthy briefs on the history and present operation of the Sterling Area, coupled with a detailed guesstimate of the area's gold and dollar balance sheet for July–September that year.[22] The historical survey described in particular how Britain had come to incur her biggest Sterling Area burden, the so-called sterling balances, or, in plainer terms, those debts (amounting to £2.7 billion at the end of 1947) run up with India, Pakistan, Burma, Ceylon and certain Middle Eastern and other countries (and, to a lesser extent, with Australia and New Zealand) for the privilege of defending them in the Second World War: debts which since the war Britain had felt herself duty-bound to pay off gradually by supplying 'unrequited exports' (that is, not currently paid for in cash or goods). In the survey's own words, since Great Britain bore 'the ultimate responsibility for the maintenance of Sterling, [the] obligation to assist in the maintenance of these great populations has in fact fallen on us and we have had to allow these drawings – not in order to encourage or assist our own trade, but in most cases in order to keep the people of these regions and their economy alive . . . .'[23]

At the same time, because out of the whole rummage-bag of Commonwealth and colonies only Malaya earned plenty of dollars, and most of the rest incurred hefty deficits, it had fallen to Britain, in the words of the draft *Economic Survey for 1948*, to provide 'dollars to the non-American world' – also 'unrequited', since this provision had to serve as another means of paying off Britain's wartime debts.[24]

On top of such crippling obligations, the Cabinet Office brief reminded the ERP representative, Britain also continued to shoulder the burden of acting as central bank for the internal transactions of the Sterling Area, 'the largest multilateral trade area in the world':[25]

It is obviously necessary for the support of such a system of multilateral trading to carry a very considerable volume of reserves in order to allow of the seasonal and other fluctuations that must take place in the Trade of the world, including changes in the price of primary products on which the economy of so much of the Sterling Area depends.

It is for this purpose that the Reserves of gold and Foreign Exchange are required to service the needs of the whole Sterling group; without adequate reserves the Group would not continue to function and this would have the most restrictive effect not only on Trade within the Group but also upon Trade between various members of the Group and the outside world. . . .[26]

And so: 'Our sheet anchor is the doctrine that our reserves must not fall in the E.R.P. Period. . . .'[27]

No wonder, then, that in September 1948 the Chancellor of the Exchequer was expressing his relief that the OEEC had agreed to lump the rest of the Sterling Area in with Britain in its proposals to be submitted to Washington for the share-out of Marshall Aid in 1948–9:

It is, of course, of great importance to our general strategy that the sterling area has been treated as a whole, and it will now be extremely difficult for E.C.A. [Economic Co-operation Administration] (even if it wishes to do so) to rule out the inclusion of the rest of the sterling area's dollar deficit in our dollar balance of payments for E.R.P. purposes.[28]

However, Whitehall intended that Marshall Aid should not only thus subsidise Britain's role as banker to the Sterling Area, but also serve – even if indirectly – to underwrite the wider costs (including military) of her pretensions as a world power. As the Cabinet Office brief for the ERA in July 1948 put it,

> It is perfectly true that if E.R.P. covers our dollar drain (and we cut down our import programme so that it does) then all our payments of gold and dollars can be regarded, by a form of marginal theory, as being financed by E.R.P. But this not only applies to the R.S.A. [Rest of Sterling Area – that is, other than the UK] deficit, but also to every conceivable gold and dollar payment we make – the Ford dividend, expenses of H.M. Embassy in Washington, legacies to American citizens, gold payments to Persia, purchase of petrol for our troops in the Middle East, every conceivable thing. One must realise that there are many items in our balance of payments unsuitable to be included in E.R.P. as such. But they must enter into our general calculations.[29]

All participants in Marshall Aid were required by the United States in drafting their long-term programmes to take as their ultimate objective the achieving by 1952–3 of what was called 'viability' (that is, independence from extraordinary economic assistance). Neither the German nor the French programmes gave great prominence to this objective, being content optimistically to claim that 'viability' would follow from industrial development and the consequent boost in exports. This blithe approach incurred British disapproval, especially because of the size of investment in industry and infrastructure contemplated by these countries. The United Kingdom Delegation to the OEEC observed of the French programme that its objectives 'may prove difficult or impossible of achievement within the period of four and a half years', and so affect 'the attainment of viability'.[30] The German programme, opined one Whitehall economic pundit, 'does not achieve the objective of viability or at least does not do so in the terms of the O.E.E.C. exercise . . .'.[31]

In contrast, the British tender in one way and another revolved round this short-term question of 'viability', or, in other words, the balance of payments – that balance as it had been, as it now was, and as

'. . . Britain's primary weakness was apparent enough – too much of her industrial strength was deployed in the old Victorian staples, too little in new technologies with fast growing markets . . .' A Lancashire cotton mill, late 1940s.

'. . . public opinion in the early postwar era was no more keen on remaking British society for the sake of success in world markets than it had been on rearming against Nazi Germany in 1933–35 . . .' Morning rush-hour on London Bridge.

'Like so much of Britain's equipment as an industrial country in 1945, the civil service elite was, in the method of its selection, its concept of its role and in its way of working, a Victorian survival overdue for root-and-branch modernization . . .'

Top Left: Sir Edward Bridges (Cabinet Secretary, 1938–46, Permanent Under-Secretary at the Treasury, 1946–56; son of the Poet Laureate; Eton and Magdalen College, Oxford; classics).

Top Right: Sir Henry Self (Permanent Under-Secretary at the Ministry of Civil Aviation, 1946–47; Bancroft's School and London University; degrees in science, mathematics, classics and philosophy; President of the Modern Churchman's Union 1947–57).

Left: Sir Donald Fergusson (Permanent Under-Secretary at the Ministry of Fuel and Power, 1945–52; Berkhampsted School and Magdalen College, Oxford; modern history).

Right: The 'Britain Can Make It' exhibition, 1946, heralding the postwar export drive. But in 1949, the year when sterling was devalued by a third against the dollar because of a balance of payments crisis, the President of the Board of Trade reported: '. . . our share of the total import trade of the USA and Canada is substantially lower than before the war . . .'

Below: '. . . as soon as the early postwar world shortage of cars was over, the foreign buyer could purchase a large, rugged and comfortable American car for less than the price of Britain's flimsier confections . . .' Assembly line for the Austin A40, Birmingham, 1949.

'. . . soot-grimed swathes of obsolescence and decay across Northern England and the Black Country, and across Southern Scotland and South Wales . . . the most intractable of all Britain's handicaps . . .' The compulsions and bribes of 'regional policy' failed to remove this handicap.

'Yet in the event "full employment", far from being the supreme social good, was to prove the most pervasively effective brake of all on the pace of technological change . . .' Workers in the London docks 'fully employed' – and fully unionised.

'. . . the one large-scale attempt to develop a major industry based on advanced technology, but founded not on industrial and commercial realism, but on the delusion that Britain with the Commonwealth was, and would remain, a power in the same league as the United States . . .' The Bristol Brabazon transatlantic airliner, the most expensive of the 'turkeys' produced by postwar aviation policy. It never entered service.

'. . . the failure to press on with major schemes of industrial development is doing irreparable harm to the national economy . . .' So wrote the President of the Board of Trade, in March 1948. Despite receiving much more Marshall Aid than either France or Germany, Britain invested a far lower proportion in modernising her industry and infrastructure. This Lancashire scene actually dates from 1954.

Left: 'A policy of parlours before plant' – £130 million more capital investment was poured into new housing in the three years 1947 to 1949 than into new construction in all industries and the country's decrepit transport and communications networks. A new block of council flats, Walthamstow, London, 1948.

Below: ' . . . a melancholy record of contrasts between what needed to be done and what was sanctioned to be done . . .' Between 1945 and 1950 the obsolete and worn-out railway system – along with the rest of the national infrastructure – was starved of investment by the Labour Government because of the competing demands of New Jerusalem and the world role.

'. . . the hazards of worn-out electro-mechanical exchanges, hard-pressed operators in unmechanised trunk exchanges, and overloaded long-distance cabling . . .' The national telecommunications network proved yet another victim of the rationing of capital investment in 1945–50.

'. . . a network which is essentially dated in configuration from the horse-drawn or even the ox-drawn era . . .' Nevertheless, not a single mile of motorway was built in 1945–50, and even urgent local improvements like new bridges were put off again and again.

Left: '. . . nationalisation, far from serving to whip progress forward, enabled Whitehall the better to rein it back.' The flag of the National Coal Board was hoisted at mines all over the country on Vesting Day, 1 January 1947.

Below: 'Britain was now once again facing the very real prospect of national bankruptcy . . .' In September 1949, and even though she was benefiting from generous Marshall Aid, Britain was compelled by a balance-of-payments crisis to devalue sterling by a third against the dollar.

it would be in 1952–3, when, according to the tender, 'viability could unquestionably be secured . . . .'.[32]

Why this anxious concern with 'viability'? It may have been because of a scrupulous regard (not shared by those ungentlemanly Europeans) for the object of Marshall Aid as formally laid down by the United States administration.[33] But it is much more probable that, like so much else, it stemmed from Whitehall's hallucination that Britain could have a future as a world power. Since living on tick was hardly consistent with being a world power, such a future clearly depended on regaining financial and economic independence as soon as possible. In a memorandum to his Cabinet colleagues in September 1948 the Chancellor of the Exchequer, Stafford Cripps, acknowledged in so many words that this was indeed the British motivation: 'The special significance of these programmes [to achieve viability by 1952–3] is that they mark the point in the curve at which we cease to live on American charity, with all that this freedom implies for national self-respect and for our independent position in the world.'[34]

How did the concern for 'viability' within four years, the 'overriding need' to conserve Britain's gold and dollar reserves, and the 'primary purpose' to maintain the level of imports together affect the amount of Marshall Aid to be invested in modernising Britain as an industrial society? The answer is that they served to relegate such investment to the mere category in the British Long-Term Programme of being 'clearly of great importance'.[35]

Germany and France in their own long-term programmes chose as their *Schwerpunkt* (or, as it might be said, overriding need or primary purpose) massive investment in industry and infrastructure, opening the way to rapid advances in production and exports.[36] The French programme in fact took the form of an enlargement of '*Le Plan*', in progress since the beginning of 1947. In its own words,

the French Government has prescribed the setting-up *of a plan* of modernisation and equipment, having as its objective to put at the disposal of French agriculture and industry the machines, techniques and methods which will enable them to achieve as high a rate of productivity as those of the most advanced countries.[37]

371

The first part of the French programme ('Exposé général') dwells entirely on modernisation, production programmes and investment. The second part, consisting of appendices on particular topics, opens with production programmes and objectives before going on to deal with the balance of payments and foreign exchanges. In the German long-term programme the topics of investment, industrial production, agriculture and manpower rate thirty pages out of fifty-two, whereas foreign trade and fiscal policy rate only twelve.[38] In short, whatever may be their incidental flaws, both these programmes are technocratic corporate plans framed in accordance with clear 'mission statements'.

In contrast, the British 'Long-Term Programme' is a prolix academic essay characteristic of the Whitehall mind of 'Our Age'. It opens with a disquisition on the role of economic planning in a democratic society, and proceeds to a tour of the wide horizon – fiscal policy, the balance of payments, multilateral trade, government efforts to persuade the nation of the need to produce and export more, the Sterling Area, full employment, the importance of international co-operation. It is indeed, as Cripps acknowledged at the time, 'a general statement' rather than 'a set of detailed plans of action',[39] or, in less polite language, a Whitehall smoke-screen. According to the British Progress Report to the OEEC in spring 1950, the 'Long-Term Programme':

> did not set out to give a comprehensive set of forecasts for every sector of the economy whose internal consistency could be tested. . . . Much of the document was in fact descriptive of the then situation of the United Kingdom and of its problems, and of the methods in use to secure objectives which were vital to the achievement of viability. . . . Moreover it was considered undesirable to be too explicit about our expectations in a document which it was anticipated would eventually be published. Consequently much of the information was presented in a form which is not readily comparable with current statistics.[40]

Relegated to third and fourth out of the seven 'chapters' of the 'Long-Term Programme' are 'Major Industrial Plans' and 'Investment in the United Kingdom', together comprising 101 paragraphs out of 226. The chapter on 'Major Industrial Plans' sets out to prove (sometimes by the dubious device of percentage increases rather than actual figures) how output and export volumes in various industries have swollen impressively over 1947 or 1938 (a poor pre-war year, and so a favourable comparison), and how they are expected to go on swelling mightily during the period of Marshall Aid. However, in striking contrast to the German approach[41] there is very little attention paid to the differences between technologies in terms of future potential, either in regard to added value, or likely return on capital or world-market share – hardly surprising, since none of the economists or politicians who drafted the 'Programme', essay-writers and committee-men all, had ever worked in a design studio or factory, or sold so much as a cake at a charity bazaar. It is very much a question of 'never mind the quality, feel the width'. This emphasis on volume attracted sharp criticism from the ECA Mission in London in its report on the United Kingdom long-term and 1949–50 programmes:

> Throughout the programmes, stress is continuously placed on the production of goods for export. Although there are some comments on increased productivity, nowhere does there appear to be concrete recognition of the growing difficulties which will face the selling of United Kingdom goods abroad as the present seller's market shifts to a buyer's market. The United Kingdom export targets during the next four years will be met only if its products can meet increasing world competition.[42]

In common with the German and French tenders, the British tender certainly laid much emphasis on developing energy supplies (coal, oil, gas and electricity) and the basic industries such as steel and agriculture. However, its picture of general manufacturing might have been painted by L. S. Lowry, all reeking chimneys, gaunt mills and thunderous workshops. For the main sections are taken up with the traditional 'heavies' such as cotton and woollen textiles, shipbuilding, bulk chemicals, mechanical engineering. Although the programme does accord rayon and terylene together one paragraph out of eight in the section on 'Textiles', there are not even passing mentions of consumer white goods, motor-vehicles, office machines, electrical and radio products or even aircraft, let alone separate sections in the main texts and in the statistical tables on investment and production. Thus the British programme does not display the same awareness of Whitehall studies back in wartime (see above, pp. 30, 170–71) that British industry stood in need of fundamental redeployment from old familiar products and their slow-growing markets to new technologies with the potential for fast export growth and high added value. In short, the British programme evinced none of the forward vision displayed by its German rival:

> New methods, material and products developed during the war may well have an effect upon capital investment and the structure of industry. New chemical processes, new methods of food processing, new uses for glass, plywood and light metals are a few developments that may need large capital expenditures, give opportunities for establishing new businesses and perhaps entire new industries, adding to the demand for capital goods.[43]

But in any case Britain simply did not propose to invest as high a proportion of her Marshall Aid (or of her GNP) in industry and infrastructure as Germany, France or, for that matter, Italy – the logical consequence of relegating such investment to third in priority ('clearly of great importance') behind keeping up imports ('a primary purpose') and the maintenance of the gold and dollar reserves ('an overriding need'). The opening paragraph of the chapter in the 'Long-Term Programme' on 'Investment in the United Kingdom', while remarking that the 'development and modernisation of industrial and agricultural equipment is one of the explicit objectives of the European Recovery Programme', immediately adds the cavil:

> A careful balance between this and other objectives must be maintained. Excessive home investment might defeat its own ends; it would endanger stability [author's note: that is, domestic price stability, already subverted by inflationary pressure, arising not least from full employment], require more imports than can be afforded and sharply limit exports. . . .[44]

Britain therefore proposed a gross fixed investment programme for all purposes (*including* housing) of about $8.4 billion a year during the period of Marshall Aid – no larger in real terms than in 1947.[45] Although the 'Long-Term Programme' bragged that this figure amounted to 20 per cent of GNP, gross fixed capital formation in 1948 in fact came to only 13–14 per cent of GNP. This compares with Germany's projected annual figure of 21.4 per cent.[46]

The ECA Mission in London proved by no means happy with the cautiousness of Britain's plans for industrial investment, nor with the concomitant priority given instead to the balance of payments:

> Within the same quality range, the British must concentrate upon lowering unit costs. And this in turn means increased productivity. The Mission believes that the United Kingdom should provide for even larger investment in the modernizing of its plants so that when E.C.A. aid terminates the country will be in a sounder competitive position. Only in this manner can viability, once achieved, be maintained. The Mission ... does not believe that a greater investment can be accomplished, however, if too much emphasis is placed upon reducing present payment deficits between now and 1952 to the detriment of plant modernisation.[47]

Direct comparisons between the British programme and, say, the French or German are not easy, since the British deliberately avoided giving a detailed forecast of how they would deploy investment between 1948 and 1952.[48] Rather, they offered catch-all totals, which in any case dealt in *gross* fixed investment instead of the more relevant *net* fixed investment (that is, new, extra, construction and kit) which France and Germany provided as well as gross figures.[49] But if British net fixed investment is taken to be 30 per cent of gross,[50] this would give a projected total for all purposes (including housing) of about $9.6 billion (or 6 per cent of GNP) for the four-year period of Marshall Aid, as against Germany's $8.1 billion (or 9.2 per cent of GNP, rising, according to the German programme, to 11 per cent by 1953).[51] The planned British effort in regard to overall net fixed investment was thus proportionately a third poorer than Germany's.

The inadequacy of British intentions with regard to investment during the four years of Marshall Aid can be expressed in another way. Britain proposed to invest for all purposes a sum equivalent to three times the Aid that she eventually received: about $9.6 billion to $2.7 billion. But the French target for overall net investment was the equivalent of four times what she eventually received in Aid: $10.7 billion to $2.7 billion. And the German target came to nearly five times the sum eventually received in Aid: $8.1 billion to $1.7 billion.[52] In other words, as things stood in 1948, an ERP dollar handed to Germany during the next four years would lead to nearly twice the

375

pay-off in terms of overall net new investment as a dollar handed to Britain.

But when it comes to comparisons of investment in industry and infrastructure *alone*, the British effort (as guesstimated in Whitehall for Whitehall eyes only) looks even more flaccid. In November 1948 the Investment Programmes Committee was reckoning such investment in the current year at about half the total of all investment, and much the same in 1949.[53] Over the four years of Marshall Aid this annual rate would give a cumulative net fixed investment in energy industries, iron and steel, factories and plant of all kinds, and transport and communications of about $5.6 billion[54] (or about 2.9 per cent of GNP) – as against Germany's $4.2 billion[55] (or nearly 4 per cent of estimated GNP).

Moreover, even though Whitehall had earlier reckoned that 1949–50 would be 'the decisive year of the whole programme',[56] the Labour Government failed to spur investment into a gallop despite the stimulus of a belly-full of Marshall Aid oats. Under the Cabinet's investment plan for 1949 the energy industries, manufacturing, and transport and communications were to receive just 3 per cent more than the guesstimated figure for 1948 (and, if shipping is included, by 1.8 per cent!)[57] – a meaningless gesture, since, as a secret paragraph (not to appear in the published version) of the draft 1949 *Economic Survey* pointed out, 'these calculations of fixed investment both for the past and for the future are extremely uncertain. The statistical material on which they are based is quite inadequate. . . .'[58] As it turned out, in the wake of the great summer sterling crisis (see above, pp. 90, 159–60) the Prime Minister actually ordered investment in all industries (energy included) and infrastructure to be *cut* by £50 million, of which £15 million was to fall on manufacturing.[59] In consequence investment in new industrial plant and machinery in 1950 was to drop by £7 million, and in new building for industry by £5 million.[60] According to Whitehall estimates in January 1950, investment in such new construction in the 'decisive' Marshall Aid years 1949 and 1950 (at £62 million and a projected £61.75 million respectively) would be a mere 3 per cent higher than in 1948 – barely ahead of inflation.[61]

In any case, the 1949 sterling devaluation serves strikingly to demonstrate that it had been without avail that Britain had been pouring Marshall Aid into the holed pot of her reserves of gold and dollars,[62] whence much of it leaked away down the drain of the Sterling Area. By now Whitehall was beginning to fear that the United States might grow weary of supplying Aid for such a purpose. Even before devaluation, Sir Oliver Franks, the British Ambassador in Washington, was reporting that it was uppermost in the minds of Dean Acheson, the American Secretary of State, and Hoffman, the ERA Administrator, that British policies should be directed at improving her 'efficiency and competitive power'.[63] The Chancellor noted at the same time that 'American attention is now turning to the internal rigidities of the British economic structure.'[64] In other words, stop asking us to keep bailing you out, and start putting yourselves in order. When on 13 December 1949 the Cabinet Economic Policy Committee met to ponder how best to angle Britain's application for Marshall Aid in 1950–1, it took note that 'the United States officials so far consulted had been unanimous in their view that Congress would not be prepared to make a large appropriation which would apparently go straight to the United Kingdom Government's reserves . . .'.[65]

Given the British Government's preference for 'wholesale' handouts under broad ERP categories which it could then spend 'retail' as it chose, it is no wonder that it should prove deeply reluctant to link receipts of Marshall Aid to particular uses – especially the technological uses on which the ERA was so keen. Whereas, for example, the Americans and the continental participants in Marshall Aid were jointly financing agreed industrial projects, to a total by June 1951 of $2.25 billion (only $565 million of which would have been directly provided by Marshall Aid),[66] His Majesty's Government, jealous of the sovereignty of a world power, stood aloof. As early as January 1948 the Cabinet Economic Policy Committee chaired by the Prime Minister had decided that it would be necessary:

> to define with great care the arrangements under which the United States Government would be furnished with information about the use of supplies provided under the European Recovery Programme. It was undesirable that any opening be given for excessive interference by United States representatives in our management of our domestic affairs.[67]

The civil servants on Whitehall's European Economic Co-operation Committee were to prove similarly cagey.[68] For example, in response to a proposal by the OEEC that such machinery imports as could be directly related to broad economic projects should be listed in the 1949–50 programme, the committee agreed that while it was 'desirable for us to seek to satisfy the views of the European Economic Co-operation Administration',

> any initiative on our side might give rise to embarrassing enquiries by E.C.A. about the end-use of E.R.P. commodities. Moreover, if information [about machinery imports] . . . were submitted as an appendage to OEEC's 1949–50 Report it would in fact show a relatively very small percentage of United Kingdom E.R.P. imports directly connected with projects. A number of other countries, in their programmes, would certainly be able to show far better percentages. . . .[69]

A rare exception was the new steel strip mill at Margam in South Wales, its components being entirely American because of the lack of the necessary engineering capability in Britain.

Yet of all the contrasts between the British deployment of Marshall Aid and the French or German deployment the most revealing lies in the use of so-called 'counter-part funds' (the proceeds in a country's own currency of selling Marshall Aid supplies on its domestic market). For France and Germany (Italy too) allotted these funds to major programmes of modernisation in industry or infrastructure. The French long-term programme in fact formally committed *all* her counter-part funds to '*Le Plan*',[70] to an eventual total of nearly $2 billion, including $724.5 million in her energy industries and $281.3 million in transportation and communications.[71] Germany invested counter-part funds to a total of $629.4 million, of which $166.6 million went to the energy industries and $84 million to machinery and light industry.[72] But Britain chose instead to devote all her $1.7 billion of counter-part funds to 'retiring' (that is, reducing) public debt.[73] Whereas the continentals benefited by a whole series of major technological developments, such as the electrification of the 317-mile main line between Paris and Lyons,[74] Britain finished up with a mere alteration of figures in a ledger.

Why did the British Government opt for so imbecilely barren a policy? It was out of fear that to spend counter-part funds on capital re-equipment would disastrously turn up the flame beneath the inflation already simmering away under the repressive lid of controls, subsidies and rationing.[75] In other words, the counter-part funds were wasted because, firstly, the Government had failed to reform the currency and cancel public debt like Germany, and secondly, because contrariwise it was stoking general inflation through commitment to the costs of both the world role and New Jerusalem ('full employment', the welfare state and costly housing programmes).

In the meantime the prime-ministerial cuts in capital investment in the productive economy in autumn 1949 had been followed in spring 1950 by the Cabinet decision to hold back such investment in the future for the sake of building more houses, so all too suitably rounding off what Whitehall had originally envisaged as the 'decisive year of the whole [Aid] programme' (see above, p. 376).[76] In the event, Britain would invest in 1950 only 9 per cent of GNP in gross fixed capital formation in plant, machinery, buildings and transport for industry and infrastructure as against Germany's 19 per cent, with the result that her actual total of such investment would amount to only 78 per cent of the German total.[77] Such was the sacrifice made by Britain for the sake of choosing as her overriding Marshall Aid objective the maintenance of the Sterling Area's dollar reserves (see above, pp. 367–9). Yet the sacrifice had proved to be in vain, for in spring 1950 these reserves were, as the Chancellor of the Exchequer reported to his colleagues, 'still at a lower level than when Marshall Aid began and lower still than when we suspended convertibility . . .'.

> In order to rebuild them to a satisfactory level we shall need to earn a steady dollar surplus over a long period at a time during which external aid will diminish and come to an end and we shall become liable to repay dollar loans ourselves. From the end of 1951 our loan obligations to the United States and Canada increase by about $200 million a year.[78]

*

Marshall Aid had offered Britain a unique opportunity to remake herself as an industrial power while time should serve. By botching this opportunity the Labour Government (abetted by the Whitehall intelligentsia) had therefore accomplished the cardinal blunder of their entire total-strategy.

For in the competition to design things, make them and sell them for a living in the markets of the world, Britain by 1950 was already beginning to lose her enormous postwar headstart over rivals hobbled at first by defeat and occupation.

CHAPTER TWENTY

'The Policy of "Take It or Leave It"'

ONCE THE sellers' market of 1946–7 had vanished, much of British industry competing in hard-currency export markets bore a gruesome resemblance to an army deficient in all the fundamentals needed for victory in the field. In the first place, it lacked up-to-date, well-made weaponry well designed for the terrain – that is to say, first-class goods tailored to the requirements of particular foreign markets. This was partly due to the prevailing technical stagnation in British industry, both in the design of products and in the plant that fabricated them. But it was also partly due to British companies' ingrained habit of manufacturing a product according to their own ideas of excellence, and then expecting the customer gratefully to buy it. For British businessmen neglected, indeed scorned, reconnaissance, or, in other words, thorough study of consumers' preferences in a given market before embarking on a sales campaign. This resemblance to an army ripe for defeat extended to a lack both of well-devised strategic plans for marketing and pricing, and of shrewd selling tactics. It extended to limp and incompetent conduct of actual marketing operations, which were characterised by late and undependable delivery, shortage of spare parts, and slow and sketchy after-sales service. In fact, British industry's postwar export record of hasty improvisation, of floundering on unfamiliar and ill-reconnoitred terrain, of the unreliability and ineffectiveness of poorly designed and untested kit, can only put a military historian in mind of such early British campaigns of the Second World War as Norway in 1940 and the Western Desert in 1941.[1]

Already in the course of 1948 British exporters were beginning to fail the rigorous test at proof presented by Switzerland, which, though small, was the epitome of a rich, technically sophisticated and highly discriminating market. If British industry could not triumph over its rivals here, it could hardly hope to do so in much bigger but similarly exacting markets in Europe or elsewhere. As the Commercial Counsellor at the British Embassy in Berne reported towards the end of 1948, 'The privileged position of the Swiss buyer tends to make competition for his favours more and more keen; every little advantage of price, quality, design and delivery is exploited to the full.'[2]

In this report the Commercial Counsellor drew attention to 'the great difference in approach of each foreign supplying country to the question of export . . .':

> In the United Kingdom . . . not only does the official rate of exchange appear to be high in the view of importers, but prices are being constantly adjusted upwards to meet increasing costs of production. Industrial associations actually have uniform export quotations for their members, and no consideration is paid to competition from other sources. On the other hand, the American supplier is prepared to cut prices radically in order to get into a market. . . . The Germans, as in pre-war days, are always willing to offer under competitors' quotations. . . .[3]

Unfortunately British pricing was not the end of it – indeed, hardly the beginning:

> The policy of 'Take it or leave it' is quite outplayed in the Swiss market, where the client insists on service and delivery to specification. . . . It is no exaggeration to say that numerous breaches of confidence by the supply of faulty or badly finished material have considerably lowered the traditional reputation of United Kingdom goods. Failure to keep to promised delivery dates, non-observance of Swiss buying seasons, unforeseen additional charges, abnormal packing expenses, delays in replying to enquiries, lack of technical literature or data in French, German or the metric system, unsatisfactory trade catalogues and apparent disinterestedness [sic] in this little market, have turned away many a good post-war client who now looks elsewhere for his needs. That a serious business transaction should be treated negligently because of shorter working hours and a five-day week is incomprehensible to the Swiss.[4]

Then again, the 'loose manner' in which British exporters made arrangements for marketing their goods in Switzerland had proved 'a frequent source of criticism':

> Preference is always given by the Swiss importer to direct purchases from the manufacturer. The approach of omnibus export agencies, often with no technical qualifications, is regarded with suspicion. They are generally considered to be not only unnecessary and expensive at a time when keen quotations mean everything, but they are an obstacle to prompt dealings and close understanding. . . .
> The appointment of unsuitable Swiss agents with little interest beyond their overall commission has also given rise to complaints. . . .[5]

While the slack British exporter to Switzerland fumbled and bumbled and lost ground, his German rival was beginning to advance again with the skill, teamwork, energy and initiative so often displayed in the past by battle-groups of the Wehrmacht. In remarking that 'the great progress recently made by Germany calls for special attention . . .', the Commercial Counsellor in Berne pointed out that it was 'distressing to the Swiss representative of United Kingdom manufacturers, who loyally lost all business during the war, to find himself beaten out by German deliveries at shorter dates and lower prices . . .'.[6]

The Counsellor's detailed comments on particular products made no more cheerful reading. Although British machinery (including machine-tools) was sometimes criticised by the Swiss for 'poor workmanship, bad finish and lack of attention to precision,' the main handicap here to sales lay, as with other goods, in 'long and uncertain deliveries', which supplied the 'decisive factor' in losing orders to America and Germany.[7] And while high British prices accounted for loss of market share in pottery, textiles, chemicals, pharmaceuticals and electrical apparatus, it was dowdy British design that depressed sales of cutlery and clothing.[8]

At the opposite end of the scale from Switzerland but just as ruthlessly dismissive of over-priced, under-designed and limply marketed products was North America, the largest market in the world in terms of buying power and geographical spread alike. It also constituted for Britain the one market that alone was vital to the achieving of 'viability' and hence those other desirables so much bandied about by politicians and bureaucrats like national independence and Britain's future as a centre of world influence and power. Yet in North America the British 'private enterprise' whose alleged virtues were constantly lauded by the Conservative Party in and out of Parliament was repeating on a continental scale the same patterns of ineptitude as it displayed in little Switzerland.

This was true even in Canada, a member of the Commonwealth. Among the chief handicaps to increasing exports of British machinery, according to a Whitehall report in February 1948, were 'long delivery dates', the 'unsuitability of our types for Canadian requirements', the 'inadequacy of our servicing arrangements', the 'inadequacy and unsuitability of the representation of British engineering industry in Canada' and the 'fear of the U.S.A. as competitors which has made some of our manufacturers hesitant about trying to get American business . . .'.[9] In the case of consumer industries, Canadians, being accustomed to American types, 'do not take readily to the United Kingdom version of the same goods . . .'.[10] Clearly it was beyond the wit of man, certainly Birmingham or Manchester man, to abandon the British version as quickly as practicable in favour of making American types, which in any case would have very likely gone down better with European customers like the Swiss as well.

A year later little had changed for the better. The President of the Board of Trade reported in March 1949 that 'the Canadian taste for American equipment plus the American ability to supply most engineering goods more quickly, and, in many cases, more cheaply than can the United Kingdom has made Canada a difficult market . . .'.[11] Overall, the value of British exports to Canada in 1948 had been about the same as the average (in 1948 prices) for the last three years before the war.[12]

It was the United States which presented at once the most splendid of all opportunities for the foreign exporter and the most daunting of challenges – the commercial equivalent, it might be said, of the Normandy invasion and the ensuing campaign in north-west Europe. For the United States had emerged from the war a far richer society than at the time of Pearl Harbor despite its colossal war production. In terms of industrial technology and also consumer goods (and consumer habits) it constituted by 1945 that future which the whole Western world would come to experience in the next half-century. This already existing future was excitingly portrayed by the editorial content and advertisements in American magazines such as *Look*, *Colliers* and the *Ladies Home Journal* which reached Britain during the war as the cultural candy within the cargoes of Lend–Lease – everything from eight-lane motorways with flyovers to self-service supermarkets and built-in kitchens complete with cabinet refrigerators, automatic washing-machines, and cookers twice the British size, all sleekly styled by professional design departments or consultant industrial designers like Raymond Loewy.[13]

To try to sell present British products, frumpishly old-fashioned as they for the most part were, to this market would be like landing Great War tanks and guns on the Normandy beaches on D-Day. Yet this is what British exporters did, at first understandably out of short-term necessity but later because of sheer dogged conservatism. New designs for the American market, such as the disastrous Austin Atlantic car (see below, p. 389), were to be the exception.

In any case, successfully to invade this market above all others required the same kind of professionalism, of thoroughness of staff work and organisation, of will to win, that the three British armed services had devoted for many months to planning and carrying out the D-Day landings. It did not receive it. Moreover, this continent-wide market also required a permanent commercial presence on the ground similar in geographical spread to the military presence now maintained in the Middle East and Far East in support of Ernest Bevin's foreign policy, even if in this case made up of managers, sales executives and engineers rather than soldiers, sailors and airmen. But it did not receive it.[14]

According to a Whitehall report in August 1948,

During 1947, the United Kingdom got off to a better start in the U.S. market than most other foreign countries but we knew that the latter were planning to develop exports to the U. S. and that they would do their utmost to compete with us. It is perhaps too soon to estimate the full force and consequences of this competition because though Japanese and German exports are being increased they are far from reaching the expected volume even in the U.S. market, but we must reckon at least with still keener Czechoslovakian, Italian and Belgian competition in the consumer goods field.[15]

The report warned that 'the progress made during the first five months [of 1948] gives little ground for complacency . . .'. Current sales, being swollen by 'windfall' items, 'do *not* represent a building up of long-term markets in the U.S.A. . . .'.[16]

These misgivings were fully borne out by a special *Time-Life* survey in summer 1948 of the American market for British consumer goods, which, in the words of a Whitehall summary, 'confirmed previous reports of the shortcomings of many United Kingdom firms, particularly their lack of understanding of the U.S. consumers' requirements and their inadequate arrangements for distribution outside the Eastern Seaboard area . . .'.

> There are criticisms [continued this précis of the *Time-Life* survey] of the lack of energy in opening up new channels of distribution to tap the large, potential markets in the South-West and North Central regions. There is evidence also of a continuing reluctance to regard the U.S. market as a desirable long-term market well worth the extra effort of establishing or expanding sales. . . .[17]

All this was further corroborated by a comprehensively scathing report by the British Consul-General in Houston, Texas, which:

> strongly criticises United Kingdom firms for delays in correspondence, poor advertising matter, unexpected price changes, reluctance to be guided by local knowledge and experience, unsuitable designs and lack of a wholehearted approach to developing trade with the wealthy S.W. region of the U.S.[18]

The melancholy conclusion was therefore drawn in Whitehall that it was:

> wishful thinking to suppose that the United Kingdom will be able to sell £70 million, or more, to the U.S.A. in those years [1949 and later] unless:
>
> (a) there is far greater determination and better marketing organisation by United Kingdom manufacturers and exporters in making a properly conceived effort to establish a wider market for their goods; and
>
> (b) more successful measures are devised to maintain or improve our competitive power.[19]

In September 1948 the Board of Trade not unjustifiably expressed the opinion that British manufacturers required 'a long and probably painful process of education, stressing the need to design goods according to American tastes, to study the market intensively and often to adopt American methods of selling . . .'.[20] Moreover, 'our merchanting foothold in the U.S.A. is extremely weak, partly because of the unwillingness of Americans to use any intermediaries and partly because of the high initial cost of gaining a footing . . .'.[21]

In December 1948 it was the turn of the Research Institute of America to indict – in a public report – the stupidity of British exporters. Apart from making the usual complaint (like the Swiss) about high prices and poor deliveries, the RIA concentrated on what it called 'Britain's Poor Salesmanship', painting an extraordinary picture of the commercial and industrial reality behind the costly façade of Britain as a first-class world power:

> More serious are the U.S. sales which British companies missed because they just didn't try. When RIA conducted its survey of the British Industries Fair last spring, many Members tried to contact British suppliers, only to discover amazing indifference. When one British manufacturer of a synthetic fabric was reached, he declared he didn't think it would be worth while to distribute in the U.S. 'since there were already several equivalent fabrics on the American market' . . . and then proceeded to name three competing U.S. products which he felt that prospect might prefer. Another British manufacturer of a resin with special properties simply told an American buyer, 'We do not think it would be economical for anyone in the U.S. to buy our material'.[22]

Then again:

> British manufacturers and exporters have also misjudged U.S. markets in several important respects:
> . . . Poor sizing. Sales of woolen suitings, knitwear and men's furnishings have been cut by Britain's failure to make uniform sizes according to U.S. standards.
> . . . Design and Style. British manufacturers have lost business by ignoring U.S. tastes. The U.K. has failed to take into account American preference for bright colours and modern designs in

haberdashery, household textiles, etc. Shoes fail to come up to U.S. standards of comfort. Summer clothing uses fabrics too heavy for American tastes. Luggage is too cumbersome. . . . Sporting goods (particularly bicycles) have ignored U.S. likes and dislikes.

And the RIA rounded off its indictment with these blistering words:

. . . Inadequate promotion and contact. Advertising in all lines except automobiles is poor; salesman contact worse. Greater emphasis on brand names is necessary. Also, more samples, fewer dog-eared catalogues, particularly in lines like china, silverware and cutlery.

. . . No repair facilities. U.S. dealers in cutlery, toys and wheel goods find this a major complaint.

. . . Bad packaging. Usually neither attractive nor strong enough. Overpacking - particularly in the case of men's furnishings - crushes goods and requires extra expense before items can be displayed.[23]

With the British manufacturer and exporter too obviously more dunce than entrepreneur, it hardly surprises that when in March 1949 the President of the Board of Trade (Harold Wilson) took stock of British prospects on the North American market he found that the proportion of exports going thence was 'still slightly lower than before the war', while the proportion 'of our share in the total import trade of the USA and Canada is substantially lower than before the war . . . '.[24] Moreover, he warned his colleagues, 'as competition from other non-American sources begins to expand, we shall be hard put to it to maintain, still less increase, the present volume of our trade . . . '. Therefore, to achieve the expansion in dollar exports from £140 million in 1948 to £185 million a year by 1952–3, or over 30 per cent up on 1948 and over 100 per cent up on 1947 (as envisaged in the British Marshall Aid programme), 'represents the most formidable task yet faced by the United Kingdom export trade . . . '.[25] He did, however, draw some comfort from what he called the 'outstanding increase' recently in the sale of British motor-cars to Americans and Canadians.[26]

And indeed motor-vehicles constituted the crucial panzer battle of world export markets. During the next half-century their production would supply the index of a nation's industrial growth and the driving force of that growth. Their exports would provide the measure of a nation's technological competence and productive efficiency.

In 1947–8 British exports of motor-vehicles, especially cars, were certainly numerically impressive. But this was only because European car industries were still on their backs and even the American car industry for the time being could not satisfy pent-up home demand. British cars themselves were pre-war models designed in conformity with a taxation system favouring a multiplicity of under-powered models, most of them consequently more suited to a weekend toddle by a British family down to the seaside than to long-distance transport. Only from 1 January 1948 was the horsepower tax replaced with a flat-rate tax. By this time, with the postwar sellers' market now almost over and foreign competition sharpening, several of Britain's postwar models had already been designed, if that is the right word for a combination of amateurish doodles and mechanical improvisation.

The Austin A30, an update of the typical pre-war British runabout, was the first of the new models to come off the production lines (in 1947), a little round tub narrow in the wheelbase and high in the body. A larger version, but similarly podgy in shape, the A40 (inspiringly named the Devon, and Dorset for the two-door version) and the A70 Hampshire, became the mainstay of Austins' exports in 1948. In this same year appeared a car that was to become a legend, if only to the British – the Morris Minor (later renamed the 1000). Designed by a Greek immigrant engineer called Issigonis, it counted as technically revolutionary because of such novel features as independent front suspension (common on American cars since the early 1930s). Because Issigonis despised 'styling', it is hardly surprising that the Minor, with a body vaguely imitative of an American car of a decade back, was as dowdy as its Austin rivals. In the words of a historian of the British car industry, the Minor 'became the stand-by of those who wanted something dependable and manageable, which would not frighten them with unduly sharp performance'.[27]

But at least the Standard Motor Company's new offering in 1948, the Vanguard, complete with wide cabin, bench seats and a steering-column gear-shift, and built in a 1930s rearmament 'shadow' factory, did represent an attempt to break free of British motoring tradition and make a 'world car' comparable to American Fords and Chevrolets. Unfortunately the bulbous American-style body was simply dropped on to the chassis, engine and suspension of a pre-war Standard 12. Rushed from the drawing-board into production and out on to the road in much the same way as a wartime British tank, it proved unequal either to European *pavé* or to the Australian outback.[28] A Standard manager later recalled:

> The Vanguard was, of course, supposed to take care of world conditions. But none of our engineers, and none of our senior sales force, had really been round the world to see what the conditions were. So we were only surmising from what we had been told by the dealers we had appointed.[29]

Yet such hurried development, with the buyer as tester, was common among the native British manufacturers, although the Labour Government, by imposing ambitious export targets backed with the sanction of steel rationing, was also to blame. Issigonis, for instance, widened the body of the Minor at the last moment before production by sawing the prototype in half and moving the two sides apart until he thought the dimensions were right.[30] Moreover, such spatch-cockery was disastrously coupled with dilettante efforts at styling by chairmen or managing directors – Sir John Black in the case of the Standard Vanguard; Leonard Lord with the Austin A90 Atlantic convertible.[31] This latter monstrosity, a provincial Briton's nightmare vision of American taste, was intended to be the flagship of Austins' export drive in the United States. The company launched the car by the public-relations gimmick of driving it round and round the Indianapolis racing circuit for nearly 12,000 miles at an average speed of 70.58 miles per hour, beating the previous stock-car record over the distance (set by a Studebaker in 1928) by 2.1 miles per hour. There followed an expensive advertising campaign. Sadly, however, the American motorist failed to buy the Atlantic despite Austins' certainty that it was the car he ought to want. In mark of defeat, unsold Atlantics were shipped back to Britain and converted to right-hand drive.[32]

Meanwhile prices of cars exported by British manufacturers remained uncompetitively high. To some extent this reflected the likewise uncompetitive cost of British steel[33] (reflecting in turn the cost of British coal). But for the most part it was the car firms' own fault in producing too many different models and components, and hence never achieving production runs long enough to yield economies of scale.[34] In 1947 Lucas, the components firm (known in North America as the 'Prince of Darkness' because their lighting equipment was so unreliable), made a vain case for standardisation by putting on display for journalists the 68 different types of distributor, 133 types of headlamp and 98 types of windscreen wiper currently demanded from them.[35] In 1948 Austins, the largest native British car exporter, still produced four different models, ranging from the small A40 (annual output: 42,500) to two-ton pseudo-Bentleys called the Sheerline[36] and the Princess (combined output: 2000). The Rootes Brothers' disparate range comprised the Sunbeam-Talbot sports-saloon, the Hillman Minx family car, and three different types of Humber, including a cumbersome coach-built colossus of stately design called the Pullman, its export price being three times greater than that of a Packard or Cadillac.[37]

In consequence, as soon as the early postwar world shortage of cars was over, the foreign buyer, whether Swiss, Arab, Australian, North American or whoever, could purchase a large, rugged and comfortable American car for less than the price of even Britain's flimsier confections[38] – and at the same time be sure of better after-sales service.

For here lay another lamentable weakness undermining the current British export drive and wounding the reputation of British cars long into the future, especially in North America. Grandees like Leonard Lord and Billy Rootes might carry out their personal tours of the market, like Chiefs of the Imperial General Staff visiting an overseas theatre, shake a few important hands and quickly stitch up deals with local distributors, but no sales-and-service organisations thoroughly trained and equipped or fully stocked with spares ever resulted.[39] For the British motor industry in its defeatism[40] saw export markets partly as a short-term necessity imposed on it by government and partly as an opportunity for a quick killing before an early return to the familiar comfortable role of supplying the undemanding British family motorist.[41] At Austins' annual general meeting in 1947, for instance, the Chairman significantly remarked that 'valuable export markets may remain open [to the company] *for a few months* [emphasis added]'.[42]

Meanwhile the European motor-vehicle industries had been preparing and launching their own export offensives. In contrast to the fragmented British scene, large-scale production was concentrated into a very few firms: Renault, Citroën and Peugeot in France; Mercedes and Volkswagen in Germany; Fiat in Italy. Again in contrast with such British firms as Austins and Morris, none of these manufacturers made the mistake of dividing their resources between a complete range of cars from runabout to sports-car and luxury saloon. Instead they concentrated on a particular class in order to gain economies of scale: Fiat, Renault, Peugeot and Volkswagen on small and medium-size utilitarian models for a mass market; Citroën and Mercedes on larger, more luxurious vehicles. Moreover, they either offered technical innovation, such as the Renault 4cv and the Volkswagen (both rear-engined and with independent suspension front and rear), or meticulous engineering and outstanding performance like the Mercedes. And lastly, they fully understood the need for well-organised and well-trained sales-and-service back-up.

No firm and its car better illustrate this profound contrast in industrial cultures between Britain and Europe than Volkswagen.[43] As is now famous, British carmakers like Rootes and Morris turned down the chance in 1945 of acquiring the bombed-out Volkswagen factory and its product, seeing no future for either. After all, the VW hardly fulfilled the 1945 British ideal of a family car to be driven by a respectable *pater familias* in a trilby hat. The British military authorities in Germany proved more open-minded, however, finding the VW wonderfully reliable and able to stand up to the worst of roads (in the guise of the *Kubelwagen*, with a Jeep-like open body, it had served in the war as Germany's equivalent of the Jeep). In December 1947 the British military appointed the forty-six-year-old Dr Heinz Nordhoff as managing director. Nordhoff's professional background could hardly have been more different from that of the jumped-up ex-apprentices – throw-backs to the self-taught entrepreneurs of the first industrial revolution – who now ran much of the British car industry, like Nuffield, Leonard Lord and Billy and Reggie Rootes. For he had graduated as a certified mechanical engineer from the Berlin-Charlottenburg Technische Hochschule, one of the pre-eminent technical institutions of the world. Since then he had worked for BMW aero-engines and for Opel (the German outstation of General Motors), running its truck factory (the largest in Europe) at Brandenburg during the war.

The difficulties confronting Nordhoff and his managers in charge of production and sales-and-service at the beginning of 1948 made

British manufacturers' complaints about such matters as shortages of steel and the policies of the Labour Government seem entirely trivial. The German economy as a whole was still a wreck, with a worthless currency and production down to 40 per cent of pre-war. The VW factory itself consisted of an ill-repaired bomb-site manned by semi-starved workers, while VW had not a single dealer within Germany or abroad. Nordhoff was to remember:

> I had to start from scratch in the real sense of the word. Seven thousand workers were painfully producing at the rate of a mere 6000 cars a year – providing it didn't rain too much. Most of the roof and the windows of the factory had been destroyed. Pools of stagnant water were under foot. . . . All the people I met at the factory were not only as poor and hungry as myself, they were desperate and without hope.[44]

On assuming command on 1 January 1948, Nordhoff set about his problems exactly like an able general taking over a defeated, disorganised and demoralised army. In his own words, 'the job of reinstalling hope and confidence in the hearts of desperate people was a much more difficult task than getting a line of presses back into operation . . .'.[45] Addressing the assembled workers as partners in a joint enterprise, he told them: 'For the first time in its history the *Volkswagenwerk* will this year have to face the necessity of standing on its own feet. It is up to us to make this largest of all German motor-car factories a decisive factor for Germany's peacetime recovery.'[46]

At the same time Nordhoff carried out a strategic analysis of world markets, began to plan a global service organization, and set on foot a production-accounting system. On test-driving his Dr-Porsche-designed product for the first time, he was pleased to discover that 'it was not just another small car . . .'. In fact, it seemed to him 'an extraordinarily amazing motor-car with a special personality [and] unlimited possibilities'.[47]

By ploughing back all receipts into the business (including into extra food for his workers), Nordhoff managed that first year to repair and enlarge the factory, rebuild more than 3 million square feet of plant and offices, and create an extra 400,000 square feet of factory space by redeploying machines. It was a major step towards Nordhoff's objective of an American-style assembly-line a mile long pumping out what was essentially a single product (for VW commercial vehicles were based on the same engine and mechanical layout as the car).[48] With the currency reform providing the essential framework for success (as with all German industries), the Volkswagenwerk turned out nearly 20,000 vehicles in 1948 (as against fewer than 9000 in 1947), and 46,000 in 1949, already up to half the output of the Austin A40, Austins' longest single production run. Next year the Volkswagen total would double again, reaching the startline for the global triumph to come.[49]

In harmony with this accelerating rhythm of the assembly line, Nordhoff was pursuing a long-term market strategy – Germany and Europe first, and then, in the 1950s, the world. He based this strategy on the concept of reliability, and not only reliability of the car itself, for each forward step of expansion was first prepared and then consolidated by setting up first-class service organisations.

Here again the British car firms made a sombre contrast, hastily tipping their vehicles into every market all at once, from North America and the Commonwealth to Europe, with consequently sketchy after-sales service. And by the latter months of 1948, with the sellers' market now over, British firms were already beginning to suffer the consequences. From Switzerland, that export testbench, the British Commercial Counsellor reported that the share of British motor-vehicles had dropped from 40 per cent in 1947 to an average of 28 per cent in the first five months of 1948,[50] while the American, French and Italian shares had all risen. 'It should be added', wrote the Counsellor, 'that since the end of May Germany has come on the scene with the Volkswagen. . . . In addition the Opel is beginning to come in from Germany again, and some Mercedes are also being imported. . . .'[51] British car prices in Switzerland, he wrote, were 'distinctly higher' (a Morris 8 cost more than a Volkswagen, and a Standard Vanguard almost as much as a Chevrolet),[52] while the cars were 'constantly criticised for their old-fashioned design. Some of them look completely out of date to the Swiss who for all their conservatism have now become accustomed to modern American design. . . .'[53] Nor was this all: 'A disability from which British cars continue to suffer in this country is lack of attention to service and spare parts.'[54]

Answers to a questionnaire sent in June 1948 to British high commissions in all Commonwealth countries and to commercial posts at embassies in foreign countries revealed that the British car manufacturer was not merely being beaten in a Swiss skirmish but stood in peril of losing a global battle: 'Comments and complaints concerning British cars are unanimous. They are old-fashioned in appearance, too low slung, unsuitably sprung, and are much smaller and lower-powered than American cars at comparable prices. . . .'[55] The Board of Trade could only conclude that 'unless and until new British models can establish themselves in their own right, the dollar shortage will be the main prop of the United Kingdom export market'.[56]

The trouble was that the pre-war designs rushed abroad for the sake of the balance of payments, coupled with poor servicing, had already inflicted lasting damage on the reputation of British cars. In October 1949, when most of the new models had gone on sale, the Canadian correspondent of *The Economist* could still write: 'The product of the British motor industry, with its narrow tracks, small luggage space, and reputed inability to stand up to bad roads has been criticised to the point of monotony.'[57] By this time too the American car industry was pouring forth its own postwar designs, instantly ageing the new British models and leading to a collapse in British car sales in the United States from 24,475 cars in 1948 to only 3600 in the first nine months of 1949.[58]

But then came the devaluation of sterling in September 1949, chopping the dollar prices of British cars by up to a third (although not, of course, the real costs of production), and lifting sales in the United States to a total of 756 in October and 1363 in November, about a fifth and a third respectively of the figure for July 1948.[59] In 1950 the cut-price exchange rate even boosted sales in America to 20,000 cars, as against 24,000 in the peak year of 1948. In fact, 1950 was to see Britain overtake America to become the world's largest exporter, so apparently contradicting all the evidence that foreign buyers thought little of British cars and their after-sales service.

Unfortunately, however, this was success only when measured according to the favourite British principle of 'Never mind the quality, feel the width', and the favourite British perspective of the short term. For, with the exception of some specialist sports models, the cars were still their dull, weakly built and ill-serviced selves. The industry was simply continuing to benefit from three great 'windfall' advantages – postwar world demand, its own two- to three-year lead over its

European rivals in getting back into production, and the temporary boost from a cheapened pound. In any case, over 50 per cent of British motor-vehicle exports went to the less exacting markets of the Commonwealth, while the largest single British exporter was Fords, an American outstation with the only factory in Britain that could compare in scale, layout and equipment with an American or modern European factory. In 1950 Ford of Britain introduced two immensely successful new models, the Consul and the Zephyr, both of them essentially American in styling and technical specification.[60] More ominous still for the native British carmakers like Austin and Morris, the sheer output of European motor-vehicles was steadily catching up on Britain's initial postwar head-start. By the beginning of 1950 France and Germany were together turning out 8000 cars per week; Britain 10,000.[61] And even now, after the lapse of five years, none of the structural and productive shortcomings identified in the March 1945 report on 'The Re-settlement of the Motor Industry' had yet been remedied. All in all, therefore, the shiny paint of current export figures only served to conceal the rust already corroding the industry's future.

At the end of November 1949 the President of the Board of Trade (Harold Wilson), visiting the United States to assess for himself the prospects for British products of all kinds in this key export theatre, found to his dismay that British 'enterprise' remained just as incorrigibly slothful and stupid as ever. Trade literature was still, he reported, 'unattractive and poorly produced and is too often sent in insufficient quantities. Moreover, many British firms seem curiously reluctant to send samples, and indeed regard the receipt of a sample as a privilege for which the potential buyer ought to be prepared to pay. . . .'[62] There was reluctance to conform with American trade practice, as in the case where a British firm, on being asked by 'a very large United States chain store' to fill in a 'Standard Specification Sheet', replied that 'they had never done any such thing before' and if the American firm 'were not willing to buy on the basis of samples, then the British firm did not wish to do business with them . . .'.[63] The President of the Board of Trade also learned that there were still 'frequent complaints that British firms do not do enough to study the particular styles which find favour in the United States . . . particularly in the textile and apparel field . . .'. In fact, 'some British firms still insist on knowing better than their customers . . .'.

In one recent instance, for example, a United States firm gave their British suppliers explicit instructions about the positioning of the seams and certain buttons on shirts which were being purchased. The British firm, however, supplied the shirts with the seams and buttons in accordance with British practice as 'they thought the shirts were more satisfactory that way'.[64]

How, then, is to be explained the paradox presented by such well-documented ineptitude on the one hand and on the other the impressive statistics of British export performance with which between 1946 and 1950 the Government dazzled the British public and American Marshall Aid administrators? For example, the Government's General Memorandum to the OEEC on Britain's 1949–50 Marshall Aid programme could trumpet that in the fourth quarter of 1948 the index of export volume stood at 147 per cent of 1938; that in 1949 it was expected to rise yet again, to 156 per cent;[65] and that the 1948 volume of exports to North America, the key to solving the problem of Britain's huge dollar deficit, stood at 27 per cent above 1938.[66]

The explanation of the apparent paradox is simple: such grandly brandished totals were in fact doubly misleading. In the first place, 1938 had been a poor year for the economy, so providing a conveniently favourable basis of comparison for postwar performance. Secondly, the annual economic surveys and the tenders for Marshall Aid were framed on Whitehall's chosen motto of 'Never mind the quality, feel the width': in other words, comparisons of volume rather than value. When the postwar British export performance is judged in terms of value (and value at constant prices) it looks, as might be expected from the reports from overseas markets, not so much brilliant as dim. For exports of goods *and* services by *value* in 1947 came to a mere 63.1 per cent of 1913 (in other words, about the same percentage as in 1899); in 1948 to 76.9 per cent of 1913 (just larger than 1905's percentage of 1913); in 1949 to 85.3 per cent of 1913 (equal to 1928's percentage of 1913); and even in 1950 to only 97.5 per cent of 1913 (just larger than 1912).[67] In any case, the *total value* of exports in 1948 was only 13 per cent greater than in 1938.[68]

There are even to be found tucked away in the voluminous *Economic Survey for 1950* other figures which demonstrate how lacklustre the British record really was. The proportion of Britain's total exports sent to the Western hemisphere in 1948 was no larger than in 1938, and in 1949 actually smaller.[69] The proportion of total exports sent to the advanced industrial countries of the OEEC in 1947–9 was in each year *lower* than in 1938.[70] For the truth was that British industry had continued to seek refuge, as it had done since the late-Victorian era, in the easy markets of the Sterling Area (above all the Commonwealth). These took 52 per cent of British exports in 1949 (partly 'unrequited' and so down the drain) as against 45 per cent in 1938.[71] Even the 'pullulating and disease-ridden' of the colonial Empire swallowed almost the same proportion of British exports in 1949 as the Western hemisphere.[72]

In spring 1950 the Chancellor of the Exchequer, peering at his tarot cards, failed to perceive a brilliant future for British exports, and especially of engineering goods, where, he wrote, 'present assumptions are already optimistic on the basis of any previous experience, and in some sectors, notably that of motor vehicles, it seems extremely unlikely that even the present level can be maintained'.[73] And he was just as gloomy about the prospects for the balance of payments, the whole *raison d'être* for frantically scrambling for exports while screwing down imports. He told his ministerial colleagues in July 1950 that in regard to the Sterling Area as a whole, 'if Marshall Aid was ignored, the year 1950–51 was expected to show a dollar deficit of over $200 million'.[74]

So it was that five years after the German war had ended, five years of living on American loans and handouts, no British industrial miracle was under way, nor even foundations laid for achieving one in the decade to come. Even the balance of payments, for the sake of which so much had been sacrificed, still lay all in doubt.

In a powerfully romantic metaphor the novelist Joseph Conrad likened the island of Britain to 'a mighty ship bestarred by vigilant lights – a ship carrying the burden of millions of lives'.[75] In summer 1950 this liner, having survived the great storm of the Second World War thanks to an American tow, was wallowing slowly ahead perilously overladen, more rusty than mighty. In need of being rebuilt from the keel up, she had instead undergone only a superficial refit, with items of new technology bolted on to her Victorian structure. Money which should have gone into such vital re-equipment as new engine-rooms had been spent instead on a costly new sick-bay, spacious new cabins for the crew and passengers, and on a worldwide public-relations campaign to proclaim the importance and prestige of a line constantly teetering on the verge of bankruptcy. The board of directors was not alone to blame for this state of things: the ship's officers and crew were so devoted to the old vessel, its worn-out machinery and its familiar routines that the very idea of adapting to a virtually new ship appalled them. The passengers too had no wish to see her drastically altered: they were fond of her in all her traditional if faded splendour; and they just wanted to enjoy a quiet, comfortable and relaxing voyage, not too disturbed by the bickerings between the officers and a lower-deck unwilling and discontented to the point of recurrent mutiny.

Nothing could therefore have been more untoward than a sudden squall threatening to roll the overladen and barely seaworthy ship on to its beam-ends.

On 23 June 1950 the army of the [Communist] People's Republic of North Korea invaded South Korea, a blatant case of aggressive war, a brutal challenge to the authority of the United Nations. Now Britain as 'a centre of world influence and power', with garrisons, naval squadrons and air forces stationed in the Far East from Malaya to Hong Kong, as a permanent member of the Security council, must decide what to do, both politically and militarily. More to the point, she must decide how much she could *afford* to do (especially by way of rearmament), given her barely convalescent economy, her need for exports, her narrow base in modern technology, the cost of New Jerusalem, and the burden of sterling.

These were fateful choices, for they signified that the turning-point was now at hand of the total strategy which the Labour Government had been pursuing for the last five years – that total strategy misbegotten of British dreams, British illusions and British overstretch.

References

PROLOGUE

1. R. B. McCallum and Alison Readman, *The British General Election of 1945* (London, Oxford University Press, 1947), p. 48.
2. PREM 8/35, CP(45)112, 14 August 1945.
3. Ibid. See also Keynes's more formal and comprehensive memorandum of 12 September 1945 in PREM 8/35, reproducing GEN 89/1.
4. H. Duncan Hall, *North American Supply* (London, HMSO and Longmans, Green, 1955), p. 530.
5. Ibid.
6. Ibid.
7. Ibid.

Chapter One:
'THE STRENGTH OF ENGLAND'

1. See Correlli Barnett, *The Collapse of British Power* (London, Eyre Methuen, 1972; paperback edn, Stroud, Alan Sutton, 1984), part IV, pp. 123–233 for an account of British imperial policy 1918–41, with special regard to grand strategy and the comparative industrial and military resources of the United Kingdom and the rest of the Empire.
2. A. G. Boycott, *The Elements of Imperial Defence: A Study of the Geographical Features, Material Resources, Communications and Organization of the British Empire* (Aldershot, Gale & Polden, 1931), p. 112.
3. B. R. Tomlinson, *The Political Economy of the Raj* (London, Macmillan, 1979), p. 56.
4. E. J. Hobsbawm, *Industry and Empire* (Harmondsworth, Pelican Books, 1969), table 33.

399

5. Study Group, Royal Institute of International Affairs, *The Colonial Problem* (London, Oxford University Press, 1937), p. 324.

6. Boycott, *Elements of Imperial Defence*, pp. 89–90.

7. W. K. Hancock, *Survey of British Commonwealth Affairs*, vol. II: *Problems of Economic Policy, 1918–1939*, part I (London, Oxford University Press, 1942), p. 27.

8. Barnett, *Collapse of British Power*, p. 109.

9. CAB 32/2, part I, E-10, cited in ibid., p. 252.

10. See Barnett, *Collapse of British Power*, pp. 83–98, 485–91. Also Correlli Barnett, *The Audit of War: The Illusion and Reality of Britain as a Great Nation* (London, Macmillan, 1986; Papermac, 1987), chs 4–6, passim. See also Dr David Edgerton, *Twentieth Century British History*, vol. 2, No. 3, 1991, pp. 360–79, 'The Prophet Militant and Industrial: The Peculiarities of Correlli Barnett'.

11. See Barnett, *Audit of War*, ch. 5, for a history of the British iron and steel industry vis-à-vis its foreign competitors in the period 1880s–1930s.

12. *History of the Ministry of Munitions* (London, HMSO, 1922), vol. II, p. 58.

13. See Barnett, *Collapse of British Power*, pp. 83–9, citing *History of the Ministry of Munitions*, passim.

14. See Barnett, *Collapse of British Power*, pp. 89–106.

15. Quoted in R. H. Heindel, *The American Impact on Great Britain, 1891–1914* (New York, Octagon Books, 1968), p. 153. For an analysis of British technological laggardliness and its causes between the 1840s and the Great War, see Barnett, *Collapse of British Power*, pp. 91–112, and *Audit of War*, passim, but especially chs 4–6 and 10–11.

16. C. 3881.

17. United Kingdom Census of Production, 1907, quoted in D. H. Aldcroft and H. W. Richardson, *The British Economy, 1870–1939* (London, Macmillan, 1969), p. 193.

18. Hobsbawm, *Industry and Empire*, pp. 191–2, and tables 28 and 33.

19. See Barnett, *Collapse of British Power*, pp. 91–106, and *Audit of War*, ch. 11.

20. C. 3966, *Endowed Schools (Schools Enquiry) Commission, Report of*, vol. I (1867–8), p. 80.

21. C. 3981, *Second Report of the Royal Commissioners on Technical Instruction*, vol. I: *Report* (1884), p. 337.

22. Ibid., pp. 213–14.

23. G. A. N. Lowndes, *The Silent Social Revolution* (London, Oxford University Press, 1937), p. 101.

24. Cited in Barnett, *Audit of War*, p. 208.

25. Barnett, *Collapse of British Power*, pp. 105–6.

26. Cd 5130, p. 90.

27. See Barnett, *Collapse of British Power*, pp. 19–68, and *Audit of War*, chs 1 and 11.

28. See Barnett, *Collapse of British Power*, part I; *Audit of War*, ch. 1.

29. See Barnett, *Audit of War*, pp. 223–7.

30. *Royal Society Yearbook for 1903* (London, Royal Society, 1903), pp. 180–95.

31. See Barnett, *Audit of War*, ch. 10. See also E. P. Thompson, *The Making of the English Working Class* (Harmondsworth, Pelican Books, 1974).

32. Cf. Henry Pelling, *A History of British Trade Unionism* (Harmondsworth, Pelican Books, 1971), pp. 64–8; John Lovell, *British Trade Unions, 1875–1933* (London, Macmillan, for Economic History Society, 1977), pp. 17, 23, 26–8.

33. *History of the Ministry of Munitions*, vol. IV, part I, p. 30.

34. Charles Loch Mowatt, *Britain Between the Wars, 1918–1940* (London, University Paperback, 1968), table p. 261.1.

35. Cmd 3282, pp. 80–1.

36. J. R. Seeley, *The Expansion of England* (London, Macmillan 1883), p. 192.

37. Cf. the Labour Party's 1918 programme, quoted in Egon Wertheimer, *Portrait of the Labour Party* (London, Putnam, 1929), pp. 59–60.

38. See Barnett, *Collapse of British Power*, pp. 166–232, for an account of vain British attempts in the 1920s to turn the 'white' Empire into a firm peacetime political and military alliance.

39. See ibid., pp. 133–66, for an account of British policy in India, 1918–35.

40. See ibid., pp. 162–4.

41. See ibid., pp. 237–98, for an account of British faith in the League of Nations, and concomitant pursuit of disarmament, in the 1920s.

42. See ibid., pp. 273–82, for an account of the delays and stoppages over construction of the Singapore base, 1924–30.

43. CAB 16/109, cited in ibid., pp. 345–6.

44. Hobsbawm, *Industry and Empire*, p. 211.

45. See Barnett, *Collapse of British Power*, pp. 419–38, for an analysis of British opinion in the early 1940s, and the influence on it of best-selling trench novels and memoirs.

46. See ibid., pp. 350–80, for an account of the Abyssinian crisis based on Cabinet and Chiefs of Staff papers.

47. Cf. CAB 53/27, COS 426, 22 January 1936.

48. See especially Barnett, *Collapse of British Power*, pp. 362–3, 365, 367–9, 379–80.

49. See ibid., pp. 394–408.

50. See ibid., pp. 402 and 407.

51. CAB 53/21, COS 560, 21 February 1937.

52. White Paper on *Statistics Relating to the War Effort of the United Kingdom*, Cmd 6564 (1944).

53. Nicholas Mansergh, *The Commonwealth Experience* (London, Weidenfeld & Nicolson, 1969), p. 126.

54. CAB 16/112, DPR(DR)9, 12 February 1936.

55. Barnett, *Audit of War*, pp. 133–4.

56. Appendix to CAB 27/648, CP 247(38).

57. See Barnett, *Collapse of British Power*, pp. 451–76, 494–556, for an account of British defence and foreign policies towards Germany, 1937–9, based on Cabinet and Chiefs of Staff records.

58. CAB 29/159, AFC1, 20 March 1939.

59. CAB 16/209, SAC4.

60. For analysis of the cost-effectiveness, or rather cost-ineffectiveness, of Britain's Mediterranean and Middle East strategy (including the Italian campaign), see Correlli Barnett, *Engage the Enemy More Closely: The Royal Navy in the Second World War* (London, Hodder & Stoughton, 1991), chs 8, 11, 12, 16, 17, 20, 21 and 22.

61. PREM 8/35, reproducing GEN 893, appendix B.

62. PREM 8/35, CP(45)112.

63. Ibid.

Chapter Two:
'A FINANCIAL DUNKIRK'

1. Cf. CAB 87/3, RP(43)25, 15 June 1943; CAB 87/14–15, files of the Official Committee on Reconstruction: Industrial Problems, March 1944–May 1945.

2. CAB 87/14, R(I)(44)5, The Long Term Prospects of British Industry, 23 June 1944.

3. Ibid.

4. White Paper on *Statistics Relating to the War Effort of the United Kingdom*, Cmd 6564 (1944), cited in Correlli Barnett, *The Audit of War*, p. 6.

5. See Barnett, *Audit of War*, part II, chs 3–9, for an analysis of Britain's wartime technological performance based on contemporary government files.

6. These figures and later ones in this chapter relating to British wartime

productivity are taken from Barnett, *Audit of War*, as calculated from, or recorded in, Cabinet or ministry files.

7. According to Ministry of Aircraft Production calculations in 1944. See AVIA 10/269.

8. CAB 87/92, CM(42)2, report by T. E. B. Young, cited in Barnett, *Audit of War*, p. 65. All quotations and statistics quoted in relation to the wartime coal industry are drawn from Barnett, *Audit of War*, ch. 4, and thence from the official records therein cited.

9. BT 28/319, 30 August 1942, cited in Barnett, *Audit of War*, ch. 6.

10. CAB 102/406, paper before the Munitions Management and Labour Efficiency Committee of the Production Efficiency Board, 17 November 1944, cited in Barnett, *Audit of War*, ch. 8.

11. BT 28/377, Report on Vickers-Armstrong (Aircraft) Ltd, Weybridge, by five expert Inspectors of Labour Supply, cited in Barnett, *Audit of War*, ch. 8.

12. CAB 102/393, Development of Jet Propulsion and Gas Turbine Engines in the United Kingdom: revised draft by Miss C. Keppel.

13. CAB 102/51, Reciprocating Aero-Engines and Engine Accessories Production and Programmes 1935–45, by Dr D. A. Parry.

14. AVIA 10/99, Fedden Mission Report, 1943.

15. John Stevenson, *British Society 1914–1945* (Harmondsworth, Pelican Books, 1984), p. 197, table 14.

16. M. P. Jackson, *The Price of Coal* (London, Croom Helm, 1974), p. 80.

17. The Minister of Fuel and Power to the House of Commons, July 1944.

18. CAB 87/9, R(44)152, 2 September 1944.

19. CAB 87/92, CM(42)2.

20. H. Wilson, *New Deal for Coal* (London, Contact Books, 1945), p. 34.

21. W. H. B. Court, *Coal* (London, HMSO and Longmans, Green, 1951), p. 283.

22. Wilson, *New Deal for Coal*, p. 127 and n. 1.

23. ADM 1/11892, Labour in Naval and Mercantile Shipyards (Report of the Barlow Committee), 1943.

24. Cited in CAB 102/407, unpublished official history study by Mrs P. Inman, Labour Requirements and Supply for the Ministries of Supply and Production.

25. BT 28/319 (Bentham Report), 30 September 1942.

26. ADM 1/11892.

27. CAB 87/63, EC(43)2, 13 October 1943.

28. See CAB 87/63, EC(43)2, CAB 102/407 and LAB 10/132, Trade Stoppages, Weekly Return to the Minister, November 1940 to December 1944.

29. CAB 102/407, to the Clyde Control Committee, 21 May 1943.

30. Ibid.

31. Mass-Observation, *Report on Behalf of the Advertising Service Guild*, no. 2: *Home Propaganda* (London, John Murray, 1941).

32. ADM 1/11892.

33. CAB 102/406.

34. Ibid.

35. See Barnett, *Audit of War*, pp. 154–6.

36. CAB 87/63, EC(43)2, 13 October 1943, report by the Ministry of Labour.

37. William Hornby, *Factories and Plant* (London, HMSO and Longmans, Green, 1958), p. 303; M. M. Postan, *British War Production* (London, HMSO and Longmans, Green, 1952), p. 304.

38. W. K. Hancock and M. M. Gowing, *British War Economy* (London, HMSO and Longmans, Green, 1949), pp. 161–2.

39. See Barnett, *Audit of War*, ch. 9, pp. 158–61.

40. Ibid.

41. AVIA 10/338, 31 March 1943.

42. ADM 1/15218, letter to Secretary of OPTEC from the RDF Board, 13 January 1943: annex to OPTEC(43)3.

43. See Barnett, *Audit of War*, p. 169, citing wartime government records.

44. See ibid., pp. 169–70, and notes.

45. Ibid., p. 205.

46. Ibid.

47. Ibid.

48. Ibid., p. 203. See the whole of ch. 11, but especially pp. 201–5, for an analysis of the British record on education and training, from elementary schools to universities, in the period before the Second World War.

49. PREM 8/35, CP(45)112.

50. Ibid. Keynes's guesstimates were as follows: government expenditure overseas down to £150 million; imports at £1450 million = total of £1600 million, balanced against exports at £1450 million; invisible income at £150 million = total of £1600 million.

51. Ibid.

52. PREM 8/35, 23 August 1945.

53. See Julian Lewis, *Changing Direction: British Military Planning for Postwar Strategic Defence, 1942–1947* (London, Sherwood Press, 1988), chs 3 and 4 passim.

54. See the telegrams between the British negotiators in Washington led by

Keynes and London in PREM 8/35.

55. PREM 8/35, CM(45)50th Conclusions, minute 3, confidential annex, 6 November 1945.

56. Ibid., CM(45)57th Conclusions, minute 3, confidential annex, 29 November 1945.

57. Ibid., CP(45)312, memorandum by Dalton, 28 November 1945.

Chapter Three:
'OUR POSITION AS A GREAT POWER'

1. CAB 131/1, DO(46)1, minute 1, 11 January 1946, Hugh Dalton, Chancellor of the Exchequer, in the course of the Defence Committee's discussion of COS(46)5(O), reviewing an earlier report (COS(45)565(O)) on the size of the armed forces as at 30 June 1946.

2. Cf. CAB 131/2, DO(46)47, 2 April 1946, COS Report on The Strategic Position of the British Commonwealth; CAB 131/1, Bevin in the course of discussion of this report in the Cabinet Defence Committee; CAB 131/6, DO(48)12, 23 January 1948, draft Defence White Paper.

3. CAB 131/5, DO(49)51(draft), 27 June 1949, Size and Shape of the Armed Forces 1950–53 (Harwood Committee Report): memorandum by the Minister of Defence on the report and the COS's comments thereon.

4. CAB 131/1, DO(46)1, minute 1, 11 January 1946, discussion of COS(46)5(O), reviewing earlier report (COS(45)565(O)) on the size of the armed forces at 30 June 1946.

5. Ibid.

6. CAB 131/1, DO(46)3rd, minute 1, 21 January 1946.

7. Ibid.

8. Ibid. COS figures in COS(46)5(O) and COS(46)9(O)(revise).

9. CAB 131/2, DO(46)66, 10 May 1946, Call-up to the Forces in the Transitional Period.

10. CAB 131/2, DO(46)20, February 1946, Memorandum on the Size of the Armed Forces – 30 June 1946 and 31 December 1946: report by the COS, appendix I, note by the Admiralty.

11. CAB 131/1, DO(46)1st, minute 1, 11 January 1946.

12. CAB 131/6, DO(48)3, 5 January 1948, Size and Shape of the Armed Forces: Report by the COS, annex II.

13. CAB 131/2, DO(46)66, 10 May 1966, annex II. CAB 131/2, DO(46)117, 9 October 1946, The Introduction of a Permanent Scheme for Compulsory

Military Service: report by the Man-Power Working Party, gives a figure of 31,000 projected for March 1947.

14. See Alan Bullock, *Ernest Bevin: Foreign Secretary 1945–1951* (London, Heinemann, 1984), part II, especially chs 5–7.

15. CAB 131/2, DO(46)66, 10 May 1946, annex II, Distribution of the Army as at 31 December 1946; annex III, Global Distribution of the RAF as at 1 January 1947; DO(46)121, 13 October 1946, The Strength of the Army December 1946–March 1947; memorandum by the Secretary of State for War, appendix B, Part II.

16. CAB 131/2, DO(46)20, February 1946, Memorandum on the Size of the Armed Forces – 30 June 1946 and 31 December 1946: report by the COS, appendix I, note by the Admiralty.

17. CAB 131/2, DO(46)117, 9 October 1946, figures as at 31 December 1946.

18. CAB 131/2, DO(46)66, 10 May 1946, figures forecast for 31 December 1946.

19. CAB 131/2, DO(46)20, February 1946, appendix I.

20. PREM 4, WP(43)30, June 1943, The Relations of the British Commonwealth to the Post-War International Political Organisation, by C. R. Attlee.

21. See Julian Lewis, *Changing Direction: British Military Planning for Post-war Strategic Defence, 1942–1947*, chs 1–4.

22. Cf. T 230/3, Civil Aviation – Summary of Developments 1941/45, pp. 6, 14 and 15; CAB 134/57, CAC(45)3rd, 23 October 1945, Civil Aviation Committee, comments by the Minister of Civil Aviation.

23. See the minutes and memoranda of the Cabinet Civil Aviation Committee, 1945–50, in CAB 134/57–9, especially CAB 134/57, CAC(45)3, CAC(45)3rd, CAC(47)2, 5, 6 and 9; CAB 134/58, CAC(48)3, CAC(48)1st, CAC(48)11, CAC(48)13; CAB 134/59, CAC(50)2, CAC(50)3.

24. CAB 129/1, CP(45)144, 1 September 1945.

25. CAB 131/1, DO(46)5th, minute 1, 15 February 1946.

26. CAB 131/2, DO(46)27, also COS(46)55(0), 2 March 1946. Future of the Italian Colonies: memorandum by the Prime Minister and Minister of Defence.

27. CAB 131/2, DO(46)40, 13 March 1946.

28. CAB 131/2, DO(46)46, 30 March 1946, Organisation of Zones of Strategic Responsibility.

29. CAB 131/2, DO(46)47, 2 April 1946.

30. The Minister of Fuel and Power was of the same mind. See CAB 131/2,

DO(46)45, 28 March 1946, Petroleum Resources in the Middle East.

31. CAB 131/5, 8th, minute 1, 14 April 1948. According to the Minister of Defence, the Haifa oil refinery produced only 1 per cent of world supplies, but was essential to Palestine and neighbouring allied states, and to British and US forces in the Middle East.

32. Citing DO(46)40.

33. CAB 131/1, DO(46)10th, minutes 2, 3 and 4, 5 April 1946.

34. CAB 134/219, EPC(48)92, 1 November 1948, report by the Colonial Development Working Party.

35. CAB 131/1, DO(46)10th.

36. Ibid.

37. CAB 131/7, DO(49)89, Defence Burdens and the Commonwealth: memorandum by the Secretary of State for Commonwealth Relations.

38. CAB 131/9, DO(50)1, 3 January 1950.

39. CAB 131/9, DO(50)13, 2 March 1950, Defence Efforts of the Several Commonwealth Countries; annex: The British Commonwealth: Population, National Income, Budgetary Revenue and Defence Expenditure.

40. The present author as a national serviceman saw this futility at first hand.

41. CAB 131/2, DO(46)113, 25 September 1946, Strategic Value of India to the British Commonwealth of Nations: report by the Commander-in-Chief in India.

42. CAB 131/2, DO(46)68, 12 June 1946, India – Military Implications of Proposed Courses of Action: report by the COS.

43. CAB 131/2, DO(46)104, 4 September 1946, Strategic Importance of India: extracts from a report by the COS.

44. CAB 131/1, DO(46) 26th, 2 October 1946.

45. CAB 131/2, DO(46)67(revise), 25 May 1946, Strategic Requirements in the Middle East.

46. See also CAB 131/1, DO(46)14th, 24 April 1946, discussion of the Anglo-American Committee of Enquiry report on Palestine, and on negotiations with Egypt for a new treaty.

47. CAB 131/2, DO(46)67(revise).

48. CAB 131/1, DO(46)17th, minute 1, 27 May 1946.

49. CAB 131/2, DO(46)80, 1 June 1946.

50. CAB 131/1, DO(46)22nd, minute 1, 19 July 1946.

51. CAB 131/3, DO(46)107, 13 September 1946, Middle East Policy: report by the COS.

52. CAB 131/1, DO(46)30th, 24 October 1946.

53. CAB 131/3, DO(46)135, 8 November 1946, Strength of the Armed Forces

at 31 December 1946 and 31 March 1948.

54. Ibid.

55. CAB 131/5, DO(47)1st, 1 January 1947.

56. CAB 131/4, DO(47)3, 6 January 1947, Palestine – Strategic Requirements: report by the COS.

57. CAB 131/5, DO(47)2nd, 14 January 1947.

58. CAB 131/4, DO(47)21, 28 February 1947, Oil Pipelines to the Mediterranean from the Middle East Oil Areas.

59. CAB 131/5, DO(47)14th, 4 June 1947.

60. CAB 131/4, DO(47)50, 2 June 1947, Location of Stores to be Moved from India and Egypt.

61. CAB 128/10, CM(47)76th, 20 September 1947.

62. CAB 131/5, DO(47)22nd, 29 September 1947.

63. CAB 131/4, DO(47)76, 9 October 1947, British Defence Committee in South East Asia: report by the COS on its composition and terms of reference.

64. CAB 128/9, CM(47)78th, minute 3, 2 October 1947.

65. CAB 131/6, DO(48)8, 15 January 1948.

66. Ibid., DO(48)27, 12 April 1948.

Chapter Four:
'WE CANNOT AFFORD EITHER THE MONEY OR THE MEN'

1. CAB 131/2, DO(46)20, Memorandum on the Size of the Armed Forces – 30 June 1946 and 31 December 1946: report by the COS.

2. Ibid.

3. Ibid.

4. CAB 132/2, DO(46)5th, minute 1, 15 February 1946.

5. Ibid., annex 1.

6. Ibid.

7. Ibid.

8. Ibid.

9. CAB 131/1, DO(46)12th, minute 3, 15 April 1946.

10. CAB 124/503, MEP(46)9, 22 October 1946, Survey of the Economic Situation, by the National Joint Advisory Council.

11. Ibid. See also CAB 134/503, MEP(46)16, 21 December 1946, *Economic Survey for 1947*, p. 3, which puts the total manpower requirements of the

armed forces and their supporting industries and services at 2.6 million in 1947, equal to one-eighth of the total British working population.

12. CAB 131/6, 23 January 1948, Joint War Production Staff Report on Supply of Arms and Equipment to Foreign and Commonwealth Countries.

13. Cf. CAB 131/5, DO(48)4th, 20 January 1948, Discussion of the Report of the Commonwealth Advisory Committee on Defence Science.

14. Kenneth O. Morgan, *Labour in Power 1945–1951* (Oxford, Clarendon Press, 1984), p. 282.

15. CAB 131/4, DO(47)5, Production, R & D Programmes: report by the Production Committee.

16. CAB 131/5, DO(47)2nd, 14 January 1947.

17. Ibid.

18 Cf. CAB 131/1, DO(46)12th, minute 3, 15 April 1946: discussion by the Defence Committee of a memorandum by the Chairman of the Manpower Committee on alternative schemes for the call-up of forces for national service as from 1 January 1947; DO(46)15th, minute 1, 3 May 1946, discussion of a memorandum by the Chairman of the Manpower Committee (CP(46)194), a memorandum by the Foreign Secretary on the 'serious implications on our foreign policy' of future contemplated strengths of the forces (DO(46)64); and a report by the COS (DO(46)66) covering a statement of location and strengths of forces, and forecasts of withdrawals and reductions.

19. CAB 131/2, DO(46)117, 9 October 1946.

20. Ibid.

21. CAB 131/1, DO(46)27th, minute 1, 16 October 1946, Introduction of Permanent Scheme for National Service.

22. CAB 131/1, DO(46)28th, minute 1, 17 October 1946. See also CAB 131/1, DO(46)27th, minute 1, 16 October 1946, comments by the three COS, and also Bevin's long discourse on Britain's world policy.

23. CAB 131/4, DO(47)9, 13 January 1947, memorandum by the Chancellor of the Exchequer on the Defence Estimates for 1947–8.

24. CAB 134/503, MEP(46)9, 22 October 1946, survey of the economic situation prepared for the National Joint Advisory Council.

25. CAB 131/4, DO(47)9, 13 January 1947, memorandum by the Chancellor of the Exchequer on the Defence Estimates for 1947–8.

26. Cf. CAB 131/5, DO(47)3rd, 14 January 1947; CAB 128/9, CM(47)9th, minute 2; 17 January 1947, CM(47)10th, 21 January 1947; CM(47)13th, minute 1, 28 January 1947.

27. CAB 128/9, CM(47)10th, 21 January 1947.

28. Morgan, *Labour in Power*, pp. 341–7.

29. CAB 131/4, DO(47)63, 2 August 1947, The Strength of the Armed Forces: memorandum by the Minister of Defence, citing CP(47)221, memorandum of 30 July on overseas military expenditure by the Chancellor of the Exchequer.

30. CAB 131/4, DO(47)68, 15 September 1947.

31. Ibid.

32. CAB 131/5, DO(47)20th, minute 1, 18 September 1947.

33. Ibid.

34. Ibid. The Cabinet endorsed these proposals on 2 October 1947. See CAB 128/9, CM(47)78th, minute 3.

35. CAB 131/6, DO(48)12, 23 January 1948, paragraph 51 of the draft Defence White Paper, 1948.

36. CAB 131/5, DO(48)3rd, 14 January 1948.

37. CAB 131/6, DO(48)3, 5 January 1948, Size and Shape of the Armed Forces: report by the COS.

38. CAB 131/5, DO(48)1st, minute 1, 2 January 1948, Defence Estimates 1948–9.

39. Ibid.

40. CAB 131/5, DO(48)2nd, 8 January 1948, statement by the Minister of Defence.

41. CAB 131/6, DO(48)20, 23 February 1948, Withdrawal from Palestine: Progress Report No. 2 by Official Committee on Palestine.

42. CAB 131/5, DO(48)9th, minute 1, 30 April 1948.

43. CAB 131/6, DO(48)49, 29 July 1948, Preparation for Defence: note by the COS.

44. Ibid., DO(48)46, 26 July 1948, The Defence Position: memorandum by the Minister of Defence.

45. Ibid.

Chapter Five:
THE COLD WAR AND TOTAL–STRATEGIC OVERSTRETCH

1. Readers should note that this chapter is not at all intended to give an account either of the Cold War or of British diplomacy and defence policy in the period 1945–50; it provides only brief summaries as background for its chosen topic of the costs of the British world role and their impact on the British economy. For a detailed account of the Cold War and Britain's

foreign policy, the reader is referred to Alan Bullock's magisterial work, *Ernest Bevin: Foreign Secretary 1945–1951* (London, Heinemann, 1984).

2. CAB 131/7, DO(49)45, 17 June 1949, citing DO(49)2nd, minute 4, 10 January 1949.

3. Ibid., DO(49)45, 17 June 1949, Western Union Defence – United Kingdom Commitment: memorandum by the COS.

4. CAB 131/6, DO(48)70, 7 October 1948, Malaya – Possibility of Australian Assistance: note by the Joint Secretaries to the Defence Committee – annex I, telegram (no. 629) from the High Commissioner in Australia. CAB 131/5, DO(48)21st, 3 November 1948: Slim as CIGS formally confirmed to the Defence Committee that Australia would not be sending troops to Malaya. For the Dominions' general unwillingness to equal Britain's per capita contribution to Commonwealth defence, see pp. 59–60.

5. Bullock, *Ernest Bevin*, p. 631.

6. CAB 131/6, DO(48)47, 26 July 1948, The Defence Position: note by the Prime Minister in circulating to the Defence Committee a memorandum by Sir Norman Brooke on defence preparedness after consultation with the Ministry of Defence, the Home Office and the Central Economic Planning Staff on the economic considerations.

7. CAB 131/5, DO(48)13th, 27 July 1948.

8. CAB 131/5, DO(48)14th, 30 July 1948.

9. CAB 131/6, DO(48)53, 11 August 1948.

10. CAB 131/5, DO(48)16th, 13 August 1948.

11. Ibid.

12. Ibid.

13. CAB 131/6, DO(48)55, 19 August 1949; CAB 131/5, DO(48)17th, 23 August 1948.

14. CAB 131/6, DO(48)83, 6 December 1948.

15. CAB 131/5, DO(48)23rd, minute 2, 8 December 1948.

16. CAB 131/7, DO(49)47, 21 June 1949, note by Joint Secretaries of the Defence Committee circulating 'Size and Shape of the Armed Forces: Report of the Harwood Working Party': 'Report of the Inter-Service Committee Working Party on Size and Shape of the Armed Forces', 28 February 1949 (Misc/P.(49)6,i).

17. Ibid.

18. CAB 134/220, EPC(49)21st, minute 5.

19. CAB 131/7, DO(49)51(draft), 27 June 1949, Size and Shape of the Armed Forces 1950–53: memorandum by the Minister of Defence on the Harwood Report and the COS's comments thereon.

20. CAB 131/7, DO(49)50, 22 June 1949, Size and Shape of the Armed Forces 1950–52.

21. CAB 131/7, DO(49)51(draft), 27 June 1949.

22. CAB 131/8, DO(49)17th, minute 6, 1 July 1949, statement by the Colonial Secretary in the course of a discussion on the size of colonial defence forces. In his words, 'the standard of living of the bulk of the colonies was low. . . . He did not see how they could meet the full bill even for internal security forces. . . .'

23. See Kenneth O. Morgan, *Labour in Power 1945–1951*, p. 384.

24. CAB 131/7, DO(49)65, 8 October 1949, Note by Secretary to the Defence Committee circulating annex I, report of Inter-Departmental Committee on Defence Estimates, and annex II, report by COS on the strategic aspects.

25. COS(49)313(final), 27 September 1949, annex II in CAB 131/7, DO(49)65, 15 October 1949.

26. See ibid., appendix I. Home Fleet: one fleet carrier, two light fleet carriers, three cruisers, sixteen destroyers; Mediterranean Fleet: one light fleet carrier, four cruisers, eleven destroyers, seven frigates; East Indies and Far East: one light fleet carrier, five cruisers, seven destroyers, fifteen frigates. The cocktail circuit on the America and West Indies and the South Atlantic stations took in another two cruisers and five frigates.

27. Ibid., appendix II.

28. CAB 131/7, DO(49)66, 8 October 1949, The Requirements of National Defence: Size and Shape of the Armed Forces 1950–53: memorandum by the Minister of Defence.

29. CAB 131/8, DO(49)19, minute 2, 9 October 1949.

30. CAB 131/7, DO(49)69, 3 November 1949, Size and Shape of the Armed Forces 1950–53: memorandum by the Lord President of the Council.

31. CAB 131/8, DO(49)20th, 15 November 1949.

32. CAB 134/220, EPC(49)39th, 21 October 1949.

33. CAB 131/8, DO(49)21st, minute 2, 21 November 1949, and DO(49)22nd, 25 November 1949.

34. CAB 131/8, DO(49)22nd, 25 November 1949.

35. CAB 131/7, JWPS(49)93(final), 21 December 1949, Service Production Programmes 1950–51: report by the Joint War Production Staffs to the Minister of Defence.

36. CAB 131/9, DO(50)47, 28 June 1950. Size and Shape of the Aircraft Industry – Need for Planning to Preserve War Potential: memorandum by the Minister of Supply.

37. CAB 131/9, DO(50)47.

38. See CAB 87/13, PR(43)98, 10 November 1943, memorandum by the Minister of Aircraft Production to the Reconstruction Programmes Committee on The Future of the Aircraft Industry.

39. See CAB 134/57–60, Civil Aviation Committee, meetings and memoranda, 1945–50.

40. Cf. CAB 134/57, CAC(45)3, CAC(45)3rd, CAC(46)4th, and CAB 134/687, SI(M)(46)1st; CAB 134/58, CAC(47)1, 2, 5 and 9, CAC(47)1st; CAB 134/689, SI(M)(48) 3 and 4, and SI(M)(48)2nd; CAB 134/58, CAC(48)3, 13, 3rd, 16 and 4th; CAB 134/59, CAC(50)1st, 4 and 6.

41. CAB 134/440, IPC(50)2, 24 April 1950, Report on Capital Investment 1951–52, p. 51, para. 172; CAB 134/242, ER(L)(49)163, 27 May 1949, General Memorandum for OEEC on United Kingdom Revised 1949–50 Programme, table 9, p. 13.

42. CAB 131/7, DO(49)8, 3 February 1949, Guided Weapons Research and Development: memorandum by the Minister of Supply (George Strauss).

43. CAB 131/7, DO(49)20, 10 March 1949, Defence Research and Production Programmes 1949–50: report by the Defence Production Committee.

44. CAB 131/9, DO(50)20, 20 March 1950, United Kingdom Contribution to the Defence of Western Europe, annex: report by the COS.

45. CAB 131/8, DO(50)10th, 25 May 1950.

46. CAB 131/9, DO(50)40, 19 May 1950. See also DO(50)40, 19 May 1950, Co-operation with Egypt: report by the COS (Field-Marshal Slim, Air Chief Marshal Sir John Slessor, and Admiral Creasy for the First Sea Lord).

47. CAB 131/7, DO(49)23, 22 March 1949, memorandum by the Secretary of State for War.

48. CAB 131/9, DO(50)40.

49. CAB 131/9, DO(50)50, 6 July 1950, appendix B: Army World-wide Order of Battle as at 3 July 1950. NB: disparate formations and units are listed, but not numbers of personnel, making exact comparisons impossible. Appendix C: Summary of Present Dispositions of the Royal Air Force. This is broken down into numbers of squadrons of different types of aircraft.

50. Cmd 7631, February 1949, para. 25.

51. CAB 134/641, 17 January 1949, *Economic Survey for 1949* (provisional draft), p. 24, table XV.

52. Figure for 1948 from *Economic Survey for 1951*, Cmd 8195 (1951), table 11; figure for 1949 from *Economic Survey for 1952*, Cmd 8509 (1952), table 2.

53. CAB 131/9, DO(50)13, 2 March 1950, Defence Efforts of the Several Commonwealth Countries.

54. International Institute of Strategic Studies, *The Military Balance 1971–2* (London, IISS, 1971), table 4.

55. CAB 134/242, ER(L)(49)163, 27 May 1949, General Memorandum for OEEC on United Kingdom Revised 1949–50 Programme, table 9, and annex I, table V. See also CAB 134/440, IPC(50)2.

Chapter Six:
'A NEVER-TO-BE-REPEATED OPPORTUNITY'

1. CAB 134/219, EPC(48)92, 1 November 1948, report by the Colonial Development Working Party.

2. Cited in Kenneth O. Morgan, *Labour in Power 1945–1951*, p. 194.

3. CAB 134/219, EPC(48)73, 19 July 1948, Compensation for War Damage and Denial Measures in Burma: memorandum by the Chancellor of the Exchequer.

4. CAB 134/220, EPC(49)45th, 18 November 1949.

5. CAB 134/219, EPC(48)92, 1 November 1948. See also CAB 134/217, EPC(48)35, 27 April 1948, memorandum by the Chancellor of the Exchequer plus a 59-page survey of the colonial Empire by the Colonial Development Working Party, long on colonial needs and short on benefits to Britain.

6. CAB 134/219, EPC(48)71, 15 July 1948, interim report by the Sterling Area Development Working Party.

7. Cf. his memorandum of 7 December 1948 on Practical Achievements in the Colonies Since the War: CAB 134/219, EPC(48)112.

8. See Correlli Barnett, *The Collapse of British Power* (London, Eyre Methuen, 1972; paperback edn, Stroud, Alan Sutton, 1984), pp. 124–33.

9. CAB 134/219, EPC(48)112, 7 December 1948. See also EPC(48)35, 27 April 1948, report by the Colonial Development Working Party, and the reference in paras 37 and 38 to the competition between British industry and the colonial service for scarce resources of trained technicians.

10. CAB 134/242, ER(L)(49)163, 27 May 1949, General Memorandum for OEEC on United Kingdom Revised 1949–50 Programme.

11. CAB 134/641, PC(49)8, *Economic Survey for 1949* (provisional draft), 17 January 1949, paras 63 and 125.

12. CAB 134/219, EPC(48)92, 1 November 1948, report by the Colonial

Development Working Party, and EPC(48)112, 7 December 1948, Practical Achievements in the Colonies Since the War. See also CAB 134/787, CCP(O)(52)8, 17 June 1952, Commonwealth Trade, note by Mr G. D. A. MacDougall of the Paymaster-General's Office.

13. CAB 134/241, ER(L)(49)93(revise), 1 April 1949, The Long-Term Programme and the Commonwealth, appendix B, para. 1.

14. Cf. CAB 133/49, ER(ECA)(48)1, 7 July 1948, The Sterling Area, annex II.

15. CAB 133/78–9, records of the Colombo Conference, 9–15 January 1950.

16. CAB 133/131, PEC(52)3, 22 July 1952, External Economic Policy: Appreciation of the Attitude of Commonwealth Governments: memorandum by a group of officials.

17. See CAB 133/49, ER(ECA)(48)1, 7 July 1948, for a succinct account of the evolution of the Sterling Area, prepared in the Cabinet Office for the enlightenment of the American European Recovery Programme representative in London. See also a memorandum by R. W. B. Clarke on the Sterling Area dated 15 December 1951 in T 236/3070.

18. See above, pp. 26–7.

19. See above, pp. 27–8.

20. CAB 134/225, EPC(50)40, 22 March 1950, Sterling Balances: memorandum by the Chancellor of the Exchequer, annex A.

21. CAB 133/49, ER(ECA)(48)1, 7 July 1948.

22. Ibid.

23. T 236/3070, RWBC/4788, 15 December 1951, The Sterling Area: memorandum by R. W. B. Clarke.

24. Cf. ibid., para. 17; CAB 133/49, ER(ECA)(48)1, The Sterling Area, 7 July 1948, p. 7.

25. CAB 133/49, ER(ECA)(48)1.

26. Ibid.

27. CAB 133/225, EPC(50)40, 22 March 1950, memorandum jointly written by the Working Parties on the Sterling Area and on Development in South and South-east Asia.

28. Ibid.

29. Donald Moggridge (ed.), *The Collected Writings of John Maynard Keynes*, vol. XXIV: *Activities 1944–46: The Transition to Peace* (London, Macmillan and Cambridge University Press, for the Royal Economic Society, 1979), p. 8.

30. See ibid., p. 64.

31. CAB 134/220, EPC(49)137, 13 November 1949. See also CAB 134/225,

EPC(50)40, 22 March 1950, memorandum on the sterling balances by the Working Parties on the Sterling Area and on Development in South and South-east Asia, para. 10.

32. Moggridge, *Collected Writings of J. M. Keynes*, vol. XXIV, p. 64.

33. Noël Annan, *Our Age: The Generation That Made Post-War Britain* (London, Fontana, 1991).

34. CAB 133/49, ER(ECA)(48)1, 7 July 1948.

35. CAB 87/95, EEP(44)2nd, 15 February 1944, Committee on External Policy.

36. CAB 87/95, WP(44)21, 18 February 1944.

37. CAB 134/220, EPC(49)24th, minute 2, 1 July 1949.

38. For a sample of the Foreign Office's frame of mind, see the despatch of Sir Edmund Hall Patch (Head of the British Delegation to the OEEC in Paris) of 23 August 1950 on the topic of the European Payments Union, in CAB 133/65, ER(P)(50)21, in which he states with becoming modesty: 'We may be apt to under-rate our capacity to exercise influence. It has often happened that the leading continental countries wished to take a line of their own because they have regarded our ideas as unhelpful; or we have had to follow a policy in the Organisation [OEEC] which rested on national interest and was sharply opposed to European policy. At such times, a combined opposition quickly appeared and forced us into isolation. . . .'

We may also relish this remark: 'There is no doubt also that it should be one of the objectives of our policy vis-à-vis the United States to become, as soon as possible, less dependent on them, and to be in a better position to speak as becomes a world power. . . .'

39. Cf. Bevin's speech of 22 January 1948 in the House of Commons. Alan Bullock, *Ernest Bevin: Foreign Secretary 1945–1951*, pp. 519–21.

40. CAB 134/217, EPC(48)34, 23 April 1948, note by the President of the Board of Trade, covering the report of the Interdepartmental Study Group on A Customs Union between all the Countries of the Commonwealth or the United Kingdom and the Colonies.

41. Ibid., annex A, para. 1.

42. CAB 134/219, EPC(48)78, 7 September 1948, Implications of a European Customs Union.

43. Ibid., annex.

44. CAB 134/236, ER(L)(48)198, 29 November 1948, instructions approved by the Foreign Secretary, Chancellor of the Exchequer and the President of the Board of Trade.

45. CAB 134/221, EPC(49)6, 25 January 1949, Our Policy to O.E.E.C. and

Our Proposals for Its Structure.

46. CAB 134/224, EPC(50)24th, item 5.

47. CAB 134/224, EPC(50)17th, item 2, 4 July 1950, The Stikker Plan.

48. Ibid., citing EPC(50)68. The Economic Policy Committee concurred in this recommendation.

49. It is not intended here to summarize the complex negotiations over the Schuman Plan, but only to bring out basic British attitudes and motivations.

50. CAB 134/293, FG(50)4, 17 June 1950, note by the Foreign Office.

51. On the constitutional issue, see CAB 134/293, FG(50)4, 17 June 1950, Committee on the Proposed Franco-German Coal and Steel Authority: Constitutional Problems Involved in a Supra-National Authority as Envisaged by M. Schuman: note by the Foreign Office.

52. Jean Monnet, *Memoirs* (trans. R. Mayne, 1978), (London, Collins, 1978), pp. 306–8.

53. Cited in Morgan, *Labour in Power*, p. 418.

54. CAB 134/224, EPC(50)15th, item 2, 25 May 1950. See also Bullock, *Ernest Bevin*, pp. 773–4 and 778–90.

55. CAB 134/293, FG(WP)(50)38, 16 June 1950, Working Party on Proposed Franco-German Coal and Steel Authority: Schuman Proposals for an International Coal and Steel Authority in West Europe: report by working party of officials.

56. CAB 134/295, FG(WP)(50)54, 24 July 1950, Working Party on the Proposed Franco-German Coal and Steel Authority: Integration of Western European Coal and Steel Industries, annex I, Draft of the United Kingdom's Proposals for Co-ordinating the Coal and Steel Industries of Europe.

57. Bullock, *Ernest Bevin*, pp. 769–70.

58. *Memoirs*, pp. 306–8.

59. See CAB 134/224, EPC(50)15th, item 2, 25 May 1950, but especially CAB 128/17, Cabinet Conclusions, 2 June 1950.

60. CAB 134/224, EPC(50)20th, item 2, 28 July 1950.

61. CAB 134/295, FG(WP)(50)55, 31 July 1950.

62. Cited in Bullock, *Ernest Bevin*, p. 782, n. 2.

Chapter Seven:
THE BRAVE NEW WORLD AND THE CRUEL REAL WORLD

1. R. H. Sherard, *The Child Slaves of Britain* (London, Hurst & Blackett, 1906), p. 85, writing of Manchester. See Correlli Barnett, *The Collapse of British*

Power, pp. 428–32 for a comparison of slum life and life in the trenches of the Western Front, based on contemporary witness. See also Correlli Barnett, *The Audit of War: The Illusion and Reality of Britain as a Great Nation*, ch. 10, on the condition of the British working class in the 1930s and 1940s, similarly based on contemporary reports and witness.

2. See Barnett, *Collapse of British Power*, part I, and *Audit of War*, ch. 1, for an analysis of the influences that went to form the character and mindset of the British governing class and intelligentsia in the nineteenth century.

3. See Barnett, *Collapse of British Power*, pp. 44–5.

4. Ibid.

5. Cited in ibid., p. 14.

6. Cited in Barnett, *Audit of War*, p. 14.

7. Noël Annan, *Our Age: The Generation That Made Post-War Britain*, p. 19. On other small-'l' liberal characteristics of the governing elite in the 1940s and 1950s, see pp. 17, 26–31, 240, 297–8.

8. Ibid., p. 240.

9. See Annan, *Our Age*, passim, for a passionate defence of his generation of the ruling elite and intelligentsia, which, though he does not appear to realise it, in fact entirely bears out the present author's critical analysis in both *The Collapse of British Power* and *The Audit of War*, and his summary in this chapter of *The Lost Victory*.

10. See William Harrington and Peter Young, *The 1945 Revolution* (London, Davis-Poynter, 1978), ch. 8.

11. Obituary in *The Times*, 16 August 1984, cited in Barnett, *Audit of War*, p. 21.

12. Cited in Barnett, *Audit of War*, p. 22.

13. *Social Insurance and Allied Services*, Cmd 6404 (1942).

14. Sir William H. Beveridge, *The Pillars of Security and Other War-Time Essays and Addresses* (London, George Allen & Unwin, 1943).

15. See Barnett, *Audit of War*, ch. 2, esp. pp. 40–5. Dr Jose Harris in an article, 'Enterprise and Welfare States: A Comparative Perspective' in *Transactions of the Royal Historical Society*, 40 (1990), pp. 175–95, criticising my account in *The Audit of War* of the origins and potentially limitless cost of the postwar Welfare State, argues that by 1950 Great Britain was spending a lower percentage of GNP on welfare than West Germany, Austria and Belgium. But none of these countries was also spending nearly 8 per cent of GNP on defence like Britain. Indeed, West Germany and Austria were not spending a penny. Moreover, West Germany did not embark on her first major postwar improvement on the welfare system inherited from the Weimar Republic

and Bismarck until 1957, when her 'economic miracle' was complete.

16. *Picture Post* editorial, New Year issue, 4 January 1941.

17. See Barnett, *Audit of War*, ch. 2, esp. pp. 44–51.

18. Quoted in W. K. Hancock and M. M. Gowing, *British War Economy*, p. 523.

19. Cited in Barnett, *Audit of War*, p. 26.

20. Cf. Nigel Nicolson's chance encounter with the great man: 'I was in a train travelling to Cambridge when an elderly man in my carriage began explaining to his companion the success of his recent report on the social services. His self-laudation continued for half an hour, and what was most remarkable about it was his anxiety to impress not only his friend, but me, a total stranger, giving sidelong glances in my direction as he completed each boastful point or anecdote. His name, of course, was Sir William Beveridge.' Article in the *Independent Magazine*, no. 252, 10 July 1993, p. 15.

21. See Barnett, *Audit of War*, pp. 26–8 and 45–8 for an account of the proceedings of this committee, based on the committee's minutes and memoranda, CAB 87/81, SIC(41) and (42) series.

22. ibid., p. 46.

23. ibid., p. 45.

24. ibid., pp. 45–6.

25. ibid., p. 47.

26. Cited in ibid., p. 47.

27. Cited in ibid., p. 27.

28. Cited in ibid., p. 47.

29. See ibid., p. 33.

30. PREM 8/35, CP(45)112.

31. John Campbell, *Nye Bevan and the Mirage of British Socialism* (London, Weidenfeld & Nicolson, 1987), p. 5.

32. CAB 134/697, SS(45) and (46) series. See especially SS(45)30, 27 November 1945, draft report of the Social Services Committee on the National Insurance Scheme for submission to the Cabinet.

33. Cf. CAB 134/697, SS(45)30, 27 November 1945, National Insurance Scheme, draft report, paras 3, 5, 9, 10.

34. What follows is not intended as even a bare summary of the Labour government's social insurance legislation and its enactment, for which see Kenneth O. Morgan, *Labour in Power 1945–1951*, ch. 4, but only as an examination of the Government's attitude to the cost in relation to Britain's postwar economic circumstances.

35. See CAB 134/697, SS(45)21, 9 November 1945, for the Government Actuary's analyses.

36. See A. W. Dilnot, J. A. Kay and C. N. Morris, *The Reform of Social Security* (Oxford, Oxford University Press, for Institute of Fiscal Studies, 1984) for an analysis of the disastrous long-term results of this strategy.

37. See CAB 134/704, CP(48)131, 26 May 1948, Social Services in Western Europe, giving details in regard to France, The Netherlands, Belgium and Italy. See also CAB 134/704, SWE(48)7, 6 April 1948, Committee on Social Services in Western Europe: The Health and Welfare Services of Belgium.

38. CAB 134/697, SS(45)1st, minute 2, 29 August 1945.

39. CAB 134/697, SS(45)21, 9 November 1945, National Insurance Scheme: Proposals for Increases in Pension and Other Benefits: memorandum by the Minister of National Insurance, circulating a memorandum by the Government Actuary, table III.

40. Ibid.

41. See CAB 134/704, CP(48)131, 26 May 1948, Social Services in Western Europe.

42. CAB 134/697, SS(45)27, 21 November 1945, National Insurance Scheme: Contributions and Costs: memorandum by the Minister of National Insurance.

43. See CAB 134/697, SS(45) and SS(46) series: meetings and memoranda of the Cabinet Social Services Committee.

44. CAB 134/697, SS(45)28, 26 November 1945, National Insurance Scheme: Report by Officials on Additional Safeguards Required if Unemployment Benefit is Made Continuous.

45. CAB 134/697, SS(45)17, 19 November 1945, Period of Unemployment Benefit in Relation to Training Schemes.

46. CAB 134/697, SS(45)11th, 26 November 1945.

47. Ibid., SS(45)12th, 29 November 1945.

48. CAB 128/4, CM(45)62nd, minute 2.

49. CAB 134/698, SS(46)1st, 15 January 1946.

50. Ibid. See also the earlier debate in the Social Services Committee about unemployment benefits and possible abuse on 26 November 1945, in SS(45)11th.

51. CAB 128/5, CM(46)6th, minute 2, 17 January 1946.

52. Ibid.

53. CAB 87/12, PR(43)12, 13 February 1943, views of the British Employers' Confederation (dated 10 February 1943) circulated to the

Cabinet Reconstruction Priorities Committee.

54. See Charles Webster, *The Health Services Since the War*, vol. I: *Problems of Health Care: The National Health Service Before 1957* (London, HMSO, 1988), pp. 78–9, and Morgan, *Labour in Power*, pp. 151–53.

55. See Campbell, *Nye Bevan*, passim, but esp. pp. xiii, xv, 14–15, 67–8, 124, 153 and 213.

56. ibid., p. 6.

57. Ibid., p. 67.

58. Cited in Morgan, *Labour in Power*, p. 124.

59. Ibid., p. 126.

60. Ibid., p. 127.

61. Ibid., p. 140.

62. The following sequence is not intended to be even a summary of the political and administrative problems and negotiations which led to the National Health Service Act of 1946, for which see Webster, *Health Services*, vol. I, ch. IV.

63. See the minutes and memoranda of the Cabinet Social Services Committee, CAB 134/697, SS(45) series. See also Morgan, *Labour in Power*, pp. 166–72; Webster, *Health Services*, pp. 84–8.

64. CAB 134/697, SS(45)33, 13 December 1945.

65. See Webster, *Health Services*, pp. 133–4; Morgan, *Labour in Power*, pp. 153–4, 167–73, 180. Professor Webster has confirmed to the present author that Bevan and his advisers carried out *no* detailed calculations of the likely demand for free medical services, and the resources needed to meet such demands. Letter of 26 July 1992.

66. CAB 134/697, SS(45)33, para. 53.

67. See Barnett, *Audit of War*, ch. 10, and esp. pp. 192–3, which briefly summarise basic health indicators in the 1930s and 1940s.

68. Webster, *Health Services*, p. 216. See also pp. 261–2.

69. Ibid., p. 133.

70. See Campbell, *Nye Bevan*, p. 180.

71. Ibid., p. 173n.

72. CAB 134/697, SS(45)15th, 17 December 1945.

73. See the files of the Social Services Committee in CAB 134/697, SS(45) series, as well as the Cabinet minutes in CAB 128/1–2 and memoranda in CAB 129/2–5. See also Morgan, *Labour in Power*, pp. 165–74; Webster, *Health Services*, pp. 80–8 and 133.

74. See Webster, *Health Services*, pp. 94–107 and 133. A separate National Health Service (Scotland) Act in broadly similar form was passed in 1947,

also with no challenge on the score of basic cost.

75. CAB 134/697, SS(45)34, 13 December 1945. The National Health Services in Scotland: memorandum by the Secretary of State for Scotland.

76. Webster, *Health Services*, p. 134.

77. CAB 129/31, CP(48)302, 13 December 1948, memorandum on the National Health Service.

78. All ibid.

79. Ibid. See also CAB 129/31, CP(48)308, 29 December 1948, memorandum by the Secretary of State for Scotland, putting the cost of the Scottish NHS to the Exchequer in 1949 at £34.5 million.

80. CAB 129/31, p. 258, and CP(48)302, p. 259, table I.

81. T 229/185, 4 January 1949, cited in Webster, *Health Services*, p. 138.

82. Ibid.

83. CAB 128/15, CM(49)37th, 23 May 1949.

84. CAB 129/34, CP(49)105, 6 May 1949. See also CP(49)106, similar memorandum by the Secretary of State for Scotland.

85. CAB 128/15, CM(49)37th, minute 1, 23 May 1949.

86. CAB 134/220, EPC(49)6, 7 July 1949.

87. CAB 129/37, CP(49)170; CAB 134/220, EPC(49)38th, 20 October 1949. See also CAB 134/220, EPC(49)111, which lists possible cuts.

88. CAB 134/220, EPC(49)35th, 14 October 1949. See also CAB 129/37, part I, CP(49)205, 20 October 1949, memorandum by the Prime Minister on Reduction of Investment Programme and Government Expenditure.

89. CAB 134/220, EPC(49)35th.

90. CAB 134/220, EPC(49)35th, 14 October 1949, the second (afternoon) meeting that day.

91. CAB 134/220, EPC(49)38th, 20 October 1949.

92. Cited in Webster, *Health Services*, p. 156.

93. CAB 134/518, NH(50)1, 22 April 1950.

94. CAB 134/518, NH(50)1st, 10 May 1950. See also Bevan's memorandum on the same topics, Measures to Intensify Control of Expenditure, NH(50)2, 6 May 1950.

95. CAB 134/518, NH(50)2, 6 May 1950.

96. CAB 134/518, NH(50)1st.

97. Ibid.

98. Ibid.

99. CAB 124/518, NH(50)3, 6 May 1950, Questions Arising Out of the New 'Ceiling' Policy: memorandum by the Minister of Health.

100. CAB 134/518, NH(50)2nd, 23 May 1950.

101. CAB 134/518, NH(50)3rd, minute 1, 28 May 1950.

102. CAB 134/518, NH(50)8, 24 June 1950.

103. Ibid.

104. CAB 134/518, NH(50)6, 23 June 1950, Condition of Expenditure [*sic*]: memorandum by the Minister of State for Economic Affairs.

105. Campbell, *Nye Bevan*, p. 218.

106. Cited in ibid., p. 219.

107. CAB 134/518, NH(50)17, circulated with a memorandum by Bevan on 15 July.

108. Ibid., statement 1.

109. Ibid., p. 5, para. 7.

110. CAB 134/518, NH(50)17.

111. CAB 124/518, NH(50)4th, 28 July 1950.

Chapter Eight:
PARLOURS BEFORE PLANT

1. *Poverty: A Study of Town Life* (London, Macmillan, 1910).

2. See Correlli Barnett, *The Audit of War*, ch. 10, for a historical summary of living conditions in industrial areas from the early nineteenth century to the Second World War.

3. *Report of the Royal Commission on the Distribution of the Industrial Population*, Cmd 6153 (1940), pp. 84–5.

4. See Barnett, *Audit of War*, p. 37; R. B. McCallum and Alison Readman, *The British General Election of 1945*, passim; also Charles Madge (ed.), *Pilot Guide to the General Election* (London, Pilot Press, 1945).

5. *Housing Policy*, Cmd 6609 (1945).

6. Morgan, *Labour in Power*, p. 163.

7. Campbell, *Nye Bevan*, p. 154.

8. Ibid.

9. Ibid., p. 158.

10. Ibid., p. 160.

11. Cf. *Economic Survey for 1947*, Cmd 7046 (1947), paras 112–13; *Economic Survey for 1948*, Cmd 7344 (1948), para. 28; CAB 134/220, EPC(49)28th, item 2, discussion of softwood imports.

12. Morgan, *Labour in Power*, p. 167.

13. CAB 134/503, MEP(46)16, 21 December 1946, Ministerial Committee on Economic Planning: *Economic Survey for 1947*: covering memorandum by

the Steering Committee, para. 46.

14. Ibid., MEP(46)15, 21 December 1946, *Economic Survey for 1947*: report by the Economic Survey Working Party, table 5.

15. CAB 134/437, IPC(47)2, 15 August 1947, citing Cabinet Conclusions 1 and 2, 1 August 1947.

16. Ibid.

17. Cf. Japan, which during the next half-century was to become the second most powerful industrial economy of the world while her workers remained ill-housed and over-crowded.

18. CAB 134/437, IPC(47)2, 15 August 1947, annex I.

19. Ibid.

20. Ibid.

21. CAB 134/437, Investment Programmes Committee, IPC(47)6th, 28 August 1947.

22. Ibid.

23. Cf. CAB 134/437, IPC(47)19th, minute 3, 15 September 1947. See also Morgan, *Labour in Power*, pp. 168–9.

24. CAB 134/437, IPC(49)9, 8 October 1947.

25. Ibid.

26. Cited in Campbell, *Nye Bevan*, p. 161.

27. White Paper on *Capital Investment in 1948*, Cmd 7268 (1948); CAB 134/637, PC(48)44, 6 April 1948, Production Committee: The Building Programme: Note by the Minister of Works.

28. CAB 134/438, IPC(48)8, 16 July 1948.

29. CAB 134/637, PC(48)44, memorandum by the Headquarters Building Committee.

30. See Barnett, *Audit of War*, ch. 12, esp. pp. 263–4.

31. CAB 134/438, IPC(48)22nd, 12 May 1948, referring to the Minister of Health's note, IPC(WP)(48)62, and IPC(48)8, 16 July 1948, Report on Capital Investment in 1949 by the Investment Programmes Committee.

32. CAB 134/438, IPC(48)8.

33. Ibid., table 52.

34. Ibid., table 47.

35. CAB 34/438, IPC(4)11, letter dated 28 October 1948, with reference to para. 159 of the Long-Term Programme.

36. CAB 134/638, PC(48)98, 22 July 1949, Report on Capital Investment in 1949: memorandum by the Chancellor of the Exchequer.

37. CAB 134/438, IPC(48)12, November 1948.

38. Ibid.

39. CAB 134/438, IPC(49)3, 12 May 1949, Report on Capital Investment in
1950–52, table I, Gross Fixed Investment 1948 and 1949.

40. Cf. letter to the author from Sir Alexander Cairncross, 24 January 1994.

41. CAB 134/438, IPC(49)3.

42. Ibid., table 17.

43. Ibid., paras 240 and 251.

44. CAB 134/660, PC(49)17th, item 2, 11 July 1949.

45. CAB 128/16, CM(49)61st, 21 October 1949.

46. CAB 129/37, CP(49)205, 20 October 1949.

47. CAB 134/438, IPC(49)6, 10 November 1949, Capital Investment in 1950.

48. CAB 134/220, EPC(49)35th, 14 October 1949.

49. Cited in Campbell, *Nye Bevan*, p. 208.

50. CAB 128/17, CM(50)21st, minute 2, 17 March 1950.

52. CAB 134/441, IPC(50)38th, 19 April 1950, briefing to the Investment
Programmes Committee by the Chairman, F. F. Turnbull of the Central
Planning Staff.

53. CAB 134/441, IPC(50)2, 24 April 1950, para. 211.

54. Ibid., para. 209.

56. Ibid., table I.

57. Ibid., para. 211.

58. CAB 134/224, EPC(50)12th, 12 May 1950.

59. CAB 134/225, EPC(50)50, 6 May 1950, memorandum by the Chancellor
of the Exchequer summarising the views of the Economic Planning Board
(EPB(50)6th and 7th) and the Official Committee on Economic Development (ED(50)3rd).

60. CAB 134/224, EPC(50)12th.

62. Only broad-brush figures can be given, for the following reasons.
Firstly, the estimates under various headings in the recommendations year
by year of the Investment Programmes Committee and its retrospective
estimates of actual spending rarely correspond, partly because of
insufficient and unreliable statistical information. Secondly, the IPC's
figures do not agree with those given in the *Economic Surveys* for 1947
(Cmd 7046), 1948 (Cmd 7344), 1949 (Cmd 7647), 1950 (Cmd 7915)
and 1951 (Cmd 8195). Thirdly, no indication is given in the *Economic
Surveys* of the rate of inflation involved in the figures, and fourthly the
breakdown into categories of investment alters from one set of annual

figures to another, especially in the *Economic Surveys*.

The cumulative totals given here are based on the *Economic Survey* figures, Cmd 7647, table 7, and Cmd 8309, table 20. Cmd 7647, table 7, breaks totals down into 'construction' and 'plant' and are at current prices; Cmd 8309, table 20, does not. I have based my guesstimated breakdowns of the totals for 1949 on the proportions of construction to plant given in the breakdowns for 1947 and 1948, which are about the same for both those years.

In regard to new housing, total investment in new housing *and* repair and maintenance in 1947 was £460 million, £475 million in 1948, and an estimated £420 million in 1949 (all from Cmd 7647). Cost of new housing in 1948 was £330 milllion, and in 1949, £298 million (Cmd 8039). New housing was thus on average 70 per cent of the total. Therefore estimated total for new housing in 1947 (otherwise not given in Cmd 7647) is £322 million. Therefore combined total for 1947, 1948 and 1949 is £950 million.

63. ROBN 7/3/3, The Long-term Programme of the Bizone of Germany, p. 51, para. 181.

64. In November 1945 the Government Actuary estimated the 1948 cost to public funds of existing social insurance and health schemes at £293 million (CAB 134/697, SS(45)21, table III). Allowing for inflation at 2.5 per cent per year, this would give a figure of £300 million for 1949: total for the two years 1948 and 1949, £593 million. The total cost of the NHS to the taxpayer for 1948 (nine months) and 1949 came to £362.7 million (report of the Enquiry into the Financial Workings of the Service by Sir Cyril Jones, CAB 134/518, NH(50)17, statement 1). The total cost to the taxpayer of social insurance handouts in those two years amounted to some £980 million (1948 figure from Cmd 7647, table 24; 1949 figure from Cmd 7915, table 12). Total cost of the NHS and social insurance to the taxpayer for the two years: £1342 million. Difference between estimated cost to public funds of existing 1945 schemes as at 1948–9 and actual costs of NHS and New Jerusalem welfare handouts: some £750 million.

Cost of new housing in 1948 and 1949 was £628 million (Cmd 8309, table 20).

Therefore total cost of New Jerusalem over the two years 1948 and 1949: £1377 million, or in round figures some £1400 million.

65. L. Pliatzky, *Getting and Spending: Public Expenditure, Employment and Inflation* (Oxford, Basil Blackwell, 1982), p. 2.

66. Cmd 7915, table 12. The figure given therein includes agricultural subsidies of some £50 million.

67. Morgan, *Labour in Power*, p. 371; Cmd 7915, table 12.

68. GNP at a combined total of £21,778,000 for both years. 1948 figure of £10,517,000 from C. H. Feinstein, *Statistical Tables of National Income, Expenditure and Output of the United Kingdom, 1855–1965* (Cambridge, Cambridge University Press, 1972), table 2; 1949 figure from Cmd 7915, table 10.

69. At £18,937,000 combined total for both years. See Cmd 7915, tables 2 and 10, for gross output of enterprises ('Manufacturing etc., transport, distribution, services and farming') in 1948 and 1949.

Chapter Nine:
THE CHARACTER OF THE NATION

1. CAB 134/218, EPC(48)66, The Balance of Payments: paper by the Central Economic Planning Staff, circulated to the Economic Planning Committee by the Chancellor on 9 July 1948.

2. Ibid.

3. Ibid., para. 19, and table V.

4. Ibid., table VII.

5. Ibid.

6. Ibid., table X.

7. See T 236/280–2 on reparations policy 1946, as also CAB 134/215–30, minutes and memoranda of the Cabinet Economic Policy Committee, 1947–9, passim. For a full analysis see Alec Cairncross, *The Price of War: British Policy on German Reparations 1941–1949* (Oxford, Basil Blackwell, 1986), and esp. his summary on pp. 229–35.

8. Churchill Archives Centre, Robinson Papers, ROBN 4/1/2, EIPS/59 of 30 January 1945, report by EIPS on Issues Affecting the Economic Obligations to be Imposed on Germany; EIPS/45, 9 February 1945, further report by EIPS, esp. appendix B, summary of working-party reports on fifteen industries.

9. ROBN 5/7 (OS), report by Miss M. E. Hill, Miss K. H. Spikes and Mr A. Fewster.

10. See above, Chapter 1; see Correlli Barnett, *Audit of War*, passim, but esp. chs 3–9 and 13. The general picture of the backwardness of British industry, not least in outlook, was confirmed by the Anglo-American Committee on Productivity, which investigated and reported on more than seventy industries in 1949–54.

11. Cf. CAB 87/3, RP(43)25, Report on the Recovery of Exports Markets, on

the excessive weight of the old Victorian staples like textiles in both the structure of British industry and the pattern of pre-war exports (these being the first industries to be developed by new industrialising countries), coupled with a weakness in new technologies and in technological research. Only 4 per cent of British exports to the United States in 1937 had been dependent on modern invention and design.

12. See Barnett, *Audit of War*, passim, but esp. ch. 11.

13. Ibid., but see also ch. 10.

14. Ibid., esp. ch. 11.

15. Ibid.

16. Other examples of pre-war neglect, especially in terms of export markets, include agricultural machinery, ball-bearings, electrical goods (including bulbs), scientific instruments, all kinds of photographic apparatus, clocks and watches, typewriters, telecommunications, radio valves and components. See ROBN 4/1/2, EIPS/59 and ROBN 4/1/2, memorandum on the Position of the German firms of Siemens and Halske, AG, and Subsidiaries throughout Europe and the World, by T. A. Eades, Managing Director of the Automatic Telephone and Electric Co. Ltd, 20 September 1944; ROBN 5/7 (OS); CAB 87/3, RP(43)25. See also above, pp. 427.

17. CAB 87/18, R(IO)(45)12.

18. CAB 87/3, RP(43)25, Report on the Recovery of Export Markets and the Promotion of Export Trade, by the Post-War Export Trade Committee: evidence to the BOT Industrial and Export Council.

19. Ibid.

20. Ibid.

21. Ibid.

22. See Barnett, *Audit of War*, passim, but esp. chs 3–9.

23. Kenneth O. Morgan, *Labour in Power 1945–1951* (Oxford, Clarendon Press, 1984), p. 503.

24. The fact of widespread overmanning and low productivity in Britain is attested by the wartime reports of the various production ministries (see Barnett, *Audit of War*, passim) as well as by the reports of the Anglo–American Committees on Productivity. In the early 1950s the present author had personal experience of the unacknowledged bargain between employers and the white-collared by which partly or wholly redundant 'jobs' for life and a pension were traded against low salaries, for he was then 'working' for a nationalised industry essentially unchanged in its culture from the pre-nationalisation private company. He can imagine the pain and indignation among his colleagues if it had been proposed

to halve the staff, and double the salaries and treble the workload of those remaining.

25. Cf. Gallup Poll in January 1946 in which 73 per cent preferred job security to higher wages. A similar poll in May 1947 found that 55 per cent thought the Government's most important task was 'to guarantee every person a steady job and a decent standard of living', as against 40 per cent reckoning that the Government's most important task was 'to make certain that there are good opportunities for each person to get ahead on their own'. George H. Gallup (general ed.), *The Gallup International Opinion Polls: Great Britain 1937–1975*, vol. I, *1937–1964* (New York, Random House, 1977), pp. 125 and 157.

26. See Morgan, *Labour in Power*, ch. 7, esp. pp. 284–6, 296–7; and p. 330.

27. Cf. Addison to Cripps, 10 March 1950: 'We are extracting £600m. a year from people, simply in order to prevent them spending it.' Morgan, *Labour in Power*, p. 407, n. 99.

28. See Morgan, *Labour in Power*, pp. 369–71. The present author lived through this era of universal rationing and remembers it well in all its dreary restrictiveness, like life in a Victorian public institution. What excitement, what queues, when news spread that a local grocer had received a small consignment of canned steak-and-kidney pudding!

29. Ibid., p. 369; J. L. Hodson, *The Sea and the Land* (London, Victor Gollancz, 1945), p. 303. However, so well-known a contemporary phenomenon hardly needs documentary proof.

30. On working-class dislike of upward social mobility, see Richard Hoggart, *The Uses of Literacy: Aspects of Working Class Life with Special Reference to Publications and Entertainments* (London, Chatto & Windus, 1971), pp. 20 and 116.

31. In July 1947, a Gallup Poll asked respondents in what career they would wish to be famous, if they had the choice. 18 per cent said 'a musician'; 9 per cent 'a scientist'; 21 per cent 'a doctor'; and only 11 per cent 'the head of a big business'. Gallup, *Gallup International Opinion Polls*, vol. I, p. 159. Asked which qualities they would wish a child of theirs to have, 57 per cent answered 'honest'; 40 per cent 'intelligent'; 25 per cent 'considerate towards others'; 22 per cent 'reliable'; 16 per cent 'affectionate'; and only 10 per cent 'ambitious'.

32. See Barnett, *Audit of War*, chs 10 and 11.

33. Hoggart, *Uses of Literacy*, p. 20.

34. Ibid., p. 116.

35. The present author was brought up in just such a house and suburb,

where his father and his friends' fathers, his uncles and all the neighbours in the road lived exactly such routine and unaspiring lives. See D. V. Glass (ed.), *Social Mobility in Britain* (London, Routledge & Kegan Paul, 1954), passim. In his editorial introduction Glass writes of British society at the time of investigation in 1949: 'the general picture so far is of a rather stable social structure, and one in which social status has tended to operate within, so to speak, a closed circuit. Social conditions have conditioned educational level, and both have conditioned social status.' See also John H. Goldthorpe, David Lockwood, Frank Bechhofer and Jennifer Platt, *The Affluent Worker* (Cambridge, Cambridge University Press, 1968), which concluded that even the affluent worker of the 1960s still knew where he 'belonged'.

36. The present author was 'trained' alongside all kinds of blue- and white-collared workers in the North Thames Gas Board in the early 1950s, and testifies to this point. He himself became no less adept at stretching a little effort over a long day.

37. Hodson, *The Sea and the Land*, p. 340.

38. Ibid., p. 356.

39. Article in a special issue of *Encounter* edited by Arthur Koestler (vol. XXI, no. 1, July 1963) and entitled 'Suicide of a Nation'.

40. Leader-page article in the issue of 2 January 1980, © Times Newspapers Limited 1980. See also Professor Leslie Hannah's inaugural lecture as Professor of Business History at the London School of Economics, 11 October 1983, on the cultural reasons for Britain's lack of business dynamism, especially want of personal ambition, in which he remarks that in Britain successful businessmen such as Sir John Ellerman are 'generally not envied or not admired or even, quite simply, not known about', in contrast to the way Germans celebrate a man like Krupp or the Japanese a man like Matsushita.

41. The Times/ORC Poll, in *The Times* for 23 June 1980, © Times Newspapers Limited 1980. The present author, as an employee of the North Thames Gas Board in the 1950s, shared in the attitudes documented by the preceding quotations once his initial burst of enthusiasm had died down.

42. Ralf Dahrendorf, *On Britain* (London, BBC Worldwide Limited, 1982), p. 49. See also article by Peter Wilby in the *Sunday Times* for 19 May 1985 on the views of graduates of various European nationalities at the European School of Management Studies. He cites their common agreement that 'the British still regard naked ambition as ungentlemanly'.

43. 21st edition of *Social Trends* by the Central Statistical Office (London, HMSO, 1991).

44. *British Social Attitudes Survey* (of 3000 voters) by Social and Community Planning Research (Aldershot, Gower Publishing, 1988); Eric Jacobs and Robert Worcester, *Typically British? The Prudential MORI Guide* (London, Bloomsbury, 1991).

45. See survey of national attitudes by Social and Community Planning Research, November 1992. To the present author, whose adult experience of British life spans the postwar era from 1945 to the present day, it hardly requires elaborate documentary evidence to establish that the temperament of the nation has been, and still remains, sluggish and lacklustre.

46. Eyewitness evidence of the present author. The late 1940s and 1950s were his twenties and thirties.

47. As a man of eighteen in 1945, the present author writes from personal observation and experience.

48. *Statistics Relating to the War Effort of the United Kingdom*, Cmd 6564 (1944).

49. In May 1948, a year after the great sterling convertibility crisis, and despite three years of Government preaching about the importance of exports, only 1 per cent of respondents to a Gallup Poll thought that production was the main problem for the Government, as against 31 per cent picking housing and 21 per cent food and rationing.

50. See David Cannadine and Simon Price (eds), *Rituals of Royalty: Power and Ceremonial in Traditional Societies* (Cambridge, Cambridge University Press, 1987), passim.

51. CAB 132/47, CIP(TR)(48)3, note by Secretary of the Committee on Industrial Productivity (Panel on Technology and Operational Research), circulating the First Interim Report of the Committee on Research and Productivity, dated 17 September 1947, as submitted to the Lord President (Morrison).

52. CAB 134/234, WR(L)(48)91, 6 September 1948, The Draft Long-Term Programme (material to be submitted by the United Kingdom to the Organisation for European Economic Co-operation), para. 26, p. 7.

53. Sir Stafford Cripps had been superintendent of a munitions factory during the Great War. Cripps had also had 'main board' experience as Minister for Aircraft Production in the Second World War. The trade unionists comprised Bevin, Ellen Wilkinson, Tom Williams, George Isaacs, George Hall and Jack Lawson.

54. Attlee (Haileybury and University College, Oxford), Lord Jowitt (Marlborough and New College, Oxford), Dalton (Eton and King's

College, Cambridge), Lord Pethick-Lawrence (Eton and Trinity College, Cambridge), and Sir Stafford Cripps (Winchester and University College, London).

55. See Correlli Barnett, *Collapse of British Power*, pp. 21–43, and *Audit of War*, ch. 11, for analyses of the origins, values and development of British governing-class education from the 1820s to the 1940s.

56. Clement R. Attlee, *The Will and the Way to Socialism* (London, Methuen, 1935), p. 6.

57. Nicholas Davenport in *The Dictionary of National Biography 1961–1970* (Oxford, Oxford University Press, 1981), p. 266.

58. Morgan, *Labour in Power*, p. 52.

59. Ibid., p. 53.

60. Annan, *Our Age*, p. 397.

61. Cf. *Report of the [Fulton] Committee on the Civil Service*, 1966–8, Cmnd 3638, vol. I (1967–8 Sessional Papers, vol. xviii, p. 129), p. 12: 'Few members of the [administrative] class actually see themselves as managers, i.e., as responsible for organisation, directing staff, planning the progress of work, setting standards of attainment and measuring results, reviewing procedures and quantifying different courses of action. One reason for this is that they are not adequately trained in management. Another is that much of their work is not managerial in this sense; so they tend to think of themselves as advisers on policy to those above them, rather than managers of the administrative machine below them.'

62. Cf. Cmnd 3638, vol. I, p. 9: 'The Home Civil Service today is still fundamentally the product of the nineteenth-century philosophy of the Northcote–Trevelyan Report. The tasks it faces are those of the second half of the twentieth century.'

63. All this was to be belatedly laid bare in paining detail in Cmnd 3638.

64. Cf. Cmnd 3638, p. 12: 'there is not enough contact between the Service and the rest of the community. There is not enough awareness of how the world outside Whitehall works. . . .'

65. See Alec Cairncross and Nita Watts, *The Economic Section, 1939–1961: A Study in Economic Advising* (London, Routledge & Kegan Paul, 1989), a remarkably self-satisfied but densely opaque account, passim.

66. C. Tennant Sons and Company. I am grateful to Lord Plowden for these details relating to his career. On the basis of this experience Lord Plowden gave his book the title of *An Industrialist in the Treasury: The Post-War Years* (London, André Deutsch, 1989).

67. Cairncross and Watts, *Economic Section*, appendix, pp. 351–7.

68. There is an exact parallel in Basil Liddell Hart, as defence correspondent of *The Times* and all-purpose strategic cham, exercising a major influence on Neville Chamberlain's thinking from 1936 onwards, and personally advising the Secretary of State for War, Leslie Hore-Belisha, on army organisation, equipment and appointments in 1937–8, with catastrophic results, for it led to the scrapping of any commitment of land forces on the continent in support of the French, so depriving Chamberlain's diplomacy of any leverage during the Munich crisis of 1938. See Barnett, *Collapse of British Power*, pp. 494–505. The present author, despite having written books on strategic history for more than thirty years, would not regard himself as equipped to serve in Whitehall as an adviser on strategy and defence policy. However, like Liddell Hart, academic economists have never doubted their omnicompetence.

69. See Cairncross and Watts, *Economic Section*, chs 8–15. See also memorandum by Austin Robinson on The Functions of the Economic Adviser, 11 June 1946, in ROBN 5/2. For inaccuracy of forecasting see J. C. R. Dow, *The Management of the British Economy 1945–60* (Cambridge, Cambridge University Press: National Institute for Economic and Social Research, Students' Edition 3), pp. 131–5, tables 5.1, 5.2 and 5.3. It makes an ironic comment on the 'planned economy' that the statistical information available to the planners was so unreliable that they were not even sure whether actual gross investment was rising or falling. Cf. letter to the author from Sir Alexander Cairncross, 25 January 1994.

70. Annan, *Our Age*, pp. 297–8.

71. Cf. CAB 134/217, EPC(48)1, 23 December 1947, draft *Economic Survey for 1948*; CAB 134/242, ER(L)(49)163, 27 May 1949, General Memorandum for OEEC on United Kingdom Revised 1949–50 Programme.

72. CAB 133/49, ER(ECA)(48)5th, 23 July 1948. See also CAB 133/59, ER(Mission)(49) series, in which again American officials press for detailed information and programmes, to which British officials respond with evasions.

73. See H. Mercer, N. Rollings and J. D. Tomlinson (eds), *Labour Governments and Private Industry: The Experience of 1945–1951* (Edinburgh, Edinburgh University Press, 1992), esp. the essay by David Edgerton, 'Whatever Happened to the British Warfare State? The Ministry of Supply, 1945–1951', which argues that the ministry was 'the scientific, technological and industrial powerhouse of the British state, and pursued the discriminatory, interventionist and technological policies which many critics have said British governments have not, but should have pursued.' However, the

evidence adduced in the essay shows that the interventionist role of the
Ministry of Supply was, apart from civil aircraft, overwhelmingly in the field
of defence procurement.

74. Cf. Keith Middlemass, *Power, Competition and the State*, vol. I: *Britain in
    Search of Balance 1940–61* (London, Macmillan, 1986), p. 12 of
    Introduction; G. Denton, M. Forsyth and M. MacLennan, *Economic
    Planning and Policies in Britain, France and Germany* (London, George
    Allen & Unwin, 1968), p. 22.

75. See Barnett, *Audit of War*, ch. 13, and its referenced sources in the CAB 87
    series: cf. esp. CAB 87/63, EC(43)4, 15 October 1943.

76. See Barnett, *Audit of War*, pp. 119–20.

77. Annan, *Our Age*, p. 17.

78. Ibid., p. 18.

79. Ibid., p. 469. See also pp. 296–7, 474–5.

80. *Economic Survey for 1947*, Cmd 7046 (1947), para. 8.

81. Ibid., paras 25 and 26.

82. Ibid., para. 27.

83. Peter Hennessy and Andrew Arends, *Mr Attlee's Engine Room: Cabinet
    Committee Structure and the Labour Governments 1945–51*, Strathclyde
    Papers on Government and Politics no. 26 (Glasgow, Strathclyde
    University, 1983).

84. CAB 134/503, MEP(46)1st, 21 January 1946.

85. CAB 134/503, MEP(47)1st, 7 January 1947.

86. See, for instance, the list of committees cited in the Bibliography of the
    present book.

87. The Investment Programmes Committee (CAB 134/437–42) came to six
    volumes; the Economic Policy Committee of 1948–51 (CAB 134/215–30)
    to fifteen.

88. CAB 134/635–52.

89. CAB 134/438, IPC(48) series.

90. Cf., among many, the Treasury T 229 series on Central Economic
    Planning, numbering some 140 files. See also, for instance, the memor-
    andum on The Functions of the Economic Adviser by Austin Robinson in
    June 1946 (ROBN 5/2), which states that the Economic Steering
    Committee operates through 'a series of Sub–Committees' of which the
    four that most concerned him were the Statistical Working Party, the
    Manpower Working Party, a Sub-Committee of the Balance of Payments
    Working Party and the Investment Working Party.

91. Cf. CAB 134/635, PC(47)11, 11 November 1947.

92. Cf. CAB 134/437, IPC(47)22nd, 28th and 29th; CAB 134/438, IPC(48) 5th and 6th.

93. Terms of reference in CAB 134/635, PC(47)1, 21 October 1947.

94. CAB 134/640, PC(49)156th, minute 1, 21 June 1949. The Production Committee similarly discussed at length whether the Ford Motor Company should be allowed to expand at Dagenham, as it wished, or be pressed to build at Kirkby, Liverpool, a 'Development Area'.

Chapter Ten:
'THE EBBING OF THE TIDE OF THE SELLERS' MARKET'

1. CAB 134/638, PC(48)74, 1 June 1948, Production Committee: Turn-round of Shipping in British Ports, report by working party appointed in September 1947. Covering memorandum by the Minister of Transport, p. 2. Main report, passim.

2. Ibid., working party report, para. 45. As late as January 1949 the Minister of Transport was reporting to his colleagues that turn-round in British ports had 'a long way to go to get back to pre-war standards'; and that more mechanisation, especially cranage, was needed. CAB 134/641, PC(49)11, 27 January 1949, Turn-Round of Shipping in the United Kingdom Ports. See also his report on the same topic on 1 June 1948, CAB 134/638, PC(48)74. See also CAB 132/34, CIP(HF)(50)11, 31 May 1950, The London Docks: A Framework for Study, report by the Field Investigation Group of the British Institute of Management, which found that 'the social pressures in dockland, alike at work and in the communities, are traditionally wholly and strongly against any deviation from the accepted norms, customs and special relationships'.

3. Cf. CAB 87/3, RP(43)25, Report on the Recovery of Export Markets, 15 June 1943. According to this, of total British exports in 1937 of £521 million, only £123 million were marketed by companies' own selling organisations. But cf. too, for example, CAB 134/44, BP(E)(47)12, 30 October 1947, Assistance to New Exporters from Merchants' Organisations.

4. ROBN 5/1, note of 3 May 1946.

5. Economic Survey for 1947, Cmd 7046 (1947), p. 11.

6. Ibid., p. 12.

7. CAB 134/503, MEP(46)10, 23 October, 1947, annex: Balance of Payments Working Party: Import Programme for 1947: note by the Treasury dated 12 October 1946.

8. CAB 134/502, MEP(46)10, 23 October 1946, annex: Balance of Payments Working Party: Import Programme for 1947: note by the Treasury, para. 7.

9. Cf. Cmd 7046, paras 12–29.

10. Ibid., para. 14.

11. Morgan, *Labour in Power*, pp. 127–9.

12. ROBN 5/1, letter from H. Townshend to A. E. Welsh, 11 January 1946.

13. CAB 134/503, MEP(46)10, 23 October 1946, Import Programme for 1947.

14. Ibid., Balance of Payments Working Party, Import Programme for 1947.

15. Ibid.

16. CAB 134/503, MEP(46)15, 21 December 1946, para. 49.

17. Ibid., para. 49.

18. CAB 134/503, MEP(46)16, 21 December 1946, *Economic Survey for 1947*: covering memorandum by the Steering Committee, para. 24.

19. Ibid., para. 30.

20. Ibid., paras 31 and 33.

21. Ibid., paras 31 and 32.

22. CAB 128/9, CM(46), 7 January 1947.

23. Morgan, *Labour in Power*, p. 340.

24. *Economic Survey for 1948*, Cmd 7344 (1948), para. 8.

25. Ibid., paras 6 and 7.

26. Peter J. S. Dunnett, *The Decline of the British Motor Industry: The Effects of Government Policy, 1945–1979* (London, Croom Helm, 1980), p. 35, table 3.1. A 6-cylinder Chevrolet cost 661 Australian pounds; a 4-cylinder Standard 14 of half the horsepower cost 720 Australian pounds. An 8-cylinder Buick cost less than a 6-cylinder Wolseley of nearly half the horsepower.

27. Ibid., p. 34.

28. CAB 134/167, E(48)14(final), 2 February 1948, Committee on Exports: Exports to Canada.

29. CAB 134/167, E(48)26(final), 6 March 1948, memorandum by the Cabinet Committee on Exports on exports to the United States of America, p. 2.

30. Ibid., p. 1.

31. Ibid.

32. T 230/134, National Union of Manufacturers: Questionnaire on Export Trade, December 1947, Summary of Replies, p. 5.

33. Ibid., appendix C.

34. Ibid., p. 6.

35. Ibid., p. 4.

36. Ibid.

37. Ibid., p. 7.

38. Ibid., pp. 3–4.

39. CAB 134/215, EPC(47)1, 9 October 1947.

40. CAB 134/635, PC(47)1, Trafalgar Day 1947.

41. CAB 134/44, BP(E)(47) series.

42. Cf. The Economic Policy Committee, with thirty-one meetings and thirty-three memoranda in the last eleven weeks of 1947, and forty meetings and sixty-eight memoranda in 1948.

43. ROBN 4/5/1, Motor Vehicle Study. The same study notes that while British car production in 1938 stood at 155 per cent of 1933, and of trucks at 161 per cent, German production in 1938 stood at 300 per cent and 543 per cent of 1933 respectively.

44. CAB 87/63, EC(43)4, 15 October 1943, cited in Correlli Barnett, *Audit of War*, ch. 13, p. 270.

45. See CAB 132/28–30, CIP(48–50) series, Committee on Industrial Productivity; and CAB 132/31–5, CIP(HF)(48–50) series, the Committee's Panel on Human Factors. This panel gave rich employment to a gaggle of academics such as sociologists and psychologists, who turned in voluminous papers full of the obvious dressed up in jargon. See, for example, the 163-page job on Royal Ordnance Factories, CAB 132/34, CIP(HF)(50).

46. CAB 134/234, ER(L)(48)91, 6 September 1948.

47. CAB 134/635, PC(47)11, 11 November 1947.

48. Ibid., para. 4.

49. CAB 87/10, R(45)8, 5 February 1945.

50. CAB 134/647, PC(50)72, 5 July 1950, Development Councils under the Industrial Organisation and Development Act 1947.

51. Ibid.

52. Cf. terms of reference in CAB 134/638, PC(48)77, 21 June 1948, Progress Report from the Committee on Industrial Productivity, annex B.

53. CAB 132/31, CIP(HF)(48) series.

54. CAB 132/44, CIP(TR)(48) series.

55. See CAB 132/28, CIP(48)27, 20 September 1948, memorandum by the Chairman of the Committee on Industrial Productivity on its future work.

56. Ibid.

57. CAB 132/29, CIP(49)9, 17 March 1949, annual report (third draft).

58. Ibid.

59. Ibid. para. 45.

60. CAB 132/29, CIP(49)13 and 24.

61. CAB 132/32, CIP(HF)(49)27.

62. CAB 132/32, CIP(HF)(49)28, 40 and 42.

63. CAB 132/28, CIP(48)43(revise).

64. CAB 132/31, CIP(HF)(48) series. The author measured the thickness of the file in the PRO.

65. CAB 132/34, CIP(HF)(50)9.

66. CAB 132/32, CIP(HF)(49)6, report by the Tavistock Institute on research at Glacier Metals.

67. CAB 132/29, CIP(49)28, 19 October 1949, The Future Work of the Committee, by Mr G. B. Blaker. See also CAB 132/30, CIP(50)11, 17 June 1950, second annual report of the Committee on Industrial Productivity, which does not really dissent from Blaker's paper.

68. CAB 134/648, PC(50)109, 8 November 1950, para. 8.

69. Ibid.

70. Quoted to the European Economic Co-operation Committee on 21 July 1948 from Washington telegram no. 3550. See CAB 134/232, ER(L)(48)13th.

71. When the author joined the North Thames Gas Board in 1952 as a 'graduate trainee', his first task was to write for the Chairman a précis of the report of the Anglo-American Productivity Team on the Gas Industry. Briefly put, the American industry belonged in all aspects, from production and distribution to customer service, to the twentieth century; the British to the nineteenth. To cite one small example, American gas meters were installed in boxes on the outside of houses along with the electricity meter so that meter-readers had no need to catch the householder at home in order to read the meter. The gas meters were also fixed by standard screw couplings, whereas in Britain lead pipes had to be bent into shape and the joints between them and the brass unions on the meter 'blown' in hot lead by a skilled gas-fitter. When the author left North Thames Gas five years later, not one of the American practices described in the report had yet been adopted.

72. Cf. CAB 132/30, CIP(50)11, 17 June 1950, second report of the Committee on Industrial Productivity, para. 5.

73. CAB 134/639, PC(48)113, 8 September 1948, memorandum by the Minister of Supply on Standardising and Simplifying Engineering Products.

74. CAB 134/222, EPC(49)72, The Dollar Situation.

75. CAB 87/9, R(44)152, 2 September 1944, memorandum by the President of the Board of Trade on the cotton industry.

76. Ibid.

77. Ibid.

78. Ibid.

79. CAB 133/58, notes of meeting on 29 July 1948 between ECA London Mission and British officials to discuss imports of textile machinery.

80. The Clynes Committee, cited in CAB 87/9, R(44)152.

81. Ibid.

82. Cotton Industry Working Party Report (London, HMSO, 1947).

83. Committee of Investigation into the Cotton Textile Machinery Industry, Report [Evershed Report] (London, HMSO, 1947).

84. CAB 132/47, CIP(TR)(48)2nd, item 2.

85. CAB 134/648, PC(50)121, 14 December 1950, note by the President of the Board of Trade circulating A Review of Progress in the Cotton Industry, address given to the Cotton Board Conference at Harrogate, 20 October 1950.

86. CAB 132/47, CIP(TR)(48)2nd, 27 February 1948.

87. CAB 134/644, PC(50)15th, item 1, 28 July 1950.

88. CAB 132/48, CIP(TR)(49)2.

89. Ibid.

90. CAB 134/647, PC(50)82, 25 July 1950, Working Party Report on Research and Development in the Textile Machinery Industry, para. 36.

91. Textile Machinery Makers Ltd at Helmshore. See CAB 134/647, PC(50)82, III, 5. See also R. Rothwell, 'Technical Innovation in Textile Machinery', in Keith Pavitt (ed.), *Technical Innovation and British Economic Performance* (London, Macmillan, 1980), pp. 126–41.

92. CAB 134/648, PC(50)121.

93. Ibid.

94. CAB 132/48, CIP(TR)(49)2, 8 July 1949.

95. CAB 132/648, PC(50)121.

Chapter Eleven:
'THE REMEDY IS PUBLIC OWNERSHIP'

1. See Samuel H. Beer, *Modern British Politics: A Study of Parties and Pressure Groups* (London, Faber & Faber, 1965), ch. V, esp. pp. 132–7, and ch. VI, esp. pp. 164–73. See p. 130 for the phrase cited from Ramsay MacDonald; p. 131 for the phrase cited from Robert Blatchford's book *Merrie England*.

2. Cited in ibid., p. 133.

3. Cited in ibid.

4. Cited in ibid., p. 137.

5. See Correlli Barnett, *Collapse of British Power*, part I, and *Audit of War*, ch. 1.

6. Cited in Alan Bullock, *The Life and Times of Ernest Bevin* (London, Heinemann, 1960–83), vol. I, p. 21.

7. C. R. Attlee, *The Labour Party in Perspective* (London, Victor Gollancz, 1937), p. 15.

8. See Barnett, *Audit of War*, ch. 5.

9. CAB 134/693, GEN 98/1–6. It is noteworthy that the official history, *The Nationalisation of British Industry 1945–51* (London, HMSO, 1975), a titanic 1059-page lump of turgidity by Sir Norman Chester (a Professor of Administration, not of industrial or technological history), is concerned with the political, parliamentary, legal, financial and administrative aspects of nationalisation, to the exclusion of the industrial and technological. Just 24 pages out of the 1059 are allotted to 'Accountability and Efficiency', and another 9 pages to 'The Early Results', which are looked at solely in terms of profit and loss accounting. This bias all too accurately reflects that of ministers and officials at the time.

10. The memorandum on Iron and Steel (CAB 134/693, GEN 98/1) by the Minister of Supply and of Aircraft Production devoted six out of seven pages to compensation, administrative structures, pricing and wages; and one short paragraph to the planning and timing of new investment. The two-and-a-half page memorandum on British Air Transport (GEN 98/2) by the Minister of Civil Aviation and the three pages on Public Utility Services (including transport) (GEN 98/5) by the Minister of War Transport were similarly proportioned. The seven and a half single-spaced foolscap pages on fuel and power by the Minister thereof (GEN 98/3), mostly concentrating on coal, devoted less than a page to the essential issues of investment and exports.

11. CAB 134/693, GEN 98/4.

12. CAB 134/693, GEN 98/6, para. 2.

13. CAB 134/693, SI(O)(45)3, section (7), para. 2.

14. CAB 134/693, GEN 98/6, paras 3 and 4.

15. CAB 134/693, GEN 98/1st, 9 November 1945.

16. See CAB 134/693, SI(O)(45)1st, 29 November 1945. Sir Bernard Gilbert of the Treasury in the chair. Other members comprised Sir Alan Barlow of the Treasury (Marlborough and Corpus Christi College, Oxford; first-class honours in Classics); Sir Donald Ferguson of the Ministry of Fuel and Power (Berkhamsted School and Wadham College, Oxford; first-class honours in Modern History (meaning from AD 410)); C. W. Evans of the Ministry of

Civil Aviation (Manchester Grammar School and Wadham College, Oxford; honours degree in Classics); H. Townshend of the Post Office (King's School, Canterbury, and Trinity College, Cambridge); James Meade of the Economic Section again; Sir Herbert Brittain of the Treasury; Sir Cyril Hurcombe of the Ministry of War Transport again; A. Johnston of the Office of the Lord President (George Heriot's School and University of Edinburgh); and Austin Robinson, academic economist and temporary civil servant, at present Economic Adviser to the Board of Trade (Marlborough and Christ's College, Cambridge).

17. CAB 134/693, SI(O)(46)12, 21 February 1946, first report.

18. See CAB 134/687, SI(M)(46) series.

19. CAB 134/688, SI(M)(47) series.

20. CAB 134/689, SI(M)(48) series.

21. See CAB 134/693, 694 and 695, SI(O)(46) series, SI(O)(47) series and SI(O)(48) series. In 1946, the committee discussed twenty-nine items and amassed forty-three memoranda, not one of which related to the long-term industrial and commercial development of the nationalised sector, or to nationalisation as a tool of technological change. In 1947 there were nineteen agenda items and twenty-seven memoranda, and in 1948 seven agenda items and seventeen memoranda, none of which in either year touched on industrial strategy and development. What occupied the committee throughout were questions of insurance, pensions, accounts, records, compensation for loss of office, plus a few glances at workers' participation and pricing.

22. CAB 134/693, GEN 98/2(revised).

23. CAB 134/690, SI(M)(49)31, 3 May 1949, Government Control over Socialised Industries.

24. CAB 134/693, SI(O)(45)3, 4 December 1945, The Problems of Socialisation, p. 4, para. 19(a) and pp. 7–8.

25. CAB 134/693, GEN 98/1, paras 24 and 26.

26. CAB 134/693, GEN 98/3, paras 21 and 23.

27. Ibid., para. 34.

28. Ibid., para. 33.

29. CAB 134/693, GEN 98/5, para. 13.

30. Ibid., para. 14.

31. Ibid., para. 13.

32. Ibid., para. 14.

33. Ibid., para. 15.

34. ROBN 5/3, 27 November 1945.

35. CAB 134/693, GEN 98/2(revise).

36. Ibid.

37. CAB 134/693, SI(O)(46)4th, item 3, 14 February 1946.

38. Ibid. See also CAB 134/693, SI(O)(46)19(revise), 11 April 1946, the second draft of the committee's Report on Price Policy in Socialised Industries, esp. paras 6 and 9.

39. CAB 134/687, SI(M)(46)8th, item 2, 14 May 1946. This followed almost word for word the official committee's report, para. 6.

40. ROBN 5/1, draft memorandum to Sir Alan Barlow at the Treasury, July 1946.

41. CAB 134/688, SI(M)(47)32, 18 July 1947.

42. CAB 134/689, SI(M)(48)32, 9 April 1948, Some Current Problems in Socialised Industries.

43. Ibid.

44. CAB 134/689, SI(M)(48)16, 20 February 1948, Examples of Industrial Organisation. On 15 December 1947 the Lord President had informed his colleagues that 'I have been reading a book, recently published, on the organisation of General Motors,' and duly circulated to them selected extracts. See CAB 134/688, SI(M)(47)50.

45. The Deputy Chairman of the North Thames Gas Board, Robert Nigel Beresford Dalrymple Bruce, had been educated at Harrow and Magdalen, Oxford (BA Hons, Chemistry). The culture of the upper reaches of the board in the 1950s when the present author was the humble author of the first draft of the board's annual report resembled a cross between a Senior Common Room, the Foreign Office and the Mess in a fashionable regiment.

46. CAB 134/688, SI(M)(47)37, 22 October 1947, Manning of Public Boards.

47. CAB 134/689, SI(M)(48)43, 14 May 1948, Manning of Public Boards.

48. CAB 134/688, SI(M)(47)37.

49. CAB 134/689, SI(M)(48)43, 14 May 1948. See also CAB 134/690, SI(M)(49)9th, item 2, 11 July 1949, on recruitment of members of boards from outside the industries, where suitable candidates from within were lacking.

50. CAB 134/688, SI(M)(47)43, 13 November 1947. See also CAB 134/690, SI(M)(49)31, 3 May 1949, Government Control of Socialised Industries: memorandum by the Minister of Transport, in which he says of the railways and road haulage, that they 'have within their ranks experts with life-long practical experience of the operations of various forms of transport who . . . should provide a body well-qualified to work out practical and economic solutions to the many problems involved.'

51. CAB 134/688, SI(M)(47)43, 13 November 1947, Taking Stock: memorandum by the Minister of Fuel and Power.

52. Ibid.

53. Ibid.

54. See, for example, CAB 134/690, SI(M)(49)9th, item 2, 11 July 1949, in regard to appointments of members of boards: 'From the point of view of the morale of the industries, it was desirable to recruit from within them when suitable candidates were available [but because of] serious shortage of men of the highest calibre . . . it was agreed that . . . Ministers must not hesitate to go outside the industries, despite the criticism which would be aroused.'

55. See CAB 134/690, SI(M)(49)30, 32 and 33, 21 and 24 May and 14 June, memoranda on Government Control of Socialised Industries, by the Ministers of Supply, Labour and National Service, and Civil Aviation.

Chapter Twelve:
'THE PRESTIGE OF THE AIRCRAFT INDUSTRY'

1. CAB 134/59, CAC(50)1, 17 January 1950, Progress of Civil Aviation Under the Present Administration: memorandum by the Minister of Civil Aviation.

2. Cf. T 230/3, June 1945, Civil Aviation – Summary of Developments 1941/45. See also CAB 87/85, AC(41)1, Interim Report of the Inter-Departmental Committee on Civil Aviation, chaired by Sir Francis Shelmerdine, 11 December 1941.

3. *British Air Transport*, Cmd 6605 (1945).

4. CAB 134/57–9, CAC(45–50) series.

5. Cf. CAB 134/59, CAC(50)3, 19 January 1950, The Aircraft Position of the Airways Corporations with Particular Reference to the Brabazon and a Replacement for the D.H.89: memorandum by the Minister of Civil Aviation.

6. CAB 134/58, CAC(47)5, 28 March 1947, Aircraft for Commonwealth and Empire Services: memorandum by the Minister of Civil Aviation, appendix IV.

7. Cf. CAB 134/59, CAC(50)1, paras 5 and 6.

8. CAB 134/59, CAC(50)1, 17 January 1950, Progress of Civil Aviation Under the Present Administration.

9. CAB 134/57, CAC(45)3, 3 September 1945, Civil Aviation Policy: memorandum by the Minister of Civil Aviation.

10. In January 1943 Air Vice-Marshal R. S. Sorley reported after a visit to the

USA that Britain was behind in all aspects of aircraft design, R and D and production: 'soon we shall be out of date . . .'. CAB 70/6, DC(S)(43)2, Defence Committee (Supply). In a lecture on 1 December 1944 to future MAP members of the Control Commission in Germany, as Special Technical Adviser to the Ministry of Aircraft Production, Fedden commented that Britain was 'so seriously short of first-rate technical people and engineers' that after the war she should learn from the German training system. ROBN 4/1/2 EIPS Papers 1944–5.

11. The Lockheed Constellation. See CAB 70/6, DC(43)2, Defence Committee (Supply), 2 January 1943: note by Secretary of State for Air on report by Air Vice-Marshal R. S. Sorley on his visit to American factories.

12. AVIA 10/106, Sir Roy Fedden's visit to USA: terms of reference: report – programme of meetings. Preliminary report circulated on 22 April 1943.

13. Ibid.

14. CAB 87/9, R(44)135, 24 July 1944.

15. CAB 134/57, CAC(45)3, 3 September 1945.

16. CAB 134/687, SI(M)(46)1st, 24 January 1946.

17. CAB 134/58, CAC(47)1, citing annex to CP(46)344.

18. CAB 134/58, CAC(47)5, 28 March 1947, Aircraft for Commonwealth and Empire Services: memorandum submitted to the Minister of Civil Aviation by the Chairman of the Interdepartmental Civil Aircraft Requirements Committee.

19. Ibid., appendix I.

20. Ibid.; see also CAB 234/58, CAC(47)2, 21 March 1947, Purchase of Foreign Aircraft for the Government Corporations: memorandum by the Minister of Civil Aviation; CAC(47)6, 28 March 1947, Tudor Aircraft: memorandum by Minister of Civil Aviation.

21. Ibid.

22. CAB 134/58, CAC(47)5, appendix I.

23. CAB 134/58, CAC(47)2, 21 March 1947, Purchase of Foreign Aircraft for the Government Corporations.

24. Ibid., appendix III.

25. CAB 134/58, CAC(47)1, 6 March 1947, Purchase of Foreign Aircraft for the Government Corporations: memorandum by the Minister of Supply.

26. Ibid.

27. CAB 134/58, CAC(47)9, Project X.

28. Ibid.

29. CAB 134/58, CAC(47)1st, 21 April 1947.

30. Ibid.

31. Ibid.

32. CP(46)344, 11 September 1946.

33. CAB 134/689, SI(M)(48)3, 8 January 1948, The Ordering of Aircraft for the Airways Corporations: memorandum by the Minister of Supply.

34. Ibid.

35. Ibid.

36. Ibid.

37. CAB 134/689, SI(M)(48)4.

38. CAB 134/689, SI(M)(48)2nd, 16 January 1948.

39. Ibid.

40. CAB 134/58, CAC(48)1st, 8 April 1948, statement by the Minister of Civil Aviation.

41. CAB 134/58, CAC(48)3, 11 March 1948, The British Civil Aircraft Position: memorandum by the Minister of Civil Aviation.

42. Ibid.

43. Ibid.

44. Ibid.

45. Ibid., annex B.

46. Ibid., annex B.

47. CAB 134/58, CAC(48)4, 23 March 1948: British Civil Aircraft for the Atlantic and Empire Routes.

48. CAB 134/58, CAC(48)1st.

49. Ibid.

50. Ibid.

51. CAB 134/58, CAC(48)11, 4 June 1948, The 'Fly British' Aircraft Policy (The Situation on Empire and South American Routes).

52. CAB 134/58, CAC(48)13, 4 June 1948. The Tudor II: memorandum by the Minister of Supply. See also the appendix: Statement by the Committee of Enquiry (chaired by Sir Christopher Courtney) into the Tudor Aircraft, which also noted that to keep it flying 'would obviate the damage to the prestige of the British aircraft industry' from cancellation.

53. Issue of 14 June 1948.

54. CAB 134/58, CAC(48)3rd, 17 June 1948.

55. Ibid.

56. Ibid.

57. CAB 134/58, CAC(48)16, 26 June 1948, The Future of the Tudors.

58. Ibid.

59. CAB 134/58, CAC(48)4th, 30 June 1948.

60. CAB 134/59, CAC(49)3, 5 April 1949, Official Working Party on the Civil Aircraft Programme.

61. CAB 134/59, CAC(49)1st, 7 April 1949.

62. CAB 134/59, CAC(50)3, 19 January 1950, The Aircraft Position of the Airways Corporations with Particular Reference to the Brabazon and a Replacement for the D.H.89.

63. CAB 134/59, CAC(50)1st, 24 January 1950.

64. CAB 134/59, CAC(50)4, 13 July 1950, The Brabazon Aircraft.

65. Ibid.

66. CAB 134/59, CAC(50)6, 27 November 1950, The Future of the Brabazon and S.R.45: joint memorandum by the Minister of Supply and the Minister of Civil Aviation.

67. Ibid.

68. Ibid.

69. Ibid.

70. CAB 134/59, CAC(50)2nd, 5 December 1950.

71. CAB 134/58, CAC(50)4, 17 January 1950.

72. CAB 131/9, DO(50)47, 28 June 1950.

73. Ibid. As it happened, the annual value of the industry's civilian work, at £11 million, was virtually the same as the annual losses incurred by the nationalised airlines.

Chapter Thirteen:
A DISASTROUS CHOICE OF PRIORITIES

1. CAB 134/440, IPC(48)12, November 1948, Estimated Gross Fixed Investment, 1948 and 1949.

2. *Economic Survey for 1947*, Cmd 7046 (1947), para. 68.

3. CAB 134/215, EPC(47)33, 23 December 1947, Report on Marshall Aid: note by the Chairman of the London Committee, para. 20(g).

4. CAB 134/217, EPC(48)1, 3 January 1948, memorandum by the Chancellor of the Exchequer covering the draft *Economic Survey for 1948*: draft Survey, para. 58(a). This paragraph did not appear in the White Paper version (Cmd 7344).

5. CAB 134/636, PC(48)15th, 23 July 1948, in discussion on the Investment Programmes Committee report on capital investment in 1949, and the Chancellor of the Exchequer's memorandum commenting on it (PC(48)98).

6. German figure from Statistisches Bundesamt, *Volkswirtschaftliche Gesamt-rechnungen*, Fachserie 18, Reihe 5.7 (Stuttgart und Mainz, W. Kohlhammer, 1985), tables 7.1. and 7.2. British figure from C. H. Feinstein, *Statistical Tables*, table 5(ii). Professor Feinstein writes to the author that on the basis of comparing pre-war with postwar at constant prices, 'there was a *decline* of approximately one percentage point in the share of GFCF [gross fixed capital formation] between 1938 and 1948. If the calculation for both years is done at 1938 prices the share falls from 11.4% to 10.2%; if it is done at 1948 prices it falls from 14.5% to 13.5%. However, the share rose after 1948 and the average for 1948–57 is 15.0% at constant 1958 prices; this can be roughly adjusted to 15.2% at 1948 prices. This average of 15.2% for 1948–57 at 1948 prices thus shows a small *increase* as compared with the 1938 share, also at 1948 prices, of 14.5%. . . .'

It appears that Professor J. C. R. Dow in table 2.1, p. 15 of *The Management of the British Economy 1945–60* includes additions to stock in his figure for gross domestic investment in 1948, an item *not* included in the 1938 figure he uses as a comparison. Additions to stock accounts for 1.7 per cent of his 1948 figure of 15 per cent which apparently compares so flatteringly with the 1938 figure of 12 per cent.

Professor Sidney Pollard on p. 32 of *The Wasting of the British Economy: British Economic Policy 1945 to the Present* (London, Croom Helm, 1982), gives the same misleading figures as Dow of 15 per cent of GNP in 1948 devoted to gross domestic investment as against 12 per cent in 1938, but gives no sources.

Professor Feinstein has written to the present author that he would not himself place the emphasis on the comparison with the single year 1948. Nevertheless, I have thought it right to let the comparison between 1938 and 1948 stand, because Dow and Pollard use these years incorrectly to suggest that postwar Britain was creditably investing more than pre-war Britain.

7. German figure of 19.04 per cent (1950) from Statistisches Bundesamt, *Volkswirtschaftliche Gesamtrechnungen*, Fachserie 18, Reihe 5.7, tables I (p. 42) and 10.1. British figure (1950) from Feinstein, *Statistical Tables*, tables 3, 40 and 41.

Chapter Fourteen:
'LUDICROUSLY INADEQUATE' –
INVESTMENT IN INFRASTRUCTURE

1. The exception being, of course, the Roman roads, the surviving traces of which stand as marvels of directness and comprehensive strategic planning amid the Anglo-Saxon wendings.

2. Barnett, *The Audit of War*, p. 272 and n. 34.

3. Ibid., p. 273.

4. CAB 134/427, IPC(47)10th, item 2, 2 September 1947.

5. Ibid.

6. See reference in CAB 134/438, IPC(48)26th, item 1, 20 May 1948.

7. Ibid.

8. See reference in CAB 134/438, IPC(48)26th, item 1, 20 May 1948.

9. CAB 134/437, IPC(47)9, 8 October 1947, Investment Programmes Committee: report, appendix 10, para. 2.

10. IPC(WP)(48)64, cited in CAB 134/438, IPC(48)26th, item 1, 20 May 1948.

11. CAB 134/438, IPC(48)26th, item 1.

12. Ibid.

13. CAB 134/439, IPC(48)8, 16 July 1948: Report on Capital Investment in 1949, para. 141.

14. CAB 134/636, PC(48)16th, item 5, 23 July 1949.

15. CAB 134/438, IPC(48)58th, 5 August 1948.

16. Ibid.

17. CAB 134/438, IPC(48)60th, item 2, 11 August 1948. CAB 134/439, IPC(48)9, 1 September 1948, para. 12.

18. CAB 134/438, IPC(48)71st, 22 December 1948.

19. Ibid.

20. CAB 134/440, IPC(48)12, Estimated Gross Fixed Investment, 1948 and 1949 (as decided by the Production Committee in PC(48)15th, item 1, and 16th, item 5, and 18th, item 1).

21. CAB 134/440, IPC(49)3, 12 May 1949, Report on Capital Investment in 1950–1952, table 47.

22. Ibid., paras 150 and 152.

23. CAB 134/440, IPC(49)62nd, item 2, 13 September 1949; ibid., IPC(49)68th, item E, 28 October 1949. As with all contemporary statistics, whether forecasts or estimates of current and past expenditure, the figures cannot be taken as literally accurate, being susceptible to considerable

adjustment. It is the trend of the arguments and decisions which is relevant.

24. CAB 134/440, IPC(49)62nd, item 2, 13 September 1949.

25. See CAB 134/440, IPC(49)5, 3 November 1949, Capital Investment in 1950: draft report by the Investment Programmes Committee.

26. CAB 134/220, EPC(49)46th, item 1, 22 November 1949.

27. Ibid.

28. CAB 134/441, IPC(50)7th, item 1, 20 January 1950.

29. Ibid.

30. Cf. CAB 134/440, IPC(49)68th, item E. See also CAB 134/220, EPC(49)46th.

31. CAB 134/441, IPC(50)7th, item 1.

32. CAB 134/646, PC(50)53, 23 May 1950, Investment in 1951 and 1952: memorandum by the Minister of State for Economic Affairs (Hugh Gaitskell); and CAB 134/644, PC(50)8th, item 1, 25 May 1950. See also CAB 134/441, IPC(50)2, Capital Investment in 1951 and 1952, table 30 and para. 135.

33. CAB 134/644, PC(50)8th, item 1.

34. The Southern Railway's Portsmouth line, part of its electrified suburban or semi-suburban network, was 70 miles long.

35. CAB 134/438, IPC(47)10th, item 4, 2 September 1947. By contrast, the author as a national serviceman on his way to Egypt in May 1946 was electrically hauled from near Paris to beyond Toulouse, a distance of some 500 miles. French plans in 1948 for investing Marshall Aid included electrifying the 317-mile-long main line between Paris and Lyons.

36. Ibid.

37. CAB 134/437, IPC(47)28th, item 3, 3 December 1947.

38. CAB 134/437, IPC(47)29th, item 1.

39. CAB 134/437, IPC(47)9, appendix 10, paras 1–5.

40. CAB 134/438, IPC(47)10th, item 4. As it was, the start-to-stop speed of steam-hauled trains on average barely exceeded 40 m.p.h, as the author well remembers.

41. Ibid.

42. CAB 134/439, IPC(48)8, para. 121.

43. CAB 134/439, IPC(48)9, 1 September 1948, Capital Investment in 1949: supplementary report, annex, para. 12.

44. CAB 134/438, IPC(48)33rd, item 2, 31 May 1948.

45. Ibid.

46. CAB 134/439, IPC(48)8, para. 117.

47. In the author's experience in the mid-1950s Euston was the gloomiest,

most haphazard and generally slummiest terminus in London – and that was in comparison with other London termini, none of which could compare in upkeep, order and cleanliness with the Gare St Lazare, let alone with Zurich or Lucerne on the Swiss Federal.

48. IPC(WP)(48)136, discussed in CAB 134/438, IPC(48)46th, item 1, 30 June 1948.

49. CAB 134/439, IPC(48)8, 16 July 1948, paras 121 and 130.

50. CAB 134/636, PC(48)16th, item 5, 23 July 1948.

51. CAB 134/438, IPC(48)58th, 5 August 1948.

52. CAB 134/438, IPC(48)60th, 11 August 1948.

53. CAB 134/440, IPC(49)23rd(revise), 14 February 1949.

54. Ibid.

55. BTC's proposals were for £97 million in 1950, £111 million in 1951 and £119 million in 1952; the IPC's figures were some £92 million in 1950 and some £96 million in 1952. CAB 134/440, IPC(49)3, table 43 and para. 144.

56. Ibid.

57. CAB 134/440, IPC(49)68th, 28 October 1949.

58. Ibid. The author can vouch for this. The 'uncut moquette' upholstery on British trains at this time was stiff and shiny with the hair-oil of twenty years, whereas a second-class coach in which the author travelled from Rouen to Dieppe in the summer of 1949 was immaculate even to freshly laundered antimacassars.

59. CAB 134/440, IPC(49)68th. See also IPC(49)5, 3 November 1949, Capital Investment in 1950: draft report by the Investment Programmes Committee.

60. CAB 134/220, EPC(49)46th, item 1, 22 November 1949.

61. CAB 134/441, IPC(50)2, 25 April 1950, paras 121 and 129.

62. CAB 134/441, IPC(50)2, para. 129; CAB 134/440, IPC(49)3, table 43.

63. At best £89.1 million in 1952 for British Railways and the London Transport railways, according to CAB 134/646, PC(50)53, 23 May 1950 and CAB 134/644, PC(50)8th, 25 May 1950; £92 million at end-1950 as at February 1950, according to CAB 134/441, IPC(50)20th, 13 February 1950.

64. CAB 134/441, IPC(50)20th, 13 February 1950.

65. Ibid.

66. Ibid.

67. CAB 134/441, IPC(50)20th.

68. Ibid.

69. CAB 134/437, IPC(47)13th, item 1, 4 September 1947.

70. CAB 134/437, IPC(47)9, appendix 9, para. 1, and appendix 14, para. 20.

71. CAB 134/439, IPC(48)8, paras 187–91.

72. Ibid., para. 193.

73. Ibid.

74. Ibid., para. 188.

75. CAB 134/440, IPC(49)65th, 26 October 1949. See also IPC(49)5, 3 November 1949, Capital Investment in 1950: draft report by the Investment Programmes Committee, para. 15.

76. CAB 134/440, IPC(49)5, 3 November 1949.

77. CAB 134/441, IPC(50)5th, item 1, 16 January 1950, discussing IPC(WP)(50)6.

78. Ibid.

79. Ibid.

80. CAB 134/441, IPC(50)38th, item k, 19 April 1950.

81. CAB 134/644, PC(50)8th.

82. Cf. CAB 134/438, IPC(48)33rd, item 1, 31 May 1948: 'While the lack of proper facilities was the chief cause of the present slow turn-round of shipping there was no doubt that some contribution to improvement could be obtained from changes in labour organisation and increased output. . . .' There were major dock strikes in 1947, 1948 and 1949, as well as continuing grotesque restrictions on productive efficiency. See below, Chapter 18.

83. See CAB 132/34, CIP(HF)(50)2, 1 June 1950, Research in the Liverpool Docks, and CIP(HF)(50)11, 31 May 1950, The London Docks: A Framework for Study, for informed insights into these mentalities and their mutually destructive interaction.

84. CAB 134/439, IPC(48)8.

85. CAB 134/437, IPC(47)9, appendix 10, para. 7.

86. CAB 134/439, IPC(48)8, table 30.

87. Ibid.

88. Ibid., para. 160.

89. CAB 134/440, IPC(48)12, citing PC(48)15th, item 1; 16th, item 5; and 18th, item 1.

90. CAB 134/438, IPC(48)68th, item 1, 19 November 1948.

91. CAB 134/440, IPC(49)3, 12 May 1949.

92. Ibid., para. 164.

93. Ibid., table 50.

94. Ibid., para. 169.

95. CAB 134/440, IPC(49)62nd, item 2, 13 September 1949.

96. CAB 134/440, IPC(49)63rd, 20 September 1950.

97. Ibid. Cf. also CAB 134/441, IPC(50)2nd, item 1, 10 January 1950.

98. CAB 134/441, IPC(50)2, 25 April 1950, table 32.

99. CAB 134/661, PC(50)53, 23 May 1950.

100. CAB 132/34, CIP(HF)(50)11, 31 May 1950; Committee on Industrial Productivity: Panel of Human Factors: The London Docks: A Framework for Study, para. 65.3.

101. Issue of 6 April 1950.

102. As reported in the *Daily Mirror* on 26 May 1950. For a detailed examination, with many examples, of the problem of the resistance of the flat-capped to mechanisation of the ports, see CAB 132/34, CIP(HF)(50)11, 31 May 1950, Committee on Industrial Productivity: Panel on Human Factors: The London Docks: A Framework for Study; and CIP(HF)(50)12, 1 June 1950, Research in the Liverpool Docks.

Chapter Fifteen:
'THE SPOTLIGHT HAS ALWAYS BEEN ON COAL'

1. CAB 134/437, IPC(47)9, 8 October 1947, pp. 34–5.

2. Ibid.

3. Ibid.

4. CAB 134/438 (p. 105 in file), Electricity Programme: note of a meeting held on 20 April 1948.

5. Ibid.

6. CAB 134/639, PC(48)146, citing PC(48)13th, item 3.

7. Ibid., PC(48)146, 30 November 1948, Electricity Generating Station Programme: memorandum by the Minister of Fuel and Power.

8. See Barnett, *Audit of War*, esp. ch. 11.

9. Ibid.

10. Ibid.

11. CAB/636, PC(48)24th, item 1, 2 December 1948.

12. Ibid.

13. CAB 134/439, IPC(48)8, 16 July 1948, para. 93.

14. Ibid., para. 91.

15. Ibid., table 14.

16. Ibid., para. 96.

17. Cf. CAB 134/440, IPC(49)3, para. 106.

18. CAB 134/440, IPC(49)10th, item 1, 19 January 1949, discussing the

Revised BEA programme for 1948/52 (IPC(WP)(48)216).

19. Ibid.

20. CAB 134/440, IPC(49)69th, item 1, 28 October 1949.

21. CAB 134/440, IPC(49)3, 12 May 1949.

22. Ibid., para. 107.

23. Ibid., table 29 and para. 112.

24. CAB 134/440, IPC(49)5, 3 November 1949, appendix 2.

25. CAB 134/441, IPC(50)2, 25 April 1950, para. 99.

26. Ibid.

27. Ibid.

28. Ibid., para. 104.

29. Ibid., para. 101.

30. CAB 134/646, PC(50)3, annex.

31. A distinguished scientist, Dr H. Roxbee-Cox, had reported to the Committee on Industrial Productivity on 12 September 1949: 'A high degree of electrification is a characteristic of efficient production, not a cause. If the Grid were to supply twice as much electricity, productivity would not, in consequence, rise. The "Causal" factors are modern management and modern equipment.' See CAB 132/29, CIP(49)27.

32. CAB 134/644, PC(50)8th, item 1, 25 May 1950.

33. CAB 134/441, IPC(50)2, 25 April 1950, para. 75.

34. The present author, as a graduate trainee with the North Thames Gas Board in 1952, had the pleasure of visiting Beckton and its Victorian splendours, as well as seeing some of the small gasworks taken over by the Board on nationalisation.

35. CAB 134/437, IPC(47)9, 8 October 1947, appendix 14, para. 16.

36. CAB 134/439, IPC(48)8, 16 July 1948.

37. CAB 134/440, IPC(49)3, 12 May 1949, para. 119.

38. Ibid., table 35 and para. 120.

39. CAB 134/440, IPC(49)5, appendices I and II. See also IPC(49)69th, item 5, 28 October 1949.

40. CAB 134/646, PC(50)53, 23 May 1950, annex.

41. The present author's first job as a graduate trainee with the North Thames Gas Board in 1952 was to write for the Chairman a précis of the committee's report.

42. CAB 134/438, IPC(48)39th, item 3, 10 June 1948.

43. Ibid.

44. Ibid.

45. See Barnett, *Audit of War*, ch. 4, for an account of the coal industry's poor

wartime record, and a summary of the industry's history back to the first industrial revolution.

46. Cmd 6610.

47. H. Wilson, *New Deal for Coal* (London, Contact Books, 1945), p. 11, quoting from Ministry of Fuel and Power, *Statistical Digest for 1948*, Cmd 6538 (1941).

48. CAB 134/440, IPC(49)3, 12 May 1949, para. 86.

49. Wilson, *New Deal for Coal*, p. 76.

50. CAB 134/438, IPC(48)34th, item 2, 1 June 1948.

51. Ibid.

52. Ibid.

53. CAB 134/218, EPC(48)65, 8 July 1948, Coal for the Railways: memorandum by the Minister of Transport.

54. Ibid.

55. CAB 134/218, EPC(48)63, 8 July 1948, Coal and Coke Exports: 1948–49. Export Availability of Solid Fuel in the Fiscal Year July 1948–June 1949: report by the Chairman of the European Economic Co-operation Committee.

56. Ibid.

57. Ibid.

58. CAB 134/218, EPC(48)64, 8 July 1948, Adjustments in Inland Coal Prices.

59. CAB 134/216, EPC(48)28th, item 1, 9 July 1948.

60. Ibid.

61. Ibid.

62. Ibid.

63. CAB 134/439, IPC(48)8, 16 July 1948, para. 67.

64. Ibid., para. 69.

65. CAB 133/58, ER(Mission)(48)10, 13 October 1948, Weekly Record of Departmental Discussions with Members of the E.C.A. Mission in the United Kingdom, Reference ER(L)(48)131.

66. Ibid.

67. See Barnett, *Audit of War*, ch. 4.

68. Morgan, *Labour in Power*, p. 106.

69. CAB 134/639, PC(48)133, 2 November 1948, memorandum by the Minister of Fuel and Power covering report by the Joint Committee on Production appointed by the National Coal Board and the National Union of Mineworkers.

70. Ibid.

71. CAB 134/639, PC(48)138, 15 November 1948.

72. CAB 134/645, PC(50)2, 11 March 1950, Progress Report on the Long-term Programme of the U.K., p. 4.

73. CAB 134/440, IPC(48)12, citing PC(48)15th, item 1; 16th, item 5; 18th, item 1.

74. CAB 134/440, IPC(49)3, 12 May 1949, para. 85.

75. Ibid., tables 20 and 21.

76. Ibid., para. 87.

77. Ibid., para. 91.

78. CAB 134/440, IPC(49)69th, item 3, 28 October 1949; CAB 134/220, EPC(49)46th, 2 November 1949, IPC(49)5, 3 November 1949, appendix 2.

79. CAB 134/441, IPC(50)13th, item 2, 2 February 1950.

80. Ibid.

81. CAB 134/293, FG(WP)(50)38, 16 June 1950, report by official Working Party on Proposed Franco-German Coal and Steel Authority, table VII.

82. Ibid.

83. Ibid.

84. CAB 134/441, IPC(50)2, 25 April 1950.

85. CAB 134/441, IPC(50)2, table 58.

86. Ibid.

87. CAB 134/645, PC(50)19, 11 March 1950, p. 14.

88. CAB 134/646, PC(50)3, 23 May 1950.

89. CAB 134/644, PC(50)8th, 25 May 1950.

90. Cf. CAB 132/29, CIP(49)13, 21 April 1949, Coal Saving: note by Dr H. Roxbee-Cox.

91. M. Gowing, *Independence and Deterrence: Britain and Atomic Energy, 1945–1952,* vol. I: *Policy Making* (London, Macmillan, 1982).

92. CAB 134/221, EPC(49)25, 21 March 1949, Coal/Oil Conversion. See also CAB 134/218, EPC(48)7, 13 July 1948, Review of Oil Situation: memorandum by the Minister of Fuel and Power.

93. Ibid.

94. Ibid.

95. Ibid.

96. CAB 132/438, IPC(47)5th, 27 August 1947.

97. Ibid.

98. See Barnett, *Audit of War,* ch. 11.

99. IPC(47)9, 8 October 1947, appendix 5.

100. See Barnett, *Audit of War,* ch. 11, for a comparison of British and German provisions for further education before the war.

101. CAB 132/438, IPC(47)5th.

102. Ibid.

103. CAB 132/438, IPC(48)23rd, item 1, 13 May 1948. See also IPC(WP)(48)79.

104. Ibid.

105. Ibid.

106. Ibid., para. 306.

107. Ibid., Table 54.

108. Ibid.

109. CAB 134/440, IPC(49)3, 12 May 1949.

110. CAB 134/642, PC(49)61, 27 May 1949, Educational Building Programme 1950–1952: memorandum by the Minister of Education.

111. CAB 134/441, IPC(50)3rd, item 1.

112. Ibid.

113. CAB 134/441, IPC(50)2, 24 April 1950.

114. CAB 134/644, PC(50)8th, 25 May 1950.

115. The topic of British education and training at all levels in the first postwar decade will be dealt with in detail in a future volume, only the course of capital investment in 1947–50 being summarised here.

Chapter Sixteen:
'A POLICY OF MAKE-DO AND MEND':
MANUFACTURING

1. CAB 134/437, IPC(47)9, 8 October 1947, para. 22.

2. CAB 134/503, MEP(46)15 and 16.

3. CAB 134/437, IPC(47)2, 15 August 1947.

4. CAB 134/437, IPC(47)9. In its final version, after chipping and polishing by ministers, published as Cmd 7268.

5. Ibid., para. 8.

6. Ibid., para. 25.

7. Ibid., para. 12.

8. Ibid., para. 15.

9. Ibid., para. 27.

10. Ibid., para. 48.

11. CAB 134/637, PC(48)44, 6 April 1948. The Building Programme: report by Headquarters Building Committee.

12. CAB 134/637, PC(48)37, 18 March 1948, Steel for Industrial Building: memorandum by the President of the Board of Trade (Harold Wilson).

13. Ibid.

14. Ibid.

15. CAB 134/439, IPC(48)8, 16 July 1948, para. 4, table I.

16. Ibid., para. 8.

17. Ibid., para. 245.

18. Ibid., para. 25.

19. CAB 87/3, RP(43)25. See note 11, p. 427 above.

20. CAB 134/440, IPC(48)9, 10 and 12, November 1948, noting decisions of Production Committee in PC(48)15th, item 1; 16th, item 5; and 18th, item 1.

21. Ibid., para. 29. The paragraph is actually sub-headed: 'Make-do and mend'.

22. Ibid., para. 245.

23. CAB 134/235, ER(L)(48)173, 17 November 1948, paras 57 and 58.

24. CAB 134/440, IPC(49)3, 12 May 1949, para. 231.

25. Ibid., para. 234 and table 68.2.

26. Ibid., table 72.

27. Board of Trade: textiles, hosiery, rayon and synthetic fibres, pottery and glassware, chemicals, dyestuffs, plastics, paper, paint, fertilisers, leather, timber and furniture, tyres and rubber manufactures, printing, films and 'others'. Ministry of Supply: aircraft, motor-vehicles, tractors, ball-bearings, explosives, radio, scientific instruments, power-station equipment, mining machinery, locomotives, rolling stock, machine-tools, aluminium, other non-ferrous metals, medical and ophthalmic equipment, refractories and general engineering. Ministry of Food: milk and milk products, oils and fats, fish, meat and livestock, grain drying and storage, cereal products (including flour mills), sugar refining, chocolate and sugar confectionery, coffee, canning, cold stores and 'miscellaneous'.

28. CAB 134/440, IPC(49)3, 12 May 1949, table 68.

29. Ibid., para. 237.

30. Ibid., para. 235.

31. Ibid., para. 237.

32. CAB 87/3, RP(43)25, 15 June 1943.

33. Ibid., table 84.

34. Ibid., tables 84 and 85.

35. Cf. CAB 134/242, ER(L)(49)163, 27 May 1949, General Memorandum for the OEEC on United Kingdom Revised 1949–50 Programme, p. 44.

36. Ibid., para. 62.

37. CAB 134/440, IPC(49)5, 3 November 1949, draft report on capital investment in 1950, in accordance with the Cabinet's instruction in

CM(49)61st, and the Prime Minister's memorandum, CP(49)205.

38. Ibid., para. 12.

39. Ibid., section 21.

40. CAB 134/440, IPC(IB)(49)2, 12 December 1949, Industrial Building Sub-Committee: draft report on industrial building, para. 10. CAB 134/441, IPC(IB)(50)1, 18 January 1950, Industrial Building at the End of 1950; IPC(50)2nd, item 2, 10 January 1950.

41. On the basis of the 'higher programme' of two offered to ministers, and chosen by them. See CAB 134/441, IPC(50)2, 25 April 1950, table 8.

42. Ibid., para. 190.

43. Ibid., para. 211.

44. CAB 134/644, PC(50)12th, 12 May 1950, citing CM(50)21st, minute 2.

45. CAB 134/646, PC(50)53, 23 May 1950, para. 6(c).

46. CAB 134/644, PC(50)8th, item 1, 25 May 1950.

47. CAB 132/29, CIP(49)20, 15 June 1949, attaching report by a visiting team to the US from the British Cotton Industry Research Association, dated 9 May 1949.

48. CAB 134/648, PC(50)121.

49. CAB 134/638, PC(48)69, 29 May 1948, Implications for the Shipbuilding Industry of Contemplated Steel Allocations for 1948–50.

50. CAB 134/440, IPC(49)9th, item 1, 18 January 1949.

51. CAB 134/642, PC(49)90, 27 July 1949, The Future of the Shipbuilding and Shiprepairing Industries.

52. Ibid., para. 19.

53. Ibid.

54. Ibid., para. 20.

55. CAB 134/640, PC(49)19th, item 1, 23 September 1949.

56. CAB 134/640, PC(49)26th, item 2, 2 December 1949.

57. CAB 134/646, PC(50)2, 6 April 1950, letter to the Chancellor of the Exchequer (Cripps).

58. CAB 134/643, PC(49)125, 1 November 1949, memorandum on ship repairs abroad, covering a report by the Overseas Negotiations Committee.

59. CAB 134/646, PC(50)52, 22 May 1950, para. 12.

60. Ibid., table II.

61. Ibid., para. 20.

62. Ibid., para 19.

63. Ibid., para. 20.

64. Ibid., para. 9.

65. Ibid., para. 40.

66. See ADM 1/11892, Labour in Naval and Mercantile Shipyards (Barlow Report), 1942. The question of strikes, demarcation disputes and over-manning in the shipyards as in other industries will be explored in full in a later volume.

67. CAB 134/644, PC(50)11th, item 2, 30 June 1950.

68. CAB 134/647, PC(50)79, 20 July 1950.

69. CAB 132/47, CIP(TR)(48)16, 23 July 1948, report on British machine-tools by L. A. Ferney, B.Sc., M.I.Mech.E.

70. Ibid., para. 4a.

71. See Barnett, *Audit of War*, pp. 133–4, 159–61.

72. CAB 132/47, CIP(TR)(48)16, para. 59.

73. Ibid., para. 66.

74. Ibid., para. 75.

75. Ibid., para 78.

76. Ibid., para. 75.

77. *Census of Production, 1948* (London, HMSO, 1953), vol. 4, Trade C, Machine Tools, table 19.

78. *Census of Production, 1951* (London, HMSO, 1955), vol. 4, Trade C, Machine Tools, table 25.

79. *Census of Production, 1948*, vol. 4, Trade C, table 15; *Census of Production 1951*, Vol. 4, Trade C, table 13. These census returns for machine-tools include a wider range of kit than the machine-tool industry in the sense used by Ferney. Ferney's figures for both operatives and value of output are alike five-eighths of those in the censuses. I have therefore adjusted the census figures downwards to accord with his usage.

80. *Census of Production 1948*, vol. 4, Trade C, table 21; *Census of Production, 1951*, vol. 4, Trade C, table 1.

81. *Statistical Abstract of the United States, 1950* (Washington, DC, US Department of Commerce, 1950), table 916: added value of metal-working machinery (excluding jigs, cutting tools and fixtures), $650,807,000. Divided by 2.80 (sterling–dollar exchange rate after September 1949) = £232,431,000. Divided by 4 (UK population 45 million; US population 200 million) = £58,107,000.

82. Barnett, *Audit of War*, p. 159, and CAB 87/3 IEP(43)49, 11 September 1943, Report on Disposal of Surplus Goods and Factories.

83. CAB 132/47, CIP(TR)(48)5, 23 February 1948, Committee on Industrial Productivity: note by the Chairman of the Panel on Technology and Operational Research on 'Future Programmes', para. 5.

84. Figures for 1951: *Historical Record of the Census of Production, 1907 to 1970*

(London, Government Statistical Service, n.d.), table 2, Standard Industrial Classification Orders in percentage terms of all manufacturing industries 1907 to 1970.

85. Figures for 1950: *Census of Production, 1951*, vol. 6, Trades A, B, C, D and I, in each case table 1.

86. Gross output of 9.3 per cent plus 7.4 per cent, as against textiles' 12.3 per cent. *Historical Record of the Census of Production, 1907 to 1970*, table 2.

87. *Statistical Abstract of the United States, 1950*, table 916: fabricated metal products, $4,921.5 million; machinery except electrical, $7,812.5 million. Total, $12,734 million. Textiles (including rayon): $5,340.9 million.

88. Ibid.

89. Ibid.

90. *Census of Production, 1948*, vol. 3, tables 6 and 8.

91. CAB 134/639, PC(48)150, 13 December 1948, Survey of Agricultural Expansion Programme.

92. £46.5 million as against £256 million. *Census of Production, 1948*, vol. 4, Trade I, tables 6 and 1.

93. £67.97 million as against £369.5 million. *Census of Production, 1951*, vol. 4, Trade I, tables 6 and 1.

94. *Statistical Abstract of the United States, 1950*, figures for 1947, table 916: Total for office machines of all kinds, $972,900,000; for refrigerating machinery, $597,486,000; for domestic laundry equipment, $161,791,000. Divide by 2.80 and again by 4.

95. CAB 132/50, CIP(WP)(49)4th, item 1, 12 February 1949.

96. American 1947 figures in *Statistical Abstract of the United States, 1950*, table 916: computing and related machines, $231,200,000; typewriters, $121,385,000. British figures from *Census of Production, 1948*, vol. 4, Trade I, table 8; *Census of Production, 1951*, vol. 3, Trade I, table 8.

97. Letter of 10 March 1987 from Professor B. W. (later Sir Brian) Oakley to the author.

98. Ibid.

99. CAB 132/44, CIP(TI)(48)13, 7 June 1948, report by Dr J. E. Holmstrom on his recent visit to the United States and Canada. He did not see a Univac computer, but only read descriptions of it.

100. *Historical Record of the Census of Production, 1907 to 1970*, table 2.

101. Ibid.

102. Ibid.

103. *Census of Production, 1948*, vol. 4, Trade K, table 1; Trade M, table 1.

104. Cf. CAB 134/440, IPC(49)3, para. 237.

105. *Statistical Abstract of the United States, 1950*, figure for 1947 in table 916: radios and related products, $231,207,000.

106. *Census of Production, 1948*, vol. 4, Trade M, table 8; *Census of Production, 1951*, vol. 4, Trade K, table 8.

107. *Census of Production, 1951*, vol. 4, Trade K, table 11; C. H. Feinstein, *Statistical Tables of National Income, Expenditure and Output of the United Kingdom, 1855–1965* (Cambridge, Cambridge University Press, 1972), table 15, T39.

108. The topic of R and D and the supply of scientific manpower and technical personnel will be fully dealt with in a later volume.

109. CAB 134/438, IPC(48)63rd, item 2, 3 September 1948, discussing IPC(WP)(48)159, the proposed 1949 programme of Research Establishments for Research Associations assisted by the Department of Scientific and Industrial Research.

110. Mr G. Bowen of the Board of Trade in ibid.

111. CAB 134/440, IPC(49)18th, item 1.

112. CAB 134/441, IPC(50)14th, item 2, 3 February 1950.

113. Ibid.

114. CAB 134/639, PC(48)119, 20 September 1948, Priority for Defence Research and Development Work: memorandum by the Minister of Defence (A. V. Alexander).

115. CAB 134/640, PC(49)1st, 14 January 1949.

116. CAB 131/8, DO(49)17th, item 4, discussing DO(49)28, 25 March 1949, Expansion of Capacity in Industry for Electronic Research and Development: memorandum by the Minister of Supply (George Strauss).

117. *Statistical Abstract of the United States, 1950*, table 916: 1947 figure for 'communication equipment', $1374 million.

118. According to CAB 134/376, IO(45)1, item 1, 10 July 1945, and IO(45)2, 20 May 1945, Report of Working Party on Future of the Scientific Instrument Industry.

119. CAB 13/376, SOI(44)7, 31 May 1944, Final Report by the Sub-Committee of the Industrial Capacity Committee on Scientific and Optical Instruments.

120. Ibid.

121. Ibid.

122. Ibid.

123. *Historical Record of the Census of Production, 1907 to 1970*, table 2.

124. In January 1949 the IPC agreed that 'it was not possible to apply the ordinary checks, such as those applied to other programmes, to the Atomic

Energy programme . . .'. CAB 134/440, IPC(49)13th, item 1, 24 January 1949. See M. Gowing assisted by L. Arnold, *Independence and Deterrence*, vol. 1, pages 168–70, 178, 217–19, 223–4, 230–1; vol. 2, appendix 16, p. 85.

125. CAB 134/642, PC(49)82, 1 July 1949, Sheet Steel and the Motor Industry: memorandum by the Minister of Supply.

126. P. J. S. Dunnett, *The Decline of the British Motor Industry*, pp. 35–41.

127. CAB 134/440, IPC(49)16th, item 1, 3 February 1949, discussing a note from the Ministry of Supply on the motor industry (IPC(WP)(49)14).

128. Ibid.

129. CAB 134/440, IPC(49)3, para. 372.

130. Ibid.

131. T 236/870, letter from S. J. Belton (? – signature illegible) of the United Kingdom Treasury Delegation to E. Rowe-Dutton, reporting conversation with a Mr Stradella, in charge of GM's external finances.

132. Ibid.

133. Cf. W. J. Reader, *Imperial Chemical Industries: A History*, vol. II: *The First Quarter-Century, 1925–1952* (London, Oxford University Press, 1975).

134. Cf. CAB 134/637, PC(48)37, 18 March 1948, Steel for Industrial Building: memorandum by the President of the Board of Trade.

135. CAB 87/10, R(45)36, 6 April 1945.

136. Ibid.

137. Ibid.

138. Ibid.

139. Ibid.

140. H. Duncan Hall, *North American Supply*, p. 94, n. 1.

141. It was only in the 1920s that the Iron and Steel Research Council was set up; only in 1944 that the British Iron and Steel Research Association followed.

142. J. C. Carr and W. Taplin, assisted by A. E. G. Wright, *History of the British Steel Industry* (Oxford, Basil Blackwell, and Cambridge, Mass., Harvard University Press, 1962), p. 31. See Barnett, *Audit of War*, ch. 5, for a succinct account of the decline of British iron and steel from the 1890s to 1939.

143. Barnett, *Audit of War*, p. 103.

144. CAB 87/10, R(45)17.

145. See N. Chester, *The Nationalisation of British Industry 1945–51* (London, HMSO, 1975), passim, but esp. pp. 15, 159–83, 308–15, 678–89.

146. See Morgan, *Labour in Power*, pp. 110–19.

147. CAB 134/687, SI(M)(46)9, 25 March 1946, Capital: Development and Future Organisation of the Iron and Steel Industry: memorandum by the

Economic Section of the Cabinet Office. The Iron and Steel Federation Report was published as Cmd 6811.

148. Howard G. Roepke, *Movements of the British Iron and Steel Industry – 1720 to 1951* (Urbana, University of Illinois Press, 1956), pp. 178–9.

149. CAB 134/687, SI(M)(46)9, para. 4(d).

150. Ibid., para. 13.

151. Cf. CAB 134/437, IPC(47)9, p. 37.

152. CAB 134/438, IPC(48)24th, item 1.

153. CAB 134/437, IPC(47)9, p. 37.

154. CAB 134/438, IPC(48)24th, item 1, 18 May 1948.

155. Ibid.

156. Ibid.

157. CAB 134/439, IPC(49)8, paras 229–30.

158. CAB 134/636, PC(48)18th, item 2, 6 September 1948, Longterm Demand for Steel, discussing PC(48)111, joint memorandum by the Chancellor of the Exchequer and the Minister of Supply covering a working party report on estimated future demand for steel.

159. CAB 134/440, IPC(49)22nd, 11 February 1949.

160. Ibid. In fact, fixed capital expenditure at current prices in 1948 amounted only to £30 million (B. S. Keeling and A. E. G. Wright, *The Development of the Modern British Steel Industry* (London, Longmans, 1964), p. 129, table 26.

161. Ibid.

162. Mr A. C. Boddis, in ibid.

163. CAB 134/440, IPC(49)3, para. 227.

164. Ibid., para. 228.

165. Carr and Taplin, *History of the British Steel Industry*, p. 597.

166. Ibid., citing CP(49)205.

167. IPC(WP)(50)36, cited and discussed in CAB 134/441, IPC(50)16th (revise), item 1, 7 February 1950.

168. CAB 134/437, IPC(47)9, p. 37.

169. CAB 134/441, IPC(50)16th.

170. Keeling and Wright, *Development of the Modern British Steel Industry*, p. 129, table 26.

171. Ibid. Old 1949 estimate: £48.8 million; new: £43.2 million. Old 1950 estimate: £45.6 million; new: £48.5 million. Old 1951 estimate: £43.2 million; new: £45.8 million. Old 1952 estimate: £37.9 million; new: £44.6 million.

172. Ibid.

173. Ibid. These comments were reproduced almost verbatim in the IPC report

on capital investment in 1951 and 1952 (CAB 134/441, IPC(50)2, 25 April 1950).

174. Ibid. Also repeated in IPC(50)2.

175. CAB 134/441, IPC(50)2.

176. CAB 134/646, PC(50)53, annex.

177. CAB 134/440, IPC(49)22nd.

178. K. Warren, *The American Steel Industry 1850–1970 – A Geographical Interpretation* (Oxford, Clarendon Press, 1973), p. 242.

179. *Economic Survey for 1950*, Cmd 7915 (1950), table 15.

180. CAB 134/217, EPC(48)1, 3 January 1948, *Economic Survey for 1948*, paras 121–41.

181. Keeling and Wright, *Development of the Modern British Steel Industry*, table 17, p. 92.

182. 1950 figure: Feinstein, *Statistical Tables*, tables 40 and 41.

Chapter Seventeen:
EXPORTS OR SOCIAL RESCUE?

1. Cf. A. Morley Dell, *The Countries of the Modern World* (London, George G. Harrap, 1935), used by the present author in 1945, chs VII–X.

2. See Barnett, *The Audit of War*, ch 10, for an account of the health, housing and personal capability of the British industrial proletariat in the 1930s and 1940s; and ch. 11 for an account of its education.

3. CAB 87/56, IEP(42)36, 26 August 1942, Nuffield College Social Reconstruction Survey on Methods of Influencing the Location of Industry.

4. CAB 87/63, EC(43)5, 18 October 1943; cf. also *Report of the First Commissioner for the Special Areas in England and Wales* (1936), quoted in CAB 87/63, EC(43)4.

5. As advocated in 1939 with regard to worn-out coalmining areas by the economist S. R. Dennison, *The Location of Industry and the Depressed Areas* (Oxford, Oxford University Press, 1939), pp. 199–200:

Unless it is desired to give an entirely new direction to the siting of industry, such as implied in the construction of large numbers of 'garden cities', it is manifestly an inappropriate policy to attempt to attract new industries to such places, for they are mostly somewhat isolated, have little economic life apart from that which depended upon their one industry, and are indeed not at all suitable for the location of expanding industries. Thus the appropriate policy here appears to be one of transference. . . .

6. CAB 87/7, R(44)66, 30 March 1944, Post-War Employment: Location of Industry.

7. As in the case of Toulouse.

8. There is a useful summary of the pre-war history of the 'Development Areas' and measures to help them, as also of the emergence of the postwar policy, in the 1948 White Paper on *Distribution of Industry Policy*, parts I and II. Draft version in CAB 134/130, DI(48)32, 6 August 1948.

9. *Report of the Royal Commission on the Distribution of the Industrial Population*, Cmd 6153 (1940), pp. 193–4.

10. See Barnett, *Audit of War*, pp. 247–56.

11. CAB 87/63, EC(43)5, 18 October 1943.

12. Ibid.

13. Ibid.

14. CAB 87/63, EC(43)13, 20 October 1943.

15. Ibid.

16. In a similar spirit to the postwar renaming of backward countries as 'developing countries'.

17. CAB 87/7, R(44)6, Report of the Steering Committee on Post-War Employment, 11 January 1944.

18. Ibid.

19. CAB 87/7, R(44)58, 22 March 1944.

20. Ibid.

21. Cited in CAB 134/130, DI(48)32, para. 19.

22. *General Report of the Select Committee on Estimates*, Session 1955/56, *The Development Areas* (London, HMSO, 1956), p. vii, cited in Gavin McCrone, *Regional Policy in Britain* (London, George Allen & Unwin, 1969), p. 112, table I.

23. CAB 134/130, DI(48)3rd, minute 6, 4 March 1948. First discussed in DO(48)2nd in February.

24. Ibid.

25. Ibid.

26. Ibid.

27. CAB 134/130, DI(48)25, 15 June 1948. General Electric Co. Valve Factory at Shaw: note by the Parliamentary Secretary of the Board of Trade.

28. Martin Adeney, *The Motor Makers: The Turbulent History of Britain's Car*

Industry (London, Collins, 1988), p. 199.

29. CAB 134/636, PC(48)130, 28 October 1948, The Production Committee: The Ford Motor Company's Proposals for Expansion: memorandum by the Minister of Supply.

30. Cited in CAB 134/636, PC(48)21st, 29 October 1948.

31. Ibid.

32. Ibid.

33. Ibid.

34. Panel A, the Distribution of Industry Committee and the Production Committee.

35. Cf. CAB 134/130, DI(49)6th, 14 December 1948; CAB 134/639, PC(48)153, 15 December 1948; PC(48)25th, 17 December 1948; CAB 134/131, DI(49)2nd, DI(49)8, 4 March 1949; CAB 134/640, PC(49)10th, minute 1, 29 April 1949; CAB 134/641, PC(49)48, 26 April 1949.

36. Panel A on 8 December 1948, as cited in CAB 134/639, PC(48)153, 15 December 1948, annex.

37. CAB 134/130, DI(48)6th, 14 December 1948.

38. Ibid.

39. Ibid.

40. CAB 134/130, PC(48)153, 15 December 1948. The Ford Motor Company's Proposals for Expansion; Note by the Economic Secretary, Treasury. This summarises the discussions in the Distribution of Industry Committee for the benefit of the Production Committee.

41. Ibid.

42. CAB 134/636, PC(48)25th, minute 1, 17 December 1948.

43. Ibid.

44. Letter reproduced as annex A to CAB 134/131, DI(49)8, 4 March 1949.

45. Ibid.

46. CAB 134/131, DI(49)8, annex C.

47. Ibid.

48. Ibid.

49. CAB 134/131, DI(49)2nd, minute 1.

50. CAB 134/641, PC(49)10th, minute 1.

51. In the words of the Joint Parliamentary Secretary to the Minister of Supply in reporting to his colleagues on the Distribution of Industry Committee. CAB 134/130, DI(48)23, 8 June 1948.

52. Ibid.

53. Ibid.

54. CAB 134/130, DI(48)5th, 18 June 1948.

55. Ibid.

56. CAB 134/130, DI(48)27, 28 June 1948, annexes A and B.

57. Quoted from the October 1943 Board of Trade Report on 'The Location of Industry', CAB 87/63, EC(43)13.

58. Facts about the company drawn from CAB 134/131, DI(49)23, 17 September 1949, Champion Sparking Plug Company Limited: note by the Parliamentary Secretary to the Board of Trade.

59. Ibid.

60. Ibid.

61. Ibid.

62. CAB 134/131, DI(49)6th, minute 2, 22 September 1949.

63. Cf. CAB 134/130, DI(48)2, 3 January 1948, Proposal by the De Havilland Aircraft Company to Erect a New Assembly Shed at Hatfield, Herts (Panel A, Case No. 1562): note by the Parliamentary Secretary to the Board of Trade.

64. CAB 134/130, DI(48)3, 3 January 1948, The Expansion of the De Havilland Aircraft Company at Hatfield, Herts: note by the Parliamentary Secretary to the Board of Trade.

65. Ibid.

66. Ibid.

67. Ibid.

68. Ibid.

69. CAB 134/130, DI(48)1st, minute 3, 13 January 1948.

70. On 21 January 1949. CAB 134/131, DI(49)4, Location of the Aircraft Industry.

71. CAB 134/130, DI(48)5th, minute 2, 18 June 1948.

72. Ibid.

73. CAB 134/131, DI(49)4, 21 January 1949, Location of the Aircraft Industry.

74. CAB 134/131, DI(49)2nd, minute 3.

75. See CAB 134/131, DI(49)24, 17 September 1949, Leavesden Airfield – De Havilland Engine Company: note by the Parliamentary Secretary to the Board of Trade.

76. Ibid.

77. Ibid.

78. CAB 134/131, DI(49)6th, minute 3, 22 September 1949.

79. Ibid. See also *Second Report of the Select Committee on Estimates*, Session 1955/56, *The Development Areas* (London, HMSO, 1956), p. vii.

80. Ibid.

81. Ibid. See also detailed figures in CAB 124/131, DI(49)7, 2 March 1949,

Report on the Progress of Government and Privately Financed Factory Building Schemes in the Development Areas: note by the Parliamentary Secretaries to the Board of Trade and the Ministry of Works, tables II and III.

82. Expenditure figure from McCrone, *Regional Policy in Britain*, p. 114; jobs total from CAB 134/130, DI(48)32, 6 August 1948, draft White Paper on *Distribution of Industry Policy*, appendix 7.

83. Cf. CAB 134/130, DI(48)32, part II, para. 42; part III, para. 5.

84. CAB 134/646, PC(50)47, 23 May 1950, Distribution of Industry: memorandum by the Ministry of Labour and National Service.

85. CAB 134/640, PC(49)13th, 20 May 1949.

86. CAB 134/131, DI(49)15, 30 May 1949. Measures to secure a geographical distribution of new industrial projects more favourable to the Development Areas. See also his note of 16 July, DI(49)19.

87. CAB 134/646, PC(50)41, 3 May 1950, Factory Building in the Unemployment Areas.

88. Ibid.

89. Ibid.

90. Even the advanced factories built by Government in the Development Areas by May 1950 came in total square-footage to only 5 per cent of all new factory buildings and extensions over 5000 square feet approved from the end of 1944 to the end of June 1948. Cf. CAB 134/646, PC(50)41, 3 May 1950, and CAB 134/131, DI(49)7, 2 March 1949, table II.

91. As at 30 September 1947, a total of 3259 applications had been approved. CAB IPC(47)10, 7 November 1947, Analysis of Approvals by Panel A and Regional Distribution of Industry Panels. A total of 1518 applications for industrial development certificates were made in the half-year 1 July–31 December 1948. CAB 134/131, DI(49)7, 2 March 1949, table II.

Chapter Eighteen:
THE PERVASIVE HARM OF 'FULL EMPLOYMENT'

1. Ian McLaine, *Ministry of Morale: Home Front Morale and the Ministry of Information in World War II* (London, George Allen & Unwin, 1979), p. 10.

2. See Barnett, *Audit of War*, ch 1, for an account of wartime attitudes towards full employment, together with relevant source references.

3. Steering Committee [Official] on Post-War Employment. See CAB 87/13, PR(43)37 and PR(43)39.

4. CAB 87/64, EC(43)6, memorandum by the Treasury on maintenance of employment, timing and planning of public investment, and control and timing of private investment, etc., 16 October 1943.

5. Ibid.

6. CAB 87/63, EC(43)6, covering note by the Treasury.

7. CAB 87/63, EC(43)9, 18 October 1943.

8. CAB 87/63, EC(43)12, 20 October 1943.

9. Leslie Jones, *Shipbuilding in Britain Mainly Between the World Wars* (Cardiff, University of Wales Press, 1957), p. 64, table XX.

10. Sir William H. Beveridge, *Full Employment in a Free Society: A Report by William H. Beveridge* (London, George Allen & Unwin, 1944), p. 29.

11. CAB 87/63, R(44)6.

12. Michael P. Jackson, *The Price of Coal* (London, Croom Helm, 1974), p. 52.

13. CAB 102/407.

14. H. M. D. Parker, *Manpower: A Study of Wartime Policy and Administration* (London, HMSO and Longmans, Green, 1957), p. 211, table 26.

15. W. K. Hancock and M. M. Gowing, *British War Economy*, p. 351.

16. Ibid.

17. Ibid.

18. See Barnett, *Audit of War*, chs 4–9.

19. CAB 87/63, EC(43)15.

20. CAB 87/63, R(44)6; also CAB 87/7, R(44)6.

21. Ibid.

22. CAB 87/5, R(44)8th, 21 January 1944.

23. Ibid.

24. Cmd 6527.

25. CAB 134/227, EPC(50)124, 1 December 1950, Wages and Prices and Full Employment: memorandum by the Chancellor of the Exchequer (Hugh Gaitskell).

26. Ibid.

27. Ibid.

28. Ibid.

29. Ibid.

30. CAB 134/503, MEP(46)9, 22 October 1946, Ministerial Committee on Economic Planning: Ministry of Labour and National Service; National Joint Advisory Council: Survey of the Economic Situation.

31. CAB 134/503, MEP(46)8, circulating LP(46)25th. See also ROBN 5/ 3, note of 17 November 1945 from Austin Robinson (Chief Economic Adviser to the Board of Trade) to Sir Charles Bruce-Gardner et al., in

reference to the previous day's meeting of the official Working Party on Manpower, saying that the likely manpower deficit over the next six months would be 2 million, of which 900,000 would fall on Board of Trade industries; and 500,000 on the metal and engineering industries, the major exporters.

32. See Morgan, *Labour in Power*, pp. 181–2 and notes.

33. CAB 134/503, MEP(46)9.

34. Ibid.

35. Ibid.

36. Ibid.

37. Leaving aside the over 2 million temporarily rendered idle by the icy winter of 1947.

38. CAB 134/503, MEP(46)16, 21 December 1946, *Economic Survey for 1947*: covering memorandum by the Steering Committee, para. 15.

39. *Economic Survey for 1948*, Cmd 7344 (1948), para. 187.

40. See T 229/85.

41. CAB 134/225, EPC(50)9, 7 January 1950.

42. CAB 134/222, EPC(49)73, 4 July 1949, The Dollar Situation: Forthcoming Discussions with U.S.A. and Canada.

43. Letter to the author, 24 December 1993.

44. CAB 134/220, EPC(49)25th, item 1, 1 July 1949.

45. CAB 234/503, MEP(47)1st, item 2, 7 January 1947.

46. Ibid.

47. T 229/85, interim report circulated 18 September 1947.

48. Ibid.

49. T 229/85, Wages Policy, 29 January 1948.

50. See LAB 10/759, Restoration of Pre-War Trade Practices Act 1942 – Restrictive Practices – General File, for the reasons why Government excluded the unions from the scope of restrictive practices examination and legislation. See Morgan, *Labour in Power*, pp. 75–81, 180–2, 371–4, for an account of the relations between the unions and the Labour Government, especially in regard to wages policy and a wage freeze.

51. Calculated from C. H. Feinstein, *Statistical Tables*, T140, table 65.

52. CAB 134/241, ER(L)(49)128(final), 26 April 1949.

53. Ibid.

54. Cf. CAB 134/222, EPC(49)72. The Dollar Situation: memorandum by the Chancellor of the Exchequer.

55. Cf. CAB 87/7, R(44)6 and CAB 134/503, MEP(46)9.

56. ROBN 6/2/1.

57. CAB 134/222, EPC(49)72. See also CAB 134/227, ER(L)(49)128(final), 26 April 1949.

58. ROBN 6/2/1.

59. Michael Balfour, *West Germany* (London, Ernest Benn, 1968), p. 154.

60. Karl Hardach, 'Germany 1914–1970', in Carlo Cipolla (ed.), *The Fontana Economic History of Europe*, vol. 6, *Contemporary Economies–1* (London, Collins/Fontana Books, 1976), p. 210.

61. CAB 134/219, EPC(48)101, 22 November 1948, Long-Term Programme of the Bizone of Germany: memorandum by the Chancellor of the Exchequer.

62. *Scala* magazine, May–June 1987, p. 22.

63. The author was at school in the London suburb of Croydon at the time.

64. ROBN 7/3/3, The Long-Term Programme of the Bizone of Germany [English-language version of the German tender for Marshall Aid], p. 14, paras 34–8. See also Balfour, *West Germany*, p. 169; Cipolla, *Fontana Economic History of Europe*, vol. 6, pp. 212–13; *Scala* magazine, May–June 1988, p. 24. Geoffrey Denton, Murray Forsyth and Malcolm MacLennan, *Economic Planning*, pp. 53–4.

65. ED 124/210, Paper YSC 9/59, Youth Service Committee: The Purchasing Power of the £: answer by Mr Erroll (Parliamentary Secretary to the Board of Trade) to a question in the House of Commons on 6 November 1958 (giving changes in the internal purchasing power of the pound from 1914 to 1957).

66. Balfour, *West Germany*, p. 174.

67. The United Kingdom received $2.7 billion, West Germany $1.7 billion. Figures from HM Treasury and the German Embassy. See next chapter, note 2.

68. Denton, Forsyth and MacLennan, *Economic Planning*, p. 52.

69. ROBN 7/3/3; CAB 134/236, ER(L)(48)222, 14 December 1948, European Economic Co-operation Committee, report on The Long-Term Programme of the Bizone of Germany.

70. CAB 134/219, EPC(48)101, 22 November 1948, Long-Term Programme of the Bizone of Germany: memorandum by the Chancellor of the Exchequer covering a report by the working party.

71. Ibid.

72. Ibid.

73. CAB 134/219, EPC(48)109, 11 December 1948, also CAB 134/236, ER(L)(48)222, 14 December 1948, The Long-Term Programme of the

Bizone of Germany: Report by the Committee on European Economic Co-operation.

74. CAB 134/219, EPC(48)101, 22 November 1948, annex 'C' (Secret), from German Section (Mr R. B. Stevens) to Berlin, sounding warning about scale of German plans and asking for views on desirability of reining it back.

75. CAB 134/219, EPC(48)109, 11 December 1948, covering memorandum by the Chancellor of the Exchequer.

76. CAB 134/236, EPC(48)109.

77. Ibid. See also CAB 134/240, ER(L)(49)45(final), 17 February 1949, report by the European Economic Co-operation Committee on The European Long Term Programme, para. 25, which observed of the Bizone's plans:

> The *Bizone* . . . cannot become viable by 1952 at a reasonable standard of living. But it must move towards viability, and the existing long-term programme is far from it. . . . If the food programme could be got right, and the industrial investment programme brought within financial possibilities, the Bizone could get within a reasonable distance of viability by 1952, and could possibly become viable by the middle 1950's. At present, there are neither the controls nor the drastic internal budgetary policy which could serve to keep the agricultural and industrial effort on the right lines.

78. CAB 134/242, ER(L)(49)186, 21 June 1949, European Economic Co-operation Committee: Plan of Action 1949/50: Other Participants' Reports on Internal Finances. Annex 'B'. Country Reports on Internal Financial Position: Report of the Bizone. Brief prepared by working party under the leadership of the Economic Section of the Cabinet Office.

79. Ibid.

80. Ibid.

81. Ibid.

82. Ibid., annex 'B'.

83. Ibid.

84. Ibid.

85. Ibid.

86. CAB 134/234, ER(L)(48)91, 6 September 1948, Draft: The Long-Term Programme (material to be submitted by the United Kingdom to the Organisation for European Economic Co-operation).

Chapter Nineteen:
THE WASTING OF MARSHALL AID

1. ROBN 7/3/3, Long-term Programme of the Bizone of Germany, p. 27, para. 75.
2. HM Treasury gave the author a figure of $2.7 billion for the British share, while the German Embassy gave $1.7 billion for the German share. But according to *The Marshall Plan and the Future of US–European Relations* (New York, German Information Centre, 1972), of the $13 billion total of Marshall Aid, roughly $3.1 billion went to Britain, $2.7 billion to France, $1.5 billion to Italy and just under $1.5 billion to West Germany.
3. In a letter of 13 December 1993 to the author, Sir Alexander Cairncross confirmed that in his judgement Britain did indeed use Marshall Aid to enable her to carry on her role of banker to the sterling area, and to meet withdrawals from her reserves by creditors. In answer to the author's question (letter of 9 December 1993) as to what might have been the impact on Britain's global military role and her economic aid to, and investment in, the Commonwealth if Britain had NOT received Marshall Aid, Sir Alexander replied: 'Drastic cuts.'
4. See T 229/136, especially minutes of a meeting in the Treasury on 16 July 1947, and papers by R. W. B. Clarke of 21 and 23 July 1947.
5. R. W. B. Clarke, paper on Alternative Courses of Action, 23 July 1947.
6. Ibid.
7. Ibid.
8. CAB 134/217, EPC(48)1, 3 January 1948, memorandum by the Chancellor of the Exchequer on the draft *Economic Survey for 1948*.
9. Para. 230. Draft circulated on 23 December 1947 as unnumbered paper with CAB 134/217, EPC(48)1.
10. Ibid., para. 232.
11. Ibid., para. 235. This did not only·apply to imports from the United States – see CAB 134/215, EPC(47)33, 23 December 1947, Report on Marshall Aid: note by the Chairman of the London Committee: 'It is crucially important to us that E.R.P. dollars should be provided to enable us to make purchases of essential food and materials in Canada and South America.'
12. CAB 134/215, EPC(47)33, 23 December 1947, note by R. W. B. Clarke, Chairman of the London Committee [on Marshall Aid], covering the report of the committee.
13. Ibid. report on Marshall Aid.
14. CAB 134/217, EPC(48)38, 10 May 1948, Prospects under E.R.P.:

memorandum by the Chancellor of the Exchequer, annex B.

15. CAB 124/217, EPC(48)19, 19 March 1948, European Recovery Programmme: Programmes to be Transmitted to the United States Authorities: report by the London Committee, paras 5 and 6.

16. CAB 124/217, EPC(48)24, 25 March 1948, memorandum by the Chancellor of the Exchequer on the European Recovery Programme. See also CAB 134/217, EPC(48)19, 19 March 1948, Submission of Programmes to the United States Authorities: report by the London Committee.

17. CAB 134/217, EPC(48)38, 10 May 1948, Prospects under E.R.P.: memorandum by the Chancellor of the Exchequer. This essential point was communicated to the Balance of Payments Committee of the OEEC, and later to the American ERP representative in London. See CAB 133/49, ER(ECA)(48)1st, 25 June 1948.

18. Ibid.

19. CAB 134/215, EPC(47)33, 23 December 1947.

20. Ibid.

21. Mr T. K. Finletter.

22. CAB 133/49, ER(ECA)(48)1, 7 July 1948: a memorandum on the origins and working of the Sterling Area (annex I); a memorandum on the Sterling Area, with special reference to the need for maintaining the Sterling Area reserves (annex II); and a table giving a detailed breakdown of the estimated gold and dollar payments and receipts for the rest of the Sterling Area and others in respect of the period 1 July 1948 to 30 September 1948 (annex III).

23. Ibid., annex I, p. 7.

24. Para. 74.

25. Ibid.

26. Ibid.

27. Ibid., annex II.

28. CAB 134/219, EPC(48)85, 15 September 1948, The 1948–49 Programme: memorandum by the Chancellor of the Exchequer.

29. Ibid. With particular regard to the sterling balances, Sir Alexander Cairncross comments in a letter of 13 December 1993 to the author: 'we used Marshall Aid largely to repay debt (ie, we used the proceeds of sale of goods supplied under Marshall Aid – the so-called counterpart funds). But on the continent these were used on projects agreed with E.C.A. – in our view adding to inflationary pressure by allowing funds already spent on imports to be spent again on investment.'

30. ROBN 7/4/2, The French Long Term Programme: note by the UK delegation.

31. ROBN 7/4/3, undated note on Bizone: Long Term Programme (Economic Aspects).

32. CAB 134/234, ER(L)(48)91, 6 September 1948, Draft Long-Term Programme, para. 212. Industrial plans and investment in the UK merited 101 paragraphs out of 226 of main text. Published as Cmd 7572.

33. Cf. ROBN 7/3/2, letter of 21 November 1948 from Austin Robinson to Richard Clarke:

> My view is yours, that the most important thing in the world is to rub the Europeans' noses in it. . . . What we want to say is that it looks very improbable that by 1952/53 Europe will be able to pay for more than 75% of the present planned imports from all overseas sources and perhaps 60% of the present planned imports from North America; we have got to think how we go about cutting down imports to make life as tolerable as it can be with that level. . . .

34. CAB 134/219, EPC(48)70, 7 September 1948, Balance of Payments and Production Programmes for 1952–53 for Submission to the Organisation for European Economic Co-operation: memorandum by the Chancellor of the Exchequer.

35. CAB 134/234, ER(L)(48)91, 6 September 1948, Draft: The Long-Term Programme (material to be submitted by the United Kingdom to the Organisation for European Economic Co-operation); final version, little altered, dated 30 September 1948, in ROBN 7/3/2.

36. ROBN 7/3/3, Long-Term Programme of the Bizone of Germany, which allotted 30 out of 53 pages of main text to industry, agriculture, transport and general investment, and 8 pages to foreign trade and the achievement of equilibrium in the balance of payments; ROBN 7/4/2, Réponse Française au questionnaire de l'Organisation Européenne de Cooperation Economique sur le Programme à Long Terme, which out of 93 pages allotted an appendix of 15 pages to the balance of payments and foreign exchange, whereas industrial modernisation and development formed the major part of the opening 'Exposé Général', and also merited 17 pages of appendices.

37. ROBN 7/4/2, Réponse Française au questionnaire de l'Organisation Européenne de Cooperation Economique sur le Programme à Long Terme, p. 13.

38. ROBN 7/3/3, The Long-term Programme of the Bizone of Germany.

39. CAB 134/219, EPC(48)79, 7 September 1948, Balance of Payments and Production Programmes for 1952–53 for submission to the Organisation for

European Economic Co-operation: memorandum by the Chancellor of the Exchequer.

40. CAB 134/645, PC(50)19, 11 March 1950.

41. Cf. CAB 133/62, ER(P)(48)95, OEEC: United Kingdom Record of the 11th Meeting of the Executive Committee Working Party, 5 and 6 November 1948, Bizone Long-Term Programme, Dr Bode's evidence and replies to questions.

42. CAB 134/235, ER(L)(48)173, 17 November 1948, Comments of the E.C.A. Mission in London on the Long Term Programme and the 1949–50 & 1948–49 Programmes of the United Kingdom, p. 10, para. 57.

43. ROBN 7/3/3, The Long Term Programme of the Bizone of Germany, p. 27, para. 77.

44. CAB 134/234, ER(L)(48)91, p. 28, para. 149.

45. Ibid., para. 154. The pound sterling is converted to dollars at $4.03 throughout the following discussion of Marshall Aid and investment.

46. C. H. Feinstein, *Statistical Tables*, T16, gives $48 billion as British GNP in 1948; acccording to ROBN 7/3/3, The Long-Term Programme of the Bizone of Germany, p. 19, table 7, her GNP in 1948 came to $24 billion. British gross capital formation as percentage of GNP in 1948 from Feinstein, *Statistical Tables*, table 5(iii); German figure from ROBN 7/3/3, p. 20 and table 9. In 1950 the actual proportion of German GNP devoted to gross capital formation was 23.2 per cent (*Statistisches Bundesamt, Volkswirtschaftliche Gesamtrechnungen*, Fachserie 18, Reihe 5.7 (Stuttgart und Mainz, W. Kohlhammer, 1985) table 7.1).

47. CAB 134/235, ER(L)(48)173, 17 November 1948.

48. CAB 134/645, PC(50)19, 11 March 1950, Progress Report on the Long-Term Programme of the UK, p. 12.

49. Cf. CAB 134/440, IPC(49)59th, item 2, 16 May 1949, comments by the Chairman of the Investment Programmes Committee (W. Strath, of the Central Economic Planning Staff) on the request of the OEEC for information 'on the main branches of economic activity including anticipated investment and its incidence on, e.g., production, employment, balance of payments, etc. . . .' In regard to manufacturing the OEEC 'hoped to see a more detailed breakdown than we could achieve . . .':

We were asked to give figures on gross fixed investments and net fixed investment. This we should be unable to do. In order to show the relative importance of projected investments and to gauge their incidence on the anticipated increase in production we were also

asked to provide a comparison of the gross value of output for each
branch of economic activity in 1948 with the estimated output after
the completion of the projected investments. This we should also be
unable to do.

50. Calculated from Feinstein, *Statistical Tables*, T106.

51. ROBN 7/3/3, The Long-Term Programme of the Bizone, p. 21, table 11.
The programme gives all figures either in dollars alone or dollars and
Deutschemarks together.

52. ROBN 7/3/3, The Long-Term Programme of the Bizone, p. 20, table 10.
ROBN 7/4/2, La Réponse Française, p. 32, table IX. The French
programme gives all figures in French francs, which for the purpose of this
discussion of Marshall Aid is converted to the dollar at the official 1948 rate of
FF215.

53. CAB 134/438, IPC(48)12. Estimate of total gross fixed investment in
1948: $8.2 billion; in industry and infrastructure for 1948: $4.2 billion.
Cabinet approved total GFI in industry and infrastructure for 1949: $4.0
billion.

54. That is, 30 per cent of $16 billion.

55. ROBN 7/3/3, p. 21, table 11.

56. CAB 134/219, EPC(48)81, 14 September 1948, Draft 1949–50
Programme for Submission to the Organisation for European Economic
Co-operation.

57. CAB 134/641, 17 January 1949, *Economic Survey for 1949* (provisional
draft), p. 17, table VIII.

58. Ibid., p. 19, para. 56.

59. CAB 134/440, IPC(49)5, 3 November 1949.

60. CAB 134/441, IPC(IB)(50)1 (also IPC(WP)(50)7), 18 January 1950, report
by the Chairman of the Industrial Buildings Committee Sub-Committee.

61. Ibid.

62. Cf. CAB 134/643, ER(L)(49)216, 22 July 1949, 1949/50 Programme
Supplementary Memorandum for Submission to OEEC, paras 6 and 21.
CAB 134/645, PC(50)19, 11 March 1950, Progress Report on the Long-
Term Programme of the UK, pp. 18, 20 and 23.

63. CAB 134/220, EPC(49)24th, item 2, 1 July 1949.

64. CAB 134/222, EPC(49)72, appendix B, para. 11.

65. CAB 134/220, EPC(49)51st, item 1, 13 December 1949.

66. W. A. Brown and R. Opie, *American Foreign Assistance* (Washington, DC,
Brookings Institution, 1953), pp. 236–7.

67. CAB 134/216, EPC(48)2nd, minute 1, 9 January 1948.

68. See CAB 134/232, ER(L)(48) series, fifty-six meetings of the European Economic Co-operation Committee (official). See also CAB 133/49, ER(ECA)(48) and (49) series, the minutes of joint meetings of British bureaucrats and the London representatives of the ECA, for vain attempts of the Americans to get details of specific industrial projects and uses of American supplies out of the adroitly evasive British. Cf., for instance, ER(ECA)(48)4th, 16 July 1948, and ER(ECA)(49)13th, 6 October 1948, when a US representative asked for 'rather more detail' about progress in particular British industries, 'particularly as regards the future', but the meeting agreed that such information 'must inevitably be restricted to generalities'.

69. CAB 134/232, ER(L)(48)43rd, minute 5, discussing ER(L)(48)62: 1949/50 Programme: Method of Presentation of Machinery Imports.

70. ROBN 7/4/2, Réponse Française.

71. Brown and Opie, *American Foreign Assistance*, p. 237.

72. Ibid.

73. Ibid., p. 244. The decision when originally taken in autumn 1948 occasioned some disquiet in the ECA Mission in London. See CAB 134/235, ER(L)(48)159, 30 October 1948, note on Drawings on Special Account, covering exchange of letters in September between T. K. Finletter (Head of ECA Mission) and Roger Makins of the Foreign Office.

74. ROBN 7/4/2, Réponse Française, p. 47. This would save 600,000 tonnes of coal a year.

75. Cf. letter of 25 January 1994 to the author from Sir Alexander Cairncross.

76. CAB 134/224, EPC(50)12th, item 2, 12 May 1950.

77. British figures from, or calculated from, Feinstein, *Statistical Tables*, table 41, which gives total investment in new plant, buildings and equipment (that is, less houses and in social and public services facilities) as £1.3 billion. GNP according to Feinstein (table 3) came to £13.3 billion. German figures from *Statistisches Bundesamt*, Fachserie 18, Reihe 5.7, p. 41, table 1, for GNP at £8.4 billion (at DM 11.75 to £); p. 86, table 10.1, and p. 88, table 11.1, for investment in new plant, buildings and equipment of £1.6 billion.

78. CAB 134/225, EPC(50)44, 27 April 1950, Fundamental Discussions with the United States: memorandum by the Chancellor of the Exchequer, annex A: Summary of Fundamentals of External Financial Policy, para. 6.

Chapter Twenty:
'THE POLICY OF "TAKE IT OR LEAVE IT"'

1. In his preface to *The Desert Generals* (London, William Kimber, 1960; 2nd edn George Allen & Unwin and Pan Books, 1984) the present author made the same analogy from the reverse point of view in regard to the Western Desert campaigns: 'The methods of thinking, organising and fighting of each side . . . adumbrate their industrial and commercial methods in the post-war era.'

2. CAB 134/170, E(P)(48)15, circulated with a note by the President of the Board of Trade, 15 December 1948. In January 1948 it was estimated that exports to Switzerland would reach £25.5 million that year. By October the total was £18.8 million, 'and there is no possibility of £25 million being reached . . .'. The report was based on enquiries to some 200 Swiss representatives of some 500 British suppliers.

3. Ibid.

4. Ibid.

5. Ibid.

6. Ibid.

7. Ibid.

8. Ibid.

9. CAB 134/167, E(48)(14(final)33, 2 February 1948, Exports to Canada: memorandum by the Exports Committee.

10. Ibid.

11. CAB 134/221, EPC(49)33, 31 March 1949, Expansion of Exports to North America: memorandum by the President of the Board of Trade.

12. Ibid.

13. The present author, reading these wartime American magazines as a teenager, found them a revelation, showing up the drab British scene (even the pre-war British scene) as belonging to a past age.

14. See, for example, CAB 134/167, E(48)26(final), 6 March 1948, Exports to the United States: memorandum by the Committee on Exports.

15. CAB 134/167, E(48)71(final), 6 August 1948, Exports to the United States: memorandum by the Export Committee Secretariat.

16. Ibid.

17. Ibid.

18. As cited in ibid.

19. Ibid.

20. CAB 134/167, E(48)89, 11 September 1948, Exports to the U.S.A.: note

by the Export Promotion Department of the Board of Trade.

21. Ibid. On this general question of limp British marketing, see CAB 134/167, E(48)92, the report by Neville Blond, Honorary Trade Adviser to the Board of Trade, 9 September 1948, which confirms the weakness of exporters' distribution systems and their ignorance of America and American taste.

22. Cited in CAB 134/167, E(48)105, 3 December 1948.

23. Ibid.

24. CAB 134/221, EPC(49)31, 29 March 1949, Expansion of Exports to North America: memorandum by the President of the Board of Trade.

25. Ibid.

26. CAB 134/221, EPC(49)33, 31 March 1949, Expansion of Exports to North America: memorandum by the President of the Board of Trade.

27. M. Adeney, *The Motor Makers*, pp. 196–7.

28. Chassis, springs and shock-absorbers all proved too weak to cope with rutted tracks, potholes and pavé. Cf. ibid., pp. 206–7. The present author was a passenger in a Vanguard on a holiday to Spain in 1948. On the first day out from Dunkirk a back spring broke on the pavé. On the way home the exhaust gasket blew, a replacement being improvised by a French garage. The mechanic scornfully compared the cat's-cradle mess of the Vanguard's engine compartment with the clear and accessible layout of a Peugeot 203 alongside.

29. Alec Dick, later Standard's managing director before its demise, cited in ibid., p. 206.

30. Ibid., p. 196.

31. See ibid., p. 198, and R. J. Wyatt, *The Austin, 1905–1952* (Newton Abbott and London, David & Charles, 1981), pp. 248–9.

32. Wyatt, *Austin*, p. 218.

33. As Billy Rootes pointed out in a report to his brother Reggie following a visit to America soon after the War. See John Bullock, *The Rootes Brothers: Story of a Motoring Empire* (Yeovil, Patrick Stephens, an imprint of Haynes Publishing, 1993), pp. 142–5.

34. See Dunnett, *The Decline of the British Motor Industry*, pp. 21–4.

35. Adeney, *Motor Makers*, p. 200.

36. The present author was a passenger in a Sheerline driven to Spain by the same owner who had previously had the Vanguard with the broken spring. The owner was mortified when on the winding N20 in Quercy his unwieldy beast, driven at maximum safe speed, was overtaken by a Peugeot 203.

37. In March 1946, the Pullman sold in the Middle East for £1250; the Packard

for £453 and the Cadillac for £403. See T 236/370.

38. For example, a 16 H.P. Austin delivered in Baghdad in 1946, £690; Ford Mercury, £303. See ibid.

39. Cf. Dunnett, *Decline of the British Motor Industry*, pp. 27–8, 37, 40; Wyatt, *Austin*, pp. 244, 248–9; Bullock, *Rootes Brothers*, ch. 19. Nonetheless the car firms' initial attempts to set up sales and service organisations in America impressed Whitehall. See CAB 134/167, E(48)26(final), 6 August 1948, Quarterly Report on Exports to the U.S.A.

40. Cf. Billy Rootes to his brother in 1945: 'When the initial world shortage of motor products has been appeased, it is difficult to see how Britain will be able to compete, because even before the war we were not competitive in the world markets so far as prices were concerned. . . .' Cited in Bullock, *Rootes Brothers*, p. 143.

41. Cf. Dunnett, *Decline of the British Motor Industry*, pp. 34, 36–7.

42. Ibid., p. 37.

43. The following summary of Volkswagen's postwar revival is based on W. H. Nelson, *Small Wonder: The Amazing Story of the Volkswagen* (London, Hutchinson, 1967), ch. 6.

44. Ibid., p. 113.

45. Ibid., p. 117.

46. Ibid., p. 115.

47. Ibid., p. 117.

48. Ibid., pp. 122–3.

49. Ibid., p. 286, table 1.

50. T 236/870, Switzerland: Report on the Market for Private Cars.

51. Ibid.

52. Ibid.

53. Ibid.

54. Ibid.

55. Ibid., Prospects of U.K. Exports of Wool and Rayon Piece Goods and Motor Vehicles.

56. Ibid.

57. Cited in Dunnett, *Decline of British Motor Industry*, p. 37.

58. CAB 134/225, EPC(50)4, 30 December 1949, Exports to the United States of America: report on his recent visit to the U.S.A. by the President of the Board of Trade (Harold Wilson), para. 14(b).

59. Ibid.

60. R. A. Church, *Herbert Austin: The British Motor Car to 1941* (London, Europa Press, 1979), p. 55.

61. Dunnett, *Decline of the British Motor Industry*, p. 43.

62. CAB 134/225, EPC(50)4.

63. Ibid.

64. Ibid. It must be remembered that at this epoch British shirts still had long fore-and-aft tails (longer aft than fore), and a vent on the chest for unbuttoning, whereas American shirts were already of the universal modern [1990s] pattern of short square tails and a button-through front.

65. CAB 134/242, ER(L)(49)163, 27 May 1949, para. 80.

66. Ibid., para. 83.

67. C. H. Feinstein, *Statistical Tables*, T22.

68. At 1948 prices. See ibid., table 5, T14–15.

69. *Economic Survey for 1950*, Cmd. 7915 (1950), table 9. 1938: 17 per cent; 1947: 15 per cent; 1948: 17 per cent; 1949: 15 per cent.

70. Ibid. 1938: 26 per cent; 1947: 24 per cent; 1948: 24 per cent; 1949: 23 per cent.

71. Ibid.

72. Ibid. 14 per cent as against 15 per cent.

73. CAB 134/225, EPC(50)46, 9 May 1950, Forecasts of National Income and Expenditure. See also Cmd. 7915, para. 58.

74. CAB 134/224, EPC(50)18th, item 1, 13 July 1950.

75. Joseph Conrad, *The Nigger of the 'Narcissus': A Tale of the Sea* (London, Gresham Publishing, 1925), pp. 162–3.

Bibliography

Unpublished Sources
Public Record Office

Admiralty (ADM series)

ADM 1/11892   Labour in Naval and Mercantile Shipyards.

ADM 1/15218   Operations and Technical Radio Committee: Papers 1–67, 1942–43 [includes papers of the Radio Board].

Ministry of Aircraft Production (AVIA series)

AVIA 10/99   Fedden Mission (to the United States) Report, dated June 1943.

AVIA 10/269   Labour Statistics 20/10/42–16/8/44.

AVIA 10/338   War Cabinet – Radio Production Committee and General Questions on the Radio Industry, 1941–1944 [includes papers of the Radio Production Executive].

Board of Trade (BT series)

BT 28/319   Report to the Machine Tool Controller on the Equipment of Shipyards and Marine Engineering Shops, by Mr Cecil Bentham, 30 September 1942.

BT 28/377   Report on Vickers-Armstrong (Aircraft) Ltd, Weybridge, by five expert Inspectors of Labour Supply.

Cabinet and Cabinet Committees: Minutes and Memoranda (CAB series)

CAB 16 series

CAB 16/109–12   Report, Proceedings and Memoranda of the Defence Requirements Sub-Committee of the Committee of Imperial Defence 1933–5.

CAB 16/209   Strategic Appreciation Committee of the Committee of Imperial Defence 1939.

CAB 27 series

CAB 27/648   Defence Programmes and Their Acceleration Committee, 1938.

CAB 29 series

CAB 29/159   Anglo–French Staff Conversations, London, 1939.

CAB 32 series

CAB 32/129   Imperial Conference, London, 1937.

CAB 53 series

CAB 53/21–54   Committee of Imperial Defence: Memoranda of the Chiefs of Staff Committee, 1937–39.

CAB 87 series   (Committees on Postwar Reconstruction)

CAB 87/1–3   Reconstruction Problems, March 1941–Oct. 1943.

CAB 87/5–10   Reconstruction, Dec. 1943–May 1944.

CAB 87/12–13   Reconstruction Priorities, Jan.-Nov. 1943.

CAB 87/14–15   Reconstruction (Industrial Problems), May 1944–June 1945.

CAB 87/17–18   Reconstruction (Official) Industrial Problems, March 1944–May 1945.

CAB 87/55–7   Post-war Internal Economic Problems, Nov.1941–Oct.1943.

CAB 87/63   Post-war Employment, July 1943–Jan. 1944.

CAB 87/64   Economic Aspects of Reconstruction Problems, Oct.1941–Feb. 1942.

CAB 87/76–82 Social Insurance and Allied Services, July 1941–Oct.1942.

CAB 102 Series   (Cabinet Office Historical Section; Official War Histories (1939–1945), Civil)

CAB 102/51   Reciprocating Aero-Engines and Engine Accessories Production and Programmes 1935–45, by D.A. Parry.

CAB 102/406   Labour Welfare and Utilisation in the Aircraft Industry, by J.B. Jeffreys; draft used by Mrs Inman in writing official history *Labour in the Munitions Industries*.

CAB 102/407   Labour Requirements and Supply for the Ministries of Supply and Production; draft by Mrs Inman for use in *Labour in the Munitions Industries*.

CAB 128–9 series   *(Meetings and Memoranda of the Cabinet, 1945–1950)*

CAB 128/1–17   Meetings of the Cabinet 1945–50.

CAB 129/1–43   Memoranda of the Cabinet 1945–1950.

CAB 131 series   *(Meetings and Memoranda of the Cabinet Defence Committee).*

CAB 131/1–9   Meetings and Memoranda of the Cabinet Defence Committee 1946–1950.

CAB 132 series

CAB 132/28–35   Sub-Committee on Industrial Productivity 1945–50.

CAB 132/40–1 and 44–6   Committees on Industrial Productivity.

CAB 132/47–8   Panel on Technical and Operational Research.

CAB 132/49–50   Working Party on Technical and Operational Research.

CAB 133 series

CAB 133/18–24   E.R.C.: Commonwealth Liaison Committee, London, 1948–51.

CAB 133/42–4   Organisation for European Economic Co-operation – United Kingdom Delegation, Paris, 1947–8.

CAB 133/46   Committee of Co-operation, Paris, 1947.

CAB 133/49   Meetings between United Kingdom and United States Economic Co-operation Administration Representatives (plus memoranda), London, 1948–50.

CAB 133/58–60   Weekly Record of Departmental Discussions with Members of the United States Economic Co-operation Administration Mission in the United Kingdom, 1948–51.

CAB 133/61–6   United Kingdom Delegation, Paris, Meetings and Papers, 1948.

CAB 133/67–8   Organisation for European Economic Co-operation – United Kingdom Delegation (General Report).

CAB 133/72–6   European Recovery Conference – British Washington Committee.

CAB 133/78–9   Records of the Colombo Conference, 9–15 January 1950.

CAB 133/94–5   European Recovery Conference – United Kingdom Treasury and Supply Delegation, Washington: meetings with participating countries.

CAB 133/131   Preparations for Commonwealth Economic Conference, 1952.

CAB 134 series

CAB 134/44   Balance of Payments; Committee on Exports, 1947.

CAB 134/45   Exchange Requirements Committee 1947.

CAB 134/ 57–60   Civil Aviation Committee 1945–50.

CAB 134/130–2   Distribution of Industry Committee 1945–1950.

CAB 134/166–70   Committee on Exports.

CAB 134/182–5   European Economic Co-operation Committee 1950–51.

CAB 134/215–30   Economic Policy Committee 1948–51.

CAB 134/232–57   European Economic Co-operation Committee (continued).

CAB 134/293–7   Committee on Proposed Franco-German Iron and Steel Authority.

CAB 134/437–42   Investment Programmes Committee.

CAB 134/443   Industrial Buildings Committee.

CAB 134/503   Ministerial Committee on Economic Planning, 1946–47.

CAB 134/509–12   Ministerial Manpower Committee.

CAB 134/518–19   National Health Service Committee, 1950–1.

CAB 134/635–52   Production Committee, 1947–51.

CAB 134/687–96   Committee on the Socialisation of Industries, 1946–51.

CAB 134/697–8 and 704–5   Social Services Committee.

Ministry of Education (ED series)

ED 124/210   Paper YSC 9/59

Ministry of Labour and National Service (LAB series)

LAB 10/536   Report of Enquiry into London Bus Dispute, 1945.

LAB 10/567   Report of Enquiry into London Dock Dispute, 1945.

LAB 10/580   Report of Enquiry into London Dock Dispute, 1945.

LAB 10/613   Dispute at Ford Motor Company, 1946.

LAB 10/665   London Dock Strike, 1947.

LAB 10/759   Restoration of Pre-War Trade Practices Act 1942 – Restrictive Practices – General File.

LAB 10/895   Troubles in the Coal Industry, 1947.

LAB 10/932   Restrictive Practices in Shipbuilding, 1950.

Treasury (T series)

T 228/90   Postwar Highways Policy, 1943–48.

T 228/94   Transport: general questions.

T 229/7   Agricultural Production – plant and machinery, 1947–48.

T 229/19   Export sales organisation in Canada, United States and Argentina; information for the Chancellor of the Exchequer's visit to America, 1948.

T 229/49   Report of Economic Cooperation Administration on United Kingdom public social services.

T 229/63   Meeting with the Federation of British Industry to discuss industry and the way to recovery, 1947.

T 229/85   National Wages Policy; Official Working Party on the stabilisation of wages, 1947–48.

T 229/94–100   Organisation for European Economic Co-operation [especially T 229/99–100: Long-term Progress Working Group, papers and minutes, 1948].

T 229/136   Marshall Proposals: alternative action in case of breakdown, 1947.

T 230/3   Civil Aviation – Summary of Developments 1941/45.

T 230/29   Re-organisation of the Coal Industry.

T 230/134   Future British Exports: prospects in connection with increasing world competition, 1946–47.

T 230/134   National Union of Manufacturers: Questionnaire on Export Trade, December 1947.

T 236/280–2   German Standard of Living and Conditions of Industry: reports by Economic Advisory Council, 1945–46.

T 236/870   Motor Vehicles (Exports), 1946–48.

T 236/3070, RWBC/4788   The Sterling Area; memorandum by R.W.B. Clarke, 15 December 1951.

T 267/3   Treasury Historical Memorandum No.3.

Churchill Archives Centre, Churchill College, Cambridge

AVAR: Earl Alexander of Hilsborough.

BEVN: Rt. Hon Ernest Bevin.

CLRK: Sir Richard Clarke.

FORB: Sir Archibald Forbes.

NBKR: Lord Noel-Baker.

ROBN: Sir Austin Robinson.

COMMAND PAPERS AND OFFICIAL PUBLICATIONS

Command Papers

C. 3966   *Endowed Schools (Schools Enquiry) Commission, Report of*, vol. I (1867–8).

C. 3981   *Second Report of the Royal Commissioners on Technical Instruction*, vol. I: *Report* (1884).

Cd 5130   *Report of the Board of Education, 1908–9* (1910).

Cmd 3282   *Final Report of the Committee on Trade and Industry* (1928–9).

Cmd 6153   *Report of the Royal Commission on the Distribution of the Industrial Population* (1940).

Cmd 6404   *Social Insurance and Allied Services* (1942).

Cmd 6502   *A National Health Service* (1944).

Cmd 6527   *Employment Policy* (1944).

Cmd 6550–1   *Social Insurance*, parts I and II (1944).

Cmd 6564   *Statistics Relating to the War Effort of the United Kingdom* (1944).

Cmd 6605   *British Air Transport* (1945).

Cmd 6609   *Housing Policy* (1945).

Cmd 6610   *Coal Mining: Report of the Technical Advisory Committee* (1945)

Cmd 7046   *Economic Survey for 1947* (1947).

Cmd 7268   *Capital Investment in 1948* (1948).

Cmd 7344   *Economic Survey for 1948* (1948).

Cmd 7433   *The Colonial Empire (1947–1948)* (1948).

Cmd 7631   *Statement on Defence 1949* (1949).

Cmd 7647   *Economic Survey for 1949* (1949).

Cmd 7915   *Economic Survey for 1950* (1950).

Cmd 7968   *The Colonial Territories (1949–50)* (1950).

Cmd 8195   *Economic Survey for 1951* (1951).

Cmd 8509   *Economic Survey for 1952* (1952)

Cmnd 3638   *Report of the Committee on the Civil Service* (1966–8), vol. I [1967–8 Sessional Papers, vol. xviii].

Official Publications

Census of Production, 1948 (London, HMSO, 1953).

Census of Production, 1951 (London, HMSO, 1955).

Historical Record of the Census of Production 1907 to 1970 (London, Government Statistical Service, n.d.).

Social Trends (London, HMSO, 1991)

History of the Ministry of Munitions, 12 vols (London, HMSO, 1922).

Committee of Investigation into the Cotton Textile Machinery Industry, Report (London, HMSO, 1947).

Cotton Industry Working Party Report (London, HMSO, 1947).

General Report of the Select Committee on Estimates, Session 1955/56, *The Development Areas* (London, HMSO, 1956).

Second Report of the Select Committee on Estimates, Session 1955/56, *The Development Areas* (London, HMSO, 1956).

American

Statistical Abstract of the United States, 1950 (Washington, DC, United States Department of Commerce, 1950).

German

Statistisches Bundesamt, *Volkswirtschaftliche Gesamtrechnungen,* Fachserie 18, Reihe 7, Lange Reihen 1950 bis 1984 (Stuttgart und Mainz, W. Kohlhammer GMBH, 1985).

SECONDARY SOURCES

Addison, P., *The Road to 1945: British Politics and the Second World War* (London, Jonathan Cape, 1975).

Adeney, M., *The Motor Makers: The Turbulent History of Britain's Car Industry* (London, Collins, 1988)

Aldcroft, D. H., and Richardson, H. W., *The British Economy, 1870–1939* (London, Macmillan, 1969).

Annan, N., *Our Age: The Generation That Made Post-War Britain* (London, Fontana, 1991).

Attlee, C.R., *The Will and the Way to Socialism* (London, Methuen, 1935).

—— *The Labour Party in Perspective* (London, Victor Gollancz, 1937).

Bacon, R., and Eltis, W., *Britain's Economic Problem: Too Few Producers* (London, Macmillan, 1978).

Balfour, M., *West Germany* (London, Ernest Benn, 1968).

Barnett, Correlli, *The Desert Generals* (London, William Kimber, 1960; second edition, George Allen & Unwin and Pan Books, 1984).

—— *The Collapse of British Power* (London, Eyre Methuen, 1972; paperback edn, Stroud, Alan Sutton, 1984).

—— *The Audit of War: The Illusion and Reality of Britain as a Great Nation* (London, Macmillan, 1986; Papermac, 1987).

—— *Engage the Enemy More Closely: The Royal Navy in the Second World War* (London, Hodder & Stoughton, 1991).

Baylis, J., *Anglo-American Defence Relations 1939–80: The Special Relationship* (London, Macmillan, 1982).

Beer, S. H., *Modern British Politics: A Study of Parties and Pressure Groups* (London, Faber & Faber, 1965).

Beveridge, W., *The Pillars of Security and Other War-Time Essays and Addresses* (London, George Allen & Unwin, 1943).

—— *Full Employment in a Free Society: A Report by William H. Beveridge* (London, George Allen & Unwin, 1944).

Boycott, A.G., *The Elements of Imperial Defence: A Study of the Geographical Features, Material Resources, Communications and Organization of the British Empire* (Aldershot, Gale and Polden, 1931).

Brown, W. A., and Opie, R., *American Foreign Assistance* (Washington, DC, Brookings Institution, 1953).

Bullock, A., *The Life and Times of Ernest Bevin*, 3 vols (London, Heinemann, 1960–83).

—— *Ernest Bevin: Foreign Secretary 1945–1951* (London, Heinemann, 1984).

Bullock, J., *The Rootes Brothers: Story of a Motoring Empire* (Yeovil, Patrick Stephens, 1993).

Cairncross, A., *The Price of War: British Policy on German Reparations 1941–1949* (Oxford, Basil Blackwell, 1986).

Cairncross, A., and Watts, Nina, *The Economic Section 1939–1961: A Study in Economic Advising* (London, Routledge & Kegan Paul, 1989).

Campbell, J., *Nye Bevan and the Mirage of British Socialism* (London, Weidenfeld & Nicolson, 1987).

Cannadine, D., and Price, S. (eds), *Rituals of Royalty: Power and Ceremonial in Traditional Societies* (Cambridge, Cambridge University Press, 1987).

Carr, J. C., and Taplin, W., assisted by Wright, A. E. G., *History of the British*

Steel Industry (Oxford, Basil Blackwell, and Cambridge, Mass., Harvard University Press, 1962).

Carver, M., *Tightrope Walking: British Defence Policy Since 1945* (London, Hutchinson, 1992).

Castle, H. G., *Britain's Motor Industry* (London, Clerke and Cocheran, 1950).

Central Statistical Office, *Social Trends*, 21st edn (London, HMSO, 1991).

Chester, D. N. (ed.), and Wilson, F.M.G., *The Organization of British Central Government 1914–1956* (London, George Allen & Unwin, 1957).

Chester, N., *The Nationalisation of British Industry 1945–51* (London, HMSO, 1975).

Church, R. A., *Herbert Austin: The British Motor Car to 1941* (London, Europa Press, 1979).

Cipolla, C. (ed.), *The Fontana Economic History of Europe*, vol. 6: *Contemporary Economies–1* (London, Collins/Fontana Books, 1976).

Clarke, R., *Anglo-American Co-operation in War and Peace, 1942–1949* (Oxford, Oxford University Press, 1982).

Cole, G. D. H., *National Coal Board* (London, Fabian Society, 1949).

Conrad, J., *The Nigger of the 'Narcissus': A Tale of the Sea* (London, Gresham Publishing, 1925).

Court, W. H. B., *Coal* (London, HMSO and Longmans, Green, 1951).

Cross, J. A., *Whitehall and the Commonwealth* (London, Routledge & Kegan Paul, 1967).

Dahrendorf, R., *On Britain* (London, British Broadcasting Corporation, 1982).

Dale, H. E., *The Higher Civil Service of Great Britain* (London, Oxford University Press, 1941).

Darby, P., *British Defence Policy East of Suez, 1947–1968* (Oxford, Oxford University Press for the Royal Institute of International Affairs, 1973).

Dell, A. M., *The Countries of the Modern World* (London, George G. Harrap, 1935).

Dennison, S. R., *The Location of Industry and the Depressed Areas* (Oxford, Oxford University Press, 1939).

Denton, G., Forsyth, M., and MacLennan, M., *Economic Planning and Policies in Britain, France and Germany* (London, George Allen & Unwin, 1968).

The Dictionary of National Biography 1961–1970 (Oxford, Oxford University Press, 1981).

Dilnot, A. W., Kay, J. A., and Morris, C. N., *The Reform of Social Security* (Oxford, Oxford University Press for Institute of Fiscal Studies, 1984).

Dow, J. C. R., *The Management of the British Economy 1945–60* (Cambridge,

Cambridge University Press: National Institute for Economic and Social Research, Students' Edition 3, 1970).

Dunleavy, P., *The Politics of Mass Housing in Britain, 1945–1975: A Study of Corporate Power and Professional Influence in the Welfare State* (Oxford, Clarendon Press, 1981).

Dunnett, P. J. S., *The Decline of the British Motor Industry: The Effects of Government Policy 1945–1979* (London, Croom Helm, 1980).

Edgerton, David, *England and the Aeroplane: An Essay on a Militant and Technological Nation* (Macmillan, in association with the Centre for the History of Science, Technology and Medicine, University of Manchester, 1991).

—— *Twentieth Century British History*, vol. 2, No. 3, 1991, 'The Prophet Militant and Industrial: The Peculiarities of Correlli Barnett'.

Feinstein, C. H., *Statistical Tables of National Income, Expenditure and Output of the United Kingdom, 1855–1965* (Cambridge, Cambridge University Press, 1972).

Finer, H., *The British Civil Service* (London, Fabian Society, 1927).

Gallup, G. H. (general ed.), *The Gallup International Opinion Polls: Great Britain 1937–1975*, vol. I: *1937–1964* (New York, Random House, 1977).

Gann, L. H., and Duignan, P. (eds), *Colonialism and Africa 1870–1960* (Cambridge, Cambridge University Press, 1969).

German Information Centre, New York, *The Marshall Plan and the Future of US–European Relations* (New York, GIC, 1972).

Glass, D.V. (ed.), *Social Mobility in Britain* (London, Routledge & Kegan Paul, 1954).

Goldthorpe, J. H., Lockwood, D., Bechhofer, F., and Platt, J., *The Affluent Worker* (Cambridge, Cambridge University Press, 1968).

Gowing, M., *Independence and Deterrence: Britain and Atomic Energy, 1945–1952*, vol. I: *Policy Making* (London, Macmillan, 1982).

Grove, E., *Vanguard to Trident: British Naval Policy Since World War Two* (London, The Bodley Head, 1987).

Guttsman, W. L., *The British Political Elite* (London, MacGibbon & Kee, 1963).

Hall, H. D., *North American Supply* (London, HMSO and Longmans, Green, 1955).

Hancock, W. K., *Survey of Commonwealth Affairs*, vol. II: *Problems of Economic Policy, 1918–1939*, part I (London, Oxford University Press, 1942).

Hancock, W. K., and Gowing, M. M., *British War Economy* (London, HMSO and Longmans, Green, 1949).

Harrington, W., and Young, P., *The 1945 Revolution* (London, Davis-Poynter, 1978).

Harris, Jose, 'Enterprise and Welfare States: A Comparative Perspective' in *Transactions of the Royal Historical Society*, 40 (1990).

Heindel, R. H., *The American Impact on Britain 1891–1914* (New York, Octagon Books, 1968).

Hennessy, P., *Never Again: Britain 1945–1951* (London, Jonathan Cape, 1992).

Hennessy, P., and Arends, A., *Mr Attlee's Engine Room: Cabinet Committee Structure and the Labour Governments 1945–51*, Strathclyde Papers on Government and Politics No. 26 (Glasgow, Strathclyde University, 1983).

Heussler, R., *Yesterday's Rulers: The Making of the British Colonial Service* (New York, Syracuse University Press, 1963).

Hobsbawm, E. J., *Industry and Empire* (Harmondsworth, Pelican Books, 1969).

Hodson, J. L., *The Sea and the Land* (London, Victor Gollancz, 1945).

Hoggart, R., *The Uses of Literacy: Aspects of Working Class Life with Special Reference to Publications and Entertainments* (London, Chatto & Windus, 1971).

Hornby, W., *Factories and Plant* (London, HMSO and Longmans, Green, 1958).

Inman, P., *Labour in the Munitions Industries* (London, Longmans, Green, 1957).

International Institute of Strategic Studies, *The Military Balance 1971–2* (London, IISS, 1971).

Jackson, M. P., *The Price of Coal* (London, Croom Helm, 1974).

Jacobs, E., and Worcester, R., *Typically British? The Prudential MORI Guide* (London, Bloomsbury, 1991).

Jones, L., *Shipbuilding in Britain Mainly Between the World Wars* (Cardiff, University of Wales Press, 1957).

Kahn, A. E., *Britain in the World Economy* (London, Pitman, 1946).

Keeling, B. S., and Wright, A. E. G., *The Development of the Modern British Steel Industry* (London, Longmans, 1964).

Knaplund, P, *Britain, Commonwealth and Empire* (London, Hamish Hamilton, 1956).

Lewis, J., *Changing Direction: British Military Planning for Postwar Strategic Defence, 1942–1947* (London, The Sherwood Press, 1988).

Locke, R. R., *The End of the Practical Man: Entrepreneurship and Higher Education in Germany, France and Great Britain, 1880–1940* (Greenwich, Conn., and London, Jai Press, 1984).

Louis, W. R., *Imperialism at Bay: The United States and the Decolonialisation of the British Empire, 1941–1945* (Oxford, Clarendon Press, 1981).

—— *The British Empire in the Middle East 1945–1951* (Oxford, Oxford University Press, 1984).

Lovell, J., *British Trade Unions, 1875–1933* (London, Macmillan, for Economic History Society, 1977).

Lowndes, G. A. N., *The Silent Social Revolution* (London, Oxford University Press, 1937).

McCallum, R. B., and Readman, A., *The British General Election of 1945* (London, Oxford University Press, 1947).

McCrone, G., *Regional Policy in Britain* (London, George Allen & Unwin, 1969).

McLaine, I., *Ministry of Morale: Home Front Morale and the Ministry of Information in World War II* (London, George Allen & Unwin, 1979).

Madge, C. (ed.), *Pilot Guide to the General Election* (London, Pilot Press, 1945).

Mansergh, N., *The Commonwealth Experience* (London, Weidenfeld & Nicolson, 1969).

—— *Survey of British Commonwealth Affairs: Problems of Wartime Co-operation and Post-war Change, 1939–1952* (Oxford, Oxford University Press, 1958).

Martin, L. W., *British Defence Policy: The Long Recessional* (London, IISS, 1969).

Marwick, A., *British Society Since 1945* (London, Allen Lane, 1982).

Mass-Observation, *Report on Behalf of the Advertising Service Guild*, no. 2: *Home Propaganda* (London, John Murray, 1941).

Mathias, P., *The First Industrial Nation* (London, Methuen, 1969).

Maxey, G., and Silberston, A., *The Motor Industry* (London, George Allen & Unwin, 1959).

Mercer, H., Rollings, N., and Tomlinson, J.D. (eds), *Labour Governments and Private Industry: The Experience of 1945–1951* (Edinburgh, Edinburgh University Press, 1992).

Middlemass, K., *Power, Competition and the State*, vol. I: *Britain in Search of Balance 1940–1961* (London, Macmillan, 1986).

Miller, J. D. B., *Britain and the Old Dominions* (London, Chatto & Windus, 1966).

Moggridge, D. (ed.), *The Collected Writings of John Maynard Keynes*, vol. XXIV, *Activities 1944–46: The Transition to Peace* (London, Macmillan and the Cambridge University Press, for the Royal Economic Society, 1979).

Monnet, J., *Memoirs* (London, Collins, 1978).

Morgan, K. O., *Labour in Power 1945–1951* (Oxford, Clarendon Press, 1984).

Morris, D. (ed.), *The Economic System in the UK* (3rd edn, Oxford, Oxford University Press, 1985).

Mowatt, C. L., *Britain Between the Wars, 1918–1940* (London, University Paperback, 1968).

Nelson, W. H., *Small Wonder: The Amazing Story of the Volkswagen* (London, Hutchinson, 1967).

Overy, R.J., *William Morris, Viscount Nuffield* (London, Europa Press, 1976).

Parker, H. M. D., *Manpower: A Study of Wartime Policy and Administration* (London, HMSO and Longmans, Green, 1957).

Pavitt, K. (ed.), *Technical Innovation and British Economic Performance* (London, Macmillan, 1980).

Pelling, H., *Britain and the Marshall Plan* (London, Macmillan, 1988).

—— *A History of British Trade Unionism* (Harmondsworth, Pelican Books, 1971).

Pliatzky, L., *Getting and Spending: Public Expenditure, Employment and Inflation* (Oxford, Basil Blackwell, 1982).

Plowden, E., *An Industrialist in the Treasury: The Post-War Years* (London, André Deutsch, 1989).

Pollard, S., *The Wasting of the British Economy: British Economic Policy from 1945 to the Present* (London, Croom Helm, 1982).

Postan, M. M., *British War Production* (London, HMSO and Longmans, Green, 1952).

Reader, W. J., *Imperial Chemical Industries: A History*, vol. II: *The First Quarter-Century, 1925–1952* (London, Oxford University Press, 1975).

Roepke, H. G., *Movements of the British Iron and Steel Industry –1720 to 1951* (Urbana, University of Illinois Press, 1956).

Rowntree, B. Seebohm, *Poverty: A Study of Town Life* (London, Macmillan, 1910).

Royal Institute of International Affairs, Study Group of, *The Colonial Problem* (London, Oxford University Press, 1937).

—— *Political and Strategic Interests of the United Kingdom* (London, Oxford University Press, 1939).

Royal Society Yearbook for 1903 (London, Royal Society, 1903).

Seeley, J. R., *The Expansion of England* (London, Macmillan, 1883).

Shanks, M., *The Stagnant Society* (rev. edn, Harmondsworth, Pelican Books, 1972).

Sherard, R. H., *The Child Slaves of Britain* (London, Hurst & Blackett, 1906).

Shonfield, A., *British Economic Policy Since the War* (Harmondsworth, Penguin Books, 1958).

Snyder, W. P., *Politics of British Defence Policy 1945–1962* (Columbus, Ohio, Ohio State University Press, 1964).

Social and Community Planning Research, *British Social Attitudes Survey* (Aldershot, Gower Publishing, 1988).

Stevenson, J., *British Society 1914–1945* (Harmondsworth, Pelican Books, 1984)

Thompson, E. P., *The Making of the English Working Class* (Harmondsworth, Pelican Books, 1974).

Tomlinson, B. R., *The Political Economy of the Raj* (London, Macmillan, 1979).

Turner, G., *The Car Makers* (Harmondsworth, Penguin Books, 1964).

Warren, K., *The American Steel Industry 1850–1970 – A Geographical Interpretation* (Oxford, Clarendon Press, 1973).

Webster, C., *The Health Services Since the War*, vol. I, *Problems of Health Care: the National Health Service Before 1957* (London, HMSO, 1988).

Wertheimer, E., *Portrait of the Labour Party* (London, Putnam, 1929).

Wettern, D., *The Decline of British Seapower* (London, Jane's Publishing, 1982).

Wilkinson, R., *The Prefects: British Leadership and the Public School Tradition* (London, Oxford University Press, 1964).

Wilson, H., *New Deal for Coal* (London, Contact Books, 1945).

Wyatt, R. J., *The Austin, 1906–1952* ((Newton Abbot and London, David & Charles, 1981).

Index